CW01263059

POLITICISING COMMODIFICATION

This book examines the new economic governance (NEG) regime that the EU adopted after 2008. Its novel research design captures the supranational formulation of NEG prescriptions and their uneven deployment across countries (Germany, Italy, Ireland, Romania), policy areas (employment relations, public services), and sectors (transport, water, healthcare). The new regime led to a much more vertical mode of EU integration, and its commodification agenda unleashed a plethora of union and social-movement protests, including transnationally. The book presents findings that are crucial for the prospects of European democracy, as labour politics is essential in framing the struggles about the direction of NEG along a commodification–decommodification axis rather than a national–EU axis. To shed light on corresponding processes at the EU level, it upscales insights on the historical role that labour movements have played in the development of democracy and welfare states. This title is also available as Open Access on Cambridge Core.

ROLAND ERNE is the author of *European Unions: Labor's Quest for a Transnational Democracy* (Cornell University Press, 2008), co-author of *New Structures, Forms and Processes of Governance in European Industrial Relations* (Eurofound, 2007), and co-editor of *Labour and Transnational Action in Times of Crisis* (Rowman & Littlefield, 2015) and *Transnationale Demokratie* (Realotopia, 1995). His research has appeared in publications such as the *British Journal of Industrial Relations*, *Cambridge Journal of Economics*, *European Journal of Industrial Relations*, *European Political Science*, *Labor History*, *Labor Studies Journal*, *Industrial Relations Journal*, *Journal of Common Market Studies*, *Journal of European Social Policy*, *Socio-Economic Review*, and *Transfer*.

SABINA STAN is the author of *L'agriculture roumaine en mutation: La construction sociale du marché* (CNRS Éditions, 2005; Open Edition Books, 2020) and co-editor of *Labour and Transnational Action in Times of Crisis* (Rowman & Littlefield, 2015) and *Life in Post-Communist Eastern Europe after EU Membership* (Routledge, 2012). Her research in economic anthropology, European health policy, patient mobility, labour migration, and corruption has appeared in *Social Science and Medicine*, *Journal of European Social Policy*, *Labor History*, *European Journal of Industrial Relations*, *Transfer*, *Journal of the Royal Anthropological Institute*, *Medical Anthropology*, *Dialectical Anthropology*, *Anthropologica*, *Anthropologie et Sociétés*, and *Material Culture Review*.

DARRAGH GOLDEN is the author of *Labour Euroscepticism: Italian and Irish Unions' Changing Preferences towards the EU* (ECPR Press, 2024) and co-editor of *Labour and Transnational Action in Times of Crisis* (Rowman & Littlefield, 2015). His research in comparative political economy, comparative employment relations, transnational labour activism, and EU transport policy has appeared in the *British Journal of Industrial Relations, European Journal of Industrial Relations, Global Labour Journal, Journal of Common Market Studies, Labor History, Rivista Giuridica del Lavoro,* and *Transfer.*

IMRE SZABÓ is the author of *The New Face of Labour Protest* (Routledge, under contract). His research in comparative political economy, labour politics, social movements, and EU water policy has appeared in *Economic and Industrial Democracy, European Journal of Industrial Relations, European Policy Analysis, Journal of Common Market Studies,* and *Transfer.*

VINCENZO MACCARRONE is the author of several articles on the international political economy, workers in the platform economy, comparative employment relations, and transnational governance appearing in the *British Journal of Industrial Relations, Economic and Industrial Democracy, European Journal of Industrial Relations, Global Labour Journal, Global Political Economy, Quaderni di Rassegna Sindacale, Rivista Giuridica del Lavoro, Transfer,* and *Work, Employment and Society.*

Politicising Commodification

EUROPEAN GOVERNANCE AND LABOUR POLITICS
FROM THE FINANCIAL CRISIS TO THE
COVID EMERGENCY

ROLAND ERNE
University College Dublin

SABINA STAN
Dublin City University

DARRAGH GOLDEN
University College Dublin

IMRE SZABÓ
Central European University, Vienna

VINCENZO MACCARRONE
Scuola Normale Superiore, Firenze

CAMBRIDGE
UNIVERSITY PRESS

CAMBRIDGE
UNIVERSITY PRESS

Shaftesbury Road, Cambridge CB2 8EA, United Kingdom

One Liberty Plaza, 20th Floor, New York, NY 10006, USA

477 Williamstown Road, Port Melbourne, VIC 3207, Australia

314–321, 3rd Floor, Plot 3, Splendor Forum, Jasola District Centre, New Delhi – 110025, India

103 Penang Road, #05-06/07, Visioncrest Commercial, Singapore 238467

Cambridge University Press is part of Cambridge University Press & Assessment, a department of the University of Cambridge.

We share the University's mission to contribute to society through the pursuit of education, learning and research at the highest international levels of excellence.

www.cambridge.org
Information on this title: www.cambridge.org/9781316511633

DOI: 10.1017/9781009053433

© Roland Erne 2024

This publication is in copyright. Subject to statutory exception and to the provisions of relevant collective licensing agreements, with the exception of the Creative Commons version the link for which is provided below, no reproduction of any part may take place without the written permission of Cambridge University Press & Assessment.

An online version of this work is published at doi.org/10.1017/9781009053433 under a Creative Commons Open Access license CC-BY-NC 4.0 which permits re-use, distribution and reproduction in any medium for non-commercial purposes providing appropriate credit to the original work is given and any changes made are indicated. To view a copy of this license visit https://creativecommons.org/licenses/by-nc/4.0

When citing this work, please include a reference to the DOI 10.1017/9781009053433

First published 2024

A catalogue record for this publication is available from the British Library.

A Cataloging-in-Publication data record for this book is available from the Library of Congress

ISBN 978-1-316-51163-3 Hardback
ISBN 978-1-009-05436-2 Paperback

Cambridge University Press & Assessment has no responsibility for the persistence or accuracy of URLs for external or third-party internet websites referred to in this publication and does not guarantee that any content on such websites is, or will remain, accurate or appropriate.

Contents

List of Figure and Tables		*page* vii
List of Tables in the Online Appendix		ix
List of Authors		xi
Acknowledgements		xiii
List of Abbreviations		xvii
1	Introduction	1

PART I ANALYTICAL FRAMEWORK

2	European Economic Governance and Labour Politics	13
3	A Paradigm Shift in Understanding EU Integration and Labour Politics	37
4	How to Assess the Policy Orientation of the EU's NEG Prescriptions	53
5	Contextualising the EU's NEG Prescriptions and Research Design	73

PART II EU ECONOMIC GOVERNANCE IN TWO POLICY AREAS

6	EU Governance of Employment Relations and Its Discontents	95
7	EU Governance of Public Services and Its Discontents	132

PART III EU ECONOMIC GOVERNANCE IN THREE SECTORS

8 EU Governance of Transport Services and Its Discontents 167

9 EU Governance of Water Services and Its Discontents 204

10 EU Governance of Healthcare and Its Discontents 231

PART IV COMPARATIVE ANALYSIS AND POST-PANDEMIC DEVELOPMENTS

11 Labour Politics and the EU's NEG Prescriptions across Areas and Sectors 269

12 The EU's Shift to a Post-Covid NEG Regime 307

13 The Policy Orientation of the EU's Post-Covid NEG Regime and Its Discontents 323

14 Conclusion 353

Glossary 359
References 363
Index 393

Figure and Tables

FIGURE

2.1 The four faces of the EU's new economic governance
(NEG) regime   *page* 34

TABLES

4.1	Analytical framework for the analysis of NEG prescriptions on employment relations	*page* 61
4.2	Analytical framework for the analysis of NEG prescriptions on public services	67
5.1	Coercive power of NEG prescriptions	86
6.1	Themes in NEG prescriptions on employment relations (2009–2019)	109
6.2	Categories of NEG prescriptions on employment relations by coercive power	110
6.3	Transnational protests politicising the EU governance of employment relations (1993–2019)	122
7.1	Themes of NEG prescriptions on public services (2009–2019)	143
7.2	Categories of NEG prescriptions on public services by coercive power	145
7.3	Transnational protests politicising the EU governance of public services (1993–2019)	161
8.1	Themes of NEG prescriptions on transport services (2009–2019)	178
8.2	Categories of NEG prescriptions on transport services by coercive power	179

8.3	Transnational protests politicising the EU governance of transport services (1993–2019)	194
9.1	Themes of NEG prescriptions on water services (2009–2019)	211
9.2	Categories of NEG prescriptions on water services by coercive power	212
9.3	Transnational protests politicising the EU governance of water services (1993–2019)	224
10.1	Themes of NEG prescriptions on healthcare services (2009–2019)	244
10.2	Categories of NEG prescriptions on healthcare services by coercive power	246
10.3	Transnational protests politicising the EU governance of healthcare (1993–2019)	260
11.1	Commodifying NEG prescriptions on employment relations and public services (cross-sectoral)	272
11.2	Decommodifying NEG prescriptions on employment relations and public services (cross-sectoral)	274
11.3	Commodifying NEG prescriptions on public services (sectoral)	286
11.4	Decommodifying NEG prescriptions on public services (sectoral)	288
11.5	Transnational socioeconomic protests in Europe (1997–2019)	300
11.6	Transnational socioeconomic protests targeting EU laws and prescriptions by sector	303
12.1	The EU's evaluation scoreboard for National Recovery and Resilience Plans	315
13.1	Transnational protests politicising the EU governance of employment relations (2020–28 February 2023)	331
13.2	Transnational protests politicising the EU governance of public services (2020–28 February 2023)	335
13.3	Transnational protests politicising the EU governance of transport services (2020–28 February 2023)	339
13.4	Transnational protests politicising the EU governance of healthcare 2020–28 February 2023)	346

Tables in the Online Appendix

Available at http://hdl.handle.net/10197/24708

- A1.1 Documents analysed
- A1.2 Interviews conducted
- A1.3 Participant observations
- A5.1 Semantic links between prescriptions to 'increase cost-effectiveness in healthcare' and other healthcare prescriptions for Germany, Italy, Ireland, and Romania, 2011–2019
- A6.1 Short quotes from NEG employment relations prescriptions for Germany, 2009–2019
- A6.2 Short quotes from NEG employment relations prescriptions for Italy, 2009–2019
- A6.3 Short quotes from NEG employment relations prescriptions for Ireland, 2009–2019
- A6.4 Short quotes from NEG employment relations prescriptions for Romania, 2009–2019
- A7.1 Short quotes from NEG public service prescriptions for Germany, 2009–2019
- A7.2 Short quotes from NEG public service prescriptions for Italy, 2009–2019
- A7.3 Short quotes from NEG public service prescriptions for Ireland, 2009–2019
- A7.4 Short quotes from NEG public service prescriptions for Romania, 2009–2019
- A8.1 Short quotes from NEG transport prescriptions for Germany, 2009–2019
- A8.2 Short quotes from NEG transport prescriptions for Italy, 2009–2019
- A8.3 Short quotes from NEG transport prescriptions for Ireland, 2009–2019
- A8.4 Short quotes from NEG transport prescriptions for Romania, 2009–2019
- A9.1 Short quotes from NEG water prescriptions for Germany, 2009–2019
- A9.2 Short quotes from NEG water prescriptions for Italy, 2009–2019
- A9.3 Short quotes from NEG water prescriptions for Ireland, 2009–2019

A9.4   Short quotes from NEG water prescriptions for Romania, 2009–2019
A10.1 Short quotes from NEG healthcare prescriptions for Germany, 2009–2019
A10.2 Short quotes from NEG healthcare prescriptions for Italy, 2009–2019
A10.3 Short quotes from NEG healthcare prescriptions for Ireland, 2009–2019
A10.4 Short quotes from NEG healthcare prescriptions for Romania, 2009–2019
A10.5 Hospitals, by form of ownership, Germany, Italy, Ireland, and Romania, 2008; 2017
A10.6 Hospital beds by hospital ownership, Germany, Italy, Ireland, and Romania, 2008; 2017
A13.1 NEG prescriptions in CSRs for Germany, Italy, Ireland, and Romania, 2019–2020
A13.2 Post-Covid NEG prescriptions in CIDs for Germany, Italy, Ireland, and Romania, 2021

Authors

Roland Erne (PhD in Social and Political Sciences, European University Institute, Florence) is Professor of European Integration and Employment Relations, School of Business, University College Dublin (UCD); Adjunct Professor of International and Comparative Labor, ILR School, Cornell University, Ithaca, NY; and Principal Investigator, ERC project 'Labour Politics and the EU's New Economic Governance Regime', School of Business and Geary Institute for Public Policy, UCD.

Sabina Stan (PhD in Social and Cultural Anthropology, University of Montreal) is Assistant Professor in Sociology and Anthropology, School of Nursing, Psychotherapy, and Community Health, Dublin City University; and former Senior Social Scientist, ERC project 'Labour Politics and the EU's New Economic Governance Regime', School of Business and Geary Institute for Public Policy, UCD.

Darragh Golden (PhD in Industrial Relations and Human Resources, UCD) is Ad Astra Fellow, UCD School of Business; and former Postdoctoral Fellow, ERC project 'Labour Politics and the EU's New Economic Governance Regime', School of Business and Geary Institute for Public Policy, UCD.

Imre Szabó (PhD in Political Science, Central European University, Budapest) is Visiting Faculty, Department of Political Science, Central European University, Vienna; and former Postdoctoral Fellow, ERC project 'Labour Politics and the EU's New Economic Governance Regime', School of Business and Geary Institute for Public Policy, UCD.

Vincenzo Maccarrone (PhD in Industrial Relations and Human Resources, UCD) is Global Marie Skłodowska-Curie Fellow, Scuola Normale Superiore, Florence; and former Postdoctoral Fellow, ERC project 'Labour Politics and the EU's New Economic Governance Regime', School of Business and Geary Institute for Public Policy, UCD.

Acknowledgements

This book is an outcome of our research project 'Labour Politics and the EU's New Economic Governance Regime' (www.erc-europeanunions.eu/), which, since 2017, has received funding from the European Research Council (ERC) under the European Union's Horizon 2020 research and innovation programme (grant agreement No 725240). We also acknowledge the funding from the Irish Higher Education Authority, which allowed us to extend our research when the Covid pandemic delayed our fieldwork. Moreover, we thank the Irish Research Council (IRC) for its Basic Research Excellence Recognition Award 2016 and a PhD scholarship grant (2016–2021); the University College Dublin (UCD) School of Business for funding our ERC research project manager; the UCD Geary Institute for Public Policy for providing us with a stimulating research environment and its facilities; UCD Research and the School of Business for seed funding; and Enterprise Ireland for its 2015 Proposal Preparation Support Scheme grant. We appreciate too the support from the European Trade Union Institute (grant No 2051-911-31), which allowed us to enhance our transnational socioeconomic protest database.

This book would not have seen the light of day without the generosity towards our work of numerous people whom we would like to sincerely thank. Above all, we are tremendously grateful to the many informants who talked to us despite their charged agendas: namely, German, Irish, Italian, Romanian, and EU-level trade union officials; national and European social movement activists; representatives of national and EU-level employers' associations; national and European members of parliament; as well as officials from the European Commission, Council of the European Union, International Monetary Fund, and national governments.

Our research profited very much too from the support and feedback that we received from practitioners and researchers alike. We are very grateful to

Maria Belizón, Anthony Brabazon, Máire Coyle, Orla Feely, Tom Gormley, Philip O'Connell, Michael O'Neill, Andrea Prothero, Bill Roche, and Tobias Theiler for their help in setting up our ERC research group. In October 2019, Stefano Bartolini, Dorothee Bohle, Lorenzo Cini, Mark Dawson, Adrienne Héritier, Brigid Laffan, Guglielmo Meardi, Devi Sacchetto, and Philippe Schmitter offered very helpful comments and suggestions at a dedicated project workshop held at the European University Institute in conjunction with the Scuola Normale Superiore in Florence. In June 2019, we discussed our research with German, Romanian, and European unionists at a fringe meeting at the 10th congress of the European Public Service Union (EPSU) in Dublin. In 2018 and 2019, we organised several UCD seminars with Nicolas Jabko, Christian Joerges, Alexandra Kaasch, Philippe Schmitter, and Martin Seeleib-Kaiser, who provided us with important insights for our research (www.erc-europeanunions.eu/events/). We also thank the discussants of the papers presenting our first research findings at subsequent workshops and international conferences (www.erc-europeanunions.eu/conference-pre sentations/) and the peer reviewers of ensuing journal articles and chapters (www.erc-europeanunions.eu/publications-1/).

Overall, we are especially indebted to the anonymous peer reviewers of this monograph and to the colleagues who carefully read one or several of its draft chapters, namely Andreas Bieler, Hervé Champin, Paul Copeland, Amandine Crespy, Colin Crouch, Gemma Gasseau, Elke Heins, Yves Hellendorff, Richard Hyman, Christian Joerges, Alkuin Kölliker, Kalle Kunkel, Imelda Maher, Paul Marginson, Silvia Rainone, and Felix Syrovatka. Nonetheless, the usual disclaimer about our responsibility for any omissions and mistakes applies.

Furthermore, we would like to pay thanks to our former IRC postdoctoral fellow Jamie Jordan and our former ERC postdoctoral fellow Jörg Nowak for their important contributions to our project (Jordan, Maccarrone, and Erne 2021; Erne and Nowak, 2022). As visiting researchers, Ludwig Zurbriggen and Felix Syrovatka made notable contributions to our ERC research at its beginning and its conclusion, respectively. Our PhD students Mary Naughton and Costanza Galanti contributed a lot to the academic life of our group, while pursuing their own research questions, as warranted for doctoral students in the social sciences. Finally, we would like to extend our gratitude to our research project manager, Bianca Föhrer, whose support was crucial for both the successful operation of our ERC project in general and the submission of this monograph in particular. A very special note of thanks also goes to Catherine O'Dea for carefully proofreading the entire draft manuscript. Many thanks are also due to Ruth Martin for her professional indexing and to Trent Hancock for his editing work during the production process.

We are very grateful to Kenneth Armstrong for suggesting writing this monograph in the first place and to Finola O'Sullivan, Marianne Nield, Sharon McCann, and Gemma Smith from Cambridge University Press for their patience and support throughout its production. Last but not least, we thank our partners, families, and friends who supported us throughout the project's journey.

Abbreviations

ABVV/FGTB	Algemeen Belgisch Vakverbond – Fédération Générale du Travail de Belgique (General Labour Federation of Belgium)
ACV/CSC	Algemeen Christelijk Vakverbond – Confédération des syndicats chrétiens (Confederation of Christian Trade Unions, Belgium)
AEMH	Association Européenne des Médecins des Hôpitaux (Association of European Hospital Doctors)
AGS	Annual (Sustainable) Growth Strategy
AIM	International Association of Mutual Benefit Societies
AMEPIP	Agenţia pentru Monitorizarea şi Evaluarea Performanţelor Întreprinderilor Publice (Agency for Monitoring and Evaluation of Public Enterprise Performance in Romania)
ATAF	Azienda Trasporti dell'Area Fiorentina (former public transport provider in Florence, Italy)
ATCEUC	Air Traffic Controllers European Unions Coordination
Attac	Association for the Taxation of Financial Transactions and for Citizens' Action
BDA	Bundesvereinigung der Deutschen Arbeitgeberverbände (Federation of German Employers' Associations)
BDI	Bundesverband der Deutschen Industrie (Federation of German Industry)
BEPGs	Broad Economic Policy Guidelines
BoP	Balance of payments
CEE	Central and Eastern Europe
CEEP	Centre Européen des Entreprises à Participation Publique (European Centre of Employers and Enterprises providing

	Public Services and Services of General Interest; until December 2020, then SGI Europe)
CEOE	Confederación Española de Organizaciones Empresariales (Spanish Confederation of Business Organisations)
CER	Community of European Railway and Infrastructure Companies
CGIL	Confederazione Generale Italiana del Lavoro (Italian General Confederation of Labour)
CGT	Confédération Générale du Travail (French General Confederation of Labour)
CID	Council Implementing Decision
CIF	Construction Industry Federation (in Ireland)
CJEU	Court of Justice of the European Union
ČMKOS	Českomoravská konferderace odborových svazů (Czech Moravian Confederation of Trade Unions)
CNE	Centrale nationale des employés (Belgian trade union)
CoE	Council of Europe
COM	Communication of the European Commission
CPSU	Civil and Public Services Union (in Ireland)
CSC	See: ACV/CSC
CSR	Country-Specific Recommendation
CT	Constitutional Treaty
DB	Deutsche Bahn (German railways)
DE	Germany
DG	Directorate-General
DGB	Deutscher Gewerkschaftsbund (German Trade Union Confederation)
DG ECFIN	Directorate-General for Economic and Financial Affairs
DG EMPL	Directorate-General for Employment, Social Affairs, and Inclusion
DG ENV	Directorate-General for Environment
DG GROW	Directorate-General for Internal Market, Industry, Entrepreneurship, and SMEs
DPER	Department of Public Expenditure and Reform (in Ireland)
DRG	Diagnostic-Related Groups
DWD	Drinking Water Directive
EAEA	European Arts and Entertainment Alliance (European trade union federation of arts and entertainment workers)
EAHP	European Association of Hospital Pharmacists
EAP	Economic Adjustment Programme

EAPN	European Anti-Poverty Network
EASA	European Aviation and Safety Agency
ECA	European Cockpit Association (European federation of pilots' trade unions)
ECB	European Central Bank
ECI	European Citizens' Initiative
ECJ	European Court of Justice
ECMT	European Conference of Ministers of Transport
ECSC	European Coal and Steel Community
EC Treaty	Other name for the Treaty establishing the European Community
EDP	Excessive Deficit Procedure
EEC	European Economic Community
EES	European employment strategy
EFBWW	European Federation of Building and Woodworkers
EFFAT	European Federation of Food, Agriculture, and Tourism Trade Unions
EFSF	European Financial Stability Facility
EHIC	European Health Insurance Card
EMCO	Employment Committee (of the EU)
EMU	Economic and Monetary Union
ENPCHSP	European Network against the Privatisation and Commercialisation of Health and Social Protection (the European Network)
EP	European Parliament
EPC	Economic Policy Committee
EPF	European Patients' Forum
EPHA	European Public Health Alliance
EPSU	European Public Service Union
ERA	European Railway Agency
ERO	Employment Regulation Orders (in Ireland)
ESF	European Social Forum
ESM	European Stability Mechanism
ETF	European Transport Workers' Federation
ETUC	European Trade Union Confederation
ETUCE	European Trade Union Committee for Education (trade union federation for education)
ETUI	European Trade Union Institute
EU	European Union
Euratom	European Atomic Energy Community

EUROCOP	European Confederation of Police (trade unions)
EURORDIS	European Organisation for Rare Diseases
FDP	Freie Demokratische Partei (Free Democratic Party, Germany)
FEMPI	Financial Emergency Measures in the Public Interest (Ireland)
FEMS	Fédération Européenne des Médecins Salariés (European Federation of Salaried Doctors)
FGTB	See: ABVV/FGTB
FNV	Federatie Nederlandse Vakbeweging (Confederation of Dutch trade unions)
FS	Ferrovie dello Stato (Italy's national railway company)
GDP	Gross domestic product
GP	General practitioner (a general medical doctor)
GUE/NGL	Confederal Group of the European United Left/Nordic Green Left (in the European Parliament)
HOPE	European Hospital and Healthcare Federation
HOSPEEM	European Hospital and Healthcare Employers' Association
HRM	Human resource management
HQ	Headquarters
IBEC	Irish Business and Employers Confederation
IDC	International Dockworkers Council
IE	Ireland
IMF	International Monetary Fund
INMO	Irish Nurses and Midwives Organisation
ISME	Irish Association for Small and Medium Enterprises
IT	Italy
ITF	International Transport Workers' Federation
ITUC	International Trade Union Confederation
KOZ	Konfederácia Odborových Zväzov Slovenskej Republiky (Confederation of Trade Unions of the Slovak Republic)
MEDEF	Mouvement des entreprises de France (Movement of the Enterprises of France; French employer federation)
MEP	Member of the European Parliament
MFF	Multiannual Financial Framework
MIP	Macroeconomic Imbalance Procedure
MoU	Memorandum of Understanding
NEG	New economic governance
NGO	Non-governmental organisation
NRRP	National Recovery and Resilience Plan

List of Abbreviations

NTA	National Transport Authority (in Ireland)
OECD	Organisation for Economic Co-operation and Development
OGBL	Onofhängegen Gewerkschaftsbond Lëtzebuerg (Luxembourgish trade union confederation)
OMC	Open method of coordination
OPZZ	Ogólnopolskie Porozumienie Związków Zawodowych (All-Poland Alliance of Trade Unions)
PD	Partito Democratico (Italian centre-left party)
PHM	People's Health Movement
P-MoU	Precautionary Memorandum of Understanding
PNL	Partidul Naţional Liberal (National Liberal Party, Romania)
PPP	Public–private partnership
PSI	Public Services International (Global federation of public service unions)
PSO	Public service obligation
QMV	Qualified majority voting
REA	Registered Employment Agreements (in Ireland)
RRF	Recovery and Resilience Facility
RO	Romania
SEA	Single European Act
SGEI	Services of general economic interest
SGI Europe	Services of General Interest Europe (European employers' association in the public sector)
SGP	Stability and Growth Pact
SME United	European Association of Craft, Small, and Medium-Sized Enterprises
SMP	Single market programme
SNCF	Société nationale des chemins de fer français (French national railway company)
SOE	State-owned enterprise
SPD	Sozialdemokratische Partei Deutschlands (Social Democratic Party of Germany)
SUD	Solidaires Unitaires Démocratiques (a radical union confederation in France)
SURE	(EU) Support (scheme) to mitigate Unemployment Risks in an Emergency
SWD	Staff working document of the European Commission
TEC	Treaty Establishing the European Community
TEEC	Treaty Establishing the European Economic Community
TEU	Treaty on European Union

TFEU	Treaty on the Functioning of the European Union
TNC	Transnational corporation
TUC	Trades Union Congress (British trade union confederation)
UIL	Unione Italiana del Lavoro (an Italian trade union confederation)
UITP	Union Internationale des Transports Publics (International Association of Public Transport)
UK	United Kingdom
ULC	Unit labour cost
UNI Europa	European trade union federation of (private sector) service workers' unions
US	United States
USSR	Union of Soviet Socialist Republics
ver.di	Vereinte Dienstleistungsgewerkschaft (United Services Union, Germany)
WFD	Water Framework Directive
WHO	World Health Organisation
Younion	Austrian trade union (of municipal, media, education, etc. workers)

1

Introduction

We know that the market didn't work. That's why we are here.[1]

1.1 AIMS AND OBJECTIVES OF THE BOOK

Until the 2008 crisis, the European Union's (EU's) influence on employment relations and public services primarily took the form of horizontal market integration rather than a vertical integration of public policies under the auspices of EU authorities (Erne, 2018). The architects of the European single market and monetary union were convinced that horizontal market pressures would bring about the desired convergence of national employment and social policies. EU member states and unions agreed to coordinate their employment and social policies across borders (Erne, 2008), but the emerging multilevel EU economic governance regime was not a vertically integrated system with the EU exerting authoritative direction over national employment relations and welfare states. For most governments and business leaders, even the mere interest of EU authorities in employment relations under the banner of EU governance represented too much intervention in their affairs (Léonard et al., 2007).

After 2008 however, Europe's political and business leaders lost faith in self-governing markets when they realised that the then-existing European single market and monetary union had generated major economic imbalances that threatened to break up the EU. Without much ado, the Commission first approved bank bailouts at odds with EU treaty provisions that were intended to

---

[1] Response of the European Commission (DG ECFIN) representative to a comment about the EU's and IMF's 'failed' neoliberal, free-market ideology. International Labour Organisation/European Commission forum: *The Governance of Policy Reform in Ireland*, Government Buildings, Dublin Castle, 7 December 2012, Roland Erne, participant observation.

prevent state aid for private corporations as well as excessive budget deficits. Subsequently, the Commission, Parliament, and Council shook off the institutional gridlocks that had hitherto prevented a vertical integration of EU policies in the social field by adopting the Six-Pack of EU laws that enabled the European Commission and Council (EU executives)[2] to prescribe policy changes in fields hitherto shielded from vertical EU interventions. Since then, all EU member states must participate in a yearly cycle of country-specific policy prescriptions, surveillance, and enforcement – the European Semester process. The Semester integrates into one document the country-specific prescriptions[3] relating to the Memoranda of Understanding (MoUs) of bailout programmes, the revised Stability and Growth Pact (SGP), the new Macroeconomic Imbalance Procedure (MIP), and the Europe 2020 strategy. Although EU member states were still able to disregard the weak Europe 2020-related recommendations (for example, those intended to 'enhance social inclusion'), bailout programme countries risked the withdrawal of financial EU assistance; eurozone countries with excessive deficits or macroeconomic imbalances risked substantial financial fines; and *all* EU member states risked the withdrawal of EU structural funding in the event of non-compliance with MoU-, SGP-, or MIP-related new economic governance (NEG) prescriptions.[4] As the Parliament and the Council have defined excessive imbalances as 'severe imbalances, including imbalances that jeopardise *or risk jeopardising* the *proper functioning* of economic and monetary union' (emphasis added) (Art. 2, Regulation 1176/2011), no aspect of social policymaking is a priori excluded from its scope (Erne, 2015). Since the financial crisis of 2008, EU governance has thus undergone what former Commission President Barroso called a silent revolution (ANSA, 2010).

Despite its vertical nature however, the NEG regime should not be objectivised, as supranational socioeconomic and political systems do not predetermine the responses of actors on the ground (Burawoy, 2000).

---

[2] Within the NEG regime, EU executive power has two sources: the supranational Commission and the intergovernmental Council of finance ministers (Figure 2.1). As they must act in conjunction to be effective, we refer to them interchangeably as EU executives and as Commission and Council.

[3] As stated in the Glossary at the end of this book, NEG prescriptions are segments of MoUs or country-specific recommendations (CSRs) that entail a specific policy instruction. This is important, as governments and/or unions typically act not on the unitary text of MoUs or CSRs but on the specific prescriptions contained in them. Our units of analysis are thus not MoUs or CSRs per se but the shortest segments of them that make sense semantically.

[4] See our typology of NEG prescriptions in terms of their 'very significant', 'significant', or 'weak' coercive power (Table 5.1).

Barroso's silent revolution from above had indeed opened contradictory possibilities for unions and social movements across Europe. On the one hand, NEG's reliance on vertical intervention and surveillance made decisions taken in its name more tangible, offering concrete targets for contentious transnational countermovements. On the other hand however, NEG mimicked the governance structures of transnational corporations (TNCs) by using key performance indicators that put countries in competition with one another, thus constituting an obstacle to transnational collective action (Erne, 2015). The NEG regime's vertical and country-specific prescriptions also raised the threat of nationalist countermovements, thus making transnational collective action of trade unions and social movements ever more vital for the future of European integration and democracy.

This monograph seeks to understand the EU's vertical economic governance regime by engaging in three analytical moves. First, we develop a new outlook on the interplay between EU economic governance, labour politics, and EU democracy by proposing a novel analytic approach that captures not only the national but also the transnational social and economic processes at work (Stan and Erne, 2021a). Second, drawing on this novel outlook and analytic approach, we assess market-driven 'horizontal' and political 'vertical' EU integration pressures on labour and public services in different areas and sectors to uncover the interrelations between these different modes of EU integration. Then, we map the policy orientation of vertical EU interventions by EU laws and NEG prescriptions in these areas along a commodification–decommodification axis. In other words, we classify EU interventions based on whether or not they attempt to turn labour and public services into commodities to be traded on the market. Most relevant to our analysis is thus the policy prescriptions' potential to advance the commodification or decommodification of employment relations and public services. Third, we analyse the responses of trade unions and new social movements to EU executives' NEG prescriptions across different policy areas and sectors. In the final chapters of the book, we compare the patterns of NEG prescriptions and countervailing protests by unions and social movements across borders and assess their feedback effects on the EU integration process in general and on the EU's NEG regime after the outbreak of the Covid-19 pandemic in particular. In short, the book aims to help scholars as well as policymakers, trade unionists, and social movement activists get a better grasp of the arcane NEG regime, as such an understanding is important if they want to change its structure and its policy orientation.

1.2 RESEARCH DESIGN AND METHODOLOGY

This monograph analyses the structure and policy orientation of the EU's much more vertical, new governance regime in employment relations and public services, from its creation after the 2008 financial crisis to its (provisional) suspension in March 2020 after the outbreak of the Covid-19 pandemic. In addition, we assess the continuity and change of the post-Covid NEG regime, which the European Parliament and Council institutionalised in 2021 when they adopted the Recovery and Resilience Facility (RRF) Regulation.

Concretely, we assess EU horizontal (market) integration pressures and vertical (political) governance interventions by EU laws and NEG prescriptions in two cross-sectoral policy areas (employment relations and public services), three public services sectors (transport, water, healthcare), in four EU member states, namely, Germany (DE), Italy (IT), Ireland (IE), and Romania (RO). In addition, we document and analyse the transnational countervailing trade union and social movement actions that they triggered, based on our database of transnational socioeconomic protest events across Europe since 1993 (Erne and Nowak, 2023).

By choosing two large (DE, IT) and two small (IE, RO) states, we avoid the common fallacy of studying the EU's NEG without considering where the state receiving *country-specific* NEG prescriptions is situated within the EU's political economy. To facilitate a deeper analysis of the cases, we assess NEG prescriptions for a set of four states as opposed to all twenty-seven. Understanding the dynamics at work in NEG requires a deep knowledge of EU-level policymaking and of the affected states, policy areas, and sectors, as well as corresponding language skills. If one classifies the NEG prescriptions simply at their face value, they often appear ambiguous; but, if we take into account the EU *and* national semantic, communicative, and policy contexts in which they are situated, their policy orientation becomes much clearer.

By comparing different policy areas and sectors, we are going beyond the traditional country-by-country comparisons that still dominate comparative industrial relations, social policy, and political economy research. Although the country-specific NEG prescriptions may indeed nationalise social conflicts, NEG is still a supranational regime, as much as the corporate governance regimes of TNCs that NEG mimics.

Our multi-sited research is based on observations at EU level and in Germany, Ireland, Italy, and Romania. This allows us not only to make *country-by-country* comparisons but also to compare different *transnational sets* of NEG prescriptions *policy-area-by-policy-area* and *sector-by-sector*. We can therefore make inferences about structural factors that favour *transnational* rather than national countervailing labour movements. By inquiring whether NEG prescriptions on employment relations and public services form similar commodification patterns across countries, we ask whether public sector unions can politicise them more easily than unions in the private manufacturing sector. Indeed, despite the latter having been exposed to horizontal EU market integration pressures for much longer, their public sector counterparts' exposure to vertical NEG prescriptions offers more concrete targets for collective action (Szabó, Golden, and Erne, 2022).

Finally, our multidisciplinary and multi-sited study relies on a great variety of primary sources gathered between 2008 and 2023, ranging from around 230 EU, German, Italian, Irish, and Romanian laws, government documents, and court cases; over 160 interviews with national and EU-level policymakers, unionists, and social movement activists; to about 60 participant observations of EU and trade union events (Online Appendix; Tables A1.1–A1.3). Given this in-depth engagement with research sites over many years, the book can be described as an outcome of a 'slow comparative research' process (Almond and Connolly, 2020).

1.3 PLAN OF THE BOOK

In Part I, we describe NEG and outline our theoretical contribution and research design. Chapter 2 describes the vertical NEG regime that EU leaders adopted after 2008. We pay a lot of attention to the intricate details of the regime – not to complicate things but rather to unveil its governance mechanisms. This prompts us to propose in Chapter 3 three conceptual innovations for our study. First, we shift from the classical distinction of negative and positive integration (Scharpf, 1999) to one that distinguishes horizontal and vertical integration modes (Erne, 2018). Second, we propose to go beyond the classical, state-centred (intergovernmental or supranational) paradigms of EU law and political science, as we have found that the EU's NEG regime mimics the corporate governance regime that TNCs use to steer the activities of their subsidiaries and their workforce (Erne, 2015). Finally, we pursue an analytical approach that complements existing EU politicisation studies, which assess the salience of Eurosceptic views in media debates, opinion polls, elections, and referenda, as we must study EU politicisation also at the meso level of interest politics (Zürn, 2016; Erne, 2023a). After all, the political cleavages that structure national politics have neither been created in individuals' minds at the micro level nor were they simply an outcome of systemic macro-level changes (Bartolini, 2000).

Chapters 4 and 5 outline our research design. In Chapter 4, we review the existing literature in the field and outline its methodological limitations: (a) the flattening of the semantic links between different policy terms used in EU executives' NEG prescriptions and (b) the neglect of the power relations between different actors involved in their production. Studies of the NEG regime must indeed give more attention to the links between the policy orientation of NEG prescriptions and concrete social groups' material interests in them. This is another good reason to study NEG in conjunction with labour politics.

Given the role of commodifying interventions as triggers of countervailing social protests (Polanyi, 2001 [1944]; Szabó, Golden, and Erne, 2022; Erne and Nowak, 2023), we then explain why the commodification–decommodification axis is the most relevant nexus of EU economic governance and labour politics. Subsequently, we operationalise these concepts in relation to employment relations and public services to guide the ensuing analysis of EU executives' NEG prescriptions across those policy areas.

As EU executives deploy NEG prescriptions unevenly across countries, time, and policy areas, our research design must also take account of their hierarchical ordering in larger policy scripts. Chapter 5 shows how we do that, that is, by assessing NEG prescriptions in their semantic, communicative, and policy context. Such an assessment, however, requires not only deep knowledge of our research sites and areas but also a comparative approach that goes beyond the traditional country-by-country design of labour and social policy research.

In Parts II and III of the book, we set the above research design to work. In the empirical Chapters 6–10, we first assess the horizontal and vertical EU integration pressures on labour or public services before 2008, and then we analyse the NEG prescriptions from 2009 to 2019 in the two areas and three sectors across the four countries over eleven years. We begin in Part II with employment relations (Chapter 6) and public services (Chapter 7).

Chapter 6 shows that workers' wages and employment relations were, until the 2008 crisis, shaped by horizontal market pressures rather than direct political vertical EU interventions in the labour policy area. That changed radically after the EU's shift to NEG. We found that the EU's NEG prescriptions on wage levels, collective bargaining, and hiring and firing mechanisms followed a consistent trajectory that furthered the commodification of labour in Italy, Ireland, and Romania, but less so in Germany. Instead, Germany received decommodifying NEG prescriptions on wage policy, which were linked to a rebalance-the-EU-economy policy rationale. Although this policy rationale was still compatible with the overarching commodifying script of NEG, the diverging policy orientation of prescriptions in this area across countries made it hard for unions to challenge NEG transnationally.

Chapter 7 shows that EU leaders had already started in the 1980s to steer the trajectory of national public services in a commodifying direction. The commodifying pressures from direct EU interventions reached a peak in 2004 with the Commission's draft Services Directive, which failed to become law due to unprecedented, transnational protest movements. After the financial crisis however, the EU's shift to NEG empowered EU executives to pursue public service commodification by new means. Our analysis reveals that the NEG prescriptions on public services for Germany, Ireland, Italy, and Romania consistently pointed in a commodifying direction, by demanding a curtailment of public resources for public services and their marketisation. Although our analysis uncovers some decommodifying prescriptions, namely, quantitative ones calling for more investment at the end of the 2010s, they were usually justified with policy rationales subordinated to NEG's primary commodifying script.

Part III assesses the NEG prescriptions across three public sectors in detail. Chapter 8 traces the EU governance of transport services from the Treaty of Rome to NEG. Initially, European public sector advocates were able to shield transport from commodification, but, over time, the Commission gradually advanced a commodification agenda one transport modality after another. Sometimes, however, the Commission's draft liberalisation laws encountered enduring resistance and recurrent transnational protests by transport workers, leading the European Parliament and Council to curb the commodification bent of the Commission's draft directives. After 2008 however, NEG provided EU executives with new means to circumvent resistance. Despite their country-specific methodology, *all* qualitative NEG prescriptions on transport services issued to Germany, Italy, Ireland, and Romania pointed towards commodification. But the more the Commission succeeded in commodifying transport services, the more the nature of counter-mobilisations changed. Accordingly, the European Transport Workers' Federation's (ETF) failed Fair Transport European Citizens' Initiative (ECI) no longer targeted vertical EU interventions but rather the social dumping pressures created by the free movement of services and fellow transport workers. This target made joint transnational collective action more difficult.

Chapter 9 analyses the EU governance of water and the countervailing mobilisations against its commodification. Initially, European law decommodified water services through the harmonisation of quality standards that took them out of regulatory competition between member states. However, from the 1990s onwards, the Commission repeatedly attempted to commodify water through liberalising EU laws. When these attempts failed, EU executives tried to advance commodification by new means, namely, through the EU's NEG prescriptions. Our analysis revealed that all qualitative prescriptions on water services issued from 2009 to 2019 to Germany, Ireland, Italy, and Romania called for their marketisation, despite recent calls to increase public investment. Like preceding attempts by draft EU directives, however, the NEG's consistent commodification script triggered transnational protests by unions and social movements that defended water as a human right and as a public service, namely, the successful Right2Water ECI.

Chapter 10 traces the EU governance of health services and its discontents. The first European interventions in the health sector facilitated mobile workers' access to health services in their host countries. This decommodified cross-border care, albeit by recourse to solidaristic mechanisms situated at national rather than EU level. Since the 1990s however, horizontal market pressures and public deficit criteria have led governments to curtail healthcare spending and to introduce marketising reforms. Thereafter, healthcare became a target of EU competition and free movement of services law. In 2006, transnational social protest movements moved EU legislators to drop healthcare from the scope of the draft EU Services Directive but, after the financial crisis, EU executives pursued commodification of healthcare through new means, as shown by our analysis of their NEG prescriptions for Germany, Italy, Ireland, and Romania. Even when commodifying prescriptions were on occasion accompanied by decommodifying ones, the latter remained subordinated to the former. Although their country-specific methodology hampered transnational protests, the overarching commodification script of NEG prescriptions led not only to transnational protests by the European Public Service Union (EPSU) but also to the formation of the European Network against the Privatisation and Commercialisation of Health and Social Protection, which unites unionists and social movement activists.

In Part IV, we compare the findings of the preceding chapters, analyse the substantial change to NEG that EU leaders adopted after the outbreak of the pandemic, and assess the policy orientation of the post-Covid NEG regime. We conclude by outlining the prospects for EU governance and labour politics. The comparisons of NEG prescriptions in Chapter 11 reveal that almost all *qualitative* prescriptions across all countries, areas, and sectors pointed in a commodifying direction, tasking governments to marketise employment relations and public services. Most *quantitative* prescriptions tasked governments to curtail wages and public expenditures too, but, over time, they not only became less coercive but also increasingly pointed in a decommodifying policy direction, tasking governments to invest more. It would, however, still be wrong to speak of a socialisation of NEG, not just given the decommodifying prescriptions' weak coercive power (Jordan, Maccarrone, and Erne, 2021) but also because of their explicit links to policy rationales that are compatible with NEG's overarching commodification script. Moreover, Chapter 11 shows that EU executives' NEG prescriptions tasked governments to channel more public resources into the allegedly more productive sectors (transport and water services) rather than into essential social services like healthcare.

Most importantly however, the NEG regime shifted the frontiers of the battle against the commodification of public services. This means that union strategies based only on fighting spending cuts would be misguided, as public services have themselves become a site of capitalist accumulation – an insight acquired by many union and social movement activists themselves. Given NEG's country-specific methodology, it is not surprising that there have been only a few instances of transnational action on specific NEG prescriptions. By contrast, the share of transnational labour protests targeting EU interventions broadly defined increased after 2008, namely, in the healthcare sector. This suggests that NEG has been altering protest landscapes, prompting unions and social movements to broaden the scope of their demands, not just at EU level (Erne and Nowak, 2023) but also locally (Naughton, 2023). This insight is all the more important given EU leaders' response to the Covid crisis, which not only led to a temporary suspension of austerity but also renewed calls for marketising reforms in public services sectors.

In Chapter 12, we show that the Covid-19 emergency and the ensuing suspension of the SGP and its sanctioning mechanisms in 2020 led to crucial changes in the NEG regime. For example, the transnational distribution of EU funds, institutionalised by the EU's RRF Regulation in 2021, meant that the post-Covid NEG regime no longer mimicked the divisive beggar-thy-neighbour tools that TNCs use to steer their subsidiaries and workforce. Even so, EU executives continue to direct the post-Covid NEG regime without much participation by national and European parliaments or unions and social movements. Instead of the financial sanctions of the suspended SGP, EU executives use the policy conditionalities attached to RRF funding to reach their objectives.

In Chapter 13, we provide a preliminary analysis of the policy orientation of the post-Covid NEG regime, to give policymakers, unionists, and social movement activists an idea about possible future trajectories of EU governance of employment relations and public services. We do that on the basis of not only the recently adopted EU laws in these two policy areas, such as the decommodifying Minimum Wage Directive, but also EU executives' post-Covid NEG prescriptions in two areas, three sectors, and four countries. Vertical NEG interventions in national wage policies paradoxically cleared the way for the decommodifying EU Minimum Wage Directive by effectively making wage policy an EU policymaking issue, but, in the area of public services, we see an accentuation of the trend of NEG prescriptions in recent years: more public investments but also much more private sector involvement in the delivery of public services.

Chapter 14 concludes the book by highlighting its major insights both for the study of European integration and labour politics and for the prospects of egalitarian democracy in Europe.

PART I

Analytical Framework

2

European Economic Governance and Labour Politics

2.1 INTRODUCTION

The 2008 financial crisis represents a major turning point for European economic governance and labour politics. The crisis triggered European Union (EU) interventions in its member states' employment relations and social policies, which had hitherto been largely shielded from coercive EU interventions. At first, this shift occurred only in countries where governments had signed bailout programmes with international and EU institutions. After the EU adopted a Six-Pack of laws on economic governance in 2011 however, no member state was outside the reach of its new economic governance (NEG) regime. This shift is significant for analysts and social actors alike. As NEG denotes a departure from the usual trajectories of EU policymaking, EU scholars must rethink their long-established analytical perspectives. The shift to NEG challenges organised labour and egalitarian democracy too, as it threatens the role that labour movements and public services have played in Europe since the making of the mid-twentieth-century class compromise between capital and labour.

Although the NEG prescriptions that the EU began issuing after the financial crisis did not affect all workers and all public service users across Europe equally, the shift to NEG has nevertheless been fundamental. The Six-Pack's new EU Regulation 1176/2011 'on the prevention and correction of macroeconomic imbalances', for example, assumes that the purpose of NEG is to ensure that member states pursue 'proper' economic policies (Art. 2). This wording mirrors a technocratic understanding of EU governance, predicated on the implementation of apparently apolitical 'regulatory' standards by European executive agencies to create an integrated marketplace, as advocated, for example, by the Italian political scientist Giandomenico Majone (1994). If, however, EU economic policymaking is reduced to an exercise that consists of the implementation of 'proper' policies, it eschews the idea of democratic interest intermediation between conflicting political priorities or social interests. After all, NEG affects not only technical standards but also *redistributive* areas of labour politics, which affect social classes differently, as happens in the case of wage bargaining or the provision of public services. NEG's technocratic assumptions, which supplant democratic choices, thus become highly problematic.

Although the single market programme (SMP) and economic and monetary union (EMU) exposed workers and labour movements to increased competitive pressures, the greater horizontal market integration caused by the SMP and EMU did not question the formal autonomy of social partners, as illustrated by the revival of neo-corporatist social pacts and social partnership agreements during the 1990s (Erne, 2008). By contrast, the shift to the much more vertical NEG regime pushed trade unions into a corner. This development seemed to leave very few options to labour movements: passive acceptance, national resistance, or transnational counter-mobilisations (Erne, 2019). Which of these responses have dominated, and why? And what have been the intended and unintended consequences of the shift to NEG for the European integration process, labour politics, and egalitarian democracy? These questions are vital for practitioners and analysts of EU governance and labour movements alike. The shift to NEG not only restructures the European political space and thereby challenges the role of trade unions but also requires new analytical tools that can adequately capture the ongoing social transformations that NEG has triggered.

In sum, in response to the upheavals caused by the 2008 financial crisis, EU policymakers adopted NEG. To understand the challenges that this new regime poses to labour politics however, we must also comprehend EU economic governance and its bearing on employment relations and public services prior to the shift to NEG. In section 2.2, we thus assess European integration dynamics already present before NEG and the ways in which labour movements positioned themselves in relation to them. Tensions between market-driven and political modes of EU integration were already apparent in the 2000s, but the shift to NEG made them much greater. NEG also unsettled EU policymakers' and scholars' core assumptions about EU economic governance and labour politics. Before we can discuss the analytical and political challenges caused by NEG however, we must first describe how it works, as we do in section 2.3.

2.2 EU ECONOMIC GOVERNANCE AND LABOUR POLITICS BEFORE THE 2008 FINANCIAL CRISIS

Economic Dynamics

According to the Treaty on European Union (TEU), the 'Union shall establish an internal market' and 'promote social justice' and 'economic, social and territorial cohesion, and solidarity among Member States' (Art. 3(3) TEU).[1] Whereas advocates of a social Europe argued that the latter EU objectives would require countervailing EU social policy interventions (Marginson and Sisson, 2004), the business-friendly promoters of the European single market project argued that its creation would produce substantial employment and welfare gains, as the free movement of capital, goods, services, and people would generate economies of scale and a decrease in prices for consumers resulting from increased competition (Cecchini, Catinat, and Jacquemin, 1988; van Apeldoorn, 2002; Jabko, 2006). Given these conflicting views, it is not surprising that the EU integration process did not follow a uniform trajectory since the adoption of the European Economic Community (EEC) Treaty in 1957. Instead, European economic and social integration has proceeded in different stages and at different speeds.

To draw a differentiated picture of the European integration process and to explain the unequal progress of its social and economic goals across time, Fritz Scharpf (1999) distinguished between the *negative* liberalising and *positive* harmonising of European laws, building on earlier works of Keynesian economic integration theory (Tinbergen, 1965; Pinder, 1968). Concretely, Scharpf distinguishes between EU interventions that (a) remove restrictions to the free movement of goods, capital, services, and people across borders (negative integration) and (b) set supranational standards to regulate goods, capital, services, and labour markets at EU level (positive integration). Negative integration *increases* market competition between firms and regulatory competition between different national governance regimes. The outcome is thus an increase in labour commodification (Streeck, 1992), which means turning labour power into a mere commodity to be bought and sold in the marketplace. In contrast, positive integration sets harmonised standards at EU level. If the harmonised standards are not set too low, positive integration curtails firms' capacity to use lower national standards to gain a competitive advantage and thus *limits* market and regulatory competition. When positive integration involves the regulation of employment relations and social protection, it functions as a market-correcting device that decommodifies labour.

---

[1] The EU's primary (or constitutional) law is specified in two treaties. Whereas the TEU sets out the objectives and principles of the EU, the Treaty on the Functioning of the European Union (TFEU) provides the organisational details and outlines the EU's policy areas. The TEU is an amended version of the Treaty on the European Union (signed in Maastricht in 1992), and the TFEU is basically the former (E)EC Treaty, signed in Rome in 1957 and amended by the Single European Act, the Maastricht Treaty, the Amsterdam Treaty, the Nice Treaty, and the Lisbon Treaty. The (E)EC Treaty became the TFEU in December 2009, after EU member states ratified the Lisbon Treaty.

The distinction between negative and positive integration enabled Scharpf (1999) to capture an essential shift in European policymaking triggered by the Single European Act (SEA) and its single market programme. After the SEA's adoption in 1986, economic integration processes went up a gear. The SEA departed from the positive (but cumbersome) integration approach based on building a level playing field for all firms through the harmonisation of national standards at European level. Instead, to remove all remaining non-tariff barriers to the internal market,[2] the SEA pursued a negative integration approach based on the mutual recognition of national standards for commodities traded across borders rather than their harmonisation at European level.

Positive regulation has always faced significant obstacles at European level. Most notably, new EU laws in the social field require a high level of consensus that is 'difficult or impossible' to reach, given the 'heterogeneity of Member State interests and preferences' (Scharpf, 2006: 854). In this context, European leaders' strategy of playing the market as a mechanism to unite Europe (Jabko, 2006) and the consequent shift to negative integration was significant: the SEA's single market programme (SMP) amplified market competition and facilitated the rise of a much more integrated European production system. The SEA rewarded companies that relocated part of their production capacities to countries with lower labour standards. In addition, economic integration went up another gear after the Maastricht Treaty (1992) launched the Economic and Monetary Union (EMU) and after the European Council opened the EU's eastwards accession process at its 1993 Copenhagen summit. Subsequently, the Maastricht EMU and the Copenhagen EU accession criteria, coupled with the increasing competitive pressures in an ever more integrated European market, increased the pressures on national budgets and unit labour costs (wages and social contributions) across old and new Europe alike.

The drafters of the Maastricht Treaty attached a social protocol to it, which was meant to facilitate the adoption of EU laws in the social field to prevent a race to the bottom in labour and social standards. Since the late 1990s however, EU policymakers have adopted only very few positive, market-correcting EU laws – although the EU did manage to adopt more of them in the social field than Fritz Scharpf (1999) and Wolfgang Streeck (1992) anticipated. Overall, those laws were not robust enough to offset competitive pressures unleashed by the SMP and the EMU (Marginson and Sisson, 2004; Maccarrone, Erne, and Golden, 2023).

---

[2] Intra-EEC tariff barriers had already been removed at the outset of the EEC.

Although the increased intra-European economic competitive pressures triggered by the SMP and EMU did not lead to the creation of a strong social Europe, neither did they lead to an end to social concertation between governments, employers, and unions at national level, as initially expected by neo-corporatist employment relations scholars (Streeck and Schmitter, 1991). Governments and employers continued to involve unions in national corporatist arrangements or social pacts – not to ensure a fair distribution between capital and labour as before but to moderate wage growth. Wage moderation was a key feature of these arrangements for two reasons: first, to improve the competitive position of countries' firms in an ever more transnational marketplace and, second, to fulfil the Maastricht Treaty's low inflation criteria to access the EMU (Grote and Schmitter, 1999; Molina and Rhodes, 2002; Erne, 2008). To access the EMU, governments also began reducing the costs of public services to meet the Treaty's public deficit criteria. They achieved that by curtailing public expenditure or shifting the costs of public services to private purses through a series of marketising reforms (see Chapters 5–10), leading to a commodification of the social welfare state, namely, employment relations, social services, and public utilities (Supiot, 2013).

After the introduction of the Euro in 1999 and the accession of ten new EU member states in 2004 however, the disciplining effects of the EMU and accession criteria on labour and the social welfare state diminished. This led EU leaders to relaunch the economic integration process by drawing on negative integration through service liberalisation. To achieve that, the Commission notably asked the European Parliament and Council in 2004 to adopt its proposal for an EU Services Directive, but these attempts were not entirely successful and, by the end of the decade, the contradictions of European economic integration became ever more apparent. Contrary to the assumptions of the proponents of the internal market programme quoted at the start of this section, European integration did not lead to market integration trickling down to social integration. Another reason for this was that the building of the single market and monetary union in an enlarged EU accentuated rather than reduced social and economic imbalances across countries and social classes (Meardi, 2013; Hugree, Penissat, and Spire, 2020).

Given the absence of substantial European industrial and social policies to reorient them, economic forces were by and large left to their own devices. As a result, the SMP, the EMU, and accession processes strengthened the productive apparatus in the EU's old core (namely, in countries that belonged to the former Deutschmark zone). In the eurozone's periphery, interest-rate convergence fuelled speculative property investments instead of productive ones, which would have allowed sustainable growth (Aglietta, 2019: 66).

This happened even in countries like Ireland, where governments included unions in social pacts and adopted policies in favour of the creation of new industrial clusters (McDonough and Dundon, 2010; Ó Riain, 2014; Roche, O'Connell, and Prothero, 2016). In contrast, firms in core countries benefitted from two mutually reinforcing trends: (1) increasing economies of scale (in the enlarged EU market) and (2) increasing agglomeration effects whereby the most innovative and productive businesses prefer existing innovation hubs to greenfield peripheral locations (Aglietta, 2019: 78). Thus, the economies in the EU's strongest economies benefitted the most from economic and monetary unification, also because the introduction of the Euro removed any danger of countervailing currency revaluations in the former Deutschmark zone (Erne, 2008: 101). In turn, the SMP and the accession process led to a restructuring of productive capacities in the EU's new eastern periphery at the price of its continued dependence on the core (Hardy, 2009; Bohle and Greskovits, 2012; Simonazzi, Ginzburg, and Nocella, 2013; Ban, 2014; Stan and Erne, 2014).

From an international political economy perspective, the making and enlargement of the internal market and monetary union led to a new transnational division of labour that affected the economies of different member states differently. From a labour perspective however, economic integration increased the competitive pressures on wages and working conditions everywhere. Workers in high-wage, core countries faced increased threats from firms that they would relocate, and economic and monetary EU integration exposed lower-paid workers from peripheral locations to increased transnational competition, not least given their employers' subordinate position in transnational supply chains. In addition, just before the advent of the 2008 crisis, the Court of Justice of the European Union (CJEU) further accentuated the imbalance between the EU's economic and social objectives by prioritising the transnational economic freedoms of corporations over workers' social rights (Dølvik and Visser, 2009; Schiek, 2012; Garben, 2017; Arnholtz and Lillie, 2019; Wagner, 2020). Thus, although economic EU integration led to a much more integrated production system on the continent, it also amplified social divisions inside countries and transnationally across Europe.

By the 2000s, economic EU integration had also become increasingly politicised (Höpner and Schäfer, 2010; Schulz-Forberg and Stråth, 2014; Zürn, 2016), with unions and social movements (Turnbull, 2006; Erne, 2008; della Porta and Caiani, 2009) and the European Parliament playing an increasingly influential role (Hix and Høyland, 2013). Calls for a more political Europe also led to the draft Treaty establishing a Constitution for Europe in 2004. Many proponents of a social and democratic Europe had already been supporting a shift from economic to political integration in the 1990s (Habermas, 1992; Erne et al., 1995; Golden, 2024). After the introduction of the Euro, some promoters of economic integration called for more political EU interventions too (Buti and van den Noord, 2004), albeit for different reasons, namely, to trigger structural reforms in member states that would consolidate the internal market and monetary union and enhance their competitiveness (Trichet, 2006). In the following, we thus assess the political dynamics of EU integration before describing the shift to the EU's NEG regime in section 2.3.

Political Dynamics

The devastation caused by fascism and World War II amplified calls, including from trade unionists (Buschak, 2014), for a democratic, federal Europe (Spinelli and Rossi, 2013 [1941]). The first attempts to create one failed though. To uphold human rights and democracy in Europe, ten countries[3] created the Council of Europe (CoE) in 1949 as an international and not a federal organisation.[4] The constitution of a Political European Community, with a directly elected Peoples' Chamber, a Senate, and a supranational Executive accountable to parliament (Karp, 1954), equally unravelled in 1954 (Griffiths, 1994). European integration thus became an economic venture, albeit one that continued to be shaped by powerful political dynamics.

In 1951, six countries[5] created the European Coal and Steel Community (ECSC), which was led, by contrast to the CoE, by a *supranational* High Authority, the latter-day European Commission. The ECSC Treaty also established a *supranational* Court, the latter-day CJEU (Art. 31, ECSC Treaty). Whereas the High Authority was subject to judicial review, the actions of the ECSC executive did not depend on a democratic, popular mandate, even though the ECSC Treaty also created an Assembly, the latter-day European Parliament, which could dismiss the High Authority by a no-confidence vote (Art. 24, ECSC Treaty). The ECSC was tasked with

---

[3] Belgium, Denmark, France, Ireland, Italy, Luxemburg, the Netherlands, Norway, Sweden, and the United Kingdom.
[4] Over time, however, the CoE – which should not be confused with either the Council of the European Union (Art. 16 TEU) or its European Council (Art. 15 TEU) – did develop some supranational features, namely, the European Court of Human Rights set up in 1959 in Strasbourg. The Strasbourg court can claim superiority over national laws, court rulings, and practices if they contravene the CoE's European Convention on Human Rights.
[5] Belgium, France, Italy, Luxembourg, the Netherlands, and West Germany.

overseeing the post-war reconstruction of the steel and coal sector not only for economic but also for political reasons. This was outlined by the French foreign minister, Robert Schuman, who proposed its creation: 'By pooling basic production and by instituting a new High Authority, whose decisions will bind France, Germany and other member countries, this proposal will lead to the realization of the first concrete foundation of a European federation indispensable to the preservation of peace' (European Commission, 2020a). According to neo-functionalist European integration scholar Ernst Haas (1958 [2004]), the promotors of the ECSC in 1951 and the EEC and European Atomic Energy Community (Euratom) in 1957 were convinced that political integration would ultimately follow from the creation of these *European communities* as a spill-over from economic integration.

Although the making of an integrated European common market and customs union required *supranational* laws, the exact dosage of supranationalism and intergovernmentalism remained a contested issue among decision makers, lawyers, and scholars from the outset. At every stage in the 'process of creating an ever closer union among the peoples of Europe' (Art. 1 TEU), different visions emerged of what the EU should be. To what extent should member states retain their autonomy and just pool their sovereignty on a case-by-case basis (intergovernmentalism) or does European integration also require supranational state structures to govern an ever more integrated economy (federalism)? During their first three decades, the European communities worked largely as an intergovernmental organisation despite the founders' federal ambitions. This changed in 1987, when the SEA extended qualified majority voting in the Council to more policy areas to facilitate the implementation of its single market programme by new EU laws. In 1993, the Treaty of Maastricht extended qualified majority voting to additional areas, including working conditions and public services, and gave the European Parliament more co-legislation rights. At long last, Haas' neo-functionalist hypothesis seemed to be confirmed. In foreign and security policy, or pay and healthcare policy, however, member states retained much of their policymaking powers. Furthermore, the Maastricht Treaty counterbalanced the power of the supranational Commission by institutionalising the intergovernmental European Council of heads of state or government and by tasking it to 'provide the Union with the necessary impetus for its development' (Art. D TEU; now Art. 15(1) TEU). In employment relations and public services, EU policymaking followed therefore neither an intergovernmental nor a supranational approach. Instead, it has been described as a multilevel governance regime that displays different combinations of intergovernmental collaboration and supranational EU authority (Marginson and Sisson, 2004).

Both intergovernmentalist and supranationalist EU scholars have focused their studies on institutional questions, addressing the question of the formation of a European polity, usually in terms of an opposition between national and supranational decision makers.[6] However, their focus on political executives, namely, the Council and the Commission, often neglects questions about democratic accountability. Regardless of whether EU decisions are made at intergovernmental Council or supranational Commission meetings, in both settings national and European parliaments and publics play a secondary role. To be able to assess also the prospects of a more democratic EU, we must enlarge our analytical perspectives. We therefore analyse not only institutional processes but also the roles played by non-governmental actors, namely, trade unions and social movements, which also contributed to the making of social and democratic states at national level. In addition, we must place EU integration within broader developments in capitalist accumulation.

As shown in historical European studies, political authority over a population included few rights at the outset (i.e., civic rights to private property) and only subsequently more fundamental political and social rights (Marshall, 1950). The establishment of European state structures has usually been a product of coercion and economic capital accumulation (Tilly, 1992). Political and social rights usually followed afterwards as ruling elites' response to countervailing social movements (Marshall, 1950; Galbraith, 1952; Habermas, 1992). Although 'soft-liners' within ruling classes often played a key role in past democratisation processes (O'Donnell and Schmitter, 2013 [1986]: xviii), Western Europe's democracies and welfare states were not created out of the blue by benevolent rulers. Rather, they were usually the outcome of the social (class) struggles and subsequent class compromises between organised labour and capital (Rueschemeyer, Huber Stephens, and Stephens, 1992).

The creation of welfare states would not have been possible without labour's struggles for a democratisation of social and economic policymaking, namely, through an extension of political rights to participation in decision making and of social rights shielding workers from market pressures and vagaries (Marshall, 1950; Foot, 2005). These struggles included calls not only for more democracy in politics and society but also for actions that *politicised* social and economic issues by bringing them into the public sphere of debate and policy intervention. After World War II, Western European labour movements therefore

---

[6] The view that the national–supranational divide would be the most significant dimension of EU policymaking shapes even EU scholars' multilevel governance approach, which tries to overcome the polarised views of intergovernmentalists and federalists.

partially succeeded in shifting the conflict between workers and employers from the marketplace to the political arena, thereby embedding liberalism (Ruggie, 1982). This stabilised the capitalist economy and led to the creation of European social welfare states (Crouch, 1999; Millward, 2005; Wahl, 2011), with three key dimensions: individual and collective labour rights, social protection, and public utilities (Supiot, 2013).

Building on Stein Rokkan (1999) and his own work (Bartolini 2000) on the formation of democratic states, Stefano Bartolini (2005) stressed that the formation of EU state structures requires not only democratic participation rights but also the building of a welfare system. Others have reached similar conclusions (Habermas, 1992; Erne et al., 1995; Schmitter, 2000; Erne, 2008). EU policymaking in employment relations and public services is thus connected to political integration as well as its democratisation and politicisation. An exclusive focus on the institutional (national/supranational) dimensions of EU policymaking would thus be too narrow in scope to understand the links between EU governance and its democratisation – hence our focus on interest groups and social movements.

As seen in the previous section on economic integration however, the creation of the internal market resulted in 'regime competition' (Streeck, 1992), which exposed employment relations and public services across Europe to increased commodifying market pressures. Workers perceived this process of renewed commodification of labour, social protection, and public utilities as resulting mostly from either impersonal market forces or interventions by national governments. Countervailing trade union action therefore usually targeted the latter rather than the more distant EU. This was possible also because the shift to negative integration, following the 1986 SEA, left the formal autonomy of national labour and social policy regimes intact. Thus, these regimes could still react differently to the pressures of the increased market and regime competition unleashed by EMU and EU accession processes. This triggered a torrent of institutionalist research about the different national 'varieties of capitalism' and labour politics (Thelen, 2001). Until the 1990s, apart from some notable exceptions (Lefébure and Lagneau, 2001; Erne, 2008), national trade unions therefore found few reasons for EU-level action and were mostly invested in concession bargaining to defend labour and social standards at national, regional, or local level as well as they could.

The obstacles to positive EU integration in social policy fields, seen in the section above, led to an inbuilt asymmetry between market-making and market-correcting EU laws, which favoured capital. Nonetheless, unions started to build – intersectoral and sectoral – European umbrella organisations (Gobin, 1996; Dølvik, 1997; Degryse and Tilly, 2013; Fischbach-Pyttel, 2017) and participated in EU policymaking in the hope of obtaining some labour and social rights at EU level in exchange for their support for the integration process (Crouch, 2000; Erne, 2008). These included the SEA's Treaty articles on occupational health and safety and the Maastricht Treaty's protocol on social policy that facilitated the adoption of directives in these fields by a qualified majority vote (instead of unanimity) in the Council (see Chapter 6). Although the EU's social legislative agenda went much further than Scharpf and Streeck had initially expected, overall, its achievements remained quite modest, also because of loopholes in many social EU directives that firms and governments could exploit to derail their application in practice.[7] By contrast, the EU laws that created the internal market and monetary union left national policymakers much less room for manoeuvre.

A few days before the Euro became an everyday reality, the European Council (2001) thus acknowledged that European citizens would be 'calling for a clear, open, effective and democratically controlled Community approach' and tasked a Convention of national and EU-level public representatives to draft a Constitution for European citizens. Despite these democratic openings, however, the European Council also restated that the 'basic issue should continue to be proper operation of the internal market and the single currency' (2001: 21).

Popular political pressures for a more democratic EU led to a partial democratisation of EU decision-making processes. In the 1980s, the Commission used its powers to open up public services to competition through the adoption of Commission Directives (Art. 106(3) Treaty on the Functioning of the European Union: TFEU). After the Commission decided to marketise the public telecommunications sector on its own, several governments challenged its power to do that before the CJEU. Although the governments lost their legal battle in court, they nevertheless won the war. In fact, the Commission thereafter felt obliged to abandon its exclusive legislative competition policy powers concerning public services 'in favour of conventional law-making processes involving the Council and Parliament' (Maher, 2021b: 832; see also Chapter 7). The marketisation of public utilities henceforth relied on inter-institutional, political compromises and thus progressed more slowly (see Chapters 7 and 8).

The democratisation of EU law-making went also beyond these institutional actors, as the Treaty of Maastricht introduced European social dialogue

---

[7] At times, however, notionally 'weaker' institutional power resources provided by EU laws can give workers more effective leverage for collective action than those provided by 'stronger' national labour laws, as shown by a transnational campaign of Ryanair pilots in 2017, which forced the Ryanair management to recognise trade unions (Golden and Erne, 2022).

with representative EU-level organisations of management and labour, giving them formal co-decision rights in EU social policymaking (Arts. 154 and 155 TFEU). The partial democratisation of EU policymaking also went beyond organised interest groups to include EU citizens at large: the European Citizens' Initiative (ECI) introduced in the Treaty of Lisbon (2007) gives groups composed of at least one million European citizens from at least seven different member states the right to make a legislative proposition to the Commission (Art. 11(4) TEU; Szabó, Golden, and Erne, 2022).

The more the EU democratised its legislative procedures, the more trade unions and social movements became aware of the threat of commodifying EU laws for employment relations and public services and mobilised against them across borders. By the mid-2000s, the Commission's attempts to deregulate public services by EU laws had run out of steam, as the countermovements that they triggered motivated the European Parliament to curb the Commission's commodifying bent through legislative amendments, for example in the case of Commissioner Bolkestein's draft Services Directive of 2004 (COM(2004) 2 final/3) (Erne, 2008; della Porta and Caiani, 2009; Crespy, 2012). The referendums on the draft Treaty establishing a Constitution for Europe (hereinafter, constitutional treaty or CT) did 'bring citizens closer to the European design and European Institutions' (CT, Preface), but without producing the desired effects. Instead of consolidating the 'proper operation of the internal market and the single currency' (European Council, 2001: 21), the French and Dutch referendum debates on the CT in 2005 and the parallel discussions on the draft Bolkestein Directive gave social movements and unions an exceptional opportunity to politicise and reject the policy orientation of the EU's economic integration processes in a European public sphere (Kohler-Koch and Quittkat, 2013; Béthoux, Erne, and Golden, 2018). The more EU governance by hard law triggered political countermovements, the more the EU relied on new governance tools.

In 2000, the European Council launched its Lisbon strategy, which aimed to turn the EU, by 2010, into the most competitive economy in the world. To achieve this objective, the EU relied on tools introduced in the previous decade, namely, the Broad Economic Policy Guidelines (BEPGs) introduced by the Maastricht Treaty (Art. 121 TFEU) and the Open Method of Coordination (OMC) introduced by the Amsterdam Treaty (Art. 148 TFEU). These procedures sought to achieve a greater convergence of national policies towards the EU's economic and social goals, namely, through a combination of numerical benchmarks, country-specific reports and recommendations, mutual learning, and peer pressure (Armstrong, 2010). Although not legally binding, these 'soft law' mechanisms nevertheless had 'practical effects' (Snyder, 1993: 32). They created stronger links between national and EU officials and crafted a new way of governing that depoliticised policymaking and strengthened policymakers' capacity to govern at a distance from popular pressures (Miller and Rose, 1990; Lascoumes and Le Galès, 2004). Even so, trade unionists hardly found these new governance mechanisms threatening. After all, the promotors of the Lisbon agenda still tried to reconcile opposing social interests, as shown by the introduction of composite terms – such as 'flexicurity' – into the Euro-speak vocabulary (Hyman, 2005: 26). The Lisbon strategy's non-binding nature also reassured those who feared commodifying EU interventions in the social field. After the crisis of 2008 however, EU leaders broke the institutional padlocks that had hitherto constrained direct EU interventions in employment and social fields without much ado and set up the much more constraining NEG regime.

2.3 THE EU'S NEW ECONOMIC GOVERNANCE REGIME AFTER 2008

The making of the EU's NEG regime marks a major shift in EU policymaking. NEG provides new tools for the European Commission and Council not only to issue policy prescriptions to member states in areas of employment relations and public services but also to enforce them. In this section, we outline the economic and political context in which NEG was set up after the 2008 financial crisis, its coercive architecture, and the mechanisms that led to its institutionalisation at the beginning of the 2010s.

A Silent Revolution from Above

Before 2008, EU laws that directly affected employment relations and public services were rare, even though the SMP and EMU exposed workers and welfare states to increased competitive market pressures. Most European business and centre-right political leaders did not think that this would be a problem. Employment relations and social policy should remain a matter for national social partners and policymakers (Léonard et al., 2007), regardless of the frictions that the making of the internal market and monetary union might entail. Although economic and monetary integration would make labour and social policy adjustments necessary, business and centre-right political leaders thought that the increased competition between different national industrial relations and welfare regimes triggered by it would suffice to ensure the EU's cohesion quasi automatically (Erne, 2008: 54).

After 2008 however, the views of European business and centre-right political leaders changed dramatically when they realised that the internal market and monetary union did not 'promote economic, social and territorial cohesion, and solidarity among Member States' (Art. 3(3) TEU) but led to threatening macroeconomic imbalances between them. In June 2010, the European organisation of organised capital therefore urged the Commission and Council to draft a 'European framework' for 'product, labour, health care and social security reforms' (Business Europe, 2010: 7). This was a major policy shift, as Europe's business leaders had perceived the mere interest of EU authorities in employment relations under the banner of governance as 'too much intervention' only a few years earlier (Léonard et al., 2007: 7).[8]

To prevent the collapse of the monetary union, which 'would lead to a chain reaction that might well bring down the European Union as a whole' (Beck, 2013: 24), the EU adopted a much more interventionist NEG regime. In these exceptional situations, the existing order 'may legitimately be suspended to defend the common good' (2013: 27). The 'impending catastrophe empowers and even forces the Europe builders to exploit legal loopholes so as to open the door to changes' (2013: 26–27). Although Ulrich Beck acknowledged that the rhetoric of the 'imminent collapse of Europe may easily result in the birth of a political monster' (2013: 28), the sociologist of the risk society condoned the route taken by EU leaders as a response necessitated by the financial crisis. This pathway involved unlocking the many constitutional padlocks that had hitherto stood in the way of a more interventionist EU governance regime in employment relations and public services.

Across the globe, the upheavals caused by the financial crisis shattered into pieces 'the sophisticated but conceptually hollow premise on which the framework of self-regulating markets had been built' (Griffith-Jones, Ocampo, and Stiglitz, 2010: 1). Within the EU, the crisis seemed to vindicate the views of heterodox economic sociologists and political economists who had long argued that the single market and monetary union would require a *gouvernement économique européen* (Albert, 1997: 584) or even a *gouvernement européen tout court* (Boyer and Dehove, 2001). At first, many centre-left politicians and trade union advisors thus welcomed the shift to a more interventionist EU governance regime (Erne, 2012a, 2012b). This shift, however, soon disappointed those who believed in 2008 that the crisis would lead to a shift away from the free-market credo towards more social policies. In fact, the failures of neoliberal theory did little to weaken the power of corporate business interests in EU socioeconomic policymaking (Crouch,

---

[8] Incidentally, this shift also shows that the widespread EU assumptions about the internal market and monetary union as a tool to achieve economic and social cohesion 'were ideologically informed' and 'baseless, empirically' (Kochenov, 2019: 218; see also de Búrca, 2015; Stan and Erne, 2021b).

2011). As political leaders considered private banks to be systemically relevant, the banks managed to turn even the threat of their 'imminent ruin' into a powerful political asset (Erne, 2020: 260; Stiglitz, 2010). After 2008, the Commission thus approved national bank bailouts of unprecedented proportion. Intriguingly, by doing this, the Commission reinterpreted, in 'a highly politicised environment' (Maher, 2021b: 833), the EU Treaties' competition policy principles that seemed to stipulate that state aid for private corporations was incompatible with the internal market (Buch-Hansen and Wigger, 2011).[9]

Facing competing pressures from business associations, unions, and governments, the European Commission and Council of finance ministers (EU executives) adopted a crisis narrative that mirrored different political concerns – as outlined below – but still went in a business-friendly direction (Syrovatka, 2022a: 211–299). First, EU executives endorsed the calls of business interests and surplus countries[10] for the curtailment of public spending. At the same time, EU executives endorsed calls for a supranational surveillance of national employment and social policies. Although this policy shift echoed long-standing Keynesian concerns of centre-left politicians and trade union economists (Erne, 2008; Delors, Fernandes, and Mermet, 2011), it did not represent a shift to the left. The EU executives just decided that the Euro's success would depend not only on the curtailment of public spending in deficit countries but also on a much more constraining pan-European strategy of employment relations and public services reforms. This conclusion mirrored the shift of Business Europe (2010) in favour of stronger EU powers in labour, healthcare, and social policy, which was supported also by the American Chamber of Commerce, southern European organised capital, and MEDEF, the movement of French enterprises (Syrovatka, 2022a: 221–224). The German employer and business associations, BDA and BDI (2010), however, remarkably did not favour it, as they feared that a more supranational labour and social policy regime would lead to EU calls for higher wages in Germany, which would counteract the export-oriented strategies of German firms (2010: 4).

A Constraining Governance Architecture

When some member states were no longer able to refinance their public debt after the crisis, the EU concluded several bailout programmes with member

---

[9] Art. 127(1) TFEU states that 'save as otherwise provided in the Treaties, any aid granted by a Member State or through State resources in any form whatsoever which distorts or threatens to distort competition by favouring certain undertakings or the production of certain goods shall, in so far as it affects trade between Member States, be incompatible with the internal market'.

[10] That is, countries with a current account balance surplus, like the Netherlands and Germany.

states in collaboration with the International Monetary Fund (IMF) and, in eurozone countries, also with the European Central Bank (ECB). These programmes made EU bailout funding conditional on the implementation of strict policy prescriptions, including in policy fields hitherto believed to be shielded from top-down EU interventions. This happened despite the EU's allegedly 'ordoliberal' (Joerges, 2013) principles that would outlaw the massive bailouts of private banks, the Treaty's no-bailout clause that would outlaw EU funding for its member states (Art. 125 TFEU),[11] and its Charter of Fundamental Rights. Regardless of their liminal legality, the EU first approved massive state aid packages for ailing private banks and then conditional state bailout programmes of around €500 billion, which is a lot more than the EU's annual budget of around €140 billion (Kilpatrick, 2017: 338).[12] Arguably, the EU could also have let banks or member states default on their debt repayments. This option was not chosen though, as EU and ECB leaders feared that even partial defaults could lead to the collapse of the Euro, which would represent a systemic risk to capitalist accumulation in general (Harvey, 2010; Tooze, 2018). In its subsequent case law, the EU's CJEU upheld the legality of the EU's NEG regime. To that end, the CJEU had to advance an interpretation of Treaty provisions that was not 'always the legally obvious' one (Barrett, 2020: 5).[13] The Memoranda of Understanding (MoUs) with

---

[11] According to Art. 125 TFEU, 'the Union shall not be liable for or assume the commitments of central governments, regional, local or other public authorities, other bodies governed by public law, or public undertakings of any Member State without prejudice to mutual financial guarantees for the joint execution of a specific project'.

[12] Eurozone finance ministers also approved an assistance programme for the Spanish financial sector under the European Stability Mechanism (ESM), which the EU leaders created after amending Art. 136 TFEU by Decision 2011/199 in 2011. Furthermore, the ECB purchased private and public assets for more than €2,500 billion between October 2014 and December 2018 to support the EU economy (Kilpatrick, 2017).

[13] In Case C-370/12 *Thomas Pringle v Government of Ireland*, 27 November 2012, for example, the CJEU ruled that the EU bailout mechanisms, such as the ESM, would be legal, despite the TFEU's no-bailout clause (Art. 125). In so doing, the CJEU reinterpreted the aim of Art. 125 TFEU as an obligation to keep member states submitted to the 'logic of the market' that apparently guided the drafters of the EU treaties (Case C-370/12, para. 135). Consequently, EU bailout mechanisms would be legal as long as they enforced that submission to the market through political demands (or 'conditionalities') favouring fiscal discipline and structural adjustment. To secure the stability of the eurozone as a whole, the CJEU also '"discovered" an ultimate objective for EMU (safeguarding the financial stability of the euro area) that had no basis in the Treaties' (Hinarejos, 2015: 125–126). Gavin Barrett (2020: 6) thus described the *Pringle* ruling 'as the case in which the European Court of Justice cautiously deferred to a revolution ... in order to save the Eurozone: a revolution, in effect to save the status quo'. Whereas 'judicial activism was needed to advance the cause of European integration' in the past, in the financial crisis 'something quite different was needed, that the law not become an obstacle. Thanks to the case-law of the Court of Justice, this need was met' (Barrett, 2020: 5–6).

three non-eurozone (Hungary, Latvia, and Romania) and four eurozone (Greece, Ireland, Portugal, and Cyprus) member states signed by the EU between 2008 and 2015 could thus include binding prescriptions on employment relations and social policies, despite EU executives' lack of legislative powers in these fields. As non-compliance would lead to a withdrawal of EU bailout funding, the level of constraint faced by a member state in relation to MoU-related prescriptions was very significant.

The strict conditionalities of MoU did not affect only bailout programme countries. The MoU's approach to budgetary discipline and policy changes also served as a general model for the silent revolution from above that the then Commission President, José Manuel Barroso, had already announced in 2010. This revolution took the form of a package of new EU laws that strengthened the EU's economic governance powers in relation to all its member states. Using a dormant Maastricht Treaty paragraph as its legal basis,[14] the European Parliament and Council adopted the Six-Pack of EU laws on EU economic governance in 2011. The Two-Pack, which they adopted in 2013, further institutionalised the powers of the Commission and the Council in national fiscal policy (Bauer and Becker, 2014).

Instead of steering member states' policies through the classical method of governing by law in accordance with the EU's ordinary legislative procedure, the Six-Pack institutionalised the NEG regime that steers member state policies through new public management tools, for example numerical benchmarks, country-specific ad hoc prescriptions, and an extraordinary policy enforcement regime. According to the Six-Pack laws, the Commission can propose fines for non-compliant states. In the event of excessive deficits, Regulation 1173/2011 allows yearly fines of up to 0.2 per cent of GDP for non-complying eurozone countries (Erne, 2012b; Bauer and Becker, 2014). In contrast to the fines foreseen in the original Stability and Growth Pact (SGP) adopted in 1997,[15] the Commission's fines apply automatically unless a qualified majority of national finance ministers vetoes them within a ten-day period. The Six-Pack thus substantially enhanced the sanctioning mechanisms behind the SGP's excessive deficit procedure (EDP), which is the corrective arm of the EU's surveillance regime that aims to ensure member states' compliance with the EU's deficit and debt criteria. Although the EU's reference values for its EDP

---

[14] 'The European Parliament and the Council ... may adopt detailed rules for the multilateral surveillance' (Art. 121(6) TFEU).
[15] Council Regulation (EC) 1466/97: On the strengthening of the surveillance of budgetary positions and the surveillance and coordination of economic policies, and Council Regulation (EC) 1467/97: On speeding up and clarifying the implementation of the excessive deficit procedure.

are clear-cut,[16] most member states exceed them most of the time; but what matters for an EDP against a state are not reference values as such but the Commission's assessment of their trajectory. This gives the Commission considerable leeway in relation to member states' budgetary policies.[17] In 2013, the Six-Pack's rules on budget deficits were strengthened further by the Two-Pack of EU laws that enhanced the Commission's control over national budgetary processes and by the Treaty on Stability, Coordination, and Governance in the Economic and Monetary Union (or Fiscal Treaty), in which EU member states committed themselves to introducing balanced budget rules and automatic fiscal correction mechanisms in their own legal systems.

In addition to the enhanced EDP, the Six-Pack laws introduced a novel Macroeconomic Imbalance Procedure (MIP), which likewise foresees fines that the Commission can enforce unless a reversed qualified majority of finance ministers vetoes them within ten days. MIP Regulation 1176/2011 allows yearly fines of up to 0.1 per cent of GDP for eurozone countries that display excessive macroeconomic imbalances and fail to enact the corresponding EU corrective action plans. Compared with the EDP, the MIP rests on an even vaguer definition of what constitutes a punishable infringement, that is, *excessive imbalances* in the MIP case. According to Art. 2 of the MIP Regulation, these 'mean severe imbalances, including imbalances that jeopardise *or risk jeopardising* the *proper functioning* of economic and monetary union' (emphasis added).[18] This definition is so all-encompassing that no employment and social policy area can a priori be placed out of its reach, as almost all employment relations and social policies restrict the apparent self-sufficient functioning of markets (Erne, 2012b).

---

[16] 'The reference values referred to in Art. 126(2) of the Treaty on the Functioning of the European Union are: 3% for the ratio of the planned or actual government deficit to gross domestic product at market prices; 60% for the ratio of government debt to gross domestic product at market prices' (Art. 1, Protocol 12, TFEU).

[17] 'The Commission shall monitor the development of the budgetary situation and of the stock of government debt in the Member States with a view to identifying gross errors. In particular it shall examine compliance with budgetary discipline on the basis of the following two criteria: (a) whether the ratio of the planned or actual government deficit to gross domestic product exceeds a reference value, *unless*: – either the ratio has declined substantially and continuously and reached a level that comes close to the reference value, – or, alternatively, the excess over the reference value is only exceptional and temporary and the ratio remains close to the reference value; (b) whether the ratio of government debt to gross domestic product exceeds a reference value, *unless* the ratio is sufficiently diminishing and approaching the reference value at a satisfactory pace' (emphasis added) (Art. 126(2) TFEU).

[18] This formulation can already be found in the Maastricht Treaty (Art. 103(4) TEC, now Art. 121(4) TFEU) but only regarding the non-binding Broad Economic Policy Guidelines and not as a basis for the issuing of financial fines in the event of non-compliance.

The scoreboard of MIP indicators, which Art. 4 of Regulation 1176/2011 tasked the Commission to set up, does not clarify the limits of MIP-related NEG interventions in employment relations and public services either. By contrast, the scoreboard confirms the encompassing remit of the MIP, as four of its fourteen headline indicators affect labour and social policy, namely, unit labour cost, unemployment, long-term unemployment, and youth unemployment rates. The inclusion of these four social indicators, however, is not a sign of a social turn in the MIP. Their use rather indicates a vision that sees labour as a troublesome factor of production that can jeopardise the proper functioning of the European economy. This is evidenced by the scoreboard's benchmark for unit labour cost increases, which defines only a ceiling but no floor for them. This is very problematic, as the unequal wage developments across the EU in the 2000s were caused not by excessive wage increases in the EU's periphery (i.e., wage increases above national inflation and productivity rates) but by excessive wage moderation policies in a core country, namely, Germany (Erne, 2008). Conversely, the scoreboard's ceilings for unemployment, long-term unemployment, and youth unemployment rates seem to point in a social direction. What matters, however, is not only the design of the MIP indicators as such. More important is the policy direction of the subsequent NEG prescriptions that the EU issues to reach them. To lower unemployment rates, for example, EU executives issued NEG prescriptions that urged the Italian government to weaken the Italian labour law, which protected workers against unjustified dismissals (Chapter 6).

The MIP thus became a significant tool for making inroads into the structural reform agenda first advanced through EU laws on the internal market and monetary union as well as the non-binding Broad Economic Policy Guidelines (BEPGs) that EU executives began to issue after the adoption of the Maastricht Treaty in 1993. However, whereas the former ran out of steam in the 2000s following the democratisation of the EU's ordinary legislative procedure, the latter lacked coercive power, as outlined in section 2.1. By adopting MIP Regulation No 1176/2011, the European Parliament de facto delegated its legislative power to define what constitutes appropriate socioeconomic policies to the Commission and the Council's Economic Policy Committee (EPC) advising it.[19] The Commission and the EPC not only designed the MIP scoreboard, which is meant to identify those

---

[19] The EPC, comprising two delegates from each member state, the Commission, and the ECB, advises the Council and the Commission by providing analyses, methodologies, and draft formulations for policy recommendations. Its proceedings are confidential, https://europa.eu/epc/.

countries whose socioeconomic policies require an in-depth review but also drafts the country-specific recommendations (CSRs) and, if necessary, corrective action plans to ensure the 'proper' functioning of the European economy.

The Commission also plays a central role in the sanctioning procedures underpinning both EDP and MIP procedures. So far however, the 'atomic bomb character' (Calmfors, 2012: 11) of the fines for non-complying member states has prevented the Commission from triggering them. Even so, the Commission succeeded in nudging reluctant member states to take NEG prescriptions seriously, namely, when they threatened to open an EDP or an MIP against those member states. This happened, for example, in 2018, when the first Italian government led by Prime Minister Conte initially declined to follow EU advice in relation to its 2019 budget law. After the Conte government was confronted with both the Commission's determination to sanction it and increasing interest payments demanded by holders of Italian government bonds, the Italian government felt obliged to revise its stance and reach an accord with the Commission (Fabbrini, 2022; Gasseau and Maccarrone, 2023).

Since 2014, all EU structural and investment funding has depended on 'sound economic governance', which means the implementation of MoU, SGP, and MIP prescriptions by the member state concerned (Art. 23, Regulation 1303/2013 of the European Parliament and of the Council of 17 December 2013). Hence, EU social and cohesion funding became conditional on the implementation of NEG's policy agenda (Costamagna and Miglio, 2021; Syrovatka, 2022a), even though local recipients of EU funding can hardly be held responsible for excessive imbalances or deficits (Jouen, 2015). This set in train a money-for-reforms approach that fundamentally reoriented the purpose of the EU's social and cohesion funding. Whereas the EEC's social funds offset the negative effects of horizontal market integration, the structural reform clause of Common Provisions Regulation 1303/2013 turned the EU's social and cohesion funding into an instrument for the further advancement of market integration.

As all facets of the NEG regime are interrelated, EU executives introduced a new policymaking process in 2011, the European Semester, which integrates all NEG interventions in one overarching procedure.

How NEG Works: The European Semester

The EU's ordinary legislative procedure understands politics as a process of democratic interest intermediation between conflicting social and political interests. To reshape member states' policies, the Commission must therefore propose specific, universally applicable laws and get them adopted by the

European Parliament and the Council. In the social policy field, the Commission must also consult the European confederations of employers and trade unions on possible directions of its proposals (Art. 154(2) TFEU). 'Should management and labour so desire', their EU-level agreements can even be 'implemented by a Council decision on a proposal from the Commission' (Art. 155(2) TFEU), making social partners 'co-legislators' at EU level (Welz, 2008: 357).

NEG does not follow this logic of democratic interest intermediation. It is instead a new policymaking space at the borderline of democracy, bypassing national and European parliaments and social partners (Habermas, 2011). Whereas labour politics had been an arena of interest intermediation between organised capital and labour – and right- and left-wing political parties, respectively – NEG frames politics in technocratic terms as a conflict between the 'right and the wrong' (Mouffe, 2011: 5). Hence, NEG gave the Commission and the Council a complementary (and arguably more efficient) policymaking tool that is less prone to parliamentary intermediations and the veto power of social partners, more holistic in terms of its overarching strategic goals, and country-specific in its focus by comparison with the EU's ordinary legislative procedure.

The EU bailout programmes, the excessive deficit procedure (EDP) of the revised SGP, and the new macroeconomic imbalance procedure (MIP) thus came to complement and overlay the EU's economic growth strategy called Europe 2020. All four mechanisms were brought together in 2011 when the EU introduced an annual cycle of country-specific policy prescriptions, surveillance, and enforcement in the guise of the European Semester (the Semester). The Semester has thus institutionalised NEG as a system of policy coordination and surveillance drawing on four legal strands: the legally binding MoU, EDP, MIP, and the non-binding Europe 2020 strategy.

The Semester begins with a strategic Commission document that outlines the EU's Annual Growth Strategy (AGS),[20] proceeds with the Commission's assessment of member states' progress in implementing the NEG agenda (in Country Reports and, if necessary, in-depth reviews), and ends with a Council Recommendation for each member state that includes several policy prescriptions outlining their tasks. As shown in Figure 2.1, the recommendations are drafted by the Commission in May and adopted by the Council (of finance ministers) in July. Each recommendation document includes several

---

[20] Since the 2020 cycle, the AGS is called Annual Sustainable Growth Strategy.

34 Analytical Framework

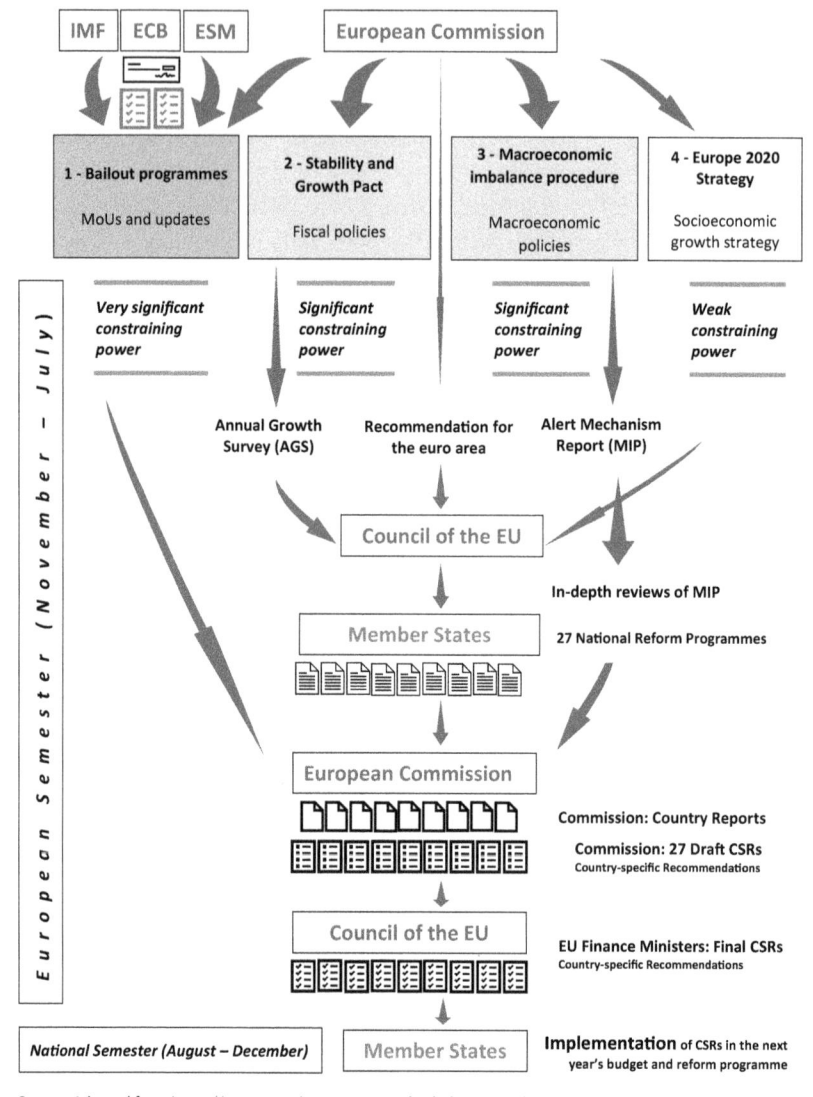

FIGURE 2.1 The four faces of the EU's new economic governance (NEG) regime

Source: Adapted from https://www.consilium.europa.eu/en/infographics/european-semester/; own illustration.

CSRs on fiscal and economic as well as employment relations and public services matters.

Figure 2.1 also shows that the Council Recommendations issued since 2011 integrated all NEG prescriptions in one document, despite their different legal foundations. Concretely, Council Recommendations include policy prescriptions based on the following strands of the NEG regime:

(1) Memoranda of Understanding (MoUs) specifying the strict conditions attached to EU bailout funding. If a member state was subject to an EU bailout programme, the Council Recommendation that it received stated that it had to implement the prescriptions specified by the corresponding MoU and its updates.
(2) The Stability and Growth Pact (SGP), which aims to discipline member states' fiscal policies (as revised by the Six- and Two-Pack laws of 2011 and 2013).
(3) The Macroeconomic Imbalance Procedure (MIP), which aims to prevent and correct macroeconomic imbalances (as introduced by the Six-Pack laws).
(4) Europe 2020, which was the EU's 'smart, sustainable, and inclusive' growth strategy for 2010–2020. It was based merely on a Commission Communication (COM [2010] 2020 final) and formally not binding. Europe 2020 replaced the Lisbon strategy (2000–2010).

The integration of policy prescriptions, emanating from different but interdependent strands, in one document appears to favour a holistic, multidimensional approach to socioeconomic governance. Yet, the social goals of the Europe 2020 strategy are subordinated to the 'meta-priority of the structural stability of monetary union' (Pochet and Degryse, 2013: 109). This becomes clear by comparing the weak constraining power of social Europe 2020 prescriptions (backed merely by the naming and shaming of non-compliant states) with the significant constraining power of SGP/MIP prescriptions (backed by fines) and the very significant constraining power of MoU-related prescriptions, given the threat of a withdrawal of financial assistance in the event of non-compliance. We therefore cannot treat all CSRs equally, as is usual among other scholars in the field (see Chapters 4 and 5). As MoU-, SGP-, and MIP-related NEG prescriptions constrain the range of national policy options, we can also no longer dismiss NEG recommendations as mere soft law (Bekker, 2021; Jordan, Maccarrone, and Erne, 2021; Rocca, 2022). In comparison with the EU's preceeding economic policy coordination tools, NEG prescriptions leave member states much less room for manoeuvre. This is true not only if a country becomes subject to an MoU programme, but also if a country faces an EDP or an MIP – as happened in the case of France, which is neither a small nor a peripheral country (Erne, 2015; Syrovatka, 2021).

Member states that received NEG prescriptions in MoUs and their updates had to implement them to receive bailout funding. It is thus not surprising that all eurozone countries that were subject to a bailout programme 'by-and-large adopted the fiscal consolidation measures prescribed by the Troika' (European Parliament et al., 2014: 6). The same study also noted that Ireland, Cyprus, Portugal, and Greece were given unevenly onerous prescriptions for 'structural reforms', depending on the different 'structural conditions' that businesses enjoyed in them before the crisis. As the structural conditions that business enjoys can always be improved further, the study finally also conceded that it was difficult to assess whether the structural reforms that a government implemented in turn would be 'sufficient' (2014: 6). As a result, national governments could never be sure in advance whether their reform programme would satisfy EU expectations (Erne, 2015) – as shown, for example, regarding the recurrent NEG prescriptions that Italy received to deregulate its employment protection laws (see Chapter 6).

The difficulty of delimitating the scope of necessary NEG reforms at the outset makes the task of assessing the implementation of NEG prescriptions difficult too. When assessing the implementation of an EU directive, the Commission usually conducts a merely formal analysis to check whether all member states have transposed it into national law. When assessing the implementation of NEG prescriptions however, the Commission evaluates member states' progress substantively, within the framework of the European Semester. Put differently, its assessment of policy implementation under NEG is qualitatively different and enlarged, increasing its scope for follow-up and further policy intervention. As there are no limits to 'growth-enhancing structural reforms', it is thus not surprising that the Commission and the European Court of Auditors (2020) were fully satisfied with the implemented changes in only a few cases. This, however, does not mean that the impact of CSRs is limited, as one may think if one relies on the CSR implementation figures provided by the Commission itself (Efstathiou and Wolff, 2018; Al-Kadi and Clauwaert, 2019). Any meaningful analysis of NEG therefore requires a research methodology that allows us to assess the policy orientation and effects of NEG prescriptions across countries and areas in their semantic, communicative, and policy context. We construct and outline such a methodology in Chapters 4 and 5.

In this chapter, to unveil its governance mechanisms, we have described the intricate NEG regime that EU leaders adopted after 2008. In Chapter 3, we review the classical approaches of scholars of EU integration and labour politics and outline why they need to be revised given the EU's shift to NEG.

3

A Paradigm Shift in Understanding EU Integration and Labour Politics

3.1 INTRODUCTION

The shift to the European Union's (EU's) new economic governance (NEG) regime after the financial crisis of 2008 questions key assumptions that guide the thinking of scholars and practitioners in the field. This prompts us to argue first for three conceptual innovations, namely, new ways to envision (1) different modes of European integration, (2) different EU governance mechanisms, and (3) the politicisation of EU governance and labour politics. After that, we outline the interests of the EU's NEG regime for employment relations and public services, as well as the need to examine the role of different structural conditions under which countervailing movements of trade unions and social movements can or cannot politicise EU integration (Erne, 2018; Szabó, Golden, and Erne, 2022).

3.2 MODES OF INTEGRATION: FROM NEGATIVE/POSITIVE TO HORIZONTAL/VERTICAL INTEGRATION

The 2008 financial crisis showed that the creation of the EU's single market and monetary union led not to economic and social convergence, as anticipated by its promoters (Cecchini, Catinat, and Jacquemin, 1988; European Commission, 1990), but to severe economic imbalances that threatened to break up the EU. To prevent that from happening, the European Commission and Council (EU executives) triggered a 'silent revolution' (Barroso cited in ANSA, 2010) and set up NEG, as shown in Chapter 2. As market forces failed to trigger the 'necessary' adjustments in member states' employment relations and social policies, EU executives had to trigger them by fiat, as a European Commission official from DG ECFIN openly admitted at a meeting of an EU–ECB–IMF Troika delegation with Irish government officals, social partners, and academics in Dublin Castle in 2012 (see Chapter 1, n. 1). In response, by introducing NEG, EU executives created a new political space located outside the EU's ordinary legislative procedure. Its legality is liminal; and, surprisingly, it is still not clear to EU lawyers whether NEG prescriptions constitute law, and, if yes, EU law (Kilpatrick and Scott, 2021: 3), despite their constraining nature. Although NEG prescriptions were spelled out in legal documents, the legal scholar Alain Supiot (2013) argued that NEG would challenge the rule of law, as the normative concept of the rule of law should not be reduced to the mere application of legal techniques of domination.

By contrast, Ulrich Beck, the sociologist of the risk society, argued that the 'impending catastrophe empowers and even forces the Europe builders to exploit legal loopholes so as to open the door to changes' (Beck, 2013: 26–27), as mentioned in Chapter 2. It is thus hardly surprising that almost all legal challenges to NEG have failed, including those of workers, unions, and left-wing parliamentarians who questioned the legality of NEG interventions in the social field by invoking social rights as set out in national constitutions, International Labour Organisation conventions, and the EU's Charter of Fundamental Rights (Kilpatrick, 2017; Bonelli and Claes, 2018; Markakis and Dermine, 2018; Barrett, 2020; Kilpatrick and Scott, 2021). After all, pundits time and again presented NEG's package of internal devaluation, austerity, and structural reforms as a 'necessary' adjustment to an 'external shock' that would leave 'responsible' governments with no other option but to implement it; even if this meant that more and more people would become detached from democratic politics (Armingeon, Guthmann, and Weisstanner, 2016; see also Mair, 2013). The EU's NEG prescriptions in areas hitherto shielded from vertical interventions have thus questioned interpretations of the EU's competences that are based on a narrow reading of its Treaties. The wording of the Treaty articles on 'pay' (Art. 153(5) TFEU), the 'protection of workers where their employment contract is terminated' (Arts. 153(1)(d) and (2) TFEU), or 'the organisation and delivery of health services' (Art. 168(7) TFEU), for example, seems to suggest that these areas would be prerogatives of member-state rather than EU laws and procedures, but this did not prevent vertical NEG interventions in these fields.

Ironically however, by creating NEG, the EU's business and political leaders unintentionally created conditions that rendered past debates about the EU's apparent lack of legal competences in essential social policy fields anachronistic (Scharpf, 1999: 10, 203; Stan and Erne, 2021a, 2021b). Until recently, the opponents of social EU laws often succeeded in preventing them by pointing to the apparent lack of EU competences in the social field

(Cooper, 2015). After a decade of recurrent EU interventions in national wage and employment policymaking (Chapter 6), however, such EU competence arguments no longer worked to prevent the adoption of the EU Directive on Adequate Minimum Wages (2022/2041) by the European Parliament and Council in October 2022 (Chapter 13).

In sum, after the financial crisis, EU legislators broke the institutional padlocks that had hitherto limited EU interventions in the employment and social policy fields by adopting, in 2011, the Six-Pack of EU laws, which enabled unrestricted interventions by EU executives in these fields. The financial crisis triggered a 'quantum leap of economic surveillance in Europe' (Commissioner Rehn, *EUObserver*, 16 March 2011) and institutionalised NEG to allow vertical EU interventions in employment and social policy areas. NEG shifted legislative powers from national and European parliaments and social partners to the Commission and Council. This 'revolution', which was meant to 'save the status quo' (Barrett, 2020: 6), was also supported by the EU's Court of Justice, the European Parliament (which approved the Six- and Two-Pack laws), and national parliaments of both deficit and surplus countries (which approved the EU's bailout programmes). Consequently, the shift to NEG achieved what institutionalist EU integration theorists, like Scharpf (1999), believed impossible for the EU to achieve, namely, the concentration of substantive policymaking and enforcement powers in the hands of EU officials in all socioeconomic areas, including pension, healthcare, and wage policies.

Given this radical shift in EU policymaking, we argue that it is time for an analytical paradigm shift that allows us to capture the emerging European system in employment relations (Erne, 2019; Jordan, Maccarrone, and Erne, 2021), social policy (Stan and Erne, 2021a, 2021b), and public service governance (Golden, Szabó, and Erne, 2021). Instead of negative and positive integration (Tinbergen, 1965; Pinder, 1968; Scharpf, 1999), we propose an alternative analytical distinction that better captures the current EU integration dynamics triggered by the shift to NEG: the distinction between horizontal (market) and vertical (political) integration. Whereas vertical integration is triggered by substantive policy prescriptions of a 'supranational political, legal or corporate authority' (Erne, 2019: 346), horizontal integration refers to the abstract, but nevertheless constraining, transnational market pressures experienced by social actors within the increasingly integrated European marketplace.

This analytical move is important for two reasons. First, once the single market had been created by law (through negative and vertical EU acts that removed national legal restrictions to the free movement of goods, capital, services, and people across borders), the resulting horizontal market pressures became an independent driver of further integration in their own right, hence the need to distinguish horizontal (market) integration from vertical (negative or positive) political integration.

Second, after the shift to NEG, earlier institutional padlocks no longer prevented EU interventions in substantive policy areas, such as employment relations and public services. To ensure structural convergence (Scharpf, 2021), the NEG regime set supranational standards also in these policy fields. This amounts to positive integration in the original, analytical sense of the term, which denotes the making of the 'system of economic regulation at the level of the larger unit' (Scharpf, 1999: 45). At the same time, the policy orientation of the NEG 'government of governments' (Scharpf, 2021: 162) hardly matches the underlying normative Keynesian beliefs of those who coined and propagated the positive/negative integration typology in the first place. Accordingly, Scharpf (2021) quietly abandoned the typology, which had informed the scholarly debate on different modes of European integration for decades. We thus distinguish between different types of vertical EU intervention in the economic and social fields, based on their (commodifying or decommodifying) policy orientation and not their (negative or positive) institutional properties.

The shift to the EU's NEG regime also questions earlier institutionalist views of EU politics, which emphasised the EU's limited legal competences and policymaking capacities in the field of employment relations and public services. We therefore go beyond earlier institutionalist thinking and take larger processes into account, especially those of capitalist accumulation and crisis (Bieler and Erne, 2015; Bieler and Morton, 2018: ch. 9). This wider perspective on transnational economic and political integration pressures helps us explain why EU leaders were able to break institutional EU padlocks when they created the NEG regime.

We acknowledge that the underlying idea of these two concepts is not new. Vertical political interventions and horizontal market pressures have been forces structuring the behaviour of modern capitalist societies since their making. Acknowledging this, however, is an asset rather than a drawback, as it gives the proposed framework for analysis an even stronger basis. After all, the social sciences were created to study the interactions between capitalist horizontal (market) and vertical (political) interventions precisely when the 'great *question sociale* (or soziale Frage) of the late nineteenth or early twentieth century: how to incorporate the industrial working class within civil society' became a salient political, economic, and social issue (Crouch, 2015: 4).

The distinction between horizontal market pressures and vertical political interventions allows us to account for both the economic and the political aspects of European integration and the ways in which they were combined during its history. After the Single European Act (SEA), European integration was driven by vertical EU laws and interventions that opened new sectors and areas to transnational competition. Although rarely a direct target of the latter, national employment relations and social protection arrangements have nonetheless been *indirectly* impacted by the horizontal market pressures unleashed by the SEA, the Economic and Monetary Union (EMU), and EU enlargements.

Given the urgency of the financial crisis and the botched attempts to pursue further liberalisation through Commissioner Bolkestein's proposal for a Services Directive in 2004 (COM (2004) 2 final/3), EU leaders did not use the EU's ordinary legislative procedure to bring about the changes in employment relations and public services that they deemed necessary (Erne, 2015). Instead, the EU turned the (soft law) socioeconomic policy coordination instruments of the early 2000s into hard and coercive policymaking tools.

The EU's shift to the NEG regime brought a new formula to EU integration, namely, *country-specific* vertical interventions by EU executives based on *supranational* EU steering and surveillance mechanisms. These interventions also *directly* targeted areas hitherto largely shielded from EU vertical interventions via the EU's ordinary legislative procedure (e.g., pay and healthcare policy). In doing so, EU executives sought to compensate for the failure of existing horizontal market pressures to bring about the desired economic convergence of national policies in these social policy areas.

In contrast to horizontal market forces, vertical NEG interventions are much more tangible, and thus politically contentious. Countervailing movements may therefore be able to politicise vertical NEG interventions much more easily than horizontal market pressures (Erne, 2018). The concentration of new powers at EU level could be seen as a near perfect example of neo-functionalist spill-over, but increased vertical (political) integration pressures can also trigger popular countermovements that may lead to the EU's downfall. In 2012, even proponents of neo-functionalist EU integration theory could therefore imagine the following scenario: 'first, the collapse of the euro; then of the EU, and, finally, of democracy in its member states' (Schmitter, 2012: 41). Thus, precisely to prevent EU disintegration from happening, the NEG regime's architects devised new EU governance tools that could not be politicised that easily.

3.3 EU GOVERNANCE: FROM STATE-CENTRED TO CORPORATE MANAGEMENT MECHANISMS

In the 1990s, governance became a widely used analytical category, as it allowed scholars to adopt a much more encompassing perspective on politics and the economy. EU scholars used the term to go beyond the classical intergovernmental and federal perspectives mentioned in Chapter 2 (Marks et al., 1996; Kohler-Koch and Rittberger, 2006). Economic sociologists used it to go beyond the dichotomy of states and markets (Hollingsworth and Lindberg, 1991; Hollingsworth and Boyer, 1997; Crouch, 2005), and industrial relations scholars used governance for both reasons (Marginson and Sisson, 2004; Léonard et al., 2007).

Since its origin however, the term 'governance' had also been used for political reasons. In its White Paper on governance, for example, the European Commission (White Paper, COM (2001) 428) used the concept to propagate a more deliberative (and less hierarchical) form of policymaking, which would allegedly allow a greater involvement of non-state actors and therefore increase its legitimacy (Joerges, 2002; Kohler-Koch and Quittkat, 2013). In addition, governance has been used to justify supranational interventions in the political affairs of notionally sovereign nation-states. After all, the World Bank and the IMF coined the term in the early 1990s precisely to legitimise their 'good governance' interventions in the Global South and Eastern Europe (Guilhot, 2005; Moretti and Pestre, 2015: 82).

Despite the shift to a much more vertical NEG regime after the crisis, most scholars who come from state-centric disciplines, such as law and political science, continue to portray governance as a non-hierarchical form of policymaking, namely, one based on mutual learning, policy coordination, and surveillance. Consequently, EU governance would be a mix (or a hybrid form) of intergovernmental and supranational mechanisms combining soft EU law with laws emanating from a hard and binding legal norm (Maher, 2021a, 2021b). Building on industrial relations and economic sociology, we propose, by contrast, an alternative analytical framework that captures NEG not as a hybrid form of intergovernmental and supranational rulemaking, but as an independent, third mechanism borrowed from the private governance found in transnational corporations (TNCs) (Erne, 2015). The vertical nature of the NEG regime rests on control mechanisms that TNCs use to govern their subsidiaries (numerical benchmarks, ad hoc prescriptions, and financial awards and penalties). This allows us to go beyond the dominant state-centred paradigms in EU integration research (e.g., intergovernmentalism or federalism) without having to abandon the focus of the political sciences on power and power relations.

The similarity of the NEG regime's *country-specific* and corporate *subsidiary-specific* policy prescriptions also allows us to go beyond the state-centric perspectives of EU scholars on differentiated integration (Kölliker, 2006; Leuffen, Rittberger, and Schimmelfennig, 2022). One can describe NEG's *country-specific* prescriptions as a case of differentiated integration but not in the usual sense of the opt-outs from EU laws that aim 'to accommodate economic, social and cultural heterogeneity' (Bellamy and Kröger, 2017: 625). State-centred differentiated integration scholars have focused their analysis on national opt-outs, which accommodate EU member states with different objectives. Alkuin Kölliker (2006: 14), for example, defined differentiation as a general term for the 'possibility of member states to have different rights and obligations with respect to certain common policy areas.' In contrast, the EU's NEG regime uses country-specific prescriptions to realign the policies of its member states along its overarching *supranational* priorities, namely, the proper functioning of the eurozone and the EU economy as a whole, as outlined above. Hence, EU executives used NEG's country-specific measures to achieve pan-European goals, as managers in headquarters (HQs) of TNCs use site-specific interventions to achieve company-wide objectives. We have thus argued that NEG can be described as a case of *reversed* differentiated integration, as its country-specific prescriptions aim to reduce (rather than accommodate) national heterogeneity (Stan and Erne, 2023).

The proposed change of perspectives on EU governance from state-centred to corporate management mechanisms represents an important analytical move, and not just because TNCs started long ago to effectively use similar governance tools to advance their agendas (Arrowsmith, Sisson, and Marginson, 2004; Erne, 2015). Equally important are the insights of studies on international human resource management and industrial relations highlighting that TNCs' vertical interventions in the affairs of their subsidiaries do not always succeed, regardless of HQs' control over investment decisions and their frequent use of whipsawing tactics that pit subsidiaries against one another (Bélanger et al., 2000; Edwards and Kuruvilla, 2005; Anner et al., 2006; Morgan and Kristensen, 2006; Erne, 2008; Pulignano et al., 2018; Clegg, Geppert, and Hollinshead, 2018; Golden and Erne, 2022).

In sum, NEG is neither a supranational nor an intergovernmental governance regime (Bauer and Becker, 2014; Bickerton, Hodson, and Puetter, 2015), as it uses mechanisms that cannot be neatly captured by either of these state-centred paradigms of European integration scholarship. If, however, we go beyond them, we can grasp the nature of the EU's NEG regime much more easily, namely, as a governance regime that mimics the corporate governance mechanisms of TNCs, which use numerical benchmarks and ad hoc prescriptions to increase the command of corporate HQs' senior management teams over their subsidiaries (Erne, 2015). Accordingly, the EU's NEG regime allows EU executives – that is, the supranational European Commission and the intergovernmental Council of national finance ministers – to shape member states' labour and social policies through key performance indicators, country-specific ad hoc prescriptions, and corrective action plans.

NEG's methods reshape member states' policies by combining governance at a distance already set up through the Broad Economic Policy Guidelines and the Open Method of Coordination (Arrowsmith, Sisson, and Marginson, 2004; Lascoumes and Le Galès, 2004; Armstrong, 2010) with the vertical punch of constraining enforcement procedures. To regulate the EU economy, including its employment relations, public services, and social policies, EU executives draw on divisive corporate governance methods that business leaders have designed to govern TNCs (Arrowsmith, Sisson, and Marginson, 2004), rather than on universal laws enacted by democratic legislators (Joerges, 2016). Yet, as the EU is not a business corporation but a political organisation that claims to 'be founded on the values of respect for human dignity, freedom, democracy, the rule of law and respect for human rights' (Art. 2, TEU), its shift to NEG also led to a severe legitimacy crisis of EU governance, which in turn would facilitate its politicisation.

3.4 POLITICISING EU GOVERNANCE AND LABOUR POLITICS

The distinction between horizontal and vertical integration and the similarities between NEG and corporate governance mechanisms described above not only enlightens us about the EU's arcane NEG dynamics but also enables us to identify potential 'levers' (Mills, 2000 [1959]: 131) by which the NEG may be challenged and changed by countervailing social actors, namely, unions and social movements. As mentioned above, we distinguish vertical and horizontal modes of EU integration based on the different types of constraints underpinning them. Horizontal market integration places societal actors (unions and social movements, but also companies) under transnational (economic) market pressures. By contrast, vertical political integration leads to them being constrained by prescriptions of a supranational political authority. This distinction is pivotal, as these two modes of EU integration offer different crystallisation points for countervailing collective action.

Horizontal (market) integration pressures first and foremost result from the exploitation of labour power in the capitalist production process. The social nature of these pressures, however, is not easily detectable. Although commodities are produced by human labour, they seem to acquire a life of their own once they are traded on the market. As a result, the 'mutual relations of the producers, within which the social character of their labour affirms itself, take the form of a social relation between the products' (Marx, 2005 [1867]: ch. 1.4). Consequently, workers often perceive market pressures as emanating from an external, even natural, mystical force. This highlights 'a paradox in Marx's account: how can there be class struggle when exploitation is not palpable but mystified?' (Burawoy, 2022). If we pose Burawoy's question in the context of increasing *transnational* market pressures, it becomes even more puzzling.

As seen above, the horizontal market pressures unleashed by the SEA and the EMU did not question the autonomy of national welfare states and trade unions. Even so, trade union experts described their national bargaining autonomy, as far back as 2004, as 'autonomy in the playpen' (Sterkel, Schulten, and Wiedemuth, 2004: 1), as national multi-employer collective bargaining agreements were no longer able to take workers' pay and conditions out of competition between different producers, given their increasing exposure to transnational market competition. At the beginning of EU economic and monetary integration, some observers therefore believed that 'as markets expanded unions had to enlarge their strategic domain to keep workers from being played off against each other' (Martin and Ross, 1999: 312); but the attempts of European trade union federations to coordinate national wage bargaining strategies across borders, to prevent a race to the bottom in wages and labour standards through the adoption of EU-level targets, largely resulted in failure. This reflected European trade unions' difficulties in revealing and politicising the hidden social relations behind horizontal market integration pressures (Erne, 2008: 189).

By contrast, vertical political pressures are more tangible than horizontal market pressures and therefore easier to politicise. Reliance on vertical state-like structures (e.g., EU institutions) makes decisions taken in their name more visible, thereby offering concrete targets for contentious transnational collective action (Erne, 2008; Erne et al., 2015). Vertical interventions are easier to politicise, albeit 'within a limited timeframe, as the impact of vertical intervention (e.g., in the case of looming liberalizing EU laws) increases horizontal competition in the medium and long term' (Szabó, Golden, and Erne, 2022: 636). In short, horizontal integration constrains transnational labour mobilisation, whereas vertical integration can act as a catalyst for it (Erne, 2008: 199–200; Erne, 2018). Crucially however, there is a significant difference between universal vertical interventions and country-specific vertical interventions, as the latter favour uneven protests across countries (Stan, Helle, and Erne, 2015).

Thus, given NEG's recourse to mechanisms characteristic of corporate governance, we can learn a lot from unions' fights against corporate whipsawing tactics that put workers from different subsidiaries in competition with one another. TNCs put workers under pressure, but, at times, workers within

TNCs can also unite across borders (Anner et al., 2006). Countervailing *transnational* movements of workers within TNCs occur when workers across different locations are victims of similar vertical corporate interventions (Erne and Nowak, 2022; Golden and Erne, 2022). Likewise, NEG interventions in labour politics must follow an overarching EU script to trigger encompassing countermovements. To be effective, these movements can either deliberately target NEG through *transnational* collective action or unintendedly trigger EU-level policy changes through the aggregate effects of their actions at local or national level if they point in the same policy direction (Nunes, 2021; for countervailing, national, and local level protests in the era of NEG see: Maccarrone, 2020; Naughton, 2023; Galanti, 2023).

But what kind of EU interventions would represent a fundamental challenge for trade unions and social movements such that it would trigger countermobilisation? The distinction between horizontal market pressures and vertical political interventions allows us to grasp the *form* of EU pressures that may or may not trigger countervailing movements. We nevertheless must also address the *substance* of these pressures and their articulation with labour politics. Otherwise said, what fundamental labour interests do these pressures threaten? We argue that labour movements are not only about struggles that limit the exploitation of workers by their companies in the production process. It is equally in the interest of labour to decommodify employment relations and public services to ensure labour's social reproduction and well-being by shielding it from the vagaries of market fluctuations and the systemic whims of transnational processes of capitalist accumulation. We thus need to see where EU integration and NEG stand in relation to them and to labour commodification.

3.5 THE INTEREST OF IT ALL: THE COMMODIFICATION OF LABOUR AND PUBLIC SERVICES

The creation of European welfare states during the twentieth century would not have been possible without labour's struggles for social rights seeking to shield workers from the vagaries of the market (Marshall, 1950). Labour's interest in engaging in such struggles can be seen as stemming from the nefarious effects that unchecked markets have on society. These effects take the form of commodification, a process whereby 'wage employment and the cash nexus [become] the linchpin of a person's existence' (Copeland, 2020: 103). Traditionally, welfare states sought to respond to commodification through decommodification, that is, the processes allowing individuals 'to uphold a socially acceptable standard of living independent of the market' (Copeland, 2020: 104; see also Esping-Andersen, 1990). Nonetheless, since the 1970s, the application of neoliberal reforms to employment relations and social protection has led to employment and welfare arrangements being used 'to both commodify and decommodify' social relations (Copeland, 2020: 103).

But why was it so, why did the mid-twentieth-century class compromise no longer do the trick? In order to respond to this question, we must address the fact that labour has an interest in social rights not only because markets dissolve meaningful social relations in society at large (Polanyi, 2001 [1944]), but also, more precisely, because the interest of the capitalists who are the players in these markets is to expand and intensify labour commodification as a way to maximise the extraction of surplus value in the productive process (Marx, 2005 [1867]; Bieler, 2021). At a macro, structural level, welfare states are thus an attempt to temper capitalist accumulation and rebalance the power relation between capital and labour. Traditionally, employment and welfare arrangements aimed to (partially) shield labour from market forces by (1) shielding workers from full exploitation and commodification (through protective employment legislation); (2) socialising the reproduction of the current and future labour force (through the provision of public services in the areas of healthcare, water, transport, but also childcare and education); and (3) socialising the risks of sickness, unemployment, and old age (through social security).

The crisis in the Fordist regime of capitalist accumulation after the 1970s unsettled the post-World War II class compromise (Harvey, 2005). Dominant classes, including European ones, used neoliberal theory – namely, its view of free markets as offering the best road to economic and social development – as a justification for attacks on the solidaristic, redistributive employment and welfare arrangements of the previous era. These attacks were driven not only by a purely ideological preference for markets over redistributive employment and welfare arrangements but also by capitalists' need to respond to the exhaustion of previous modes of capitalist accumulation by conquering new areas for capitalist expansion and commodification – in this case, social reproduction processes hitherto shielded from capitalist accumulation through solidaristic, redistributive employment and welfare arrangements.

Labour's loss of power in the context of stagflation (since the 1970s) and then the demise of communist regimes in Eastern Europe (since the 1990s) emboldened neoliberal free-market approaches to employment and welfare arrangements. At the same time, during neoliberal times, capitalist accumulation came to rely extensively on predatory practices reminiscent of Marx's 'primitive accumulation' (2005 [1867]: part 8) as an antidote to the exhaustion of spatial–temporal fixes relying on expanded reproduction in the form of capital delocalisation and long-term investment in new productive assets. This is what Harvey (2003) aptly calls *accumulation by dispossession*, a process that involves not only using financial mechanisms and intellectual property rights in asset stripping but also, and importantly, 'enclosing the commons' (Bieler and Jordan, 2018: 75) of previously socialised, decommodified areas of social reproduction. Indeed, one of the key mantras of contemporary global capitalism is the privatisation of state assets, state companies, and public services (Harvey, 2003).

Given the variegated character of neoliberalisation (Brenner, Peck, and Theodore, 2010) and the uneven realisation of the single market programme across the EU, the commodification of employment and welfare arrangements proceeded to different degrees and at a different pace across countries and sectors. This was already apparent in the 1990s and 2000s when EU leaders sought to construct the single market as a space for extended capitalist accumulation. The single market put national employment and welfare arrangements under increasing horizontal market pressures. These pressures triggered different responses at different times in different member states. The single market programme, EMU, and accession processes placed governments under budgetary and competitive pressures that led to their adopting various mixes of commodifying employment and welfare measures to lower public expenditures and unit labour costs. These pressures also led to a greater integration of productive capacities across Europe, most notably by transnational manufacturing firms opening subsidiaries in the EU's eastern periphery. This was paralleled in the area of social reproduction by the rise of TNCs engaged in public service provision, including in water, transport, and healthcare, and informal private arrangements in the form of transnational 'care chains' (Hochschild, 2000). As a result, workers were set in competition with one another not only through regulatory competition between national systems but also through competition between public and private service providers as well as subsidiaries and suppliers of TNCs.

Although these commodification pressures are thus linked to broader restructuring processes within the capitalist world system that preceded the EU's shift to NEG, they also needed to be enforced politically (Burawoy, 2000), especially when horizontal market integration did not lead to the desired economic convergence of national labour and social policies as outlined above. This explains our book's focus on EU executives' NEG prescriptions on employment relations and public services and the social countermovements that they might trigger. In section 3.6, as a last conceptual move, we outline our approach to countervailing protests of unions and social movements, including their potential role as agents of the EU's democratisation.

3.6 NEG AND TRANSNATIONAL COLLECTIVE ACTION: FROM AGENT-CENTRED TO STRUCTURAL FACTORS

The formation of political authority in nation-states typically preceded their democratisation through political and social rights. Accordingly, the formation of a more vertical EU polity through NEG may paradoxically also lead to a transnational democracy. After all, 'democracy requires not only a people (*demos*) but also binding rules (*kratos*)' (Erne, 2008: 18). There is a dialectical relationship between popular mobilisations and the creation of political authority (Tilly, 1992). Nonetheless, the vertical nature of the EU's NEG regime may not only trigger popular demands for more voice but equally lead to popular calls to exit the EU, as became apparent in the UK's Brexit referendum debate. This has also been emphasised in many EU politicisation studies that analysed the salience of Eurosceptic positions in opinion polls, elections, referenda, or EU-related media debates (for a review, see Zürn, 2016).

To understand the growing politicisation of the EU integration process however, we must go beyond the scope of existing EU politicisation studies that assess the salience of EU-related issues in media debates, opinion polls, election, or referendum campaigns. To capture the restructuring of the European political space, we must study not only these micro- and macro-level processes but also activities that take place at the (meso) level of interest-group politics (Zürn, 2016). After all, the creation of the left–right cleavage in European politics has also been driven by the *organisational networks* of the labour movement (Bartolini, 2005).

The restructuring of the European political space remains a social process (Saurugger, 2016). Individual attitudes become a social force only if they are mobilised and reinforced by intermediary associations; this in turn depends on the organisational networks of interest groups and social movements in the forecourt of party politics. EU politicisation studies should therefore look below the macro level of public debates as presented in mass media and above the micro level of survey results and election outcomes (Zürn, 2016). This explains our interest in European trade unions and social movements, as they play a key role not only in the formation of the left–right cleavage but also in the democratisation of social and economic policymaking (Rueschemeyer, Huber Stephens, and Stephens, 1992; Bartolini, 2000; Foot, 2005; Erne, 2008).

The shift to a much more vertical NEG regime offers contradictory options for labour. EU executives' vertical NEG interventions make decisions taken in the EU's name more tangible, offering concrete targets for countervailing, transnational collective action. At the same time however, NEG's technocratic, numerical benchmarks and its country-specific, ad hoc interventions put countries in competition with one another. This constitutes a deterrent to transnational collective action. Thus, the shift to NEG may also favour the politicisation of EU politics along national culturalist rather than transnational class lines (Erne, 2019). This is partly because some pro-European politicians – such as former Commissioner Bolkestein (Béthoux, Erne, and Golden, 2018) – like to portray their critics in cultural terms as nationalists (Statham and Trenz, 2013: 132) and partly because Eurosceptics believe that the restoration of national social states' formal autonomy would solve workers' social and economic problems.

NEG thus risks being a supranational regime that nationalises social conflict (Erne, 2015). Does this mean that transnational counterreactions to NEG are doomed from the start, as some Eurosceptic analysts of the EU's democratic prospects think? For Wolfgang Streeck, for example, the 'growing feeling among the citizens of Europe that their governments are not taking them seriously' (2014: 160) mirrors capitalists' diminished interest in democratic interest intermediation: 'All capital still wants from people is that they give back to the market ... the social and civil rights they fought for and won in historic struggles' (2014: 159). Even so, we do not assume that 'constructive opposition is impossible', as this would indeed imply that 'irrational' outbursts of rage would be the only option left to people (2014: 160). Nor do we share the false optimism of global labour scholars who assume, following a partial reading of Polanyi (2001 [1944]), that transnational market fundamentalism will inevitably produce a transnational countermovement, as if 'society' would 'summon up its own defence in the face of a market onslaught' (Burawoy, 2010: 302).

In this study, we avoid Polanyi's under-theorised notion of society and analyse concrete social actors instead, namely, those engaged in social protests that contest the commodification of public services, such as water provision, and those engaged in social protests that target the exploitation of workers in the production process. Polanyi's approach suffers from another limitation: that of missing the 'complex interplay' between 'state and society' (Burawoy, 2010: 302). Thus, we do not focus our analysis on the actor-centred factors that explain why some labour alliances have succeeded in politicising European integration pressures across borders (Szabó, Golden, and Erne, 2022). Instead, we try to unpack the relationships between the structures of the EU's NEG regime and countervailing collective action.

Indeed, scholars of social protests have acknowledged the role played by structural explanations in triggering them, such as political opportunity structures faced by social movements (Tarrow, 1994) or long waves of economic boom and bust in which they act (Kelly, 2012 [1998]). Nevertheless, social movement scholars usually explain successful instances of collective action in terms of actor-centred factors, such as activists' interactions with allies and the public (Diani and Bison, 2004), the use of bottom-up organising strategies (McAlevey, 2016), or activists' capacity to foster alliances across workplaces and union organisations at different levels (Brookes, 2019). Although these social interactions are certainly critical, the options available to actors to build successful countervailing movements are also shaped by structural factors, as neatly summarised by union organiser and industrial relations scholar Jane McAlevey (2016: 3): 'Even understanding whom to target – who the primary and secondary people and institutions are that will determine whether the campaign will succeed (or society will change) – often requires a highly detailed power-structure analysis.' This explains our interest in the different forms of European integration pressures that unions and social movements have been facing.

Hence, we analyse the making and operation of the EU's NEG regime across time, locations, and sectors to identify the internal contradictions that could serve labour movements as crystallisation points for countervailing collective action (Poulantzas, 1980; Bieler and Erne, 2014; Bruff, 2014; Cox and Nilsen, 2014; Panitch, 2015). This is important, as the biggest challenge that we are facing is hardly the absence of studies that deplore the decline of the mid-twentieth-century class compromise that laid the foundations for solidaristic, redistributive employment and welfare arrangements in Europe. The biggest challenge is rather the scarcity of ideas about the potential 'levers' (Mills, 2000 [1959]: 131) that countervailing movements could pull to turn the page of austerity politics. In this book, we therefore aim not simply to add a novel, conceptually driven depiction of the EU's NEG regime, its operation, and its outcomes, but also to identify such potential levers or points of intervention for trade unions and social movements that the EU's NEG regime may unintentionally have created for them.

Certainly, these interventions are far from easy, as NEG concentrates decision-making powers in the hands of EU executives and uses technocratic governance-by-numbers techniques to insulate policymaking from popular demands. At the same time, we also know that the more policymaking institutions are insulated from democratic interest intermediation mechanisms, the more they risk becoming targets for countervailing mobilisations (Bruff, 2014; Erne, 2018) or calls to simply exit them (Hirschman, 1970). The EU's much more vertical NEG regime may offer unions and social movements a tangible target for its politicisation to defend decommodified labour and welfare arrangements. Yet, NEG's politicisation is likely to happen across national borders only if its country-specific prescriptions are informed by a commodifying pan-European policy script. As such a script is a necessary (albeit not sufficient) condition for countervailing collective action, we outline in Chapters 4 and 5 a novel methodology to assess the policy direction of NEG prescriptions in the social field across countries and years that goes beyond the decontextualised pea counting of EU executives' country-specific recommendations that has so-far dominated the research in the field.

4

How to Assess the Policy Orientation of the EU's NEG Prescriptions?

4.1 INTRODUCTION

In this chapter, we first present the existing studies of the EU's new economic governance (NEG) policy prescriptions and then discuss the methodological challenges that they pose to their assessment. We show that these studies flattened both (a) the semantic relationships between the different policy terms used in them and (b) the power relations between different actors involved in their production. We set up instead a research design that accounts for (a) the links between the policy orientation of NEG prescriptions and the material interests of concrete social groups and (b) the hierarchical ordering of prescriptions in larger policy scripts unevenly deployed across countries, time, and policy areas. We address the first point in this chapter and the second in Chapter 5.

In section 4.2, we identify commodification as the most relevant NEG policy orientation for analysing the nexus between EU economic governance and labour politics. Before the EU's shift to NEG, EU interventions had triggered countervailing social protests specifically when they pointed in a commodifying policy direction, as shown in Chapter 3 and Chapters 6–11. In section 4.3, we thus operationalise the concept of commodification in the areas of employment relations and public services and outline the corresponding analytical framework against which we assess the policy orientation of NEG prescriptions in these two policy areas.

4.2 ASSESSING THE POLICY ORIENTATION OF NEG AND ITS METHODOLOGICAL CHALLENGES

Following the establishment of the European Semester (see Chapter 2), an increasing number of scholars have assessed the frequency and policy orientation of NEG prescriptions in the social field, that is, those targeting areas such as employment relations, education and training, equality policy, health and long-term care, pensions, and poverty and social exclusion (Bekker, 2015; Darvas and Leandro, 2015; de la Porte and Heins, 2016; Clauwaert, 2018; Copeland and Daly, 2018; Dawson, 2018; Zeitlin and Vanhercke, 2018; Al-Kadi and Clauwaert, 2019; Crespy and Vanheuverzwijn, 2019; Copeland, 2020). Two major views have emerged. One sees NEG as becoming increasingly social over time, given the increase in the *number* of prescriptions addressing employment and social policy issues as well as a postulated change in their policy *orientation*. The other view questions these conclusions, arguing that social prescriptions have been mostly subordinated to fiscal discipline objectives.

Prominent among the first camp are Zeitlin and Vanhercke (2018), who argue that a progressive socialisation of the European Semester has occurred since its establishment in 2011. According to them, this socialisation is manifested at two interdependent levels. At the governance *mechanisms* level, it takes the form of an increasing involvement of social policy actors (i.e., the Commission's DG for Employment, Social Affairs, and Inclusion; the Employment, Social Policy, Health, and Consumer Affairs Council; and so on) in the formulation of country-specific recommendations (CSRs) and in the EU's multilateral surveillance of national reforms implemented in response to these recommendations. This involvement is accompanied, at policy *orientations* level, by an increasing presence of social objectives in NEG documents, affecting the share not only of prescriptions in the social field in general but also of those geared towards social investment objectives more particularly.

Proponents of the socialisation thesis highlight processes of 'strategic *agency*, reflexive learning and creative adaptation' (emphasis added) (Zeitlin and Vanhercke, 2018: 149) to account for social policy actors' apparently successful uploading of social objectives to the European Semester. Offering a complementary position to that of Zeitlin and Vanhercke (2018), Greer and Brooks (2021: 71) argue that 'opponents to a narrow fiscal governance agenda' of the European Semester – Zeitlin and Vanhercke's (2018) social policy actors – have managed not so much to *socialise* the Semester as to *weaken* it. The two authors take the example of healthcare and argue that, by broadening the goals of the Semester, expanding the scope of conflict around it, and disputing and diversifying the data on which it rests, social policy actors in the European Commission and Council have undermined the efficacy of its fiscal governance agenda in this area.

In response to these stances that privilege agency, other scholars propose a more balanced view of the structure–agency nexus (Copeland, 2020). They point out that social policy actors' agency is limited by a series of *structural* constraints inbuilt in the architecture of the European Semester (Copeland and Daly, 2018; Dawson, 2018). Most notably, their subordination to economic and financial policy actors (i.e., the DG for Economic and Financial Affairs, the Economic and Financial Affairs Council) has led to social policy continuing to be displaced and marginalised by fiscal policy in the Semester's policy process (Dawson, 2018; Copeland, 2020). This has contributed neither to the Semester's socialisation (Zeitlin and Vanhercke, 2018) nor to the weakening of its fiscal governance objectives (Greer and Brooks, 2021). It has resulted instead in the capturing of social policy actors' agenda in economic policy actors' 'wider logic of competitiveness and market fitness' (Dawson, 2018: 207; see also Degryse, Jepsen, and Pochet, 2013). Therefore, the increase in the number of social prescriptions in NEG documents does not reflect a move to a socially progressive orientation of NEG's structural reform but rather a mostly cosmetic (discursive) move to address social discontent generated by austerity policies in the aftermath of the crisis (Crespy and Schmidt, 2017; Crespy and Vanheuverzwijn, 2019).

How can we test these opposing claims, that is, how can we assess empirically the orientation of policy prescriptions included in NEG documents? Such an endeavour poses certain methodological challenges. As seen in Chapter 2, the NEG regime is largely shielded from democratic control. NEG prescriptions are formulated in a technocratic jargon that is both precise enough to trigger the desired political effects and ambiguous enough to diminish the risk of their politicisation (Moretti and Pestre, 2015). As scholars critical of the socialisation thesis have shown, the language of NEG documents in social areas has been vague (Dawson, 2018) and ambiguous (Crespy and Vanheuverzwijn, 2019; Miró, 2021) or has mixed orientations (Copeland and Daly, 2018). This reflects a classical domination method whereby documents are peppered with jargonistic language to make them incomprehensible to non-expert readers and thus immune from popular critique (Orwell, 2013 [1946]; Lanchester, 2014).

Two main methodological approaches have emerged on how to assess the orientation of NEG prescriptions in the employment and social policy areas. One approach draws on the history of policy ideas and neo-institutionalism and upgraded analyses of social policy at *national* level to study policymaking at the *supranational* EU level. It considers that, as the national institutional framework would be articulated around a few path-dependent, self-reproducing traditions or varieties of welfare capitalism (namely, liberal, conservative, and social democratic, see Esping-Andersen, 1990), so EU social policy is informed by various policy paradigms or philosophies of welfare reform (namely, liberal, Third Way, and social democratic, see Daly, 2012). This approach therefore proceeds by considering given sets of distinct policy paradigms (Daly, 2012), models (Heimberger, Huber, and Kapeller, 2020), objectives (Zeitlin and Vanhercke, 2018), or orientations (Copeland and Daly, 2018) and then tracking them down in policy documents.

The second approach draws on post-structuralist discourse theory to capture not so much the path-dependency and stability of policy paradigms, as the possible indeterminacy and change across time of the meaning of policy terms (Crespy and Vanheuverzwijn, 2019; Miró, 2021). It asks whether NEG's key policy terms are not inherently ambiguous and open and thus function like empty signifiers. Concretely, this approach mobilises semantic analysis to map the semantic connections between ambiguous policy terms (e.g., structural reform or competitiveness) and distinct policy objectives (Crespy and Vanheuverzwijn, 2019) or frames (Miró, 2021). Crespy and Vanheuverzwijn (2019) thus map the links between structural reform and social investment versus social retrenchment policy objectives. In turn, Miró (2021) maps the connections between competitiveness and quality versus cost policy frames.

Certainly, policy paradigms are not as coherent and stable as implied by varieties-of-welfare studies. The change across time in the content of policies adopted under a certain banner (social democratic, for example) and the convergence and overlap between different social policy approaches (Copeland, 2020) question these studies' assumptions that specific policy prescriptions can be assigned to distinct and stable social policy paradigms. Nonetheless, seeing policy terms as inherently indeterminate and constantly shifting is equally problematic in methodological and analytical terms. Indeed, although the two studies mentioned above show that key policy terms are associated with contradictory objectives (i.e., structural reforms with social retrenchment *and* social investment, see Crespy and Vanheuverzwijn, 2019) and frames (i.e., competitiveness with cost *and* quality, see Miró, 2021), they have difficulty solving the resulting conundrum – namely, given the presence of contradictory policy orientations, how can we assess which one is most significant from an analytical point of view, and how can we then explain why it reveals the deeper character of NEG employment and social policies?

The two studies show that more progressive policy objectives or frames are consistently (i.e., quality competitiveness) or even increasingly (i.e., social investment) present in policy documents. This indicates a discursive turn away from austerity policies and is a finding that seems to confirm the socialisation thesis. At the same time, both studies engage in a critique of the socialisation thesis by stressing the continuous importance across time of socially regressive orientations within NEG prescriptions. They thus highlight that structural reform has retained an ideological core of 'typically neoliberal policy recipes' (Crespy and Vanheuverzwijn, 2019: 94) and that competitiveness is seen mostly in terms of cost rather than of quality (Miró, 2021).[1]

To explain why it is the repeated occurrence of socially *regressive* rather than socially *progressive* policy orientations that reveals the deeper character of NEG policies, both sets of authors had to mobilise factors such as the deployment of policy reforms over time and the coercive power of policy prescriptions, which lie outside discourse per se. This analytical move is not surprising. Thinking in terms of empty signifiers may help give a name to the presence of contradictory orientations and frames but has little to offer towards explaining the centrality of particular types of policy orientations in NEG policy processes. At the 1997 EU summit in Amsterdam, the newly elected socialist French government succeeded in adding Growth to the name of the Stability Pact. However, this amendment reoriented the pact only at a discursive level, as the renamed Stability *and Growth* Pact still focused on fiscal restraint (Heipertz and Verdun, 2010). Discourse theory rests on underlying assumptions of semantic indeterminacy, disconnection between language and social groups' material interests, and flat power relations (Turner, 1994). This results in an analytic design that likewise flattens the semantic relationships between different policy terms: the latter are 'ambiguous' only if the analysis gives equal weight to the opposing policy orientations with which these terms are semantically linked. Moreover, this analytic design eludes a consideration of how policy prescriptions promote or inhibit the interests of concrete social groups (and most particularly social classes) and are thus embedded in the struggles waged by these groups over prescriptions' meaning.

We thus need a research design that accounts for (a) the links between the orientation of NEG prescriptions and the interests of concrete social groups and (b) the hierarchical ordering of NEG prescriptions in larger transnational policy scripts, which are unevenly deployed across countries, time, and policy areas. This results in a research design that (1) links the policy orientation of prescriptions to the material interests of labour (i.e., in opposing the *commodification* of labour and social reproduction) – to account for the embeddedness of NEG prescriptions in social (class) conflict; (2) captures the uneven *semantic context* of prescriptions – to map the ways in which prescriptions form larger hierarchical taxonomies; (3) captures the uneven *communicative*

---

[1] Steering away from discourse analysis, Copeland and Daly (2018) run into a similar analytical dead end. They classify NEG's social prescriptions in three categories, namely, market-making, market-correcting, and mixed. The mixed category in particular muddles up the analytical bases that would allow us to assess the overall direction of NEG's social prescriptions.

context of prescriptions – to account for the differentiated allocation of coercive power to different types of prescriptions across countries, time, and policy areas; and (4) captures the uneven *policy context* of prescriptions – to account for the embeddedness of NEG prescriptions in an uneven European political economy, their national and supranational EU-level path-dependency, and their differentiated deployment across countries and time. Such a research design allows us to link the dots between macro-level theory and processes (e.g., neoliberalism), meso-level operational categories of policy orientation (e.g., commodification and decommodification), and systematic empirical analysis (i.e., the classification, comparison, and assessment of NEG prescriptions in terms of their policy orientation).

In Chapter 5, we situate NEG prescriptions in their semantic, communicative, and policy contexts and draw their implications for our case selection, data collection, and analytical strategies. In section 4.3, we address the issue of linking the policy orientation of NEG prescriptions to the material interests of labour. We argue that commodification is the most relevant dimension for our analysis of the nexus between NEG and labour politics. We then operationalise the concept in the specific policy areas of employment relations and public services.

4.3 TOWARDS A NOVEL APPROACH FOR ASSESSING THE POLICY ORIENTATION OF NEG PRESCRIPTIONS

By looking at the material interests of the social groups that might benefit from NEG prescriptions, or be hurt by them, we can also more fundamentally question the analytical relevance of the policy orientations selected in the two studies discussed in section 4.2: are social investment and quality competitiveness indeed socially progressive and, if yes, for whom? As some analysts have already argued, social investment policies may contribute both to decommodifying labour (e.g., active labour policies provide increased resources for training) and to recommodifying it (e.g., the same policies link welfare payments to work activation) (Greer, 2015; Copeland, 2020; McGann, 2021). Likewise, the promotion of quality competitiveness relies on quality quantification, thus expanding rather than curtailing technocratic governance over employment and social policy areas. In both cases, the decommodifying potential of policy prescriptions is subordinated to a larger commodifying logic. Neither thus truly serves labour's interests in decommodified, solidaristic employment relations and public services.

In contrast, and as argued in Chapter 3, looking at whether NEG employment relations and public services prescriptions promote the further *commodification* of these policy areas allows us to capture the nexus between NEG and labour politics. It does so, more particularly, by addressing labour's interest in opposing commodification and in defending solidaristic, redistributive, decommodified employment relations and public services. Therefore, rather than assessing whether NEG prescriptions follow social investment or social retrenchment objectives, or again quality or cost competitiveness frames, we consider that the policy orientation most relevant to our analysis is the policy prescriptions' potential to advance the commodification or decommodification of employment relations and public services.

In Chapter 3, we follow Harvey (2004) in considering the renewed commodification of employment relations and public services as participating in processes of accumulation by dispossession. This also allows us to operationalise the concept of commodification, most notably by capturing the connections between the *curtailment* of employment relations and public services (dispossession) and their *marketisation* (accumulation) (see also Mercille and Murphy, 2016, 2017; Stan and Toma, 2019; Hermann, 2021). This is highly relevant for our study of NEG interventions in employment relations and public services, as Business Europe and the European Commission and Council regarded both austerity (curtailment) and structural reform (marketisation) as the two main dimensions of NEG, as outlined in Chapter 2.

We thus consider that the commodification of employment relations and public services is two-sided, inasmuch as it combines a *quantitative* attack on the level of workers' wages and on the level of resources and coverage of public services (curtailment) with the *qualitative* marketisation of governance mechanisms in employment relations (bargaining mechanisms and hiring and firing rules) and in public services (at sectoral and provider level). In the opposite direction, decommodification too combines quantitative and qualitative dimensions. The policy developments in this decommodifying direction include, respectively, increasing wage levels, resource levels for public services, and coverage levels of public services and de-marketising, that is, making the governance mechanisms of employment relations and public services more solidaristic and redistributive.

The dynamics of curtailment and marketisation are interlinked. If workers have to live on lower wage levels (curtailment), they are also more vulnerable when facing employers' pressures to flexibilise the employment relations mechanisms that had hitherto protected them from employers' discretionary decisions (marketisation). Likewise, decreased state funding for public services (curtailment) opens up new opportunities for private companies' involvement in these services (marketisation). In transport, state underfunding for British Rail, for example, led to the latter's wholesale privatisation in the 1990s

(Dyrhauge, 2013: 45). In healthcare, decades of underfunding of public health services paved the way for increasing numbers of private hospitals, for example, in Romania in the 2010s (Stan, 2018). In the water sector, the combination of public budget restraints and the need to meet environmental standards was used by governments to justify infrastructure upgrades through public–private partnership (PPP), which gave private capital investors a crucial role (Boda and Scheiring, 2006; Hall and Lobina, 2007).

We understand commodification as a *process* rather than as a condition (i.e., commodity) that social relations can enter or leave (Appadurai, 1986; Hermann, 2021). This is most relevant for assessing the commodification of employment relations and public services. Indeed, in the areas of labour and social reproduction more largely, full commodification has rarely been achieved. In fact, both labour and social reproduction are fictitious commodities (Polanyi, 2001 [1944]; Hermann, 2021). For us, therefore, commodification and decommodification are matters of *relative degree*. This means that, in looking at NEG prescriptions, we assess their potential for *increasing* or *decreasing* commodification in a particular area of intervention. Categorising prescriptions as having a potential for commodification or decommodification thus indicates their potential not so much to fully commodify or decommodify a certain policy area, as to increase its commodification or decommodification *relative to the status quo*. This also allows us to overcome the need to predefine, like Copeland (2020), a series of points on the continuum between decommodification and commodification.

In the following two subsections, we outline the conceptual framework against which we assess the potential of NEG prescriptions to further commodify or decommodify employment relations and public services. This framework is theoretically driven inasmuch as it draws on our theoretical perspective on the nexus between NEG and labour politics but also on existing theoretical discussions of the dimensions of commodification of employment relations and public services.

Analysing the Policy Orientation of NEG Prescriptions in Employment Relations

Within employment relations, we focus on NEG prescriptions that affect workers' terms and conditions *while in employment* (see also Copeland, 2020). This means that we exclude prescriptions on workers' *social wage*, most notably the payments provided by states outside of employment that enable workers' subsistence (e.g., unemployment benefits or pensions, see de la Porte and Natali, 2014) or their employability (e.g., education and training).

TABLE 4.1 *Analytical framework for the analysis of NEG prescriptions on employment relations*

		Policy orientation	
Categories	Dimension	*Commodification*	*Decommodification*
Wage levels	Quantitative	Curtail	Increase
Bargaining mechanisms	Qualitative	Marketise	De-marketise
Hiring and firing mechanisms	Qualitative	Marketise	De-marketise

Source: Our own.

Concretely, we distinguish between three categories that are central to the relationship between management and labour: (1) wage levels, (2) bargaining mechanisms, and (3) hiring and firing mechanisms. Whereas wage levels represent the most significant quantitative feature of employment relations, the latter two areas stand for its most significant qualitative features: bargaining mechanisms determine the operation of employment relations, and hiring and firing mechanisms determine the conditions for the creation and dissolution of employment relationships. Table 4.1 operationalises what commodifying and decommodifying prescriptions mean in each of these three areas of intervention.

Under the **wage levels** category, we distinguish between *commodifying* prescriptions that curtail wage levels and *decommodifying* ones that increase them. Wages are the price that workers receive from employers in exchange for their labour power. At the same time, labour is 'a human activity which goes with life itself' (Polanyi, 2001 [1944]: 75) and not a good produced for sale on the market. Labour is a *fictitious* commodity (Polanyi, 2001 [1944]), inasmuch as it not only has a price but also is vital for securing workers with their subsistence and social reproduction. In the event of wages falling, workers cannot withhold their labour power from the market in the same way that a manufacturer can withhold products until their price increases (Esping-Andersen, 1990: 37). Instead, given wages' importance in ensuring workers' subsistence and social reproduction, workers become even more dependent on selling their labour power to employers, for example by working longer hours or taking up a second job. This may result in a race to the bottom in wage levels. At the extreme, the subordination of labour to a fully self-regulating market threatens not only its social reproduction but also that of society (Polanyi, 2001 [1944]).

To prevent such a development from happening, all European employment relations systems include *decommodifying* political interventions, which ensure that wage levels do not decline below a certain floor (Nowak and Erne, 2024). Sometimes, governments set this wage floor directly by introducing a statutory national minimum wage, or employers and trade unions determine it in collective bargaining agreements. Other times, governments back up wages indirectly by keeping unemployment and welfare benefits as well as public sector wages relatively high, thereby incentivising private sector employers also to provide higher wages. Furthermore, the EU and its member states recognise workers' rights to defend their interests collectively by allowing them to form trade unions, which provide workers protection against arbitrary dismissals. All government decisions in the area of employment relations have therefore a signalling role for the entire labour market and thus – directly or indirectly – also for workers' wage levels. Interventions that aim to roll back these features that workers have achieved over 'years of bargaining and political activity', point in a *commodification* direction, as they increase wage and labour market flexibility under the guise of 'economic efficiency' (Stiglitz, 2002: 13). For the sake of clarity, however, we must assess the quantitative NEG prescriptions that curtail wages directly and the qualitative prescriptions on employment relations mechanisms separately. Under the heading of wage levels, we therefore assess only NEG prescriptions that curtail wage levels directly, either in general or in the public sector in particular.

Furthermore, we must highlight another insight of employment relations research: we cannot assess wage developments in isolation. Our analysis of country-specific prescriptions on wage levels must thus also take the corresponding national inflation and productivity developments into account (Erne, 2008: part II).

Finally, it is also important to note that not all NEG prescriptions that mention wages fall into our quantitative wage levels category. Some prescriptions demand wage increases to be linked to *company-level* productivity developments rather than to overarching sectoral or national benchmarks. Depending on the particular productivity rate in a given company, these prescriptions may (or may not) curtail wage levels. We have nevertheless classified them as commodifying – not because they curtail wages but because they call for a decentralisation of multi-employer bargaining structures. This leads us to consider the qualitative dimension of employment relations, namely, the central mechanisms governing them.

Under the **bargaining mechanisms** category, we distinguish between *commodifying* prescriptions that call for a decentralisation and individualisation of bargaining mechanisms between employers and workers that expose workers to increased market pressures and *decommodifying* prescriptions that favour solidaristic collective agreements (Schulten, 2002). The decentralisation and individualisation of bargaining mechanisms marketise bargaining mechanisms by making labour more like a commodity to be bought and sold on the market. In contrast, solidaristic collective bargaining institutions (such as multi-employer bargaining arrangements) de-marketise bargaining mechanisms by setting collectively agreed standards that apply to all employers covered by the agreement, thus taking workers' wages and working conditions out of competition (Pontusson, 2006).

Individualisation and decentralisation both matter when it comes to deciding whether the bargaining logic is decommodifying (solidaristic) or commodifying (individualistic) (Schulten, 2002; Thelen, 2014). Individualisation is a more radically commodifying process in which collective agreements are abolished altogether and employees are left to negotiate individually with the management. Decentralisation is still within the domain of collective employment relations, but we consider it as a step on the way towards individualisation, thus participating in the further commodification of employment relations. Decentralisation means a downward shift in the dominant level of bargaining. The dominant level means the level of the economy at which the negotiations on core employment issues take place. This can be the firm (company), the industry, the sector, or the entire economy – the latter three are also called multi-employer bargaining because more than one employer's participation is needed for their functioning. Negotiations can occur at multiple levels, but what matters is the hierarchy of these levels. In centralised bargaining systems, actors at the lower level (for example, in a single firm) have only limited space to deviate from the terms set at the higher level. Following decentralisation, these higher levels lose their relevance and give way to the lower levels in determining the key parameters of wages and working conditions. Negotiations at national, sectoral, or industry level may disappear altogether. They may also just be hollowed out, meaning that they no longer set enforceable targets for lower levels, only propose broad guidelines, or allow a broad range of exemptions on various grounds.

Until recently, the policy orientation of collective bargaining has coincided with the level on which bargaining takes place: the higher the level at which the bargaining takes place, the more solidaristic the logic (hence enhancing decommodification). If there is no collective agreement, contracts will be by default negotiated (or even imposed in the case of vulnerable workers such as undocumented immigrants) at individual level, hence pointing to the deepest possible commodification of bargaining mechanisms. Examples include bargaining mechanisms in the United States or Britain, which have consistently led to much more differentiated and therefore more unequal wage policy outcomes, as they reflect the lack of centralised, multi-employer bargaining systems in these liberal market economies (Crouch, 1999; Thelen, 2001; Pontusson, 2006). In turn, company-level agreements illustrate a slightly less extreme form of commodification: if they adopt the solidaristic principle of setting employment conditions at company level, they limit competition between workers inside it (decommodification); however, workers still find themselves in competition with workers from other companies active in the sector (commodification). At the next level, sector-level bargaining may diminish competition in terms of wages and working conditions between companies in a sector and thus contribute to further decreasing labour commodification. Finally, national-level collective bargaining can provide the most elaborated version of solidaristic, decommodified wage policy. An example is the Rehn-Meidner model, named after two Swedish trade union economists, which used 'deliberate, centrally controlled force to counteract ... the centrifugal force of the market, i.e., its tendency towards wage differentiation' (Meidner and Heldborg, 1984: 71 cited in Schulten, 2002: 174).

Although the bargaining level remains a widely used industrial relations indicator,[2] its significance has been undermined by the radical changes undertaken by a number of EU countries. More specifically, multi-employer collective bargaining agreements have increasingly allowed local deviations from collectively agreed standards over time. This happened, for instance, in Germany in 2004 when the opening and hardship clauses of a new sector-wide agreement allowed company-level agreements to derogate from collectively agreed sectoral wage standards (European Commission, 2010a). These changes led to bargaining levels and policy orientations of collective bargaining mechanisms starting to diverge.

Therefore, as the bargaining level per se can no longer capture the decommodifying and commodifying potential of bargaining mechanisms, we distinguish instead between *more* solidaristic and *more* individualistic mechanisms to set workers' terms and conditions. The first mechanisms de-marketise bargaining mechanisms by decreasing competition between workers (decommodification). The second marketise these mechanisms by increasing competition and thus workers' exposure to market pressures or, better said, to the power of capital (commodification).

We define solidaristic collective bargaining narrowly, meaning mechanisms to ensure the equality of wages within one country across different employee groups. The narrowness of this definition implies that the equality of wages

---

[2] See the OECD/AIAS ICTWSS database (OECD, 2022).

may go together with overall wage moderation. We therefore regard NEG prescriptions in favour of centralised collective bargaining as *decommodifying*, although national collective bargaining institutions have often been used to moderate wages to get an international competitive advantage within an ever more integrated European economy (Molina and Rhodes, 2002; Erne, 2008). This conceptualisation is also analytically consistent and ensures that our categories do not overlap. Our first category on wage levels captures calls for the curtailment of wages as *commodifying* interventions. In turn, we classify NEG prescriptions that call for centralised collective bargaining structures under the bargaining mechanisms category as prescriptions with a *decommodifying* policy orientation.

Governments rarely intervene directly in the content and mechanisms of bargaining – except when they are themselves the employers – but they can still influence them indirectly. This is particularly relevant for our study, as it is neither employers nor trade unions who receive NEG prescriptions but member state governments. The formal rules for government intervention in collective bargaining vary across the EU, but governments in general are capable of changing the legal framework in which bargaining takes place between employers and trade unions. In this context, *commodifying* prescriptions ask governments to promote bargaining decentralisation. In turn, prescriptions are *decommodifying* if they call for an expansion and strengthening of these supports.

Our third category in employment relations covers **hiring and firing mechanisms**, which refer to the rules that determine employment boundaries and employers' discretion in setting them. Prescriptions under this category may either decrease workers' protection in this respect, and thus lead to a higher exposure of workers to market vagaries and the power of employers (*commodification*), or increase workers' protection vis-à-vis such vagaries and power (*decommodification*). This category includes prescriptions relative to the duration of employment as well as those relative to (collective) dismissal rules. The first may seek to *commodify* labour by reducing contract durations (e.g., fixed-term and temporary agency work versus permanent contracts), the second by favouring more flexible dismissal rules (e.g., by abolishing rules on unfair dismissal, adopting rules that are less protective on notice periods, compensation in the case of dismissal, reinstatement rights, and so on).

Protections on the duration of employment and on dismissal rules may overlap. A lower contract duration (e.g., fixed-term) may serve as a functional equivalent to easier firing: they both serve to increase management's discretion vis-à-vis workers. In theory, workers also may benefit from increased flexibility – as easier firing means also easier hiring according to the advocates of employment reforms. However, as workers must work to ensure their subsistence, even workers enjoying trade union collective bargaining rights are 'typically in a disadvantageous position in labour markets': 'It is far easier for an employer to replace recalcitrant workers than for employees to "replace" a recalcitrant employer, especially when the unemployment rate is high' (Stiglitz, 2002: 13).

Finally, we should note that prescriptions in the areas of wage levels, bargaining mechanisms, and hiring and firing mechanisms may also focus more closely on public sector employment relations. This is possible because governments are also the employers in the public sector. In that role, they can act as *decommodifying* model employers promoting higher wages, more encompassing collective bargaining mechanisms, and more protective hiring and firing mechanisms (Szabó, 2018). Alternatively, they can use the signalling role of public sector employment relations to drive down private sector wages, decentralise bargaining, and lower the protection offered by hiring and firing mechanisms – therefore promoting *commodification*.

In the next subsection, we turn to the ways in which we have operationalised the potential of NEG prescriptions to further commodify or decommodify public services.

Analysing the Policy Orientation of NEG Prescriptions on Public Services

The commodification of public services may affect both their provision and users' access to them. In this study, we therefore consider NEG prescriptions that affect both the *provision* of public services and *access* to them, as this allows us to capture the degree to which these prescriptions may affect both workers and users – and thus have the potential to trigger counter-reactions from both organised labour and users. Although provision and access are interlinked, we nonetheless distinguish between prescriptions affecting first and foremost provision and those affecting first and foremost access. We combine in a single table (see Table 4.2) the categories that we used to assess the potential for commodification or decommodification of NEG prescriptions on the provision of public services and on access to these services.

Among prescriptions affecting the **provision of public services**, we distinguish three categories, namely, one with a quantitative dimension (resource levels) and two with a qualitative dimension (sector-level as well as provider-level governance mechanisms).

Among NEG prescriptions on **resource levels**, we consider those requesting the curtailment of these resources as *commodifying*. Curtailment measures in this area include attacks either on the levels of expenditure on public services

TABLE 4.2 *Analytical framework for the analysis of NEG prescriptions on public services*

	Categories	Dimension	Policy orientation	
			Commodification	*Decommodification*
Provision of public services	**Resource levels**	Quantitative	Curtail	Increase
	Sector-level governance mechanisms	Qualitative	Marketise	De-marketise
	Provider-level governance mechanisms	Qualitative	Marketise	De-marketise
Access to public services	**Coverage levels**	Quantitative	Curtail	Increase
	Cost-coverage mechanisms	Qualitative	Marketise	De-marketise

Source: Our own.

(e.g., cuts in the budget allocated to the sector) or on the material infrastructure needed for the provision of services (e.g., cuts in the number of hospitals or hospital beds, of railway and bus lines, or of water infrastructure and water provision levels). The curtailment of resource levels may also be a result of what some analysts see as 'implicit privatisation' (Schmid et al., 2010: 459), namely, the shift of expenditure and service levels from areas where services are provided mostly by public providers to areas where private providers play a more prominent role (e.g., the shift from inpatient to outpatient care). In the opposite direction, we consider prescriptions seeking to increase the levels of expenditure and the material infrastructure available to public service providers as *decommodifying*. This classification is warranted inasmuch as such an increase channels resources towards public providers. The degree to which this happens can, however, be evaluated only by looking at the larger context, namely, the extent to which public services have already been commodified. Indeed, in cases where private providers have already entered the sector following previous commodification waves (more specifically by marketising their sector- and provider-level governance mechanisms, see below), increased public resource levels could be used to bolster the private provision of these services (and hence commodification).

NEG prescriptions may *commodify* public services also by marketising their **sector-level governance mechanisms**. Among these, we first distinguish those seeking to establish sector-wide regulatory and service-purchasing independence. Regulatory independence involves moving the regulation of the sector (i.e., the terms and conditions for the use of public infrastructure as well as the relations between service providers) from democratic government control (i.e., relevant ministries) to a regulatory authority that is independent of the state (e.g., transport, water, or healthcare agencies). Likewise, service-purchasing independence involves the establishment of bodies (e.g., national healthcare funds or national transport authorities) that manage public service funds and contract public services out to (private or public) service providers. These regulatory bodies are called independent, as they are not subject to democratic control (i.e., relevant ministries and parliaments). Both regulatory and purchasing independence are portrayed as technocratic fixes that place decisions beyond the influence of politics to ensure a conducive environment for competition (De Francesco and Castro, 2018). The declared goal of independent regulators and purchasers is to make all service providers (including publicly owned ones) behave like private companies, as well as to ensure access to the sector for private providers and to fight monopolies.

Prescriptions seeking to marketise sector-level governance mechanisms (and thus *commodify* public service provision) may also include those seeking to open the sector to private providers. These measures have been known in the literature as leading to the liberalisation of public services.[3] Liberalisation can be achieved by allowing sector-level purchasers to buy services from private providers as well as by introducing competitive tendering mechanisms in the sector (Hermann and Verhoest, 2012). Decision makers qualify competitive tendering, also known in the EU as procurement, as a way to increase the cost-efficiency of public services by increasing competition among service providers (Kunzlik, 2013). In addition, private service providers can enter public services sectors through PPPs. PPPs are long-term contractual agreements where private companies make an initial investment (usually in infrastructure) that the state subsequently repays over the life of the project (Ménard, 2009; Mercille and Murphy, 2016). In turn, sector-level governance may be *decommodified* by making sector-level regulators and purchasers subject to greater democratic government control and by decreasing the opening of the sector to competition from private providers. The latter involves re-erecting barriers to private providers' entry into the sector.

NEG prescriptions may *commodify* public services also by marketising their **provider-level governance mechanisms**. Among these prescriptions, we first distinguish those that seek to change the legal status of public providers. Thus, prescriptions may seek to transfer providers' assets from public ownership into private hands (e.g., selling to private companies publicly owned hospitals, water utility companies, or public bus or railway companies). This is what is generally understood by the privatisation of public services and what Krachler, Greer, and Umney (2022: 2) aptly term 'material privatisation'. Other prescriptions seeking to change the legal status of public providers may give private companies the right to contract out services with the latter, resulting in what Krachler, Greer, and Umney (2022: 2) call 'functional privatisation'. This involves, in a first step, the division of public services into core and secondary services, with the first remaining to be provided in-house by public providers and the second being, in a second step, outsourced to private providers (e.g., the contracting out of ancillary cleaning, catering, and diagnostic services in healthcare or the leasing of marginal rail lines in transport). Sometimes, outsourcing secondary services has prepared the ground for outsourcing core services. Finally, a change in public providers' legal status may entail their corporatisation. This involves incorporating public service providers under private company law although their ownership remains public

---

[3] While acknowledging its normative connotations (e.g., its positive association with 'freedom'), in this book we use the term liberalisation in a descriptive manner, as including measures that seek to increase the opening of a sector to competition from private providers.

(e.g., the transfer of responsibilities from local authorities to a water utility; changing the status of public hospitals to autonomous commercial units). Corporatisation moves providers from the public services sector to the semi-state sector, whereby they are subject to EU competition rules. It may sometimes be a first step towards full (material) privatisation. Corporatisation also normally means that workers are not governed by collective public service agreements. This shows that the commodification of employment relations and of public services are interconnected and have feedback effects.

NEG prescriptions that commodify public services by marketising their provider-level governance may also affect providers' internal operation. This may happen, most notably, by promoting the introduction of models imported from the private business sector, namely, new public management or managerialism (Clarke, Gewirtz, and McLaughlin, 2010). Managerialisation may include corporate governance reforms that strengthen the power of company management and reduce the influence of public service workers and trade unions on the day-to-day management of the company. Managerialisation may also include managerial reforms that centralise financial control, monitoring, and surveillance in the hands of managers. This rests on 'governance by numbers' (Supiot, 2017), which involves segmenting services into tasks that are priced in the light of cost-benefit calculations; increasing the visibility of financial flows (e.g., by introducing e-health measures such as user identifiers); introducing methods for financing providers on the basis of fixed-priced reimbursement rates (e.g., the diagnostic-related-groups [DRG] method in healthcare) (Krachler, Greer, and Umney, 2022); or introducing performance-based payment, wage, and fund-allocation systems. These measures serve to place workers in competition with one another and increase managers' control of them (Friedberg et al., 2010).[4] Increased managerial control at provider level is a precondition of increasing central managerial control at sector level (as seen above).

In the opposite direction, prescriptions seeking to de-marketise provider-level governance mechanisms (and thus *decommodify* public services provision) may do so by favouring a public status for providers. This can be achieved, for example, through the public repossession of privatised facilities and assets or by reverting to the in-house provision of outsourced services. An example is the re-municipalisation of water services, whereby local authorities take back direct

---

[4] Some of these measures, such as fixed-priced reimbursement rates or performance-based payments, may enhance competition not only inside but also among public service providers and thus may affect not only provider-level but also sector-level governance. We, however, have classed them under the first, as this is where changes have to be effected first.

control of services previously contracted out to private providers (Kishimoto, Gendall, and Lobina, 2015). Decommodification may also follow prescriptions seeking to move public providers away from market-like technocratic management to public service administration, most specifically by increasing workers' and citizens' democratic oversight over decision making.

Among prescriptions affecting users' **access to public services** (see lower part of Table 4.2), we distinguish between prescriptions on coverage levels (quantitative) and those on coverage mechanisms (qualitative dimension).

Prescriptions on **coverage levels** with a potential for *commodification* include those seeking to curtail the scope of services or again the range of the population covered by public schemes (e.g., in the first case, by reducing the range of services covered by public schemes and, in the second, by excluding some categories of people from automatic coverage). In the opposite direction, access to public services may be *decommodified* by increasing the scope of services and the range of population covered by public schemes.

Prescriptions seeking to *commodify* access to services by marketising **cost-coverage mechanisms** include those seeking to make these mechanisms more dependent on users' private means (e.g., by introducing co-payments and private insurance for accessing healthcare services or water charges and cost-recovery mechanisms for accessing water services). In the opposite direction, access to public services may be *decommodified* by reintroducing redistributive mechanisms (such as progressive taxation or social insurance) to cover the cost of public services to users and by making access free at the point of delivery.

The privatisation of service provision, the managerialisation of service organisation, sector-level regulatory and purchasing independence, the opening of public services sectors to private providers, competitive tendering, and recourse to cost-coverage mechanisms putting a premium on private means all contribute to the *marketisation* of public services.[5] Policymakers who promote marketising policies claim that the latter increase competition and thus lead to a more cost-efficient allocation of resources and an

---

[5] As mentioned above, marketisation includes measures that seek to make public services more market-like and give private actors more space in the funding, provision, and management of these services. For us, marketisation is thus but one component (namely, accumulation) of the two sides of the commodification coin, the other being attacks on the commons of public services (i.e., dispossession). In this, we differ from Crespy (2016: 35), who sees marketisation as a synonym of commodification, or from Krachler, Greer, and Umney (2022: 2), who define it as the 'introduction or intensification of cost based competition among service providers' and 'a property of the transaction between purchaser and provider'. The latter authors place marketisation at the micro level and assume that it leads to increased competition. In contrast, we understand marketisation as a meso-level process, involving institutional arrangements facilitating capitalist accumulation in public services.

improvement in service quality. Nonetheless, in practice, marketisation often far from lives up to these promises. Managerialisation may lead to public service providers playing with numbers in a bid to increase the costs reimbursed by public funders (e.g., hospitals allocating patient cases under higher-priced DRGs) (Krachler, Greer, and Umney, 2022). Public service providers may also seek to reach cost-cutting managerial targets by increasing the pace of service delivery, resulting not only in increased workloads and worsening working conditions for public services workers (Flecker and Hermann, 2012; Galetto, Marginson, and Spieser, 2014; Kunkel, 2021) but also in lower service quality for users (Mihailovic, Kocic, and Jakovljevic, 2016; Armstrong et al., 2000; Hermann, 2021). Likewise, the privatisation of service provision may foster the selective appropriation of more profitable services by private providers – leaving more costly ones to be provided by generally underfunded and overloaded public providers (Krachler, Greer, and Umney, 2022). In turn, this may lead, over time, to increased capital concentration rather than competition among providers (Buch-Hansen and Wigger, 2011).

In our analysis, we classify prescriptions in the different categories detailed in this section according to whether the *object* rather than the *aim* of prescriptions fits a particular category. By looking at what prescriptions address in the first instance (object) rather than at what they might allegedly realise in policymakers' view (aims), we seek to avoid conceptual fuzziness and analytical uncertainty. Indeed, as many prescriptions have multiple aims, classifying them according to their aims would be difficult, if not impossible. For example, prescriptions on cost-coverage mechanisms (e.g., introduce co-payments for medical services) aim in the end to curtail healthcare expenditure (and hence resource levels available for public service provision) but concern in the first instance the cost of services to users. We therefore classify these prescriptions under access to public services and its cost-coverage mechanisms category rather than the category of resource levels under provision of public services.

Having operationalised the concept of commodification in the areas of employment relations and public services, we now turn to the analytical strategies that we adopt in assessing the patterns of NEG prescriptions across countries, time, and policy areas.

5

Contextualising the EU's NEG Prescriptions and Research Design

5.1 INTRODUCTION

In Chapter 4, we highlighted the need for a research design that acknowledges the links between the policy orientation of new economic governance (NEG) prescriptions and the material interests of different social groups. We thus identified commodification as the policy orientation most relevant to our analysis of the nexus between EU economic governance and labour politics and developed a corresponding analytical framework to assess NEG prescriptions in the areas of employment relations and public services. Before engaging in this assessment, however, we need to understand their meaning, for which we must make an additional analytical move.

The meaning of NEG policy prescriptions depends not only on their wording but also on their location in larger policy scripts and their uneven coercive power across countries, time, and policy areas. Hence, NEG prescriptions are embedded in larger semantic fields and taxonomies, in power struggles over the definition of appropriate solutions to social problems, and in the uneven European political economy. This chapter thus first explains the semantic, communicative, and policy contexts in which we situate NEG prescriptions and then outlines the implications of this analytical move for our research design, including case selection, data collection, and comparative approach.

5.2 HOW TO MAP THE PATTERNS OF PRESCRIPTIONS ACROSS COUNTRIES, TIME, AND POLICY AREAS?

In Chapter 4, we argued that, to assess NEG prescriptions, we need not only to link them to the interests of concrete social groups (in our case, labour and its interest in opposing the commodification of employment relations and public services) but also to account for the hierarchical ordering of prescriptions in larger policy scripts unevenly deployed across countries, time, and policy areas. In order to address the latter point, we highlighted that we need a research design that captures (1) the uneven *semantic context* of prescriptions – to map the ways in which prescriptions form larger hierarchical taxonomies; (2) the uneven *communicative context* of prescriptions – to account for the differentiated allocation of coercive power to different types of prescriptions across countries, time, and policy areas; and (3) the uneven *policy context* of prescriptions – to account for the embeddedness of NEG prescriptions in an uneven European political economy, for their national-, supranational-, and EU-level path-dependency, and for their differentiated deployment across countries, time, and policy areas. In this section, we look at each of these contexts and then draw their implications for our research design.

Semantic Contexts and Hierarchical Taxonomies

The semantic context of policy prescriptions refers to how the meaning of prescriptions emerges from their relations with other prescriptions found in the policy documents of which they are part. Approaching policy prescriptions in this way reflects a core insight from linguistics: namely, that the relationship between symbols (including written ones, i.e., words), what they stand for (e.g., objects, actions, ideas), and the meanings that they carry with them (e.g., literal and metaphorical) are *arbitrary* (Lavenda and Schultz, 2020). Indeed, symbols, what they stand for, and their meanings vary from society to society and even from social group to social group, as well as across time. Therefore, to fully grasp the meaning of words (in our case, policy terms) rather than simply and solely look at the content signified by the symbols, we need to consider the semantic *relationships* established between them in a given symbolic field (e.g., a language or, in our case, the set of policy texts produced in a certain policy area).

Semantic interconnections between words are nonetheless far from random but cluster in more complex taxonomies. Taxonomies are systems of classification that organise *hierarchically* the sets of terms and concepts used to name and understand specific areas of reality. Classical taxonomies include those developed by botanists and zoologists since the eighteenth century, yet all human societies develop their own 'folk' taxonomies (Vanpool and Vanpool, 2009) in relation to the various aspects of reality. The latter include not only flora and fauna but also the desired solutions to the social problems of human societies, of which employment and social policies are modern welfare state variants. Taxonomies are not universal but reflect time- and place-specific understandings of reality. In turn, when mobilised in actual social practices of linguistic performance (e.g., policy documents), they provide the symbolic classifications and thus lenses through which social actors perceive reality.

By seeing policy formulations as part of larger policy taxonomies, we do not need to assume that the latter are fully coherent or that they are perfectly self-contained and distinct from other taxonomies. Even the most polished social policy taxonomies, namely, social policy paradigms, share policy terms and solutions with other paradigms and in this sense overlap with one another and have fuzzy boundaries. This does not make them indeterminate or ever changing, as taxonomies point to hierarchical connections between terms that have a certain degree of consistency across policy documents produced in different spatial and temporal locations. Moreover, seeing policy formulations as organised in folk (rather than scientific) taxonomies highlights their strangeness and thus unsettles their proponents' claims that the solutions they offer to social problems are logical, natural, or universal. Policy responses are as folk, as strange, and as exotic as the Medio period (1200–1450) fauna classifications from northwest Mexico documented by Vanpool and Vanpool (2009). Bringing hospital case-based financing and active labour market policies together under the same banner of structural reforms responding to the 2008 financial crisis is as strange as grouping owls, rattlesnakes, and shamans under the category of night creatures (Vanpool and Vanpool, 2009). Both classifications reflect understandings of reality that are specific to a certain time, place, and social location rather than universal.

To assess the meaning of policy prescriptions found in NEG documents and the connections that link them with one another, we draw on ethno-semantic analysis developed by linguistic anthropologists (Vanpool and Vanpool, 2009; Spradley, 2016). Ethno-semantic analysis assesses 'the underlying semantic *connections*' between words (emphasis added) (Vanpool and Vanpool, 2009: 529) to map the *patterns* of word usage across texts produced in different locations and periods in time and their grouping in the hierarchically ordered and more encompassing semantic domains (or *categories*) that, in turn, form larger taxonomies. This type of analysis thus allows us to map the articulation of NEG prescriptions on employment relations and public services in larger policy taxonomies as well as cross-country and cross-time patterns. For the purpose of this book, we draw on the theoretically driven categories, depicted in Chapter 4, of commodification and decommodification of employment relations and public services to uncover NEG taxonomies and patterns in these areas.

Before looking at how ethno-semantic analysis can be applied to the analysis of NEG documents, let us define the units of our analysis. Several scholars and European Commission analysts have pointed out that most country-specific recommendations (CSRs) contain not one but several policy statements that may apply to quite distinct areas of intervention. They have hence divided CSRs into several sub-parts, components, policy measures (Efstathiou and Wolff, 2018), policy issues (Copeland, 2020), and sub-recommendations (Darvas and Leandro, 2015; Clauwaert, 2018). It follows that it does not make much sense to assess the policy orientation of whole CSRs (Copeland and Daly, 2018). Instead, we need to look at their smaller and policy area-specific sub-components. Our units of analysis are therefore policy prescriptions, which we define as the shortest policy statements that make sense from a semantic point of view.

If the meaning of NEG prescriptions cannot be understood in isolation but only by considering the other prescriptions to which they are semantically linked, we can then use ethno-semantic analysis to map their deployment across NEG documents in a systematic manner. This presupposes mapping the semantic relations between each prescription and the concentrical textual fields of which it is part. These are formed first by all prescriptions accompanying it in the CSR of which it is part and then by all prescriptions found in the CSRs issued in the corresponding country- and year-specific Council Recommendation.

To illustrate such an approach, let us take as an example the prescription to 'increase cost-effectiveness' in healthcare, issued to Ireland in 2014 (Council Recommendation Ireland 2014/C 247/07). This prescription may be seen as ambiguous and thus illustrating the empty signifier approach to NEG seen in Chapter 4. Indeed, we could understand its meaning in two different ways: to increase the number of healthcare services provided while keeping the level of expenditure constant or to keep the level of healthcare services constant while reducing the level of expenditure. However, although these possible readings have divergent takes on the fate of healthcare expenditure, they both involve an intensification of service provision that is detrimental to workers' employment conditions and users' service quality (and thus commodifying). Moreover, this prescription takes an even clearer meaning if we consider the other prescriptions surrounding it in the document. We discover that the prescription sits in CSR2, where it is accompanied by prescriptions on increasing central financial control in healthcare and on introducing e-health measures. The latter two prescriptions thus explain what the 2014 Council Recommendation for Ireland meant by increased cost-effectiveness: a process that is about enhancing managerial control over financial flows in the healthcare sector rather than about improving health outcomes. The juxtaposition of these different prescriptions signals the semantic connections between them and thus their belonging to a common semantic category. Looking further afield, we notice that CSR1 from the same document includes prescriptions on the need to achieve 'fiscal adjustment' by enforcing binding government expenditure ceilings and that both CSR3 and CSR4 include a series of prescriptions in the area of active labour market policies. The prescription to increase cost-effectiveness in healthcare acquires therefore new shades, as it becomes one component of a larger package prioritising the curtailment of state funding (through fiscal adjustment) and the further marketisation of labour (through its activation, see Greer, 2015; McGann, 2021) – rather than better and more evenly distributed health services and health outcomes.

Looking at textual fields *closest* to prescriptions gives us an intimation of what ethno-semantic analysis achieves in terms of unearthing the meanings of prescriptions and grouping them in semantic categories. A systematic analysis, though, also needs a consideration of *wider* textual fields. In our case, the latter include the field formed by all policy prescriptions issued since the start of the NEG for the EU member state under consideration. This helps us uncover the whole range of meanings with which ambiguous prescriptions are associated in NEG documents and thus get closer to uncovering their core meaning. Of importance for ambiguous prescriptions are the more precisely formulated prescriptions with which they are semantically linked. For example, the prescription to increase cost-effectiveness in healthcare is associated mostly with prescriptions seeking more explicitly to commodify healthcare (see map of semantic links in Table A5.1 in the Online Appendix). Likewise, we can trace the meaning of vague prescriptions by uncovering their semantic links to similarly but more precisely formulated prescriptions present in Council Recommendations issued for the same country in other years. For example, we can elucidate the meaning of the prescription to 'open up the services sector to further competition, including ... *professional services*' (Council Recommendation Italy 2011/C 215/02, emphasis added) issued for Italy between 2011 and 2015 by looking at all similarly formulated prescriptions across all documents issued in the years under study for the same country. Italy received a similar prescription in 2016, whereby healthcare was explicitly included in a longer explanatory list: 'increase competition in *regulated professions* [and the] ... *health sector*' (Council Recommendation Italy 2016/C 299/01, emphasis added). This can help us see that healthcare may have been implicitly targeted by commodifying NEG prescriptions requesting increased competition in the sector even before the term was explicitly mentioned in relation to that. The meanings of apparently ambiguous or vague prescriptions are therefore not floating above actual NEG documents, freely associating with one or another prescription (as empty signifiers). Instead, they are sedimented in temporally successive layers that pull them in certain directions rather than others (i.e., commodification or decommodification).

A consideration of prescriptions' widest textual field, namely, the one formed by all prescriptions issued for all countries and years under consideration, allows us to document whether prescriptions display any common *patterns* across countries and years and to assess on this basis their position in NEG taxonomies. For example, prescriptions with similar formulations to the one issued to Ireland in 2014 (to increase cost-efficiency in healthcare) were issued twelve times for the four countries under study in the period 2009–2019; namely, four times to Germany (2011–2014), five times to Ireland (2014–2016, 2018–2019), and three times to Romania (2013–2014, 2019). That these prescriptions are also richly linked semantically to a whole set of commodifying prescriptions indicates that their dominant meaning is a commodifying rather than a decommodifying one. It also indicates that cost-efficiency may be one of the threads connecting a number of NEG prescriptions in healthcare in a common commodifying *script* (see also below).

A consideration of the semantic context of NEG prescriptions allows us to unearth the larger *taxonomies* of which they are part and the *patterns* that they form across countries, time, and policy areas. We need, however, to move a step further in our analytical strategy to link these taxonomies and patterns with social (class) conflict. As seen in section 3.3, focusing on commodification allows us to capture the nexus between NEG and labour politics. But how can the deployment of NEG prescriptions across countries, time, and policy areas be accounted for in terms of the struggles among concrete social actors and their interests? To answer this question, we now turn to the communicative context of prescriptions.

Communicative Contexts and Struggles over the Naming of Reality

The communicative context of prescriptions refers to how their meanings emerge in the specific practices of communication that inform the production of policy documents. Drawing on the sociology of the state and policymaking, we understand the production of policy documents as involving 'symbolic struggles' over 'the power to produce and to impose the legitimate vision of the world' (Bourdieu, 1989: 20). Indeed, policy documents imbue with symbolic legitimacy (and, in the case of NEG documents, also with legal power) the policy terms on which they draw. These terms are nonetheless not neutral or natural but rather an outcome of the symbolic struggles that social actors[1]

---

[1] By contrast to Zeitlin and Vanhercke (2018), we use the term 'social actors' in its original sociological sense, as referring to groups of people in a society engaged in collective action. Accordingly, we refer to Zeitlin and Vanhercke's largely institutional 'social actors' as social *policy* actors.

wage over the definition of social problems and what are to be considered as their adequate solutions. In these struggles, social actors are differently positioned in terms of economic, political, and cultural capital (Bourdieu, 1994) and hence have different efficacy in imprinting their views on policy documents and their key terms.

In these struggles, social actors rally behind various approaches to social policy to advance their own interests. In practice, these approaches coagulate around a limited range of social policy paradigms. The share and the relative pre-eminence in policy documents of concepts informed by one or another paradigm are an outcome of symbolic struggles among social actors. Paradigms, however, function not simply as pre-existing, stable reference points that actors mobilise in symbolic struggles. They are themselves the object of symbolic struggles whereby some social actors (most notably policymakers and social policy scholars) seek to reinforce the coherence and stability of paradigms, whereas others seek to challenge them. In this process, some actors might seek to build on the inherent arbitrariness of language to enhance the ambiguity of policy terms and make the boundaries between paradigms more porous. Otherwise said, coherence and ambiguity are moving stakes, not fixed outcomes.

We therefore consider the production of NEG policy prescriptions as a communicative process whereby variously situated actors struggle to impose their own views of the problems encountered by EU member states after the 2008 crisis and of the measures needed to respond to them. Most studies of NEG prescriptions on employment and social policy have concentrated on the actors most closely involved in the production of NEG documents (namely, the European Commission and the Council as addressers and member state governments as addressees). Thus, as seen above, scholars participating in the socialisation debate concur to distinguish between economic and social policy actors at EU and national level but come to different conclusions regarding the outcome of their struggles for the orientation of NEG in employment and social policy.

We argue that, although valuable, these studies gloss over several aspects of the symbolic struggles waged by social actors over policy documents and terms – aspects that are crucial for analysing the deployment of NEG prescriptions across countries and time. As seen in Chapter 4, we need to enlarge our perspective on NEG (and its documents) by taking into consideration that its production is the result of struggles not only among institutional actors at national and supranational EU level (discussed in the socialisation debate) but also among *interest groups* – most notably organised labour and capital (Erne, 2023a). Moreover, the production of policy documents involves social actors struggling not only to impose certain views of the world, and thus certain policy orientations through language, but also to enhance the *coercive power* of language. In our case, and as several analysts have pointed out (Erne, 2015; Baeten and Vankercke, 2016; de la Porte and Heins, 2016; Crespy and Schmidt, 2017; Dawson, 2018; Bekker, 2021), this enhancement goes beyond the use of language per se to include the assignation of *legal bases* to individual NEG prescriptions.

The coercive power of a prescription depends on its legal basis and on the location of the receiving country in NEG's enforcement regime, which is determined by struggles over the state's inclusion or exclusion in disciplinary NEG procedures (Figure 2.1; Table 5.1). Critical scholars in the socialisation debate have found this process to be far from neutral, as the prescriptions with the strongest legal bases have been structurally linked to conservative fiscal and economic objectives (Baeten and Vanhercke, 2016; Crespy and Schmidt, 2017; Dawson, 2018). The struggles have thus typically been over the extent of austerity and most particularly over the curtailment and marketisation of employment relations and public services to achieve these objectives. These scholars thus saw the battle over 'the lens under which policy should be examined' (Dawson, 2018: 203) as having resulted in a lose-lose game for labour and social policy: social prescriptions were based either on the non-binding Europe 2020 strategy, which may accommodate socially progressive objectives but provides a weak legal base, or on disciplinary procedures, in which case they acquire significant coercive power, but only by at the same time being geared towards socially regressive objectives (Dawson, 2018). However, precisely because NEG prescriptions target different countries and policy areas differently in terms of their frequency and coercive power, we need to adopt a research design that is also able to capture these differences empirically.

The assignment of coercive power to prescriptions during the production of NEG documents reveals power differentials between different member states, and between them and EU executives, and in the ways in which they are drawn upon in NEG's vertical policymaking and surveillance process. We thus need a research design that allows us to map the patterns of prescriptions across countries and time and, in so doing, capture variations in terms of both their meaning (and thus location in NEG taxonomies and spatial–temporal patterns) and their coercive power. Hence, continuing with the example provided in the previous subsection, just counting the frequency of prescriptions 'to increase cost-effectiveness in healthcare' is not enough; we also need to capture their varying coercive power from country to country and year to year, as well as the patterns of their coerciveness across countries and time. By highlighting the combination of this pattern of coerciveness and the consistent semantic association of these prescriptions with other more clearly commodifying prescriptions, our research design thus also allows us to question their signifying emptiness. Instead, rather than confirming their ambiguity, our analysis reinforces our previous insight on the dominant orientation of these prescriptions being the commodification rather than the decommodification of healthcare.

A consideration of how policies are patterned across time and countries is crucial if we want to understand the overall orientation and therefore deeper nature of NEG prescriptions in a specific policy area. Thus, the repeated occurrence of prescriptions oriented towards the commodification of healthcare, which, at the same time, usually had significant coercive power (Chapter 10), signals the channelling of NEG interventions in healthcare into a strong commodifying policy flow rather than an indeterminate policy drizzle mixing commodifying and decommodifying raindrops. To see how and why this flow may follow an overarching script rather than being a simple accumulation of similarly oriented prescriptions, we need, last but not least, to also take into consideration the policy context of NEG prescriptions.

Policy Contexts and the Uneven Deployment of NEG Prescriptions

The policy context of NEG prescriptions refers to how their content and coercive power relate to other current and past policies adopted at national and EU level. Studies in the varieties-of-welfare tradition draw on neo-institutional approaches to highlight the importance of institutional trajectories in understanding current social policies (Esping-Andersen, 1990). In doing so, they highlight path-dependency as one of their important dimensions, document how social policies coalesce at national level in distinct pathways or varieties (Hall and Soskice, 2001), and then use these varieties to make country-by-country comparisons.

Thinking in terms of varieties, however, raises important methodological and analytical questions, given that, at the outset, these varieties were far from isolated from one another and that, in the last decades, they have been pushed in a similar commodifying direction (Crouch, 2005; Copeland, 2020; Hermann, 2021). This push towards the commodification of employment relations and public services has also been the result of policymakers at national and EU level participating in a common transnational policy space in which neoliberal approaches have become ever more powerful (Blyth, 2013; Ban, 2016). In a European context, it is not only national governments but also EU institutions (and most notably the Commission and the Council) that have played a crucial role in the adoption and imposition of these approaches as appropriate solutions to the social policy challenges of the day (Greer, Jarman, and Baeten, 2016). The policy context of NEG prescriptions therefore includes past policies situated at both *national* and *supranational* (EU) level and their impact on the extent to which specific policy areas have been commodified in specific countries and at specific junctures.

Hence, the history of employment and social policies in the EU is not one of *distinct* pathways taken by different groups of countries, but rather of meandering yet *interconnected* trajectories that, although diverging at times, flow nonetheless in a common direction. National governments have deployed commodifying interventions unevenly across countries and time, given the uneven power relations between different member states, between them and EU institutions, and, as seen in Chapter 2, the uneven unfolding of horizontal market pressures across the EU in anticipation of economic and monetary union and EU accession processes. This unevenness has manifested itself in terms both of the specific policy mixes that EU member states adopted at different junctures and of the pace and intensity with which they implemented these interventions. A consideration of the history of unevenly deployed policies and of their impact on the commodification of employment relations and public services is crucial for accounting for why NEG prescriptions in a specific policy area targeted, at a specific juncture, some countries rather than others. For example, as shown in Chapter 10, NEG commodifying prescriptions in healthcare targeted mostly Ireland and Romania; this can be accounted for by the fact that, before NEG was introduced, healthcare (and especially hospital) commodification was less advanced in these two countries than in the other two countries in our dataset, Germany and Italy. This points to NEG commodifying prescriptions in healthcare amounting to something more than simply a set of prescriptions displaying a common commodifying orientation. Rather, it points to their participation in an overarching transnational policy *script* that follows a common *logic* in its deployment across countries and time.

Therefore, taking into consideration the time-specific unfolding of policies across countries allows us to uncover not only and simply NEG's semantically hierarchical ordering of prescriptions in employment relations and public services (i.e., taxonomies) but also their uneven deployment as overarching *scripts* encoded in NEG documents produced in different years and for different countries. Moreover, by going further back in time and considering pre-2008 EU interventions in a particular policy area, we may discover the deeper temporal sediments of EU economic governance and thus the precursors of NEG's commodifying script in this area.

Our analytical strategy thus aims to uncover the policy scripts that inform NEG documents and NEG prescriptions in selected employment and social policy areas. By seeing these documents and prescriptions as outcomes of the symbolic struggles waged by social actors over the legitimate naming of reality, our analytical strategy allows us to acknowledge the existence of a plurality of agendas that may inform NEG prescriptions in a particular policy area. As shown in Chapters 6–11, we have identified a dominant commodifying script across all policy areas, despite the occasional presence of NEG policy prescriptions that pointed in a decommodifying direction. Moreover, when analysing the semantic links of the much less constraining and less frequent decommodifying prescriptions to the policy rationales underpinning them, we found that they did not constitute a countervailing policy script. Instead, most of those policy rationales were compatible with the overarching commodification script of NEG (Tables 11.2 and 11.4).

Having looked at the semantic, communicative, and policy contexts of NEG prescriptions and their implications for our research design, we now turn to our comparative and analytical strategy, case selection, and data collection.

5.3 RESEARCH DESIGN

As seen in the previous section, traditional country-by-country comparison *à la* varieties of capitalism (Hall and Soskice, 2001) or varieties of welfare state (Esping-Andersen, 1990) aims to uncover clusters (varieties) among countries. In this perspective, each variety displays a distinctive and coherent *national* institutional configuration in employment and social policy areas (Brenner, Peck, and Theodore, 2010).

Our analysis seeks instead to capture *transnational* dynamics at work in NEG. We argue that this is a particularly relevant level for analysing NEG prescriptions in employment relations and public services – and trade-union and social-movement reactions to them (Jordan, Maccarrone, and Erne, 2021; Stan and Erne, 2021a). As outlined in Chapter 3, the NEG regime may nationalise social conflict through its *country-specific* recommendations (Erne, 2015). The EU-wide reach of the NEG documents that guide them – namely, the Annual Growth Survey and the Recommendations for the euro area (see Figure 2.1), as well as the institutionalisation of NEG and its sanctioning procedures in EU laws – namely, the Six-Pack of EU laws on economic governance – bring member states nonetheless under the same *supranational* regime of multilateral policymaking and surveillance (Erne, 2015).

Case Selection and Analytical Strategy

As this study goes beyond the methodological nationalism that characterises traditional comparative studies in social sciences, we employ a different rationale for case selection. Positivist research designs rely on Mill's method of induction, selecting most-different or most-similar cases (Przeworski and Teune, 1970), with the aim of isolating the presumed causal factors for the observed outcomes, similar to what would happen in a natural experiment. Implicit in such an approach 'is the assumption that nations or societies are aggregates of variables which can in principle be isolated analytically' (Hyman, 2001: 208). However, in a transnationally integrated regime such as NEG, it is not possible to 'seal' national boundaries in order to compare countries. Neither is it possible to separate policymaking into supranational EU and national policy production processes (Brenner, Peck, and Theodore, 2010), given that the two levels are interconnected, as outlined in Chapter 3.

By choosing countries and sectors differently positioned within the EU and its NEG regime, we have instead selected our cases as 'vantage points' (Bieler, 2021: 4) that allow us to uncover the deployment of NEG and commodification in the uneven and integrated European political economy. We expect this deployment to be uneven among countries located at different points relative to the EU's core and periphery. We also expect it to be uneven among policy areas, as these have been differently affected by EU governance and integration processes prior to, as well as after, the establishment of the NEG regime. Finally, we expect this deployment to draw on an already established commodifying stream in EU policymaking. We therefore compare country-specific NEG prescriptions not only in terms of these countries' past trajectories in the adoption of policies commodifying employment relations and public services but also in terms of whether they follow a *common* commodifying *script* in these areas. These comparisons seek thus to find *transnational* dynamics. Consequently, we selected four countries (Germany, Italy, Ireland, and Romania) that cover contrasting poles in terms of member state size (and thus votes in the Council) and economic power in the uneven EU political economy. This operationalises more abstract considerations of core–periphery divisions and helps us capture the uneven power relations involved in the production of NEG documents, in the allocation of countries to sanctioning procedures, and in the assigning of different legal bases (and hence different degrees of coercive power) to NEG prescriptions. It also allows us to assess whether policy prescriptions reflect an overarching commodifying script while being unevenly deployed across countries. The central question for us is whether commodification is indeed the dominant script in the policy areas under consideration, to what extent alternative, decommodification prescriptions can be identified, and whether the latter coalesce in a countervailing decommodifying script.

Rather than considering all prescriptions issued in the social field, our study focuses on a limited *set of policy areas*, namely, at cross-sectoral level (employment relations and public services) and at sectoral level (transport, water, and healthcare public services). Doing so allows not only for an *in-depth* consideration of the semantic, communicative, and policy contexts within which NEG prescriptions are situated but also for the fine-tuning of our account of the uneven deployment of NEG across countries, time, and policy areas. This is a value added with respect to those studies of NEG that, by assessing all CSRs (in employment and social policy areas) for all EU countries, can map the trends taken by NEG prescriptions only at a very general level.

To account for the *semantic context* of NEG prescriptions, we grouped them in a series of ever more encompassing semantic categories. First, we grouped country-specific prescriptions that use slightly different formulations to convey the same policy measure (e.g., prescriptions issued for Romania in 2013 – 'improve efficiency and effectiveness in the healthcare system' and 'pursue health sector reform to increase its efficiency' [Council Recommendation Romania 2013/C 217/17], in 2014 – 'step up reforms in the health sector to increase its efficiency' [Council Recommendation Romania 2014/C 247/21], and in 2019 – 'improve ... cost-efficiency of healthcare' [Council Recommendation Romania 2019/C 301/23]) under a common *theme*, for which we used a standardised formulation (e.g., 'increase cost-efficiency of healthcare').

Second, we classified prescriptions (by drawing on the above themes) under the *categories* of the conceptual framework developed in Chapter 4. This conceptual framework operationalised the commodification and decommodification potential of prescriptions on employment relations and public services. The aim of this framework is to make the classification of prescriptions according to their policy *orientation* (commodification or decommodification) more intelligible and then to use these categories to give a finer-tuned picture of the policy taxonomies and of the patterns formed by the deployment of NEG prescriptions across countries and time.

To account for the *communicative context* of NEG prescriptions, our analysis took into account their different *coercive power*. Following Jordan, Maccarrone, and Erne (2021: 9), we considered this power to range from *very significant*, for prescriptions enunciated in Memoranda of Understanding (MoUs) for countries under bailout programmes; to *significant* for Stability and Growth Pact (SGP)- *or* Macroeconomic Imbalance Procedure (MIP)-related prescriptions for states with excessive deficits *or* excessive macroeconomic imbalances; and to *weak*, for prescriptions underpinned by the Europe 2020 strategy, or by the EU's SGP or MIP if countries did not experience excessive deficits or excessive imbalances, as outlined in Table 5.1.

TABLE 5.1 *Coercive power of NEG prescriptions*

Legal basis of NEG prescription	Enforcement mechanisms	Coercive power
MoU strand of NEG: NEG prescriptions related to MoUs and Precautionary-MoUs	Withdrawal of financial assistance[a] Withdrawal of EU structural funding[b] Financial fines[c, d] Naming and shaming[e]	*Very significant*
Corrective SGP/MIP strand of NEG: SGP- and MIP-related NEG prescriptions for states with excessive deficits or excessive macroeconomic imbalances	Withdrawal of EU structural funding[b] Financial fines[c, d] Naming and shaming[e]	*Significant*
Preventive SGP/MIP strand of NEG: SGP- and MIP-related prescriptions for states with no excessive deficits or excessive macroeconomic imbalances **Europe 2020 strand of NEG:** Prescriptions related to the EU's Europe 2020 growth strategy	Naming and shaming[e]	*Weak*

Source: Adapted from Stan and Erne (2018/2019), Jordan, Maccarrone, and Erne (2021), and Stan and Erne (2023).

[a] According to the European Stability Mechanism (ESM) and the European Financial Stability Facility (EFSF) for euro area states created in 2012 and 2011, respectively, as well as the Balance of payments (BoP) assistance facility created in 2002 for non-euro area states, EU financial assistance is conditional on the implementation of the economic adjustment programme (EAP) spelled out in the corresponding MoU and its updates.

[b] Since 2014, EU structural and investment funding to all member states is conditional on 'sound economic governance', i.e., the implementation of EAP-, SGP-, and MIP-related NEG prescriptions (Art. 23, Regulation No 1303/2013 of the European Parliament and of the Council of 17 December 2013).

[c] Since 2011, a member state of the euro area that has not 'taken effective action to correct its excessive [budget] deficit', risks 'a fine, amounting to 0.2% of the Member State's GDP in the preceding year' (Art. 6, Regulation No 1173/2011 of the European Parliament and of the Council of 16 November 2011).

[d] Since 2011, a member state of the euro area that 'has not taken the corrective action [against excessive macroeconomic imbalances] recommended by the Council' risks an 'annual fine of 0.1% of the GDP in the preceding year of the Member State concerned' (Art. 2, Regulation No 1174/2011 of the European Parliament and of the Council of 16 November 2011).

[e] Since the adoption of the Maastricht Treaty in 1993 and the Amsterdam Treaty in 1997, the Council adopts Broad Economic Policy Guidelines (Art. 121(2) TFEU) and Employment Policy Guidelines (Art. 148(2) TFEU), which are non-legally binding recommendations for policymaking.

To account for the *policy context* of NEG prescriptions, we looked at the latter from a historical perspective. We thus placed NEG prescriptions against the canvas of EU interventions in employment relations and public services and national-level reforms that happened before the financial crisis of 2008. In doing so, we aimed to uncover continuities and differences between the latter and subsequent NEG prescriptions, most notably in terms of the commodification of employment relations and public services. As NEG did not replace but only complemented the ordinary EU governance method by law, we analysed not only the NEG prescriptions in our fields issued by EU executives since the financial crisis but also the EU laws that the Commission proposed after 2008 in accordance with the EU's ordinary legislative procedure.

In sum, when considering NEG prescriptions in their semantic, communicative, and policy contexts, we thus pursued an analytical strategy based on the following steps:

1. grouping all individual NEG prescriptions that refer semantically to a common policy measure in common *themes*, that is, standardised formulations;
2. identifying the explicit and implicit *semantic links* of apparently ambiguous and vague prescriptions to prescriptions found in other EU and national policy documents to uncover their *deeper meaning* and then mapping the larger policy taxonomies mobilised in NEG documents;
3. assessing the NEG prescriptions' potential to foster the commodification or decommodification of their respective policy areas and then classifying these prescriptions according to the *categories* of the analytical framework developed in Chapter 4;
4. identifying the *coercive power* of prescriptions and mapping the uneven attribution of this power to prescriptions going in commodifying and decommodifying directions;
5. tracing the *patterns* across countries and years formed by NEG prescriptions issued in each cross-sectoral and sectoral policy area;
6. assessing whether NEG prescriptions issued in each cross-sectoral and sectoral policy area follow, across countries and years, an overarching *commodification script*;
7. identifying the semantic links between *decommodifying* prescriptions and the *policy rationales* informing them and assessing their articulation with NEG's commodification scripts;
8. *comparing* the patterns of commodifying and decommodifying NEG prescriptions *across* cross-sectoral and sectoral policy areas.

Data Collection and Sources

Our study focuses, in a *first* instance, on whether NEG prescriptions follow an overarching transnational commodifying script across countries, time, and policy areas. Identifying this script is important, as it may offer potential crystallisation points for transnational countermovements, as shown in Chapter 3.

Our analysis of NEG prescriptions draws on (a) prescriptions included among the conditions listed in MoUs and their subsequent updates for Ireland (2010–2013) and Romania (2009–2013) and (b) prescriptions included in the CSRs listed in country-specific Council Recommendations issued between 2011 and 2019 for our four countries, namely, Germany, Italy, Ireland, and Romania. To better understand the semantic, communicative, and policy contexts of selected NEG prescriptions, we also draw on the Commission's annual Country Reports and member states' annual National Reform Programmes, as well as Annual Growth Surveys, Euro-area Recommendations, and Joint Employment Reports. Moreover, as understanding the policy contexts informing NEG policy prescriptions requires a deep knowledge of the policy context in the affected member states and corresponding language skills, our analysis is based on a long-term engagement with our cases (Almond and Connolly, 2020), which we know very well (Erne, 2008; Stan and Erne, 2014; Golden, 2015; Stan and Erne, 2016; Stan, 2018; Szabó, 2018; Maccarrone, Erne, and Regan, 2019; Maccarrone and Erne, 2023; Stan and Toma, 2019; Jordan, Maccarrone, and Erne, 2021; Golden and Erne, 2022; Szabó, Golden, and Erne, 2022). For each country selected, at least two of the book's authors are familiar with its national language. This allowed us to complement NEG documents (available in English) with studies and grey literature on employment relations and public services published both in English and in national languages. We examined NEG prescriptions by drawing mainly on document analysis, which we enriched with semi-structured interviews conducted with policymakers, for example, Commission officials involved in the operation of the European Semester process. For the purpose of mapping NEG policy prescriptions, we analysed MoUs, Council Recommendations, Commission's Country Reports, and other policy documents (Online Appendix, Table A1.1), conducted interviews with national and EU policymakers (Online Appendix, Table A1.2), and engaged in participant observations of trade-union, social-movement, and EU policy meetings (Online Appendix, Table A1.3). We participated in about sixty events organised by the abovementioned groups to make observations and maintain relationships with past and potential interviewees.

In a *second* move, our study analyses *transnational* counterreactions to NEG, based on a novel database of transnational socioeconomic protests since 1997 reported by national *and* EU-level labour-related sources, which we also compiled in the framework of our ERC project (Erne and Nowak, 2022, 2023).

Another protest database of events across thirty European countries reported in English-language newswire reports from 2000 to 2015 confirmed the return of socioeconomic grievances as the most important driver of protests across Europe (Kriesi et al., 2020). Within the economic protest cluster, political or 'public' protests 'targeting the economic crisis management of governments' clearly outnumbered the 'private' protests targeting 'private actors, above all business corporations' (Kriesi and Wüest, 2020: 280), by contrast to those that took place in the 1970s (Crouch and Pizzorno, 1978). Unfortunately, Kriesi et al.'s (2020) database does not record *transnational* protests, given its traditional country-by-country methodology. This motivated us to compile our own database (Erne and Nowak, 2023) to enable us to assess the role of the EU executives' commodifying interventions by (draft) EU laws and by NEG prescriptions as drivers of transnational socioeconomic protests during the two distinct historical periods – before and after the EU's shift to the NEG regime.

Our database captures transnational protest events related to socioeconomic grievances, including demonstrations, strikes, boycotts, and direct democratic European Citizens' Initiatives (ECIs) (Erne and Nowak, 2023). Its geographical scope includes protests across all European countries irrespective of EU membership, except Turkey, Belarus, and Russia, which we excluded for practical reasons. We collected the data on these protest events from a wide range of European *and* national websites, newsletters, and media outlets specialised in labour politics published in English, French, German, or Italian. The selection of sources in these languages exposes us to the risk of missing some protests, but we are confident that almost all transnational protests are captured by at least one of our sources.[2]

Our analysis of transnational socioeconomic protests since 1993 included in our database (Erne and Nowak, 2022, 2023) had two goals. We aimed,

---

[2] European sources: EBR-News, ETUI Collective Bargaining Newsletter; Eurofound: EIRO database and European Restructuring Monitor; European Commission: ECI Register, newsletters of the ETUC's sectoral European trade union federations and their predecessors (EAEA, EUROCOP, EFBWW, EFFAT, EFJ, IndustriAll, EPSU, ETF, ETUCE, UNI-EUROPA), IR share, planetlabor, Staff Union of the European Patent Office; German source: Labournet; French sources: Liaisons Sociales, Métis Europe, Clés du social; Italian source: Rassegna; Central and East European Source: LeftEast. We also added information on protest events based on academic publications and general news media.

firstly, to identify transnational collective action by unions and social movements and, second, to link these to pressures following from EU economic governance both before and after the establishment of the NEG regime. Trade unions and social movements are the main social actors examined in the area of contentious politics. When studying the making and operation of the NEG regime however, we also considered the activities and policy statements of employer associations.

Our *data collection* was multi-sited, as it took place at two main levels. At EU level, we looked at the interaction between EU institutions and European-level trade unions. Brussels serves not only as the main headquarters of EU institutions but also as the seat of the European Trade Union Confederation (ETUC) and of European sectoral trade union federations, such as the European Public Service Union (EPSU) and the European Transport Federation (ETF). Therefore, our Brussels field trips were the starting point for our investigation of transnational labour reactions to NEG. Furthermore, cognisant of the country-specific methodology and impact of NEG prescriptions, we also conducted fieldwork in the four selected countries of Germany, Ireland, Italy, and Romania, where we talked with representatives of national and sectoral unions on the topics of the impact of NEG on employment relations and public services and of unions' counterreactions to NEG-driven interventions.[3]

In our data collection on trade-union and social-movement collective action, we applied a step-by-step approach aiming to map first trade unions' views on NEG pressures and then their counterreactions to these pressures. In other words, we first explored trade unions' positions regarding NEG pressures and then focused on their actions at transnational level. Regarding collective action, we distinguished between the formal engagement of trade unions with European institutions through technocratic mechanisms and more contentious forms of collective action politicising European economic governance (Erne, 2008).

We adopted a historical perspective and sought to capture trade union responses to EU economic governance both before and after 2008. For this purpose, we relied on a combination of sources. We drew on documents published by unions, including articles, policy briefs, press statements, and reports. We also conducted around 160 interviews with trade unionists, social movement activists, employers' representatives, and public representatives at

---

[3] Unfortunately, fieldwork among trade unions and social movements was seriously impacted by the Covid-19 pandemic. Even so, we managed to compensate for the barriers to in-person access to our research fields through phone or online conversations, observation of online actions, and an in-depth engagement with trade-union and social-movement documents.

EU level and in the countries under analysis. We participated at events relating to the European Semester (e.g., the consultations with social partners on the Annual Growth Survey), union demonstrations, seminars and congresses (e.g., the 2019 congresses of ETUC, EPSU, and ver.di), and social movement actions (Table A1.3, Online Appendix). Our participation in these actions allowed us to gather further information through direct observation, informal interviews (Spradley, 2016), and the collection of documents otherwise not accessible online.

At the same time, during fieldwork at national level, we had to come to terms with the fact that NEG per se may not have been perceived by national trade unions as a factor directly impacting on national reforms. We noticed in more than one instance that sectoral unions delegate EU issues to general confederations to save resources or to ensure a unified view on European governance. Moreover, many interview partners had no direct engagement with NEG documents in their day-to-day organising work, but they had firsthand experience of how NEG-driven policies affected the employees and public service user groups that they represented. To talk about this impact, we drew on the categories identified in our conceptual frameworks (see Chapter 4) that had an immediate meaning for trade unions. For example, asking mid-level trade union representatives in the public sector in Romania about the impact of EU economic governance provoked a 'don't know or not relevant' answer. By contrast, asking them about the impact of a specific NEG prescription, for example how they experienced and responded to expenditure cuts in healthcare, was a discussion opener. This approach also allowed us to link back our findings from the country-specific fieldwork sites to NEG prescriptions at EU level and make findings comparable across the different countries and policy areas examined in this book.

Finally, to get a comprehensive picture of transnational countermobilisations of unions and social movements in response to EU governance interventions, we drew on our transnational socioeconomic protest database (Erne and Nowak, 2023). In each empirical Chapters (6–10), we extracted from this database a list of protests in the respective policy areas. Having outlined our conceptual framework and research design, we now assess EU economic governance interventions and the countermovements that they triggered. In each ensuing chapter, we first assess the commodifying or decommodifying policy direction of vertical EU interventions before and after the EU's shift to NEG and then analyse the transnational union and social-movement reactions to the EU's economic governance interventions.

PART II

EU Economic Governance in Two Policy Areas

6

EU Governance of Employment Relations and Its Discontents

6.1 INTRODUCTION

Most union leaders knew that the single market project and monetary union could expose workers' pay and working conditions to increased horizontal market integration pressures. Even so, European unions by and large supported the Single European Act (SEA) (1986) and the Maastricht Treaty (1993). Most European trade unionists thought that these treaties not only promised higher overall growth rates but also seemed to provide a basis for social EU laws and some protection against the most radical forms of capitalist globalisation (Bieler, 2006).

Although the idea of a European social model successively gained some traction among European policymakers, *vertical* EU interventions in the social field that improved working and living conditions remained an exception. Accordingly, a multilevel system of European employment relations emerged (Marginson and Sisson, 2004) that included some EU-level labour laws but continued to be shaped primarily by *horizontal* market integration pressures and different responses to them by governments, employers, and unions at national level. As the increased European horizontal market integration pressures would put workers and national employment relations regimes in competition with one another, French and German business leaders already predicted in 1997 that unions would 'lose their role in wage negotiations' after the introduction of the Euro (Erne, 2008: 54).

Until 2008, national social partners formally remained autonomous in the key areas of employment relations, namely, wage and collective bargaining policy. After the 2008 financial crisis however, the picture changed dramatically. The EU's new economic governance (NEG) regime empowered the European Commission and Council to issue vertical country-specific prescriptions also in the social field to ensure a 'proper functioning' of the EU economy (Chapter 2). This meant that European unions were confronted not only with commodifying horizontal market integration pressures but also with vertical NEG prescriptions in employment relations (Erne, 2019).

Before the shift to NEG, unions and social movements were at times able to successfully contest commodifying draft EU directives, as in the case of the Services Directive. Transnational counter-mobilisations against NEG prescriptions, however, are more difficult, given NEG's technocratic structure and the *country-specific* deployment of its prescriptions. NEG thus risks being a supranational regime that nationalises social conflict (Erne, 2015), unless labour realises that NEG is informed by an overarching, commodifying policy script that affects workers across countries similarly. In this chapter, we therefore assess whether NEG prescriptions on employment relations across our four countries point in a similar, commodifying policy direction, regardless of the different location of Germany, Ireland, Italy, and Romania in the EU political economy.

Before we can do so however, we must first discuss the EU's role in employment relations prior to the 2008 financial crisis. In section 6.2, we identify three main historical phases. In each of them, horizontal market pressures and vertical EU interventions played a different role in shaping employment relations and trade union action.

Section 6.3 then turns to the changes brought by the EU's shift to the NEG regime. First, we explain why employment relations became a primary target of NEG prescriptions. Then, our in-depth analysis of NEG prescriptions for our four countries shows how the NEG regime allowed the Commission and the Council of finance ministers (EU executives) to commodify policy areas hitherto shielded from direct, vertical EU interventions, namely, wage levels, collective bargaining mechanisms, and hiring and firing mechanisms. However, EU executives also issued some decommodifying prescriptions concerned with the rebalancing of the EU economy. The uneven orientation of NEG prescriptions, in turn, made it more difficult for European trade unions to put forward a common transnational response.

In section 6.4, we assess European unions' responses to the shift from horizontal market integration pressures (which did not challenge the formal autonomy of national industrial relations institutions) to the much more vertical, but also country-specific, NEG regime. We also discuss the most recent directives on employment relations and their potential to cause a shift in the orientation of EU governance in this field.

6.2 EU GOVERNANCE OF EMPLOYMENT RELATIONS UNTIL THE 2008 CRISIS

Before the shift to NEG, we distinguish three phases of EU interventions in employment relations. Until the 1980s, economic EU integration and the development of national labour and social policies were mutually supportive (Phase one). Following the relaunch of European integration by the single market programme (SMP) and economic and monetary union (EMU), horizontal market integration led to ever-increasing commodifying pressures on workers, trade unions, and national industrial relations systems. These pressures were at least partially moderated by the introduction of vertical decommodifying laws aimed at strengthening the EU's social dimension (Phase two). In the 2000s, the political will to introduce decommodifying EU labour laws faded away (Phase three). Instead, the Commission proposed commodifying legislation, such as the draft Services Directive in 2004, which would have undermined the autonomy of national wage-setting and collective bargaining systems. Although the political allies of trade unions and social movements in the European Parliament were able to alter the Commission's draft EU laws, it was the Court of Justice of the EU (CJEU) that struck the blows against labour rights at national level just before the outbreak of the 2008 global financial crisis.

Phase One: The European Common Market and National Labour Systems

Until the 1970s, the scope for European interventions in employment relations was very confined. The Treaty of the European Economic Community (TEEC) of 1957 focused on the free movement of goods, capital, services, and people, and the space it devoted to labour issues was limited. Art. 118 TEEC tasked the European Commission 'to promote close collaboration between member states in the social field, particularly in matters relating to employment, labour legislation and working conditions, occupational and continuation training, social security, protection against occupational accidents and diseases, industrial hygiene, the law as to trade unions, and collective bargaining between employers and workers'.

The flimsiness of these social EEC Treaty provisions, however, did not indicate a subordination of social issues to a market logic. The EEC abolished tariffs within the common market, but its member states also built strong industrial relations systems and social welfare states that ensured the social reproduction of labour. As social progress relied also on economic growth, produced inter alia by the making of the *European* common market, the EEC did not impinge on, but rather supported, the development of the social welfare state at *national* level (Milward, 1999). This virtuous cycle between European economic integration and social progress at national level supported the class compromise between organised capital and labour that shaped Western Europe after World War II (Giubboni, 2006; Ashiagbor, 2013; see Chapter 2). The EEC Treaty nevertheless also empowered the Commission to propose legislation on labour issues linked to the making of the common market, namely, to guarantee workers' freedom of movement within the EEC (Arts. 48–51 TEEC). In the following two decades, this led to the adoption of EU legislation in the social security field, as well as access to cross-border healthcare (see Chapter 10). Other labour-related articles in the EEC Treaty reflected French employers' preoccupation that the more advanced labour law provisions in their country could negatively affect their competitive position within the common market (Allais, 1960). Its Art. 119 therefore urged member states to enforce the principle of equal pay for equal work between men and women, as already enshrined in French legislation, and Art. 120 TEEC required member states to maintain 'equivalence' with respect to their regimes of paid holidays.

By the early 1970s however, the mid-twentieth century class compromise between capital and labour started to run out of steam when unemployment and inflation were on the rise and when companies' profit margins declined across advanced capitalist economies (Glynn, 2006). National governments' initial response was more state intervention at national level. After Denmark, Ireland, and the United Kingdom joined it in 1973, the EEC became more important. Within the EEC, organised labour also attempted to put forward a *supranational* social-democratic response to the crisis. In 1973, Western European trade union confederations founded the European Trade Union Confederation (ETUC), inter alia, to advance economic and industrial democracy in transnational corporations (TNCs). This was crucial, as TNCs had started to relocate production to lower-wage countries (Petrini, 2013). The cause of labour was also favoured by the rise in electoral support for socialist and social-democratic parties, which altered the balance of power within the Council towards labour. Accordingly, in 1972, the Council asked the Commission to propose legislation on labour protection.

In turn, organised labour obtained several decommodifying EEC laws, such as the directives that increased workers' rights in the event of collective redundancies (Directive 75/129/EEC) or the transfer of undertakings to a new employer (Directive 77/187/EEC). These issues were made even more urgent by business restructuring processes triggered by increased economic integration within the common market (Rainone, 2018). The growing participation of women in the labour market, along with the rise of feminist movements, brought the issue of gender equality back on the European political agenda too. At long last, the Commission acted on Art. 119 of the EEC Treaty, drafting two directives on equal pay and equal treatment between men and women that the Council approved in 1975 (Directive 75/117/EEC) and 1976 (Directive 76/207/EEC). By the end of the 1970s however, the balance of power within the Council became less favourable to labour (Petrini, 2013: 159). The ideological shift towards neoliberalism, combined with the staunch opposition of business associations on both sides of the Atlantic, led to a watering down of the most ambitious proposal put forward by the ETUC, namely, a directive on workers' information, consultation, and co-determination rights within TNCs.

Phase Two: The Single Market, Monetary Union, and Social Legislation

In the mid-1980s, European integration received a new impetus under the aegis of the Commission led by the French socialist, Jacques Delors. Taking place in the context of the rise of neoliberalism, this phase of integration centred primarily on market expansion. Even so, Delors' Commission promised to add a social dimension to the European integration process, which was crucial to get trade unions' support for the SEA and the Maastricht Treaty (van Apeldoorn, 2002; Bieler, 2006; Jabko, 2006; Erne, 2008; Golden, 2015).

The SEA of 1986 kickstarted the process with its SMP. Whereas the EEC Treaty tried to eliminate non-tariff-related barriers to cross-border trade through the adoption of European product standards, the SMP pursued this aim through the mutual recognition of national standards. The latter effectively put national product standards – and by implication also national welfare states and industrial relations regimes – in competition with one another (Streeck, 1998). The SEA was followed by the signing of the Maastricht Treaty in 1992, which created the legal basis for the EMU by the end of the decade.

In the 1980s, the EEC broadened its borders further, with the accession of Greece, Portugal, and Spain. The accession treaties for these countries imposed an initial limitation on workers' freedom of movement up to seven years, but they did not foresee any restriction on the circulation of services (Comte, 2019). As the new Southern members had lower labour costs, this raised the issue of how to regulate the terms and conditions of workers sent by their employer to provide services in another member state (Comte, 2019). This issue would be addressed by a directive only in the 1990s (see below).

After the fall of the Berlin Wall in 1989, the dissolution of the USSR in 1991, and the creation of the European Union in 1993, Austria, Sweden, and Finland joined in 1995, bringing the number of EU member states to fifteen. As these were countries with strong trade unions and collective bargaining institutions, their accession raised hopes for a strengthening of the EU social dimension (Dølvik, 1995). Scandinavian unions, however, also showed scepticism towards the enhancement of binding supranational legislation in the social field, which they feared could impact on the autonomy of their collective bargaining systems.

Despite their early interest in joining the EU after the fall of the Berlin wall in 1989, the first eight Central and Eastern European (CEE) countries became EU member states, together with Malta and Cyprus, only in 2004, with Romania and Bulgaria joining in 2007 and Croatia in 2013. Before being accepted as members, they had to prove that they fulfilled the political and economic criteria for accession set out by the European Council at a summit held in Copenhagen in June 1993. The Copenhagen criteria included having a functioning market economy able to withstand competitive pressures within the single market and the state's capacity to absorb the EU's entire body of laws (*acquis communautaire*). As most EU legislation is related to the single market and its four freedoms, the Commission's pre-accession strategy was 'basically about disciplining the candidate members in terms of free market integration' (Holman, 2001: 180–181). Although CEE countries also had to transpose the EU's social *acquis* into their national laws, this did little to enhance workers' rights in the new member states because of the minimalist transposition approach taken and the lack of enforcement of the EU's social *acquis* on the ground (Meardi, 2016).

The intensification of interfirm and interstate competition in the single market and monetary union led to increased horizontal market pressures on national industrial relations institutions to become more competitive (Marginson and Sisson, 2004). Furthermore, the Maastricht Treaty introduced strict national convergence criteria on public finances, inflation, exchange, and interest rates to join the EMU. These pressures affected wage bargaining dynamics, even though national bargaining systems formally remained autonomous (Streeck, 1998).

Across several member states, governments sought to conclude bi- or tripartite corporatist arrangements to moderate wage increases. Such arrangements emerged even in countries that were thought to lack the conditions for the emergence of corporatist agreements, such as Italy and Ireland (Schmitter and Grote, 1997). In contrast to the classical neo-corporatist agreements that had emerged during the era of embedded liberalism, these competitive corporatist agreements (Rhodes, 2000) were not meant to reconcile economic growth and social equality. Instead, these arrangements advocated wage moderation to increase the attractiveness of the country as a location for foreign capital investment – as happened, for example, in the case of the seven social partnership agreements that Irish governments, employer organisations, and unions signed from 1987 to 2007 (Roche, 2007; Erne, 2008: 71). Furthermore, governments sponsored social pacts that advocated wage moderation to secure eurozone membership in line with the low-inflation benchmarks set by the Maastricht Treaty, like in Italy after 1993 (Erne, 2008: 73; Pulignano, Carrieri, and Baccaro, 2018).

The growing transnational market integration triggered by economic Europeanisation and globalisation processes led to increased commodifying pressures on national employment relations systems. To alleviate them, Jacques Delors thought to complement the SMP and EMU, as well as the EU's future eastward enlargement, with European social flanking measures. After all, trade unions and left-wing parties still exerted some influence in EU politics that EU policymakers had to accommodate. Thus, the promise of a social dimension was instrumental in getting social democrats and trade unions on board for the relaunch of EU integration in the 1990s (van Apeldoorn, 2002; Bieler, 2006; Jabko, 2006; Erne, 2008; Golden, 2015).

The SEA had introduced qualified majority voting (QMV) in the Council on health and safety matters. The Maastricht Treaty extended QMV to other issues, namely, working conditions and workers' information and consultation rights. The social provisions of the Maastricht Treaty were based on a social policy agreement, which EU governments attached as a separate protocol to allow the conservative UK government to opt out of it. As the social policy agreement had been drafted by the ETUC and Europe's major employers' associations, it is not surprising that it also institutionalised the European social dialogue between management and labour at intersectoral or sectoral level.[1] This means that, before making any legislative proposal in the social policy field, the Commission must not only consult the European confederations of trade unions and employer associations but also give them up to nine months to negotiate their own agreements on the matter if they wish to do so (Art. 154 TFEU). If so, the European social partners could task their members

---

[1] At intersectoral level, the Commission recognised the ETUC, Business Europe (Europe's largest employer organisation), SME United (an association of small and medium-sized enterprises), and SGI Europe, which represents employers in the public sector, as representative organisations of labour and management.

at national level to implement the agreement autonomously or ask the Commission and Council to implement the agreement by an EU directive.

The social provisions of the SEA and the Maastricht Treaty led to the adoption of several EU directives that pointed in a decommodifying policy direction. The Council's ability to adopt EU health and safety laws by QMV meant that the Commission and the Council were able to overcome the conservative UK government's veto to adopt the Working Time Directive (93/104/EC) in 1993. The directive introduced a maximum ceiling of forty-eight working hours per week, a minimum of an eleven-hour-long rest break between two work shifts, at least four weeks of paid leave, and other provisions for night work for health and safety reasons. On the same basis, the Council adopted a directive granting basic labour rights to pregnant workers (Directive 92/85/EEC), including a protection against dismissal and at least fourteen weeks of maternity leave.

After Maastricht, the European social dialogue led to EU directives on parental leave (Directive 96/34/EC), part-time work (Directive 97/81/EC), and fixed-term work (Directive 1999/70/EC). These directives included a non-discrimination clause that gave workers holding such contracts equal labour rights while in employment. Conversely, they legitimised the use of flexible contracts as an alternative to permanent, full-time employment (Sciarra, 2003). EU policymakers also adopted labour laws according to the EU's ordinary legislative procedures, for example, when employers vetoed an equivalent social dialogue agreement. This happened, for example, in the case of the directives establishing European Works Councils (Directive 94/45/EC), on employee involvement within a company established under EU law known by its latin name of 'Societas Europaea' or SE (Directive 2001/86/EC), and on information and consultation of employees in companies at national level (Directive 2002/14/EC).

In 1996, the EU adopted the Posting of Workers Directive (96/71/EC), which is based on both the Treaty's social provisions and those on the free movement of services. The directive did not go as far as to provide equal rights to workers temporarily sent ('posted') by their employer from one member state to another to provide services there, but it granted at least a set of core labour rights guaranteed by the laws of the host country, such as a minimum wage, work and rest periods, paid annual leave, and health and safety rules.

Most importantly, however, the Maastricht Treaty did not touch key areas of national industrial relations, such as pay and collective bargaining mechanisms, despite the increasing horizontal market pressures to which the making of the EMU exposed them. The social policy agreement attached to the EC Treaty in Maastricht explicitly excluded the issues of pay, the right of association, and the right to strike from its remit. When the British government led by Tony Blair agreed to incorporate the social policy agreement into the body of the EC Treaty at the 2007 Amsterdam summit, it also made sure that these exclusions were maintained.

Phase Three: Towards a Multilateral Surveillance of Employment Relations

After the launch of the Euro in 1999, commodifying horizontal market pressures on wages and working conditions increased further. Without the possibility of using the devaluation of national currencies, labour costs became an adjustment variable for firms and countries with lower levels of productivity to remain competitive within the EMU (Martin and Ross, 1999). The tight monetary policy regime of the European Central Bank (ECB), designed to keep inflation levels below 2 per cent, also meant that wage growth had to be contained. Furthermore, German labour policymakers were able to adopt more assertive beggar-thy-neighbour wage moderation policies, as the introduction of the Euro excluded the risk of any counterbalancing revaluation of the Deutschmark against Southern European currencies (Erne, 2008).

At the turn of the new millennium, not only conservative but also New Labour policymakers (Taylor, 1999) and their advisors (Pautz, 2008) used the horizontal market integration pressures linked to economic globalisation and Europeanisation to justify their calls for radical labour market reforms. Subsequently, German social partners agreed to moderate wages to an even greater extent (Erne, 2008: 99–103; Lehndorff, 2015), and the *Neue Mitte* government of Gerhard Schröder pushed through its Hartz labour market reforms unilaterally despite fierce social movement and union opposition (Bruff, 2010: 416). Threats of further unilateral action by the Schröder government, combined with those of firms to relocate their production to cheaper locations also swayed unions to accept opening clauses in collective bargaining agreements, as in the 2004 Pforzheim agreement in the metal and electrical engineering industry (Bispinck and Schulten, 2010). Increased horizontal market integration pressures, however, did not have the same impact everywhere; this is not surprising given the EU's integrated but also unequal political economy (Bieler, Jordan, and Morton, 2019). In countries with very low wages, labour policymakers and social partners were not too concerned about wage moderation and continued to endorse decommodifying labour laws and practices. Despite the introduction of the Euro, Portuguese and Greek real wages broadly followed national productivity developments during the late 1990s (Erne, 2008: 64). In the EU's southeastern periphery, Romania's social democratic government even introduced a new Labour Code in 2003, which provided strong collective bargaining rights 'as a quid pro quo for the social peace needed to polish Romania's EU accession dossier' (Ban, 2016: 96). This code remained in place, despite the victory of a centre-right coalition in 2004 and despite Romania following a neoliberal trajectory in most fields in the run-up to 2007 EU accession (Stan and Erne, 2014; Ban, 2016).

Horizontal European market integration pressures were not strong enough to trigger major labour market reforms in countries with average labour costs either. Whereas social partners agreed to moderate wages to support Italy's accession to the Euro in 1999, its largest trade union confederation, the Confederazione Generale Italiana del Lavoro (CGIL), in 2002 staged a successful general strike against the labour market reforms proposed by the centre-right Berlusconi government that were meant to weaken the protections against unjustified dismissals granted by Art. 18 of the Italian Workers' Statute (Ferrera and Gualmini, 2004: 158).

Even so, the EMU and the EU's 2004 and 2007 eastward enlargements increased horizontal market integration pressures on employment relations, also because the impetus for introducing vertical decommodifying EU flanking measures faded away. This happened even though, by the end of the 1990s, centre-left governments held the majority in the Council. Indeed, with supply-side economics becoming popular among Third-Way social democratic parties such as Tony Blair's New Labour in the UK and Schröder's *Neue Mitte* in Germany, there was little support for decommodifying EU labour laws (Menz, 2015). Legislative activity focused on the revision of existing directives rather than on new initiatives. In the absence of a threat of legislative action by the Commission, employers' associations virtually stopped signing EU social dialogue agreements (Léonard et al., 2007). Instead, 'softer' mechanisms to coordinate EU member states' economic and employment policies gained prominence.

To better coordinate the policies of EU member states in the run-up to EMU, the Maastricht Treaty tasked the Commission and the Council of finance ministers to issue broad economic policy guidelines (BEPGs). Responding to increased horizontal market integration pressures, high unemployment figures, and protest movements by the unemployed (Balme and Chabanet, 2008), EU governments agreed at the 1997 Amsterdam summit to integrate employment policy aims into the EC Treaty (now Title IX TFEU). This led to the European employment strategy, which was meant to promote 'a skilled, trained, and adaptable workforce and labour markets responsive to economic change' (Art. 145 TFEU) and secure a 'high level of employment' (Art. 147 TFEU). At the Lisbon summit in 2001, EU executives furthermore agreed to henceforth coordinate member state policies in other areas also, such as pensions, healthcare, and social inclusion (Armstrong, 2010; see also Chapter 10).

Following Milena Büchs (2007), we discuss these coordination tools, including the BEPGs, under the same heading: the Open Method of Coordination (OMC). This makes sense, as, since 2005, EU executives have integrated their BEPGs and EU employment strategy recommendations in one document. Although these recommendations to the member states were not legally binding, they still had practical effects (see Chapter 2). Ironically, precisely the soft-law character of OMC prescriptions enabled the Commission and the Council to gradually build up governance capabilities in areas in which they did not possess formal legislative competences, including pay and healthcare (Marginson and Sisson, 2004; Büchs, 2007; Chapter 10).

The policy orientation of OMC prescriptions echoed the shift from demand- to supply-side economic policies that increasingly shaped European labour policymaking (Büchs, 2007). OMC prescriptions stressed the need to increase workers' employability and propagated a new 'flexicurity' approach, which was meant to reconcile employers' need for a flexible workforce with workers' need to secure durable employment, even if that meant keeping wage growth below productivity developments at firm level. Nevertheless, the coercive power of OMC prescriptions was weak, as they lacked any enforcement mechanism other than peer pressure from European institutions and other countries' governments (Marginson and Sisson, 2004). Yet national executives still used OMC prescriptions to discursively legitimise commodifying labour reforms, as in the case of Schröder's Hartz reform (Büchs, 2007).

A much more decisive push for further labour commodification came from the Commission's 2004 proposal for a Services Directive (COM (2004) 2 final/3). The proposed EU law envisaged liberalising the provision of all services, public and private, across borders (see also Chapter 7). The threat for labour came from the country-of-origin principle contained in the draft law, which would have made service providers subject to the provisions of their home country, rather than those of their host country. This would have given service providers from states with lower labour and product market standards a major competitive advantage, also considering the EU's concurrent inclusion of CEE countries, which had lower wages and weaker trade unions and employment protection institutions. European trade unions therefore feared that the directive would unleash a race to the bottom in working conditions and employment relations and waged a transnational campaign with social movements (Bieler, 2007; Parks, 2015; Chapter 7) that convinced the European Parliament and Council to remove the country-of-origin principle from the final text of the Services Directive (2006/123/EC).

The EU's first attempts to commodify labour through direct interventions in the area of employment relations failed, either because they were too weak (in the case of OMC) or because they triggered strong countermovements (in the case of the Services Directive). In the mid-2000s, some of its leading scholars thus concluded that EU industrial relations were 'evidently not a vertically integrated system, with the European supranational level exerting authoritative direction over national systems, that would facilitate top-down policymaking and implementation' (Leisink and Hyman, 2005: 280). In 2007 however, these arguments were called into question by the CJEU's four Laval Quartet rulings (Dølvik and Visser, 2009).[2]

With its rulings in the *Laval* and *Vikings* cases, the CJEU limited unions' capacity to take national and transnational strike action. In *Laval*, a Swedish union took secondary strike action to compel Laval, a Latvian construction company that had won a contract to renovate a school, to sign a Swedish collective agreement. In *Vikings*, a Finnish seafarers' union and the International Transport Workers' Federation called for strike action against the decision of the Finnish ferries company Vikings to reflag its ferries to Estonia to lower wages and labour standards. In both cases, the companies launched legal challenges in national courts against the unions' actions, which were brought to the CJEU in turn. In *Laval*, the Swedish employers' organisation Svenskt Näringsliv funded the court case, which it then used as a strategic opportunity to curb Swedish trade union rights (Woolfson and Sommers, 2006: 61). In *Vikings*, the Finnish company brought the case to a UK court, using the Federation's location in London to bypass the more labour-friendly Finnish courts. In both cases, the CJEU found that the use of the right to strike guaranteed by national labour laws and the EU's Charter of Fundamental Rights had unduly restricted the economic freedoms of firms guaranteed by EU treaties, namely, the freedom of establishment (*Vikings*) and of providing services across borders (*Laval*). The Court also interpreted the Posting of Workers Directive restrictively, as setting a ceiling of rights granted to posted workers, rather than a floor (Höpner and Schäfer, 2010: 354).

In *Rüffert*, the Court found that the social clause in the procurement law of Lower Saxony in Germany would violate companies' freedom to provide services across the EU. The clause stipulated that public contracts should be

---

[2] C-341/05 *Laval un Partneri* [2007] ECR I-11767; C-438/05 *The International Transport Workers' Federation and The Finnish Seamen's Union* [2007] ECR I-10779; C-346/06 *Rüffert* [2008] ECR I-01989; C-319/06 *Commission v. Luxembourg* [2008] ECR I-04323.

awarded only to companies that abided by the wage rates set by collective agreement. Finally, the Commission pushed 'the new market-oriented doctrine further' (Garben, 2017: 35), bringing Luxembourg to the CJEU as its transposition of the Posting of Workers Directive had gone too far. The Commission argued that Luxembourg was incorrectly applying the 'public policy provisions' provided by Art. 3(10) of the directive to give posted workers greater protections than the set of rights stated by the directive itself. In *Commission v. Luxembourg*, the CJEU upheld most of the Commission's arguments, providing a restrictive interpretation of the public policy exception.

The shift in the CJEU's jurisprudence in its Laval Quartet rulings sanctioned much more vertical, commodifying EU interventions in employment relations. Only a few months afterwards, in response to the 2008 financial crisis, the EU created its NEG regime, which complemented and overlayed the OMC's soft multilateral policy coordination tools with new governance instruments that enabled further vertical EU policy intervention in the field.

6.3 THE EU'S NEW ECONOMIC GOVERNANCE (NEG) OF EMPLOYMENT RELATIONS

As outlined in Chapter 2, the making of the EU's NEG regime after the 2008 crisis gave EU executives greater policy intervention powers in employment relations (Erne, 2012b, 2019). These interventions followed two logics.

First, the Commission's DG for Economic and Financial affairs (ECFIN) and the Council of finance ministers identified growing nominal unit labour costs (ULC) as a major cause of the great macroeconomic imbalances between EU member states (Schulten and Müller, 2015). EU executives henceforth treated wage policy as a major economic governance issue. Accordingly, they added a nominal ULC indicator to the scoreboard of the macroeconomic imbalances procedure (MIP) established by the Six-Pack of EU laws, which aim to ensure the 'proper functioning' of the European economy (see Chapter 2). Although excessively low wage rises also cause macroeconomic imbalances, the MIP scoreboard sets a ceiling only for nominal ULC rises (+9 per cent for eurozone, +12 per cent for non-eurozone, states over three years). This suited employers from both peripheral and core EU countries, which had no interest in curbing the strategies of wage repression that they had pursued in the decade prior to the 2008 crisis (Bieler and Erne, 2014; Baccaro and Benassi, 2017; Celi et al., 2018). By contrast, governments from countries with a current account surplus, like Germany, had to accept that the MIP scoreboard's indicator for current account imbalances would also include a floor, even if this irked their employer organisations (Syrovatka, 2022a; see Chapter 2). Nevertheless, the corresponding MIP scoreboard thresholds still left more space for the countries in surplus (+6 per cent of GDP) than for those in deficit (−4 per cent of GDP).

The inclusion of wage policy in the MIP is striking, as the EU has no legislative powers on 'pay' (Art. 153(5) TFEU) and must consider 'the diverse forms of national practices, in particular in the field of contractual relations' and respect social partners' 'autonomy' (Arts. 151 and 152 TFEU). The Commission's DG ECFIN, however, had already outlined in 2010 how the tension between its calls for wage and labour market flexibility and the protections granted by national and EU laws to social partners' bargaining autonomy could be overcome: 'In most Member States, wages are formed in a collective bargaining process without formal involvement of governments. Nevertheless, policymakers can affect wage-setting processes via a number of ways, including the provision of information on wage rules, changes to wage-indexation rules and the signalling role played by public sector wages. In addition, reforms of labour markets should also contribute to making wage-setting processes more efficient' (European Commission, 2010a: 41). As we shall see, NEG prescriptions focused extensively on these aspects.

A second rationale behind NEG that affected employment relations is the emphasis on public spending constraints related to the Stability and Growth Pact (SGP) (Syrovatka, 2022b; see Chapters 2 and 7). As the public sector wage bill constitutes a significant share of states' budgets, public sector industrial relations were thus affected directly by policy prescriptions but also indirectly by the strengthened EU fiscal constraints (Bach and Bordogna, 2013).

Our four countries received several NEG prescriptions on employment relations in country-specific recommendations (CSRs) of the European Semester process and Memoranda of Understanding (MoUs), Precautionary MoUs (P-MoUs), corresponding addendums and updates, and economic adjustment programmes (EAP) (see Chapter 2; see also Rocca, 2022).

In this section, we assess the policy orientation of NEG prescriptions in three central areas of employment relations issued to Germany, Ireland, Italy, and Romania between 2009 and 2019 to see whether they are informed by an overarching, transnational commodifying script. This is crucial to see whether they have the potential to trigger not only national but also transnational countervailing actions by unions. We have analysed all NEG prescriptions that affect workers while in employment, focusing on three major employment relations areas: wage levels, bargaining mechanisms, and hiring and firing mechanisms. As outlined in Chapter 4, we then distinguish between commodifying and decommodifying prescriptions. Accordingly, we have classified NEG prescriptions as commodifying if they urge member states to curtail wage levels, marketise bargaining mechanisms, or marketise hiring and firing mechanisms. Inversely, NEG prescriptions are decommodifying if they point in the opposite direction. Table 6.1 gives an overview of the categories and concrete themes of NEG prescriptions on public services that emerged from our analysis, as well as of their policy orientation.

As outlined in Chapter 4, we take the different degrees of coercive power of different NEG prescriptions into account, based on their legal basis and the status of the targeted state in NEG's enforcement regime. Accordingly, the coercive power of NEG prescriptions is 'very significant' if they are issued to countries that are subject to an MoU. The coercive power of NEG prescriptions is 'significant' if they are based on the SGP or MIP *and* target countries with excessive deficits or countries experiencing excessive imbalances. Finally, in all other circumstances, the coercive power of NEG prescriptions is weak.

Table 6.2 classifies all NEG prescriptions issued to the four countries under analysis between 2009 and 2019 on wage levels (triangles), bargaining

TABLE 6.1 *Themes in NEG prescriptions on employment relations (2009–2019)*

Categories	Policy orientation	
	Decommodifying	*Commodifying*
Wage levels	Sustain wage growth (DE) Reinstate national minimum wage (IE)	Reduce national minimum wage (IE) Reduce public-sector wage bill (IE, RO) Reduce new entrants' pay in public sector (IE) Establish a unified pay scale in public sector (RO) Curtail public sector wages (RO) Reduce wages in the public sector (RO) Establish objective criteria for minimum wage-setting (RO) Monitor impact of national minimum wage on employment (DE)
Bargaining mechanisms	Improve social dialogue (RO)	Decentralise collective bargaining from sector to firm level (IT) Reform sectoral wage-setting mechanisms (IE) Implement reforms to the wage-setting system to align wages with (company-level) productivity (RO)
Hiring and firing mechanisms	Facilitate transition from precarious to more stable employment contracts (DE)	Adopt legislation on the revision of employment contracts (IT) Ease legislation regulating dismissals for open-ended contracts (IT) Increase the use of fixed-term contracts (RO)

Source: Council Recommendations on National Reform Programmes; Memoranda of Understanding. See Online Appendix, Tables A6.1–A6.4.
Country code: DE = Germany; IE = Ireland; IT = Italy; RO = Romania.

TABLE 6.2 *Categories of NEG prescriptions on employment relations by coercive power*

	Decommodifying					Commodifying			
	DE	IE	IT	RO		DE	IE	IT	RO
2009					2009				▲³
2010		▲			2010		▲³ ■		▲³
2011	△				2011		▲² ■	□ ○	▲² ■ ●
2012	△ ○				2012		▲ ■	◉ ■	▲ ■ ●
2013	△ ○				2013		▲ ■	□ ○	▲³ ■ ●
2014	○				2014	△		◉ ■	△
2015					2015			◉ ■	△
2016	○				2016				△
2017	△ ○				2017			◉ ■	△
2018	△			□	2018				△
2019	△				2019				△

Source: Council Recommendations on National Reform Programmes; Memoranda of Understanding. See Online Appendix, Tables A6.1–A6.4.
Category symbol: △ = wages, □ = bargaining mechanisms, ○ = hiring and firing mechanisms.
Coercive power (see Table 5.1 and Figure 2.1): ▲■● = very significant, ▲■● = significant, △□○ = weak.
Superscript number equals number of relevant prescriptions. Country code: DE = Germany; IE = Ireland; IT = Italy; RO = Romania.

mechanisms (squares), and hiring and firing mechanisms (circles). The coercive power of a prescription is indicated by different colours: black for very significant, grey for significant, and white for weak coercive power.

Table 6.2 shows that most NEG prescriptions are concentrated on the right-hand side of the table. This visualises how NEG has pushed member states in a commodifying direction. The right-hand side of the table also contains the most coercive prescriptions. Nevertheless, the table documents also a set of prescriptions with a decommodifying policy orientation, namely, those for Germany on both wage levels and employment protection rules (on the left-hand side of the table). They have only a weak coercive power though.

Although EU executives may have used NEG to pursue other policy objectives also, such as greater social inclusion, as suggested by advocates of the socialisation hypothesis (Zeitlin and Vanhercke, 2018; see Chapter 4), Table 6.2 highlights that NEG prescriptions in employment relations hardly become more social over time. Although the number of NEG prescriptions and their constraining power diminished over time, Italy continued to receive commodifying prescriptions until 2017 and Romania until 2019. We now analyse the NEG prescriptions in depth, taking both their national and European semantic contexts into account.

NEG Prescriptions on Wage Levels

As Table 6.2 illustrates, most prescriptions under this category called for a curtailment of wages in both the public and the private sector. The two countries targeted by the prescriptions are Ireland and Romania, which were both subject to the conditionalities specified in MoUs of a bailout programme. By contrast, since 2012, Germany consistently received prescriptions to increase wage levels.

Before entering into the bailout programme, the Irish government had already implemented wage cuts as part of what the IMF itself defined as one of the most severe adjustment programmes in modern times (Whelan, 2014). The Commission praised the substantial wage cuts in the public sector in 2009, which 'helped to initiate the necessary change in labour costs' (European Commission, 2010a: 67). Hence, the first MoU signed in November 2010 did not require additional public sector wages cuts for existing employees on top of the cuts that the Irish government had already implemented unilaterally in 2009. It did, however, urge an additional 10 per cent wage cut for new entrants to the public service (MoU, Ireland, 28 November 2010); this is remarkable given the Commission's recurrent criticism of labour market segmentation (see NEG Prescriptions on Hiring and Firing Mechanisms below). The austerity measures adopted by the government depressed the Irish economy so much that it became impossible to reach the deficit/GDP targets agreed in the MoU. In 2013, the government therefore persuaded the Irish public sector unions to agree to further wage cuts in a new national public sector agreement. This was done under the duress of the Financial Emergency Measures in the Public Interest (FEMPI) Acts, which allowed the government to cut public sector wages unilaterally, in the event of union opposition (Szabó, 2018; Maccarrone, Erne, and Regan, 2019).

The MoU also asked the Irish government to reduce the minimum wage by €1 per hour, which amounted to a 12 per cent reduction (MoU, Ireland, 28 November 2010). The Irish government implemented the cut without further delay within a month, causing widespread uproar among unions and social justice NGOs. In spring 2011, Ireland's new Fine Gael–Labour government reversed the minimum wage cut in agreement with the Commission and the IMF. To offset the effect of the reinstatement of the minimum wage on nominal ULC, the government reduced employers' social contributions accordingly (MoU, Ireland, 1st update, 28 April 2011). Between 2010 and 2012, Irish wage (and social contribution) cuts contributed to a 12.8 per cent drop in nominal ULC (Erne, 2015: 353). This is astounding, as the MIP scoreboard would have allowed a 9 per cent ULC increase over this period. Ultimately however, the NEG regime does not hinge on numerical benchmarks per se but on political ad hoc interventions that use them instrumentally (see Chapter 2; Cova, 2022; Syrovatka, 2022b).

In the case of Romania, subsequent MoU addendums urged the government to first freeze public sector salaries (MoU, Romania, 1st addendum, 22 February 2010), then to cut them altogether through a reduction in wages and bonuses (MoU, Romania, 2nd addendum, 2 August 2010). By contrast to Ireland, NEG prescriptions continued to target Romanian wage policy even after the country left the bailout programme. In 2014, the Romanian government was invited to 'establish, in consultation with social partners, clear guidelines for transparent minimum wage setting' (Council Recommendation Romania 2014/C 247/21). As the prescription refers to social dialogue with unions and employers, it might appear as socially oriented (Zeitlin and Vanhercke, 2018). However, the meaning of the prescription becomes clearer if we analyse it within its semantic context. Indeed, the Commission's 2014 Country Report emphasises that 'establishing clear guidelines, in effective consultation with social partners, *should contribute to the evolution of the minimum wage in line with the underlying cyclical conditions*' (emphasis added) (Commission, Country Report Romania SWD (2014) 424: 15). Thus, rather than being concerned with the involvement of social partners in policymaking per se, the prescription aimed to prevent the unilateral minimum wage increases planned by the new social democratic government, as demanded by Romanian employer organisations.

As Italy does not have a statutory minimum wage, unlike Ireland and Romania, it did not receive explicit NEG prescriptions on wage levels for the private sector (Afonso, 2019). The Italian government did not receive any prescription to restrain wages in the public sector either. It did, however, receive prescriptions to curtail public spending (see Chapter 7), thereby putting public sector workers' wages under pressure (Bach and Bordogna, 2013).[3]

In contrast to the other three countries, from 2012, the German government received prescriptions to promote higher wage growth almost every year. In 2012, the prescription was formulated in a rather flimsy way, asking the German government to 'create the conditions for wages to grow in line with productivity' (Council Recommendation Germany 2012/C 219/10), as German wage levels were even below that. After 2013 however, the prescriptions became more clearly decommodifying, requesting Germany to 'sustain conditions that enable wage growth to support domestic demand' (Council Recommendation Germany 2013/C 217/09). Similar decommodifying prescriptions were issued between 2017 and 2019.

Although these prescriptions supported German unions' demands for higher wages (Lübker, 2019: 19), they were only partially related to a concern for enhancing social inclusion. Instead, from 2013, they were increasingly linked to Germany's core position in the European political economy and the need to rebalance the European economy. Analysing the German prescriptions on wage levels in their semantic, communicative, and policy context, we can see that they relate to the MIP's focus that also targets countries with current account surpluses, such as Germany. Accordingly, the Commission and the Council agreed that wage growth in surplus countries might have positive spill-over effects on the whole EU economy by generating demand for goods produced by other EU countries. Higher German wages would therefore contribute to a rebalancing of the eurozone and the entire EU economy (Council Recommendation Germany 2017/C 261/05; Buti and Turrini, 2017). EU executives continued to issue similar prescriptions until 2019, demanding higher German wages, indicating that the actions undertaken by German policymakers were seen to be insufficient. Given the prescriptions' weak coercive power, however, German labour policymakers were not too concerned about that.

Our comparison of all NEG prescriptions on wage levels exposed their differing policy orientations across countries. This divergence is related to countries' different position in the integrated but also uneven EU economy. On the one hand, EU executives urged Ireland and Romania to cut the public sector wage bill and national minimum wages. As both countries were subject

---

[3] In August 2011, the then Italian prime minister, Silvio Berlusconi, received a confidential letter from the chairmen of the ECB and the Bank of Italy that urged his government to 'significantly reduc[e] the cost of public employees, by strengthening turnover rules and, if necessary, by reducing wages' (Draghi and Trichet, 2011) to meet the terms of the ECB's bond-buying programme.

to MoU conditionality, the coercive power of these prescriptions was very significant. EU executives justified their prescriptions with the countries' need to curtail public spending and wages to regain national competitiveness and to consolidate public finances. On the other hand, EU executives urged Germany to promote wage growth, to expand its internal demand, and to reduce its current account surplus with the aim of correcting the corresponding macroeconomic imbalances within the EU economy. As the coercive power of these prescriptions was weak, the German government was effectively able to ignore them. The diverging orientation of NEG prescriptions on wages across countries at the core and at the periphery of the uneven EU economy made it very difficult for European trade unions to challenge these NEG prescriptions jointly in countervailing transnational collective action.

NEG Prescriptions on Bargaining Mechanisms

Bargaining mechanisms refer to the procedures for the negotiation of terms and conditions of employment between employers and workers, often collectively represented by trade unions. All countries, except Germany, received at least one prescription under this category. All the prescriptions, bar one, had a commodifying orientation, aimed at marketising bargaining mechanisms by fostering a less solidaristic logic of bargaining.

In 2011, the prescriptions of the EU–IMF bailout programme urged Romania to 'implement reforms to the wage-setting system allowing wages to better reflect productivity developments in the medium term' (MoU, Romania, 28 June 2011). The centre-right government implemented its demands unilaterally by a new Social Dialogue Act in 2011, which it adopted as a decree-law, to prevent any labour-friendly amendments in parliament. The law led to a profound decentralisation of Romania's collective bargaining system. Whereas Romania's 2003 labour code supported multi-employer collective bargaining at national level, the 2011 Social Dialogue Act abolished the provisions supporting cross-sectoral bargaining and limited extension mechanisms for sectoral agreements (Marginson and Welz, 2015; Trif, 2016). The result was a dramatic drop in the coverage of bargaining, from 98 per cent in 2010 to 35 per cent in 2011 (Trif and Paolucci, 2018). In 2018, EU executives finally acknowledged that drop, albeit without mentioning their active role in fostering the fall. In their 2018 round of CSRs, they urged the Romanian government to 'improve the functioning of social dialogue' (Council Recommendation Romania 2018/C 320/22). The coercive power of this decommodifying request was weak however, by contrast to the commodifying prescriptions on bargaining mechanisms issued when Romania was subject to the MoU conditionalities of the bailout programme.

In 2009, Ireland's long-standing system of tripartite *national* wage bargaining known as social partnership had collapsed following the government's decision to unilaterally cut wages in the public service before it signed up to the EU–IMF bailout programme (Maccarrone, Erne, and Regan, 2019). Even so, the first MoU urged the government to review the only existing *sectoral* wage-setting mechanisms still in place, namely, the Employment Regulation Orders (ERO) and the Registered Employment Agreements (REA) (MoU, Ireland, 28 November 2010). Simultaneously, several employers challenged the ERO- and REA-systems in court. In turn, the Irish High and Supreme Courts declared the ERO- and REA-related provisions that had been in place since 1946 [sic] unconstitutional (Maccarrone, Erne, and Regan, 2019: 319) and declared all existing EROs and REAs invalid. Subsequently, the government nevertheless reintroduced similar provisions in labour law, but these provisions allowed companies in financial difficulties to opt out from the terms determined at sectoral level (Maccarrone, Erne, and Regan, 2019). This echoed the concerns of the Commission, which demanded that the reform must 'ensure that wages are adequately linked to productivity levels' (EAP, Ireland, Autumn 2012 Review, 25 January 2013: 37–38).

The NEG prescriptions for Italy also included demands to introduce clauses allowing opt-outs from sectoral bargaining. Since 2011, the Italian government had repeatedly been told to ensure 'that wage growth better reflects productivity developments as well as local and firm conditions, including clauses that could allow firm level bargaining to proceed in this direction' (Council Recommendation Italy 2011/C 215/02). In the summer of 2011, under pressure from both the Commission and the ECB, the Italian centre-right government pushed through an emergency decree-law that would have foreseen a disorganised decentralisation of collective bargaining from sectoral to firm level. This motivated even Italy's largest employer confederation, Confindustria, to oppose the reform, as it would have undermined its raison d'être as an organisation conducting collective bargaining on the employers' side (Meardi, 2014; Bulfone and Afonso, 2020). In response, unions and employers signed an autonomous agreement that reaffirmed the importance of sectoral bargaining at national level. This rendered the government's decree-law ineffective (Meardi, 2014; Bulfone and Afonso, 2020). Collective bargaining decentralisation nonetheless remained high on NEG's agenda, as NEG prescriptions continued to request a greater use of firm-level bargaining until 2017.

Germany is the only country in our sample that did not receive any NEG recommendations on collective bargaining. On the one hand, the lack of any NEG prescription on collective bargaining decentralisation is not surprising, given the opt-out clauses introduced by the pathbreaking 2004 Pforzheim agreement in the metalworking and electrical industry and a similar agreement in the chemical sector, which unions and employers concluded in response to ever-increasing horizontal market integration pressures. After all, the Commission had already cited these agreements as virtuous examples in 2010 (European Commission, 2010b: 39, 132). On the other hand, Germany did not receive decommodifying NEG prescriptions in this field, despite the fact that the recitals accompanying the NEG prescriptions in favour of higher wages (see above) also acknowledged the fall in collective bargaining coverage.

Hence, the NEG prescriptions on bargaining mechanisms went in a commodifying direction, except for the weak 2018 prescription for Romania that called for improved social dialogue. The coercive power of the commodifying prescriptions was very significant (Ireland and Romania) or significant (Italy). The prescriptions for Ireland, Italy, and Romania demanded a further decentralisation of collective bargaining from cross-sectoral and sectoral level to firm level, to better align workers' wages and conditions to their employers' productivity levels to foster national competitiveness.

NEG Prescriptions on Hiring and Firing Mechanisms

Hiring and firing mechanisms are a key dimension of employment relations, as they define the boundaries of employment. Commodifying prescriptions under this category aimed to increase labour market 'flexibility', thus exposing workers to the vagaries of the market. Policymakers can increase labour market flexibility in two ways: either by increasing the use of more flexible (i.e., more precarious) forms of employment contracts or by making permanent contracts more flexible (i.e., less stable) by easing workers' protection against dismissals. Whereas Italy and Romania received only commodifying prescriptions in this field, Germany received some decommodifying prescriptions aimed at reducing the use of precarious contracts.

The NEG prescriptions issued to Romania emphasised the need to use more flexible employment contracts. In 2011, its government was urged to 'widen the set of cases for use of fixed-term contracts' (P-MoU, Romania, 29 June 2011). The centre-right Romanian government implemented this prescription in turn, with a radical reform of the Labour Code that greatly expanded the use of atypical employment contracts and reduced the scope for collective bargaining (Trif, 2016). The government pushed these changes through unilaterally by means of a decree-law, which enabled it to sideline social dialogue with trade unions and to preclude labour-friendly amendments by the Romanian parliament. When the subsequent social democratic Romanian government was considering reversing some of these changes however, the EU executives and the IMF urged them to ensure 'that any further amendment to labour legislation will be undertaken *in consultation with all stakeholders* through ordinary legislative procedures' (emphasis added) (P-MoU, Romania, 6 November 2013) to prevent the adoption of measures that would go against employers' interests.

In the Italian case, EU executives cited the segmentation of its labour market, created by several waves of liberalisation of precarious contracts since the end of the 1990s, as a compelling reason to reduce the protection of workers with permanent contracts against unjustified dismissals provided by the country's Workers' Statute (Council Recommendation Italy 2011/C 215/02). As mentioned above, in 2002, an earlier attempt by the Berlusconi government to dismantle such protections had failed as a result of strong labour opposition. In response to the corresponding 2011 NEG prescription, the former EU Commissioner Mario Monti's technocratic government managed to weaken the protection against unjustified dismissal granted by Art. 18 of the Italian Workers' Statute. As the Monti government depended on support from centre-left Partito Democratico (PD), which had links to the union movement, the scope of the deregulation nevertheless remained limited.

Only two years later however, EU executives threatened the opening of an excessive deficit procedure against Italy. In response, the new centre-left government led by the PD's Matteo Renzi pushed through a new Jobs Act (and a public sector reform, see Chapter 7) to get more flexibility from EU executives under the SGP in exchange. This was possible, as the Juncker Commission agreed to interpret the SGP more flexibly if the respective member state implemented a major structural reform instead (see Chapter 2). The ensuing Jobs Act introduced a new type of open-ended employment contract with fewer protections against dismissals (Rutherford and Frangi, 2018). As in the Romanian case mentioned above, the reform was approved through an executive decree-law that prevented any labour-friendly amendments in parliament. Following its approval, the Commission argued that 'swift implementation of the "Jobs act" should improve entry and exit flexibility, enhance labour reallocation and promote stable open-ended employment, most notably for the young' (Commission, Country Report Italy SWD (2015) 31: 32).

As Ireland was already one of the EU states with the lowest employment protection, there was little scope for further EU intervention in that area, during the bailout programme or afterwards (Prosser, 2016). As we shall see, EU executives and the IMF nevertheless urged the Irish government to change the few sectoral wage-setting mechanisms that existed there to achieve even greater 'labour market flexibility' (EAP, Ireland, Autumn 2011 Review, 28 November 2011).

In contrast, from 2013, Germany received several NEG prescriptions that urged its government to 'facilitate the transition from non-standard employment such as mini jobs into more sustainable forms of employment' (Council Recommendation Germany 2013/C 217/09). These prescriptions point in a decommodifying direction, as they reflect a concern for the increase of in-work poverty following the growth of precarious contracts such as mini-jobs (Commission, Country Report Germany SWD (2013) 355). Mini-jobs were based on a particular type of part-time employment contract with a tax-free wage up to €450 per month but without any entitlements to unemployment and health insurance or pension payments. The widespread use of these mini-jobs was facilitated by the Hartz labour market reforms of the Schröder Government in the 2000s, mentioned above. Although the NEG prescriptions on mini-jobs addressed some of the negative effects associated with their widespread use, the Commission still welcomed the Hartz reforms that propagated them in the first place (Commission, Country Report Germany SWD (2013) 355: 19).

The NEG prescriptions on hiring and firing mechanisms point in two diverging directions, as also happened in the case of those on wage levels. The prescriptions for Italy and Romania were commodifying, as they exposed workers to greater market pressures. EU executives justified their calls for more labour market flexibility in these countries to increase companies' competitiveness, to increase the number of people in employment, and to reduce labour market segmentation between more and less protected workers (Rubery and Piasna, 2016). The coercive power of these prescriptions was significant. Ireland did not receive any prescription in this area, as its hiring and firing mechanisms were already very lax. By contrast, NEG prescriptions urged the German government to foster the transition from precarious mini-job contracts to more stable forms of employment. As their coercive power was weak however, the German government did not feel obliged to enforce them.

NEG: Fostering Vertical Interventions on Employment Relations

The shift to the NEG regime increased the salience of EU vertical interventions in employment relations. The analysis of NEG prescriptions in their semantic context highlights the salience of a commodifying script that aims to increase companies' and countries' competitiveness through the curtailment of wages and the marketisation of bargaining and hiring and firing mechanisms. This script informed all commodifying prescriptions issued to Ireland, Italy, and Romania across the three categories, whether they had a merely quantitative (wage levels) or qualitative (bargaining and hiring and firing mechanisms) dimension. By contrast, there was little need for commodifying NEG prescriptions for Germany, as German policymakers had already moderated wages and decentralised collective bargaining mechanisms in the 2000s in response to increased horizontal market integration pressures, as outlined above.

Whereas most NEG prescriptions in employment relations follow a commodification script, some of them point towards decommodification. Thanks to our analysis of NEG prescriptions in their semantic context (Chapter 5), we could also map the policy rationales that informed them (Online Appendix, Tables A6.1–A10.4). From 2012, Germany's policymakers received several prescriptions that urged them to increase wages. These decommodifying prescriptions are only partially related to a social concern though. It is instead Germany's position in the integrated but also uneven EU economy that informs most of these prescriptions. EU executives considered Germany's consistent current account balance surpluses as a problem that might threaten the proper functioning of the EU economy. The decommodifying NEG prescriptions issued therefore aimed to nudge German policymakers to increase German wages to contribute to a rebalancing of the EU economy. This policy rationale, however, does not clash with the commodifying script that we have detected above. Instead, it rather complements it, as both scripts follow a similar economic logic, which sees increased competitiveness as a function of wage levels and flexible employment contracts.

We also detected another decommodifying prescription on wage levels, which does not contradict the commodifying script either, namely, the 2012 NEG prescription that allowed the Irish government to reverse the cut to the national minimum wage that the MoU had previously mandated. This measure did not contradict the commodifying script, as it was accompanied by a concomitant reduction in employers' payroll taxes to offset its impact on ULC, according to a logic that sees a reduction in ULC as necessary to increase competitiveness.

The prescriptions that demanded the German government to increase the transition from precarious contracts to more stable forms of employment are semantically linked to concern about labour market segmentation. Neither is this script in contradiction with the commodifying script. Indeed, it mirrors the (stronger) commodifying prescriptions addressed to Italy and Romania on hiring and firing mechanisms that demanded that their employment contracts be made more precarious under the same stated rationale.

The single prescription addressed to Romania to 'improve social dialogue', which recognises the fall in (sectoral) collective bargaining coverage as problematic, is semantically linked to a policy rationale concerned with enhancing social concertation. From 2018, the prescription addressed to Germany to increase wage growth was also semantically linked to a concern for the fall in collective bargaining coverage. Albeit related to few prescriptions, this script is relevant, as it marks the beginning of a shift in the EU executives' view on the role of social dialogue and solidaristic wage-setting institutions, which became more prominent from 2019 onwards, as we discuss in the concluding section.

The few prescriptions related to this policy rationale are also the only ones among all NEG prescriptions issued in the decade 2009–2019 that we could link to a social concern with a more equal distribution between labour income and capital profit. This is striking, as a more equal distribution of wage and capital incomes has historically been a key concern of European trade unions' wage policy (Erne, 2008). Instead, commodifying prescriptions on wage levels, bargaining mechanisms, and hiring and firing mechanisms dominated the picture, even after the most acute phase of the financial crisis.

In comparison with the previous phases of EU governance of employment relations, the establishment of the NEG regime highlights a qualitative shift. Until 2008, the process of EU integration had exercised only indirect – albeit strong – *horizontal* commodifying pressures on national industrial relations. Although the impetus for *vertical* decommodifying legislation had run out of steam at the end of the 1990s, even a sceptical observer of social Europe such as Wolfgang Streeck conceded that 'there have also been few examples, if any, of European regulation mandating deregulation of industrial relations at national level' (Streeck, 1998: 435). Throughout the 2000s, *vertical* interventions by EU executives aimed at commodifying wages and workers' rights were not successful either, either because of protests by labour and social movements (e.g., in the case of the draft Services Directive) or because commodifying EU interventions were embedded in non-binding policy coordination processes, such as the OMC.

Whereas the CJEU opened the way for *vertical* commodifying interventions on labour policy in its Laval Quartet rulings, it was the adoption of the NEG regime that allowed the EU's *executive* arms, namely, the Commission and the Council, to intervene in employment relations more directly and much more broadly. In turn, national governments often implemented NEG prescriptions through unilateral acts, such as emergency decree-laws, which limited organised labour's capacity to influence national policymakers. Although some scholars have argued that 'there is not and never will be' any coordination of wage policies in Europe (Höpner and Seeliger, 2018: 415, our translation), this coordination now exists; but as a result of the EU's NEG regime rather than transnational union action. Section 6.4 thus analyses European unions' responses to NEG interventions in employment relations and to the horizontal market pressures and vertical EU interventions that preceded them.

6.4 EUROPEAN UNIONS: FACING HORIZONTAL AND VERTICAL EU INTEGRATION PRESSURES

Historically, most unions supported the European integration process, while also demanding a more social EU (Horn, 2012). As outlined above, Delors' pledge to complement market integration with a *Social Europe* was fundamental for getting unions' support for the relaunch of the EU integration process in the 1990s. The ETUC, along with Europe's centre-left parties, supported Delors' idea of a supranational, social EU as a tool to govern market forces in a context of an increasingly globalised economy (van Apeldoorn, 2002).

Whereas the ETUC became a social partner at EU level, many of its affiliates were part of national-level corporatist agreements that aimed to make their national economies more competitive in an increasingly transnational marketplace (Rhodes, 2000), as the EU integration process did not question their formal autonomy. When EU policymakers nevertheless tried to commodify employment relations directly, for example in 2004 through the draft Services Directive, trade unions' coordinated transnational collective actions successfully challenged them (Bieler, 2007; Parks, 2015). In 2000, the ETUC tried to contain the increased transnational market pressures on national wage bargaining rounds through the adoption of a joint wage bargaining benchmark equivalent to the sum of productivity growth and inflation. This European coordination attempt, however, largely failed, because its affiliates were not implementing it in practice (Erne, 2008).

As Laura Horn (2012: 579) noted, until the 2008 financial crisis, European unions had 'been over-reliant on the institutional structures of the European Union, and concomitant hopes for a European social model'. The EU's response to the crisis led to a more confrontational approach by the ETUC. Despite having supported previous developments in European economic governance, the confederation opposed the Six-Pack laws as an attempt to force 'member states to undertake a coordinated contraction of demand' (Erne, 2015: 352). On the same grounds, the ETUC opposed the Fiscal Treaty (Béthoux, Erne, and Golden, 2018). Besides lobbying the European Parliament, the confederation promoted Euro-demonstrations and action days that targeted austerity policies and the NEG regime. This increase in the ETUC-led mobilisations and demonstrations since 2008 politicising the EU governance of employment relations is shown in Table 6.3, with data extracted from our Transnational Socioeconomic Protest Database (Erne and Nowak, 2023).

Table 6.3 includes protest events on employment relations targeting political authorities, using the database's political level category, excluding actions at company, sectoral, and systemic level.

TABLE 6.3 *Transnational protests politicising the EU governance of employment relations (1993–2019)*

Date	Locations	Action Type	Topic	Coordinators
2 April 1993	Brussels, multi-sited	Demonstration	'Together for employment and social Europe'	ETUC
28 May & 10 June 1997	Brussels, multi-sited	Strike, demonstration	'Europe must work' campaign	ETUC
14 April–14 June 1997	Multi-sited	Demonstration	'Employment is a right, we're entitled to an income'	Euromarches
16–17 June 1997	Amsterdam	Demonstration	EU summit	Social movements, unions
20 November 1997	Luxembourg	Demonstration	'For a social Europe and full employment'	ETUC
8 May 1998	Strasbourg, multi-sited	Demonstration	Action day of the unemployed	Social movements, unions
13 June 1998	Cardiff	Demonstration	No to Business Europe	Social movements, unions
24–29 May 1999	Cologne	Demonstration	Counterdemonstration EU summit	Euromarches, social movements
10–11 December 1999	Helsinki, multi-sited	Demonstration	European Day of Action against workfare and for a guaranteed income	Social movements, unions
23–24 March 2000	Lisbon	Demonstration	Counterdemonstration EU summit	Social movements, unions
9–11 June 2000	Brussels	Demonstration	Counterdemonstration European business summit	Social movements, unions
19 June 2000	Porto	Demonstration	'For full employment in Europe'	ETUC
31 October 2000	Brussels	Demonstration	European Works Council (EWC) Directive	ETUC
6–7 December 2000	Nice	Demonstration	'For employment in Europe and social rights'	ETUC, social movements, unions
15 June 2001	Gothenburg	Demonstration	'For another Europe'	Social movements, unions
16 June 2001	Multi-sited	Demonstration	'For another Europe'	Social movements, unions
21 September 2001	Liege	Demonstration	'More Europe, a more social, democratic and citizens' Europe'	ETUC

Date	Location	Type	Slogan/Theme	Organizers
19 October 2001	Ghent	Demonstration	'For social Europe and solidarity'	ETUC, Belgian unions
13 December 2001	Brussels	Demonstration	Europe that's us!' – 'The euro arrives... and employment?' campaign	ETUC
14 March 2002	Barcelona	Demonstration	'Europe that's us!'	ETUC
16 March 2002	Barcelona	Demonstration	'Against a Europe of capital, another Europe is possible'	ETUC
22 June 2002	Sevilla	Demonstration	'Against the Europe of capital and war'	Social movements, unions
21 March 2003	Brussels, multi-sited	Demonstration	'For a democratic citizens' Europe'	ETUC
20 June 2003	Thessaloniki	Demonstration	Counterdemonstration EU summit	Social movements, unions
22 June 2003	Sevilla	Demonstration	'Against the Europe of capital and war'	Social movements, unions
4 October 2003	Rome	Demonstration	'For social Europe'	ETUC
2–3 April 2004	Multi-sited	Demonstration	'Our Europe – Europe that's us!' for workers' rights	ETUC
5 June 2004	Brussels	Demonstration	'Non à la directive Bolkestein – Oui à l'Europe sociale'	ETUC, social movements, unions
24 November 2004	Brussels	Demonstration	'Bolkestein Directive = Frankenstein Directive'	ETUC, social movements, unions
19 March 2005	Brussels	Demonstration	'More and better jobs - Defending social Europe - Stop Bolkestein'	ETUC, social movements, unions
21 March 2005	Brussels	Demonstration	Bolkestein Directive	Social movements
15 October 2005	Multi-sited	Demonstration	Services Directive, European Day of Action	ETUC, social movements, unions
25 October 2005	Strasbourg	Demonstration	Counterdemonstration Services Directive	ETUC, social movements, unions
11 February 2006	Strasbourg, Berlin	Demonstration	Counterdemonstration Services Directive	DGB, ETUC, Attac

(*continued*)

TABLE 6.3 (*continued*)

Date	Locations	Action Type	Topic	Coordinators
14 February 2006	Strasbourg	Demonstration	Euro-demonstration: Services Directive 'Services for the people'	ETUC
20 June 2007	Brussels	Demonstration	'On the offensive with the ETUC – Defend fundamental rights, social Europe, and more and better jobs'	ETUC
5 April 2008	Ljubljana	Demonstration	'More pay – more purchasing power – more equality', protest against stagnation in salaries and rising inequality	ETUC
5 July 2008	Luxembourg	Demonstration	European trade union assembly against the rulings of the EU Court of Justice on the posting of workers	ETUC
7 October 2008	Brussels, multi-sited	Demonstration	1st World Day of Action 'For decent work and decent pay'	ITUC, ETUC
16 December 2008	Strasbourg	Demonstration	Working Time Directive: 'Priority to workers' rights, not longer working hours', against longer working hours	ETUC
14–16 May 2009	Multi-sited	Demonstration	'Fight the crisis – Put people first' campaign, against austerity	ETUC
29 September 2010	Brussels, multi-sited	Strike, demonstration	'No to austerity – Priority for jobs and growth'	ETUC
15 December 2010	Multi-sited	Demonstration	'No to austerity for everyone and bonuses for a happy few'	ETUC, unions
24 March 2011	Brussels, multi-sited	Demonstration	'No to austerity plans in Europe'	ETUC
9 April 2011	Budapest	Demonstration	'No to austerity – for a social Europe, for fair pay and for jobs'	ETUC
21 June 2011	Luxembourg	Demonstration	Euro-demonstration: 'No to austerity – For a social Europe, for fair pay, investments and jobs', and against the type of economic governance that the European Union wants to impose on workers in Europe	ETUC

Date	Location	Type	Claim	Organisers
17 September 2011	Wroclaw	Demonstration	'Yes to European solidarity – Yes to jobs and workers' rights – No to austerity'	ETUC, Polish unions (OPZZ)
30 November 2011	Brussels, multi-sited	Strike, demonstration	European Day of Action against austerity measures	EPSU
29 February 2012	Multi-sited	Demonstration	'Enough is enough! – Alternatives do exist – For employment and social justice' campaign	ETUC
14 March 2012	Luxembourg	Demonstration	Against the absence of minimum standards in terms of wages, social insurance, and pensions	ETUC
19 May 2012	Frankfurt	Demonstration	Against EU's NEG regime	Blockupy
23 May 2012	Brussels	Demonstration	'Growth and investment for jobs – No to deregulation'	ETUC
14 November 2012	Brussels, multi-sited	Strike, demonstration	'For jobs and solidarity in Europe – No to austerity'	ETUC
23 January 2013	Brussels	Demonstration	Posting of Workers Directive and in favour of European social identity card	Unions
13–14 March 2013	Brussels, multi-sited	Strike, demonstration	'No to austerity! Yes to jobs for young people!'	ETUC, unions, social movements
15 May 2013	Multi-sited	Demonstration	Against weakening of Posting of Workers Directive	Unions
28 May 2013	Brussels	Demonstration	Demanding that EU rules on public procurement fully respect workers' rights	Belgian unions, UNI, ETUC, EFFAT, EFBWW
1–2 June 2013	Multi-sited	Demonstration	Against EU's NEG regime	Unions, social movements
3 July 2013	Berlin	Demonstration	Youth employment	DGB, ETUC
4 April 2014	Brussels	Demonstration	Against unemployment	ETUC
7 March 2014–30 January 2015	Online	European Citizens' Initiative	New Deal 4 Europe. For a European special plan for sustainable development and employment	newdeal4europe
11 February 2015	Multi-sited	Demonstration	Change Greece – Change Europe	Unions, social movements
18 March 2015	Frankfurt	Demonstration	Against EU's NEG regime	Blockupy

(*continued*)

125

TABLE 6.3 (continued)

Date	Locations	Action Type	Topic	Coordinators
21 June 2015	Multi-sited	Demonstration	Solidarity with Greece	Unions, social movements
15 October 2015	Multi-sited	Demonstration	EU summit	Euromarches
22 May 2016–22 May 2017	Online	European Citizens' Initiative	Let us reduce the wage and economic differences that tear the EU apart	Jobbik
16 June 2016	Luxembourg	Demonstration	Posting of Workers Directive	EFBWW
23 June 2017	Multi-sited	Demonstration	'Public sector workers need a pay rise'	EPSU, ETUCE
26 April 2019	Brussels	Demonstration	'A fairer Europe for workers'	ETUC

Source: Transnational Socioeconomic Protest Database (Erne and Nowak, 2023). For its methodology see Erne and Nowak (2022).

In November 2012, following a motion presented by the Spanish trade union confederations at the 2011 ETUC congress, the ETUC promoted a European strike and action day against the EU's austerity measures. This led to simultaneous general strikes in four countries (Greece, Italy, Portugal, and Spain), and demonstrations and symbolic actions took place in other member states (Dufresne and Pernot, 2013).

Nevertheless, this heterogeneity in the forms of mobilisation highlights how difficult it was to transnationally coordinate national union movements against commodifying NEG prescriptions in employment relations (Bieler and Erne, 2014). Traditional obstacles to transnational union action include national trade unions' different ideological orientation and attitude towards mobilisation, as well as their power resources, which were all relevant in this case. It was, however, the diverging orientations of NEG prescriptions on employment relations highlighted in section 6.3, as well as the fact that national governments implemented similar commodifying labour market reforms at different times, that played a crucial role in reducing the incentive for a timely coordinated labour action at European level.

Despite these difficulties in coordinating transnational action, the ETUC's increased role in Euro-mobilisations led some scholars to wonder whether it had shifted its approach to a more confrontational one (Horn, 2012). In 2014 however, the ETUC had already participated in a review by the Commission of its NEG instruments and agreed to become involved in the new architecture of European economic governance (Erne, 2015). The ETUC also proposed changes, such as greater fiscal flexibility under the SGP, greater involvement of social partners, and a rebalancing of some of the MIP scoreboards. Yet, as Erne (2015: 356) notes, 'it is very unlikely that technical discussions about indicators will increase European unions' capacity to inspire transnational social mobilizations'.

During the tenure of the Juncker Commission (2014–2019), which promoted a rhetorical shift away from austerity and attempted to increase the 'ownership' of NEG prescriptions by national governments and social partners, the ETUC increased its efforts to promote a better involvement of trade unions *within* the European Semester rather than leading a more confrontational approach vis-à-vis commodifying NEG labour-policy prescriptions. This is also shown in our database of protest events, which reveals a drop in ETUC-led mobilisations politicising the EU governance of employment relations since 2014 (Table 6.3). In autumn 2015, Jean-Claude Junker launched the idea of a European Pillar of Social Rights in turn, first in the European Parliament and then at the ETUC congress in Paris, in which the EU would reaffirm its social principles and values. In 2017, the EU institutions adopted the Social Pillar at their social summit in Göteborg.

At the subsequent ETUC congress in Vienna in 2019, delegates therefore gave Juncker a very warm welcome. The ETUC congress also noted NEG's persistent 'market bias' (ETUC, 2019: 45) but hoped that this could be corrected by a greater involvement of social partners in it (Golden, 2019). The ETUC congress' action programme only tasked its affiliates to seek 'an adequate level of dialogue with their governments and improve their influence on the drafting and implementation of national reform programmes, stability/convergence programmes and CSRs' (ETUC, 2019: 48), even though it was quite unlikely that the force of argument without the argument of force would tilt the balance of power within the NEG framework in favour of labour and its decommodifying objectives (Bieler, Jordan, and Morton, 2019).

Simultaneously, however, the ETUC urged EU policymakers to reaffirm their social commitments through directives adopted via the EU's ordinary legislative procedure, which involves the more labour-friendly European Parliament. This strategy bore more results. They included a revision of the Posting of Workers Directive, which had been undermined by the Laval Quartet of CJEU judgments (see section 6.2). The revision process happened in two steps: first, through an Enforcement Directive (2014/67/EU), which aimed to prevent a circumvention of the posting rules, and then a revision of the entire directive, which was finalised in 2018 (Directive 2018/957).[4] The revised directive extended the core of employment rights granted to posted workers from a minimum wage to all aspects of remuneration. Although governments from CEE states opposed the revision in the interest of CEE employers, unions from CEE countries supported it in line with the ETUC's position (Furåker and Larsson, 2020).

EU policymakers also revised older EU directives on employment rights of precarious workers and women in pregnancy, leading, respectively, to the Transparent and Predictable Working Conditions Directive (2019/1152) and the Work–Life Balance for Parents and Carers Directive (2019/1158). These interventions followed the proclamation of the European Pillar of Social Rights mentioned above, which aimed to reaffirm the EU's existing social principles and values. Accordingly, these acts did not seek to enlarge the scope of workers' rights at EU level. The Work–Life Balance Directive, for example, added only ten days of paid paternity leave to the existing four months of unpaid leave. Eventually, however, the shift to NEG unintentionally helped the adoption of EU directives in new areas also, namely, the

---

[4] Labour's standing in this process was also strengthened by the *Elektrobudowa* and *Regiopost* cases, which the CJEU used to readjust its Laval Quartet judgments (Garben, 2017).

2022 Directive on Adequate Minimum Wages, as we discuss in the conclusion to this chapter.

6.5 CONCLUSION

This chapter has described the evolution of the EU governance of employment relations. Until the 2008 financial crisis, EU influence on member states' employment relations was felt mostly as the result of horizontal market pressures triggered by the relaunch of the integration process at the end of the 1980s. Although the SEA and the Maastricht Treaty enlarged the scope for decommodifying EU directives in the field of labour and social policymaking, EU legislators did not intervene in key employment relations areas such as pay, collective bargaining, and the right to strike, which are outside the fields outlined in Art. 153 (1) TFEU. In any case, the impetus for introducing market-correcting EU legislation faded away throughout the 1990s, with supply-side economics becoming popular even among centre-left parties. In turn, direct commodifying EU prescriptions on employment protection legislation and wage bargaining arising from new governance mechanisms like the OMC had little coercive power. The Commission's attempts to intervene in national industrial relations via its 2004 draft Services Directive also failed as a consequence of the countervailing transnational labour protests and the subsequent legislative amendments that they triggered.

Until the 2008 crisis, only the CJEU had intervened directly in member states' collective bargaining systems, via its Laval Quartet judgments. The establishment of the NEG regime after 2008, however, gave EU executives greater intervention capacities in employment relations in both the private and the public sector. This chapter has shown how employment relations became a prime target of NEG prescriptions during the last decade. In our in-depth analysis of NEG prescriptions on wage levels, bargaining, and hiring and firing mechanisms for Germany, Italy, Ireland, and Romania, we have highlighted these interventions' different policy orientations, which we related to the different positions of these countries in the integrated but also uneven EU economy. Although NEG commodifying interventions in employment relations led to an increase in Euro-mobilisations, these diverging orientations limited the capacity of European trade unions to politicise and contest NEG prescriptions across borders, even at the height of the eurozone crisis. In 2014, the ETUC shifted its strategy to a classical inside lobbying approach, even though such an approach to NEG hardly promised to tilt the balance of power within the NEG framework in favour of labour.

Following the new challenges brought by the outbreak of the Covid-19 pandemic however, the European governance of employment relations might be ready for new changes. After member states agreed to set up a recovery and resilience fund to be financed through a joint bond issue, a broader revision of the SGP and the MIP might be in sight (see Chapter 12). However, the most significant developments for European employment relations might come from a new impetus for EU directives in the social field, promoted by the European Commission led by Ursula von der Leyen. At the start of her mandate in autumn 2019, von der Leyen announced the intention to introduce 'a legal instrument to ensure that every worker in our Union has a fair minimum wage' (von der Leyen, 2019: 9). Eventually, in 2020, the Commission decided to propose a legally binding directive (COM (2020) 682 final) to establish a framework for adequate minimum wages across member states.

As Art. 153(5) TFEU excludes pay from the remit of EU law, Business Europe questioned the legal basis for the proposed directive. Their EU competence argument nevertheless failed to gain traction in the EU policymaking process. After the CJEU, in its extensive jurisprudence on NEG (see Chapter 3), justified EU executives' *commodifying* ad hoc interventions on wage levels through NEG prescriptions, one would find it hard to argue that EU legislators would not also possess the competence to *decommodify* EU interventions in this field. The legal services of the European Commission, Council, and Parliament thus agreed to use the EU's right to propose directives in the field of 'working conditions' (Art. 153(1)(b) TFEU) as the legal basis for the proposed directive.

To overcome the objections of the member states with no statutory minimum wage (e.g., Denmark, Sweden, Austria, and Italy), the Directive on Adequate Minimum Wages (2022/2041) does not oblige all states to introduce one. Instead, it suggests a two-fold approach for granting adequate minimum wages. For countries with statutory minimum wages, the directive first defines a framework for setting adequate minimum wage levels, suggesting various procedures to do so, such as proposed reference values, timely revisions, indexation, or consultations with social partners. Secondly, as states with higher collective bargaining coverage rates tend to have fewer low-wage workers, the directive also promotes collective bargaining 'in particular at sector or cross-industry level' (Art. 4) and requires those member states with a collective bargaining coverage lower than 80 per cent to establish an action plan to increase such coverage.

Although the effects of the directive will depend on its implementation, even its adoption signals a paradigm shift after a decade of commodifying

NEG interventions on wages and workers' rights. Moreover, the Minimum Wage Directive is not the only new area of employment relations where the Commission has decided to intervene.

EU legislators also acted to enforce the principle of equal pay for work of equal value, as enshrined in EU legislation. In May 2023, the European Parliament and the Council adopted a directive on pay transparency (2023/970) that requires companies with more than 100 employees to provide information on the pay gap between their female and male employees. If such a gap is greater than 5 per cent, and the company cannot justify this on 'objective' reasons, the company will have to carry out an equal pay assessment with its workers' representatives to correct the gender pay gap.

With the United Kingdom's exit from the EU, labour-friendly forces might find it easier to achieve even more new EU directives in the future. Although commodifying NEG prescriptions on wages will be less likely if they go directly against the new directive on adequate minimum wages, it remains to be seen whether the new decommodifying EU laws will be able to protect wages and workers' rights better against the increased horizontal market pressures that workers have been facing since the late 1980s.

7

EU Governance of Public Services and Its Discontents

7.1 INTRODUCTION

The provision of public services was a key element of the post-World War II class compromise. Despite some national variations in their organisation, public services and utilities became an integral component of the social welfare states across Western Europe (Ruggie, 1982; Wahl, 2011; Supiot, 2013). Even after the rise of neoliberalism at the end of the 1970s, the provision of public services remained a key feature of the European social model. The relationship between European integration and public services is nevertheless complex. Since the adoption of the European Economic Community (EEC) Treaty in 1957, there was an inherent tension between the provision of public services and the rules governing the European common market. This set the scene for subsequent conflicts between political actors with different conceptions of the balance between market and state in the provision of public services. Such was their divisiveness over this matter that Mario Monti (2010) described them as a 'persistent irritant'.

This chapter analyses EU governance interventions from the EEC Treaty until the Covid-19 pandemic and the countermovements by European unions and social movements that they triggered. It is structured in three sections. First, we analyse the articulation between European integration and public services from 1957 to the 2008 crisis. In this period, we identify three phases across which *vertical* EU interventions put public services increasingly under pressure. Then, we assess the new economic governance (NEG) regime in public services, which the EU set up after the 2008 crisis. Our analysis of NEG prescriptions on public services for Germany, Ireland, Italy, and Romania between 2009 and 2019 indicates the presence of a consistent EU commodifying script across all countries. We also detect a few decommodifying predictions that indicate the presence of other rationales. However, these rationales remain subordinated to the script of public service commodification that we have detected. Finally, we assess the responses of unions and social movements to both types of vertical EU interventions in the field, namely, the universal (draft) EU laws issued in line with the ordinary legislative procedure and the country-specific prescriptions issued in line with the NEG regime.

7.2 EU GOVERNANCE OF PUBLIC SERVICES UNTIL THE 2008 FINANCIAL CRISIS

In the period before the 2008 crisis, we identify three phases in the relationship between the European integration process and public services. Initially, European integration and the making of public services at national level grew in parallel (Esping-Andersen, 1990; Crouch, 1999; Milward, 1999). After the mid-1980s, EU governance began to impinge on this policy area. This encroachment reached new heights by the 2000s and compelled unions and social movements to develop new action repertoires in response to it.

Phase One: Common Market and National Public Services

The Treaty of Rome, which created the EEC in 1957, referred to public services and public companies only marginally. Even so, the Treaty already contained the seed for the tensions between member states' capacity to provide public services and the rules governing the EU common market that would emerge later.

The drafters of the Treaty had to contend with different traditions of public services, for example, the French *service public*, the Italian *servizi pubblici*, the German *Daseinsvorsorge*[1] (Schweitzer, 2011). To avoid contentious debates, they coined a new term, *services of general economic interest* (SGEI), but failed to define it given the unequal boundaries between the public and private sectors across member states (Art. 90(2) TEEC, now Art. 106 TFEU). As the governments of West Germany and the Benelux countries feared that the widely nationalised French and Italian industries could gain unfair trade advantages, Art. 90(2) TEEC made all SGEIs subject to European competition law (Pollack, 1998). Moreover, Art. 90(3) TEEC (now Art. 106(3) TFEU) empowered the Commission to apply competition provisions of the Treaty through adopting Commission Directives without member states' approval in the Council. Even so, Art. 90(2) TEEC also stated that

---

[1] Literally, providing for [one's] existence.

competition law shall not be used to prevent public services from delivering on their objectives. Hence, if there is a conflict of interpretation, competition law should be secondary to the public interest and the delivery of public services (Cremona, 2011). Finally, the Treaty acknowledged that public services could be provided by either publicly or privately owned undertakings: 'This Treaty shall in no way prejudice the system existing in Member States in respect of property' (Art. 222 TEEC, now Art. 345 TFEU).

During the first two decades of the European integration process, the inherent tension between the provision of public services and the EEC competition rules remained dormant. Neo-mercantilist views in favour of interventionist industrial policies prevailed, even within the European Commission (Buch-Hansen and Wigger, 2011; Warlouzet, 2018). The Commission adopted a permissive stance towards state aid for public and private enterprises, as greater competitive pressures might create 'intolerable social tensions' (European Commission, 1972: 12). Accordingly, European integration and national public services developed in parallel: the EEC removed the tariff barriers between member states, and national governments constructed welfare states and supported their industries, relying also on the proceeds of free trade. Nationalisations, such as the establishment of the energy supplier ENEL in Italy in the 1960s, went unchallenged (Millward, 2005: 187), as did the nationalisation of British Leyland and British Shipbuilders in the United Kingdom in the 1970s (Warlouzet, 2018: 101). This happened despite the opposition of Italian, German, and Dutch employers who lobbied the Commission in vain to prevent the ENEL nationalisation (Petrini, 2010: 20). In 1981, the Commission did not prevent the ambitious nationalisation programme of the French socialist government either, which brought eight industrial conglomerates and almost all French banks into public ownership (Gélédan, 1993: 48–49). Hence, during this phase, the notion of what was considered an SGEI expanded considerably.

Phase Two: Public Services in the Single Market and Monetary Union

The second phase in the relationship between European integration and public services is linked to the rise of neoliberalism in the 1980s, when 'rolling back the state' became a dominant mantra. Neoliberal voices also became louder within the European Commission.

In 1980, the Commission adopted Directive (80/723/EEC), which forced member states to inform the Commission about the amount of state aid that they provided to their public undertakings. Although the French, Italian, and UK governments challenged the Commission's use of Art. 90(3) TEEC as a basis for its directive, the Court of Justice of the European Union (CJEU) ruled in favour of the Commission.[2] In 1982, the Dutch centre-right Competition Commissioner Frans Andriessen saw state aid to enterprises as akin to 'woodworms eating away the carcass of the ship of integration' (cited in Buch-Hansen and Wigger, 2011: 77). Andriessen's successor, the neoliberal Irishman Peter Sutherland, adopted an even more confrontational approach to prevent member states from aiding their companies (Warlouzet, 2018: 171–174). Under his tenure, the Commission not only named and shamed member states by publishing reports on the amount of aid granted to their companies but also began using its powers to ban state aid in important individual cases (Buch-Hansen and Wigger, 2011). According to the head of the Commission's legal service at the time, 'none of the commissioners since have tried to row back on what Peter achieved, so it was a clear victory for Peter and for neoliberal thinking' (Claus Dieter Ehlermann cited in Walsh, 2019: 106).

In 1986, national governments adopted the Single European Act (SEA), which revised the EEC Treaty. The SEA enabled the implementation of the Commission's single market programme through adopting corresponding EU laws by a qualified majority of the Council. Following the SEA, the Commission and Council opened several public network industries to competition, namely, telecommunications, road haulage, railways, electricity, gas, and postal services. In the case of the telecommunications industry, the Commission used once again the provisions of Art. 90(3) TEEC to liberalise the sector unilaterally by a Commission Directive. As in the case of the Commission's Transparency of Financial Relations Directive (80/723/EEC), several governments (Spain, France, Belgium, and Italy) challenged the Commission's prerogatives to do so in the European Court of Justice but again without success.[3] Despite the Commission's victories in these court battles however, the Commission effectively lost the war given the strong political opposition encountered from governments. It therefore stopped issuing liberalising Commission directives. Instead, it used the slower, but more inclusive, legislative procedures involving the Council to pursue its liberalisation agenda in other network industries, such as energy and postal services (Schmidt, 1996; Pollack, 1998).

As a result, the process of public service liberalisation was gradual and uneven across sectors. Whereas the Commission and Council gradually

---

[2] C-188–190/80 *France, Italy and United Kingdom v. Commission* [1982] ECR 02545.
[3] C-202/88 *France v. Commission* [1991] ECR I-123; C-271, 281, and 289/90 *Spain, Belgium and Italy v. Commission* [1992] ECR I-5833.

opened one public network industry after another to competition, other public services, such as water and healthcare, remained almost untouched throughout this period (see Chapters 9 and 10). After all, the Commission acknowledged that workers and unions would oppose the commodification of public services because this would entail the 'risk of job destruction' and compromise people's 'access to essential services at affordable prices' (1999, cited in *Transfer*, 2002: 293).

In 1992, European governments signed the Treaty of Maastricht that established the EU and amended the EEC Treaty (then called Treaty establishing the European Community, TEC) to accomplish an economic and monetary union (EMU) by the end of the decade. The Treaty introduced the convergence criteria for member states to join the Euro (Art. 109(j) TEC), and its protocol on the excessive deficit procedure (EDP) established reference values that member states must respect, that is, a public debt/GDP ratio of 60 per cent and a public deficit/GDP ratio of 3 per cent. In many cases, the adjustment required to meet these criteria was substantial: Italy's deficit at the beginning of the 1990s was around 10 per cent of its GDP (Leibfried, 2015). In 1997, the Council also adopted the Stability and Growth Pact (SGP), which operationalised the use of the convergence criteria and the EDP in secondary EU law.

As public services consume a significant share of public spending, the new EU fiscal constraints motivated European governments to curtail their spending on them directly. In addition, governments tried to make savings through marketising public services reforms, which shifted the financial burden of public services from the state budget to the service users. These reforms often included the full or partial privatisation of former public undertakings too. The reason to do so was twofold. Firstly, the immediate revenues from sales could go towards reducing public debt. Secondly, the balance sheet of former state companies would be excluded from future public budgets (Bieler, 2006). Although some EU countries, for example the United Kingdom, had already begun privatising public services in the 1980s, most EU member states launched their privatisation programmes only after the ratification of the Maastricht Treaty in 1993 (Clifton, Comín, and Díaz Fuentes, 2006: 742). However, as the EU initially issued only overall debt and deficit benchmarks without linking them to concrete policy prescriptions, the ensuing public sector curtailment and marketisation processes unfolded at an uneven pace and intensity across countries and sectors.

Whereas Western European public services had been put under pressure by the EMU convergence criteria, in Central and Eastern Europe (CEE) the EU accession process fuelled the commodifying pressures on public services.

According to the European Council's Copenhagen EU accession criteria, EU candidate countries must have 'a functioning market economy as well as the capacity to cope with competitive pressures and market forces within the Union' (Presidency Conclusions Copenhagen European Council, 21–22 June 1993). The Commission monitored candidate countries' progress in meeting this criterion very closely, emphasising the need for further privatisations and liberalisations, even though CEE governments had already privatised most state-owned enterprises (SOEs) in the transition from state socialism to capitalism in the 1990s (Appel and Orenstein, 2018: 65–89).

To make public service delivery allegedly cheaper, governments in turn promoted public sector reforms, that is, the introduction of market-like new public management practices. The pressure to curtail the spending on public services in national budgets also incentivised member states to increasingly rely on public–private partnership (PPP) agreements to fund their projects (Kunzlik, 2013) and to use procurement rather than in-house provision of public services (Fischbach-Pyttel, 2017). In 1996, the Commission argued that 'buying goods and services by effective purchasing systems can make significant savings for governments . . . . Such considerations are all the more relevant in view of the *strong pressures* to cut budget deficits in line with the Maastricht convergence criteria' (Green Paper, COM (96 583: 4, emphasis added). In practice however, these reforms have often 'led to results almost directly opposite to neoliberalism's claims', as the substitution of public monopolies by rent-seeking private service providers with oligopoly market and significant political power allowed the latter to extract extra profits (Crouch, 2016: 156). Even so, the EMU and EU accession criteria motivated governments to adopt public sector reforms that both curtailed and marketised them, albeit in a manner that was uneven across time and space (Keune, Leschke, and Watt, 2008; Frangakis et al., 2009; Crouch, 2011, 2016). Compared with employment relations reforms however, increased horizontal market pressures played a more limited role in triggering commodifying public sector reforms (Chapter 6). After all, (public sector) markets first need to be created by vertical policy interventions before they can set in train the horizontal market pressures that will push the commodification agenda further (Szabó, Golden, and Erne, 2022).

The uneven spread of marketising reforms across countries also reflected the opposition that they faced from social forces. Furthermore, neo-mercantilist ideas did not disappear completely from the action repertoire of some governments (Buch-Hansen and Wigger, 2011). Throughout the 1990s and the 2000s, the governments of several member states intervened to protect large national companies from bankruptcy or hostile takeovers, challenging the EU's new restrictive approach to state aid. The French government led this approach, with the then centre-right Minister for Economics and Finance Nicolas Sarkozy arguing that 'it is not a right for the state to help industry. It is a duty' (cited in Buch-Hansen and Wigger, 2011: 193). When governments intervened to save companies, they often did so when they were under political pressure. In the Alstom case, even the European Commission's DG Competition yielded to these pressures when it approved its re-nationalisation. This did not happen merely because of Sarkozy's neo-mercantilist ideas but rather because Alstom's unions and European Works Council succeeded in politicising the Alstom case not only in France but also across Europe through transnational collective action (Erne, 2008; Chapter 9).

A few years earlier, in December 1995, France had already witnessed a major strike wave in its public transport sector, which observers and activists alike portrayed as the first 'revolt against globalisation' and the Europe of 'Maastricht' and as a trigger for Europe's alter-globalisation movement (*Le Monde*, 7 December 1995; Ancelovici, 2002; Bourdieu, 2008). This motivated the French government to seek a better status for public services in the EC Treaty. In turn, the drafters of the Amsterdam Treaty of 1997 amended the EC Treaty, recognising the 'place occupied by services of general economic interest in the *shared values* of the Union as well as their role in promoting social and territorial cohesion' (emphasis added) (Art. 16 TEC, now Art. 14 TFEU). In doing so, they responded to the concerns of public sector companies organised in the Centre Européen des Entreprises à Participation Publique (CEEP, now SGI Europe), which feared the negative effects of further public service liberalisations (Héritier, 2001). Overall however, the mitigating effect of this Treaty change was quite limited, as the recognition of public services as a 'shared value' is merely aspirational. In fact, Art. 14 TFEU states neither what public services should be provided, nor for whom, and at what service coverage levels.

Phase Three: Frontal but Unsuccessful Assaults on Public Services

Throughout the 1980s and 1990s, the Commission followed a sectoral approach to push for the liberalisation of public services (Crespy, 2016). This changed in the early 2000s, after the successful launch of the Euro in 1999 and the CJEU's growing reluctance to consistently endorse the Commission's public service commodification agenda in its rulings (Héritier, 2001). Subsequently, the Commission began to seek *cross-sectoral* vertical legislative interventions that went 'further than explicitly mentioned in the European Treaties' (Höpner and Schäfer, 2010: 352). In 2004, Frits

Bolkestein, a neoliberal Dutch Commissioner in charge of the internal market, proposed an encompassing directive that aimed to liberalise the entire services sector, both public and private (Crespy, 2016; see also Chapter 6).

As mentioned in Chapter 6, the most contentious item in the draft Bolkestein Directive (COM (2004) 2 final/3) was the introduction of the country-of-origin principle. This radically reinterpreted the Treaty provisions on the free movement of services (Höpner and Schäfer, 2010) by moving the responsibility for regulating service providers from the country in which they were operating to providers' home country. By creating different sets of laws relating to access to, and exercise of, a service activity depending on the national location of the provider's headquarters, the Commission wanted to give providers from states with lower labour and consumer protection standards a competitive advantage, arguably to make the EU more competitive.

In the name of the free movement of services, the draft directive also included public services that had hitherto been excluded from EU internal market and competition policy, such as healthcare, social services, and non-mandatory education (Crespy, 2016). This time however, the Commission's bold cross-sectoral liberalisation drive managed to do what most sectoral EU vertical interventions had thus far avoided, namely, trigger a broad transnational countermovement of unions, left-wing parties, and social movements. The protest movement included major Euro-demonstrations against the draft directive held in Brussels and Strasbourg (della Porta and Caiani, 2009; Crespy, 2012, 2016; Copeland, 2014; Parks, 2015). Opposition to the Services Directive also played a significant role in French voters' rejection of the EU Constitution in 2005 (Béthoux, Erne, and Golden, 2018). On the legislative front, the fight happened mostly within the European Parliament, which was now granted co-legislative power under the ordinary legislative procedure. In the Parliament, two poles emerged: a liberal-conservative one in favour of liberalisation and a centre-left one favouring social regulation (Copeland, 2014; Crespy, 2016). The pro-liberalisation camp initially seemed to hold the majority within the EU institutions, but the arguments of the Stop Bolkestein coalition dominated the public debate (Copeland, 2014). Two years after the publication of the first draft directive, members of the European Parliament (MEPs) across the major political groups reached a compromise to secure the Parliament's adoption of a revised directive. Most MEPs went further than the Parliament's Internal Market Committee and removed the country-of-origin principle from the directive. The adopted directive (Directive 2006/123/EC) also explicitly excluded healthcare from its remit (see Chapter 10), along with other public services such as childcare. Even so, the provisions of a closed list of sectors that were exempted from the scope of the directive meant that other services remained amenable to liberalisation (Crespy, 2016: 44).

Shortly before launching the proposed Services Directive, the Commission had started to work on a major revision of EU legislation on public procurement. Given that public purchases constitute a sizable share of Europe's economy – in 2008, they accounted for 18 per cent of the EU's GDP (Monti, 2010: 76) – it is unsurprising that the EU focused its interventions in this area. This included several directives that aimed to coordinate and harmonise national procurement legislation (Kunzlik, 2013). In line with the development of the EU's single market, the main aim behind the legislation was to open competition for public contracts above a certain value to all firms in the EU. The Commission had already argued in 1985 that 'Community-wide liberalisation of public procurement in the field of public services is vital for the future of the Community economy' (White Paper, COM (85) 310: 23–24). Successive EU legislative interventions followed and were consolidated in two directives approved in 2004, regulating public (Directive 2004/18/EC) and utilities (Directive 2004/17/EC) contracts. These directives imposed increasing requirements on contracting authorities in terms of announcing tenders and criteria for awarding contracts (Kunzlik, 2013: 313). The 2004 procurement directives now explicitly included public services, such as healthcare, which had hitherto been relatively untouched by EU competition policy (see Chapter 10).

During the legislative process that led to the procurement directives, a broad coalition of unions and NGOs pushed for the inclusion of social and environmental criteria in the awarding guidelines (Fischbach-Pyttel, 2017). Despite the coalition's lobbying effort, the reference to the social and environmental aims of procurement was relegated to the directive's (non-binding) recital (Bieler, 2011: 171). The weak protection for social standards in EU procurement law became then evident when the CJEU issued the *Rüffert* judgment in 2008,[4] which meant that social clauses that seek to secure adequate wage rates within national or local public procurement laws can violate companies' freedom to provide services across the EU.

Other initiatives throughout the 2000s that aimed to protect public services from the realm of competition policy also failed, for example the attempt to establish an EU framework directive to define once and for all the role of SGEIs and exclude them from competition policy (Crespy, 2016). Thus, the trajectory of EU vertical interventions on public services in the 2000s remained a commodifying one, although the transnational countermovements against the Commission's draft Services Directive also showed the limits of commodifying EU interventions that

---

[4] C-346/06 *Rüffert* [2008] ECR I-01989.

also require the democratic support of the European Parliament. These limitations are even more significant if one considers that the increased horizontal market pressures played a limited role in triggering commodifying public sector reforms compared with labour market reforms (Chapter 6).

7.3 NEG: PURSUING PUBLIC SERVICE COMMODIFICATION BY NEW MEANS

EU leaders used the 2008 financial crisis to establish the NEG regime that enabled vertical EU interventions in public services by new means (see Chapter 2). This happened in a two-fold way. First, as expenditure on public services constitutes a significant share of member states' budgets, the pressure to reduce the public services' bill increased significantly during the financial crisis. Second, European policymakers coupled austerity measures with interventions that were meant to increase the EU's and the member states' competitiveness. This led to renewed calls for more competition in services (public and private) to reduce prices and thus boost an export-led recovery (Wigger, 2019). The two issues were related, as the pressure to curtail public expenditure also acted as a catalyst for the further marketisation of public services (Crespy, 2016; see also Chapter 4), as shown by the subsequent analysis of the EU's NEG prescriptions on public services for Germany, Ireland, Italy, and Romania from 2009 to 2019.

Building on the analytical approach developed in Chapters 4 and 5, we analysed all prescriptions that explicitly targeted public services as part of either an EU/IMF Memorandum of Understanding (MoU) with a bailout programme country or the EU's annual country-specific recommendations (CSRs) within the European Semester process. Concretely, we looked at prescriptions on the *provision of public services*, which we analysed under the headings of resource levels as well as sector-level and provider-level governance mechanisms. We also analysed the prescriptions pertaining to people's *access to public services*, namely, under the headings of coverage levels offered by public services and cost-coverage mechanisms used to recover their costs, including co-payments by service users, as the latter may exclude poor people from accessing them. We then distinguished between prescriptions with commodifying or decommodifying policy orientations, depending on whether their aim was to turn public services more (or less) into commodities to be traded in the market (Chapter 4). We also distinguished prescriptions based on their coercive strength, which we established by looking at the prescriptions' legal base and the location of a given country in NEG's policy enforcement regime at the time (see Table 5.1).

Public services encompass a vast array of sectors and subsectors. In this chapter however, we include only prescriptions on public services *across* sectors, namely, those dealing with the entire public sector at different levels (national, regional, local) and those that targeted at least two subsectors of the public service (e.g., education and healthcare). In subsequent chapters, we analyse a meaningful set of sector-specific prescriptions, namely, those on public transport (Chapter 8), water (Chapter 9), and healthcare (Chapter 10) services.

As we focus our analysis in this chapter on prescriptions with a cross-sectoral scope, we have excluded from the analysis prescriptions on *prioritising* certain sectors over others in terms of public spending. Whereas such prescriptions may point in a decommodifying direction from the perspective of the sector targeted by the prescription, the opposite is true for other sectors that would lose funding in turn. From a cross-sectoral perspective, it is thus not possible to assign a policy direction to these policy prescriptions. (We nonetheless collected these prescriptions and, where relevant, analysed them in the sectoral chapters.) Following the same logic, we also did not include prescriptions on the absorption of EU funds. As EU funds usually require member states to co-finance an EU-funded project, a higher absorption rate implies a re-allocation of national funds from one area to another.[5]

Table 7.1 gives an overview of the themes of NEG prescriptions that emerged from our analysis and of their policy orientation. As emerges clearly from Table 7.1, commodifying prescriptions dominate the picture across all categories, except for one, coverage level. The latter category however, includes very few prescriptions. There are some decommodifying prescriptions in the resource levels category, albeit fewer than commodifying ones. Commodifying prescriptions also generally have a greater coercive power.

Table 7.2 goes a step further and summarises the NEG prescriptions on public services received by the four countries under analysis from 2009 to 2019. The different symbols represent prescriptions according to the five categories used to guide our analysis. Triangles represent prescriptions on resource levels. Circles stand for those on sector-level governance mechanisms. Squares represent prescriptions on provider-level governance mechanisms. Finally, prescriptions on coverage levels are represented by stars and those on cost-coverage mechanisms by diamonds. The coercive strength of a prescription is shown by its shade: the more significant a prescription's strength, the darker the symbol's shade. Tables containing short quotes for each prescription are available in the Online Appendix (Tables A7.1–A7.4).

---

[5] The promise of EU funds, for example, motivated centre-left and centre-right local councillors in Romania to invest their municipalities' limited resources in tourism infrastructure projects, such as a ski resort on Vârful Ghiţu (Argeş), despite the lack of basic local water and sanitation services.

TABLE 7.1 Themes of NEG prescriptions on public services (2009–2019)

	Categories	Policy Orientation	
		Decommodifying	Commodifying
Provision of public services	Resource levels	Increase public investment (DE) Ensure adequate investment at all levels of government (DE) Enhance social infrastructure (IE) Extend basic infrastructure (RO) Invest in public employees' skills (IT) Upgrade infrastructure capacity (IT)	Reduce public spending (IE) Reduce spending on goods and services (RO) Cut transfers to local government (RO) Reduce subsidies to public enterprises (RO) Reduce capital spending (IE/RO) Reduce goods and services spending (RO) Reduce public sector wage bill (IE/RO) Reduce new entrants' pay in public sector (IE) Establish a unified pay scale in public sector (RO) Curtail public sector wages (RO) Reduce public sector employment numbers (IE) Reduce operating expenditure of SOEs (RO) Reduce personnel expenditure of SOEs (RO) Implement enforceable spending ceilings (IE/IT/RO) Streamline number of schools and hospitals (RO)
	Sector-level governance mechanisms		More competition in network industries (IT/RO) More competition in local public services (IT) Foster competition in services (IT) Adopt and enforce annual competition law (IT) Enforce competition law (DE) Establish single contact point for external firms (RO) Fewer constraints to infrastructure investment (DE)

(continued)

143

TABLE 7.1 (continued)

Categories	Policy Orientation	
	Decommodifying	Commodifying
		Improve coordination across government layers (IT/RO)
		Improve spending monitoring across sectors (IT)
		Improve central monitoring of local authorities (RO)
		Strengthen public investment monitoring (RO)
		Strengthen monitoring of SOEs (RO)
		Strengthen monitoring of public–private partnerships (RO)
		Increase value of public contracts open to procurement (DE)
		Enhance the efficiency of public procurement (IT)
		Review public procurement procedures (RO)
Provider-level governance mechanisms		Privatise SOEs (IE/IT/RO)
		Reform governance of SOEs (IT/RO)
		Reform local public services (IT)
		Reform public administrations' human resource management (IT/RO)
		Improve the efficiency of public administration (IT)
Access to public services	Coverage levels	Improve access to integrated public services (RO)
		Increase coverage levels of social services (RO)
	Cost-coverage mechanisms	Increase tariffs of SOEs (RO)

Source: Council Recommendations on National Reform Programmes; Memoranda of Understanding. See Online Appendix, Tables A7.1–A7.4.
Country code: DE = Germany; IE = Ireland; IT = Italy; RO = Romania. SOE = state-owned enterprise.

TABLE 7.2 *Categories of NEG prescriptions on public services by coercive power*

	Decommodifying				Commodifying				
	DE	IE	IT	RO	DE	IE	IT	RO	
2009								▲[8]●■[2]	2009
2010						▲[6] ■		▲[8]●[3]■	2010
2011						▲[6] ■	△ ○[3]	▲[5]●[4]■[3]◆	2011
2012			◀			▲[4] ■	◀●[2]	▲●[2]	2012
2013	△[2]		△		○[2]	▲[3] ■	△ ○[4] □	▲[5]●[4]■[5]	2013
2014	△[2]				○	◀	◀●[4]■	○[3] □[2]	2014
2015	△[2]					△	●[3]■[2]	□	2015
2016	△			△☆	○		●[3]■[4]	□[2]	2016
2017	△	△		☆			●■[3]	○	2017
2018	△	△					●[2]■[2]	○	2018
2019	△		◀	☆			●[2]■	○	2019

Source: Council Recommendations on National Reform Programmes; Memoranda of Understanding. See Online Appendix, Tables A7.1–A7.4.
Categories: △ = resource levels; ○ = sector-level governance mechanisms; □ = provider-level governance mechanisms; ☆ = coverage levels; ◊ = cost-coverage mechanisms.
Coercive power: ▲●■◆ = very significant; ▲●■ = significant; △○□☆ = weak.
Superscript number equals number of relevant prescriptions.
Country code: DE = Germany; IE = Ireland; IT = Italy; RO = Romania.

In the early years of NEG, Ireland and Romania received the bulk of commodifying prescriptions, although Germany and Italy received some too. Commodifying prescriptions continued to be issued until 2019, targeting Italy and Romania. From 2014 however, Germany also received decommodifying prescriptions. This was also the case in our other three countries, albeit to a lesser extent. In what follows, we analyse the prescriptions more thoroughly, category-by-category, taking their specific semantic context into account.

Provision of Public Services

Resource levels: Under MoU duress, both Ireland and Romania received several NEG prescriptions to curtail resources for public services. Firstly, both countries received the prescription to cut the public sector wage bill by reducing or freezing public sector wages and/or by reducing employment numbers by partial or full recruitment bans (MoU, Ireland, 28 November 2010; MoU, Romania, 23 June 2009).

We have already analysed the impact of these measures on employment relations in Chapter 6. Here, we highlight their impact on public services. Reducing the number of public employees also reduces service quality, in terms of staff/service user ratio and so forth. This is especially the case during an economic crisis when users' need for public services usually increases. The demand to reduce the number of workers directly employed by the state might also backfire, as it can incentivise recourse to agency work, which comes with overheads and may prove more expensive than direct employment on the government payroll, as happened in the Irish health service during the Troika years (Burke et al., 2014). It is worth noting that Romania received more detailed prescriptions than Ireland on how to implement the reduction of the public sector wage bill. This mirrors the fact that, when the Troika arrived, the Irish government had already cut the public sector wage bill (see Chapter 6).

Although Italy did not receive any explicit prescription to cut the public service pay bill, it received constraining prescriptions to reduce its public expenditure between 2012 and 2014, with the stated rationale of improving 'the efficiency and quality of public expenditure' (Council Recommendation Italy 2012/C 219/14). In turn, these prescriptions motivated the Italian government to pause collective bargaining in the public sector (Bach and Bordogna, 2013). Indeed, successive Italian governments put in place a pay freeze until 2017, coupled with a partial hiring freeze, which meant that public service providers were no longer able to replace departing or retiring staff members. The pay freeze might have lasted even longer had unions not successfully challenged it in the Italian Constitutional Court. Although the government's attorneys argued that the pay freeze measure was taken 'to reduce public expenditure, in fulfilment of the obligations arising from membership of the European Union', the Court upheld the unions' constitutional collective bargaining rights.[6] By contrast, in some parts of the public sector, the hiring freeze regulations that reduced the replacement rate remained in place until 2019.

Beyond prescriptions to reduce the public sector pay bill, the MoU for Ireland demanded general budget cuts that impacted on the delivery of public services and that of Romania requested a cut in expenditure for goods and services. The MoU for both countries requested specific cuts on capital expenditure. Romania received also more specific requests for spending cuts. The second addendum of the 2009 MoU tasked the Romanian government to cut transfers to local governments and to 'streamline' (i.e., to reduce) the number of schools and hospitals; this in turn reduced the availability of key public services in disadvantaged rural areas (MoU, Romania, 2nd addendum, 20 July 2010; see Chapter 10). Several prescriptions for Romania targeted SOEs. The 2009 MoU asked the government to reduce subsidies to public enterprises, and the third addendum requested that SOEs cut 'operating expenditure, including personnel' (MoU, Romania, 3rd addendum, 19 January 2011).

Prescriptions on expenditure levels related to the binding ceilings on public spending that national governments had to introduce following the strengthening of the SGP by the Six-Pack and Two-Pack laws as well as the Fiscal Treaty (Chapter 2). Accordingly, not only Ireland and Romania but also Italy received a prescription to this aim (Council Recommendation Italy 2011/C 215/02). The spending ceilings in turn curtailed investment in public services further.

Commodifying prescriptions on resource levels prevailed from 2009 to 2013, but the picture started to change after 2014. After Ireland and Romania left the conditional financial assistance programme at the end of 2013, they ceased to receive prescriptions requesting direct spending cuts on public services. From 2014 onwards, Germany got prescriptions to increase public investment. Until 2019, the wording of these prescriptions for Germany became gradually more explicitly decommodifying. The 2014 prescription that asked Germany to increase public investment also urged it to make its public services more 'efficient'. In the following European Semester cycles, this specification disappeared when the German government was urged to deliver a 'sustained upward trend in public investment' (Council Recommendation Germany 2016/C 299/05). Prescriptions for Germany also requested more investments 'at all levels of governments', including the *Länder* and local level (Council Recommendation Germany 2014/C 247/05). The accompanying recitals noted a significant backlog in investment, albeit without acknowledging the role played by the opening of an EDP against Germany in 2010 (Council Decision Germany

---

[6] Corte Costituzionale, sentenza n. 178, 23 July 2015.

2010/285/EU) and the debt brake that its government applied across all government levels to reduce the public debt and deficit.

We classified the prescriptions for more investments as decommodifying, as they have the potential to increase resources for public services (Chapters 4 and 5). Nonetheless, the prescriptions' decommodifying policy orientation could also be informed by an overarching commodifying script. Increased public spending could go towards private service providers also, namely, in a context where NEG prescriptions demand a further marketisation of public services, as we shall see below. The recital accompanying Germany's prescription for more investment in 2016 noted that 'a more efficient use of public procurement could also have a positive impact on investment' (Council Recommendation Germany 2016/C 299/05). The recital also deplored the fact that 'alternative instruments to traditional state funding of transport infrastructure, including through public-private partnerships, are used only to a limited extent' (Council Recommendation Germany 2016/C 299/05). Finally, the Commission's Country Report linked the need to increase investment with the need 'to maintain Germany's competitive advantage' (Commission, Country Report Germany SWD (2019) 1004: 47). Tables A7.1–A7.4 in the Online Appendix therefore show the semantic link to the policy rationale informing these decommodifying prescriptions.

EU executives also issued decommodifying prescriptions on resources for public services to the other three countries but in a less consistent way. In 2012 and 2013, the Italian government was asked to 'upgrade infrastructure capacity with a focus on energy interconnections, intermodal transport and high-speed broadband in telecommunications, also with a view to tackling the North-South disparities' (Council Recommendation Italy 2013/C 217/11). Similarly, in 2016 the Romanian government was urged to 'Extend basic infrastructure ... in particular in rural areas' (Council Recommendation Romania 2016/C 299/18). The accompanying recitals cited transport and broadband networks as examples of lacking infrastructures that foster disparities between urban and rural areas. In 2017, a prescription urged the Irish government to 'enhance social infrastructure, including social housing and quality childcare' (Council Recommendation Ireland 2017/C 261/07). A similar prescription was present in the 2018 CSRs, but with a broader scope, including also transport and water (Chapters 8 and 9), which the Irish government planned to support through the adoption of a National Development Plan (Council Recommendation Ireland 2018/C 320/07).

As these prescriptions asked governments to increase the resources for public services, we classified them as decommodifying. Compared, however, with the earlier, opposite prescriptions issued within the MoU, their constraining power was weak. The prescriptions were also vaguer. They did not specify that increased services should be provided by *public* service providers, leaving open the question of private providers stepping in to benefit from increased investment. Neither did they acknowledge the negative effects that the previous, more coercive, NEG prescriptions on public-spending curtailment had had on the dire state of Italian, Irish, and Romanian public services. As in the case of Germany, the prescriptions on public spending levels must furthermore be assessed in their semantic context, including the enduring commodifying prescriptions on the provision of public services, as analysed below. The recitals of the 2016 CSRs for Italy, for example, ascribed the low public investment to 'uncertainty associated to the transition to the new code of public procurement and concessions' (Council Recommendation Italy 2016/C 299/01). This indicates that these notionally decommodifying prescriptions on more public spending were semantically subordinated to overarching, commodifying policy objectives.

Finally, a similar conclusion can be drawn in relation to the 2019 prescription for Italy, which urged its government to invest in the skills of public service employees (Council Recommendation Italy 2019/C 301/12). The call to invest more resources in public service employees also points in a decommodifying direction. However, the 2018 Country Report linked the issue of Italian public employees' apparently 'low skill profile' to a commodifying discourse that suggested relating wages more closely to performance evaluation (Commission, Country Report Italy SWD (2018) 210 final: 45–46).

Sector-level governance mechanisms: As discussed above, the NEG prescriptions on expenditure levels differed across time and country, reflecting countries' different locations in the EU political economy and the NEG policy enforcement regime at a given time. Nonetheless, not only Italy and Romania, but also Germany, received prescriptions that urged their governments to change the governance mechanisms for public services at sectoral level. All of them were commodifying, demanding increased competition among public service providers, as well as tightened financial monitoring and surveillance of their operations. By contrast, Ireland did not receive any general prescriptions in this category, only sector-specific ones for the healthcare sector (Chapter 10).

In Germany, the NEG prescriptions in this category focused on public procurement. To shape the institutional framework towards more competition, the 2013 and 2014 prescriptions urged the German government 'to significantly increase the value of public contracts open to procurement' (Council Recommendation Germany 2013/C 217/09) under EU procurement legislation. In its assessment of Germany's progress regarding the 2013 Council Recommendation, the Commission noted that 'further efforts are needed to identify the reasons behind the low publication rate and to open public procurement to EU-wide bidding' (Commission, Country Report Germany SWD (2014) 406 final: 23). In 2017, the call to increase public investment in

Germany was accompanied by a prescription to 'address capacity and planning constraints', which also implied the use of 'private sector know-how' and the speeding up of investment approval procedures by public authorities (Council Recommendation Germany 2017/C 261/05 and 2018/C 320/05).

Almost all MoUs and Council Recommendations for Romania issued between 2009 and 2019 demanded more effective public procurement procedures. In 2011 and 2012, Romania received another prescription aimed at fostering competition in the EU single market, namely, the request to set up a single contact point to help foreign firms to enter Romania or for cross-border provision of services, echoing provisions of the Services Directive. As in the case of prescriptions on public procurement, it is noteworthy how the Commission used NEG prescriptions here to further advance by new means its commodification agenda, which had already underpinned its legislative agenda in the Services Directive case.

Calls for increased competition in public services featured prominently in the NEG prescriptions for Italy. Between 2012 and 2016, NEG prescriptions recurrently called for more competition in the private and the public services sector. In 2014, for example, a prescription tasked Italy to 'remove remaining barriers to, and restrictions on, competition in the professional and local public services, insurance, fuel distribution, retail, and postal services sectors' (Council Recommendation Italy 2014/C 247/11). In 2013 and 2014, the government was asked to 'improve coordination between layers of government' (Council Recommendation Italy 2013/C 217/11). Although the meaning of this prescription is not immediately accessible, its commodifying policy direction becomes very clear when it is analysed in its semantic context (see Chapters 4 and 5). The 2013 Country Report noted that 'insufficient coordination between the central and local levels of government and lack of clarity on the division of responsibilities across them' (Commission, County Report Italy SWD (2013) 362 final: 32) hampered the implementation of liberalising EU law, namely, the Services Directive.

A 2013 prescription for Germany urged its government to improve the enforcement of competition law and to remove restrictions to competition (Council Recommendation Germany 2013/C 217/09). Like Romania and Germany, Italy received commodifying prescriptions concerning public procurement. A 2013 prescription focused on local public services, 'where the use of public procurement should be advanced, instead of direct concessions' (Council Recommendation Italy 2013/C 217/11), and the detailed 2014 prescription requested 'streamlining procedures including through the better use of e-procurement, rationalising the central purchasing bodies and securing the proper application of pre- and post-award rules' (Council Recommendation Italy 2014/C 247/11). Successive recommendations for Italy issued between 2015 and 2019 called for the adoption of an annual 'competition' law 'to address the remaining barriers to competition' (Council Recommendation Italy 2016/C 299/01). The lack of competition in Italian local public services was also deplored in the prescriptions issued in 2014, 2015, and 2018. Furthermore, Italian public network industries attracted the attention of EU executives, with two prescriptions issued in 2012 and 2013 mandating Italy to improve the 'market access condition' in the energy and transport sectors (Council Recommendation Italy 2013/C 217/11). Romania received a similar prescription for these two sectors in 2014 (Council Recommendation Romania 2014/C 247/21).

In this sector-level governance mechanisms category, another theme also emerged, as several NEG prescriptions called for the tightening of central control over public spending across different government levels and departments. The Italian government received prescriptions corresponding to this aim in 2011 and then in 2015–2016, and the Romanian government received them throughout the MoU period. Not only did the MoUs call for central financial control across all government levels, but also the Romanian 2011 P-MoU requested a stricter monitoring of SOEs and PPP agreements (P-MoU, Romania, 29 June 2011).

Provider-level governance mechanisms: Under this category, we identified two main types of prescriptions that all pointed in a commodifying direction: namely, calls for the privatisation or marketisation of SOEs and calls for reforms to render public service providers' governance mechanisms more market-like. Germany was the only country of the four not to receive prescriptions in this area.

As referenced in section 7.2, the EU 'Treaties shall in no way prejudice the rules in Member States governing the system of property ownership' (Art. 345 TFEU). Nevertheless, the European Commission and Council issued several prescriptions for Ireland, Italy, and Romania, which called not only for marketisation but also for privatisation of their SOEs. This is another example of how the NEG regime increased EU executives' capacity to intervene in areas in which they have no formal policymaking powers. In their MoU, both the Irish and the Romanian governments were tasked to privatise state assets to consolidate public finances. As the Irish government had already announced privatisation plans prior to the bailout (Palcic and Reeves, 2013; Mercille and Murphy, 2016), it did not receive precise indications on *which* state assets should be disposed of (MoU, Ireland, 28 November 2010). In contrast, the prescriptions for Romania were more precise. In 2010, for instance, the Romanian MoU included the prescription to take concrete steps towards the privatisation of SOEs in the energy and transport sectors (MoU, Romania, 2nd addendum, 20 July 2010). In the case of Italy, privatisations had already been part of successive government plans to reduce public debt. Between 2014 and 2017 however, Italian governments recurrently received NEG prescriptions that demanded the implementation of the plans (Council Recommendation Italy 2014/C 247/11).

In addition, governments received commodifying prescriptions urging them to render the governance mechanisms of providers that remained in public ownership more market-like. While subject to the MoU programme, in 2011 the Romanian government adopted an emergency ordinance on the governance of SOEs 'with inputs from the IMF, the World Bank and the European Commission' (European Commission, 2016a: 85). The reform entailed: '(i) the applicability of company law on SOEs, (ii) the separation between the ownership and the regulatory function of the authorities, (iii) the transparent and professional selection of board members and management, (iv) the concept of performance monitoring, and (v) the strengthened protection of minority shareholders' (European Commission, 2016a: 86). These themes also featured in subsequent NEG prescriptions; for example, in 2019, when the Romanian government was tasked to 'strengthen the corporate governance of State-owned enterprises' (Council Recommendation Romania 2019/C 301/23).

Similarly, Italy received a prescription in 2017 inviting the government to 'improve the efficiency of publicly-owned enterprises' (Council Recommendation Italy 2017/C 261/11). The accompanying recital explained what improved 'efficiency' would mean, namely, corporate governance reforms that ensure that publicly owned companies will 'operate under the same rules as privately-owned entities' (Council Recommendation Italy 2017/C 261/11).

Requests to marketise public administrations' governance mechanisms also featured consistently in the NEG prescriptions for Italy and Romania. In addition to cuts to the public sector wage bill (see Chapter 6), the 2009 MoU tasked the Romanian government to implement a reform 'aimed at increasing the effectiveness of the public administration' (MoU, Romania, 23 June 2009). The NEG prescriptions in this area included not only the demands on sector-level governance analysed above but also specific, commodifying demands for public service providers, for example, in relation to their human resource management (HRM). As in the case of their NEG prescriptions on SOEs, EU executives continued to prescribe public administration reforms in the HRM area, even after the end of Romania's MoU programme, until 2017.

From 2013, EU executives recurrently issued NEG prescriptions that tasked the Italian government to reform its public administration. In turn, the centre-left government led by Matteo Renzi (2014–2016) adopted the Madia reform package, which included several decree-laws on a wide range of issues, including administrative digitalisation, administrative reorganisation, and the introduction of new HRM practices. As in the case of its commodifying Jobs Act (Chapter 6), the Renzi government implemented the Madia reform to obtain greater fiscal space from EU executives in exchange, following the more 'flexible' interpretation of the SGP by the Juncker Commission and the Council. Subsequently however, the Italian Constitutional Court annulled several parts of the reform as they were unconstitutional;[7] this explains why EU executives continued to issue corresponding NEG prescriptions until 2019.

The Irish MoU did not contain any specific prescriptions on the reform of public companies or administrations, arguably because the Irish government had already started reforming them before the arrival of the Troika in December 2010. Successive governments managed to keep public services reform largely outside contentious politics (Hardiman and MacCarthaigh, 2011) – from the heydays of Irish social partnership agreements in the 2000s (Roche and Geary, 2006; Doherty and Erne, 2010) to the Croke Park public sector collective bargaining agreement of 2010 (Maccarrone, Erne, and Regan, 2019; Chapter 6). After the Troika's arrival however, the Irish government established a new government department, the Department of Public Expenditure and Reform, which privatised several public companies and pursued reforms that strengthened its control over all levels of government (MacCarthaigh, 2017). These unilateral government actions were tightly monitored by the Troika (Commission, Economic Adjustment Programme for Ireland, Spring 2012 Review), even though the policy preferences of the Troika and the Irish government were largely congruent (Dukelow, 2015). The latter thus exploited the crisis and MoU as an opportunity to implement reforms that would not have been possible in other circumstances (MacCarthaigh and Hardiman, 2020).

Users' Access to Public Services

Coverage levels: The only country that received NEG prescriptions on the coverage level of public services in general was Romania. In 2016 and 2017, Romania received decommodifying prescriptions that urged its government to 'improve [users'] access to integrated public services' (Council Recommendation Romania 2016/C 299/18). The theme of prescriptions is broad in scope and refers to the unequal access for service users living in rural areas to education, health services, and basic utilities. These prescriptions

---

[7] Corte Costituzionale, sentenza n. 251, 25 November 2016.

were clearly decommodifying but had only weak coercive power as they were based on the merely aspirational Europe 2020 strategy. The prescriptions acknowledged users' unequal access to services but failed to mention that these inequalities resulted from earlier, much more binding NEG prescriptions that commodified public transport and health services (Chapters 8 and 10) and curtailed public spending more generally, especially throughout the period of MoU conditionality (2009–2013). A 2019 prescription nevertheless urged the Romanian government even more explicitly to 'increase the coverage and quality of social services' (Council Recommendation Romania 2019/C 301/23), after the recital for the abovementioned 2017 prescription on users' access to integrated public services deplored the fact that 'over 45% of Romania's population live in rural areas' with very limited access to 'social services' (Council Recommendation Romania 2017/C 261/22). This indicates the presence of policy rationales that are not aligned to NEG's primary, commodifying objectives.

Cost-coverage mechanisms: There is only one prescription under this category concerning cross-sectoral public services, addressed once again to Romania. In this case, the prescription had a clearly commodifying policy orientation. Among the measures indicated to reduce SOEs' arrears (discussed in the section on resource levels above), the third addendum to the 2009 MoU dated 19 January 2011 also tasked the Romanian government to instruct its SOEs to increase their tariffs for service users. This obviously limited poorer users' capacity to access public services. In addition, we must note that the prescriptions on the curtailment of resource levels for all countries, discussed above, frequently forced public service providers to compensate their losses of public funding by increasing their charges for service users.

NEG: A New Avenue to Foster Commodifying EU Interventions in Public Services

Our analysis of the EU's NEG prescriptions on public services for Germany, Ireland, Italy, and Romania issued between 2009 and 2019 has shown the broad range of issues affected by NEG. Overall, commodifying NEG prescriptions clearly dominated the picture. Over the years, EU executives also issued a few decommodifying NEG prescriptions on resource levels, especially for Germany, but to a lesser extent to the other three states. However, whereas the coercive power of commodifying prescriptions was very significant or significant, echoing the countries' location in the NEG enforcement regime at a given time, the coercive power of the decommodifying prescriptions was weak.

Hence, the shift to the NEG regime intensified the EU's commodifying pressures on public services. Our analysis uncovered a consistent pattern of commodifying NEG prescriptions, which tasked the receiving member states to curtail their public spending on public services and render the governance mechanisms at both the sectoral and the provider level for public services more market-like. This indicates the presence of a consistent policy script in favour of public sector commodification deployed through corresponding NEG prescriptions across all four countries. The presence of a common commodification script however, did not lead to the issuing of equal prescriptions for the four countries across all categories at the same time. By contrast, the NEG regime's country-specific prescriptions enabled EU executives to nudge all member states in a commodifying policy direction, while also taking their unequal public services commodification trajectories into account. The unevenness of the commodifying NEG prescriptions issued to the four countries across time thus echoed different commodification trajectories followed by them before and after the EU's shift to the NEG regime, rather than the application by EU executives of a different policy script across them.

In addition to the consistent pattern of commodifying NEG prescriptions, we identified some decommodifying ones. As we were analysing the NEG prescriptions in their specific semantic context however, we were able not only to establish their concrete commodifying or decommodifying policy orientation but also to link the detected decommodifying prescriptions to the policy narratives informing them. When analysing the decommodifying NEG prescriptions in the field, we thus detected semantic links to the following policy rationales.

First, some decommodifying prescriptions to increase public investment were semantically related to another concern, namely, to boost competitiveness and growth. This policy rationale is linked to the ailing infrastructure's negative effects on the member states and the EU's competitiveness. Several NEG prescriptions to increase public investment for Germany, Italy, Ireland, and Romania were semantically linked to this policy rationale.

A second policy rationale linked to the decommodifying prescriptions to increase public investment was a commodifying one, namely, to enhance private sector involvement in public services. This was the case for the prescriptions addressed to Germany in 2016 and 2019, which linked the need for more investment to more private sector involvement through PPP or public procurement. Also, the prescriptions addressed to Italy in 2012–2013 to upgrade infrastructure capacity were semantically linked to the need to open network industries to competition.

Third, since 2017, few decommodifying prescriptions aimed at increasing public investment concerned the required shift to a green economy. These semantic links were visible in only a few decommodifying prescriptions that tasked the German and the Irish government to increase public investments.

Fourth, some decommodifying NEG prescriptions that urged the German government to increase public investment were linked to the policy rationale of rebalancing the EU economy, as already detected in Chapter 6. This policy rationale relates specifically to Germany's position at the core of the EU economy. As in the case of higher German wages, increased public investments would boost domestic demand in Germany. This would in turn increase its imports from other EU states and contribute to a more balanced European economy (Council Recommendation Germany 2017/C 261/05).

A fifth policy rationale that emerged from our analysis concerns the issue of increasing efficiency. This informs only one decommodifying prescription, namely, the one addressed to Italy about the need to invest in public employees' skills.

A few decommodifying prescriptions to increase public investment and the coverage of public and social services were semantically linked to concerns about social inclusion. This policy rationale concerns spatial inequalities (between regions and between urban and rural areas) and social cohesion. It informed a few prescriptions for Romania but was also visible in Irish and Italian prescriptions. Yet, compared with the policy rationales discussed above, the social inclusion rationale played a very marginal role. Indeed, the prescriptions informed by this policy rationale were so scarce and so weak that we can hardly speak of a socialisation of the European Semester (Zeitlin and Vanhercke, 2018). The prescriptions addressed to the Irish government in 2017–2018 to enhance social infrastructure, in particular childcare, relate to a sixth policy rationale, that is, to expand (female) labour's market participation.

In sum, in line with our methodological approach outlined in Chapters 4 and 5, we have classified all NEG prescriptions based on their primary policy orientation. Accordingly, we have detected a consistent pattern of commodifying NEG prescriptions. Not only were there fewer decommodifying NEG prescriptions, they were also weaker. In a second step, we assessed the semantic links between the decommodifying prescriptions and the policy rationales informing them. We detected that most decommodifying prescriptions were semantically linked to policy rationales that did not contradict the commodifying policy script informing most NEG prescriptions. Furthermore, when we analysed the decommodifying prescriptions to increase public investment in the context of the commodifying prescriptions in favour of marketising public sector reforms, the decommodifying prescriptions also became a vector of commodification, namely, when increased public money was channelled towards private coffers following marketising reforms of public services. This is indeed what we observed in our analysis. Calls for increased public investment have consistently been accompanied by commodifying prescriptions on public procurement, concessions, and PPP. By contrast, prescriptions on the coverage of public services were not semantically linked to commodifying prescriptions on the marketisation of public services, but they were residual as a share of all prescriptions.

Finally, all decommodifying prescriptions related to quantitative measures on public services resource and coverage levels, but there were no decommodifying prescriptions with a qualitative dimension, either on sector- and provider-level public service governance or on cost-coverage mechanisms that shape people's access to public services. Hence, whereas EU executives agreed to pause and even reverse some curtailment measures after the recovery from the financial crisis, NEG prescriptions continued to call for (qualitative) 'structural reforms' over the entire decade 2009–2019.

Vertical EU Interventions in Public Services after the Shift to NEG

The shift to the NEG regime enabled EU interventions in public services by new means, but it has not supplanted 'older' tools of vertical governance interventions by EU law. Between 2009 and 2019, the EU adopted several new laws that affect public services. First, the EU's *sectoral* liberalisation agenda led to the adoption of new EU directives in the postal, energy, and railway sectors (Crespy, 2016; Chapter 8). In addition to these laws targeting already broadly liberalised sectors, the Commission tried to advance its public services commodification agenda in new areas through sector-specific EU laws, for example, Directive 2011/24/EU on cross-border healthcare (Stan and Erne, 2021a; Chapter 10) or cross-sectoral EU laws, for example, Directive 2014/23/EU on the award of concession contracts and Directives 2014/24/EU and 2014/25/EU on public procurement. In 2016, the Commission proposed a Services Notification Procedure Directive (COM (2016) 821 final), which would have obliged local, regional, and national governments to ask the European Commission for prior approval before implementing any laws, regulations, or administrative provisions on public services covered by the 2006 Services Directive. The Commission's proposal failed to become law, however, because of opposition in the European Economic and Social Committee, the European Parliament, and the Council, and protest letters from municipalities, unions, and social movements (Hoedeman, 2020; Szypulewska-Porczyńska, 2020).

In this context, EU executives used their NEG prescriptions to reinforce commodifying pressures emanating from legislative interventions through the ordinary legislative procedure. Some of the areas targeted in NEG prescriptions, such as public procurement, were already part of the EU's *acquis communautaire*, but, in other areas, such as the governance of public administration and of SOEs, EU policymakers had no explicit legislative competences. Thus, EU executives used NEG to advance their agenda in areas thus far spared from EU interventions.

Moreover, as we shall see in more detail in Chapters 8–10 on sector-specific NEG interventions, NEG prescriptions have been issued not only in sectors already deeply affected by the EU's single market agenda (e.g., railways, see Chapter 8) but also in sectors that until the 2008 financial crisis had been partially shielded from direct EU interventions, such as water and healthcare (Chapters 9 and 10, respectively).

This push towards further commodification of public services did not go unchallenged however. For instance, water was excluded from the Concessions Directive thanks to the successful Right2Water European Citizens' Initiative (Szabó, Golden, and Erne, 2022; see Chapter 9). Moreover, due to the effort of unions and social movements, a binding social clause was inserted in the revised 2014 directive on public procurement. Yet, although the EU's ordinary legislative procedure still offers clear targets for transnational contestation, given that it involves the European Parliament, the NEG technocratic structure makes the emergence of transnational countermobilisation much more difficult.

7.4 PUBLIC SERVICES COMMODIFICATION AND THE COUNTERMOVEMENTS THAT IT TRIGGERED

Before 2008, commodifying EU interventions on public services often triggered social countermovements. Initially, union-led mobilisations against the commodification of public services took place mostly at local and national level, with varying success (Crespy, 2016). This is hardly surprising. Not only are European unions organised in national and local branches (Gumbrell-McCormick and Hyman, 2013) but also the effects of EU laws often become visible for a wider public only when national and local policymakers try to implement them on the ground (Kohler-Koch and Quittkat, 2013).

In the 2000s, ever more commodifying vertical EU interventions in public services triggered countermovements that politicised them in the European public sphere, namely, in the case of the EU-wide union campaign against Commissioner Bolkestein's Services Directive. His draft directive gave unions a visible supranational target, and its wide scope allowed them to build broad alliances with social movements. The coalition-building process was aided by the emergence of the alter-globalisation movement at the end of the 1990s. Combining lobbying activities in the European Parliament with national and Euro-demonstrations, organised labour was able to limit the directive's commodifying drive (see section 7.2).

Other imminent EU laws, namely, the directives on public procurement, also triggered union and social-movement alliances (Bieler, 2011). The EPSU's Coalition for Green and Social Procurement and several NGOs campaigned to insert social and environmental standards in the 2004 directives on public procurement. However, as mentioned in section 7.2, they succeeded in including them only in its recitals. This outcome echoed structural factors, namely, the relative disadvantage of labour and social interests vis-à-vis business interests, especially in the institutional context of the EU (Offe and Wiesenthal, 1980; Erne, 2020). Andreas Bieler (2011) also highlighted the limitations of the coalition's strategy, which relied mainly on direct lobbying activities and failed to trigger public contestation, which instead took place in the subsequent Services Directive case, when transnational mobilisation took place not only at cross-sectoral but also at sectoral level (Erne and Nowak, 2023; Chapters 8–10). European unions also used instruments of direct democracy to protect public services. To provide greater EU-level protection for public services, they proposed a decommodifying framework directive on public services, as mentioned in section 7.2. In November 2006, ETUC and EPSU launched a corresponding petition demanding 'high quality public services, accessible to all' (Crespy, 2016: 128). Although the petition preceded the adoption of the EU's official European Citizens' Initiative (ECI) procedure in 2012, it can be seen as a pilot ECI (Szabó, Golden, and Erne, 2022: 637) given the ETUC's and EPSU's declared target to collect one million signatures. Eventually however, the petition had been signed by only about 700,000 people (Crespy, 2016: 129), which was not enough to compel the Commission to draft a corresponding directive on public services.

As mentioned in Chapter 6, the responses of national governments and EU executives to the financial crisis triggered a wave of countervailing demonstrations and strikes. The comprehensive database of national protest events across Europe compiled by Hanspeter Kriesi and colleagues (2020) confirmed the resurgence of economic claims as the most important trigger of protests. Between 2000 and 2015, 38.1 per cent of all protests reported in national newswires across Europe were motivated by economic claims towards public institutions or private employers (Gessler and Schulte-Cloos, 2020: Table 6.1). Most anti-austerity protests occurred at local and national level in Southern Europe (Dufresne, 2015; Rone, 2020). The European trade union organisations, ETUC and EPSU, however, also coordinated transnational protest actions against the austerity cuts and the marketising public services reforms prescribed by the commodifying NEG prescriptions. This led to numerous Euro-demonstrations and coordinated action days politicising the EU governance of public services, as shown in Table 7.3.

After 2014 however, the number of ETUC-led transnational mobilisations targeting NEG fell notably, although EU executives continued to issue country-specific, commodifying NEG prescriptions. This fall is due to actor-centred and structural factors. Once the Commission agreed to consult European social partners before issuing its annual NEG prescriptions (Erne, 2015), the ETUC stopped organising transnational protests and returned to its traditional social partnership and lobbying approach (Bieling and Schulten, 2003; Hyman, 2005). In response to the rise of far-right Eurosceptic parties, the ETUC adopted a more social partnership-oriented and Europeanist stance. Before the 2014 European Parliament elections, the ETUC (2013) formulated its own alternative plan for investment, sustainable growth, and quality jobs. Ahead of the 2019 elections however, it signed a joint statement of the European social partners to defend 'democracy, sustainable economic growth and social justice' and 'the European project' (ETUC et al., 2019).

Structural factors also contributed to the fall in European trade union protests against NEG. By its nature, the NEG framework is 'a supranational regime that nationalises social conflict', as its *country-specific* and *asynchronous* character makes it very difficult for unions to politicise NEG at EU level (Erne, 2015: 355). That proved to be true, although our analysis showed that all qualitative NEG prescriptions on the governance of public services urged all member states to render their public services more market-like, regardless of their location in the uneven European economy. These findings show that the sweeping statements on the socialisation of the European Semester were standing on shaky ground (Zeitlin and Vanhercke, 2018). The ETUC nevertheless felt comforted by EU leaders' endorsement of a European Pillar of Social Rights in 2017 and the emergence of quantitative NEG prescriptions in favour of more public investments (de la Porte and Natali, 2018; Pochet, 2019; Ferrera, 2021), even though the latter were semantically linked to policy rationales that did not question NEG's commodifying policy direction (see section 7.3).

European unions' difficulties in politicising NEG are also linked to the marginal role that the European Parliament plays in the NEG regime (Erne, 2015). This makes unions' interventions much more difficult. After all, the transnational protests against the draft Services Directive were successful only

TABLE 7.3 *Transnational protests politicising the EU governance of public services (1993–2019)*

Date	Locations	Action type	Topic	Coordinators
5 June 2004	Brussels	Demonstration	Services Directive, 'Non à la directive Bolkestein – Oui à l'Europe sociale'	ETUC, social movements, unions
24 November 2004	Brussels	Demonstration	Services Directive, 'Bolkestein Directive = Frankenstein Directive'	ETUC, social movements, unions
19 March 2005	Brussels	Demonstration	'More and better jobs – Defending social Europe – Stop Bolkestein'	ETUC, social movements, unions
21 March 2005	Brussels	Demonstration	Services Directive	European Antipoverty Network
15 October 2005	Multi-sited	Demonstration	Services Directive, European Day of Action	ETUC, social movements, unions
25 October 2005	Strasbourg	Demonstration	Services Directive	ETUC, social movements, unions
11 February 2006	Strasbourg, Berlin	Demonstration	Services Directive	DGB, ETUC, Attac
14 February 2006	Strasbourg	Demonstration	Services Directive, Euro-demonstration 'Services for the people'	ETUC
14–16 May 2009	Brussels, multi-sited	Demonstration	'Fight the crisis – Put people first' campaign, against austerity	ETUC
29 September 2010	Brussels, multi-sited	Strike, demonstration	'No to austerity – Priority for jobs and growth'	ETUC
15 December 2010	Multi-sited	Demonstration	'No to austerity for everyone and bonuses for a happy few'	ETUC, unions
24 March 2011	Brussels, multi-sited	Demonstration	'No to austerity plans in Europe'	ETUC
9 April 2011	Budapest	Demonstration	'No to austerity – For a social Europe, for fair pay and for jobs'	ETUC

(continued)

TABLE 7.3 (continued)

Date	Locations	Action type	Topic	Coordinators
21 June 2011	Luxembourg	Demonstration	'No to austerity – For a social Europe, for fair pay, investments and jobs'	ETUC
17 September 2011	Wroclaw	Demonstration	'Yes to European solidarity – Yes to jobs and workers' rights – No to austerity'	ETUC, Polish unions (OPZZ)
30 November 2011	Brussels, multi-sited	Strike, demonstration	European Day of Action against austerity measures	EPSU
29 February 2012	Multi-sited	Demonstration	European Day of Action: 'Enough is enough! – Alternatives do exist – For employment and social justice'	ETUC
19 May 2012	Frankfurt	Demonstration	Against EU's NEG regime	Blockupy
23 May 2012	Brussels	Demonstration	'Growth and investment for jobs – No to deregulation'	ETUC
14 November 2012	Brussels, multi-sited	Strike, demonstration	'For jobs and solidarity in Europe – No to austerity'	ETUC
13–14 March 2013	Brussels, multi-sited	Strike, demonstration	EU summit: 'No to austerity! Yes to jobs for young people!'	ETUC, social movements, unions
28 May 2013	Brussels	Demonstration	Demanding that EU rules on public procurement fully respect workers' rights	Belgian unions, EFFAT, UNI, ETUI, EFBWW
1–2 June 2013	Frankfurt, multi-sited	Demonstration	Against EU's NEG regime	Blockupy
7 March 2014–30 January 2015	Online	ECI	New Deal 4 Europe. For a European Special Plan for Sustainable Development and Employment	newdeal4europe
18 March 2015	Frankfurt	Demonstration	Against EU's NEG regime	Blockupy

Source: Transnational Socioeconomic Protest Database (Erne and Nowak, 2023).
The table includes transnational protest events across at least two public sectors, as recorded in the database's intersectoral and the national and local public services 'public nat/loc' categories, excluding protest events of European public servants (public EU).

162

because of the Parliament's role as a co-legislator that gave the protest movements a lever to change the directive (Copeland, 2014; Crespy, 2016). In the case of the new Concessions Directive (2014/23/EU) and the revised Procurement Directives (2014/24/EU, 2014/25/EU), the unions were able to shift the balance of power thanks to their allies in the Parliament, which included 'social clauses' in them (Fischbach-Pyttel, 2017: 167).

However, although the ETUC stopped contesting NEG at cross-sectoral level over time, European public service trade unions in sectors hitherto only marginally affected by commodifying EU prescriptions (e.g., water and healthcare) renewed their attempts to politicise them across borders, as we shall see in the next chapters of the book.

7.5 CONCLUSION

In this chapter, we have analysed the European governance of public services and is discontents, before and after the EU's shift to its NEG regime. Initially, European integration and the making of social welfare states with public utilities and services developed in unison. Since the launch of the European single market and monetary union however, EU integration has put public services more and more under pressure. This happened through two channels: commodifying EU laws that were part of the single market agenda and indirect pressures on public budgets related to EMU. In the 2000s however, the European Commission's public service liberalisation agenda seemed to run out of steam as a result of transnational protests and related European Parliament amendments. After 2008 however, the shift to NEG gave EU executives new opportunities to advance their agendas.

The NEG prescriptions for Germany, Ireland, Italy, and Romania from 2009 to 2019 consistently pointed in a commodifying policy direction. Across all countries and times, all NEG prescriptions on the mechanisms governing public services tasked member states to marketise them, regardless of their location in the integrated, but also uneven, EU economy. As the latter determined NEG prescriptions' unequal constraining power, their impact differed across countries. Until 2013, EU executives' NEG prescriptions tasked the Irish, Romanian, and Italian governments to curtail their public spending. That changed over time; after all, countries in our sample received a few decommodifying prescriptions for higher public investments, namely, to boost Europe's competitiveness and to rebalance its economy. Given these semantic links, even these decommodifying prescriptions remained subordinated to NEG's primary commodifying agenda. Only the Romanian government was asked to spend more for social reasons. Thus, the shift to NEG significantly augmented EU pressures on public services beyond those already directed by commodifying EU laws.

These commodifying pressures triggered countermovements by unions and social movements. Initially, most mobilisation took place at national level. After 2004 however, the Commission's draft Services Directive triggered major transnational protests, effectively curbing the Commission's ambitions. The shift to NEG also triggered widespread labour protests. Despite the consistent commodifying bent of NEG prescriptions on public services across countries, unions and social movements still found it more difficult to politicise them, given the exclusion of the European Parliament from the supranational NEG regime and NEG's country-specific and asynchronous methodology that hampered transnational union action.

PART III

EU Economic Governance in Three Sectors

8

EU Governance of Transport Services and Its Discontents

8.1 INTRODUCTION

The question of transport was central to the original design of European economic integration. However, the inclusion of a specific Transport Title in the Treaty of Rome generated fierce debate on state–market relations. A fundamental source of conflict, which has not fully abated, had to do with the primacy of public services with clear social goals over economic freedoms and competition. Other sources of conflict stem from the existence of different modalities – road, rail, air, and sea. Over the decades, each modality has developed its own technology, management, and operating procedures in a bid to increase its competitiveness and gain market share, usually at the expense of other modalities. Hence, the liberalisation of one modality, be it at national or at EU level, directly impacts the functioning of another (Héritier, 1997). Today, the EU governance of transport can be characterised as 'recent, gradual, uneven, complex and crisis-driven' (Kaeding, 2007: 35).

This chapter examines the extent to which EU governance interventions have been prescribing a commodification of (public) transport services. First, we assess the EU governance of the transport sector prior to the onset of the 2008 financial crisis. In this period, the adoption of a growing number of EU laws, through the ordinary legislative procedure, led to the gradual commodification of transport services, even though the Treaty establishing the European Economic Community (EEC) exempted transport services from its free movement of services provisions (Art. 61(1) TEEC, now Art. 58 TFEU) and emphasised the relevance of the 'concept of a public service' in the transport sector (Art. 77 TEEC, now Art. 93 TFEU). Despite this, the EU has over time succeeded in commodifying many transport services, particularly in road haulage, aviation, and shipping (Héritier, 1997; Stevens, 2004; Kaeding, 2007; Kassim and Stevens, 2010). In the port, rail, and local public transport sector however, several commodification attempts by the Commission did not fully succeed because of mobilisations by European transport workers and their unions that found allies in the European Parliament and the Council of transport ministers. In a second step, we analyse the prescriptions issued under the new economic governance (NEG) regime (Chapter 2). Analysing the country-specific prescriptions for Germany, Ireland, Italy, and Romania in their semantic, communicative, and policy contexts (Chapters 4 and 5), we are able to show that the commodification of transport services, having stalled in the 2000s, was targeted afresh under the aegis of the NEG regime. Thirdly, we address the extent to which European transport workers' unions were able to oppose the commodifying governance pressures exerted by ordinary EU laws, the enhanced horizontal market pressures that they in turn triggered, and the EU's NEG interventions.

8.2 EU GOVERNANCE OF TRANSPORT SERVICES BEFORE THE SHIFT TO NEG

After 1945, most policymakers thought that European reconstruction could not be left entirely to the market and that public utilities should remain in public ownership (Millward, 2005). Thus, the drafters of the EEC Treaty gave transport special treatment.

Protecting Transport from the EEC Treaty's Liberalisation Bent

In the 1950s, the transport sector accounted for a fifth of the combined gross national product of the six original EEC countries and employed 16 per cent of the workers in the industrial sector (Lindberg and Scheingold, 1970: 142). Because of this and explicit political commitments to social and regional cohesion, the question of transport was bedevilled by fierce debates between governments, their transport ministries, and the European Conference of Ministers of Transport (ECMT), established in 1953, whose 'opinions counted as authoritative' (Schot and Schipper, 2011: 283). A clear division emerged over whether transport should be treated as any other economic sector or whether its peculiarities, such as the public service aspect, should be addressed by emphasising cooperation over competition. Already there were concerns 'that only a European authority would be able to close unprofitable railway lines because it alone could operate free from national public service considerations' (Henrich-Franke, 2008: 67). The ECMT, on the other hand, 'feared that transport integration would be misused for a political purpose, and that supranational European integration could lead to wasteful or ruinous competition' (Patel and Schot, 2011: 399).

The extent of these concerns was so grave and progress so slow that its drafters 'faced the choice to delay the Treaties or to exclude transport' (Schot and Schipper, 2011: 274). Neither option was considered acceptable. Thus, a separate Transport Title was included in the EEC Treaty that envisaged a common transport policy; however, there was 'a great deal of disagreement over how such a policy would be constructed' (Aspinwall, 1995: 480). Provisions were put in place to safeguard isolated inland modes of transport from its overall liberalising bent, and aviation was excluded altogether on national security grounds.[1]

Additional safeguards included the permissibility of state aid insofar as such subventions were for the 'co-ordination of transport or if they represent reimbursement for the discharge of certain obligations *inherent in the concept of a public service*' (emphasis added) (Art. 77 TEEC). Also, unanimity was required where transport was 'liable to have a serious effect on the standard of living and on employment in certain areas and on the operation of transport facilities' (Art. 75(3) TEEC). This provision protected the interests of transport users and workers in the sector and remained in force until the Lisbon Treaty. According to most member states, the separate Transport Title in the EEC Treaty protected the transport sector from the application of other Treaty articles governing such matters 'as competition, state aids and the freedom to provide services' (Stevens, 2004: 44). Despite the Commission's enthusiasm for creating a common transport market (Commission, Memorandum, COM (61) 50 final; Tindemans, 1976), the Council staunchly defended decommodified transport services. In the 1970s, the Council exempted, for instance, the question of transport from the first wave of procurement directives. Whereas EEC policymakers reached 'almost magical compromises' in the agricultural sector, which was also governed by a specific Treaty Title, there was an 'almost total deadlock' in the transport sector (Lindberg and Scheingold, 1970: 163).

Towards the Commodification of Transport Services by EU Law

Following the first EU enlargement in 1973, liberalising transport became again a political issue. UK governments, along with Dutch ones, spearheaded

---

[1] Art. 84(2) TEEC treated air and sea transport separately from road, rail, and inland waterways. Although the Article empowered the Council to adopt European laws on shipping and aviation if unanimously agreed, bilateral intergovernmental agreements remained the modus operandi there until the mid-1980s.

the deregulatory drive but, with unanimity voting prevailing in the Council, their efforts were initially readily prevaricated. The application of neoliberal paradigms to transport, however, was also assisted by developments that originated outside Europe, namely, the deregulation of US aviation in the late 1970s (Kassim and Stevens, 2010). Following this, the Commission, in the first half of the 1980s, published three reports on inland (1983), maritime (1984), and air (1985) transport with the objective of launching 'an irreversible liberalisation process' that 'was intended to work like a snowball getting both larger and faster as it rolled down hill' (Stevens, 2004: 57).

For the reasons cited, civil aviation and maritime transport were excluded from the EEC Treaty (and therefore fatefully also from the protections of its Transport Title) and were instead regulated by intergovernmental agreements. In an important European Court of Justice (ECJ) case, known as *Nouvelles Frontières*,[2] inter-airline agreements were found to be illegal 'in the absence of any Community regulation exempting them from the normal application of Treaty competition rules' (Stevens, 2004: 58). This case was a 'turning point for EU aviation' (Kaeding, 2007: 47), which received a further boost when the European Parliament, along with the Dutch government, brought the Council before the ECJ, which ruled that the Council had infringed the Treaty by failing to ensure freedom to provide services in the sphere of international transport.[3] Constituting a 'watershed for supranational transport policy' (Kerwer and Teutsch, 2001: 29), this ruling meant that the Council could no longer insist on harmonisation as a precondition to liberalisation (Erdmenger, 1983; Héritier, 1997). This emboldened the pro-commodification advocates reorganising themselves at European level (Jensen and Richardson, 2004).

In 1985, the Commission (White Paper, COM (85) 310: 27) once again emphasised that transport was 'of prime importance' for the internal market and framed it as a normal economic activity without mentioning its role as a public service. That said, the rail sector was spared and considered as being 'not of direct relevance to the internal market' (White Paper, COM (85) 310: 30). Under the Single European Act, qualified majority voting was extended to many areas including aviation and maritime. This change 'made it harder to resist the neoliberal agenda embedded in the Treaties' (Stevens, 2004: 246), but not impossible. The successful adoption of three liberalisation packages between 1987 and 1992 created the single European aviation market. Buoyed by this, the EU turned its liberalisation sights on road haulage, rail, and other

---

[2] C-209-213/84 *Ministère Public v. Asjes* [1986] ECR 01425.
[3] C-13/83 *European Parliament v. Council of the European Communities* [1985] ECR 01513.

network industries (Chapter 7). The liberalisation of road haulage was contentious on the question of cabotage (the operation of non-resident hauliers in foreign markets); however, on account of the 'weakened position of the anti-liberalization actors' (Héritier, 1997: 541), agreement on a liberalisation package between member states was possible, formally at least (Schmidt, 2002). Several member states, including Italy and Germany, regulated road haulage to protect their railways from intermodal competition. The latter proposed a road toll for trucks from other member states to protect its railways and contribute to road-building costs. This, at the behest of the Commission, was deemed illegal by the ECJ. Hence, railways were to be susceptible to competition from road haulage, thereby contributing to its liberalisation.

Regarding the question of rail liberalisation, Directive 91/440/EEC 'is the most important Community measure to improve the competitiveness of rail transport' and required the organisational separation of railway operations and infrastructure management (Commission, Communication (1998) 202/final). This separation is also important in the context of monetary union, a point we return to below. In the 1990s, EU rail legislation (e.g., the Directives 95/18/EC on licensing of railway undertakings or 95/19/EC on railway infrastructure capacity) constituted a false start, as it focused on 'less demanding' reforms (Knill and Lehmkuhl, 2002: 272) and was characterised by a high degree of ambiguity, which mirrored the resistance by governments, such as the French (Kerwer and Teutsch, 2001: 46), and by the state-owned railway companies, represented by the Community of European Railway and Infrastructure Companies (CER). To overcome that resistance, the Commission (White Paper, COM (96) 421) first favoured a 'big bang' liberalisation; but, once the Commission realised that support from the Council was not forthcoming, it adopted a more gradual approach (Dyrhauge, 2013: 56). Hence, rail liberalisation really began in earnest only in the 2000s. By then however, the Amsterdam Treaty had enhanced the status of the European Parliament in EU transport policymaking. Subsequently, the Parliament became a co-legislator with the Council; this also meant becoming a target for both pro- and anti-commodification groups (see section 8.4).

Under their Lisbon growth agenda for the 2000s, EU leaders envisaged greater service liberalisation as well as the curbing of state aid (European Council, 2000: 20). The conservative Spanish EU Transport Commissioner Loyola de Palacio spearheaded this endeavour and sought to liberalise the rail sector, public transport, and port services, with mixed results. All three legislative attempts triggered countermovements by unions and other public sector advocates. Regarding railways, three packages of EU railway laws were agreed, between 2001 and 2007, with the emphasis placed first on rail freight given its role in the movement of goods and its lesser political standing in terms of public salience. The first package envisaged competition on Trans European Rail Freight Network routes from 2003 and for all international rail freight from 2008. The second package, adopted in 2004, accelerated the liberalisation of rail freight services by fully opening the rail freight market to competition as of January 2007. The third package, adopted in 2007, aimed to open international passenger transport to market mechanisms by 2010. We return to the rail *acquis* below, but first let us consider one of the most overlooked pieces of EU legislation for public transport (Finger and Messulam, 2015: 4).

Public services obligations (PSOs) have been central to the state's provision of public transport services and 'can best be described as an activity carried out in the public interest, either directly by the authorities or by private undertakings under the control or supervision of the public authorities' (Degli Abbati, 1987: 21). Questions pertaining to state aid and competition come under the remit of the Commission's DG Competition, which by the 2000s was no longer 'a sleepy, ineffectual backwater of Community administration' (Wilks and McGowan, 1996: 225).[4] Building on both the 2001 transport White Paper (COM (2001) 370) and the 2004 White Paper on services of general economic interest (COM (2004) 374), the Commission proposed a new Regulation that sought to streamline rules governing state aid by introducing compulsory competitive tendering in public transport. A protracted process ensued, involving three attempts by the Commission to have the regulation adopted. Following a landmark case[5] on state aid in the public transport sector, the ECJ ruled that 'where subsidies are regarded as compensation for the services provided by the recipient undertakings in order to discharge public service obligations, *they do not constitute state aids*' (emphasis added) (Bovis, 2005: 572). This Altmark ruling, along with amendments introduced by the European Parliament and the Council, meant that PSO Regulation 1370/2007 allowed for the possibility both of direct award and of competitive tendering, that is, member-state discretion in the awarding of public contracts prevails. This was welcomed by pro-public services advocates, such as the European Transport Workers' Federation (ETF) and several member states, as the adopted regulation differed from the Commission's original market-oriented proposal (ETF, 2010).

---

[4] The Barroso II Commission transferred the responsibility for state aid for transport services from its Directorate General (DG) for Transport to DG Competition.
[5] C-280/oo *Altmark Trans GmbH and Regierungspräsidium Magdeburg v. Nahverkehrsgesellschaft Altmark GmbH, and Oberbundesanwalt beim Bundesverwaltungsgericht* [2003] ECR I-07747.

Rail liberalisation followed the same logic as other network industry liberalisations, such as telecommunications and electricity (Chapter 7). This logic centres on privatisation, regulatory independence, unbundling, and competition (Florio, 2013). EU legislators are limited by Art. 345 TFEU regarding privatisation (Akkermans and Ramaekers, 2010), but the dividing of services from infrastructure, that is, unbundling and fostering competition, overseen by an independent regulator, remain paramount to EU liberalisation, which can indirectly, but not unintentionally (Clifton, Comín, and Diaz Fuentes, 2003), put pressure on governments to pursue (partial) privatisation. This gradual approach seeks to foster competition by establishing a regulatory framework that ensures that national governments stay at arm's length. Here, the Commission, in relation to unbundling, has a clear and long-standing preference for vertical separation 'as a more effective means to alleviate the infrastructure monopoly problem, ensure neutrality and allow new entrants on the market of train operations' (van de Velde, 2015: 53). However, alternative governance structures also exist (Dyrhauge, 2013: 42–50).

The three rail liberalisation packages sought to restrict state interference by promoting vertical separation, which concretely involves (1) splitting up the state-owned railway company into separate passenger and freight units; (2) establishing an infrastructure manager to oversee non-discriminatory charging and the granting of access to the rail network, based on an economic rationale rather than social needs; and (3) creating an independent rail regulator 'to whom applicants can appeal if they consider that the rules have not been applied fairly' (Stevens, 2004: 99). The Commission depends on disgruntled private enterprises taking anti-competition cases (Kelemen, 2011) to ensure liberalisation. However, cases taken by private rail companies challenging state-owned rail companies' (alleged) abuse of position have not materialised.

Following the Swedish and British national liberalisation processes, the Commission pushed for vertical separation. Each of its three legislative liberalisation packages ended in conciliation between the European Parliament and Council (Dyrhauge, 2013: 88). In the legislative process, vertical separation was resisted by key member states, notably Germany and Italy, ensuring a degree of heterogeneity. In 2010, the Commission nonetheless filed actions against thirteen member states, including Germany[6] and Italy,[7] for having allegedly breached the first railway package. Most member states undertook only a minimum separation, thereby allowing the preservation of national rail holding groups, such as Deutsche Bahn. The Commission argued that the rail

---

[6] C-556/10 *Commission v. Germany* [2013] ECLI 116.
[7] C-369/11 *Commission v. Italy* [2013] ECLI 636.

acquis means that the infrastructure manager, such as Deutsche Bahn Netz, cannot form part of a holding company that also comprises the railway undertakings. In other words, holding companies, such as Deutsche Bahn, were problematic. In addition, the Commission was critical of the fact that the German and the Italian infrastructure operator's independence was not supervised by an independent agency. Following the opinion of Advocate General Niilo Jääskinen, the Court of Justice of the EU (CJEU) rejected the Commission's complaint regarding Germany and Italy. Moreover, the Court noted that the rail *acquis* requires only legal and accounting separation, which are present in the holding company model (*Rail Gazette*, 7 September 2012). Despite evidence to the contrary (van de Velde, 2015), the neoliberal Estonian EU Transport Commissioner Siim Kallas said after the ruling that the Commission 'remains convinced that a more effective separation between an infrastructure manager and other rail operations *is essential* to ensure non-discriminatory access for all operators to the rail tracks' (emphasis added) (*Politico.eu*, 28 February 2013).

Another key development in EU transport governance is the Lisbon Treaty (Schweitzer, 2011: 52), which abolished the unanimity requirement in the Council for transport sector-specific laws that 'might seriously affect the standard of living and level of employment in certain regions' (Art. 75(3) TEEC). When adopting EU laws in the field, EU legislators are henceforth tasked only to consider the following: '*account shall be taken* of cases where their application might seriously affect the standard of living and level of employment in certain regions, and the operation of transport facilities' (emphasis added) (Art. 91(2) TFEU). In other words, a significant institutional safeguard that protected the initial social purpose of European transport service governance was finally removed. Whereas the Commission's (MEMO/09/531) corresponding explanatory memo simply failed to mention it, trade unionists overlooked this change in the Lisbon Treaty debates (Béthoux, Erne, and Golden, 2018). This modification was still very much welcomed by pro-commodification advocates, as it facilitated the adoption of new EU laws in the field, which we assess at the end of the post-financial crisis developments section below. Before turning to the EU's response to the 2008 crisis and its implications for public transport services, we must assess a precursor to the NEG regime that is bound up in economic and monetary union (EMU). We briefly consider this next.

EMU and the Commodification of Public Transport Services

The EMU accession criteria involved a forensic surveillance process resulting in a strong conditioning effect on state–market relations, especially on public transport infrastructure (Savage, 2005). To join the eurozone, national governments had, among other things, to have a public deficit of less than 3 per cent of GDP. Albeit indirect, pressures arising from the EMU criteria were particularly relevant for the rail sector, which 'had become a growing burden on the public finances' (Finger and Messulam, 2015: 1). In addition to liberalisation, EU rail legislation accordingly sought 'to reduce railway debt to a level that does not impede sound financial management' (Commission, COM (1998) 202 final: 2). Here, member states devised novel ways to manage public debt, which included reforming the transport sector. For some member states, reforms constituted a significant reversal of the entire post-World War II policy paradigm (Clifton, Comín, and Diaz Fuentes, 2003). Italy, for example, topped the OECD privatisation ranking between 1995 and 1999 (Savage, 2005: 129). These initiatives, all in the name of meeting the EMU criteria, were complemented by a hiring freeze, hospital closures (see Chapter 10), and reduced rail subsidies.

In this context, the Commission promoted three interrelated measures of immediate relevance for public transport services and their gradual commodification. The first has already been mentioned above in terms of establishing an environment for competition, namely, the separation of infrastructure managers from incumbent rail companies so as 'to prevent state subsidies for public service obligations being used to finance commercial activities' (Dyrhauge, 2013: 85–86). Secondly, there was the creation of independent regulatory agencies, and once again there was a fiscal aspect. For instance, in the rail sector, regulatory agencies were envisaged as operating not only to 'prevent conflict of interests' and enhance competition but equally importantly 'to reduce its reliance on public financing' (Dyrhauge, 2013: 54). Thirdly, there was the question of EU cohesion funds, which went towards the construction of infrastructural projects. Although often portrayed as a side-payment to the EU's periphery in exchange for EMU (Hooghe and Marks, 2001), the cohesion funds were 'anything but a value-free pursuit' (Nanetti, 1996: 60). Rather, they were a vehicle for 'stimulating the mobilisation of domestic private capital and attracting private capital from outside the country' (1996: 66). This was achieved by public–private partnership (PPP), which can 'dramatically improve the deficit position of member states' (Savage, 2005: 149).

The question of excessive deficits never really went away; however, EU executives lacked the teeth to deal with member states in troubled fiscal waters in the first half of the 2000s (Heipertz and Verdun, 2010). Following the 2008 crisis, EU leaders remedied this weakness through the adoption of the NEG regime (Chapter 2). From the above, it is clear that the liberalisation of rail and local public transport has faced numerous obstacles, including diverging member-state preferences and counter-mobilisations (see section 8.4). On rail liberalisation, Helene Dyrhauge (2013: 160) writes that 'EU railway market opening is not a highspeed train which is quickly reaching its destination ... instead it is a slow regional train stopping at all stations'. Such 'stations' include a general transposition deficit (Kaeding, 2007), a lack of infringement proceedings by private litigants against incumbents, failed infringement proceedings by the Commission, and consequently persistent regulatory heterogeneity regarding both the degree of independence of the regulator and the degree of vertical separation. Might the NEG regime provide the Commission and national finance ministries with a new avenue whereby awkward national transport ministries, the European Parliament, a not always reliable CJEU, and recalcitrant transport unions can be circumvented?

8.3 GOVERNING THE TRANSPORT SECTOR THROUGH COMMODIFYING NEG PRESCRIPTIONS

In this section, we assess the extent to which the EU's NEG regime allowed the Commission to circumvent the strong anti-commodification contingent that it inevitably faces in the more democratic governance mechanisms of the EU's ordinary legislative procedure. Here, we analyse the policy orientation of NEG prescriptions relevant for transport. Hundreds of country-specific recommendations (CSRs) have been issued by the EU but, rather than attempting to analyse all NEG prescriptions contained in CSRs for all countries from 2009 to 2019 without regard to their context-specific meaning (see Chapters 4 and 5), our focus is on Germany, Ireland, Italy, and Romania, which we know very well and are in different positions in the EU's integrated but also uneven political economy. The objective is to determine whether the prescriptions further a commodification agenda across countries, whilst taking into consideration prescriptions' coercive power, which relates to the position of a country within NEG's enforcement regime at a given time (Chapter 5). Doing so enables us to go beyond broad-brush, macro-theories of neoliberalism and commodification (Bruff, 2014; Baccaro and Howell, 2017; Hermann, 2021) and offers a more nuanced understanding of the mechanisms underpinning the Commission's transport-related policies across space and time.

Following the analytical framework outlined in Chapters 4 and 5, we first identified the NEG prescriptions on the provision of public transport services and people's access to them, identifying common themes (i.e., common formulations of semantically similar prescriptions). In contrast to the water (Chapter 9) and the healthcare (Chapter 10) sectors, EU executives issued no prescriptions relating to people's access to transport services. We therefore assessed the transport-related NEG prescriptions in terms only of the remaining three categories of our analytical framework, pertaining to (a) resource levels and the (b) sector- and (c) provider-level governance mechanisms for the provision of public transport services. Whereas the resources category has a quantitative dimension, the sector- and provider-level mechanisms categories have a qualitative dimension. Together, these dimensions can shed light on whether we can speak of a transnational commodification script informing the EU's NEG prescriptions in transport and, if so, along what dimensions it has been applied.

Table 8.1 presents the themes of all transport-related NEG prescriptions for Germany, Ireland, Italy, and Romania from 2009 to 2019. We assess not only the prescriptions that mention transport services explicitly but also those for network industries and local public transport services where there is a semantic link to transport, typically in CSRs' recitals.

Table 8.2 represents all transport-related NEG prescriptions across our four countries and time, based on the categories to which they belong, their policy direction, and their coercive power.

A simple glance at Tables 8.1 and 8.2 reveals that *all* qualitative NEG prescriptions on sector- or provider-level governance mechanisms point in a commodifying policy direction. It is equally noteworthy that Germany, Italy, and Romania received commodifying prescriptions. Regardless of the countries' unequal locations in the EU's political economy, the Commission and the Council of finance ministers clearly tasked all governments to foster the marketisation of the public transport sector but, whereas the constraining power of the NEG prescriptions for Germany was weak, those for Romania and Italy were much more constraining, as indicated by the respective black and grey colours of the symbols in Table 8.2 (see Chapter 2).

Contrariwise, most quantitative, resource-level-related prescriptions point in a decommodifying direction. By contrast to the commodifying prescriptions mentioned above, the coercive power of the decommodifying ones has always been weak, with two exceptions. We must reiterate that transport services were also affected by the intersectoral prescriptions on employment relations and public services in general, discussed in Chapters 6 and 7. This is significant, as most NEG prescriptions on the curtailment of spending on public services were intersectoral. This was also relevant in the Irish case.

Table 8.2 indicates that EU executives issued only decommodifying NEG prescriptions for Ireland. This, however, does not indicate a lack of commodifying policy interventions in Irish transport services. Sure, Ireland's island location reduced the relevance of its domestic transport networks for the European single market. Because of this, Ireland had already received a derogation from the liberalising EU rail *acquis* before the financial crisis. More important for the single market, however, were Ireland's ferry and air links to the United Kingdom and the continent. As successive Irish governments had already commodified

TABLE 8.1 *Themes of NEG prescriptions on transport services (2009–2019)*

Categories	Policy Orientation		
		Decommodifying	Commodifying
Provision of public services	Resource levels	Increase public investment (RO/DE) Improve infrastructure capacity (IT) Prioritise public investment (IE) Focus investment in infrastructure quality (IT)	Close railway lines (RO)
	Sector-level mechanisms		Restructure Transport Ministry and regulatory agency (RO) Strengthen regulator's independence (RO/DE) Lease railway lines (RO) Increase efficiency of rail passenger services (RO) Increase efficiency in railway planning (RO) Reform rail sector to make it more attractive for cargo (RO) Promote competition in the transport sector (RO/IT/DE) Implement performance management scheme (RO) Promote competition in the local transport sector (RO/IT/DE) Set-up regulatory authority (IT) Operationalise regulatory authority (IT)
	Provider-level mechanisms		Privatise state-owned company (RO) Reduce payment arrears of state-owned rail company (RO) Restructure state-owned enterprises (RO/IT) Restructure local public services (IT)
Access to public services	Cost-coverage mechanisms Coverage levels		

Source: Council Recommendations on National Reform Programmes; Memoranda of Understanding. See Online Appendix, Tables A8.1–A8.4.
Country code: DE = Germany; IE = Ireland; IT = Italy; RO = Romania.

TABLE 8.2 *Categories of NEG prescriptions on transport services by coercive power*

	Decommodifying				Commodifying			
	DE	IE	IT	RO	DE	IE	IT	RO
2009								●[4]
2010								●[2] ■
2011					O^2			▲●[18] ■[2]
2012			▲		O		●	▲●[12] ■[2]
2013			△		O		O^3	●[6] ■[6]
2014					O		●[3]	□
2015				△	O		●[2]	□
2016	△	△		△			●[2] ▨	O
2017		△					●[2]	
2018		△		△			●[2] ▨	□
2019	△	△	▲	△			●[2]	□

Source: Council Recommendations on National Reform Programmes; Memoranda of Understanding. See Online Appendix, Tables A8.1–A8.4.
Thematic area: △ = resources; O = sector-level governance; □ = provider-level governance.
Country code: DE = Germany; IE = Ireland; IT = Italy; RO = Romania.
Coercive power: ●▲■ = very significant; ○△▨ = significant; ○△□ = weak.
Superscript number equals number of relevant prescriptions.

179

aviation and ferry services (Sweeney, 2004: 35; Mercille and Murphy, 2016: 697), there was no need for corresponding NEG prescriptions. Irish governments had also increased the role of private operators in local public transport services, 'not by head-on confrontation with the unions, but by ensuring that the existing state companies only play a limited role in new services' (Wickham and Latniak, 2010: 163). In 2004, for example, the government increased the competitive pressures on Dublin Bus by conceding the operation of Dublin's new light rail service to the French transnational corporation Veolia. For the same reason, Irish governments also supported Aer Lingus' low-cost competitor, Ryanair, at crucial moments of its history (Allen, 2007: 226–227; Golden and Erne, 2022).

After the financial crisis, the commodification of Irish public transport services gained even more traction, even before the arrival of the Troika in Ireland in December 2010. In 2009, Irish legislators had already transferred the task of public transport governance from both the national transport ministry and the Dublin Transportation Office to an independent National Transport Authority (NTA). In July 2010, the Irish finance minister tasked a Review Group on State Assets and Liabilities (2011: 1) to propose a list of measures 'to de-leverage the state balance sheet through asset realisations'. In 2011, the Group recommended 'that the *Aer Lingus* shares' (2011: 87) and stated-owned 'bus businesses competing directly with private operators should be disposed of' (2011: 99). Furthermore, the government should seek 'to limit the level of public subsidy' for public transport providers and the amount of 'capital to be invested in further transport projects' and envisage 'the privatisation of all or part *of Dublin Bus*' (2011). In turn, the NTA conceded 10 per cent of Dublin's bus routes to private operators (Mercille and Murphy, 2016: 697), but Irish governments curtailed public transport expenditure so radically that even EU executives felt obliged to issue countervailing NEG prescriptions after 2016, as we shall see below.

Hence, the absence of commodifying NEG prescriptions for Ireland does not indicate EU support for decommodified public transport services but rather overzealous spending cuts and marketising reforms by Irish governments that made such NEG prescriptions needless. This once more shows that the meaning of NEG prescriptions can only be understood in their specific semantic, communicative, and policy context. To make better sense of the NEG regime's quantitative and qualitative dimensions in the transport sector across all our four countries, we now assess the orientation of all transport-related NEG prescriptions in more detail category-by-category.

Prescriptions on the Provision of Services

Resource levels: This section speaks to NEG's quantitative dimension and to the question of commodification and decommodification. From Table 8.2 we can see that on the right, commodification side of it there is a singular, but repeated, resource-level-related commodifying prescription, which tasked the Romanian government to 'identify and close ... lowest cost recovery segments of the railway lines' (P-MoU, Romania, 29 June 2011: 12). Subsequently, around 1,200 km of line were closed or leased out (European Commission, 2013: 51). The upshot of this was to restrict users' access to (rural) transport services either because of cessation of the service or via an increase in prices, which were implemented (European Commission, 2014a: 17). In essence, their closure put important public services and goods beyond even commodification, all in the name of cost reduction. In 2015, the Commission nevertheless lamented that some 'unsustainable railway lines are still not closed' (Commission, Country Report Romania SWD (2015) 42: 27). Hence, Romania's line closures represent 'a real cautionary showcase' (*Global Railway Review*, 24 September 2015) that unwittingly contradicted the enhanced role for rail laid out in the EU's 2011 White Paper on transport.

After the 2008 financial crisis, the Irish Government also cut its capital expenditure on public transport, from €900m in 2008 to a low point of €254m in 2012, and its current expenditures from €343m in 2008 to a low point of €236m in 2015 (Hynes and Malone, 2020). These cuts, however, were triggered not by explicit, transport-related NEG prescriptions but by the intersectoral NEG prescriptions on public expenditure cuts and the Irish government's turn to austerity that predated the arrival of the Troika (see Chapter 7). The Italian and German governments equally curtailed their public spending on transport to such an extent that EU executives in turn felt obliged to later issue countervailing prescriptions.

Looking at the left side of Table 8.2, we see that all countries under study also received prescriptions on resource levels that pointed in a decommodifying direction. Between 2012 and 2019, EU executives repeatedly tasked governments to increase or prioritise public investment in transport. For instance, the German government received an NEG prescription to 'achieve a sustained upward trend in public investment, especially in infrastructure' (Council Recommendation Germany 2016/C299/05) on account of Germany's 'sound fiscal position overall' (Commission, SWD (2014) 406 final: 3). Despite federal spending on transport infrastructure having increased from an average of around €10bn annually over the period 2010–2014 to €12.3bn in 2016, EU executives stated that this 'still falls short to meet the additional annual public investment requirement' (Commission, Country Report Germany SWD (2016) 75: 46). Here, it needs to be borne in mind that Germany's enduring underinvestment in transport preceded the debt break, enacted in its federal constitution in 2009, and German finance ministers' proclaimed goal of a *Schwarze Null*: 'black zero'. Consequently, 'spending on public infrastructure has been on a downward trend *for a long time*' (emphasis added) (Commission, SWD (2014) 406 final: 7), with 'transport infrastructure' being 'affected in particular' (2014: 9). The upward investment is seen as necessary to 'maintain and modernise Germany's public infrastructure' (2014: 9), which is 'crumbling' (*Economist*, 17 June 2017).

Ireland too received transport-related decommodifying prescriptions on an annual basis between 2016 and 2019, but the gist of these prescriptions differed from those issued to Germany. The NEG prescriptions issued to the Irish government were: 'Enhance the quality of expenditure ... by *prioritising* ... public infrastructure, in particular transport' (emphasis added) (Council Recommendation Ireland 2016/C 299/16) and better 'target government expenditure, by *prioritising* public investment in transport' (emphasis added) (Council Recommendation Ireland 2016/C 299/16; Council Recommendation Germany 2017/C 261/07). As these decommodifying prescriptions tasked the government to divert public money away from other public sectors towards maintaining and upgrading public transport infrastructure however, they were still speaking to the austerity doctrine of doing more with less (Hermann, 2021). After the continued deterioration in the financial positions of Ireland's transport providers triggered waves of strike action in 2016 and 2017 at Luas, Bus Éireann, and Iarnród Éireann, respectively (Palcic and Reeves, 2018; Maccarrone, Erne, and Regan, 2019), the government at last increased its spending on public transport once again. Since then, capital investment rose to €496m and current spending to €302m in 2019 (Hynes and Malone, 2020).

In 2019, all four countries received a transport-oriented decommodifying prescription. These came in the wake of the Italian Morandi Bridge disaster in August 2018, which killed 43 people and left 600 people homeless. A symbol of Italy's *miracolo economico*, the Morandi bridge had been privatised in the late 1990s along with 4,000 miles of toll roads in the context of satisfying the Maastricht public deficit criteria (*New York Times*, 5 March 2019). The prescription urged the Italian government to focus on 'the quality of infrastructure' (Council Recommendation Italy 2019/C 301/12). Consequently, EU executives granted Italy an allowance of €1bn to secure its infrastructure, as the 'state of repair is a clear source of concern' (Commission, Country Report Italy SDW (2019) 1011: 52). The ailing state of transport infrastructure also informed the corresponding prescriptions for the other three countries. Furthermore, the 2019 prescriptions on public investments in transport infrastructure were linked semantically to another emerging policy script, namely, the looming climate emergency and the transition to a greener economy (von der Leyen, 2019). As seen above however, these concerns had hardly been a priority in the preceding years.

Sector-level governance mechanisms: Prescriptions under this category are the most prevalent, recurring in tranches across Germany, Italy, and Romania.

This prevalence arises because EU public sector liberalisation occurred primarily at sectoral level (Héritier, 1997; Schmidt, 2002; Smith, 2005: Leiren, 2015). At the same time, liberalisation attempts were limited, as EU legislators were able to prescribe only new regulatory frameworks that sought to foster competitive dynamics by gradually removing the exclusive rights of public operators (Florio, 2013). Thus far however, the power of the supranational, regulatory governance agencies that have emerged in the transport sector is very limited.[8] Hence, the governance of the sector, namely, in rail and local public transport, still resides predominately with member states. This has produced mixed results with regard to the independence of transport governance from partisan, democratic governments – hence, the focus of NEG prescriptions on public transport governance across three of the four countries under study.

Romania received numerous prescriptions on the sectoral governance of rail. For instance, EU executives tasked the Romanian government to 'pursue the restructuring of the Ministry of Transport' (MoU, Romania, 23 June 2009: 5), with similar prescriptions returning in follow-up (supplementary) agreements (MoU, Romania, 1st addendum, 22 February 2010; MoU, Romania, 2nd addendum, 20 July 2010: 8; P-MoU, Romania, 29 June 2011: 12). Additionally, 'a strong and independent regulatory body for the railway sector' (P-MoU, Romania, 29 June 2011: 12) was envisaged. Another prescription insists that 'the regulator has the necessary powers to request data and to take independent decisions on infrastructure charges' (MoU, Romania, 2nd supplemental, 22 June 2012: 32).

Similarly, EU executives tasked the Italian government to set up 'the Transport Authority *as a priority*' (emphasis added) (Council Recommendation Italy 2013/C 217/11, see also Council Recommendation Italy 2014/C 247/11). Following these prescriptions, national legislators established new transport authorities in Italy (Autorità di Regolazione dei Trasporti) and Romania (Autoritatea pentru Reformă Feroviară), which became operational in 2016. By contrast, the NTA set up by Irish legislators in 2009 had begun operating in 2011; this explains the absence of corresponding NEG prescriptions for Ireland.

The primary objective of these agencies is to ensure competitive neutrality in the transport sector and to bring about organisational change and cost-cutting in state-owned operators so that they behave like private companies. Increasing the power of the infrastructure manager must also be seen as part of

---

[8] The European Aviation and Safety Agency (EASA) or the European Railway Agency (ERA) deal with technical issues, such as vehicle authorisation and safety certifications, rather than broader economic governance issues (van de Velde, 2015). In December 2017 however, the EASA nonetheless made EU industrial relations history; namely, when Ryanair pilots leveraged the staff shortages caused by an EASA decision to enforce the EU flight time limitations regulation also in Ireland to threaten transnational strike action. This transnational collective action by Ryanair pilots incidentally forced Ryanair to recognise trade unions (Golden and Erne, 2022).

the vertical separation between the state-owned rail company and the management of the state-owned infrastructure. Interestingly, the objective was to 'end political interference in tariff setting and to allow the rail infrastructure company (CFR Infrastructura) to independently determine rail track access charges' (European Commission, 2013: 51). A euphemism for preventing practices of corruption, the prescription implies that fully liberalised sectors are free of such meddlesome sins, but as Helene Dyrhauge (2013: 111–112) showed, such processes can be 'precarious ... even when there is no state-owned incumbent' (see also Crouch, 2016).

Despite the existence of a regulatory agency for network industries, EU executives told the German authorities to 'strengthen the supervisory role of the Federal Network Agency in the rail sector' (Council Recommendation Germany 2011/C 212/03). For some time, the EU had been deeply suspicious of the German integrated governance structure in the rail sector and the power of the German incumbent, Deutsche Bahn, to thwart competition and maintain its almost 90 per cent market share in passenger services and almost 80 per cent of the freight market (Dyrhauge, 2013: 45–50). In 2013, 2014, and 2015, NEG prescriptions thus tasked the German government to 'take further measures to eliminate the remaining barriers to competition in the railway markets' (Council Recommendations Germany 2013/C 217/09; 2014/C 247/05) generally, and in 'long-distance rail passenger transport' in particular (Council Recommendation Germany 2015/C 271/01).

There were also several prescriptions on the subject of PSOs and competitive tendering. The prescriptions that targeted Romania urged its government to 'continue competitive tendering in the public service obligation contract' (P-MoU, Romania, 29 June 2011: 12) and to 'improve the efficiency of public procurement' (Council Recommendation Romania 2019/C 301/23). The prescriptions for Italy directed its government to promote competition in local public transport services through 'the use of public procurement ... instead of direct concessions' (Council Recommendation Italy 2013/C 217/11). Uncoincidentally, most of the public transport service contracts between the incumbent stated-owned operator (Ferrovie dello Stato) and Italy's regional governments expired at the end of the following year. Similar prescriptions were repeatedly issued to the Italian government in 2015 and 2016. The latter was more explicit and stated: 'take further action to increase competition in ... transport ... and ... the system of concessions' (Council Recommendation Italy 2016/C 299/01). In 2011, an Italian law that imposed compulsory competitive tendering for all local utilities was repealed through a popular abrogative referendum initiated by the Italian water movement, unions, and other public sector advocates (see Chapter 9). Even so, the EU continued to push its commodifying agenda in the field by repeatedly advocating the adoption of a controversial, national competition law (2015, 2017, 2018, 2019). As most Italian legislators remained confident that EU executives would not dare fine Italy for non-compliance, they resisted implementing the prescription. On 2 August 2022 however, the Italian Parliament adopted the Annual Law No. 118/2022 on Market and Competition as requested, after the EU made its post-Covid resilience and recovery funding conditional upon the execution of its NEG prescriptions, as discussed in Chapter 13.

On the surface, some sector-level governance prescriptions seemed rather innocuous, but on closer inspection a different story emerged. For instance, the Romanian government was urged to adopt 'a comprehensive long-term transport plan' and 'implement' it (MoU, Romania, 2012: 32; Council Recommendation Romania 2016/C 299/18). Although this might appear to be a perfectly understandable request, it was private capital that benefitted immediately, with US consulting company AECOM, 'the world's premier infrastructure firm', being awarded the €2.2m contract to develop the masterplan (*Railway Gazette*, 20 April 2012). More ominously however, the adoption of the master plan was 'an ex-ante conditionality for EU funding of transport infrastructure in Romania during the 2014–20 EU funds programming period' (European Commission, 2015b: 33). Hence, EU executives used the cohesion funds as a carrot to further a commodification agenda according to Common Provisions Regulation 1303/2013 (Chapter 2) – prefiguring the conditionalities attached to the EU's post-Covid resilience and recovery funding (Chapter 12). It was by no means a coincidence that such enticement came at a time when the degree of coercion of NEG prescriptions for Romania had significantly diminished, as Romania was no longer involved in any very significant or significant NEG enforcement procedure. Hence, EU executives deployed other mechanisms to ensure compliance, using Romania's dependence on EU structural and investment funding.

Provider-level governance mechanisms: The clearest form of commodification in the provider-level governance mechanisms category is privatisation. To this end, the MoU of 2010 tasked the Romanian government to take concrete steps towards the privatisation of CFR Marfă (MoU, Romania, 2nd addendum, 20 July 2010: 8), the state-owned rail freight company. The Romanian government in turn put up CFR Marfă for sale, but its privatisation collapsed in 2013 after the winning bidder, Grup Feroviar Roman, pulled out of the deal. EU executives nonetheless largely succeeded in turning freight transport into a private affair, as the opening of the sector to competition from private rail and road operators reduced CFR Marfă's market share to less than 20 per cent (ADZ.ro, 7 July 2021).

As documented in Chapter 7, EU executives tasked Italy to 'swiftly and thoroughly implement the privatisation programme' (Council Recommendation

Italy 2015/C 272/16). Although this prescription did not mention Trenitalia's parent company, Ferrovie dello Stato, explicitly, the intended target became clear shortly afterwards when the Italian government announced its plan to sell up to 40 per cent of the company (*Financial Times*, 18 November 2015). This proposal, however, provoked mayhem, not only within its workforce but also within its senior management, and led to the resignation of the entire company board, as its members could not agree on how to privatise the railway, thereby stalling the government's privatisation plans. This, however, did not prevent Italy's state-owned railway company – like its German (DB) and French (SNCF) counterparts – from buying up privatised rail companies elsewhere in the EU (Gevaers et al., 2015).

Other than privatisations, NEG prescriptions promoted the corporatisation of state-owned rail operators. EU executives tasked the Romanian railway management company, CFR Infrastructura, 'to complete the present business plan with market-oriented information' (MoU, Romania, MoU, 2nd supplemental, 22 June 2012: 32; P-MoU, Romania, 29 June 2011: 12). The following year, 2013, they tasked the Romanian government to continue their 'corporate governance reform of state-owned enterprises' in the 'transport sector' (Council Recommendation Romania 2013/C 217/17). With progress being too slow and 'insufficient' (European Commission, 2014b: 4), EU executives urged the government yet again to accelerate the corporate governance reform of state-owned enterprises in the 'transport sectors and increase their efficiency' (Council Recommendation Romania 2014/C 247/21). As outlined above, increasing efficiency meant reducing costs through either labour shedding or line closures, both of which negatively affected the quality of public services. Even so, the NEG prescriptions echoed this approach in 2016 and 2019.

The 2016 prescription for the Italian government tasked it to implement 'all necessary legislative decrees', namely, those 'reforming publicly-owned enterprises' local public services' (Council Recommendation Italy 2016/C 299/01). The latter included local public transport companies, whose 'inefficiency' was identified as being 'particularly critical' (European Commission, 2015a: 57). Unsurprisingly, publicly-owned (local) enterprises were targeted again by NEG prescriptions in 2019. In response, the Italian government introduced a new legislative framework that 'aims to regulate systematically state-owned enterprises in line with the principles of efficient management, protection of competition and the need to reduce public expenditure' (Commission, Country Report Italy SWD (2016) 81: 66). Furthermore, the government of Prime Minister Renzi announced that the number of publicly owned *enti locali* would be significantly reduced from 8,000 to 1,000 (*Il Foglio*,

13 January 2016). As the national government tasked its regions with the regulation of its local public transport and water services, different regional governance patterns emerged (Di Giulio and Galanti, 2015). Nonetheless, even the centre-left government of Tuscany, once a heartland of Italian communism, awarded the operation of all public transportation services in the region in a single bundle to the French RATP Group 'with subsidies amounting to €4bn' (2015: 9). This put Tuscany's municipal public transport providers (e.g., the Azienda Trasporti dell'Area Fiorentina: ATAF) out of business.

Prescriptions on Users' Access to Services

As outlined above, several NEG prescriptions explicitly targeted the provisions of transport services. By contrast to those on water (Chapter 9) or healthcare services (Chapter 10), EU executives did not issue any NEG prescription that targeted primarily users' access to public transport services, either on cost-coverage mechanisms (user charges) or on coverage levels (scope) of public services. That said, the constraints caused by the general NEG prescriptions on the curtailment of public spending (Chapter 7) or on the closure of unprofitable lines (discussed above) did affect users' access to public transport services, albeit indirectly. Take Ireland for example. The Irish government radically reduced its subsidies for public transport providers. In the case of Dublin Bus, its public service obligation subsidy decreased from an already comparatively low figure of 29 per cent in 2009 to 20 per cent in 2015 (Unite, 2016), resulting in substantial ticket price increases (*Irish Times*, 19 October 2018).

NEG: Commodifying Public Transport Services by New Means

In sum, the transport sector was the subject of numerous NEG prescriptions. Most of them were qualitative in character and all of those went in a commodifying policy direction. By contrast, there was a dearth of quantitative prescriptions on the curtailment of spending on public transport services, save that issued in the singular to Romania in 2011/2. This finding is hardly surprising however, as the curtailment of public expenditure usually occurs at intersectoral level (Chapter 7). The exception here is healthcare, which constitutes a significant chunk of government expenditure (Chapter 10). There were also some quantitative prescriptions relating to resources, which pointed in a decommodifying direction. This suggests that some prescriptions were motivated by an alternative policy rationale, which does not fit the dominant commodification policy script that informs all qualitative NEG prescriptions on transport services issued across all countries from 2009 to 2019. We come back to this in this chapter's conclusion. Before that, however, we discuss EU executives' qualitative NEG prescriptions on transport services, which are striking as they repeatedly went beyond the *acquis* of EU law in the field, most explicitly by pushing a privatisation agenda.

Sector-level governance as a category featured most regularly, and these prescriptions chimed with the evolving rail *acquis*, which has been slow and tortuous. In a sector bedevilled by transposition deficits, regulatory heterogeneity, and (unsuccessful) infringement proceedings (section 8.2), the shift to the NEG regime provided EU executives with an opportunity to put the creation of the European rail market back on track. Sector-level prescriptions included enhanced independence for the regulator and the infrastructure manager from the publicly owned rail company and the national government; this technocratic fix is synonymous with ending political interference. For it to succeed, partisan, democratic decision making must be portrayed 'as slow, corrupt, and ultimately irrational' (Radaelli, 1999: 47).

For the Commission, the German rail market is critical with regard to creating the single European rail market, as this 'has an impact on the whole European railway system, given Germany's central geographical position' (Council Recommendation Germany 2012/C 219/10: Recital 15). However, the Commission remained frustrated with the lack of competition in German rail and rather suspicious of its governance structure, not least regarding financial transparency and cross-subsidisation. Deutsche Bahn has an integrated governance structure, which the Commission considered an obstacle to competition. Pursuing a parallel two-pronged approach vis-à-vis Germany, EU executives repeatedly issued prescriptions for the elimination of barriers to rail competition, with the Commission on a constant basis lamenting the lack of 'progress in removing the remaining barriers to competition in the railway markets' and identifying the 'existing legal framework' as 'impeding competition' (Commission, Country Report Germany SWD (2017) 71: 48). The Commission's regular misgivings reflect the weak coercive power that the German NEG prescriptions were having. For this reason, the Commission was obliged also to continue making use of its traditional governance powers by law and through court proceedings, as outlined in the next subsection. Even so, the clearly commodifying bent of the NEG prescriptions issued to Germany on the provision of transport services is remarkable, as it confirms the existence of an overcharging commodifying policy agenda targeting all countries, irrespective of their location in NEG's policy enforcement regime.

Romania and Italy, on the other hand, not only received prescriptions that went deeper than sectoral level governance but were also obliged to take them much more seriously. Both countries created independent transport authorities with substantial regulatory powers to further the liberalisation process. Ireland would have been obliged to take such prescriptions seriously, given its location in NEG's policy enforcement regime. However, there was no need for them as Irish legislators had already set up the NTA in 2009.

EU executives also tasked the Romanian government to enhance the regulatory powers of the independent infrastructure agency in relation to its charges to railway, metro, or tram companies for their use of the rail network. Infrastructure charges are one resource, along with state subsidies, to finance rail infrastructure but have been 'the subject of serious political and economic debates and decisions *since the very origin of railways*' (emphasis added) (Messulam and Finger, 2015: 323). More importantly, they remain 'one of the main barriers' to implementing commodifying rail reforms in Europe (2015: 325). The drafters of Directives 95/19/EC and 2001/14/EC tried to resolve the rail access charge issue, but the final directives 'failed to deliver' (2015: 325). To this end, the EU's shift to the NEG regime provided EU pro-market actors with an opportunity to resolve this question in their favour. Whereas the European Parliament and the Council of transport ministers had been able to curb the commodifying bent of the Commission's earlier universal legislative proposals in the field, typically in response to transnational strikes and demonstrations triggered by the Commission's proposals (see below), their country-specific NEG prescriptions enabled the Commission and Council of finance ministers to pursue a commodification agenda that went beyond the transport *acquis*.

In sum, the shift to the NEG regime enabled EU executives to cajole reluctant member states – particularly those subject to constraining prescriptions – into accepting the Commission's preferences, which EU legislators often watered down in the ordinary legislative procedures pertaining to transport laws. It is unequivocal that NEG prescriptions pursued the Commission's long-standing commodifying policy preferences, namely, vertical separation in rail, regulatory independence, tendering for PSOs in transport services rather than direct concessions, and increased competition between transport providers. In other words, NEG provided EU executives with a new avenue to commodify transport services. Where NEG prescriptions' coercive power was weak or began to wane however, EU executives continued to use the ordinary EU legislative procedures by law to advance their objectives.

EU Laws on Transport Services after the Shift to NEG

After most member states exited the corrective arms of the NEG regime, EU executives began to use another power resource to enforce their country-specific prescriptions, namely, the ex ante conditionality of EU cohesion funding (Chapter 2). This was the case in Romania, where EU executives used the carrot of EU cohesion payments (rather than the stick of financial sanction) to further their policy agenda in the transport sector. This enforcement power resource, however, works only for countries that depend on EU cohesion funding. Although EU executives also tasked the German government to reform the existing governance framework for public transport to increase competition, the weak constraining power of NEG prescriptions in this case meant that Germany could largely ignore them. To advance its policy objectives, the Commission therefore continued to use its ordinary legislative powers as initiators of EU laws as well as its legal powers in state aid and infringement proceedings.

In 2011, the Commission released another White Paper on transport (COM (2011) 144 final), which set the making of a true internal market for rail services as a priority. To that end, it proposed the structural separation between infrastructure management and service and the mandatory award of public service contracts under competitive tendering for public passenger transport. Already in 2010, the Commission had proposed replacing Directive 91/440/EEC with a recast directive, which sought to 'avoid distortion of competition and preferential treatment of the incumbent' by strengthening the independence of regulatory bodies from partisan politics and in particular the transport ministry (Dyrhauge, 2013: 86). Importantly however, the final Recast Single European Railway Directive (2012/34/EU) of the European Parliament and Council 'did not require organisational separation, thus complete vertical separation was not necessary' (Dyrhauge, 2013: 86). Despite this setback, the Commission continued to pursue its commodifying objectives, not only through NEG prescriptions but also by proposing a fourth package of EU railway laws.

The 2016 fourth railway package is the Commission's most ambitious to date, as it aimed to introduce vertical separation and competition in the passenger market, including rail services under PSOs. Regarding governance structure, a blocking Council minority of national transport ministers (including Austria, Germany, Italy, and France) resisted vertical separation along with Community of European Railways (CER) and European transport workers' unions (Scordamaglia and Katsarova, 2016). The CER (2011) argued that a one-size-fits-all model for all countries would be unrealistic given the variation between them in structural characteristics. In addition, competition would work no better with vertical separation than with a holding company. The final package adopted by the Parliament and Council thus allowed for vertically integrated rail companies but introduced Chinese walls to restrict financial flows between the infrastructure manager and the rail operator in the overarching holding company. According to the package's Compliance Verification Clause, the Commission can prevent rail companies that are part of a vertically integrated structure from operating in other member states if fair competition in their home market is not possible.

The ETF (2014) feared that cherry-picking lucrative contracts would lead to the neglect of less profitable rail routes and argued that direct award should remain the member states' prerogative. To this end, the ETF (2014) petitioned members of the European Parliament (MEPs) and transport ministers to curb the Commission's enthusiasm for competitive tendering by respecting the freedom of choice guaranteed under the PSO Regulation (1370/2007) discussed in section 8.2. Regarding the outcome, the ETF was pleased that governments had not accepted the Commission's 'dogmatic' approach (ETF, 2015a), although concerns about social and employment conditions remained. The legislative amendments of the European Parliament and the Council of transport ministers to the fourth railway package somewhat curbed the commodification bent of the Commission's initial legislative proposal, but this prevented neither the Commission and the Council of finance ministers from issuing NEG prescriptions that went further than the EU's legal *acquis* (as discussed above), nor the Commission from using its significant powers as an enforcer of EU law to advance its aims.

In March 2011, the Commission conducted dawn raids on Deutsche Bahn offices. However, the latter brought a case to the CJEU, which deemed the Commission's actions to be illegal.[9] It was against this backdrop that the Commission proposed its fourth package of EU railway laws. As mentioned above however, a Franco–German alliance in the Council, coupled with European Parliament lobbying by the CER and the ETF, thwarted the Commission's push for 'radical policy change' (Dyrhauge, 2022: 866). In 2017 however, the CJEU condemned Germany for failing to take all the necessary measures to ensure the transparency of accounts between Deutsche Bahn and its subsidiaries,[10] some of which operate in other member states. Hence, in the German case, policy change resulted from a CJEU ruling rather than NEG prescriptions or the adoption of new EU laws.

---

[9] C-583/13 P *Deutsche Bahn v. European Commission* [2015] ECLI 404.
[10] C-482/14 *European Commission v. Germany* [2017] ECLI 499.

Finally, the Commission used its dual role as investigator and decision maker in EU competition law to advance its commodification agenda. This happened in the case of the privatisation of the freight train company CRF Marfă, which failed despite the MoU-related NEG prescription discussed above. In turn, the Commission brought CRF Marfă to the brink of insolvency when it ordered it to pay back the €363m of state aid that it had received, in agreement with the Council and the IMF, to facilitate its privatisation (Commission Decision 2021/69, Recital 107).[11]

8.4 EU TRANSPORT GOVERNANCE AND TRANSNATIONAL COUNTERMOVEMENTS

From the pre- and post-2008 scenarios outlined above, it is clear that the commodification of transport services has been a long-standing policy preference of the Commission. However, the more there was a public service aspect, the more commodification became contentious; this explains why Mario Monti (2010) described the slow pace of EU service liberalisation as a 'persistent irritant'. This reflects the resistance by anti-commodification forces, including transport workers' unions and social movements (Turnbull, 2000, 2010; Gentile and Tarrow, 2009; Hilal, 2009; Fox-Hodess, 2017). Understanding this resistance and the form it takes is important, as 'the extent to which non-capitalist space is incorporated also depends on the level of resistance against this expansion' (Bieler and Morton, 2018: 41). In this section, we discuss transport workers' resistance to EU prescriptions and their consequences.

Most European transport workers are represented at EU level by the ETF, especially in the public railway sector (Traxler and Adam, 2008). The ETF's raison d'être, since 1999, is, simply put, to add the argument of force to the force of argument (Turnbull, 2010). This is done by combining outsider strategies (European demonstrations and transnational strike actions) with insider strategies (lobbying MEPs and European transport ministers) that seek

---

[11] Tellingly, the Commission admitted that a successful privatisation would have 'alleviated' its state-aid concerns (Commission Decision 2021/69: Recital 263). After all, the Commission agreed to state aid for the Greek state company TrainOSE (Commission Decision 2018/1040), as its acquisition by Trenitalia 'definitely cut the links between [Greece's] rail infrastructure manager and its rail operator' (Commission Decision 2021/69: Recital 333). Hence, the Commission used its competition policy powers to enforce NEG prescriptions, as also shown by the following newswire 'Without the sale' for €45m to Trenitalia, TrainOSE 'would have had to return more than 700 million euros in state aid to the European Union, forcing it to shut' (Reuters, 14 July 2016).

to protect transport workers' interests and to prevent a further commodification of transport services. To date, transnational protest actions by European transport workers have made a difference, albeit to varying degrees, depending on the transport modality in question.

Table 8.3 presents a list of transnational transport-related social and economic protests politicising the EU governance of transport services (Erne and Nowak, 2023). The list documents the capacity of the ETF, the International Transport Workers' Federation (its global sister organisation), and transnational grassroots alliances of European dockworkers to orchestrate transnational strikes and days of action against commodifying EU interventions. The apogee is undoubtedly 'the war on Europe's waterfront' where docker strikes were 'timed to coincide with Council deliberations on the [Port Services] Directive' (Turnbull, 2010: 341), but other transport modalities have also been defended against EU liberalisation attempts, albeit to a lesser degree (Hilal, 2009; Crochemore, 2014; Harvey and Turnbull, 2015; Golden and Erne, 2022; Szabó, Golden, and Erne, 2022). This can be explained not only by the Commission's unwavering bent for the commodification of the sector but also by its incremental liberalisation strategy, which targeted each modality one by one (Héritier, 1997; Szabó, Golden, and Erne, 2022). Whereas the transnational strikes of dockers (Fox-Hodess, 2017) – and to some extent also railway workers (Hilal, 2009; Crochemore, 2014) – were quite effective, other transnational union campaigns were less successful, including those politicising the EU public procurement directives in the 2000s, as 'the organisation of strikes [or demonstrations] was [either] not considered [or failed to materialise]' (Bieler, 2011: 175).

As EU executives pursued the commodification of transport generally, and rail in particular, through a combination of manifold approaches including new EU laws, such as the fourth railway package, infringement proceedings, and, as demonstrated above, NEG prescriptions, it proved difficult to mount resistance, albeit to different degrees across these different modes of EU governance. Additionally, there is the horizontal market pressure aspect that intensified significantly following the EU's Eastern enlargements, thereby increasing intramodal competition between the rail and the road haulage sector, through the establishment of letterbox companies in countries with lower labour standards and the subsequent posting of drivers from those countries to countries with higher labour standards (ETF, 2012). As we shall see, the politicisation of such developments can prove challenging.

Different modes of EU integration differently affect organised labour's capacity to politicise them. Vertical integration through direct EU interventions unintentionally also offers targets for countervailing social movements.

TABLE 8.3 *Transnational protests politicising the EU governance of transport services (1993–2019)*

Date	Location	Action Type	Topic	Coordinators
7 March 1994	Multi-sited	Strike	Against deregulation of the European air transport sector	ETF
19 November 1996	Brussels, Italy	Strike, demonstration	Against white book on transport	ETF
9 June 1997	Multi-sited	Strike	International Day of Action in road transport	ETF/ITF
18 June 1998	Luxembourg	Demonstration	Against white book on transport	ETF
8 September 1998	Multi-sited	Strike	International Day of Action in road transport	ETF/ITF
23 November 1998	Multi-sited	Strike, demonstration	Against EU plans for rail privatisation	ETF
5 May 1999	Multi-sited	Strike	International Day of Action in road transport	ETF/ITF
29 March 2000	Multi-sited	Demonstration	Against first rail package	ETF
1 October 2000	Luxembourg	Demonstration	Against Working Time Directive for road transport	ITF/ETF
29 March 2001	Multi-sited	Demonstration	International Day of Action in support of rail safety	ITF/ETF
25 September 2001	Multi-sited	Strike	Against proposed port package	ETF
15 October 2001	Multi-sited	Demonstration	International Day of Action on road transport	ETF/ITF
6 November 2001	Multi-sited	Strike	Against proposed port package	IDC
26 March 2002	Brussels	Demonstration	International Day of Action of railway workers	ETF/ITF
14 June 2002	Strasbourg, multi-sited	Strike	Against port package	IDC
19 June 2002	Multi-sited	Strike	Air traffic controllers against a single European airspace	ETF
17 January 2003	Multi-sited	Strike	Against port package	ETF
17 February 2003	Brussels	Demonstration	Against port package	ETF
10 March 2003	Strasbourg, multi-sited	Strike, demonstration	Against port package	ETF/IDC
14 March 2003	Multi-sited	Demonstration	International Day of Action of railway workers	ETF/ITF

194

18 March 2003	Multi-sited	Strike	Against EU plans towards privatisation of rail freight transport	Various
8–12 and 29 September 2003	Multi-sited	Strike	Against port package	ETF
13 October 2003	Multi-sited	Strike, demonstration	International day of road transport	ETF/ITF
19 November 2003	Multi-sited	Strike	Against port package	ETF/IDC
31 March 2004	Lille	Demonstration	European Day of Action against the liberalisation of railways	ETF
21 November 2005	Multi-sited	Strike	Against port package	ETF
11–12 January 2006	Multi-sited	Strike	Against port package	ETF
16 January 2006	Strasbourg	Demonstration	Against port package	ETF
2 March 2006	Multi-sited	Strike	European railway strike against meeting of EU traffic ministers	ETF
13 November 2008	Paris	Demonstration	Against rail privatisation	ETF
5 October 2009	Multi-sited	Demonstration	Against (weak) EU safety regulations	ETF/ECA
13 April 2010	Lille	Demonstration	Against liberalisation and privatisation of railways	ETF
24 May 2011	Brussels	Demonstration	European Day of Action against Recast Directive on railways	ETF
8 November 2011	Multi-sited	Strike, demonstration	European Day of Action against liberalisation of railways	ETF
9–13 January 2012	Lisbon, multi-sited	Strike, demonstration	Solidarity with Portuguese dockworkers	ETF/IDC
24 September 2012	Brussels	Demonstration	Against social dumping in the road transport sector[a]	ETF
9 October 2012	Brussels	Demonstration	Against social dumping in the road transport sector[a]	ETF

(*continued*)

TABLE 8.3 (*continued*)

Date	Location	Action Type	Topic	Coordinators
5 November 2012	Multi-sited	Demonstration	Against airport package	ETF
29 November 2012	Lisbon	Demonstration	Against plans by the Portuguese government to change labour rules	IDC
22 January 2013	Multi-sited	Demonstration	Against (weak) EU safety regulations	ETF/ECA
12 June 2013	Multi-sited	Strike	Against a single European airspace	ETF
9 October 2013	Multi-sited	Demonstration	Railway workers against fourth railway package	ETF
10 October 2013	Brussels, multi-sited	Demonstration	ETF Road Transport Section against social dumping	ETF
14 October 2013	Brussels	Demonstration	Against package on Single European Sky	ETF
29–30 January 2014	Multi-sited	Strike	Against package on Single European Sky	ETF/ATCEUC
4 February 2014	Multi-sited	Strike	Solidarity with Portuguese dockworkers	ETF/IDC
25 February 2014	Strasbourg	Demonstration	Against fourth railway package	ETF
3 May 2014	Multi-sited	Demonstration	European protest day of truck drivers[a]	Various
8 October 2014	Luxembourg	Demonstration	Against fourth railway package	ETF
14 September 2014–14 September 2015	Online	ECI	Fair Transport Europe – equal treatment for all transport workers	ETF
5–11 October 2015	Multi-sited	Demonstration	Global rail and road action week, including opposition to the EU's planned fourth railway package	ITF/ETF
13–14 January 2016	Sines	Demonstration	Precarious labour in the port of Sines	IDC
7 July 2016	Multi-sited	Strike	Global day of docker action[a]	IDC/ITF/ETF
5 December 2016	Brussels	Demonstration	Against fourth railway package	ETF
12 December 2016	Strasbourg	Demonstration	Against fourth railway package	ETF

10 March 2017	Multi-sited	Strike	Solidarity with Spanish dockworkers	IDC, ITF
26 April 2017	Brussels	Demonstration	End social dumping in road haulage	ETF
17 May 2017	Strasbourg	Demonstration	Campaign for a social Road Initiative	ETF
8 June 2017	Luxembourg	Demonstration	Against road package	ETF
9–11, 19, and 29 June 2017	Multi-sited	Strike	Solidarity with Spanish dockworkers	IDC
20–24 November 2017	Multi-sited	Demonstration	Action on Posting of Workers Directive	ETF
29 May 2018	Strasbourg	Demonstration	Against mobility package	ETF
2 October 2018	Multi-sited	Demonstration	Working conditions at airports	ETF
3 December 2018	Brussels	Demonstration	Working conditions for drivers	ETF
7–9 January 2019	Multi-sited	Demonstration	Action for fair mobility package	ETF
26–27 March 2019	Brussels	Demonstration	Action week for Fair Transport	ETF

Source: Transnational Socioeconomic Protest Database (Erne and Nowak, 2023).

The table documents protest events targeting political authorities in relation to transport services, using the database's political level category, excluding actions at company and systemic level. These events also include protests on EU laws regarding the private sector, e.g., truck drivers. In addition, [a] indicates transnational events that targeted employers at the sectoral level.

The more socioeconomic decisions are taken by tangible political and corporate elites rather than abstract market forces, the easier it might be for social movements and unions to mobilise discontent (Erne, 2012c: 124). Accordingly, European transport workers' unions were able to delay and curb the EU-law commodification of some transport modalities by combining their lobbying activities with transnational strikes and demonstrations across Europe as well as outside the European Parliament before important votes (Turnbull, 2010; Scordamaglia and Katsarova, 2016). Thus, since the mid-1990s, the impending threats caused by looming commodifying EU laws have triggered countervailing union protests across countries, as shown in Table 8.3.

The more EU laws succeed in commodifying the provision of public services however, the more difficult it becomes for unions to organise countervailing actions, as the resultant increasing horizontal market integration pressures are opaque and increase competitive tensions between workers across countries that may hamper transnational collaboration. Despite its vertical nature, the NEG regime did not lead to a notable increase in transnational protests, with the exception of transnational solidarity strikes by Northern European dockworkers in support of their Spanish and Portuguese colleagues, who were striking against the implementation of commodifying, country-specific NEG prescriptions in their countries (Table 8.3; Fox-Hodess, 2017). Although these European dockworkers understood that the country-specific NEG prescriptions had been informed by an overarching, commodifying policy script (as documented above), the ETF did not politicise the NEG regime, delegating the issue of EU economic governance to the ETUC. Instead, the ETF tried to politicise both the looming threats caused by the draft fourth package of EU railway laws (official 1, ETF rail section, 10 August 2017, telephone interview) and the social dumping caused by increased competition in the road haulage sector (official 2, ETF secretariat, 14 September 2018, Brussels). To that end, the ETF used a novel tool, the European citizens' initiative (ECI), which EU leaders introduced into the draft EU Constitution and the Lisbon Treaty in response to calls to make the EU more democratic (Szabó, Golden, and Erne, 2022).

According to Art. 11(4) TEU, any group that can collect one million signatures of EU citizens from at least seven member states within the time frame of one year can urge the Commission to address the gist of concerns outlined in their ECI. Hoping to follow the success of the Right2Water ECI launched by EPSU (see Chapter 9), the ETF launched its own Fair Transport ECI, even though the ETF is – like EPSU – an under-resourced organisation with only a small secretariat of around fifteen staff members (Müller and Platzer, 2017) and an organisation with a high degree of internal heterogeneity (Szabó, Golden, and Erne, 2022). Different sections within the ETF supported the idea of an ECI for different reasons: either to challenge the Commission's unrelenting agenda for further commodifying EU laws or to highlight the negative effects of earlier commodifying EU laws. These concerns varied from sector to sector. With regard to road haulage, which had already been fully liberalised, the proliferation of social dumping cases has been the source of union concerns in Northern Europe. The ETF's rail section, however, aimed to curb further commodifying vertical EU laws and was much less concerned with social dumping (Erne and Blaser, 2018). Bridging these diverging views within the ETF, however, would ultimately blur the focus and meaning of the ECI and contribute to the ETF's failure to gather the required one million signatures (Szabó, Golden, and Erne, 2022).

The Fair Transport ECI was designed to complement an eponymous ETF (2015b) campaign that encompassed all modalities, including local public transport, but emphasised the problem of social dumping. With over 200 affiliates, representing over five million workers, one might be forgiven for thinking that a successful outcome for the ECI was certain, although any hard-nosed campaigner might well caution that, regarding the orchestration of campaigns from the local to the transnational, nothing is inevitable. Despite the quorum being met in Denmark, Sweden, and Belgium, the necessary criterion for an ECI to be deemed successful was not even nearly satisfied, with an estimated 200,000 signatures collected (ETF, 2016). This disappointing result stands in contrast to its campaigns against the draft Port Services Directives in the 2000s and the successful Right2Water campaign coordinated by EPSU, which was supported by a social movement united by a shared view on water as a common good (Chapter 9). In contrast to EPSU's successful Right2Water campaign, the EFT failed to align itself with social movements that might also be against the closure of railway lines and in favour of public transport services, such as the Campaign for Better Transport in the United Kingdom. Instead, by narrowly framing the campaign on 'social dumping and working conditions' (ETF, 2015b), the ECI largely failed to capture the public imagination.

In hindsight, ETF officials acknowledged this aspect (official 1, ETF rail section, 10 August 2017, telephone interview; official 2, ETF secretariat, 14 September 2018, Brussels). In a letter to affiliates seen by the authors, the ETF (2016) nevertheless claimed that the campaign had 'been successful in putting social dumping issues on the agenda in European politics' thanks to a sop by the Commission President Juncker in his state of the union address, 'that workers should get the same pay for the same work in the same place' (Juncker, 2016). This concession is a low benchmark for evaluating success and differs from the experience of the Right2Water campaign, which measured success in terms of the exclusion of water from the scope of the commodifying Concessions Directive (2014/23/EU) (Chapter 9). Conversely, road haulage workers were excluded from the decommodifying, revised Posting of Workers Directive (2018/957), despite the ETF's involvement in its drafting (Seeliger and Wagner, 2020). Eventually however, this disappointment was reversed in the deliberation about the EU's Mobility Package laws, introduced in 2017, which sought to further commodify road haulage. Here, the ETF (2018) scored a major victory when most MEPs rejected outright the proposed weakening of European transport workers' terms and conditions: on pay for posted workers, on driving and rest time, and on cabotage. In July 2020, the European Parliament finally adopted the amended Mobility Package and paid homage to the essential transport workers who kept Europe moving during the Covid-19 pandemic.

8.5 CONCLUSION

Transport policy is important in fulfilling broader policy goals beyond transport itself: to supply public goods such as regional development, equal opportunities, and social cohesion, but this logic has been questioned by the rise of the neoliberal paradigm. Already in its 1996 white paper, the European Commission had argued that 'in the future the railways must behave much more like normal businesses, that endeavour to satisfy their customers' requirements in the knowledge that, if they fail to do so, someone else will and they will lose the business'. In short, transport 'should be first and foremost a business' (COM (96) 421: 10). After the EU liberalised the aviation and road haulage sectors, rail became a key target of its transport policy. Given the resistance to rail services commodification articulated by public railway companies, unions, and a blocking Council minority of transport ministers, the EU laws that were meant to commodify rail did not go as far as the Commission wanted (Dyrhauge, 2013) – hence the interest of the Commission and Council in pursuing its commodification by new means, namely, the country-specific NEG prescriptions that they began to issue after the 2008 crisis.

Our analysis shows that EU executives' NEG prescriptions were informed by a consistent commodification script, pushing privatisation, corporate restructuring, competitive tendering, and even line closures. As shown in Tables 8.1 and 8.2, all NEG prescriptions across all countries under study on the sector- or provider-level governance of public transport services pointed in a commodifying direction, thereby compromising their role in fostering social and territorial cohesion. Another key finding is that some NEG prescriptions went further than the *acquis* of EU laws in the field, disregarding democratic norms at both national and EU level. Two examples neatly demonstrate this.

Firstly, there was scant regard for the freedom of choice principle, enshrined in PSO Regulation (and the fourth package of EU railway laws), which allows the awarding of concessions for public services in-house (Commission, SWD (2013) 53 final/2: 19). Despite this principle, EU executives regularly issued NEG prescriptions that pressured governments to amend this practice in favour of competitive tendering. In the Italian case, such NEG prescriptions ignored the will of the Italian people, as expressed in the 2011 abrogative referendum, which rescinded the law that had introduced competitive tendering for all utilities provided by municipalities. The referendum campaign focused mainly on water as a public good (Chapter 9), but the rescinding of the law limited the commodification of the local public transport sector also, until NEG prescriptions and regional laws reintroduced the commodification agenda.

Secondly, the NEG prescriptions that tasked member states to privatise public transport operators went far beyond Art. 345 TFEU, which stipulates that the EU 'shall in no way prejudice the rules in member states governing the system of property ownership'. NEG's call for privatisations over the past decade revealed a penchant for high-order commodification to 'improve public debt sustainability' (Council Recommendation Italy 2016/C 299/01, Recital 13). This echoes the privatisation wave in the late 1990s triggered by EMU convergence criteria on public debt and deficits but fails to remember a key source of deficits: the massive public bailouts of private banks during the financial crisis, which had been approved by the Commission despite Art. 107 TFEU, which in principle prohibits state aid 'favouring certain undertakings' and despite the bank bailouts' contributing to deficits well in excess of the -3 per cent benchmark deficit criterion, for example, -32.1 per cent in 2010 in the Irish case (Eurostat: GOV_10DD_EDPT1). By contrast, the Commission brought the Romanian public railway company, CRF Marfă, to the brink of insolvency when it ordered it in 2021 to pay back the aid it had received from its government to facilitate its privatisation, as requested by NEG prescriptions, as its privatisation failed.

Whereas all qualitative prescriptions on the governance of transport were commodifying, some quantitative prescriptions on resource levels pointed in the opposite policy direction. When analysing the latter in their semantic, communicative, and policy context however, we discovered a number of caveats that we must also address. Firstly, the latter prescriptions did not feature prominently before 2016 and were issued consistently only to Ireland, as shown in Table 8.2. However, Ireland's post-crisis economic recovery was driven by the transnational corporation sector and foreign direct investment rather than by the austerity policy associated with NEG (Regan and Brazys, 2017). Secondly, compared with the commodifying ones, decommodifying NEG prescriptions had a much weaker coercive power. Thirdly, most decommodifying NEG prescriptions were informed by a complementary policy rationale that did not contradict the commodifying bent behind the qualitative NEG prescriptions. The prescriptions that tasked the German government to spend more on its crumbling transport infrastructure, for example, were informed by a concern about the effects of underinvestment on its competitiveness. This means that they were informed by a policy rationale that Mariana Mazzucato (2013) related to the entrepreneurial state, which drives growth through more investments in its infrastructure. This rationale also featured prominently in the justifications for the NEG prescriptions for Ireland after 2016, although the ensuing actual spending increases failed to fully reverse the government's dramatic post-2008 cuts for capital and current spending on transport of 72 and 31 per cent, respectively (Hynes and Malone, 2020). In addition, EU executives in their calls for more public investments frequently made a link between such investments and PPPs – implying commodification (Mercille and Murphy, 2017). Social or ecological concerns, however, motivated only a few NEG decommodifying prescriptions. Transition to the green economy, a cornerstone of von der Leyen's (2019a) agenda, informed the 2019 prescriptions issued to Germany and Italy; and the aim of social cohesion, an issue that gained prominence again in Juncker's (2016) declarations, informed the 2016 and 2019 prescriptions on resources for Romanian transport services. Overall however, most of the prescriptions that urged governments to spend more on transport emphasised its function in a properly functioning European economy rather than its contribution to social inclusion or the transition to a green economy.

Until the 2000s, European transport workers and the ETF were relatively effective in resisting the EU's commodification of transport services. Their resistance was most effective when opposing liberalisation attempts broached via the EU's ordinary governance-by-law approach, as in the case of the first draft Port Services Directive or the PSO Regulation. Many pieces of draft EU legislation in the sector have triggered transnational strike action (see Table 8.3) as well as intense lobbying that stemmed the commodification of transport services, notably on Europe's waterfront and, to some extent, also in rail (Dyrhauge, 2022). Protest actions proved less effective, however, in the face of more abstract horizontal market pressures that followed earlier successful, liberalisation attempts by law (Szabó, Golden, and Erne, 2022). Paradoxically, the ETF's initial successes in delaying many EU-law commodification attempts prevented it from forging broader alliances with user movements in the defence of public services. This absence became particularly visible during the ETF's Fair Transport ECI, which failed to entice the necessary support from at least one million EU citizens, by contrast to EPSU's successful Right2Water ECI (see Chapter 9). At the same time, the different fate of the two ECIs mirrors different aims and targets. Whereas the Fair Transport ECI aimed primarily to counter the horizontal market pressures that resulted from the commodification of transport services in the road haulage sector (ETF, 2015a), the Right2Water ECI pre-empted looming vertical commodification attempts by the Commission (see Chapter 9). As horizontal market pressures put service providers and workers in competition with each other, the failure of the ETF to galvanise enough support across borders for its ECI therefore also reflects the wider spread of the commodification agenda in the transport compared with the water or healthcare sectors (Chapter 11).

Compared with their success in politicising the EU's liberalising draft laws, the ETF and its affiliates found it much more difficult to politicise the country-specific NEG prescriptions across borders, despite their overarching, commodifying policy orientation and their vertical nature. This reflects their very technocratic nature and their asynchronous implementation across different modes of transport and countries. The EU portrayed its European Semester as a tool of macroeconomic governance, although its NEG prescriptions can be, as we have seen, very sector specific. To some extent, the sectoral ETF fell prey to this portrayal, as the ETF left the questions of EU governance to the ETUC to deal with. Consequently, in the transport sector, NEG triggered only a few instances of transnational protests explicitly targeting NEG prescriptions, namely, transnational solidarity strikes with Spanish and Portuguese dockers who went on strike against the implementation of commodifying NEG prescriptions (Table 8.3). The multi-scalar alignment of the dockers' transnational protest campaigns (Fox-Hodess, 2017) suggests that the dockworkers must have understood well the overarching dynamics behind NEG's country-specific prescriptions. This is not surprising, given European dockworkers' long-standing confrontations with the Commission's port services commodification agenda. Overall, however, the increased commodification pressures triggered by EU executives' vertical NEG prescriptions, the proposals for new EU rail laws, and the increased horizontal market pressures caused by earlier EU laws led to an encompassing European trade union response, the ETF's Fair Transport campaign, which failed, however, by contrast to the parallel Right2Water ECI.

9

EU Governance of Water Services and Its Discontents

9.1 INTRODUCTION

In this chapter, we analyse the EU governance of water services and its discontents. We investigate the extent to which EU leaders called for a commodification of water through EU laws and new economic governance (NEG) prescriptions; and we assess the transnational countermovements of unions and social movements that they triggered. In addition, we assess the interactions of these vertical EU governance interventions with horizontal market pressures triggered by the making of a European market in the sector.

In the water sector, horizontal market integration has been advancing relatively slowly because of significant physical barriers to trade. As opposed to other public network industries (including transport), water supply and distribution systems are typically contained within sub-national borders. The distribution of water (except bottled water) remains a local issue, making tap water a non-tradable good. Nonetheless, water services were hardly insulated from neoliberal demands to commodify public services across the globe (Dobner, 2010; Bieler, 2021; Moore, 2023). From the 1980s onwards, water-related technologies, governance ideas, and, most importantly, capital have become ever more transnational. Water services became a target of mobile capital across borders. The operation of water supply networks and participation in water-related infrastructure projects (the improvement of sanitation systems, for example) represented lucrative business opportunities for transnational corporations (TNCs), especially given the scale and know-how requirements of these tasks (Hall and Lobina, 2007: 65). The expansion of water TNCs, however, has also triggered the emergence of countervailing protest movements defending the commons, especially in countries where the arrival of TNCs meant direct privatisation and price increases (Sultana and Loftus, 2012; Bieler and Erne, 2014; Bieler, 2021).

Whereas horizontal (market) integration processes are relatively uniform in their commodifying impact, vertical (political) EU interventions can go in two opposite directions: they can either decommodify water services through setting EU-wide environmental and quality standards or commodify them through EU laws and governance prescriptions that curtail public spending and marketise the sector. In this chapter, we analyse the EU governance of the water sector throughout two time periods. Section 9.2 outlines the developments before the 2008 crisis, focusing on the EU's ordinary policymaking procedures through EU laws and court rulings. In section 9.3, we analyse the policy orientation of the EU's *country-specific* NEG prescriptions for Germany, Ireland, Italy, and Romania, which the European Commission and Council of finance ministers (EU executives) began issuing after 2009 (see Chapters 2, 4, and 5). Water services is an area where EU-level commodification through EU laws and court rulings had advanced moderately before 2008. The EU's shift to NEG after the financial crisis therefore opened up opportunities for further water service commodification, as shown in section 9.3. Section 9.4 outlines and assesses the counterreactions triggered by vertical EU interventions in the water sector, most importantly, the first successful European citizens' initiative (ECI) on the Right2Water. In the conclusion, we discuss the links between different modes of integration, commodification, and countervailing mobilisations by unions and social movements in the water sector.

9.2 EU GOVERNANCE OF WATER SERVICES BEFORE THE SHIFT TO NEG

In most EU member states, water provision is the task of local authorities that operate under a national regulatory framework. EU governance has nevertheless made significant inroads in the area in recent decades. A significant part of the EU's *acquis communautaire* deals with water services from an environmental perspective, but the economic aspects of water management have also gained an increasingly European dimension. We use the distinction between environmental and economic management for analytical purposes but, as we shall see, the environmental governance of water has also substantial economic implications, in terms of whether the legislation prescribes market or non-market solutions as the most appropriate way to ensure the sustainability and quality of water resources.

Phase One: Preventing Regime Competition on Water Quality

Community legislation targeting the water sector started to appear in the 1970s, with specific directives on quality standards (Directive 75/440/EEC, Directive 79/869/EEC). Taking a more comprehensive approach, in 1980 the Council adopted Directive 80/778/EEC on the quality of water intended for human consumption, commonly known as the Drinking Water Directive (DWD). As their basis, the directives invoked Art. 2 of the Treaty establishing the European Economic Community (EEC Treaty), which outlined the Community's central aims.[1] These directives stated that the approximation of laws across member states was needed, as the differences in national legislation might create differences in the 'conditions of competition and, as a result, directly affect the operation of the common market' (Directive 80/778/EEC, Preamble). The directives aimed to tackle the disparities in quality standards across member states, which could have been exploited as unfair competitive advantage. Despite the directives' semantic links to the common market project, they pointed in a decommodifying policy direction, as they took water quality out of regulatory competition.

The DWD was first updated in 1998, catching up with some of the new developments in the sector since 1980, including quality standards for bottled water. Nevertheless, some of the more ambitious quality goals, such as odour, taste, or colour, were dropped from the final text of the directive because of objections by water suppliers. For these reasons, the cost implications of the Water Framework Directive (WFD) were relatively modest and were spread out over a long timeframe (Hall et al., 2004: 11–12).

Phase Two: Towards the Commodification of Public Water Services

By contrast to the DWD case discussed above, the implementation of the Urban Waste-Water Treatment Directive (91/271/EEC) entailed much higher costs, transforming the financing models of water investment and also strengthening the position of the private sector. The infrastructural developments needed to comply with the waste-water directive amounted to 'arguably the largest common infrastructure project undertaken by the EU in its history' (Hall and Lobina, 2007: 65). This strained the budgets of municipalities and national governments that were under pressure to fulfil the Maastricht deficit and debt targets in the run-up to the introduction of the Euro (see Chapter 7). Implementing the directive was also challenging financially in Central and Eastern European countries that joined the EU in the 2000s. Subsequently, a large share of European regional and cohesion funds was used to meet this challenge. Overall, the financing needs of waste-water investment combined with EU-wide austerity contributed to strengthening the role of water TNCs, especially in Central and Eastern Europe, including one of our

---

[1] 'It shall be the aim of the Community, by establishing a Common Market and progressively approximating the economic policies of Member States, to promote throughout the Community a harmonious development of economic activities, a continuous and balanced expansion, an increased stability, an accelerated raising of the standard of living and closer relations between its Member States' (Art 2. EEC Treaty).

country cases, Romania (Hall et al., 2004: 13; Hall and Lobina, 2007: 66). Private companies usually undertook these projects in public–private partnership (PPP) and concessions arrangements (Ménard, 2009).

EU-level legislation in water services obtained a much more explicit legal base with the Treaty of Maastricht in 1992. Art. 130s TEC (now Art. 192 TFEU) established the EU's competence for setting environmental standards in the area, thereby enabling EU legislators to adopt EU laws concerning the management of water resources. Building on these new powers, in 2000 the EU adopted the WFD as the main and most comprehensive piece of European legislation in water services. The directive has the ambition to cover all relevant aspects of water management in Europe, the protection of drinking water being only one objective. Unlike the DWD or the Waste-Water Treatment Directive, the WFD contains few direct technical targets but operates at a more general level, setting guidelines and principles for a variety of connected stakeholders.

The WFD embodies the contradictions of the Europeanisation of the water sector. The preamble to the directive declares that water 'is not a commercial product like any other but, rather, a heritage which must be protected, defended and treated as such' (Directive 2000/60/EC, Recital 1). The above decommodification principle stands in contradiction to the directive's embrace of the idea that market mechanisms, in particular pricing, can be used effectively to achieve the goal of sustainable water management. The WFD is couched in market-based terminology, such as supply and demand, and requires member states to prepare economic analyses of water use in their areas.

A significant element of the directive is the cost recovery principle, which demands an adequate financial contribution from water users and polluters to cover the costs of the environmental protection of water. Art. 9 of the directive (titled Recovery of costs for water services) prescribes that 'Member States shall ensure by 2010 that water-pricing policies provide adequate incentives for users to use water resources efficiently, and thereby contribute to the environmental objectives of this Directive' (Directive 2000/60/EC, Art. 9). Art. 9 also includes a derogation from the adequate water-pricing principle on the basis of 'established practices' that allowed Ireland to continue financing water services from general taxation.

To sum up, our review of the relevant documents suggests that EU environmental legislation in the field of water management has assumed an increasingly commodifying character over time, even though this happened gradually and has not flipped the balance of policymaking, which is still dominated overall by ideas of regulating rather than expanding the market. Two mechanisms propelled the limited commodification of environmental rules.

First, private actors dominated the infrastructural investment projects needed to achieve the standards set out in the Waste-Water Treatment

Directive. Second, the WFD introduced an overarching theme into water-related EU legislation that considers the market mechanism as an effective way of solving environmental problems. Even though this formulation is vague in the text of the directive, the Commission and the European Environment Agency recurrently interpreted the provision in their communications and reports in a commodifying way, for example by emphasising the responsibility of individual households to protect water resources by paying the market price for drinking water (Page and Kaika, 2003: 339–340; Kirhensteine et al., 2010; European Commission, 2012; European Environment Agency, 2013).

Phase Three: Frontal but Unsuccessful Attempts to Commodify Water

The shift towards more commodification in environmental legislation in the early 2000s was matched by the first direct attempts in European economic governance to liberalise water provision. Until in the 2000s, sector-specific liberalising directives did not target drinking water and sanitation services, although other network industries (such as electricity, gas, transport, and telecommunication) were made part of the EU internal market (see Chapters 7 and 8; Bieling and Deckwirth, 2008: 242; Crespy, 2016: 43).

With the appointment of the neoliberal Dutchman Frits Bolkestein as Commissioner for Internal Market and Taxation in 1999, pro-commodification actors started to show more interest in the water sector. Bolkestein championed an outspoken, radical, and comprehensive agenda of service liberalisation, stating explicitly that such an agenda should include water. This view on water is documented not only in the Commissioner's speeches but also in Commission-sponsored policy studies and a Commission communication (Bolkestein, 2002; Gordon-Walker and Marr, 2002; European Commission, 2003).

Bolkestein advocated the commodification of the water sector as 'a practical instrument for establishing the correct relationship between price, quality and the standard of the service provided' (Bolkestein, 2002: 6). Following up on this, the Commission's Communication on Internal Market Strategy Priorities 2003–2006 stated that the Commission would launch a comprehensive review of the sector and consider 'all options', including legislative proposals in the area of competition law, while respecting neutrality of ownership and public service obligations (European Commission, 2003: 13–14).

Despite the radically pro-commodification attitude of the Commissioner and the ambitious tone in the reviewed policy documents, the text of the directive proposed by the Commission on the Services in the Internal Market eventually treated the water sector as an exception. The Commission's proposal, published in March 2004, allowed for derogations for non-economic services of general interest (including water) from the country-of-origin principle, the most controversial part of the directive (see Chapter 7). The scope of the Services Directive in its final form (2006/123/EC) is even more restrictive, excluding not only 'water distribution' but also 'water distribution and supply services and wastewater services'. EU legislators finally excluded water services from the final directive as a result of transnational protests in favour of people's access to water as a human right – a claim that found support in the European Parliament and among central member state governments (Crespy, 2016). We discuss the development of vital countermovements in more detail in section 9.4.

9.3 EU GOVERNANCE OF WATER SERVICES AFTER THE SHIFT TO NEG

In section 9.2, we have shown that the exclusion of water services from the EU Services Directive prevented an EU-wide commodification of the water sector, even though amendments to the EU directives on drinking water and wastewater gradually introduced new provisions in favour of user charges and an increasing involvement of private capital in the sector. In this section, we assess the EU governance of water services after the 2008 financial crisis, which ushered in the NEG era in EU policymaking, first in the form of immediate crisis management in specific countries and then perpetuated in time and extended to all member states by the European Semester (Erne, 2018, 2019).

As outlined in Chapter 2, the European Semester is a yearly process of coordination, scrutiny, and correction of member states' economic and social policies. The Semester targets these policies in a bid to avoid fiscal and macro-economic imbalances and to promote structural reforms. The main legal acts of NEG are the Council Recommendations on National Reform Programmes that the Council issues every year to each member state in the Semester process. These acts of the Council contain a set of country-specific recommendations (CSRs) on the measures that each member state should implement to achieve NEG's goals. For those member states that received bailout packages, the Council Recommendations prescribed that they should follow the instructions of the Memoranda of Understanding (MoUs) and their updates, that is, the legal documents attached to their financial assistance (bailout) programmes.

Given the country-specific methodology of the NEG regime, in this book we limit our analysis to four countries that represent the diversity of the EU in terms of size, geographical location, and economic development (including development of water infrastructure): Germany, Ireland, Italy, and Romania. Ireland and Romania were both subject to bailout programmes, so, in their case, the NEG framework gained an extra layer of importance.

How does the water sector feature in the NEG regime? First, the increasing surveillance of member states and the tighter integration of fiscal policies with structural reform in NEG enables EU-level actors to pursue a commodification agenda targeting the water sector by new and more efficient means (Golden, Szabó, and Erne, 2021). Second, the presence of the water sector in CSRs gives further proof of NEG's comprehensive nature. Despite being relatively small in terms of GDP and employment share, water services feature in MoUs and CSRs, and the prescriptions are much more detailed than any previous legal instrument.

In the following, we present the findings of our analysis of NEG prescriptions relevant to the water sector in Germany, Ireland, Italy, and Romania. Our basic unit of analysis is the NEG prescription, that is, a specific statement calling on a member state to implement a certain policy measure or to achieve a specific policy goal (Chapter 5). We extracted these prescriptions from the NEG documents mentioned above: the country-specific Council Recommendations as well as the MoUs and their updates. As the water sector is not targeted only in explicit NEG documents, we extended our analysis to NEG prescriptions that target broader areas of which the water sector is part: that is, local public services, network industries, and public utilities.[2] We inferred whether these general prescriptions had relevance for the water sector by looking at supplementary information: the recitals of the Council Recommendations and Country Reports issued by the Commission as part of the Semester process. When analysing the policy orientation of a specific NEG prescription, we also considered its policy- and country-related semantic context (Chapters 4 and 5).

In this section, we analyse the policy orientation of NEG prescriptions in water services: whether they advocated commodification or decommodification and to what extent they added up to an overarching script. To achieve this goal, we first grouped the prescriptions using the categories of coverage levels and cost-coverage mechanisms (pertaining to people's access to services) and of resource levels, provider-level governance, and sector-level governance (on the provision of services). These categories reflect the broad thematic target areas of NEG prescriptions, and commodification can mean different things in each of them, as demonstrated in Table 9.1, which summarises the main themes of the prescriptions. Following the discussions provided in our methodological Chapters 4 and 5, we recall here that the two main channels of commodification are linked to either a decrease in resources (curtailment) or the introduction of structural reforms (marketisation). The latter covers commodifying prescriptions in the categories of access and service-level and provider-level governance.

---

[2] If a prescription was targeting another subsector in these broader fields (for example, transport within network industries), we did not include the prescription in the analysis.

We provide an Online Appendix with the text of the policy prescriptions as they appeared in the NEG documents (Tables A9.1–A9.4). We have grouped them in tables according to the categories mentioned above and the main themes of the prescriptions. Before doing so, we analysed the recitals of the corresponding Council Recommendation and the Commission's Country Report, also taking into account our own country-specific knowledge regarding the management of the water sector and its discontents. This analytical, context-specific approach enabled us to reveal the policy orientation of country-specific NEG prescriptions and the overarching policy scripts informing them. Table 9.2 accounts for the different degrees of coercive

TABLE 9.1 *Themes of NEG prescriptions on water services (2009–2019)*

		Policy orientation	
	Categories	*Decommodifying*	*Commodifying*
Provision of services	Resource levels	Increase public investment (DE) Prioritise public investment (IE) Extend basic infrastructure in rural areas (RO)	
	Sector-level governance mechanisms		Foster market access (IT) Remove restrictions to competition (IT) Rectify in-house awards (IT) Increase the value of public contracts open to procurement (DE) Address planning constraints (DE)
	Provider-level governance mechanisms		Create water utility (IE) Increase efficiency and quality of public enterprises (IT)
Access to services	Cost-coverage mechanisms		Introduce water charges (IE)
	Coverage levels	Improve access to integrated public services (RO)	

Source: Council Recommendations on National Reform Programmes; Memoranda of Understanding. See Online Appendix, Tables A9.1–A9.4.
Country code: DE = Germany; IE = Ireland; IT = Italy; RO = Romania.

TABLE 9.2 *Categories of NEG prescriptions on water services by coercive power*

	Decommodifying				Commodifying			
	DE	IE	IT	RO	DE	IE	IT	RO
2009								
2010						◆		
2011						◆■		
2012						◆■	●	
2013					○	◆■	○	
2014					○		●	
2015	△						●	
2016	△	△		△ ☆			●■	
2017	△	△			○		●	
2018	△	△		△			●■	
2019	△	△					■	

Source: Council Recommendations on National Reform Programmes; Memoranda of Understanding. See Online Appendix, Tables A9.1–A9.4.
Categories: △ = resource levels; ○ = sector-level governance; □ = provider-level governance; ☆ = coverage levels; ◊ = cost-coverage mechanisms.
Coercive power: ▲●■◆ = very significant; ▲●■★ = significant; △○□☆◊ = weak. Country code: DE = Germany; IE = Ireland; IT = Italy; RO = Romania.

212

power of these NEG prescriptions in a given year and country, with MoU prescriptions having the strongest enforcement power and prescriptions issued without any reference to specific correction and sanctioning mechanisms having the weakest enforcement power (see Chapter 2; Jordan, Maccarrone, and Erne, 2021).

Table 9.2 presents the summary of the findings from our analysis. Commodification is the overarching theme that connects the NEG prescriptions across countries and over time. Of the four countries analysed here, only Romania did not receive prescriptions in the NEG framework to commodify its water sector. However, the lack of commodification prescriptions for Romania can be explained by the fact that the most profitable segments of the country's water infrastructure were already in private hands. Since 2000, for example, a subsidiary of the French utilities TNC Veolia has been operating Bucharest's water services under a twenty-five-year-long concession contract (Hall and Lobina, 2007: 70; PPI Project Database, 2016).

Germany, Ireland, and Italy all received commodification prescriptions, although with different thematic focuses, with varying degrees of coercive power and varying persistence over time. Ireland received prescriptions with very significant coercive power linked to bailout conditionality between 2010 and 2013. These prescriptions covered the categories of access to services and provider-level governance. The prescriptions issued to Germany and Italy addressed predominantly questions of competition between providers. The coercive power of the prescriptions for Italy was significant, except those issued in 2012 and 2013, whereas the coercive power of all prescriptions issued to Germany was weak throughout the whole period.

Table 9.2 also reveals that the main channel through which the NEG regime advanced commodification in the water sector was marketisation. There were no specific, commodifying prescriptions issued for the water sector in the quantitative, resource-level category. Even so, public water services were affected by the cross-sectoral prescriptions to curtail public spending (see Chapter 7). Instead, the water-specific commodifying prescriptions were all about making the management of water services more market-conforming, through structural reforms in the categories of cost-coverage mechanisms and provider-level and sector-level governance, starting with the MoU conditionality of the Irish bailout programme in 2010 to introduce water charges, all the way to Italy's 2019 NEG prescription to make local public services more efficient.

Overall, decommodifying NEG prescriptions on the water sector were much less prominent. They had a shorter and a less persistent presence and a much weaker coercive power. Decommodification prescriptions started appearing only in 2015. They did not overwrite commodification prescriptions but rather ran parallel to them (commodification prescriptions continued to be issued to Italy up until 2019); this calls into question claims of scholars who saw a shift towards social prescriptions after 2014 (Zeitlin and Vanhercke, 2018). We now proceed to analyse the prescriptions in more detail, across the four categories, in the order that they first appeared in CSRs or MoUs, starting with users' access to services.

Prescriptions on Users' Access to Water Services

Cost-coverage mechanisms: Among the four countries under study here, Ireland received the most detailed and explicit NEG prescriptions to commodify its water sector through the introduction of household water charges. The primary goal of the charges was to make user access conditional upon payment; therefore, these prescriptions fall under the category of access to services in general and cost-coverage mechanisms in particular. The establishment of a commercial relationship between service providers and users had links to the categories of resources for providers and provider-level governance. The original MoU of 2010 and its updates until 2013 repeated two general goals for Irish governments to follow: the transfer of responsibilities from local authorities to a national water utility (later to be named Irish Water; now Uisce Éireann) and the introduction of water charges.[3] The introduction of water charges is a clear example of how the NEG regime interpreted environmental principles in a commodifying way and how it used fiscal policy tools to promote marketising structural reforms.

The MoU signed in December 2010 committed the Irish government 'to move towards full cost-recovery in the provision of water services' (MoU, Ireland, 16 December 2010: Memorandum of Economic and Financial Policies, 8, paragraph 24), despite Ireland having received a derogation from the cost recovery principle in the EU WFD in 2000 to protect its system of financing water provision for domestic users from general taxation. The introduction of water charges in the bailout programme would have put an end to this derogation recognised in EU law.

The sixth update of the MoU committed the Irish authorities to 'consider and provide an update on the general government debt and deficit treatment implications of establishment of Irish Water' (MoU, Ireland, 6th update, 13 September 2012). The seventh and eighth updates demanded that, over time, the Irish government's budget plans should 'be based on Irish Water

---

[3] In Ireland, water provision has been financed from general taxation since 1996. Private households do not pay any charges, unlike commercial users of water services (Murphy, 2019).

becoming substantially self-funded' (MoU, Ireland, 7th update, 25 January 2013; 8th update, 12 April 2013).

The discussion of water charges in the context of cost recovery and government deficit would suggest that the main purpose of the introduction of the charges was related to the curtailment of public spending. Given the small share of the sector in government spending however, revenues expected from the introduction of domestic water charges would have provided only a small contribution to fiscal adjustment (European Commission, 2014c: 30). The primary goal of charging for water was therefore not to ensure the environmental protection of water, and not even to balance budgets, but to marketise access to water and introduce the cash nexus into the relationship between users and providers.

Updates to Ireland's MoUs between 2011 and 2013 prescribed ever more detailed measures towards the introduction of water charges, including the collection of precise data on the progress of water meter installation. The ninth and tenth updates of the 2013 MoUs contain numerical annexes on 'the quantum of pre-installation surveys completed, and water meters installed by geographical area' (MoU, Ireland, 9th update, 3 June 2013; MoU, Ireland, 10th update, 11 September 2013). Nevertheless, the Troika left Ireland before the introduction of water charges and even before the installation of water meters had finished. The introduction of water charges triggered a long wave of social-movement and union protests in Ireland in 2014 and 2015, including a water bill boycott campaign supported by large sections of the Irish population, which eventually forced the government to suspend the charging system in 2016 (Hilliard, 2018; Bieler, 2021; Moore, 2023). After 2013, the EU's NEG prescriptions no longer mentioned water charges, even though the Commission's Country Reports continued to monitor Irish governments' attempts to introduce them. By contrast, EU executives issued no prescriptions to Germany, Italy, and Romania on user access, as their water systems were already financed mainly by user charges and tariffs (Armeni, 2008; ver.di, 2010).

Coverage levels: Only Romania received a decommodifying prescription in the access to services category, pertaining to coverage levels. In 2016, Romania received an NEG prescription that urged the Romanian government to improve people's access to integrated public services in disadvantaged rural areas where water and waste-water services are often simply lacking (Council Recommendation Romania 2016/C 299/18).[4] If one assesses this prescription

---

[4] In 2020, only 67 per cent of Romania's rural population had access to safely managed drinking water services, compared with Slovakia: 98 per cent, Hungary: 89 per cent, Brazil: 72 per cent, Algeria: 69 per cent, or Bangladesh: 62 per cent (United Nations, SDG statistics indicator 6.1.1. https://sdg6data.org/en/maps).

in its semantic context, it appears to have been motivated by genuine concerns about social inclusion, but, compared with NEG's countervailing commodifying prescriptions, this social prescription was much less specific. Neither the NEG prescription nor the corresponding Country Report (Commission, Country Report Romania SWD (2016) 91) outlined how such an extension of people's access to public services could be financed. The prescription was also merely aspirational given its weak enforcement power, by contrast to those related to MoU-, excessive deficit-, or excessive macroeconomic imbalance procedures.

Prescriptions on the Provision of Water Services

Provider-level governance mechanisms: Marketising structural reforms formulated within the NEG framework did not only aim to set up new market-conforming rules for users' access to water services. They also intervened in the ownership and internal operation structure of the public entities that provide these services. Here, we see a break with the methods of the ordinary legislative procedures that formally respected the neutrality of ownership principle laid out in Art. 345 TFEU (Golden, Szabó, and Erne, 2021). Breaking with this tradition, NEG prescriptions explicitly declared that governments should copy the more efficient private sector as the operating model for the water sector, even though they stopped short of calling for direct privatisation.

In Ireland, local governments provided water services until 2013, when, as part of MoU conditionality, a new law transferred water services to the newly incorporated national utility firm, Irish Water (Hilliard, 2018). Although water charges were abolished in 2017 after sustained mass protest, the corporate model of service provision remained intact, with important commodifying implications for water workers who were going to lose local government employee status and the protections laid down in public sector collective agreements. To fend off this threat, in 2022, Irish unions secured an agreement at the Irish Workplace Relations Commission, whereby Irish Water and local authorities pledged that there would be no compulsory transfer of staff from local authorities to Irish Water (ICTU, 2022). This agreement, however, does not stop Irish Water from hiring new staff members on worse terms and conditions.

In Italy, NEG prescriptions outlined how the government should transform the operation of state-owned enterprises. In this area, the two most frequently repeated goals were the reform of publicly owned enterprises, on the one hand, and efficiency improvements, on the other, fitting the general principles of new public management (Kahancová and Szabó, 2015).

Sector-level governance mechanisms: Within the broader issues of sector-level governance, the introduction of market relations between providers dominated the prescriptions issued to Germany and Italy. The two countries received similar NEG prescriptions about improving market access and promoting competition between service providers. The prescriptions condemned the allegedly high share of in-house awards for the delivery of public services and promoted the opening up of these contracts to procurement procedures and concessions. Another NEG prescription, issued to Germany in 2013, called for an increase in the value of public contracts open to procurement (Council Recommendation Germany 2013/C 217/09). Although the content was similar, the tone of the 2014 prescription was less sharp, as it demanded only that the German government should 'identify the reasons behind the low value of public contracts open to procurement under EU legislation' (Council Recommendation Germany 2014/C 247/05). Germany continued to receive recommendations to enhance competition between 2014 and 2017 but with a specific focus on the railway sector (see Chapter 8) and, later, professional and business services. German local public services received one more commodifying prescription in 2017, when the CSRs identified planning constraints as a hindrance to investment.

The Italian case provides the most consistent example of how the NEG regime advanced commodification of the water sector through marketising reforms. Unlike in the German and the Irish CSRs, the commodifying prescriptions in the Italian CSRs were not counterbalanced by decommodifying prescriptions, and they formed a coherent theme even after the alleged social turn of the European Semester in 2014 (Zeitlin and Vanhercke, 2018). Calls to open up local public services and network industries to competition appeared first in the Italian CSRs in 2012, prescribing the adoption of specific laws to achieve this goal. In particular, the 2013 Country Report for Italy picked water services as a negative example where no progress had been made in the promotion of competitiveness and efficiency, whereas it welcomed the separation of the operator from the network manager in the gas sector (Commission, Country Report Italy SWD (2013) 362). The Commission's criticism came after Italian citizens voted in June 2011 by a more than 95 per cent majority to repeal the law that allowed the private sector to manage local public services. Incidentally, the centre-right Berlusconi government tried to invalidate this abrogative referendum in favour of public water services by calling on citizens to boycott it, but the Italian social movements and trade unions that had launched the referendum nevertheless succeeded, as it exceeded the 50 per cent participation quorum laid down in Italian law (Bieler, 2015). The abrogation of the law by referendum, however, did not prevent both centre-right and centre-left governments from reintroducing similar laws at national and regional level afterwards (Di Giulio and Galanti, 2015; Erne and Blaser, 2018).

Resources for public water services: The decommodifying prescriptions issued for Germany, Ireland, and Romania focused on resources for providers. By contrast, Italy did not get any decommodifying prescriptions on water services. After 2015, Germany received prescriptions that tasked its government to increase investment in public infrastructure, particularly at local level. The emphasis on municipalities is crucial from the perspective of the water sector, as in Germany the provision of water services is the responsibility of municipalities, and at the same time municipalities were under severe fiscal pressure from the German debt brake (*Schuldenbremse*) and EU deficit rules (Bajohr, 2015).

Investment in water also featured in NEG prescription issued to Ireland. Four of them directly and specifically dealt with the water sector between 2016 and 2019, tasking the Irish government to invest more in water services. Investment in water was never a stand-alone item but rather part of a broader productive, public infrastructure agenda. We labelled these prescriptions as decommodifying as seen in Table 9.2. Although the direction of NEG prescriptions on the resources for water was decommodifying, we must qualify this assessment on two counts.

First, the corresponding Irish NEG prescriptions from 2016 and 2017 used the term 'prioritise government expenditure' in the water sector, implying that additional public investment in the water sector must be counterbalanced by cutbacks in other areas (Council Recommendations Ireland 2016/C 299/16 and 2017/C 261/07). The same holds true in the Romanian case, where the 2016 NEG prescription on infrastructure projects in the waste-water sector called for a 'prioritisation' of investment in them (Council Recommendation Romania 2018/C 320/22).

Second, EU executives linked the need for increased investment to water charges as a potential source of extra funding (Commission, Country Report Ireland SWD (2016) 77: 62). The Commission's Country Report also justified the need for more resources to compensate for the preceding 'seven years of sharply reduced government investment' that 'have taken a toll on the quality and adequacy of infrastructure' (Commission, Country Report Ireland SWD (2016) 77: 4 and 61). The report, however, is oblivious of the reasons why there was underinvestment in the first place. It did not mention that the MoUs' cost-cutting recommendations had played their part in underinvestment.

Pursuing the Commodification of the Water Sector through NEG Prescriptions

To summarise the findings of our analysis of NEG prescriptions: we uncovered a transnational agenda of commodification in the water sector in

Germany, Ireland, and Italy. We explained the absence of commodifying prescriptions for Romania by the fact that its government had already achieved the commodification of its lucrative urban water services in the run-up to EU accession. In the other three countries, NEG prescriptions continued the commodifying agenda that had its roots in the Commission's legislative agenda preceding NEG, starting with the commodification turn of EU environmental laws and Commissioner Bolkestein's attempts at water services liberalisation in the early 2000s. EU executives linked the introduction of water charges in Ireland explicitly to the WFD's cost recovery principle, even though Ireland had secured an opt-out from it in EU law. NEG prescriptions targeted the Irish system of financing public water provision from general taxation, which the European Commission (2003: 14) had already denounced in 2003. EU executives also formulated the NEG prescriptions for Germany and Italy to open up local public water services to external competition in the spirit of Commissioner Bolkestein's draft Services Directive (COM (2004) 2 final/3). The European Commission and the Council of finance ministers could do that, as the shift to the NEG regime empowered them to pursue an agenda that had been rejected by the European Parliament when it comprehensively excluded the water sector from the final Services Directive (2006/123/EC). Our analysis also revealed that commodifying prescriptions exclusively targeted qualitative characteristics of water governance through marketising structural reforms. By contrast, there were no water sector-related prescriptions that tasked member states to curtail the resources for them. We must, however, reiterate here that water services had also been affected by the prescriptions that tasked governments to cut public spending in general (see Chapter 7).

Concretely, all qualitative NEG prescriptions that targeted water services governance mechanisms, namely, those on cost-coverage mechanisms and provider-level and sector-level governance, pointed in a commodifying policy direction across all years and all countries. This means that they were informed by an overarching policy script of commodification. We also observed a few decommodifying prescriptions that called for quantitative changes, namely, more public resources for the German, Irish, and Romanian water sectors and an expansion of service coverage levels in Romania. These decommodifying prescriptions, however, were not only scarce and weaker in terms of their coercive power but also informed by a reasoning that did not contradict the overarching commodifying policy script of NEG, with one exception. All qualitative NEG prescriptions on the governance mechanisms for water services followed a common logic of commodification across countries and time, with the exception of Romania, which, as explained, had already privatised the lucrative water services in its urban areas in the run-up to its EU accession. Hence, NEG's overarching commodification script extended to all country cases, regardless of their location in the EU's political economy. At the same time, the coercive power of the corresponding NEG prescriptions still differed across them, ranging from very significant in the Irish case during the MoU period, to significant in the Italian case in the face of excessive economic imbalances, to weak in the German case, mirroring their different locations in the NEG enforcement regime at a given time.

Whereas all commodifying NEG prescriptions served the same overarching policy agenda, the decommodifying prescriptions received by Ireland, Germany, and Romania were semantically linked to other aims, namely, boosting competitiveness and growth, rebalancing the EU economy, social inclusion, or transition to a green economy. In the Irish case, EU executives linked several decommodifying prescriptions for more investments in the ailing water sector to investment prioritisation to boost competitiveness and growth. Hence, the aims that informed these prescriptions were compatible with further austerity in other areas that were not deemed as so critical to achieving this objective. The aim of boosting competitiveness and growth through more investments in water services also played a key role in Germany. By contrast to Ireland however, the investment turn in German NEG prescriptions was unqualified, as it extended to the entire public sector and to all levels of government. This echoes the presence of another objective in the German case, namely, NEG's rebalancing of the European economy agenda. As increased public investments would boost domestic demand in Germany, they would also contribute to a reduction of the trade imbalance between Germany and other countries located in more peripheral positions of the EU economy (see Chapters 6 and 7). At the same time, EU executives continued to issue commodifying prescriptions that urged the German government to reform the mechanisms governing the water sector in a market-conforming way. In turn, the German government added a greater involvement of private capital and know-how in municipal infrastructure projects as a priority in its 2017 national reform programme (Bundesministerium für Wirtschaft und Energie, 2017: 17). Hence, the decommodification prescriptions that aimed to boost competitiveness and growth and/or to rebalance the EU economy did not go against NEG's overarching commodification script (Chapter 11).

Romania and Ireland also received decommodifying prescriptions, which did not contradict NEG's overarching commodification script. In 2018 and 2019, the Irish prescriptions on the prioritisation of public investment mentioned the role of 'improved infrastructure' as a 'critical enabler' for the 'enhancement of private investment and productivity growth' and not just for 'balanced regional economic development' and Ireland's 'transition towards a low-carbon and environmentally resilient economy' (Council Recommendation Ireland 2018/C 320/07: Recital 12). The policy rationale of enhanced social inclusion, which clearly goes against NEG's overarching commodification script, guided NEG water prescriptions only once, namely, in the case of the 2016 prescription that tasked the Romanian government to extend basic infrastructure 'in particular in rural areas' (Council Recommendation Romania 2016/C 299/18) to reduce Romania's key development disparities 'between urban and rural areas' (2016: Recital 17). When EU executives repeated this 2016 prescription in 2018 however, they stressed the benefits of quality infrastructure for economic growth rather than social inclusion (Council Recommendation Romania 2018/C 320/22: Recital 19), even though large parts of Romania's rural population still had no access to safe drinking water, by contrast to all EU countries and even many developing countries (see footnote 4). If we consider the scarcity and the weak coercive power of the prescriptions that were at least partially informed by social concerns, we can hardly speak about a social turn of the NEG regime (Zeitlin and Vanhercke, 2018). Likewise, the equivocal semantic links between the weak 2018 and 2019 prescriptions on the prioritisation of public investment in water services for Ireland and the transition to a green economy hardly warrant speaking about an ecological shift in the NEG regime either. Whereas these semantic links prefigured the growing importance of a green agenda in the post-Covid NEG regime (Chapter 12), our preceding analysis of the market terminology in the WFD indicates that the growing salience of green concerns does not necessarily lead to a policy shift in a decommodifying direction.

EU Governance of Water Services by Law after the Shift to NEG

EU executives pursued a water services commodification agenda already before 2009, but their NEG prescriptions went further, as the scope of NEG interventions was much more ambitious. NEG prescriptions in the water sector targeted areas that were considered taboo during earlier phases of EU integration, such as directly prescribing a change in the legal status or operating principles of public services. We should add, however, that the interaction between ordinary legislative procedures and NEG went in both directions. NEG has not replaced the traditional sources of EU authority. The EU's ordinary legislative processes run parallel with NEG mechanisms, including in the water sector. There have been four prominent cases of intervention or intervention attempts by ordinary EU laws in the water sector since the shift to NEG after the financial crisis: namely, the Concessions Directive (2014/23/EU), the revised

Procurement Directives (2014/24/EU, 2014/25/EU), and the recast of the Drinking Water Directive (2020/2184).

A concession is a long-term contractual relationship between a contractor and a service provider, a step beyond the short-term (one-off) and unidirectional relationship of procurement. As the contractor is typically a public body and the provider is a private firm in these relationships, the legal form of the concession is closely linked with the increased use of PPPs (Porcher and Saussier, 2018). In 2011, the Commission proposed a stand-alone directive on concessions, which would have facilitated the use of the concession model in water services across the EU. The Concessions Directive would have benefitted French water TNCs, as concessions law was the legal framework that contributed to their successful long-term operation in France (Guérin-Schneider, Breuil, and Lupton, 2014). The spread of the concession model to other parts of the EU would have vested these companies with a competitive advantage over other service providers that were used to a different legal regime. In reaction to the success of the Right2Water ECI, however, the Commission excluded water from the final scope of the directive (see section 9.4). The parallel development of the NEG regime and policymaking by ordinary EU laws is also shown by the fact that Germany received NEG prescriptions to increase the value of contracts open to public procurement in 2013 and 2014, that is, the same years when EU legislators revised the Procurement and Concessions Directives.

Whereas the draft Concessions Directive attempted to commodify water services through ordinary EU laws, the recasting of the Procurement Directives and the DWD also included potentially decommodifying policy features. The legislative procedure for the Concession Directive ran in parallel with the recasting of the Procurement Directives. Pressure from unions and social movements, including the European Federation of Public Service Unions (EPSU), forced the inclusion in the Procurement Directives of stipulations about social and environmental clauses in procurement calls (see Chapter 7; Fischbach-Pyttel, 2017). Likewise, the recast DWD dealt with a social question in detail, namely, that of people's access to drinking water. Art. 16 of the directive advances the decommodification of water by obliging member states to improve or maintain access to safe drinking water for all, with a focus on the most vulnerable social groups. The non-binding Pillar of Social Rights adopted by all EU institutions in 2017 included water as an essential service with access rights for everybody, but the new DWD gave a more tangible expression to this principle (EPSU, 2021).

Both the exemption of water from the Concessions Directive and the inclusion of water access rights in the DWD were prompted by the pressure that social movements exerted on EU policymakers, namely, through the Right2Water ECI coordinated by EPSU. The transnational countermovements fighting for the right to water at European level, however, started much earlier. They are the subject of section 9.4.

9.4 TRANSNATIONAL COUNTERMOVEMENTS AGAINST THE COMMODIFICATION OF WATER

So far, we have assessed EU executives' attempts to commodify water services, either through the EU's ordinary legislative procedure or its country-specific NEG prescriptions. We now assess the protests by social movements and unions that they triggered. National and transnational protest movements successfully blocked several commodification attempts; for example, the inclusion of water and sanitation services in the commodifying EU Services Directive and the introduction of water charges, as requested by the NEG prescriptions for Ireland (Moore, 2018, 2023; Bieler, 2021). In contrast, these countervailing protest movements were less effective in advancing a proactive agenda of enshrining the right to water in EU law.

EPSU had played an important role in the transnational countermovements in the sector since the mobilisations against Commissioner Bolkestein's plan to include water in the services directive. The Bolkestein Directive had been important, as it was then that the 'Commission first showed its true colours' (interview, member of the European water movement and EPSU official, Brussels, December 2018). Since then, EPSU has been co-organising several transnational mobilisations politicising the EU governance of water services, namely, for the right to water and against the privatisation of water services, as shown in Table 9.3, which is based on the transnational protest database (Erne and Nowak, 2023).

The transnational protest events in the European water sector targeted EU executives' vertical attempts in favour of water commodification, starting with Commissioner Bolkestein's proposal for an EU Services Directive in 2004. In comparison with the transport sector, which had already been facing commodifying EU interventions much earlier, we did not find any evidence of transnational protests in the water sector before that date (see Chapter 8). In the Bolkestein case, EPSU was a leading organiser within a broad coalition against this directive. EPSU also used its links to members of the European Parliament, convincing it to push back against the Commission's most radical proposals and to remove the most controversial elements of the directive (Crespy, 2016). Bolkestein's failed attempt to commodify water services also shaped subsequent struggles. The experience of mobilisation against

TABLE 9.3 Transnational protests politicising the EU governance of water services (1993–2019)

Date	Location	Action type	Topic	Coordinators
5 June 2004	Brussels	Demonstration	Bolkestein Directive, 'Non à la directive Bolkestein – Oui à l'Europe sociale'	ETUC, other unions, social movements
24 November 2004	Brussels	Demonstration	Bolkestein Directive, 'Bolkestein Directive = Frankenstein Directive'	ETUC, other unions, social movements
19 March 2005	Brussels	Demonstration	Bolkestein Directive: 'More and better jobs - Defending social Europe - Stop Bolkestein'	ETUC, other unions, social movements
21 March 2005	Brussels	Demonstration	Bolkestein Directive	European Anti-Poverty Network
15 October 2005	Multi-sited	Demonstration	Bolkestein Directive, European action day	ETUC, other unions, social movements
25 October 2005	Strasbourg	Demonstration	Bolkestein Directive	ETUC, other unions, social movements
11 February 2006	Strasbourg, Berlin	Demonstration	Bolkestein Directive	DGB, ETUC, Attac
14 February 2006	Strasbourg	Demonstration	Bolkestein Directive: 'Services for the people', Bolkestein Directive	ETUC
22 March 2006	Brussels	Demonstration	World Water Day: against water privatisation	EPSU, environmental groups, water activists, developmental organisations

19 March 2007	Brussels	Demonstration	Against water privatisation	EPSU, NGOs, participants of World Water Assembly
10 May 2012 – 1 November 2013	Multi-sited	European Citizens' Initiative	Water and sanitation are a human right! Water is a public good, not a commodity! (Right2Water)	EPSU, other unions, social movements
22 March 2015	Brussels, Dublin, multi-sited	Demonstration	World Water Day: Human right to water services. Against water privatisation	EPSU, other unions, social movements
22 March 2017	Multi-sited	Demonstration	World Water Day: Water and sanitation are human rights	EPSU, European Water Movement

Source: Transnational Socioeconomic Protest Database (Erne and Nowak, 2023).
The table includes protest events targeting political authorities in relation to the European governance of water services, using the database's political level category, excluding socioeconomic protests at company, sectoral, and systemic level.

Bolkestein played a significant role in EPSU's decision to launch its ECI on the right to water, which turned out to be the first successful ECI in EU history (Fischbach-Pyttel, 2017: 187; Bieler, 2017; Szabó, Golden, and Erne, 2022).

The Commission registered EPSU's ECI on the right to water in May 2012 under its full title: 'Water and sanitation are a human right! Water is a public good, not a commodity!'. EPSU was the first organisation to be able, in close collaboration with social movements, to collect the one million signatures required to make this new instrument of direct democracy legally valid at EU level. The final number of signatures submitted to the European Commission in December 2013 was 1,659,543, surpassing the ECI's national-level signature thresholds in thirteen countries (Szabó, Golden, and Erne, 2022), even though ECIs must reach the thresholds, which are linked to population size, in only seven EU member states to be legally valid.

As the full title of the initiative indicates, EPSU mobilised the public by uniting defensive and proactive goals: defending water from commodification, on the one hand, and securing the human right to water, on the other. By focusing its struggle on the fight against commodification and privatisation, EPSU identified concrete negative practices against which popular discontent could be targeted: the pro-commodification policy ideas of the Commission and the lobbying of big TNCs active in water services, such as Veolia and Suez.

The other leg of the Right2Water campaign, fighting for water to become a human right, was encompassing enough to form the basis of a broad coalition, as the campaign united actors with different ideas on the details of water management and financing. Many organisations in the campaign were against water charges altogether. Others, such as the German union ver.di, one of the most active national organisations in the campaign, had a much more nuanced view on the subject. Ver.di supports domestic water charges if they guarantee the independence of non-commercial, local public providers, sustainable water management, the provision of good quality service, and decent working conditions in the sector (ver.di, 2010).

What did the Right2Water ECI achieve in substantive terms, apart from obliging the European Commission to issue a formal response? The defensive aspect of the campaign was successful, as the Commission excluded water from the scope of its draft Concessions Directive in June 2013 (Directive 2014/23/EU: Art. 12) even before the official conclusion of the ECI campaign. Although this was not a pre-defined target of the ECI campaign, the Concessions Directive caught campaigners' attention, especially in Germany (Parks, 2015: 72). In contrast, the proactive goal of securing water as a human right at European level proved to be a more challenging task for the initiative's organisers. EPSU's ultimate goal was to include strong legal guarantees of water decommodification with strong enforcement power. In other words, EPSU wanted to ensure EU laws that contained detailed mechanisms securing affordability and access to water for everyone. By contrast to the Commission's swift move to exempt water from the Concessions Directive, the revision of the DWD in a decommodifying direction was a drawn-out process of fits and starts, where EPSU often found itself on the margins of power struggles between EU institutions. Although EPSU submitted the ECI in December 2013, it took eight years to revise the DWD. Eventually, EPSU commended EU legislators' inclusion of access rights to safe drinking water in the recast DWD as a step in the right direction but still considered it insufficient (EPSU, 2021).

What is the relationship between the Right2Water ECI campaign and the NEG regime? The collection of signatures for the ECI took place over the years 2012–2013, coinciding with the peak of EU executives' commodifying NEG prescriptions for member states' water sectors. As shown in Table 9.2, in 2013, Germany, Ireland, and Italy simultaneously received commodifying NEG prescriptions that were relevant for their water sector. Even so, the ECI campaign did not achieve equal levels of support across the three countries.

The ECI received the strongest support in Germany out of all the EU member states in terms of absolute number of signatures and also regarding the number of collected signatures versus the required national validity threshold (1,236,455 versus 74,250, respectively, meaning that, if there had not been a requirement to pass the threshold in other member states too, Germany alone would have been able to carry the entire initiative). The German field operation of the ECI campaign relied on a broad coalition of unions and NGOs, many of which had long-standing experience in local struggles against water privatisation (Erne and Blaser, 2018; Moore, 2018; van den Berge et al., 2018). Furthermore, the signature collection received a boost from a popular TV show (*Die Anstalt*), which mentioned the campaign and linked it to looming threats coming from the proposed Concessions Directive (Parks, 2015). We also noticed a link between the plans for a Concessions Directive and the 2013 NEG prescriptions for Germany demanding an increase in the value of public contracts open to procurement. Concessions and procurement are separate mechanisms but have similar goals: they both target the relationship between public and private service providers.

The ECI organisers also had strong links to activists in Italy. The Italian Water Movements Forum (Forum Italiano dei Movimenti per L'acqua) was the main force behind a national referendum that repealed a law allowing private management of local public services in 2011, as mentioned above (Bieler, 2021 and 2017). Nonetheless, the ECI barely passed the threshold of 54,750 signatures in Italy with a final tally of 65,223. This could be due to organisers' fatigue and because abrogative Italian referendums do not preclude the reintroduction of similar laws by regional and national lawmakers afterwards (Di Giulio and Galanti, 2015; Erne and Blaser, 2018). EU executives' subsequent NEG prescriptions therefore recurrently tasked the Italian government to introduce such legislation to increase competition in local public services, despite the negative result of the 2011 referendum (Bieler, 2021: 87; van den Berge et al., 2018: 237).

Despite Ireland receiving several coercive NEG prescriptions between 2010 and 2013 that explicitly demanded measures to commodify its water sector, the few Irish Right2Water ECI campaigners at the time did not collect enough signatures to pass the required national ECI threshold. We attribute this in part to the time lag between the issuing of NEG prescriptions and their implementation by the Irish government. As discussed in section 9.3, the Troika left Ireland before the introduction of water charges and before the installation of water meters had been completed. The Irish Right2Water protests against the installation of water meters and the introduction of water charges intensified only gradually over the course of 2014, with a water charges boycott campaign and mass demonstrations at the end of that year (Bieler, 2021; Moore, 2023). The abolition of newly introduced water charges also became a central issue during the 2016 general election campaign; thus, water charges were in effect abolished in 2017 (Hilliard, 2018). Despite this apparent disconnect in the timing of popular mobilisation in mainland Europe and Ireland, there were significant links between the Irish and European campaigns. First, the Irish campaign borrowed its Right2Water slogan directly from the Right2Water ECI. Second, Sinn Féin's Lynn Boylan, member of the European Parliament in the left-wing GUE/NGL group between 2014 and 2019, was not only directly active in the Irish campaign but also coordinated the EU work on the follow-up to the Right2Water ECI as European Parliament rapporteur.

9.5 CONCLUSION

Vertical EU interventions in the governance of the water sector combine internal market rules and environmental policy. In this chapter, we have analysed the policy orientation of EU interventions in both areas before and after the EU's shift to its NEG regime in 2009.

EEC legislators had already started intervening in the water sector in the 1970s and 1980s to set harmonised standards on water quality. The first European directives related to the creation of the common market but nevertheless pointed in a decommodifying direction, as they aimed to guarantee a level playing field by taking water quality standards out of regulatory competition between member states. In the 1990s, ecological concerns and neoliberal views became an important motivation for the adoption of EU water and waste-water directives, which increasingly pointed in a commodifying policy direction. Despite the increasing interest of private capital in water management, however, the role of horizontal market pressures as a driver of water service commodification remained limited. In most member states, public administrations continued to manage water as a public service. In some cases, municipalities even brought them back under public management after having privatised them beforehand (Hall and Lobina, 2007; Kishimoto, Gendall, and Lobina, 2015). At the same time, most attempts by EU executives to create a European water services market by law failed, principally as a result of popular protests that led to the exclusion of the water sector from the final version of the 2006 Services Directive.

The financial crisis of 2008, however, ushered in a new era in water politics, as the shift to NEG gave EU executives new powers to pursue commodifying policy reforms. Although the amount of public spending on water was tiny in comparison with that for other public sectors, such as healthcare (see Chapter 10), all countries in our sample received commodifying NEG prescriptions; except Romania, which had already privatised its lucrative, urban water services in the run-up to its EU accession. Strikingly, all qualitative NEG prescriptions on the governance of water services or people's access to them pointed in a commodifying direction, regardless of time or the different positions of Germany, Ireland, and Italy in the EU's political economy. Even under NEG however, the proponents of water commodification found it difficult to realise their ambitions. EU executives failed to commodify water services even where they could rely on NEG prescriptions with very significant coercive power, namely, in Ireland during the Troika years. After 2015, EU executives began issuing quantitative NEG prescriptions on water services that pointed in a decommodifying direction. Most of them tasked member states to increase or prioritise public investments, not for social reasons but to rebalance the European economy and to increase its competitiveness. Concerns about enhanced social inclusion played a role in only one case, namely, the 2016 NEG prescriptions for Romania that tasked its government to improve users' access to integrated public services in disadvantaged rural areas. During the same period, EU legislators continued to exclude water services from commodifying EU directives, as happened in the case of the Concessions Directive (2014/23/EU). As discussed in Chapter 7, political countermovements forced the Commission to abandon its draft Services Notification Procedure Directive (COM (2016) 821 final), which would have obliged public authorities (including municipalities) to seek Commission approval before implementing any national or local laws, regulations, or administrative provisions on services covered by the 2006 Services Directive.

The main obstacle holding up these commodifying EU interventions was the rise of social movements and unions defending public water services at both EU and national level. EU executives' vertical commodification attempts triggered transnational countermovements for water as a human right, culminating in the successful Right2Water ECI. Commodifying NEG prescriptions on water services also ignited strong popular resistance, as the backlash against the introduction of water charges in Ireland has shown. Hence, the overarching commodifying policy orientation of vertical EU interventions in the water sector triggered successful, national and transnational, countermovements (Bieler, 2021; Szabó, Golden, and Erne, 2022; Moore, 2023). The failed water commodification attempts by both EU laws and NEG prescriptions until 2019, however, did not stop EU executives from pursing these goals by new means afterwards. Although the post-Covid pandemic NEG regime substantially increased the space for public investments, member states' access to EU recovery and resilience funding remained conditional upon the implementation of further commodifying public sector reforms, as we discuss in Chapters 12 and 13.

10

EU Governance of Healthcare and Its Discontents

10.1 INTRODUCTION

After 1945, European welfare states developed national healthcare systems to ensure universal access to health services through either national healthcare systems or national sickness funds. Until recently, policymakers and analysts alike therefore regarded healthcare as a preserve of national welfare states. However, although health services were initially hardly subject to vertical EU interventions, the pursuit of European market integration has increasingly given EU institutions room to intervene in the sector (De Ruijter, 2019; Stan and Erne, 2021a). In this chapter, we examine the policy orientation of EU interventions in healthcare and their impact on healthcare workers and users. Were EU interventions seeking to commodify health services and what union and social-movement counterreactions did they trigger?

First, we assess the European Treaties and the European laws adopted through the EU's legislative procedures, the community method. Here, we focus on regulations, directives, and Court of Justice of the European Union (CJEU) rulings affecting healthcare both before and after the 2008 financial crisis. Subsequently, we assess the policy direction of the EU's new economic governance (NEG) regime in healthcare.

Since the 1990s, the policy direction of EU laws affecting healthcare has shifted towards commodification. This trend continued when the European Commission and Council of finance ministers (EU executives) pursued their policy agenda primarily through NEG, despite the European Parliament and Council having excluded healthcare from the remit of the EU Services Directive. Our assessment of NEG healthcare prescriptions issued for Germany, Italy, Ireland, and Romania from 2009 to 2019 shows that EU executives consistently requested member states to contain public health expenditure and to marketise healthcare services.

EU interventions also triggered countervailing movements, as we show in section 10.4. The more unions realised that healthcare systems in different countries were affected by similar commodification pressures, the more they joined forces. The European Parliament and Council would not have excluded health from the scope of the Services Directive in 2006 if hundreds of thousands of protesters across Europe had not criticised the Commission's proposal beforehand. By contrast, the technocratic and *country-specific* methodology of the NEG regime made it more difficult for unions and social movements to politicise it across borders (Erne, 2015). Nonetheless, the Commission and the Council suspended one of NEG's disciplinary arms, the Stability and Growth Pact, in March 2020, when the Covid-19 pandemic vindicated those who had warned that the commodification of healthcare would entail fatal consequences (Stan and Erne, 2023).

10.2 THE GOVERNANCE OF HEALTHCARE BY EUROPEAN LAWS AND COURT RULINGS

Since the creation of the European Economic Community (EEC) in 1957, European policymakers have gradually gained more room to intervene in the healthcare sector. This process is rooted in three legislative strands: the internal market, public health, and fiscal governance (Greer, 2014). Of these, the internal market strand was the first to materialise. Hence, EU law affected healthcare long before healthcare was mentioned in European treaties. This means that any study of European healthcare governance must adopt an analytical perspective that encompasses all historical phases and legislative strands mentioned above.

Phase One: Decommodifying Cross-border Care to Create a European Labour Market

In the 1950s, EEC policymakers agreed to create a common market, while also building national welfare states that gave people access to health services without having to rely on the market. Although European policymakers across countries built different types of decommodified health and welfare services (Esping-Andersen, 1990), they agreed to foster workers' mobility across borders (Haas, 1958 [2004]). Consequently, the EEC facilitated the free movement of workers across borders by adopting regulations that gave them access to health services in their host countries. Hence, European law effectively decommodified access to cross-border care, although that was done to create a common labour market.

Although the EEC Treaty did not include healthcare among the Community's competences, it stipulated that 'The Council, acting by means of a unanimous vote on a proposal of the Commission, shall, in the field of social security, adopt the measures necessary to establish the free movement of workers' (Art. 51 TEEC, now Art. 48 TFEU). This led to the adoption of the EEC's third regulation (Regulation 3/58), which sought to build a common labour market by ensuring that workers' social security rights were safeguarded if they moved to another member state. These rights included 'the acquisition, maintenance, and recovery of the right to [medical] benefits' (Regulation 3/58). Although stopping short of harmonising social security systems (Hatzopoulos, 2005), the regulation recognised the public, solidaristic character of health services in EEC member states and sought to reconcile this with the treaty's articles on the free movement of workers. As seen in Chapter 4, solidaristic welfare provisions (including in healthcare) aimed to support capitalist accumulation by partially shielding labour from market forces. Likewise, the regulation aimed to create a European labour market by seeking to increase migrant workers' protection in the event of sickness, thus partially decommodifying their social reproduction.

In the next decades, the regulation's remit was extended from mobile workers to 'all nationals of Member States insured under social security schemes for employed persons' (Regulation 1408/1971) and, further, to self-employed persons, civil servants, students, and third country nationals. These extensions resulted in a patchy, category-specific coverage (Fillon, 2009) but went hand in hand with the building, since the Maastricht Treaty, of European citizenship (Kostakopoulou, 2007). By the mid-2000s, these developments had culminated in the adoption of the Citizens' Rights Directive setting out the conditions for the exercise of the right of free movement (2004/38/EC), a new amendment to Social Security Regulation (631/2004), and a new Regulation (883/2004) 'on the coordination of social security systems'. The amendment aligned the rights of the different categories of people introduced by previous extensions, thus reshaping what we could call a social security route to cross-border care along non-discriminatory lines.

The contribution of social security regulations to the decommodification of access to cross-border care has nonetheless not been without contradictions. Under the regulations, reimbursement of cross-border care has been at the charge of the country of origin (rather than of the host country or a European health fund). Thus, although the regulation recognises the principle of solidarity, it limits it to the country of origin. Moreover, as shall be seen below, since the 1980s, the CJEU has progressively encroached on the regulations' (and thus member states') dominion over access to cross-border care and its reimbursement (Fillon, 2009). In response, governments used the Amsterdam Treaty (1997) to state that European actions in public health should respect member states' 'responsibilities ... for the organisation and delivery of health services and medical care' (Art. 152 TEC, now 168 TFEU). This treaty change did not, however, prevent the EU from playing an ever-greater role in European healthcare governance, as outlined below.

In response to CJEU rulings, the Council and the European Parliament amended the social security regulations. The bone of contention was governments' use of pre-authorisation of cross-border care to keep healthcare expenditure under control. Pre-authorisation featured in the regulations as a condition for accessing care on changing residence to another member state as well as for accessing planned cross-border care, that is, care for which patients travel on purpose to another member state. Under pressure from CJEU case law, EU social security regulations had to stipulate the conditions under which member states may not refuse the authorisation (and thus the reimbursement) of cross-border care. Over time, these have moved from cases where competent (paying) countries cannot provide the treatment in question (Regulation 1408/1971), to those where they cannot provide it 'within a time limit which is medically justifiable' (Regulation 883/2004). In the process, member states' leeway in refusing the authorisation of cross-border care was reduced.

In addition, social security regulations allowed for coverage of unplanned cross-border care occurring during a temporary stay abroad. In this case, as no pre-authorisation was stipulated, the governance of access to cross-border care was left to medical professionals, who were to assess whether a migrant worker's 'condition ... necessitates immediate benefits' (Regulation 1408/1971) and, later on, whether insured persons needed 'medically necessary' care (Regulation 883/2004). The span of coverable care was consequently extended beyond strict emergencies.

The regulations further facilitated access to unplanned cross-border care by the introduction, in 2004, of the European Health Insurance Card (EHIC) (Regulation 631/2004). The card reflects the contradictory contribution of social security regulations to the decommodification of cross-border healthcare in Europe. Thus, on the one hand, the EHIC contributes to it inasmuch as it gives mobile Europeans who are insured in their home country access to health services in their host country under the same conditions as host country residents. The redistributive mechanisms on which decommodification is based remain, however, at national rather than EU level: it is the country of origin (rather than an EU healthcare fund) that bears the costs of cross-border care and of administering the card. As a result, care price differentials between poorer and richer countries and large differences in healthcare expenditure between countries entails EHIC being a notable financial burden for poorer member states, whereas the richer states profit from it (Stan, Erne, and Gannon, 2021). Given the unequally distributed means to engage in international travel across the EU (Hugree, Penissat, and Spire, 2020), the card's use has been uneven between different social classes and regions in the EU. EHIC use thus sustains rather than reduces healthcare inequalities across the EU; this goes against the EU's stated ambition to foster territorial and social cohesion (Stan and Erne, 2021b).

Through the social security regulations, EU law thus generated a limited, but definite, decommodifying potential for cross-border healthcare. From the 1990s onwards however, the single market, economic and monetary union (EMU), and EU accession processes put new pressures on healthcare spending, thereby triggering commodifying policy changes in the sector.

Phase Two: Single Market, EMU, and Healthcare Commodification

In a second phase, which shaped the 1990s, national health services began to be exposed to European market integration pressures – despite the introduction of a decommodifying public health title into the Maastricht Treaty in 1993. The treaty's EMU convergence criteria, however, were more consequential, as they led governments to restrain healthcare expenditure and to introduce reforms marketising their health services. In countries with healthcare services directly financed by state budgets, as in Italy and Ireland, these reforms were meant to help those countries meet the public debt and deficit criteria to join the eurozone. In countries where healthcare is financed through payroll taxes for sickness funds or health insurances, as in Germany, healthcare reforms were meant to contain unit labour costs to boost the country's competitiveness. In Central and Eastern Europe (CEE), the Copenhagen EU accession criteria exerted similar economic and fiscal adjustment pressures. As a result, the more policy reforms commodified healthcare services, the more they became subject to EU competition law, and corresponding Commission and CJEU actions.

Fiscal governance and healthcare commodification: In 1993, the Maastricht Treaty introduced 'ensuring a high level of health protection' among the objectives of the Community (Art. 3(o) TFEU) and the competences it shared with member states (Art. 4(k) TFEU). Although 'health protection' seems broad enough to include healthcare, the treaty's new health title referred only to public health (Art. 168 TFEU), implying that the EU may adopt legislation to prevent diseases rather than to treat them. Crucially however, the treaty not only mentioned public health but also urged a tighter coordination and convergence of member states' fiscal and macroeconomic economic policies. This treaty introduced debt and deficit convergence criteria and placed the Commission at the steering wheel of the multilateral surveillance process underpinning convergence (Arts. 121 and 126 TFEU). In a parallel process, the Copenhagen EU accession process created similar multilateral surveillance procedures. The resulting fiscal governance strand in EU healthcare law was thus born.

The fiscal convergence criteria placed increasing pressure on healthcare expenditure in EU member and accession states. In countries with taxation-financed health systems (like Italy and Ireland), convergence criteria put pressure on public budgets, which then trickled down to their healthcare component. This was the case for Italy, where public health expenditure fell from 6.6 per cent of GDP in 1991 to 5.3 per cent in 1995. Although it recovered thereafter, it was still below 6 per cent by 2000 (France, Taroni, and Donatini, 2005: 191–192). In response to increased international competition prompted by the European single market and EMU, many governments sponsored social pacts and other corporatist arrangements with social partners to moderate unit labour costs (Erne, 2008). In countries with payroll tax-financed health systems, governments also acted unilaterally to contain them. In Germany for example, the Schröder government not only curtailed wage growth with its Hartz labour market reforms (Chapter 6) but also cut payroll taxes for sickness funds by 0.9 per cent to boost Germany's competitiveness (Schulten, 2006). Thereafter, German sickness funds faced increased constraints, even though their budgets were not directly affected by national or EU debt-brake rules.

In response to pressures on healthcare expenditure, governments across Europe adopted healthcare reforms that sought to reduce their responsibility for funding and providing health services. These reforms took similar pathways, irrespective of whether healthcare was financed through national health systems or sickness funds. This was done either directly by curtailing resources for public healthcare or indirectly by making provider-level governance more market-like, by opening the sector to competition from private providers, and by privatising access to health services. In 2003 and 2004 for example, the Schröder government introduced the case-based (diagnostic-related groups: DRG) payment method for financing hospitals, reduced sickness funds' basic benefits package, and introduced co-payments for medical services (Busse and Blümel, 2014; Kunkel, 2021). Furthermore, many regional *Länder* and local governments privatised and corporatised their public hospitals in response to the fiscal constraints that they were facing, despite trade union and social-movement protests (Schulten, 2006; Erne and Blaser, 2018). Major publicly funded but privately owned for-profit healthcare operators emerged in turn. In Italy, healthcare reforms during the 1990s and 2000s transformed local healthcare providers into enterprises, opened the national health service to contracting with private providers, introduced from 1995 onwards the DRG method for hospital financing, and limited the basket of services in 2001 (Ferre et al., 2014; France, Taroni, and Donatini, 2005). During the 1990s and the 2000s, Ireland's healthcare system continued to be strongly reliant on private provision, with around half of the population having recourse to private insurance to access quicker treatment and doctors being allowed to treat private patients in private beds situated in public hospitals (McDaid et al., 2009). At the turn of the millennium, the Romanian government transformed its healthcare system from a state-funded national health system into an insurance-funded one and introduced the DRG method for financing hospitals. In 2006, a new law allowed the externalisation of services to private contractors and the opening of the national health fund to contracts with private providers (Stan, 2018; Stan and Toma, 2019).

The increased horizontal market integration pressures triggered by the European single market, EMU, and EU eastward enlargement led governments to commodify healthcare, albeit along varying dimensions and to different degrees. By doing that, governments sought not only to cut costs but also to use a governance-by-numbers approach (e.g., DRG financing methods) to insulate healthcare from democratic policymaking (Lascoumes and Le Galès, 2004; Kunkel, 2021). As shall be seen in section 10.3, this became relevant for the ways in which NEG was deployed across member states from 2008 on.

Healthcare and EU competition policy: As outlined in Chapter 7, since the launch of the single market programme by the Single European Act of 1986, the Commission has pushed for the commodification of public services, notably in network industries. Initially however, it excluded health services from this process. Nonetheless, the more healthcare reforms led to the commodification of health services, the more the CJEU could bring in EU competition law and treat health providers and insurers as undertakings engaged in commercial activities (Arts. 101–106 TFEU) (Hatzopoulos, 2005; Hervey and McHale, 2015). At the same time, the CJEU had to consider the notion of 'services of general economic interest' (SGEI) (Art. 106(2) TFEU), which provides a basis for exempting healthcare providers from competition rules (Hatzopoulos, 2005). In so doing however, the CJEU used 'purely economic' criteria in its assessment (2005: 159) and granted SGEI exceptions only on a case-by-case basis. As a result, it became 'almost impossible to know in advance with any degree of certainty whether EU competition rules will apply at all, and, if so, between which entities and to what degree' (2005: 160). These legal ambiguities allowed private healthcare operators and governments to instrumentalise EU competition law to promote the further commodification of healthcare systems (Kunkel, 2021).

In the 2005 legislative package adopted in response to the Altmark court case (Chapter 8), the Commission clarified the exemptions to EU restrictions on 'state aid' (Art. 107 TFEU) if an undertaking is paid for fulfilling a 'public service obligation' (Directive 2005/81/EC). The package specifically exempted compensations for hospitals providing SGEI from the notification procedure. Seven years later, the 2012 Almunia package extended this exemption from hospitals to 'health and long-term care more generally' (Decision 2012/21/EU), but only if SGEIs are provided at a cost that reflects 'the needs of an efficient undertaking' (Hervey and McHale, 2015: 250). Thus, while largely exempting healthcare providers from state-aid rules, these packages opened arrangements for the compensation of public health services to the Commission's and the CJEU's scrutiny.

Member states' capacity to use overriding reasons of general interest as grounds for shielding healthcare entities and activities from EU state-aid law depends on the degree of commodification of their health systems (Hatzopoulos, 2005). The opening up of 'previously publicly owned and managed hospitals to the private sector' and the more general experimenting 'with changes to ... health systems that involve the state acting as an economic operator' (seen in the previous subsection) led to the increasing 'likelihood that EU competition and free movement law will apply to hospitals within the health system' (Hervey and McHale, 2015: 247–248, 235).

Since the late 1990s, the scope for plaintiffs who aim to further liberalise health services through litigation has increased. However, as the application of EU competition law to healthcare entities on a case-by-case basis remained very laborious, the Commission began to seek a more straightforward avenue for commodifying healthcare, namely, by proposing new EU legislation on public procurement and the freedom of movement of services.

Phase Three: Failed Frontal Commodification Assault and Return to Incrementalism

In a third phase, in the 2000s, the Commission added to its laborious, case-by-case approach to health services a legislative programme with an explicit commodification objective. This happened despite the Amsterdam Treaty explicitly shielding the organisation of national healthcare services from EU intervention. In 2006 however, Commissioner Bolkestein's draft Services Directive (COM(2004) 2 final/3), which included health services, failed, given the unprecedented countermovements that it triggered. Subsequently, the Commission pursued an incremental healthcare commodification approach, for example with its 2008 draft directive on patients' rights to cross-border care (COM (2008) 414 final) (see below). This mirrored its earlier approach to liberalising public network industries (see Chapters 8 and 9).

Creating a European market for health service providers: In a first step, Commission and CJEU activism brought procurement to bear more forcefully on health entities (Hatzopoulos, 2005). Until the 1990s, procurement directives did not explicitly mention health and only rarely included health bodies among contracting bodies. In 1998 however, a European court ruling[1] confirmed that 'healthcare entities are subject to the rules of public procurement' (Hatzopoulos, 2005: 165). Subsequently, the Commission used the revision of public procurement directives as a more straightforward attempt to open public services, and thus healthcare, to market forces. This met with resistance from the European Federation of Public Service Unions (EPSU) and a social movements' coalition (Fischbach-Pyttel, 2017). As a result, the 2004 Procurement Directive (18/2004/EU) did cover 'health and social services' but only as non-priority services to which more flexible rules applied. The directive even so confirmed that public hospitals and healthcare authorities (Hatzopoulos, 2005) and 'the purchase of devices and equipment within health systems' may be subject to EU procurement rules (Hervey and McHale, 2015: 272).

Cross-border care offered another avenue for Commission and CJEU activism for a further commodification of health services. During the 1990s, the healthcare reforms triggered by the financial constraints discussed above increasingly framed patients as consumers in search of the best deal. Some patients thus came to seek reimbursement for cross-border care outside the scope of the social security regulations, through several CJEU rulings.[2] In its rulings, the CJEU 'established that there is no *general* exclusion for healthcare (or other welfare) services' from provisions on the free movement of services (Hervey and McHale, 2015: 77, their emphasis). The rulings thus reframed access to cross-border care from an issue of collective solidarity (as in social security regulations) to one of individual patients' rights. During the 2000s, the CJEU applied this view[3] to various member states, 'irrespective of the

---

[1] Case C-76/97 *Walter Tögel* v. *Niederösterreichische Gebietskrankenkasse* [1998] ECR I-05357.
[2] Including Case C-158/96 *Raymond Kohll* v. *Union des caisses de maladie* [1998] ECR I-01931; Case C-368/98 *Abdon Vanbraekel and Others* v. *Alliance nationale des mutualités chrétiennes (ANMC)* [2001] ECR I-05363; Case C-157/99 *B.S.M. Geraets-Smits* v. *Stichting Ziekenfonds VGZ and H.T.M. Peerbooms* v. *Stichting CZ Groep Zorgverzekeringen* [2001] ECR I-05473.
[3] Case C-385/99 *V.G. Müller-Fauré* v. *Onderlinge Waarborgmaatschappij OZ Zorgverzekeringen UA and E.E.M. van Riet* v. *Onderlinge Waarborgmaatschappij ZAO Zorgverzekeringen* [2003] ECR I-04509; Case C-372/04 *Yvonne Watts* v. *Bedford Primary Care Trust and Secretary of State for Health* ECR I-04325; Case C-444/05 *Aikaterini Stamatelaki* v. *NPDD Organismos Asfaliseos Eleftheron Epangelmation (OAEE)* [2007] ECR I-03185; Case C-173/09 *Georgi Ivanov Elchinov* v. *Natsionalna zdravnoosiguritelna kasa* rulings [2010] ECR I-08889.

organisation of their health system' (2015: 195). This is how a commercial route to cross-border care based on CJEU case law came to complement the social security route (Fillon, 2009). Patients were now encouraged to adopt a consumerist approach and choose between having cross-border care reimbursed at rates in the country of destination using the social security route or at those in their home country, through the commercial route (Hatzopoulos, 2005).

To further liberalise healthcare, the Commission envisaged proposing new legislation (Hervey and McHale, 2015). In its Internal Market Strategy for 2003–2006, the Commission included 'a well-managed application of Internal Market rules to the health care sector' among its legislative priorities (COM (2003) 238 final). The strategy praised the benefits to patients and providers of cross-border care CJEU case law, as it would make 'the most efficient possible use of resources across the EU'. In 2004, David Byrne, the then Health Commissioner, committed the Commission to 'integrating health into the Lisbon agenda as a driver of competitiveness' (*Euractiv.com*, 16 July 2004) and then stated, like his successor Markos Kyprianou one year later, that improving health should be regarded as an '*economic* priority' (emphasis added) (*Euractiv.com*, 28 July 2005). Accordingly, the Commission included healthcare in its draft Services Directive. As outlined in Chapter 6, the directive reinterpreted the EC Treaty's free movement of services provisions by the application of the country-of-origin principle. It also included provisions on the 'assumption of costs of cross-border-care' (Art. 23), which aimed to enshrine CJEU case law on cross-border care in EU law. The proposal also deemed the public financing of hospitals 'irrelevant for the purposes of classifying such care as hospital care' (Art. 4(10)). The intention was to give mobile patients the right to be reimbursed for care obtained abroad from both private and public providers by their home country's public healthcare funds. As, however, shown in Chapter 7, an unprecedented transnational countermovement of a trade union–social movement coalition motivated the European Parliament and Council to remove health services from the remit of the 2006 Services Directive (della Porta and Caiani, 2009; Crespy, 2016).

Creating cross-border patient markets: In response to the Commission's activism to create a European market for health services, several states sought to oblige all EU institutions to mainstream health concerns across all EU policy areas and activities (Bartlett and Naumann, 2021) and to make the national competence for the organisation of health services more explicit. In response, the drafters of the Lisbon Treaty of 2007 added to the treaty's public health title provisions that 'a high level of human health protection shall be ensured in the definition and implementation of all Union policies and activities' (Art. 168 (1) TFEU) and the recognition of 'the responsibilities of the Member States' not only 'for the organisation and delivery of health services and medical care' (as stated in the Amsterdam Treaty) but also 'for the definition of their health policy' (Art. 168(7) TFEU).

Undeterred by these provisions and by the Services Directive setback, the Commission continued in its attempts to build a European healthcare market, albeit by pursuing a more incremental, sectoral approach, as previously applied to the transport industry (Chapter 8), and proposed a directive 'on the application of patients' rights in cross-border healthcare' (Cross-Border Care Directive). The proposal (COM (2008) 414 final) reinstated many of the provisions on the assumption of costs in cross-border care that were part of the draft Services Directive. In 2011, the European Parliament and Council adopted a slightly amended directive (2011/24/EU), responding to the extensive 'rivalry' between economic and health policymakers involved in EU healthcare policy (Vanhercke, 2016: 296), the tensions between solidarity-based and marketising approaches to cross-border care (Crespy, 2016), and the criticism of European trade unions via EPSU (Fischbach-Pyttel, 2017). Tellingly, the treaty's new health mainstreaming and national responsibility clauses, mentioned above, did not prevent EU policymakers from basing the Cross-Border Care Directive not only on public health (Art. 168 TFEU) but also on Article 114 TFEU, which sponsors EU legislation with the objective of the 'establishment and functioning of the internal market' as a legal basis for the new directive.

The directive has been described as 'the first explicit measure to address the market's role in health services' (Brooks, 2016: 97) and a 'prime example of liberalisation in healthcare' (Crespy, 2016: 42). By allowing, in line with the draft Services Directive, public coverage of private cross-border care, it further develops the commercial route to cross-border care, notably in areas not shielded by pre-authorisation (i.e., non-hospital, low and mid-priced care, and day hospital care). This introduces competition between (domestic) public healthcare providers and (foreign) private ones, thus allowing horizontal market integration to exert pressure on public health services (Martinsen and Vrangbaek, 2008; Greer and Rauscher, 2011). On its web site, the Commission's Directorate General in charge of the internal market tellingly called the Cross-Border Care Directive a 'Medical Tourism Directive' (European Commission, 2011), thus framing it as a tool for developing profit-oriented patient mobility. The directive, in fact, further commodifies access to health services, as it treats patients not only as citizens with access to (social) benefits but also as consumers in pursuit of the best deals (Baeten, 2012; Mainil, 2012; Crespy, 2016; Stan, Erne, and Gannon,

2021). Given patients' need to pay upfront for travel *and* health services, the Cross-Border Care Directive furthermore favours better-off patients and those from richer states even more than the EHIC route to cross-border care discussed above.

In parallel with their work on the Cross-Border Care Directive, EU legislators adopted a new Insurance Directive (2009/138/EC). Although the directive 'explicitly exempted social health insurance schemes from its scope', it subjected supplementary health insurance 'to the rules of the market' (Hervey and McHale, 2015: 241); and, in 2011, the Commission renewed its attempt to bring healthcare more straightforwardly under EU procurement law. The ensuing 2014 Procurement (2014/24/EU) and Concessions (2014/23/EU) Directives for the first time explicitly mentioned health services in their body rather than just in their annexes. Following objections from EPSU (Fischbach-Pyttel, 2017), healthcare was still framed as 'services to the person' to which a 'light regime' continued to apply (OECD, 2016: 4). This means that 'Member States and public authorities remain free to provide those services themselves or to organise social services in a way that does not entail the conclusion of public contracts' (Directive 2014/24/EU) or concessions (Directive 2014/23/EU) and that there is a higher threshold above which the notification procedure should kick in. Although, in this case, 'liberalisation was accompanied by a fair level of re-regulation' (Crespy, 2016: 105), like previously with the 2004 Procurement Directive, the new directives reconfirmed that public hospitals and national healthcare authorities may be subject to their rules (Hervey and McHale, 2015). Thus, these directives entail not so much decommodification as what we may call contained commodification.

In the 2000s, the Commission's drive to promote the commodification of healthcare services became clearly visible. However, its bold attempt to create an EU healthcare market through its draft Services Directive failed dramatically. In response, EU executives used the EU's ordinary legislative procedures more carefully to pursue incremental changes, for example through the Cross-Border Care Directive. The shift to the NEG regime after 2008, however, gave EU executives also new tools to pursue their commodifying policy objectives.

10.3 PROMOTING COMMODIFICATION BY NEW MEANS: NEG PRESCRIPTIONS ON HEALTHCARE

In 2010, EU leaders described 'the health sector as a lever for controlling government debt, public expenditure and the sustainability of national finances' in their Europe 2020 economic growth strategy (Brooks, 2016: 11). In the same year, a joint report on health systems by the Commission and the Council's Economic Policy Committee articulated this view even more clearly.

The EU's 'first dedicated health report to be prepared' by the Commission's Directorate General for Economics and Finance (2016b: 111) framed healthcare as a 'productive sector' with an 'impact on economic growth' and 'a potential for high-skilled and flexible employment' that should be driven by goals of cost-containment and efficiency (European Commission, 2010c: 7–8). According to a national Deputy Permanent Representative who was in charge of European healthcare policy in the Council at the time, this shift amounted to a 'silent revolution' (De Ruijter, 2019: 1). Written during the crucial, founding moments of the EU's NEG regime, the report justified the inclusion of health policy in the ensuing NEG prescriptions (Stamati and Baeten, 2015). Given the importance of health services as a share of public spending (EU average of 14.6 per cent in 2011), they thus became one of NEG's key targets.

Following our methodology outlined in Chapters 4 and 5, we analysed the EU's NEG prescriptions in healthcare issued to Germany, Italy, Ireland, and Romania from 2009 to 2019 to assess their policy orientation. Accordingly, we classified all prescriptions in terms of their (commodifying or decommodifying) policy orientation in five thematic categories. As outlined in Table 10.1, three categories concern the provision of healthcare services (resource levels, sector-level governance, and provider-level governance) and two pertain to people's access to them (coverage levels and cost-coverage mechanisms).

Tables 10.1 and 10.2 reveal that most prescriptions in healthcare pointed in a commodification direction, and few of them may be seen as favouring decommodification.

Table 10.2 also shows that the coercive power of most commodifying prescriptions was very significant or significant, whereas most decommodifying prescriptions were weak in this respect. Among the commodifying prescriptions, most aimed to curtail resource levels and marketise sector- and provider-level governance. Only a few sought to curtail coverage levels and marketise cost-coverage mechanisms. Romania and Ireland were most affected by commodifying prescriptions, although Germany and Italy also received some. Italy and Romania also received a few decommodifying prescriptions. We now analyse the NEG healthcare prescriptions by considering them in more detail category by category.

Provision of Healthcare Services

Resource levels: Most prescriptions under this category were issued for Romania and targeted both healthcare expenditure and the material infrastructure of hospitals. In 2010, the second update of the 2009 Memorandum of Understanding (MoU) tasked the government to 'streamline' the number of hospitals (MoU, Romania, 2nd addendum, 20 July 2010). Then, the

TABLE 10.1 *Themes of NEG prescriptions on healthcare services (2009–2019)*

	Categories	Policy orientation	
		Decommodification	Commodification
Provision of services	Resource levels	Increase the budget for primary care (RO) Remedy low funding in healthcare (RO) Improve provision of long-term care (IT)	Contain health expenditure (IE) Contain hospital expenditure (RO) Streamline the number of hospitals (RO) Reduce bed capacity in hospitals (RO) Focus on prevention, rehabilitation, and independent living (DE) Shift to outpatient care (RO)
	Sector-level governance mechanisms		Streamline financial management in healthcare (IE) Increase government control over hospital budgets (RO) Increase competition in the health sector (IT) Remove restrictions to competition in medical services (IE) Enhance efficiency of public spending on healthcare and long-term care (DE) Increase cost-effectiveness of healthcare (IE) Improve cost-efficiency of healthcare (RO)

Provider-level governance mechanisms		Introduce case-based funding in public hospitals (IE)
Reduce payment arrears in healthcare (RO)
Introduce performance-based payments in primary care (RO)
Implement e-health systems (IE)
Implement e-health solutions (RO)
Access to services	Coverage levels	Revise the basic benefits package (RO)
	Improve access to long-term care (IT)
Increase access to healthcare (RO)	
	Cost-coverage mechanisms	Introduce co-payments for medical services (RO)
Establish private supplementary health insurance market (RO)
	Adjust health insurance contributions (RO)
Curb informal payments in healthcare (RO)	

Source: Council Recommendations on National Reform Programmes; Memoranda of Understanding. See Online Appendix, Tables A10.1–A10.6.
Country code: DE = Germany; IE = Ireland; IT = Italy; RO = Romania.

TABLE 10.2 *Categories of NEG prescriptions on healthcare services by coercive power*

	Decommodification				Commodification				
	DE	IT	IE	RO	DE	IT	IE	RO	
2009									2009
2010							●	◆	2010
2011					○		●	◆ ■ ◀	2011
2012		◀			○		◀	◆ ■ ● ◀	2012
2013		△		◆ ☆ ◀	△○		● ■² ◀	◆ ★ ■³ ●² ◀³	2013
2014		◀		☆ ◇²	○		■² ●²	○²	2014
2015				△ ☆			■ ●		2015
2016				◇		●	○	△	2016
2017				◇				△	2017
2018				☆			○	△	2018
2019		★		☆			○	△ ○	2019

Source: Council Recommendations on National Reform Programmes; Memoranda of Understanding. See Online Appendix, Tables A10.1–A10.6.
Categories: △ = resource levels; ○ = sector-level governance; □ = provider-level governance; ☆ = coverage levels; ◇ = cost-coverage mechanisms.
Coercive power: ▲●■★◆ = very significant; △●■☆◆ = significant; △○□☆◇ = weak.
Superscript number equals number of relevant prescriptions.
Country code: DE = Germany; IE = Ireland; IT = Italy; RO = Romania.

246

Provisional MoU (P-MoU) of 2011 committed the Romanian government to 'check that the aggregate figures for hospital budgets are consistent with the expenditure programmed' (P-MoU, Romania, 29 June 2011: 9), a request reiterated one year later (P-MoU, Romania, 2nd supplemental, 22 June 2012). In 2013, the second P-MoU reiterated the request not only to rationalise 'the hospital network' and to streamline 'hospital services' but also to continue 'the reduction of bed capacity in in-patient acute care hospitals' and to shift 'resources from hospital-based care towards primary care and ambulatory care' (P-MoU, Romania, 6 November 2013).

Thereafter, NEG prescriptions for Romania repeatedly reiterated the request to 'shift to outpatient care' (Council Recommendations Romania 2016–2019).[4] Although this shift was to be accompanied by an increase in the primary care budget (P-MoU, Romania, 6 November 2013), it involved, in the context of a contraction in overall healthcare spending, a curtailment of hospital expenditure, favouring commodification. Moreover, these measures redirected resources to an already strongly privatised outpatient sector (Chivu, 2011), favouring commodification. Hence, Romania's hospital sector and overall healthcare were heavily targeted by NEG's prescriptions. Most of them occurred between 2010 and 2013 and had a very significant coercive power as they were included in the MoUs and their updates. The invitation in 2015 to remedy 'low funding and insufficient resources' in healthcare (Council Recommendation Romania 2015/C 272/01), although potentially decommodifying, not only obscured NEG's previous resource-curtailing prescriptions for Romania but also had weak constraining power.

Ireland, Germany, and Italy also received one prescription each under the resource levels category. Thus, in 2012, the sixth update of the 2010 MoU tasked the Irish government to 'eliminate the spending overrun' in the health sector by the end of the year (MoU, Ireland, 6th update, 13 September 2012). The 2013 reiteration of this prescription was accompanied by the precise request to 'contain health expenditure next year to within the €13.6 billion departmental ceiling for 2013' (MoU, Ireland, 7th update, 25 January 2013). In turn, Council Recommendation (2013/C 217/09) asked the German government in 2013 to place a 'stronger focus on prevention and rehabilitation and independent living'. This measure echoed the shift to outpatient care requested from Romania and was intended to shift resources towards an already heavily privatised homecare sector (Lutz and Palenga-Mollenbeck, 2010). Both Ireland's and Germany's prescriptions point in a

---

[4] Council Recommendations Romania 2016/C 299/18, 2017/C 261/22, 2018/C 320/22, and 2019/C 301/23.

commodification direction. In turn, in order to 'incentivise labour market participation of women' (Council Recommendation Italy 2012/C 219/14), between 2012 and 2014 the Council Recommendations[5] tasked the Italian government to increase the provision of long-term elder care. Although these prescriptions thus pointed in a decommodification direction, their coercive power was significant in 2012 and 2014 but weak in 2013. More importantly, as Italy's system of elder care relies not so much on public as on private residential care (Basilicata, 2021), measures seeking to increase long-term care provision usually favour private provision and, hence, commodification.

To these prescriptions directly targeting healthcare resource levels, we must add those targeting the public sector in general, most notably in terms of the curtailment of public spending, public sector wages, and employment levels (Chapter 7). Between 2010 and 2019 for example, the Italian government subtracted €37bn from the national health service (Servizio Sanitario Nazionale): €25bn between 2010 and 2015 through direct expenditure cuts and €12.11bn between 2015 and 2019 through reduced service levels (Cartabellotta et al., 2019). Given the importance of healthcare in public spending and employment, the impact of these prescriptions on the sector has been considerable.

Sector-level governance mechanisms: The countries that received sector-level governance prescriptions are Romania, Ireland, and Italy. All these prescriptions affected the internal operation of the sector rather than the legal status of sector regulators and service purchasers.

EU executives tasked both Romania and Ireland to adopt measures seeking to tighten the government's financial control in healthcare. As seen above, their 2011 P-MoU requested Romania to contain hospital expenditure by strengthening central control over hospitals budgets. In so doing, the P-MoU also shifted the location and rationale behind government control from the objective of improved health outcomes enforced by the Ministry of Health to the objective of financial discipline and cost-containment enforced by the Ministry of Finance. Thus, the Ministry of Finance was tasked to 'take action' so that 'the aggregate figures for hospital budgets are consistent with the expenditure programmed' (P-MoU, Romania, 29 June 2011; P-MoU, Romania, 1st supplemental, 14 December 2011). In 2012 and 2013, EU executives reiterated this request (P-MoU, Romania, 2nd supplemental, 22 June 2012; P-MoU, Romania, 6 November 2013). The second P-MoU spelled out more clearly the resulting 'budget control mechanisms', which were to include 'improved reporting and monitoring frameworks, in particular with regard to hospitals' and 'monthly hospital budget reporting' (P-MoU,

---

[5] 2012/C 219/14, 2013/C 217/11, and 2014/C 247/11.

Romania, 6 November 2013). In 2014, EU executives reiterated the need for tighter managerial controls in healthcare, highlighting the need for 'proper management and control systems' (Council Recommendation Romania 2017/C 261/22).

The Irish government also received prescriptions that called, like those for Romania, for tighter central managerial control over hospital and healthcare expenditure. In 2013, EU executives urged the Irish government to 'streamline and consolidate multiple and fragmented financial management and accounting systems and processes' (MoU, Ireland, 9th update, 3 June 2013; MoU, Ireland, 10th update, 11 September 2013), a request that was reiterated the following year (Council Recommendation Ireland 2014/C 247/07). The coercive power of the NEG prescriptions for the ministries of finance and public expenditure to tighten central financial control in the healthcare sector was very significant for both Romania and Ireland up to 2013 and significant for Ireland and weak for Romania thereafter.

In addition, EU executives tasked both the Irish and the Italian government to increase economic competition in the healthcare sector. The 2010 MoU committed the Irish government to 'remove restrictions to trade and competition in sheltered sectors including ... medical services'. This included primary care, as the government was tasked to eliminate 'restrictions on the number of GPs qualifying' and to remove 'restrictions on GPs wishing to treat public patients' (MoU, Ireland, 16 December 2010; 1st update, 28 April 2011; 2nd update, 3 September 2011). The prescription points to a move from one form of commodified provision of healthcare to another, namely, from a limited to a greater number of private GPs with national health service contracts. In turn, in 2016, Council Recommendation (2016/C 299/01) tasked the Italian government to 'increase competition in regulated professions [and the] ... health sector'. This prescription occurred in the context of repeated and more general requests for increased competition in 'professional services' (Council Recommendations Italy 2011/C 215/02, 2013/C 217/11), 'services' (Council Recommendations Italy 2012/C 219/14, 2018/C 320/11), and 'all the sectors covered by the competition law' (Council Recommendation Italy 2015/C 272/16). Prescriptions for both Ireland and Italy under this rubric fostered further commodification in healthcare. As shown in Table 10.2, their coercive power was either significant or very significant.

In addition to these more targeted prescriptions, the governments of Ireland, Germany, and Romania received more encompassing prescriptions with the common theme of increasing the cost-efficiency of their healthcare systems. They affected healthcare governance at both sector- and provider-level, but, for convenience, we classed them under the first, more encompassing category. These prescriptions occurred four times in the German (2011–2014), five times in the Irish (2014–2016, 2018–2019), and three times in the Romanian (2013, 2014, 2019) case, thus contributing to making this theme the most frequent one in our dataset of NEG healthcare prescriptions. Although their exact formulation varies across countries – 'further enhance efficiency of public spending on healthcare and long-term care' (Germany), 'increase the cost-effectiveness of the healthcare system' (Ireland), 'improve cost-efficiency of healthcare' (Romania) – these formulations are all linked to a common quest for cost-efficiency in the sector. As mentioned in Chapter 5, these prescriptions could be understood in two different ways: (1) as requesting an increase in the level of health services provided while keeping the level of expenditures constant or (2) as requesting the level of health services to be kept constant while reducing the level of expenditures. As prescriptions to increase the cost-efficiency of healthcare were semantically linked to the more concrete prescriptions discussed above and below that sought a curtailment of resource levels and structural reforms along marketisation lines (see also the discussion in Chapter 5), the commodifying direction of these apparently ambiguous prescriptions is very evident (see also Stan and Erne, 2023).

Provider-level governance mechanisms: The two countries that received prescriptions under this category are Ireland and Romania. All these prescriptions concern the internal operation of providers rather than their legal status.

The first MoU for Romania already saw payment arrears of public healthcare providers to private suppliers as a key factor hindering financial discipline in public hospitals (MoU, Romania, 23 June 2009). In 2011, the third update of the 2009 MoU obliged the Romanian government to engage in 'major action' to prevent the re-emergence of arrears in the healthcare sector, a request reiterated in 2011, 2012, and 2013 (MoU, Romania, 3rd addendum, 19 January 2011; 4th addendum, 8 April 2011; P-MoU, Romania, 29 June 2011; 1st supplemental, 14 December 2011; 2nd supplemental, 22 June 2012; P-MoU, Romania, 6 November 2013). The payment of arrears meant redirecting the already scarce resources of public healthcare providers towards private creditors and away from supporting current services. It also consolidated the involvement of private healthcare operators and the increased marketisation of hospitals. The request to implement 'e-health solutions' (P-MoU, Romania, 6 November 2013) was also meant to facilitate this transformation, as it enhanced managerial control over expenditure at both provider and sector level. Moreover, as seen above, the 2013 P-MoU urged the government to increase the primary care budget, while simultaneously inviting it to make savings in the sector through the 'use of performance-based payments'. This questions the decommodifying potential of the prescription to increase resource levels in primary care, as performance-based payments foster the commodification of health services by increasing competition among service providers (Friedberg et al., 2010).

In its turn, the Irish government had to commit to introduce a 'case-based payment system for public hospitals' (MoU, Ireland, 9th update, 3 June 2013; MoU, Ireland, 10th update, 11 September 2013). The 2014 Council Recommendation (2014/C 247/07) reiterated the need to 'roll out activity-based funding throughout the public hospital system'. This meant aligning Irish hospital financing with the DRG method, which introduces competition both inside and between public healthcare providers and thus marketises their governance at both provider and sector level. Moreover, in 2013 and 2014, NEG prescriptions committed the government to implement 'e-health systems' (MoU, Ireland, 8th update, 12 April 2013; MoU, Ireland, 9th update, 3 June 2013; MoU, Ireland, 10th update, 11 September 2013) and to 'roll out individual health identifiers' (Council Recommendation 2014/C 247/07) needed to implement an e-health system. This is important, as effective e-health systems are needed for the operation of a case-based hospital financing system and for enhancing, more generally, central managerial control over both provider-level and sector-level expenditure, as we saw in section 10.2.

By contrast, there was no need to issue any commodifying prescriptions on healthcare services to the Italian and German governments. After all, they had already implemented crucial healthcare reforms before, including the introduction of the DRG method of hospital financing (see section 10.2).

Users' Access to Healthcare Services

Coverage levels: Romania and Italy are the countries that received prescriptions under the coverage levels category. In 2013, Romania received a prescription affecting the scope of services covered by the National Health Fund, namely, to 'define, by end-September 2013, the publicly reimbursable basic benefits package based on objective, verifiable criteria, to be financed within the limitations of available funding' and to subsequently revise it 'based on a cost-effectiveness analysis' (P-MoU, Romania, 6 November 2013). This prescription basically tasked the government to reduce the scope of services covered by national health insurance. It resulted in some health services no longer being covered by the National Health Fund. Patients thus henceforth had to fund them by private means, thereby increasing the commodification of healthcare.

Romania received one prescription under the coverage levels category that points in a decommodification direction. In 2013, the Romanian government was asked to increase the 'accessibility, in particular for disadvantaged people and remote and isolated communities', to health services (Council Recommendation Romania 2013/C 217/17), a request reiterated in 2014, 2015, 2018, and 2019. This prescription had decommodifying potential, as it aimed to increase the range of population covered by the National Health Fund. However, it failed not only to define what 'accessibility' was supposed to mean but also to acknowledge NEG's role in curtailing the level of Romania's healthcare resources and patients' service coverage levels. The prescriptions moreover failed to outline how to increase people's access to healthcare in a context of diminished resources and service levels.

Italy received one prescription under the coverage levels category. Thus, after previously deploring the 'limited availability of affordable care services' (Council Recommendation Italy 2016/C 299/01: Recital 16), EU executives in the 2019 Council Recommendation (2019/C 301/12) urged the Italian government to improve not only, as between 2012 and 2014, the provision of long-term care, seen above under the resource levels category, but also access to it, as a way to support women's participation in the labour market. Notwithstanding its decommodifying potential, its vague formulation eschews the question of the resources needed to improve access. This compromises its potentially decommodifying impact, just as in the case of the similar prescription for Romania. Moreover, neither the prescription for Italy nor that for Romania effectively mentions whether improved access involves the increased availability of public as opposed to private healthcare. This is significant, as, as we have already seen, both Italian long-term care and Romanian outpatient care had been significantly privatised already prior to the introduction of NEG. As shown in Table 10.2, the constraining power of the prescriptions with a decommodifying potential in this category was again weaker compared with the constraining power of commodifying prescriptions in this category.

Cost-coverage mechanisms: Romania is the only country that received prescriptions under the cost-coverage mechanisms category. Thus, Romania received two prescriptions that sought to balance cuts in public healthcare expenditure with increasing reliance on private means to cover the cost of public health services. In 2010, the second update of the 2009 MoU tasked the Romanian government to introduce 'a co-payment system on medical service' (MoU, Romania, 2nd addendum, 20 July 2010). This request was reiterated in 2011 (MoU, Romania, 3rd addendum, 19 January 2011; 4th addendum, 8 April 2011; P-MoU, Romania, 29 June 2011; 1st supplemental, 14 December 2011) and 2012 (P-MoU, Romania, 2nd supplemental, 22 June 2012). In 2013, the second P-MoU committed the government to 'establish the framework for a private supplementary insurance market' (P-MoU, Romania, 6 November 2013). The introduction of both co-payments and private insurance as cost-coverage mechanisms amounts to the marketisation of healthcare access, most notably by making the coverage of costs dependent on patients' private means, hence favouring commodification.

Romania received two prescriptions on cost-coverage mechanisms that pointed in a decommodification direction. Thus, in 2013, the Romanian government was tasked to 'adjust health insurance contributions' (P-MoU, Romania, 6 November 2013) in a bid to reduce labour costs. The prescription was reiterated in the 2014 Council Recommendations for Romania. Although this reduction implied lower costs for patients, favouring decommodification, it curtailed the funds available to the National Health Fund, favouring commodification. In 2014, the government was asked to 'curb informal payments' in the healthcare system, a prescription that was reiterated in 2016 and 2017 (Council Recommendations Romania 2014, 2016, 2017).[6] Curbing informal co-payments in the public healthcare system reduces patients' costs to access it; this points in a decommodifying policy direction. Successive Romanian governments, however, have used this prescription to justify a further privatisation of the healthcare system, which, instead of eliminating informal co-payments by patients, would have just formalised them (Stan, 2018). As shown in Table 10.2, the coercive power of the commodifying prescriptions in this category was again more significant than in the case of the decommodifying ones.

Pursuing a Healthcare Commodification Scrip through NEG Prescriptions

Our analysis shows that, overall, NEG prescriptions on healthcare favoured more often and more strongly commodification than decommodification. Not only were commodifying prescriptions more numerous, they were also more precise and had a stronger coercive power. In contrast, decommodifying prescriptions were fewer, vaguer, and weaker. At times, they accommodated commodification through the back door. Although the coercive power of NEG healthcare prescriptions decreased with the end of bailout programmes and countries coming out of executive deficit procedures, in 2015 the Annual Growth Survey still included health under 'structural reforms', signalling the 'acceptance of the treatment of health as an *economic* sector' (emphasis added) in the European Semester process (Brooks, 2016: 138).

The predominance of commodifying NEG healthcare prescriptions is noteworthy given the notable differences between the four countries under

---

[6] 2014/C 247/21, 2016/C 299/18, 2017/C 261/22.

study. Our sample includes larger/smaller and richer/poorer states and states with different modes of healthcare financing. The four national healthcare systems had also been affected to differing degrees by prior commodifying reforms. Accordingly, NEG prescriptions targeted our four countries differently. We can thus describe NEG as a case of differentiated integration, but not in the usual sense of the opt-outs from EU legislation that aim 'to accommodate economic, social and cultural heterogeneity' (Bellamy and Kröger, 2017: 625). On the contrary, NEG seems to be a case of reversed differentiated integration (Chapter 3), which uses country-specific prescriptions to pressure reluctant states to accept policies seeking to boost the convergence of health policies along the lines of an overarching commodification policy script.

The nature of this script becomes apparent when one tries to understand why NEG targeted different countries differently in terms of the number and coercive power of commodifying healthcare prescriptions. To account for this, different modes of healthcare financing across countries do not seem to matter, as the two states most targeted by NEG (Ireland and Romania) finance their public healthcare systems differently. Whereas Ireland finances its healthcare system (like Italy) directly out of the state budget, Romania's health system is funded (like in Germany) through pay-roll tax contributions. Given NEG's dual aim to curtail both public spending and unit labour costs, it is hardly surprising to see that those different modes of healthcare financing did not matter in NEG's approach to healthcare.

Our analysis shows instead that the different ways in which NEG prescriptions targeted member states depended on their progress on the path towards healthcare commodification before 2008. In all four countries, governments had already adopted commodifying healthcare reforms before the EU's shift to NEG, albeit to different degrees. The countries most heavily targeted by NEG (Ireland and Romania) were also those where healthcare commodification, most notably in the hospital sector, lagged behind compared with those less targeted by it (Germany and Italy).

Pre-NEG private for-profit hospitals came to play an important role in Germany and Italy: by 2008, they accounted for 40 per cent of the total number of hospitals in Germany and 54 per cent in Italy (OECD, 2020). In contrast, in the same year, 18 per cent of hospitals were private for-profit in Ireland (Mercille, 2018) and only 5 per cent in Romania (Romair Consulting, 2009: 8). Ireland was also the only country in our dataset that by 2008 had not yet adopted the DRG method of financing hospitals. NEG prescriptions for Ireland and Romania sought to accelerate the commodification of health services in these two countries not only by targeting healthcare expenditure (in common with pre-2008 fiscal governance) but also by directly prescribing the marketisation of health service governance. The result was, amongst others, a rise in the importance of private for-profit hospitals. By 2017, 19 per cent of Ireland's hospitals were private for-profit (Mercille, 2018), whereas a staggering 36 per cent (representing a 9.5-fold increase from 2008) were so in Romania (INS, 2018). These findings are not of academic interest only, as the curtailment of public hospital beds and the rise in private for-profit hospitals negatively affected member states' capacity to respond to the Covid-19 pandemic.

The way in which NEG healthcare prescriptions targeted each of the four countries under study therefore responds to NEG's agenda to advance healthcare commodification across member states by accelerating it in countries where it lagged prior to NEG's advent. Because it is doing this, we may say that NEG uses country-specific rules to promote convergence towards an overarching transnational script of healthcare commodification. Thus, because they display a common *logic* in their deployment across countries and time, commodifying NEG healthcare prescriptions participate in an overarching policy *script*.

However, although most NEG prescriptions in healthcare follow a commodification script, some of them point towards decommodification. To assess whether decommodifying prescriptions manage to challenge the commodification script, we need to map the larger *policy rationales* that inform their formulation. In healthcare, decommodifying prescriptions are semantically linked to four policy rationales: enhance social inclusion, reduce payroll taxes, expand labour market participation, and improve efficiency.

The two latter rationales point to larger commodification agendas deployed, respectively, in the cross-sectoral areas of employment and public services. In turn, the rationale of reducing payroll taxes points in a decommodifying direction, but only partially. Indeed, as we have seen above, it is linked to a prescription to adjust healthcare contributions, which also involves an overall reduction in collected healthcare funds, and hence commodification.

The only rationale that more clearly points in a decommodifying redistributive direction, and can be understood as reflecting social policy actors' attempts to alter the dominant commodifying orientation of NEG documents, is that of enhancing social inclusion. This rationale was invoked in relation to the inclusion of disadvantaged groups and low-income earners in several prescriptions issued for Romania, namely, to increase access, adjust healthcare contributions, remedy low funding, and curb informal payments in healthcare. However, even this conjunction between decommodifying prescriptions and a more clearly decommodifying policy rationale does not manage to make decommodification an alternative script informing NEG prescriptions in healthcare. Indeed, two of the four prescriptions in this set are also informed by commodifying rationales (increase efficiency); and the only prescription that seems to hold on to a purely decommodifying agenda (increase access) has consistently had poor constraining power (Online Appendix, Figure A10.4). Thus, decommodifying prescriptions were backed by policy rationales that either served commodifying agendas or, if not, did not have significant coercive power. We thus conclude that decommodifying prescriptions, although present in NEG documents, were subordinated to, rather than challenged, the dominant commodification script.

Overall, EU executives' NEG prescriptions and legislative agendas in healthcare reveal a striking continuity of policy preferences. Since the 1990s, EU legislation on cross-border care has shifted from a decommodifying to a commodifying approach, whereby patients have been increasingly conceived of as consumers and EU executives have increasingly understood healthcare providers as commercial undertakings. Furthermore, the multilateral surveillance regime set up in view of the single market, EMU, and accession processes led governments to adopt a series of commodifying healthcare reforms. When the Commission wanted to commodify health services in a more straightforward way however, it failed, as the European Parliament used its role in the EU's ordinary legislative procedure to exclude health services from the scope of the Services Directive. By contrast, the country-specific methodology of NEG and the Parliament's self-inflicted exclusion from the formulation of NEG prescriptions allowed EU executives to issue NEG prescriptions in healthcare that went 'far beyond the mandate intended in the founding treaties' (Brooks, 2016: 110).

Horizontal market and vertical political integration pressures have played an intertwined role since the outset of EU health policymaking. European executives' creation of the European internal market and EMU amplified horizontal market integration pressures, leading national executives to adopt commodifying healthcare reforms in turn. This not only increased the exposure of health services to EU competition and free movement law but also amplified private cross-border patient mobility (medical tourism) and the rise in healthcare corporations (Lethbridge, 2013). Transnational healthcare corporations grew most in states where healthcare commodification was already proceeding apace before the EU's shift to NEG, for example in Germany and Italy. The more they grew in size, the more political clout they gained, which they and their organisations (e.g., European Union of Private Hospitals) used in strategic legal battles and the lobbying of national and EU institutions (Kohler-Koch and Quittkat, 2013) – incidentally, not with the aim of fully privatising health services but rather for private for-profit providers to gain access to public healthcare funds (Stan, 2018). The predominantly commodifying policy orientation of EU executives' healthcare governance interventions by law (see section 10.2) or NEG prescriptions (see above) attests a convergence between them and the interests of transnational healthcare corporations. But how have trade unions and social movements reacted to them in turn? We turn to this issue in section 10.4.

10.4 EU HEALTHCARE GOVERNANCE AND TRANSNATIONAL COLLECTIVE ACTION

The extraordinary countermovements triggered by Commissioner Bolkestein's draft Services Directive motivated the European Parliament to exclude healthcare and other public services, such as water (Chapter 9), from it. The very encompassing threat that the draft directive posed to workers' rights and people's access to public services united a wide range of social movements and unions across different regional and political backgrounds in transnational collective action (Chapter 7). Once the Commission scaled its encompassing commodification strategy back to a more incremental, sectoral approach (Fischbach-Pyttel, 2017), European unions and social movements found it difficult to sustain the momentum created by their struggles against the Services Directive – despite the Commission henceforth applying its sectoral commodification approach not only to transport (see Chapter 8) but also to water (see Chapter 9) and health services (see section 10.2).

EPSU framed the draft Cross-Border Care Directive as a 'Bolkestein Directive' for health that would open up healthcare provision to private actors (EPSU, 2008) and increase 'competition in the health sector' (Fischbach-Pyttel, 2017: 88). The reframing of the reimbursement of cross-border care as an issue of 'patients' rights' (Baeten, 2012), however, made alliances between unions and other social actors more difficult. Not only patient organisations, but also 'some representatives within the European trade union movement' and 'the Socialists and Democrats Group of the European Parliament' (Fischbach-Pyttel, 2017: 115) welcomed the Commission's new focus on patient rights. Nevertheless, the objections from EPSU and several member states led to legislative amendments to the initial Commission proposal, changing it 'from a fairly crude market approach to an overall much more balanced text' (2017: 120). However, whereas the struggles around the Cross-Border Care Directive ensured that healthcare continued to figure prominently on EPSU's agenda during the 2000s, EPSU focused its attention in the following decade on another public service area – public water services (see Chapter 9).

In 2013, EPSU feared that the Commission's draft Concessions Directive would open the gate for the externalisation (and thus commodification) of public services and demanded the 'broad exclusion of public services' from it (EPSU Circular, 27 February 2013). The Commission's draft, however, challenged primarily public water services, and health services were listed solely in a longer list of services, mirroring its designation as a 'non-priority' service in the Procurement Directive (2004/18/EC). EPSU's reactions to the provisions on healthcare in the new draft Procurement and Concessions Directives therefore aimed primarily to preserve the status quo. EPSU achieved that objective in 2014, when the final Procurement and Concessions Directives listed health services among 'services to the person' to which a lighter regime applies (see section 10.2).

This suggests that, after the 2008 financial crisis, EPSU's activities in the area of healthcare continued to be shaped by Commission proposals for ordinary EU laws rather than the EU's country-specific NEG prescriptions, despite, as we have seen in section 10.3, the latter putting public health services under direct vertical commodification pressures. In the 2010s, union protests about health services therefore occurred primarily at local or national, rather than transnational level. Across Europe, local and national unions responded to wage cuts, employment ceilings, increased workload, and service closure (see Chapter 6) but also to more outright attempts to privatise health services, for example in Romania (Kahancová and Szabó, 2015; Stan and Erne, 2016; Adascalitei and Muntean, 2019; Szabó, 2020). In Germany, healthcare unionists were absorbed in intricate company-level battles for union recognition and better wages and working conditions, after the widespread privatisation of healthcare services meant that most healthcare workers were no longer covered by sectoral collective bargaining agreements for public sector workers (Artus et al., 2017; Krachler, Auffenberg, and Wolf, 2021). By contrast, most Irish and Italian healthcare workers continued to be covered by national collective agreements for the public sector. However, whereas the Irish Nurses and Midwives Organisation (INMO) gathered widespread popular support for its 2017 national nurses' strike after a decade of austerity cuts (Naughton, 2021), its sister unions in the largely privatised Irish long-term care sector were absorbed in endless company-level battles for union recognition and better wages and working conditions (Murphy and O'Sullivan, 2021). Nonetheless, even in Ireland, which historically has not been a central location for transnational EU-level trade union activism (Golden, 2015), calls for a coordinated European trade union response against the commodification of the healthcare emerged after the Covid-19 pandemic (Murphy and O'Sullivan, 2021).

In the early 2010s, unions from Germany, France, Great Britain, Ireland, Poland, and Sweden gathered in a series of conferences (Amsterdam and Katowice in 2011, Nanterre and Warsaw in 2012) to establish the basis for a common fight against the privatisation and commercialisation of healthcare and for the defence of public healthcare systems everywhere in Europe. After laying out a charter and plan of action at the 2012 Warsaw conference, these unions two years later created the European Network Against Privatisation and Commercialisation of Health and Social Protection (the Network) (ENPCHSP, 2014a). The Polish August 80 and the French SUD-Health Social unions were the drivers behind the first two meetings, and the Belgian Platform for Action on Health and Solidarity and the Belgian EPSU-affiliate CNE, which is the most left-wing union in the Christian union confederation ACV-CSC (Faniel, 2012: 26), played a central role in the next two meetings and the constitution of the Network and its subsequent actions, including the organisation of several European days of action against the commercialisation of healthcare (see Table 10.3).

The core membership of the Network was formed by Belgian, French, Italian, Spanish, and Dutch unions and social movements. The Network also established close relations with People's Health Movement-Europe. This mirrors CNE's social-movement unionism approach and its capacity to build bridges across political divisions, for example by allying itself in the Belgian Platform for Action on Health and Solidarity with the socialist ABVV/FGTB union confederation. CNE's militantism resonates with that of other unions and social movements that are part of the Network, such as the Spanish Marea Blanca or the SUD-Health Social: the first is a post-2010 social movement coalition fighting against healthcare austerity in Spain; the second is a rank-and-file union affiliated to the radical French trade union confederation SUD, which, unlike the other unions in the Network, is not part of EPSU.

The Network's main objective is the convergence of 'social movements and struggles' (ENPCHSP, 2014b). Since its creation in 2014, these efforts have coalesced around yearly European days of action under the banner 'our health is not for sale'. Organised around the World Health Day on 7 April, these actions sought to create a European Day 'against the commercialisation of health and social protection'. The most important action day took place in 2019. It started with a demonstration in Brussels, where more than a thousand people walked between the Belgian Ministry of Health and the European Parliament. The Belgian CSC and FGTB, which supplied the largest contingent of demonstrators, were joined by the Belgian Platform for Action on Health and Solidarity, Belgian networks

TABLE 10.3 *Transnational protests politicising the EU governance of healthcare (1993–2019)*

Date	Location	Action Type	Topic	Coordinators
5 June 2004	Brussels	Demonstration	Bolkestein Directive: 'Non à la directive Bolkestein – Oui à l'Europe sociale'	ETUC, other unions, social movements
24 November 2004	Brussels	Demonstration	Bolkestein Directive, 'Bolkestein Directive = Frankenstein Directive'	ETUC, other unions, social movements
19 March 2005	Brussels	Demonstration	Bolkestein Directive: 'More and better jobs - Defending social Europe - Stop Bolkestein'	ETUC, other unions, social movements
21 March 2005	Brussels	Demonstration	Bolkestein Directive	European antipoverty network
15 October 2005	Multi-sited	Demonstrations	Bolkestein Directive, European Day of Action	ETUC, other unions, social movements
25 October 2005	Strasbourg	Demonstration	Bolkestein Directive	ETUC, other unions, social movements
11 February 2006	Strasbourg, Berlin	Demonstrations	Bolkestein Directive	DGB, ETUC, Attac
14 February 2006	Strasbourg	Demonstration	Bolkestein Directive: 'Services for the people'	ETUC
28 May 2013	Brussels	Demonstration	EU rules on public procurement to fully respect workers' rights	FGTB, UNI Europa, ETUI, CSC, EFFAT, EFBWW
7 February 2014	Brussels	Demonstration	European Day of Action against privatisation and commercialisation of health	ENPCHSP
15 May 2014	Multi-sited	Demonstrations, strikes	European Doctors' Action Day: 'Let's stop them! We want to defend the right to health'	FEMS, AEMH, EPSU

7 April 2016	Brussels, multi-sited	Demonstration	European Day of Action against the Commercialisation of Health and Social Protection: 'Our health is not for sale'	ENPCHSP, EPSU, PHM, Alter Summit
24 October 2016	Multi-sited	Demonstrations, strikes	European Doctors' Action Day: 'Let's defend our health!'	FEMS
7 April 2017	Multi-sited including Brussels	Demonstrations	European Day of Action against the Commercialisation of Health and Social Protection: 'Our health is not for sale'	ENPCHSP, EPSU
20 October 2017	Multi-sited including Brussels	Demonstrations, strikes	European Doctors' Action Day: 'Let's defend everybody's health'	FEMS
7 April 2018	Multi-sited including Brussels	Demonstrations	European Day of Action against the Commercialisation of Health and Social Protection: 'All for health'	ENPCHSP, PHM Europe
2 April 2019	Multi-sited including Brussels	Demonstrations	European Day of Action against the Commercialisation of Health and Social Protection: 'Our health is not for sale'	ENPCHSP, EPSU, PHM

Source: Transnational Socioeconomic Protest Database (Erne and Nowak, 2023).
Table 10.3 includes protest events targeting political authorities in relation to the European governance of healthcare services, using the database's political level category, excluding socioeconomic protests at company, sectoral, and systemic level.

of health centres, unions and patient collectives from Belgium, Netherlands (FNV), France (SUD Health Social, CGT), and Poland (August 80), and activists from People's Health Movement's chapters in Belgium, Italy, Croatia, and France. In view of upcoming European Parliament elections in 2019, the demonstration was followed by several European Parliament members and candidates signing a pledge for the defence of public health systems and then a conference supported by the Greens/European Free Alliance in the European Parliament. The European Network's action days were, however, relatively small scale and had a weak media echo and a weak political impact. It remained a very small organisation that relied on voluntary action. An official on a half-time contract coordinated the initiatives of Network members across the EU, and a board of union and social movement activists from four countries (Belgium, France, Italy, and Spain) led it (interview, Network activist, December 2018).

Mirroring the Network's action days were those of the European Federation of Salaried Doctors (Fédération Européenne des Médecins Salariés: FEMS), a European organisation comprising doctors' trade unions and professional organisations from fourteen EU member states. In 2014, FEMS organised its first European action day under the banner 'Let's stop them! We want to defend the right to health' and coordinated country-level actions responding to austerity-driven policies with requests for quality health for all European citizens and for decent salaries and working conditions for all European doctors. The action was replicated in 2016 and 2017, but its scale diminished in time and was not continued thereafter.

EPSU supported both FEMS' and the Network's action days but placed the onus on its members to mobilise for their actions. The EPSU official for health and social protection usually also participated in the Network's action day events. In 2016 for example, EPSU supported the Network's action day and organised a joint press conference, seminar, and demonstration in Brussels. EPSU and the Network also organised a joint roundtable against austerity for the 2017 action day. In 2019, EPSU's health sector official took part in the demonstration and spoke at the subsequent conference in the European Parliament organised by the Network. Finally, at its 2019 Congress in Dublin, EPSU echoed the Network's objectives by including the fight against healthcare privatisation among its principal objectives.

EPSU participated in the Network's action days in a spirit of partnership, as requested by its Belgian affiliates. Even so, EPSU did not become a major driver of transnational counter-mobilisations against healthcare commodification. There are several explanations for this situation. After its fight to amend the Cross-Border Care Directive, EPSU directed most of its energies to other areas, most notably to its campaign against water privatisation (see Chapter 9). Furthermore, it was engaged in sectoral European social dialogue procedures with HOSPEEM, the European Hospital and Healthcare Employers' Association. This led in 2009 to a European Framework Agreement on 'prevention from sharp injuries in the hospital and healthcare sector', which became one of the last agreements that the Commission implemented through a binding EU directive (Directive 2010/32/EU) before it stopped doing that in the mid-2010s (Golden, 2019; Tricart, 2019; Syrovatka, 2022b). Moreover, EPSU's limited resources and differences in its affiliates' militancy levels may explain its sympathetic but cautious stance vis-à-vis the Network and the latter's anti-privatisation agenda. Finally, it is important to note that, before NEG, countermovements against the commodification of healthcare were possible because the adoption of laws by the EU's ordinary legislative procedures (i.e., the community method) requires the consent of both the European Parliament and Council. This provided union–social movement coalitions with an opportunity to influence the policymaking process, namely, when they were able to politicise draft Commission proposals in the public sphere, as happened most notably in the case of the draft Services Directive. By contrast, under NEG, unions and social movements have lost this opportunity, as the European Parliament can neither veto nor amend the NEG recommendations, which are proposed by the European Commission and approved by the Council.

Most importantly however, the commodifying effects of the EU's country-specific NEG prescriptions affected workers and patients across Europe in a disjointed way, depriving EPSU of an urgent, tangible target that could unite unions and social movements across Europe in collective action, as previously happened in the case of the draft Services Directive. Importantly, so far, no German trade union has become a leading member of the Network or otherwise embraced the cause of transnational responses to healthcare commodification, despite the growing awareness among German healthcare trade unionists and activists of the European drivers of healthcare commodification (Bündnis Krankenhaus statt Fabrik, 2020). This mirrors the fact that healthcare reforms had already significantly commodified German health services during the 2000s, leading both to a fragmentation – local-hospital-by-local-hospital (Böhlke, Greer, and Schulten, 2011) – of industrial mobilisations by healthcare workers and to a political focus of their mobilisations on the German government. If one compares EPSU's difficulties in politicising the EU's NEG interventions in healthcare with its successful mobilisations against the draft Services Directive or its successful Right2Water European Citizens' Initiative (see Chapter 9), however, one can hardly explain them by its leadership's lack of interest in transnational collective action. Thus, European unions' difficulties in politicising NEG can be better explained by the structure of the supranational NEG regime that facilitates a nationalisation of social conflicts (Erne, 2015). However, the constitution of the Network in 2014, their yearly European days of action, and EPSU's sustained support for these actions over time reveals an increasing awareness among trade unions and social movements of the significance of EU NEG interventions in the healthcare sector.

10.5 CONCLUSION

The first EU laws on healthcare focused on cross-border care and respected the solidarity principle of national welfare states as the central criterion for accessing it. Since the 1990s, commodifying approaches to healthcare have increasingly shaped the EU's legislative agenda, culminating in Commissioner Bolkestein's draft Services Directive. Transnational countermovements by European unions and social movements largely succeeded in resisting its thorough liberalisation agenda. EPSU later managed to contain the commodification of healthcare by the Procurement and Concessions Directives and, albeit only partially, to limit healthcare commodification by the Cross-Border Care Directive. Compared with the encompassing liberalisation agenda of the Bolkestein Directive however, the impact of the Cross-Border Care Directive on both workers and patients has to date been relatively small, given patients' still limited use of cross-border care.

Despite this, since the late 1990s, healthcare commodification has gathered pace across the EU. In countries with a state-financed public health system, the fiscal convergence criteria for the EMU and accession processes constrained health expenditure, motivating governments to implement commodifying healthcare reforms. Countries with health systems financed by wage-based sickness fund contributions were also put under pressure, as the increased horizontal integration pressures on wages and payroll taxes in the enlarged single European market (Erne, 2008) also indirectly constrained health budgets.

After the 2008 crisis, the EU's NEG regime furthermore enabled the European Commission and Council to issue binding country-specific policy prescriptions, thereby enabling the promotion of healthcare commodification without having to fear any countervailing amendments by the European Parliament. Whereas the Commission's draft Services, Cross-Border Care,

Procurement, and Concessions Directives provided European trade unions and social movements with a clear target, EU executives' NEG prescriptions in healthcare were neither very visible nor did they affect all countries at the same time. This made any coordinated transnational action against them very difficult. Although trade unions and social movements fought against the fallout of commodifying healthcare reforms in all our four countries, EPSU concentrated its efforts at EU level on the public water sector, which was threatened by the EU's draft Concessions Directive. This left the reactions to NEG to the intersectoral European Trade Union Confederation, which began lobbying the Commission to render its NEG prescriptions more social after the Commission incorporated the European social partners in its European Semester process in 2014 (Erne, 2015).

As shown by our detailed analysis of NEG healthcare prescriptions issued for Germany, Ireland, Italy, and Romania from 2009 to 2019, these prescriptions were informed by a common commodification script. So far however, unions and social movements have failed to trigger a transnational countermovement against them at the scale of their preceding, and successful, counter-mobilisations against the draft Services Directive. Despite their vertical orientation, the country-specific methodology of commodifying NEG prescriptions and their invisibility to the greater public effectively hampered a transnational countermovement against them. In addition, the (self-inflicted) exclusion of the European Parliament as a co-decision maker in NEG dramatically reduced the opportunities for collective movements to make themselves heard inside the EU's governance system. Instead, unions and social movements in all four countries under analysis recurrently contested commodifying healthcare measures at national and/or local hospital level, as mentioned in section 10.4. For sure, unionists and social movement activists from several countries realised at the beginning of the 2010s that they were facing a common healthcare commodification agenda and therefore created the European Network to coordinate their struggles. The Network saw the links between healthcare privatisation and commercialisation and the EU's NEG interventions in the field. So far however, the Network, EPSU, and the involved unions and social movement organisations have not succeeded in building an encompassing countermovement able to effectively confront NEG and its healthcare commodification agenda.

Early in 2020, a leading scholar in the field concluded that 'we cannot expect EU institutional actors to reverse stability rules and numerical targets that have become embedded in their practices as well as touted in their discourses – even in the unlikely event that there were to be a shift in the political orientation of the EP and the Council' (Schmidt, 2020: 303). And yet, only a few weeks later, the Commission and Council suspended the Stability and Growth Pact when they realised the huge human costs that a continuation of NEG's austerity regime would entail for public health services faced with the Covid-19 pandemic. Instead, EU leaders agreed to create a €672.5bn Recovery and Resilience Facility (RRF) to support, inter alia, the resilience of European healthcare systems through loans and grants. In response to the Covid-19 emergency, European leaders have thus adopted policies that only a few weeks earlier seemed unthinkable (see Chapters 12 and 13). Although some of these measures were afterwards reversed, such as the subsumption of private hospitals under public authority in Ireland (Mercille, Turner, and Lucey, 2022), there is now strong support for public healthcare throughout Europe. When the pandemic highlighted the importance of public health services, the immediate pressure to commodify healthcare declined. Even so, there is no guarantee that the commodification of healthcare is about to stop. First, private providers will certainly do their best to get as much Recovery and Resilience Facility funding as possible for themselves (Chapters 12 and 13). Second, the EU's commodifying NEG interventions were hardly a result of a conspiracy of detached EU elites, as one might have thought listening to Brexit campaigners, but rather a reflection of a general propensity within capitalist systems to open up new areas for capitalist accumulation (see Chapters 2, 3, and 14). The transnational struggles over healthcare commodification are therefore set to continue.

PART IV

Comparative Analysis and Post-Pandemic Developments

11

Labour Politics and the EU's NEG Prescriptions across Areas and Sectors

11.1 INTRODUCTION

In this chapter, we compare the policy orientation of the new economic governance (NEG) prescriptions that the European Commission and Council of finance ministers (EU executives) issued to Germany, Ireland, Italy, and Romania (2009–2019) across our two cross-sectoral policy areas (employment relations and public services) and three public services sectors (transport, water, and healthcare). To what extent have they been informed by an overarching policy script that sought to commodify labour and public services? This question is crucial from this book's labour politics perspective, as the presence of a commodifying script is a necessary (albeit not sufficient) condition for transnational countermovements that could alter the setup and policy direction of the EU's NEG regime.

Certainly, commodifying EU interventions as such do not necessarily trigger countervailing protest movements, especially not transnational ones (Dribbusch, 2015). Successful social movements depend also on activists' ability to construct a shared sense of injustice among people and to identify fitting targets for their grievances (Kelly, 2012 [1998]). Agency-oriented factors, such as activists' framing of the problem and their interactions with workers, allies, and the public in general, are important for successful labour and social movements, including in the case of transnational collective action (Diani and Bison, 2004; Erne, 2008; Nunes, 2021; Szabó, Golden, and Erne, 2022). This does not, however, mean that labour activists can build transnational movements as they please.

The policy direction of the NEG prescriptions and the nature of the NEG regime shape the prospect of countervailing protests too (Erne, 2015). Many commodifying EU laws have passed unchallenged (Kohler-Koch and Quittkat, 2013), but most transnational protests in the socioeconomic field have been triggered by commodifying EU laws (Erne and Nowak, 2023), for example by the Commission's draft Services Directive or its draft Port Services Directives (Chapters 6–10). When draft EU laws favoured labour, unions usually endorsed them, for example in the case of the EU Working Time Directive in 1993 (Chapter 6). This shows that unions are primarily concerned not about the national or the EU level of policymaking but rather about its substantive outcomes and policy direction.

The key role of interest groups in policyformation processes has been acknowledged by both neo-functionalist and intergovernmentalist EU integration scholars (Haas, 1958 [2004]; Moravcsik, 1993, 1998; Niemann, Lefkofridi, and Schmitter, 2019). Even so, EU integration scholars from both traditions have focused their attention on institutional actors (Stan and Erne, 2023). However, whereas intergovernmentalists look at the relations between national governments, as they aggregate different societal interests into a single national interest (Moravcsik, 1993: 483), neo-functionalists focus on the European Commission, as it is trying to strengthen its role in the EU polity in collaboration with *transnational* interest groups (Niemann, Lefkofridi, and Schmitter, 2019). This explains the dominant focus in the EU integration literature on national or supranational institutions (Bauer and Becker, 2014; Bickerton, Hodson, and Puetter, 2015); but, if one approaches EU integration from a labour politics perspective, the policy orientation of EU laws and NEG prescriptions is as important as the EU's and the NEG regime's institutional setup.

Accordingly, we have gone beyond the EU governance literature's dominant institutional focus and analysed the – commodifying or decommodifying – policy orientation of EU governance in two cross-sectoral policy areas (employment relations and public services) and three public service sectors (transport, water, and healthcare). Concretely, in Chapters 6–10, we first outlined EU governance in these fields prior to the shift to NEG. Then, we analysed the policy orientation of EU executives' NEG prescriptions for Germany, Ireland, Italy, and Romania (2009–2019) in their particular semantic, communicative, and policy contexts. Finally, we drew on our novel transnational European socioeconomic protest database (Erne and Nowak, 2023) to relate unions' and social movements' transnational protest actions to commodifying EU interventions since 1997 in all five empirical chapters.

This chapter summarises the findings of the preceding empirical chapters and compares the policy orientation of NEG prescriptions across time, countries, policy areas, and sectors, following the comparative research design outlined in Chapters 4 and 5. We distinguish between qualitative and quantitative prescriptions, as this distinction captures two key dimensions of commodification: the quantitative dimension of curtailment (of workers' wages and public services' resources) and the qualitative dimension of marketisation (of employment relations and public services). We discuss quantitative and qualitative prescriptions separately, as this allows us to compare those on employment relations with those on public services more easily.

Concretely, section 11.2 compares the commodifying and decommodifying patterns of quantitative and qualitative NEG prescriptions in our two cross-sectoral policy areas of employment relations and public services (Chapters 6–7). Section 11.3 replicates this approach and applies it to our findings for the transport, water, and healthcare sectors (Chapters 8–10). These comparisons reveal the pre-eminence of commodification in terms of the number of NEG prescriptions and their coercive power, policy rationale, and logic of deployment. Apart from a few exceptions, all qualitative NEG prescriptions across all countries and sectors pointed in a commodifying direction, tasking governments to market-ise employment relations and public services. Most quantitative prescriptions of EU executives equally tasked most national governments to curtail wages and public expenditures. Over time, however, quantitative NEG prescriptions not only became less coercive but also progressively pointed in a decommodifying direction, for example, by tasking governments to invest more in public services. It is nevertheless misleading to speak of a gradual socialisation of the NEG regime (Zeitlin and Vanhercke, 2018); not just because of the much weaker coercive power of decommodifying prescriptions (Jordan, Erne, and Maccarrone, 2021; Stan and Erne, 2023) but also given their explicit semantic links to policy rationales that are compatible with commodification (rebalance the EU economy, boost competitiveness and growth, enhance private sector involvement, expand labour market participation) and their scant links to policy rationales that may counterbalance NEG's dominant commodifying script (enhance social inclusion, shift to green economy) (see Tables 11.2 and 11.4).

In section 11.4, we summarise the consequences for labour politics of the shift to NEG. Did the latter trigger transnational countermovements by unions and social movements, as one might expect, given the commodifying policy script that had obviously been shaping EU executives' NEG prescriptions since 2009? Or did NEG's country-specific methodology effectively prevent the prescriptions' politicisation across borders – at least until March 2020 when the spread of the coronavirus across borders compelled the Commission and Council to suspend the Stability and Growth Pact (SGP)? In section 11.4, we thus assess how transnational collective actions of trade unions and social movements challenging NEG fared comparatively in the two cross-sectoral policy areas and the three public services sectors.

11.2 NEG PRESCRIPTIONS ON EMPLOYMENT RELATIONS AND PUBLIC SERVICES

Tables 11.1 and 11.2 group the commodifying and decommodifying prescriptions received by the four countries from 2009 to 2019 under the categories

TABLE 11.1 *Commodifying NEG prescriptions on employment relations and public services (cross-sectoral)*

Quantitative prescriptions

Employment relations

	DE	IE	IT	RO
2009				▲³
2010		▲³		▲³
2011		▲²		▲²
2012		▲		▲
2013		▲		▲³
2014	△			△
2015				△
2016				△
2017				△
2018				△
2019				△

Quantitative prescriptions

Public services

	DE	IE	IT	RO	
				▲⁸	2009
		▲⁶		▲⁸	2010
		▲⁶	△	▲⁵	2011
		▲⁴	▲	▲	2012
		▲³	△	▲⁵	2013
		▲	▲		2014
		▲			2015
		△			2016
					2017
					2018
					2019

Qualitative prescriptions

Employment relations

	DE	IE	IT	RO
2009				
2010		■		
2011		■	□	●■
2012		■	●	●■
2013		■	○	●■
2014			● ■	
2015			● ■	
2016				
2017			■	
2018				
2019				

Source (employment relations): Table 6.2; Online Appendix, Tables A6.1–A6.4.
Categories: △ = wage levels; □ = bargaining mechanisms; ○ = hiring & firing mechanisms.
Coercive power: ▲■● = very significant; ■● = significant; △□○ = weak.
Country code: DE = Germany; IE = Ireland; IT = Italy; RO = Romania.

Qualitative prescriptions

Public services

	DE	IE	IT	RO	
				■² ●	2009
		■		■³ ●³	2010
		■		■⁴ ●⁴ ◆³	2011
		■	○	●²	2012
	○²	■	○² ●	■⁴ ●⁵	2013
	○		○⁴ □ ●	○³ □²	2014
			■³² ●	□	2015
	○		■³⁴ ●	□²	2016
			■³ ●	○ □	2017
			■² ●²	○ □	2018
			●²	○ □	2019

Source (public services): Table 7.2; Online Appendix, Tables A7.1–A7.4.
Categories: △ = resource levels; ○ = sector-level governance mechanisms; □ = provider-level governance; ◇ = cost-coverage mechanisms.
Coercive power: ▲●■◆ = very significant; ▲●■ = significant; △□○ = weak.
Superscript number equals number of relevant prescriptions.

TABLE 11.2 *Decommodifying NEG prescriptions on employment relations and public services (cross-sectoral)*

Quantitative prescriptions

Employment relations

	DE	IE	IT	RO
2009				
2010				
2011		▲^{i}		
2012	△^{a}			
2013	△$^{a\ b}$			
2014				
2015				
2016				
2017	△^{b}			
2018	△^{bc}			
2019	△^{bc}			

Quantitative prescriptions

Public services

	DE	IE	IT	RO	
					2009
					2010
					2011
			△^{cj}		2012
			△$^{a\ cj}$		2013
△$^{2\ bc}$					2014
△$^{2\ bc}$					2015
△$^{2\ bcj}$				△^{a} ☆^{a}	2016
△$^{d\ bc}$	△$^{a\ cg}$			☆^{a}	2017
△^{bc}	△$^{ad\ c}$				2018
△$^{d\ bcj}$			▲^{c}	☆^{a}	2019

274

Qualitative prescriptions

Employment relations

	DE	IE	IT	RO
2009				
2010				
2011				
2012				
2013	O[f]			
2014	O[f]			
2015				
2016	O[f]			
2017	O[f]			
2018				□[e]
2019				

Source (employment relations): Table 6.2; Online Appendix, Tables A6.1–A6.4.
Categories: △ = wage levels; □ = bargaining mechanisms; O = hiring & firing mechanisms.
Coercive power: ▲ = very significant; △□O = weak.
Figures in superscript = number of prescriptions.
Semantic link to policy rationale: a = Enhance social inclusion; b = Rebalance EU economy; e = Enhance social concertation; f = Reduce labour market segmentation; i = Reduce payroll taxes.
Bold letters = semantic link to commodification script.

Public services

	DE	IE	IT	RO
2009				
2010				
2011				
2012				
2013				
2014				
2015				
2016				
2017				
2018				
2019				

Source (public services): Table 7.2; Online Appendix, Tables A7.1–A7.4.
Categories: △ = resource levels; ☆ = coverage levels.
Coercive power: ▲ = significant; △☆ = weak.
Figures in superscript = number of prescriptions.
Semantic link to policy rationale: a = Enhance social inclusion; b = Rebalance EU economy; c = Boost competitiveness and growth; d = Shift to green economy; g = Expand labour market participation; j = Enhance private sector involvement.
Country code: DE = Germany; IE = Ireland; IT = Italy; RO = Romania.

operationalised in Chapter 5. In these tables, we present the quantitative and qualitative NEG prescriptions separately to facilitate the comparison of those on employment relations with those on public services.

In employment relations, we distinguished a quantitative category of NEG prescriptions (wage levels) and two qualitative ones (bargaining mechanisms and hiring and firing mechanisms). In public services, we distinguished two quantitative categories: resource levels for public services provision and coverage levels, which defines the scope of public services that users can access or the population covered by public schemes. The three qualitative categories include two on the mechanisms that govern their provision (sector-level and provider-level governance mechanisms) and one on users' access to them (cost-coverage mechanisms).

The different shades of category symbols in Tables 11.1 and 11.2 depict NEG prescriptions' coercive power as very significant (black), significant (grey), or weak (white), as operationalised in Chapter 5. In Table 11.2, the superscript figures indicate the number of prescriptions in that category in a given year; the superscript letters signify the semantic links between the decommodifying NEG prescriptions and the policy rationales informing them. The bold superscript letters indicate semantic links to policy rationales that are compatible with NEG's overarching commodification script; the regular letters refer to policy rationales that may run contrary to NEG's commodification script and thus indicate potential institutional change (Crouch and Farrell, 2004).

A bird's-eye comparison based on Tables 11.1 and 11.2 reveals the dominance of commodifying NEG prescriptions in terms of their number and, most importantly, their coercive power. The tables also show that the NEG prescriptions on public services pointed more consistently than those on employment relations in commodifying policy directions across our selected countries.

The latter finding mirrors pre-NEG developments in the two areas. In employment relations, pre-NEG EU interventions by laws often pointed in a decommodifying direction (Chapter 6). By contrast, EU leaders had already promoted the commodification of public services through vertical EU interventions by law before the EU's shift to NEG (Chapter 7). That said, the horizontal market pressures unleashed by the making and enlargement of the internal market and monetary union also commodified employment relations, albeit much more indirectly. Increased competitive horizontal market integration put pressure on unit labour costs (ULC). The Europeanisation of product markets also put pressure on national multi-employer collective bargaining systems, which had been designed to take workers' terms and conditions out of competition (Chapter 6). As the increasing horizontal market pressures affected different locations differently, market integration led not to social and territorial convergence but to severe imbalances between core and more peripheral locations in the EU's political economy. This explains the radical policy shift of national political and business leaders, who previously rejected EU governance interventions in collective bargaining and wages policy (Léonard et al., 2007), towards vertical NEG interventions in this field after 2008 (Chapters 2 and 3).

By contrast, decommodified public services are not subject to horizontal market pressures, except when financed through payroll taxes given their impact on ULC, as in the case of German sickness funds (Chapter 10). Decommodified public services had typically been sheltered from horizontal market pressures, but EU policymakers made public expenditure subject to the fiscal constraints set by the Maastricht Treaty's debt and deficit criteria, as operationalised by the EU's SGP. In addition, EU executives advanced the exposure of public services to market pressures through commodifying EU laws and court rulings. The Commission's commodification attempts remained nevertheless incomplete because of transnational protests and the ensuing legislative amendments by the European Parliament and Council. In the 2000s, the European Parliament increasingly used its new powers as a co-legislator to curb the Commission's enthusiasm for public service commodification (Chapter 7). The creation of the NEG regime after 2008 thus provided EU executives with a new governance mechanism to advance public service commodification, namely, one that circumvents the potential roadblocks caused by countervailing legislative amendments by the European Parliament (Chapter 3).

Tables 11.1 and 11.2 show that the patterns of commodification and decommodification in our two cross-sectoral policy areas differed across countries and over time. Moreover, commodification advanced through different channels, with implications for the countervailing actions of unions and social movements. We thus assess the prescriptions in these areas in more detail, starting with those that target the quantitative aspects of employment relations and public services. After that, we compare the prescriptions that intervene qualitatively in these areas.

Curtailing Wages and Public Expenditure

Cutback measures first targeted Ireland and Romania, two countries that were subject to bailout conditionality. Their governments signed Memoranda of Understanding (MoUs) with EU institutions and the IMF, which set out in detail the conditions that these governments needed to fulfil to receive financial assistance to prevent them from defaulting on their sovereign debt.

As Table 11.1 shows, the Irish and Romanian governments received very coercive commodifying prescriptions on both wages and public service resource levels every year between 2009 and 2013 (Romania) and from 2010 to 2013 (Ireland). The superscript numbers in the table indicate that the Irish and Romanian governments received more than one such prescription per year. The dark black shade of the symbols for Ireland and Romania demonstrates that the coercive power of these prescriptions was very significant in that period. If they had not stuck to their commitments to cut wages and public spending, the countries would have risked not getting the next tranche of their bailout package, directly threatening them with default. Prescriptions in both cross-sectoral areas followed the same underlying logic of using curtailment as a tool not only to restore budget balance but also to promote international competitiveness. Linking wage and public service resource cuts, calls for wage reductions for workers in the public sector featured prominently in both countries. Prescriptions set detailed targets on how much governments should save on public sector workers' wages and specified measures on how to achieve these savings.

Table 11.1 also shows that NEG prescriptions to cut wages and public service resources extended beyond the period of immediate crisis management and beyond the countries under direct bailout conditionality. Whereas EU bailout programmes targeted wages and public service resources in an ad hoc manner, after 2011 the European Semester process provided a systematic framework for the EU governance of wages and public service resources (Chapter 2).

First, the Six-Pack of EU laws strengthened the coercive power of the excessive deficit procedure (EDP) of the EU's SGP. Second, the Six-Pack's new Macroeconomic Imbalance Procedure (MIP) subjected national wage policy for the first time to a coercive EU surveillance and sanctioning regime by including a ceiling for ULC increases on the MIP scoreboard (Chapter 2). After 2012, EU executives could thus issue ULC-related NEG prescriptions to curtail wage growth. As the MIP's ULC indicator did not include a floor, EU executives could not issue ULC-related prescriptions in favour of higher wages (Chapter 2), although the excessively low wage increases in surplus countries like Germany during the 2000s caused excessive macroeconomic imbalances within the EU (Erne, 2008). Given the biased setup of the MIP's ULC indicator, it is hardly surprising that deficit countries like Ireland depressed wages more than required under the MIP scoreboard's nominal ULC-increase ceiling (Jordan, Erne, and Maccarrone, 2021: 202). In designing the NEG regime, EU policymakers thus not only strengthened the pressures to curtail public spending through the revised EDP but also opened the possibility to curtail wages through the new MIP, which set a ceiling but no floor for nominal ULC increases (see Chapter 6).

Table 11.1 reveals the continuation of commodifying prescriptions in wages and public service resources for Ireland until 2016 (three years after Ireland exited its bailout programme) and for Romania until 2019. From 2011 to 2014, Italian governments also received a string of prescriptions to cut public service resources, although Italy was running primary budget surpluses in these years. Conversely, Germany received one prescription on the curtailment of public service resources and none on the curtailment of wages. After 2016, only Romania continued to receive commodifying prescriptions on wages levels, whereas the other countries received prescriptions to increase wages (Germany) and public service resource levels (Germany, Ireland, and Italy).

Boosting Wages and Public Investment

To repeat, the revised EDP and the inclusion of a nominal ULC indicator in the MIP scoreboard gave EU executives powerful tools to pursue commodification through cutting back wages and public service resources. Conversely, the MIP included a current account imbalances indicator, thereby opening the way for decommodifying prescriptions in both areas. In the case of current accounts, EU executives singled out not only deficits but also surpluses as a potential source of EU-wide macroeconomic imbalances. The coercive power of their expansionary NEG prescriptions for surplus countries was weak, as the European Commission never attempted to open an MIP against a surplus country that pursued overly restrictive wage and fiscal policies.

From 2012 onwards, EU executives nevertheless started looking at wages and public spending through the lens of current account surpluses also. Table 11.2 shows that Germany was the first to get decommodifying prescriptions to increase wages and fiscal resources for public services. The Commission interpreted the tightness of the German labour market and wage moderation not only as a success of earlier commodifying reforms but also as a source of EU-wide macroeconomic imbalances (Commission, Country Reports Germany SEC (2011) 714: 2, SWD (2012) 305: 19). Consequently, from 2013 onwards, Germany received a string of expansionary NEG prescriptions to increase wages that were semantically linked to the policy rationale to 'rebalance the EU economy', as outlined in Table 11.2. After the Commission identified Germany as a state causing macroeconomic imbalances, albeit not excessive ones, its government also started receiving a string of weak NEG prescriptions that asked it to use its available fiscal space to increase public investment.

Subsequently, EU executives issued resource-related decommodifying prescriptions to Ireland, Italy, and Romania too. Whereas Romania received its first expansionary prescriptions on public services in 2016, the prescriptions on public service resources issued to Ireland changed their policy direction in 2017. In 2019, Italy also received a decommodifying prescription on public service resources. As opposed to Germany, none of these three countries received any prescriptions calling for higher wages to 'rebalance the EU economy'. The expansionary prescriptions for Ireland, Italy, and Romania were semantically linked to other policy rationales that were typically subordinated to, rather than challenging NEG's commodifying logic (Table 11.2). Whereas the prescriptions for Romania on greater public investments were meant to 'enhance of social inclusion', which is a decommodifying rationale, those for Italy and Ireland were meant to 'boost competitiveness and growth' and to 'enhance private sector involvement' in the provision of public services; these are rationales that support rather than challenge NEG's commodification script. The latter two rationales also featured in the German case, and the Italian and Irish prescriptions with explicit semantic links to the 'boost competitiveness and growth' rationale were implicitly also related to the 'rebalance the EU economy' rationale. After all, greater German demand (boosted by more expansionary German wage and fiscal policies) must be complemented by a concomitant upgrading of the productive apparatus in the EU's periphery to achieve the stated goal of a more balanced EU economy (Chapter 2; Aglietta, 2019).

To summarise, the curtailment of wages and public service resources was the dominant theme of NEG prescriptions in our two cross-sectoral policy areas until 2016. In decreasing numbers and with weakening coercive power, they kept appearing until 2019. Over time however, we see a shift towards more expansionary NEG prescriptions on both wage and public service resource levels. This seems to lend support to those who identified a shift to a more social Semester process after the inauguration of Jean-Claude Juncker as president of the Commission in 2014 (Chapter 4). If, however, we take into account the unequal coercive power of these decommodifying prescriptions and their semantic links to their underlying policy rationales, we can see how such prescriptions can still be compatible with NEG's overarching commodification logic.

In all cases, the coercive power of decommodifying prescriptions was weak, by contrast to commodifying ones. Most expansionary prescriptions on wages or resources for public services were linked to rationales that were subordinated to NEG's overarching commodifying script. Their decommodifying orientation represents a side-effect rather than an indicator of a countervailing policy script. Neither the wage increases nor the public investment recommendations for Germany were about social concerns but about rebalancing the EU economy, that is, boosting internal demand in Germany to create greater export opportunities for firms from other EU countries. Likewise,

NEG prescriptions on greater public investment were frequently linked to calls for greater private-sector involvement in the provision of public services. When governments were tasked to spend more money on public services, this expenditure was typically not meant for (in-house) public services providers and public services workers. Rather, the EU executives' NEG prescriptions incentivised the funnelling of public funds towards private actors through marketising arrangements. This picture becomes very clear when we analyse the policy orientation of the *qualitative* NEG prescriptions in our two cross-sectoral areas, which we do next.

Marketising Employment Relations and Public Services

Tables 11.1 and 11.2 reveal a much more consistent commodification pattern among the qualitative NEG prescriptions in our two cross-sectoral policy areas compared with the quantitative ones discussed in the previous section. *All* qualitative NEG prescriptions on public services across *all* four countries point in a commodifying direction. National differences matter only in terms of the prescriptions' coercive power, given the different locations of our four countries in the EU's NEG enforcement regime. In the area of employment relations, all countries except Germany received very constraining (Ireland, Romania) and constraining (Italy) NEG prescriptions that tasked governments to commodify their collective bargaining systems and workers' hiring and firing mechanisms through reforms of their labour laws (Ireland, Italy, Romania). Germany by contrast did not receive any qualitative prescription that pointed in a commodifying direction, as EU executives were satisfied with the labour market reforms that the Schröder government (1998–2005) had already introduced to increase national competitiveness before the EU's shift to the NEG regime. Accordingly, EU executives stopped issuing additional commodifying NEG prescriptions on collective bargaining and hiring and firing mechanisms once the receiving governments had implemented them, as happened in case of Italy with the Jobs Act adopted by the Renzi government in 2015.

By contrast, public services were targeted in a much more sustained manner by qualitative commodifying prescriptions. The commodifying NEG prescriptions on how to govern public service providers and users' access to these services were not only far-reaching across all countries but also spanned the entire NEG period from 2009 to 2019, as Table 11.1 demonstrates. These prescriptions concerned the operational modes of public services and ownership structures. EU executives prescribed, inter alia, corporate governance reform of state-owned enterprises, performance-related pay in public administration, and the corporatisation of (local) public service providers. NEG prescriptions for Romania and Italy explicitly tasked their governments to privatise public services too. These prescriptions show that the NEG's drive to commodify public services went further than any previous attempts at commodification through the EU's ordinary legislative procedure. EU executives put indirect pressures on governments to balance budgets by selling off public assets in the run-up to economic and monetary union (EMU), but privatisation officially constituted a taboo during the pre-NEG history of EU integration, as its 'Treaties shall in no way prejudice the rules in Member States governing the system of property ownership' (Art. 345 TFEU). Even so, EU executives issued NEG prescriptions with very significant and significant coercive power to both Romania and Italy, forcing them to implement privatisation plans.

It is also important to compare the trajectories of quantitative and qualitative commodifying NEG prescriptions. Whereas the prescriptions on curtailing and marketising measures went hand in hand in the first years of the NEG regime, the focus of NEG prescriptions gradually moved away from curtailment towards marketisation, mirroring the Commission's increased flexibility concerning the EU's deficit and debt targets in exchange for more ambitious structural reforms. The corresponding shift in the centre of gravity of NEG prescriptions from curtailment towards marketisation, however, hardly represented a softening – or socialisation – of NEG, as acknowledged by Mario Monti, the former Italian prime minister and EU Commissioner:

> The task of government is harder when reforms directly affect the interests of well-organised groups, businesses, professionals or public service employees..... That is why I welcome the recent reorientation of EU policy – not away from fiscal policy but towards emphasis on country-specific recommendations on structural reforms.
> (Mario Monti, *Financial Times*, 19 December 2013)

Accordingly, all NEG prescriptions across all four countries and all years tasked governments to marketise public services, despite the presence of decommodifying NEG prescriptions on resources for public services after 2013. In turn, NEG prescriptions tasked all governments except Germany's to implement marketising reforms in employment relations, as the Schröder government had already implemented far-reaching reforms before 2008 (Chapter 6).

By contrast, and as Table 11.2 shows, decommodifying qualitative prescriptions were almost entirely absent, except in a very few employment relations cases. Although EU executives welcomed the Hartz labour market reforms in Germany in the 2000s, they acknowledged that they went too far in one aspect, as the flourishing of tax-exempt mini-jobs would draw young and old workers away from seeking full-time employment. To reduce the segmentation of the German labour market, they asked the German government from

2013 onwards to facilitate the transition from mini-jobs to standard employment. In 2018, EU executives implicitly accepted that the dismantling of multi-employer collective bargaining in Romania also went too far and issued a (weak) prescription that asked its government to enhance social dialogue.

An Overarching Commodification Script across the Two Cross-sectoral Policy Areas?

Our analysis shows that NEG prescriptions across the two cross-sectoral policy areas were largely informed by an overarching commodification script, especially in the case of the prescriptions belonging to our *qualitative* analytical categories.

Much of the debate on the EU's NEG regime has so far typically focused on austerity – in other words, on the curtailment of wages and public resources (Blyth, 2013). As outlined in Chapter 4, the relevant discussion has revolved around the question of whether or not successive rounds of NEG prescriptions turned away from austerity. Our study has revealed that austerity is neither the only channel of commodification of employment relations and public services nor the most prominent one. Our analysis has revealed that the NEG prescriptions across the two cross-sectoral policy areas are informed by an overarching commodification script. However, the connective glue that holds NEG prescriptions together over time and across countries is not the push to curtail spending through austerity measures but rather the pressure to commodify public services and employment relations through marketising structural reforms. In this sense, it would be wrong to construct a dichotomy between fiscal retrenchment before 2014 and the expansion of public investment after that.

By comparing the NEG prescriptions in the two cross-sectoral policy areas, our study also revealed that NEG's commodifying prescriptions targeted the governance of public services across all four countries, whereas the same did not happen in employment relations. In this area, Germany received one commodifying NEG prescription and several decommodifying ones. We must look beyond NEG to find the reasons for this. To explain these differences, we put the NEG regime in each cross-sectoral area and the three sectors into the historical perspective of EU integration in these fields (Chapters 6–10).

In employment relations, increased horizontal pressures triggered by the creation of the European internal market and monetary union were the main drivers of commodification before NEG. By contrast, horizontal market pressures played a much more limited role in public services. Correspondingly, the majority of EU law-making through the ordinary legislative procedure in employment relations served the purpose of correcting the commodifying effects of horizontal market integration by establishing minimum standards for workers across the EU. Each milestone of EU market and monetary integration was accompanied by decommodifying laws that established a plinth of EU labour standards across all member states in the areas of labour mobility, social policy coordination, occupational health and safety, and working conditions. These measures, however, were unable to counterbalance the market pressures unleashed by EU economic and monetary integration. Consequently, the EMU legitimised wage moderation and commodifying reforms of employment relations in many EU economies in the 2000s, most notably in Germany, which reported the highest ULC of all our four countries. German production sites faced particularly strong competitive pressures in the much more integrated European and global economy as a result of the growth of new transnational supply chains in the former Eastern bloc. In turn, the Schröder government, employers, and industrial relations scholars used the increased horizontal market pressures to legitimise wage moderation and the commodifying Hartz welfare and labour market reforms in the early 2000s, which subsequently also informed EU executives' NEG prescriptions elsewhere (Chapter 6).

In public services, commodification through horizontal market integration advanced slowly. The main channel of commodification in this policy area had been vertical interventions by commodifying EU laws on public services and the debt and deficit benchmarks set by the Maastricht Treaty and the SGP. Following on from a series of sectoral liberalisation directives and court rulings, in 2004 Commissioner Bolkestein presented a draft Services Directive that aimed to deregulate services across all sectors in one go, including the laws governing the transnational posting of service workers. However, unprecedented transnational social-movement and union protests and the legislative amendments by the EU's legislators curbed Bolkestein's ambitions. Conversely however, the anti-Bolkestein protest movement was unable to turn the energy of its mobilisations into a sufficiently strong movement for a decommodifying EU Directive on Services of General Interest. This enabled EU executives to pursue their commodifying public service agenda further, through new sectoral service liberalisation directives as well as corresponding NEG prescriptions (Chapters 7–10).

In sum, EU executives' NEG prescriptions on public services and employment relations generally pointed in a commodifying policy direction but not to the same degree across all categories, countries, and years. These variegated patterns of NEG prescriptions do not reflect their drafters' conflicting – commodifying or decommodifying – policy objectives but rather the unequal progress of commodification across countries and policy areas. At times, EU executives also issued decommodifying prescriptions, but their coercive power was much weaker. In addition, decommodifying prescriptions were usually linked to policy rationales that were compatible with the overarching logic of commodification. We revealed a strong overarching commodifying logic in NEG prescriptions in qualitative public services categories (sector-level governance mechanisms, provider-level governance mechanisms, cost-coverage mechanisms). In these categories, all prescriptions across all four countries and all eleven years clearly pointed in a commodifying direction, even though their coercive power differed depending on the countries' location in the NEG policy enforcement regime at a given time (Tables 11.1 and 11.2). Can we say the same about the NEG prescriptions for the three specific public services sectors: transport, water, and healthcare services?

11.3 COMPARING NEG PRESCRIPTIONS ON TRANSPORT, WATER, AND HEALTHCARE SERVICES

By comparing NEG prescriptions for Germany, Ireland, Italy, and Romania (2009–2019) across the public transport, water, and healthcare services sectors, we pursue two objectives. First, we map the patterns of their commodifying or decommodifying policy orientation (Chapters 4, 8–10). Second, we assess the extent to which prescriptions across the sectors mirror an overarching commodification script. We do that because the manifestation of a *pan-European* commodification script informing NEG's *country-specific* policy prescriptions is a necessary (but not sufficient) condition for the emergence of countervailing *transnational* movements.

Tables 11.3 and 11.4 reveal the dominance of commodifying NEG prescriptions across all three sectors and four countries, especially in our qualitative categories. NEG's focus on qualitative policy reforms is crucial, as reforms are more difficult to reverse than the quantitative curtailment of resources for the provision of public services.

As the profitable segments of the Romanian water sector had already been privatised in the 2000s, EU executives focused their sector-specific prescriptions instead on the Romanian transport and health sectors. By contrast, EU executives focused their sector-specific prescriptions for Ireland on the water and healthcare sectors, as Irish governments had already turned Ireland's public transport companies into formally independent, semi-state corporations. After 2008, Irish governments simply cut their subsidies to them, as part of their attempts to curtail public expenditure in general (Chapters 7 and 8).

Tables 11.3 and 11.4 show that EU executives issued only a few decommodifying prescriptions. Most of them appeared after 2016, tasking governments to invest more in transport and water but not in healthcare services. Despite their decommodifying orientation, most of these prescriptions did not question NEG's

TABLE 11.3 *Commodifying NEG prescriptions on public services (sectoral)*

Quantitative prescriptions

	Transport			Water					Healthcare				
	DE	IE	IT	RO	DE	IE	IT	RO	DE	IE	IT	RO	
2009													2009
2010												◀	2010
2011				◀								◀	2011
2012				◀						◀		◀	2012
2013									△	◀		◀[3]★	2013
2014													2014
2015													2015
2016												△	2016
2017												△	2017
2018												△	2018
2019												△	2019

Qualitative prescriptions

	Transport				Water				Healthcare			
	DE	IE	IT	RO	DE	IE	IT	RO	DE	IE	IT	RO
2009				●[4]								
2010				●[2] ■[2]		◆						◆
2011	○[2]			●[18] ■[4]	○	◆ ■				●		◆ ■ ●
2012	○		●	●[12] ■[2]	○	◆ ■	●			●		◆ ■ ●
2013	○		○[3]	●[6] ■[5]	○	◆ ■	○		○	●[2] ■[2]		◆[3] ■[2] ●[3]
2014	○		●[3]	□ ○	○		●		○	●[2] ■[2]		○[2]
2015	○		●[2]	□			●			■		
2016			■	□ ○	○		●			○	●	
2017			●[2]				●					
2018			■				■			○		
2019			●[2]	□			■			○		○

Source: Tables 7.2–10.2; Online Appendix, Tables A7.1–A10.6.
Categories: △ = resource levels; ☆ = coverage levels; ○ = sector-level governance mechanisms; □ = provider-level governance mechanisms; ◇ = cost-coverage mechanisms.
Coercive power: ▲★■◆ = very significant; ●■◆ = significant; △□○◇ = weak.
Superscript number equals number of relevant prescriptions. Country code: DE = Germany; IE = Ireland; IT = Italy; RO = Romania.

TABLE 11.4 *Decommodifying NEG prescriptions on public services (sectoral)*

Quantitative prescriptions

	Transport					Water					Healthcare					
	DE	IE	IT	RO		DE	IE	IT	RO		DE	IE	IT	RO	
2009															2009
2010															2010
2011															2011
2012			▲^{ch}										▲^{g}		2012
2013			△$^{a\,j}$										△^{g}	▲^{h} ☆$^{a\,h}$	2013
2014													▲^{g}	☆^{a}	2014
2015						△^{bc}								△$^{a\,h}$ ☆^{a}	2015
2016	△^{bj}	△^{c}		△^{a}		△^{bcj}	△^{c}		△^{a} ☆^{a}						2016
2017		△^{c}				△^{b}	△^{c}								2017
2018		△$^{ad\,cj}$		△^{ch}		△^{b}	△$^{ad\,cj}$		△^{c}					☆^{a}	2018
2019	△$^{d\,j}$	△$^{ad\,cj}$	▲$^{d\,hj}$	△^{ad}		△^{bcj}	△$^{ad\,cj}$						☆^{g}	☆^{a}	2019

288

Qualitative prescriptions

	Transport				Water				Healthcare				
	DE	IE	IT	RO	DE	IE	IT	RO	DE	IE	IT	RO	
2009													2009
2010													2010
2011													2011
2012													2012
2013												◆[a i]	2013
2014												◇[2a h]	2014
2015													2015
2016												◇[a]	2016
2017												◇[a]	2017
2018													2018
2019													2019

Source: Tables 7.2–10.2; Online Appendix, Tables A7.1–A10.6.
Categories: △ = resource levels; ☆ = coverage levels; ◇ = cost-coverage mechanisms.
Coercive power: ▲◆ = very significant; ▲★ = significant; △☆ = weak.
Semantic link to policy rationale: **a** = Enhance social inclusion; **b** = Rebalance EU economy; **c** = Boost competitiveness and growth; **d** = Shift to green economy; **g** = Expand labour market participation; **h** = Improve efficiency; **i** = Reduce payroll taxes; **j** = Enhance private sector involvement.
Bold letters = policy rationale linked to commodification script.
Country code: DE = Germany; IE = Ireland; IT = Italy; RO = Romania.

commodifying logic. As in the case of the cross-sectoral prescriptions for public services (Table 11.2), the expansionary prescriptions for water and transport services had weak coercive power. They were also usually linked to policy rationales that were subordinated to an overarching logic of public service commodification. Finally, most expansionary prescriptions linked their calls for more resources for public services to the term 'resource prioritisation'. This meant that any increase in public resources for some public services had to be matched with cuts elsewhere. In the following paragraphs, we compare NEG prescriptions for transport, water, and healthcare in more detail.

Curtailing Public Spending for Transport, Water, and Healthcare Services

The turn to austerity in general also curtailed public spending for the three public services sectors under consideration. EU executives thus issued *sector-specific* prescriptions that tasked governments to curtail the resource levels for specific public services as well as the coverage levels of specific public services that users could access.

In the water services sector, EU executives issued no commodifying prescription in the two quantitative categories, as Table 11.3 illustrates. In the transport services sector, EU executives issued such prescriptions only for Romania in 2011 and 2012. Even so, the Irish government, for example, cut its capital spending on transport services between 2008 and 2012 by 72 per cent and its current spending until 2015 by 31 per cent, as outlined in Chapter 8. Most sector-specific quantitative prescriptions that pointed in a commodifying policy direction affected healthcare services. Only Italy did not receive such prescriptions. Italian governments nonetheless cut €37 billion from Italy's national health service between 2010 and 2019 (Chapter 10) and implemented significant commodifying healthcare reforms (Galanti, 2023) – once more highlighting the impact of the cross-sectoral prescriptions on resource and coverage levels in specific sectors.

EU executives issued specific commodifying prescriptions on public healthcare services, as 'public expenditure on health *absorbs* a significant and growing share of EU countries' resources' European Commission, 2016b: 12, emphasis added). Romania received such prescriptions almost every year from 2010 until the advent of the Covid pandemic. When Romania was subject to very coercive MoU-related NEG prescriptions (2010–2013), EU executives tasked the Romanian government to contain hospital expenditure by reducing the overall number of hospitals and by reducing their bed capacity. Subsequently, EU executives tasked the Romanian government to make savings by shifting healthcare services from hospital to outpatient care (2016–2019). In 2013, Germany received a similar prescription, although EU executives never asked its government to curtail its public spending in general (see Table 11.1). In 2012 and 2013, EU executives tasked the Irish government to contain its health expenditure while the country was subject to a very constraining MoU.

In 2013, EU executives issued a prescription that tasked the Romanian government to 'revise the basic benefits package', curtailing the coverage levels of the public healthcare system for its users. As outlined in Chapter 10, these commodifying qualitative prescriptions led to deteriorating service levels, hospital closures, and a reduction in staffing levels, which in turn worsened the working conditions of healthcare workers as well as the welfare of patients in the public system. Incidentally, EU executives must have anticipated the negative effects of these measures on the public healthcare system too when they tasked the Romanian government in 2013 to 'establish the framework for a private supplementary insurance market' (Chapter 10). We return later in the chapter to this qualitative prescription.

In sum, given the dearth of commodifying quantitative prescriptions in the water and transport sectors (Chapter 7), the corresponding healthcare-specific NEG prescriptions do not simply mirror the application of austerity measures across all public services sectors. This becomes clear on assessing EU executives' prescriptions for Germany (2013) and Romania (2016–2019) that tasked these governments to make savings by shifting healthcare from hospital to outpatient care at a time when the two governments were not tasked to curtail the resource levels for their public services in general (Tables 11.1 and 11.3). In the Romanian case, EU executives even issued prescriptions that simultaneously tasked the government to increase spending elsewhere, including in the water and transport sectors. This suggests that the NEG prescription drafters from the Commission's DG ECFIN, quoted above, were not concerned primarily about public deficit figures (European Commission, 2016b: 12). More plausibly, the simultaneous calls for expansionary measures in other public sectors suggest that EU executives just assumed that public investments elsewhere would be more productive. The tension between allegedly (unproductive) social and (productive) economic services informing their NEG prescriptions is even clearer in the case of the decommodifying prescriptions in favour of greater public investment, which we discuss next.

Investing in (Productive) Public Services

Table 11.4 (as in Table 11.2, the superscript figures indicate the number of prescriptions in a given year; the superscript letters specify the semantic links between decommodifying NEG prescriptions and the policy rationales informing them) reveals that decommodifying NEG prescriptions in our two quantitative categories (resource levels and coverage levels) became more prevalent over time. Strikingly however, their unequal distribution patterns across sectors remained remarkably stable. As seen above, the commodifying prescriptions in these two categories targeted healthcare rather than water and transport services. Equally, the expansionary prescriptions that appeared after the alleged social investment turn in 2016 (Chapter 4) outnumbered the commodifying ones in the transport and the water but not the healthcare services sector. These sectoral differences are even more striking if we look also at the different policy rationales behind these decommodifying NEG prescriptions. Whereas NEG documents justified greater public spending on the network industries and their infrastructure as a productive, economic investment, this was not the case in healthcare. Regardless, the coercive power of all expansionary prescriptions was weak in almost all cases (Table 11.3).

The superscript letters accompanying the prescriptions in Table 11.4 specify the links between the prescriptions and the policy rationales informing them. The bold superscript letters on the right denote the semantic links to policy rationales that are compatible with the NEG's overarching commodification script, whereas the nonbold superscript letters on the left indicate policy rationales that may deviate from this script.

Table 11.4 shows that the decommodifying prescriptions were linked to different policy rationales. This is not all that surprising, as decommodifying public policies can serve different objectives, such as 'enhance social inclusion' or a 'shift to a green economy'. Policymakers created decommodifying public services also for economic reasons, for example to boost economic growth or to address market failures. Good examples of the latter can be found in public network industries that not only serve social goals but also provide key facilities for economic operators (Chapters 8–9). Europe's public healthcare systems perform economic functions not only by contributing to the reproduction of labour in general but also by facilitating the greater participation of women and mobile workers in the EU labour market in particular (Chapter 10). Marianna Mazzucato (2013) thus argued that the scope and scale of public services should increase in tandem with the creation of the EU's internal market and monetary union.

As Table 11.4 reveals, however, only a few decommodifying prescriptions were linked to social and ecological policy rationales. The 'shift to a green economy' rationale came to the fore but only after the 2018 cycle and only in decommodifying prescriptions for the water and transport sectors. The 'enhance social inclusion' rationale had appeared earlier across all sectors in prescriptions for Romania on transport, water, and healthcare services. This is hardly surprising considering the exceptionally low share of Romanian households with access to running water and sanitation (Chapter 9) and the exceptionally low share of Romanian public healthcare spending as a share of GDP of 3.9 per cent in 2015 (as compared with 5.3 per cent in Ireland, 6.6 per cent in Italy, and 9.5 per cent in Germany) (OECD, 2023a). The coercive power of these social prescriptions was weak, however, unlike the MoU prescriptions that tasked the Romanian government to increase the co-payments of healthcare users (2010–2013) and to shrink the scope of health services covered by its public healthcare fund (2013). In the other three countries, EU executives linked their decommodifying NEG prescriptions only rarely to social policy rationales. Instead, they related them to rationales compatible with NEG's commodifying script, as Table 11.4 shows.

Most expansionary NEG prescriptions targeted the infrastructure in the two network industries rather than in healthcare. After 2016, all four countries received such prescriptions, which stressed the contribution of greater investment to growth and increased competitiveness. In the German case, the expansionary prescriptions (2015–2019) were linked to the 'rebalance the EU economy' rationale, given the expected spill-over effects of a more expansionary public investment policy in surplus countries like Germany for the economies in the rest of the EU (see also section 11.2). After 2016, all four countries received expansionary prescriptions, albeit with a twist, mandating governments to prioritise infrastructure investment. This meant diverting public spending away from other areas towards infrastructure projects, inter alia, in the water and transport sectors.

In healthcare, Italy received a series of decommodifying prescriptions on resource levels to improve the provision of long-term care to incentivise greater labour market participation by women. Although the policy orientation of this prescription was decommodifying, it was linked to a policy rationale that does not question NEG's commodification script. This becomes even more apparent when we consider the predominantly private provision of long-term care services in Italy and elsewhere (Chapter 10). In NEG prescriptions on transport and water services, the link between greater public investments and the need to enhance the involvement of the private sector in public services was even more explicit, as shown in Table 11.4. As in the case of their expansionary cross-sectoral prescriptions for the public sector, EU executives incentivised the channelling of public funds towards private firms in their sectoral prescriptions too. This commodifying logic is even clearer in their *qualitative* prescriptions for the three sectors, which we discuss next.

Marketising Transport, Water, and Healthcare Services

Tables 11.3 and 11.4 reveal an extremely consistent commodification pattern across all qualitative categories of NEG prescriptions. All prescriptions on the mechanisms governing the provision of services across all sectors and countries pointed in a commodifying policy direction. Apart from four prescriptions for Romania, the same was also true concerning the prescriptions on cost-coverage mechanisms, which specify the conditions for users' access to public services.

As Chapters 8–10 discuss in detail, the degree of commodification of public services before 2008 varied from sector to sector and country to country. This explains the different deployment of marketising qualitative prescriptions across sectors and countries. In the transport sector, EU executives' prescriptions on sector-level governance mechanisms targeted mainly the regulatory framework for railways in the member states. The existing EU railway laws still enabled member states to shield their state-owned railway companies to some extent from unbridled competition thanks to union protests and the ensuing amendments by the European Parliament and the Council of transport ministers, which curbed the commodifying bent of the Commission's draft railway directives (Chapter 8). To overcome these limitations, the Commission and the Council of finance ministers issued railway-related prescriptions on a constant basis between 2009 and 2019 across all three countries, with the exception of Ireland – because Irish Rail arguably plays only a marginal role in EU transport networks. Hence, as Table 11.3 shows, EU executives sought to stimulate competition in the railway sector across the other three countries, regardless of their location in NEG's enforcement regime. As much as the coercive power of the prescriptions differed across countries, their impact differed too. Whereas the Romanian government was constrained to implement almost all MoU-related prescriptions it received, the same did not happen in the German case, given the weak coercive power of the prescriptions for Germany (Chapter 8). Table 11.3 documents similar patterns pertaining to prescriptions on transport services in the provider-level governance mechanism category. Both Romania and Italy received prescriptions to implement railway privatisation plans, albeit with different degrees of vagueness, reflecting their unequal location in the NEG regime (Chapter 8). By contrast, EU executives did not issue any prescriptions that instructed the German government to privatise DB Cargo or its parent company Deutsche Bahn.

In the water sector, commodifying NEG prescriptions targeted the sector- and provider-level mechanisms too, as also the cost-coverage mechanisms governing Irish users' access to water services. Only Romania did not receive any commodifying prescription for this sector, as its government had already privatised the lucrative water networks in the 2000s (Chapter 9). Whereas the MoU-related prescriptions tasked the Irish government to create a water corporation and to introduce charges for individual water users also, the less constraining prescriptions for Italy and the weak ones for Germany targeted the sectors' governance mechanisms to marketise water services (Chapter 9). This happened although water was not, according to the EU Water Framework Directive (2000/60/EC), 'a commercial product like any other but, rather, a heritage which must be protected, defended and treated as such' (Recital 1).

By contrast to NEG prescriptions in the area of employment relations and the healthcare sector, NEG prescriptions on water services were accompanied by simultaneous policy debates about a looming commodifying EU law, the EU Concessions Directive. This meant that water users and workers in all countries faced not only the same commodifying NEG script but also a looming EU law that would be, unlike NEG prescriptions, equally constraining across all countries. The same was not the case for public passenger transport services, which the Commission totally excluded from its Draft Concessions Directive, nor in health services, which the Commission at least excluded from its full application (Art. 5(g) and Recital 21 Draft Concessions Directive COM (2011) 897).

Compared with our other two public services sectors, healthcare services came within the reach of commodifying EU laws much later, as Chapter 10 outlines. This, however, did not stop EU executives from issuing commodifying NEG prescriptions on the mechanisms governing healthcare services. Romania's and Ireland's healthcare sectors in particular received several commodifying NEG prescriptions on sector- and provider-level governance mechanisms. This happened although European 'Union action shall respect the responsibilities of the Member States for the definition of their health policy and for the organisation and delivery of health services and medical care' (Art. 168(1) TFEU) – highlighting once more the fallacy of a too narrow, literal reading of such Treaty articles on the EU's legislative competences in the sector and the importance of the EU executives' political will. After all, Article 121 TFEU on multilateral surveillance and the ensuing Six-Pack of EU laws of 2011 allow corrective EU interventions whenever member states pursue policies that '*risk* jeopardising the *proper functioning* of the economic and monetary union' (emphasis added) (Art. 121(4) TFEU), as discussed in Chapters 2 and 3. When subject to MoU conditionality, the Irish and Romanian governments received specific and very constraining prescriptions, which centralised control over hospitals' budgets. Moreover, MoU-related NEG prescriptions forced the Irish government to shift the funding mechanisms for its hospitals from a system based on patients' needs to a delivery-oriented case-based system. The latter prescriptions were particularly important from a commodifying healthcare policy perspective, as diagnosis-related group (DRG) funding methods are a precondition for the making of healthcare markets. Whereas Germany, Italy, and Romania had already introduced the DRG financing method before the EU's shift to NEG, the Irish healthcare system lagged behind in this respect (Chapter 10). The governments of Ireland and Romania also had to introduce e-health systems, which are tellingly also needed for the operation of DRG healthcare financing methods. Conversely, the EU executives acknowledged the measures that the German government had taken earlier to improve the cost-efficiency of its hospitals and long-term care. They nevertheless asked the German government to go further, as the implemented reforms would be insufficient to contain the expected future healthcare cost increases. Promoting competition between healthcare providers was another regular theme in the prescriptions issued to Italy and Ireland. Finally, several MoU-related prescriptions on cost-coverage mechanisms committed the Romanian government to introduce co-payments for healthcare services (2010–2012) and to establish a private supplementary insurance market (2013), as mentioned earlier.

In contrast, and as Table 11.4 shows, decommodifying qualitative prescriptions were almost entirely absent, apart from four prescriptions for the Romanian healthcare sector that mandated the Romanian government to adjust health insurance contributions for low- and middle-income earners and to eradicate the practice of informal user payments to healthcare practitioners. Although the latter prescriptions pointed in a decommodifying direction, Romanian governments used them not to eradicate patients' co-payments to access healthcare services *tout court* but rather to justify the replacement of informal by formal co-payments (Chapter 10). The prescription to adjust health insurance contributions for low- and middle-income earners was likewise linked to a policy rationale that does not collide with NEG's overarching commodification script. The prescription benefitted the targeted workers as reduced payroll taxes increased their net pay, but, at the same time, it reduced companies' nominal ULC. Altogether however, this measure once more reduced the funds available for public healthcare.

An Overarching Commodification Script across All Four Countries and Three Sectors

In sum, in all three public services sectors, all NEG prescriptions on both sector- and provider-level governance mechanisms pointed in a commodifying direction. Substantive deviations from this pattern occurred only when such prescriptions were not issued because of the implementation of earlier reforms (e.g., the prior introduction of the DRG healthcare funding method in Germany, Italy, and Romania or the prior privatisation of water services in Romania) or their irrelevance (e.g., railway services in Ireland). Given the countries' different locations in the NEG enforcement regime, the overarching commodification script behind these qualitative prescriptions did not threaten the service users and workers in all four countries equally, except when prescriptions were accompanied by simultaneous draft EU laws, as happened in the case of the 2011 draft EU Concessions Directive. The same conclusion applies when we compare qualitative NEG prescriptions across the two cross-sectoral policy areas (employment relations, public services) and across the three public services sectors. All prescriptions across all four countries that tasked governments to implement structural reforms pointed in a commodifying policy direction across all years.

The more the public finances recovered from the financial crisis, the less constraining NEG prescriptions became. The slow recovery of European economies in the late 2010s led to an increase in prescriptions that pointed in a decommodifying policy direction, namely, quantitative prescriptions calling for greater public investments. Given their underlying rationales however, most decommodifying prescriptions were subordinated to NEG's overarching commodification script. Certainly, labour movements and public service users very much welcomed the more expansionary NEG prescriptions. At the same time, our analysis reveals that EU executives' NEG prescriptions mandated governments to channel more public resources into the allegedly more productive services (transport and water) rather than into essential social services like healthcare. Moreover, most decommodifying prescriptions on public service resources or wage levels were linked to commodifying rather than decommodifying policy rationales. Most importantly however, almost all *qualitative* NEG prescriptions pointed in a commodifying policy direction across the two policy areas, three sectors, and four countries, albeit with different coercive powers (depending on the countries' location in the NEG's policy enforcement regime) and in an asynchronous manner (depending on the prior progress of commodification in each site).

Our analysis has thus shown that the EU executives' country-specific NEG prescriptions had less to do with the configuration of employment relations or public services in a country than with the location of its employment relations or public services on a commodification trajectory before NEG. The NEG regime could thus be described as a case of differentiated integration but not in the usual pre-NEG sense of EU laws that aim 'to accommodate economic, social and cultural heterogeneity' (Bellamy and Kröger, 2017: 625). Instead, EU executives' country-specific NEG prescriptions followed a logic of *reversed* differentiated integration (Stan and Erne, 2023; Chapter 3), as they targeted different countries differently to pursue an overarching commodification agenda.

This leads us to the question of whether NEG's commodification script triggered an increase in transnational union and social-movement protests, or whether NEG's country-specific nature (Chapter 2) effectively precluded an upsurge in transnational action. Given EU executives' totalising aspiration to do everything necessary to ensure the 'proper' functioning of the EU economy and to put that in a few short policy documents, we assess whether the EU's shift to NEG in turn prompted unions and social movements to respond to EU executives' broad aspirations by broadening the scope of their own demands and by scaling up their countervailing collective actions.

11.4 NEG'S COMMODIFICATION SCRIPT AND TRANSNATIONAL COLLECTIVE ACTION

In this section, we problematise the impact of the EU's shift to NEG on European labour politics. We do that by assessing the patterns of transnational protests by trade unions and social movements in Europe on socioeconomic issues across two distinct historical periods. The first period spans the time from 1997, when the EU leaders agreed the original SGP in the run-up to EMU, until the advent of the financial crisis in 2008. The second period begins in 2009 and ends in 2019, that is, before EU executives opened a new era of NEG in March 2020 when they suspended the SGP's fiscal constraints after the advent of the Covid-19 pandemic (Chapter 12).

We proceed with our analysis in two steps. First, we present and discuss our general findings, comparing the salience of transnational, socioeconomic protest events at company, sectoral, political, and systemic level across the two time periods. This comparison reveals that transnational protests targeting EU legislators (EU law) or EU executives (NEG prescriptions) clearly outnumbered the protests targeting private employers, national governments, European public employers, global trade agreements, or the transnational capitalist system in general. This highlights the salience of EU interventions as an important trigger of countervailing protests by trade unions and social movements and confirms that it is easier for them to politicise vertical EU interventions rather than horizontal market integration pressures.

Second, we further differentiate the protests targeting EU legislators (EU law) or EU executives (NEG prescriptions) to assess in more detail the effects of the shift to NEG on labour politics. First, we split the protest category targeting EU law in two, distinguishing protests with a *narrow focus* on a particular law (e.g., EU Services Directive) from those with a *broad focus* on an entire thread of EU laws and policies (e.g., NEG regime). Second, we classify the protest events in the resulting categories by public service sector also. This allows us to relate the protests to the unequal patterns of commodification across public services sectors by specific EU laws, clusters of EU laws, and NEG prescriptions across the two distinct periods.

Transnational Protests on Socioeconomic Issues across Europe (1997–2019)

Table 11.5 confirms the key role of vertical EU interventions as a driver of transnational protests on socio-economic issues in Europe. In the pre-NEG period (1997–2008), we counted on average 6.8 such protests per year targeting EU institutions; this means that 62 per cent of all transnational protests belong to this *political* protest category (see Erne and Nowak, 2023). In the subsequent period (2009–2019), we counted roughly the same number of such protests per year, namely, on average 6.4 events per year targeting EU interventions by law and 0.6 events per year targeting NEG prescriptions.

If we add all political protests together, including those against the European Commission's attempts to sign global trade agreements and those of European civil servants against their supranational public employers, the number of political transnational protests as a share of all transnational protests remained roughly at similar levels during the two time periods (1997–2008: 64 per cent; 2009–2019: 59 per cent). This is noteworthy, also considering the significant increase in transnational protests overall after the 2008 crisis, from on average 11.0 (1997–2008) to on average 25.9 (2009–2019) transnational protests per year. Before assessing the patterns of transnational protests targeting EU legislators and executives and their relationship to the EU's shift to NEG in detail, we must explain the dearth of transnational protests targeting employers in the private sector. The latter is all the more puzzling as there are more transnational corporations (TNCs) than supranational governmental institutions in Europe, meaning that the number of protests targeting the former should, all other things being equal, be greater.

Explaining the scarcity of 'private' transnational protests on socioeconomic issues: In 1999, labour-friendly scholars were already advising European trade unions to 'enlarge their strategic domain to keep workers from being played off against each other' (Martin and Ross, 1999: 312). Nonetheless, most scholars of labour politics predicted that collective bargaining, social policymaking, and, thus, also union action would remain confined to the nation state (Thelen, 2001). Although greater economic and monetary integration would put unions and social policies under increased horizontal market pressures, these competitive adjustment pressures would not end the autonomy of national labour policymakers, at least not formally. Accordingly, social pacts and other national corporatist arrangements reappeared in the 1990s – albeit for novel reasons, for example, to enhance a country's competitiveness or to help it meet its EMU convergence criterion of low inflation (Chapter 6). Certainly, European unions tried to coordinate their bargaining policies across borders to curb the pursuit of beggar-thy-neighbour strategies,

TABLE 11.5 *Transnational socioeconomic protests in Europe (1997–2019)*

Levels	Targets	Protests from the adoption of the SGP until the EU's shift to NEG (1997–2008)			Protests from the EU's shift to NEG until the Covid pandemic (2009–2019)		
		Total	Per year	Share of protest	Total	Per year	Share of protest
Company	Individual employers	25	2.1	19%	60	5.5	28%
Sectoral	Multiple employers	1	0.1	1%	8	0.7	4%
Governmental	National governments	0	0	0%	1	0.1	0%
	EU institutions: EU laws	82	6.8	62%	71	6.5	33%
	EU institutions: NEG prescriptions	–	–	–	7	0.6	3%
	European public employers	0	0	0%	39	3.5	18%
	Global trade agreements[a]	3	0	2%	10	0.9	5%
Systemic	Transnational capitalist system	21	1.8	16%	20	1.8	9%
Total		132	11.0	100%	216	26.1	100%

Source: Erne and Nowak (2023).
a This category includes protests that targeted the European Commission, which negotiates and signs global trade agreements.

but these attempts largely failed (Erne, 2008). Thus, labour politics remained more a national than a European affair (Dølvik, 2004). Mirroring the varieties-of-capitalism paradigm in political economy and labour studies (Hall and Soskice, 2001), most European trade unions stressed the advantages of national coordinated employment relations systems, including in export-oriented industries. Although the corresponding competitive corporatist arrangements involved concession bargaining, it gave union leaders a seat at policymaking tables. However, the more transnational horizontal market dynamics put national bargaining systems (designed to take wages out of competition) under pressure, and the more the senior management of TNCs used whipsawing tactics that put workers from different sites in competition with one another (Greer and Hauptmeier, 2016), the more hitherto combative national industrial unions adopted collaborative stances to increase the competitiveness of 'their' production sites and companies. Transnational union protests against private employers occurred only very rarely, namely, when management adopted very uncompromising stances *and* union activists found levers in the EU institutional framework that they could use as a catalyst for transnational action (Erne, 2008; Golden and Erne, 2022). The making and enlargement of European goods and capital markets as such did not trigger transnational protests, as shown by the low number of protests targeting employers at company or sectoral level (see Table 11.5). However, whereas the increased transnational horizontal market pressures and the whipsawing games of TNCs allowed corporate executives to contain labour movements, EU executives were not as effective in preventing transnational protests by unions and social movements.

Explaining the salience of political transnational protests on socio-economic issues: In the 2000s, EU executives started to propose ever more EU laws that attempted to commodify both labour and public services. This is important, as EU labour law had hitherto pointed in a decommodifying direction (Chapter 6) and public services had been shielded from horizontal (market) integration pressures triggered by the making of the European single market (Chapters 7–10).

By contrast to the earlier European Community laws that created an integrated goods and capital market, several draft EU laws that sought to commodify labour provisions or public services in the 2000s caused counter-vailing protests by unions and social movements across borders. Having been confronted with intensified neoliberal restructuring brought about by the commodification of public utilities and the curtailment of public spending as a consequence of EMU's debt and deficit criteria from the mid-1990s onwards, public service unions started coordinating their actions at EU level as well. In the transport sector, that happened through not only the European

Transport Workers' Federation (ETF) but also the International Dockworkers Council (IDC), a transnational rank-and-file network of dockworkers (Chapter 8). The European Public Service Union (EPSU) coordinated the transnational union actions across the public sector in general, and the other two sectors (water and healthcare services) that are part of our study in particular (Chapters 7, 9–10). These transnational public sector union networks found an institutional ally in the European Parliament, and together they blocked the European Commission's commodification of port services on two occasions and at least moderated its commodification drive in relation to rail, water, and healthcare services (Crespy, 2016). By the mid-2000s, European public service unions had become quite adept at both EU protest politics and lobbying, matching similar trends in the broader social movement sphere (Parks, 2015). By adopting both action repertoires, they became quite effective at adding the argument of force to the force of argument. Both the ETF and EPSU participated in European Social Forums, and some union activists joined the transnational protests of anti-systemic alter-globalisation movements that targeted the transnational capitalist system as a whole (see Table 11.5).

EPSU sought out alliances with social movements that opposed much more strategically the EU's efforts to commodify public services. By strengthening linkages with other unions and movements, EPSU adopted a strategy that not only helped curb the commodifying direction of EU legislation on procurement but also helped thwart Commissioner Bolkestein's draft EU Services Directive (Chapters 7, 9–10). The ETF, on the other hand, could rely on the greater industrial strength of its transport workers, given their strategic position at critical junctures in the capitalist production process, their ability to organise very contentious protests politicising EU interventions, and the ETF's links to union-friendly EU legislators (Chapter 8).

In the private sector, industrial unions coordinated their activities across borders too but rarely protested against commodifying EU laws. After all, Europe's manufacturing industries had been opened up to transnational competition much earlier than services. Instead, industrial unions joined forces in their sectoral European union federation, industriAll Europe, to coordinate collective bargaining, to assist their affiliates' members in European Works Councils and to influence the EU's labour and industrial policies. Conversely, private sector unions active in sectors that are less integrated in the international goods markets, for example, the European Federation of Building and Woodworkers, often joined the protests of their public sector counterparts, namely, against the Bolkestein Directive and to ensure equal pay for equal work at the same location for local and mobile workers (Chapter 6; see also Table 11.6).

TABLE 11.6 *Transnational socioeconomic protests targeting EU laws and prescriptions by sector*

Targets	Sectors	Protests (1997–2008) Total	Per year	Per cent	Protest (2009–2019) Total	Per year	Per cent
EU laws (narrow focus)	Intersectoral	11	0.9		4	0.4	
	Private sector	6	0.5		10	0.9	
	Public sector (national/local)	28	2.3		20	1.8	
	– (of those in public transport)	(23)	(1.9)		(19)	(1.7)	
	Subtotal	45	3.8	55	34	3.1	44
EU laws (broad focus)	Intersectoral	35	2.9		24	2.2	
	Public sector (national/local)	2	0.2		13	1.2	
	– (of those in public water)	(2)	(0.2)		(3)	(0.3)	
	– (of those in public healthcare)				(8)	(0.7)	
	Subtotal	37	3.1	45	37	3.4	47
EU NEG prescriptions	– Transport services	–	–	–	7	0.6	–
	Subtotal	–	–	–	7	0.6	9
All	Total	82	6.8	100	78	7.1	100

Source: Erne and Nowak (2023).

64 per cent of all transnational protest events on socio-economic issues between 1997 and 2008 politicised draft EU laws (see Table 11.5). As shown in more detail in our analysis of the countervailing protests politicising EU governance interventions on employment relations (Chapter 6), public services in general (Chapter 7), and transport (Chapter 8), water (Chapter 9), and healthcare services (Chapter 10), transnational union action was usually triggered by draft EU laws that pointed in a commodifying policy direction. Accordingly, we would expect that EU executives' NEG prescriptions would also trigger transnational countermovements if they were informed by a consistent script in favour of commodification. As portrayed in the preceding sections of this chapter, this was the case for qualitative NEG prescriptions that tasked the governments of Germany, Ireland, Italy, and Romania to implement commodifying structural reforms of public services.

As Table 11.6 shows among all protests in our database, we identified only seven countervailing *transnational* protests against a *specific* NEG prescription across all four countries and three sectors between 2009 and 2019. This is a very low number, given the more than 200 commodifying NEG prescriptions that EU executives issued to Germany, Ireland, Italy, and Romania alone during that period – in only two cross-sectoral policy areas and three public services sectors (Tables 11.1 and 11.3). None of the transnational protests targeted NEG prescriptions issued to our four countries. As Chapter 8 illustrates, the IDC and the ETF organised the seven transnational strikes and demonstrations in support of Portuguese and Spanish dockworkers' struggles against the implementation of specific NEG prescriptions, which tasked their governments to commodify their port services (see also Fox-Hodess, 2017).

Does this mean that NEG's country-specific methodology, which mimics the corporate governance mechanisms and labour control regimes of TNCs (Chapter 3), effectively shielded EU executives from countervailing protests by unions and social movements? Our answer is no, for the following reasons.

Certainly, the EU's shift to the NEG regime after the 2008 financial crisis constitutes a paradigm shift in terms of both policymaking and enforcement. Even so, NEG's country-specific methodology did not preclude social actors from politicising EU executives' commodifying policy agenda, as the return of grievances about socioeconomic issues as the most important driver of contentious politics after 2008 shows (Kriesi et al., 2020). The difficulty was the politicisation of NEG across borders because EU executives' country-specific deployment of (seemingly) ad hoc prescriptions hampered transnational activism – even though the logic of reversed differentiated integration of EU executives' NEG prescriptions targeted different countries differently to pursue an overarching commodifying agenda.

Tellingly, the presidents of the European Commission, the European Council, the Eurogroup, the European Central Bank, and the European Parliament themselves acknowledged this agenda when they noted that the NEG prescriptions 'should be seen as part of a *political package* ... instead of being conceived as independent from each other' (Juncker et al., 2015: 7, emphasis added). As we have established in detail above, the script informing that package was one of commodification, albeit one apparently tempered by decommodifying prescriptions. However, decommodifying prescriptions were not only less consistent, vaguer, quantitative rather than qualitative, and with less coercive power than commodifying prescriptions but also were linked to policy rationales that did not contradict NEG's overarching commodification script. This suggests that the real limitation of the NEG regime as a driver of transnational countervailing action is not its apparently ambiguous policy orientation but rather the uneven coercive power of NEG prescriptions, which depends on a country's location in the NEG's policy enforcement regime.

This uneven, country-specific NEG policy enforcement regime confronted EU executives who wanted to advance a commodification agenda with two opposing dilemmas. EU executives could indeed impose commodifying prescriptions much more easily in countries that were in a weaker position in NEG's country-specific policy enforcement regime. In doing so however, they contributed to raising the level of Euroscepticism in these EU member states among the popular classes, who were most negatively affected by commodification. EU executives could not afford to ignore this trend forever without undermining their legitimacy (Schmidt, 2020), by contrast to supranational corporate executives of TNCs who do not depend on the democratic consent of their local subsidiaries or workers. However, whereas a subsidiary of a TNC cannot hold a referendum if its workers no longer want to be governed by the numerical key performance indicators and ad hoc prescriptions of its TNC headquarters, people in EU member states can elect Eurosceptic public representatives, veto EU Treaty changes, and even campaign to leave the EU. This shows that the managerial labour control regimes of TNCs cannot simply be transferred to EU public policymaking without risking the EU's disintegration.

The uneven coercive power of NEG prescriptions also presents EU executives wanting to advance the commodification of labour and public services with another major problem that has implications for transnational labour movements. Governments of surplus countries, like Germany, were able to ignore EU executives' NEG prescriptions, even when they pointed in a commodifying direction. This explains why EU executives could not afford to give up the classical governance methods by commodifying EU laws, as we have seen in the case of the Commission's 2011 draft Concessions Directive's planned commodification of water services. As soon as European trade unions and social movements from both surplus and deficit countries were confronted with an equally threatening vertical EU intervention in favour of water commodification, they joined forces across borders executing the Right2Water European Citizens' Initiative (ECI), which, in turn, forced EU legislators to exclude water services from the remit of the final 2014 EU Concessions Directive (2014/23/EU).

Most importantly however, the EU's shift to the NEG regime also shifted the frontiers of the battles against the marketisation of public services more generally, and of transport, water, and healthcare services in particular. Confronting austerity is not as easy as it sounds. As Huws (2012: 65) stated, 'a political strategy based only on "fighting the cuts" risks giving the impression that it is simply the scale of state expenditure that is in contest, rendering invisible the underlying logic of commodification and the new reality that public services themselves have become a site of accumulation'. The much more consistent focus of NEG prescriptions on structural marketising reforms across countries captured the attention of unions and social movements, namely, in public services.

As Table 11.6 shows, there were almost as many transnational protests per year targeting specific EU laws in the 2009–2019 period as in the 1997–2008 period. At the same time, the share of protests that targeted EU governance interventions broadly defined increased, namely, in the public sector including water and healthcare services, whereas the number of protests targeting specific EU laws decreased. The yearly 'Our health is not for sale' action days initiated by the European Network against Privatisation and Commercialisation of Health and Social Protection and supported by EPSU (Chapter 10) and the successful Right2Water ECI of EPSU and the European water movement (Chapter 9) are good examples of such transnational protest actions with a broad scope. The ECI not only convinced EU legislators to exclude water services from the EU Concessions Directive in 2014 (Szabó, Golden, and Erne, 2022) but also prefigured the Irish Right2Water movement, which forced the Irish government to reverse the introduction of water charges despite such charges having been requested by MoU-related NEG prescriptions (Chapter 9). That said, EPSU's and the ETUC's long-standing policy objective of securing a stronger legal basis for decommodified public services in general through an EU framework directive has so far proved to be a bridge too far (Chapter 7).

Overall, the EU executives' shift to a vertical NEG regime unleashed a plethora of socioeconomic protests, namely, in the public services that had been exposed to commodifying EU interventions more consistently across countries. Unions and social movements politicised economic governance interventions not only at national and local level but also transnationally (Chapters 6–10). Most importantly, unions and social movements framed their protests with reference to transnational political divides along the commodification–decommodification axis, rather than to divides along a national versus EU politics axis.

After the advent of the Covid-19 pandemic, the EU leaders unanimously suspended NEG's most important corrective mechanism in March 2020, namely, the SGP-related sanctions of the Six-Pack of EU laws that had institutionalised NEG in 2011. In October 2020, the European Commission furthermore proposed a decommodifying EU directive on adequate minimum wages in the European Union (COM/2020/682). Whether these events constitute a fundamental change in NEG's policy direction or a false dawn for those who perceive labour as not a commodity and public services as a common good is the focus of the next and final chapters of this book.

12

The EU's Shift to a Post-Covid NEG Regime

On 11 March 2020, the World Health Organisation recognised the Covid-19 outbreak as a global pandemic. On the same day, the *Financial Times* reported that the 'Coronavirus "tsunami" pushes Italy's hospitals to the breaking point', despite the greater number of critical care beds per person in Italy compared with most European Union (EU) member states (Johnson and Ghiglione, 2020). To prevent the collapse of their healthcare systems, European governments implemented strict containment measures, colloquially known as lockdowns. Governments also massively increased their public spending to fight the Covid-19 outbreak and to counteract the social and economic side effects of lockdown measures.

EU executives actively supported this policy response. On 17 March 2020, Commission President Ursula von der Leyen told the EU heads of states and governments at a European Council video conference that activation of the general escape clause of the Stability and Growth Pact (SGP) was imminent. In 2011, EU legislators had introduced this clause to allow the Council, on the recommendation of the Commission, to suspend the application of the preventive and corrective arms of the SGP in a situation of generalised crisis caused by a severe economic downturn in the eurozone or the EU as a whole (see Regulation (EC) 1466/97, Arts. 3(5), 5(1, 2), and 9(1), as revised by the Six-Pack of EU laws of 2011). On 20 March 2020, the Commission published its Communication (COM/2020/123 final), which called for activation of the clause. On 23 March 2020, the Council endorsed this request at a video conference and published a corresponding press 'Statement of EU ministers of finance on the Stability and Growth Pact in light of the COVID-19 crisis' (Council of the EU, 2020). The suspension of the application of both the preventive and the corrective arms of the SGP for all member states was remarkable, as a leading institutionalist scholar of the NEG regime had argued just before the outbreak of the pandemic that 'we cannot expect EU institutional actors to reverse stability rules and numerical targets that have become embedded in their practices as well as touted in their discourses' (Schmidt, 2020: 303). Yet, this is precisely what happened.

The activation of the dormant *general escape clause* articles of Regulation 1466/97 allowed EU executives to shift the trajectory of NEG's policy enforcement regime without having to change a single article of either primary or secondary EU law. Who would have thought that this would be possible? After all, EU scholars from very different intellectual traditions agreed that suspending the SGP rules would be virtually impossible, given that they were deeply ingrained in the discursive practices of EU executives (Schmidt, 2020) or given the *constitutional* nature of EU neoliberalism (Gill, 1998). Nonetheless, EU executives not only effectively suspended the SGP but did so based on tools that are formally very weak, namely, a Commission Communication (which is a *non-binding* legal instrument of the EU) and an informal press statement by the Council of the EU (2020) endorsing the Commission's Communication. Although the Council's decision arguably marked the start of a new era in EU economic governance, the corresponding Council document, because of its informal nature, does not feature on the official EUR-Lex website of EU laws and documents of EU institutions.

As in the case of the EU's shift to the NEG regime after 2008 (Chapter 2), EU executives again invoked a state of exception to break the existing trajectory of the EU's economic governance regime and to justify the shift to a new post-Covid version of it. This time, however, the EU executives' 'transnational exceptionalism' (Kreuder-Sonnen and White, 2022) did not lead to the same societal backlash against them, given its different policy orientation (Schmidt, 2022). EU finance ministers justified the suspension of the SGP rules as a necessary step to ensure 'the needed flexibility to take all necessary measures for supporting our health and civil protection systems and to protect our economies' (Council of the EU, 2020). Like in the NEG case, EU executives first responded to the Covid crisis with ad hoc measures before EU legislators institutionalised the EU's crisis response. In this chapter, we thus first assess EU executives' initial ad hoc interventions after the outbreak of the pandemic. In section 12.2, we describe the institutionalisation of the EU's crisis response in the form of the Recovery and Resilience Facility (RRF) Regulation (2021/241). Given our overarching interest in EU governance and labour politics as drivers of the social, economic, and political restructuring of Europe, we discuss in the chapter's conclusion whether we can still describe the post-Covid NEG regime as a system that mimics 'corporate governance structures that aim to hamper transnational trade union solidarity through the use of whipsawing tactics that put workers from different subsidiaries in competition with one another' (Erne, 2015: 358).

12.1 PREVENTING THE EU'S DISINTEGRATION BY NEW MEANS?

By suspending the SGP sanctioning regime for all member states, EU executives implicitly recognised the commodifying NEG prescriptions' negative impact on public services in general, and healthcare services in particular (Chapter 10). As outlined in Chapter 11, EU executives had perceived healthcare expenditure as a threat to healthy public finances rather than as a productive infrastructure investment that would boost the EU's growth and competitiveness. This perception changed, however, after the outbreak of the pandemic, when the role of healthcare as an essential public service became strikingly evident for everyone. At long last, EU executives seemed to recognise that the cuts in public hospital beds, along with the managerialisation of healthcare services resulting from NEG prescriptions (Chapter 10), reduced the capacity of national healthcare services to cope with the steep rise in patient hospitalisations during the pandemic (Stan and Erne, 2023).

After the advent of the Covid pandemic, the Commission also effectively suspended its competition policy rules limiting state aid, as it had done in 2008 to allow member states to bail out insolvent banks (Chapter 2). This time however, the relaxation of the EU's state aid rules benefitted not only private businesses but also public service providers. In fact, the relaxation of state aid rules allowed governments to cover the heavy losses that public service providers suffered as a consequence of the containment measures, for example in the public transport sector.

In terms of setting up a common EU fiscal response to the pandemic, the reaction of EU leaders was much slower. Initially, the European Council was divided on the issue, replicating the same fault lines between surplus and deficit countries as during the 2008 financial crisis. In March 2020, the governments of Belgium, France, Greece, Ireland, Italy, Luxembourg, Portugal, Slovenia, and Spain called for the creation of Corona bonds to address the consequences of the pandemic by issuing joint EU debt. However, the governments of many surplus countries firmly opposed them: Austria, Denmark, the Netherlands, and Sweden. The German government, led by a grand coalition of Christian and Social Democrats at that time, initially sided with the latter.

In April 2020, the Eurogroup of eurozone finance ministers reached a first compromise on a joint EU stimulus package that totalled approximately €540bn (Eurogroup, Press Release, 9 May 2020). The package had three main components. Firstly, a fund run by the European Investment Bank would be able to raise up to €200bn on the markets to finance loans to private companies. Secondly, the SURE (Support to mitigate Unemployment Risks in an Emergency) programme, run by the Commission, aimed to aid member states to finance temporary short-time work schemes through up to €100bn in (cheap) loans (Andor, 2020). This measure was meant to prevent mass layoffs as a result of the shutdown of EU economies, modelled on the German *Kurzarbeitergeld* that had contributed to the speedy recovery of the German economy after the 2008 crisis (Schulten and Müller, 2020).

Finally, a Pandemic Crisis Support of up to €240bn in loans from the European Stability Mechanism (ESM) was available to all eurozone states to cover pandemic-related healthcare costs up to 2 per cent of their GDP. The ESM credit line was the most contentious element of the package, given the strong MoU conditionalities attached to ESM loans issued after the financial crisis (see Chapter 2). The final agreement reached by the Eurogroup foresaw lighter conditionality and stipulated that member states should use the money to pay for 'direct and indirect healthcare, cure and prevention-related costs due to the COVID 19 crisis' (Eurogroup, Press Release, 9 May 2020). Given the ESM's role during the financial crisis (Chapter 2), however, ESM loans were still politically toxic in most member states, and this explains why no government dared apply for an ESM pandemic credit. Moreover, the total amount of the package agreed by the Eurogroup was small in light of the magnitude of the economic crisis that had hit the global economy, especially compared with the responses adopted by other advanced economies such as the United States. The Eurogroup thus also mentioned the idea of a joint EU Recovery Fund, if only the European Council could work out a corresponding agreement (Eurogroup, Press Release, 9 May 2020).

As had happened previously (Anderson, 2009), it was a Franco–German deal that broke the deadlock. On 18 May 2020, Chancellor Merkel and President Macron issued a joint call for the creation of a €500bn Recovery Fund, which, crucially, would be composed of grants rather than loans. Whereas the French government had been supporting the idea of Corona bonds since March, the shifting position of the Merkel government was notable, given its enduring opposition to any form of debt mutualisation at EU level. In the midst of the eurozone crisis in 2012, Chancellor Merkel had declared that sharing debt liability would be 'economically wrong and counterproductive' (*Reuters*, 26 June 2012). Now, she was willing to support a deal that foresaw the EU borrowing cash on financial markets to distribute as grants to member states.

One explanation for this sudden shift in Merkel's position relates to a court judgment that the German Constitutional Court had delivered only two weeks earlier. In the judgment, the court found that the bond-buying programme implemented by the European Central Bank (ECB) since 2015 would be illegal under German law, unless the ECB provided an acceptable justification for it. Although the court also stated that the judgment did not affect the ECB's new pandemic purchase programme, many observers, including within the German government, thought otherwise and therefore demanded a more stable, political solution to tackle the social and economic crisis caused by the pandemic (Mallet, Chazan, and Fleming, 2020). More important, however, were the economic reasons behind Merkel's policy shift, namely, the renewed importance of the EU internal market for the German manufacturing sector, given the disintegration of transcontinental supply chains and growing difficulties in accessing Asian export markets in times of strict Covid restrictions (Schneider and Syrovatka, 2020; Ryner, 2023; Schneider, 2023). Furthermore, the Federation of German Industry (BDI), the leading organisation of German industrialists, but also prominent entrepreneurs of export-oriented family businesses such as Reinhold Würth (2020), supported the EU debt mutualisation programmes in order to prevent a repeat of the 'mega catastrophe' of Berlin's 'small-minded' stance in the financial crisis, which divided the EU and only aided Europe's competitors in China, Russia, and the United States (Würth 2020: 7; see also Syrovatka, 2022a: 460), and to foster structural reforms in member states receiving EU funds (Schneider, 2023). This is notable, as the BDI supported the imposition of EU austerity programmes in the financial crisis but not the shift to a new EU economic governance regime, as the BDI predicted that the shift to NEG would lead to a shift of national competences in labour and social policy to EU level (Chapter 2). The northern European business associations and metalworkers' trade unions supported the idea of EU debt mutualisation too, not least because they thought that increased RRF funding would benefit their export-oriented industries, despite the opposite views of many Scandinavian politicians on EU fiscal federalism (Ekman, Møller Stahl, and Ryner, 2023). Business Europe (2020a), which had stood behind the EU's shift to NEG after the 2008 crisis (Chapter 2), publicly endorsed the shift in favour of EU debt mutualisation too.

Crucially however, EU leaders in general and the Merkel government in particular changed their positions on the matter of EU debt mutualisation for political reasons also. The national and EU institutions' imposition of austerity and commodifying structural reforms after the 2008 crisis substantially increased workers' and citizens' dissatisfaction with their political leaders at national and EU level (Armingeon, Guthmann, and Weisstanner, 2016; Bojar et al., 2022), especially in countries that had received the most constraining, commodifying NEG prescriptions. This had led to significant national and transnational protest movements, growing Euroscepticism among trade unions and workers, as well as a rising share of votes for Eurosceptic parties in successive national and EU elections (Chapter 11; van Middelaar, 2021; chapter 4; Béthoux, Erne, and Golden, 2018). Hence, if EU executives had failed to agree to an expansive response to the economic fallout caused by the pandemic, they would have jeopardised the prospects of EU integration, which was still recovering from yet another low-point – Brexit.

The Franco–German deal on debt mutualisation broke the impasse and paved the way for a corresponding European Commission (2020b) plan that was part of its proposal for the next seven-year EU budget outline, the Multiannual Financial Framework (de la Porte and Jensen, 2021). The Commission's Next Generation EU plan added €250bn in loans to the €500bn in grants as suggested by France and Germany. In July 2020, final agreement was reached at a special European Council meeting. The total amount of the package was left unchanged, but the share of grants was lowered to €390bn (European Council, Conclusions, Brussels, 21 June 2020) to secure its unanimous approval. The final Next Generation EU package includes seven programmes and is partly a repackaging of pre-existing structural and investment funds,[1] but its cornerstone is the RRF, endowed with €360bn in loans and €312.5bn in grants. The RRF is meant to finance reforms and investments in member states from 2020 until 2026, and its funds are to be distributed to EU member states based on criteria that only partially reflect the impact of the pandemic, namely, member states' GDP, size, and unemployment levels.

The Next Generation EU package was meant to be temporary and did not imply any mutualisation of existing debt. Even so, the then SPD finance minister (and future German chancellor) Olaf Scholz hailed this decision by the EU member states as Europe's Hamiltonian moment, akin to the agreement reached in 1790 by Alexander Hamilton, the then US Secretary of Treasury, to federalise the debts of the nation's united states. Be that as it may, the political agreement in favour of the package still had to be institutionalised and integrated into a coherent post-Covid NEG regime.

12.2 THE RRF REGULATION: INSTITUTIONALISING THE EU'S POST-COVID NEG REGIME

After the 2008 crisis and the EU's shift to the NEG regime, the European Semester process became a key tool of EU economic and social policymaking

---

[1] Beyond the Recovery and Resilience Facility (€672.5bn), these are: React EU (€47.5bn), Horizon Europe (€5bn), Invest EU (€5.6bn), Rural Development (€7.5bn), Just Transition Fund (€10bn), and Resc EU (€1.9bn). All amounts are expressed in 2018 prices.

(Chapter 2). After the 2020 Covid emergency however, the Semester's role in the EU's NEG regime changed significantly. In 2020, EU executives continued issuing country-specific recommendations (CSRs), even though the suspension of the SGP's preventive and corrective arms meant that almost all NEG prescriptions had lost their coercive power. This pandemic context also affected the policy orientation of the prescriptions, as we shall see in section 12.3 and in Chapter 13.

In 2021, the Commission and Council went even further, as they did not issue any CSRs at all in that year. This, however, did not mean that their impact on national economic and social policymaking vanished. Instead of drafting any country-specific NEG prescriptions, the Commission asked the governments to draft National Recovery and Resilience Plans (NRRPs) and to apply for RRF funds. To get any RRF funding, each government must convince the Commission that its plan complies with the criteria set by the RRF Regulation of the European Parliament and Council (2021/241). If this happens, then the Commission will send draft NRRPs for adoption to the Council. As a result, the Commission has further increased its leverage in EU policymaking. By contrast, the European Parliament has no say on the content of NRRPs, despite the plans' strategic role as a central steering tool of EU policy-making. The European Parliament's negligible role in the post-Covid NEG regime is largely self-inflicted, as was its marginal role in the NEG regime after the financial crisis (Chapter 2). After all, the Parliament was a co-legislator in both cases, when it approved the Six-Pack laws in 2011 (which institutionalised the NEG regime) and when it approved the RRF Regulation in 2021 (which institutionalised the post-Covid NEG regime), in both cases by very large majorities.

Each NRRP needs to detail the measures that a member state will implement to meet the conditions laid out in the regulation for RRF funding and the concrete targets and milestones for their implementation. The latter are crucial, as EU executives can freeze or withdraw RRF funding even after having approved an NRRP if the Commission concludes that a member state has failed to meet the agreed implementation targets and milestones specified in it. The targets and milestones are meticulously detailed in the annex to each country-specific Council Implementing Decision (CID). The Council's CID thus not only endorses the Commission's evaluation of the NRRPs, which gives the Commission the green light to start disbursing RRF funds to a given country, but also specifies the policy conditionalities for the disbursement of subsequent RRF tranches. In this respect, the CIDs and their annexes very much mirror the Memoranda of Understanding (MoUs) and their updates for countries under bailout conditionality.

At first sight, this similarity might not seem threatening for labour and public services. Whereas MoUs prescribed austerity cuts, NRRPs are framed as investment plans, but, as countries received MoU bailout funding only if they also implemented the NEG prescriptions specified in MoUs and their updates, RRF funding equally depends on the implementation of accompanying policy prescriptions outlined in CIDs and their annexes. This means that the coercive power of all CID-related NEG prescriptions is very significant for all countries, irrespective of their location in the pre-pandemic NEG policy enforcement regime. However, whereas EU executives were free to add to a given MoU whatever ad hoc conditionality they pleased, EU legislators have at least specified some criteria that the Commission must use when assessing an NRRP and the implementation of the corresponding NEG prescriptions.

Article 19(3) RRF Regulation sets out the broad assessment criteria for the Commission's evaluation of the national plans. These are further detailed in the regulation's Annex V. According to the Annex's Art. 3, a member state must get an A grade from the Commission in four areas to get RRF funding (see Table 12.1), as well as at least an A and a B grade in two additional areas.

The crucial four core assessment areas are the following. Firstly, all NRRPs must *address* 'all or a significant subset' of challenges identified in the CSRs issued within the European Semester (Art. 19(3) RRF Regulation). This condition is important, as it ties the RRF firmly to the EU's NEG regime. Notably, the RRF regulation does not specify which Semester cycles shall be considered. The Commission (SWD (2021) 12 final) thus specified that governments should consider not only the post-pandemic 2020 CSRs when drafting their NRRP but also those issued in 2019. The link to the 2019 NEG prescriptions is important, as they pointed much more clearly in a commodifying policy direction (Chapter 11). It is thus hardly surprising that Klaus Regling (2021), the then director of the ESM, was pleased to note that the RRF would still be geared towards structural reforms. Whereas before 2021 member states could disregard NEG prescriptions whose coercive power was weak (see Chapter 2), this was no longer the case after the EU's shift to the post-Covid NEG regime, as the Commission linked the payment of RRF funds to *all* CSRs. In so doing, the Commission increased the coercive power of *all* NEG prescriptions, regardless of their legal base or the country's location in the NEG enforcement regime (Chapter 2). According to Article 10 of the RRF Regulation, the disbursement of RRF funds is conditional not only on the particular NRRP targets and milestones that a member state must reach but also on its 'sound economic governance' in general. This means that the Commission can propose to suspend all or part of the RRF funding to penalise governments that fail to adequately implement EU macroeconomic or fiscal corrective action plans.

TABLE 12.1 *The EU's evaluation scoreboard for National Recovery and Resilience Plans*

	Core areas				Additional areas	
Assessment area	Implementation of CSRs	Economic, social, and territorial cohesion	Green transition	Digital transition	Balanced contribution across six areas	Do no significant harm
Definition	NRRP effectively **addresses** 'all or a significant subset of challenges' identified in CSRs 'including fiscal aspects thereof and the Macroeconomic Imbalance Procedure.[a]	NRRP effectively **contributes** 'to strengthening the growth potential, job creation, and economic, social and institutional resilience.'[b]	NRRP effectively **contributes** 'to the green transition' and allocates '*at least 37 %*' of its funds to that goal.[c]	NRRP effectively **contributes** 'to the digital transition' and allocates '*at least 20 %*' of its funds to that goal.[d]	NRRP 'represents a ... balanced response **contributing**' to all six pillars; (a) green transition; (b) digital transformation; (c) smart, sustainable, and inclusive growth; (d) social and territorial cohesion; (e) health, economic, social, and institutional resilience; (f) policies for the next generation (education and skills).[e]	NRRP measures ***do*** no '*significant harm*' to environmental objectives'.[f]
Grades needed	An A grade is necessary in all four areas				Either A & A, A & B or B & A grades in these two areas	

Source: RFF Regulation (EU) 2021/241, own adaptation, emphases added.
[a] Annex V, Art. 2(2);
[b] Annex V, Art. 2(3);
[c] Annex V, Art. 2(5). Annex VI defines what counts as corresponding contributions;
[d] Annex V, Art. 2(6). Annex VII defines what counts as corresponding contributions;
[e] Annex V, Art. 2(1);
[f] Annex V, Art. 2(4). The principle 'do no significant harm' is defined by Regulation (EU) 2020/852.

Secondly, NRRPs need to get an A score in a social assessment criterion. Concretely, an NRRP must include measures that strengthen 'the growth potential, job creation, and economic, *social* and institutional *resilience* of the Member State, *contributing to* the implementation of the European Pillar of Social Rights' (emphasis added) (Art. 19(3c) RRF Regulation). Compared with the first criterion, which links RRF funding to the *implementation* of concrete NEG prescriptions, the wording of the second criterion is far less constraining, as the plans must only *contribute* to the implementation of the European Pillar of Social Rights. This vague wording gives EU executives and governments a lot of leeway (Rainone, 2022).

A third criterion, also requiring an A grade, is linked to the shift to a green economy. At least 37 per cent of an NRRP's funds must be allocated to foster the green transition. This mirrors the rise in the number of NEG prescriptions semantically linked to a 'shift to the green economy' policy rationale after 2018, as outlined in Chapter 11. The criterion's clear numerical benchmark also facilitates its evaluation, as member states must simply direct 37 per cent of their RRF spending to investments that the Commission considers to be green. The regulation also states that all NRRP measures must respect the 'do no significant harm' principle (Art. 5 RRF Regulation), which stresses the role of green objectives in the post-Covid NEG regime. As outlined in Table 12.1, the no significant harm principle is an additional assessment criterion on its own – one, however, in which getting a B grade may be sufficient. This suggests that the EU's green transition NRRP assessment criterion is not linked to ecological rationales only.

As shown in Chapter 9 with regard to water charges, the pursuit of a green agenda can indeed also go hand in hand with the commodification of natural resources. As Adam Tooze wrote in a *Financial Times* editorial, just putting 'money into the NextGenEU kitty is an evasion' (Tooze, 2023). If EU executives want to bring the population with them, the green transition must include 'some element of public ownership', for example, a 'much closer involvement of trade unions in framing industrial policy ... as a counterweight to business influence, but also because labour is so crucial to the transition' (2023). Tooze's critique is very warranted, as the European Green Deal strategy, which Commission President Ursula von der Leyen unveiled in December 2019 (Commission, Communication, COM (2019) 640 final), followed the ecological modernisation leitmotif, which is compatible with EU executives' commodifying NEG policy script. Instead of seeking social change, EU executives linked the green transition to technological innovations (e.g., hydrogen and carbon dioxide removal technologies) to improve the global competitiveness of the EU economy (Haas, Syrovatka, and Jürgens,

2022: 247). Accordingly, the high share of RRF funding that EU legislation allocated to the green transition thus also mirrors the intense lobbying of 'green' energy and technology corporations, such as Shell, which also wanted to profit from the EU's green RRF funding (European Commission, 2023a). Although the Commission's DG EMPL recently also set up a unit on Fair, Green, and Digital Transitions Research in its DG Employment, Social Affairs and Inclusion, the fair transition elements in the EU's green transition policy remain very weak. The Council Recommendation on 'ensuring a fair transition towards climate neutrality' (2022/C 243/04) that followed on a corresponding Commission proposal of 14 December 2021 merely *'invited'* member states to 'adopt and implement, in close cooperation with social partners *as relevant*, comprehensive and coherent policy packages, addressing the employment and social aspects to promote a fair transition ... as well as to make optimal use of public *and private funding*' (Art. 2, emphasis added). As the latter indicates, EU executives proceeded to semantically link their calls for green investments to commodifying policy rationales, as they did in earlier NEG prescriptions on public services generally and on transport and water services in particular (Tables 11.2 and 11.4).

The fourth criterion is that NRRPs must funnel at least 20 per cent of the RRF funds towards the digital transition of the European economy.[2] As mentioned in Chapter 10, digitalisation was a policy goal that already appeared in NEG prescriptions in 2013 as a necessary tool for the operation of case-based (rather than needs-based) funding mechanisms in hospitals. In her candidacy speech for the position of Commission President, Ursula von der Leyen (2019: 4) also pledged that 'Europe must lead the transition to a healthy planet and *a new digital world*' (emphasis added). Concretely, she committed herself to 'prioritise investments in Artificial Intelligence, both through the Multiannual Financial Framework and through the increased use of *public–private partnership*' (2019: 13, emphasis added). The lobbyists from Digital Europe, the association of both the national and the global digital tech industry in Brussels, were thus knocking on an open door when they demanded that a dedicated amount of RRF funding must be set aside for their industry (Digital Europe, 2020). In view of the fact that the digital technology industry corporations were already among the major economic winners of the pandemic, given the increased demand for IT equipment and services during the lockdown consequent to the shift to online shopping, distance education,

---

[2] As an expenditure item can contribute to both the green and the digital transition, Annexes VI and VII in the RRF Regulation outline the method that must be used to determine whether it contributes to the green and/or the digital transition.

and remote working arrangements, the decision of the European Parliament and Council to award up to €134.5bn of public RRF funding to the information technology sector was breathtaking. By contrast, all pleas by European unions and social NGOs to the European Commission, Parliament, and Council to include a minimum target for social expenditure in the RRF Regulation failed (Vanhercke and Verdun, 2021), even though the pandemic put member states' social services, particularly healthcare, under the greatest stress. Before the pandemic, EU executives had already issued NEG prescriptions that tasked governments to prioritise public spending for the allegedly more productive network industries rather than on healthcare services, as revealed in Chapter 11. Hence, European unions' and social NGOs' failure to secure an RRF quota for social (including healthcare) expenditure after the pandemic is all the more striking. This observation is of both practical and academic interest, as the absence of binding social spending benchmarks questions the 'social' investment paradigm that has moulded many contributions to the NEG and social policy literature (see Chapter 5).

The RRF's structural anti-social services bias is even more apparent in the RRF Regulation clause that delimits the range of eligible RRF expenses, leaving unchanged the principles of earlier EU budget cycles: 'Support from the Facility shall not, unless in duly justified cases, substitute recurring national budgetary expenditure' (Art. 5(1) RRF Regulation). As public services are typically financed through recurring national budgetary expenditure, EU legislators nominally barred recurring public sector expenditures, namely, public sector wages, from RRF funding. This provision mirrors a very formalistic view on the division of competences between the EU and its member states (Commission official, intervention, UCD–Cornell study trip, Brussels, 18 November 2022). Accordingly, member states are not allowed to use RRF funds to address the acute staffing crisis in public healthcare services, as the 'organisation and delivery of health services and medical care' is – according to Art. 168(7) TFEU – an exclusive competence of member states. Such EU competence arguments, however, did not stop EU executives from issuing NEG prescriptions that tasked governments to curtail public sector workers' wages, as shown in Chapters 6, 7, and 10. Hence, EU competence arguments are typically political arguments that policymakers use instrumentally to justify the EU's inaction in a field (Chapter 3; Stan and Erne, 2021b). When policymakers want to see EU action in a field, however, EU competence arguments quickly lose their currency. Incidentally, of all governments, it was the nationalist Orbán government that called for greater EU involvement in the provision of national public services: the Hungarian government submitted an NRRP that dedicated some RRF funds to personnel rather than infrastructure costs, given the acute staff shortage crisis in public services (Szabó, 2022), which is virulent stark not only in Hungary but across the entire EU (EPSU, 2022a).[3] Conversely, the left-wing Spanish government accepted the RRF's funding bias for private suppliers but then – paradoxically – tried to turn that pro-business bias into an advantage for labour, by telling Spanish capitalists that they would be the biggest losers if the EU froze its RRF funding. In December 2021, Spain's left-wing labour minister, Yolanda Díaz, would hardly have been able to get the consent of the Confederación Española de Organizaciones Empresariales for her decommodifying labour market reform had Spanish business not feared missing out on RRF funding (Wise, 2021).

Given our interest in EU economic governance interventions and countervailing protests that they might trigger as drivers of the political restructuring of Europe, we must take a step back to see the broader features of the post-Covid NEG regime. We do this in section 12.3.

12.3 EU GOVERNANCE AFTER COVID: STILL MIMICKING TRANSNATIONAL CORPORATIONS?

As outlined in Chapters 2 and 3, the NEG regime that the EU adopted after the financial crisis did not follow the classical state-centred (intergovernmental or federal) governance paradigms that still dominate the EU legal and political science literature. Instead, the NEG regime mimicked the corporate governance mechanism of transnational corporations (TNCs), which steer their subsidiaries' activities using whipsawing tactics, coercive comparisons, and subsidiary-specific ad hoc interventions (Erne, 2015). As shown in Chapter 11, adopting this corporate governance strategy helped EU executives constrain *transnational* protests by unions and social movements, as the methodology of the European Semester makes strikes against specific NEG prescriptions 'almost impossible' (CGIL union official, cited in Maccarrone, 2020: 259). However, the social and economic measures that governments adopted at national and local level to implement NEG prescriptions still triggered significant union and social-movement protests (Maccarrone, 2020; Naughton, 2023). After 2008, most protests in Europe were triggered by economic rather than culturalist grievances (Kriesi et al., 2020). Given the

---

[3] The Commission accepted the very cautious wording of the draft NRRP in this regard but froze the RRF payments, as the Orbán government did not 'effectively address the country-specific recommendations addressed to Hungary in relation to the rule of law' and also failed to take the required measures 'to protect the financial interests of the Union' (European Commission, 2022).

protests' clear socioeconomic motivations however, EU executives could no longer dismiss them as objections of eternal nationalists (van Middelaar, 2021: chapter 4), as happened in the case of the mobilisations against Commissioner Bolkestein's EU Services Directive and the French, Dutch, and Irish referendums on the EU constitution and the Lisbon Treaty (Béthoux, Erne, and Golden, 2018). To prevent the EU's disintegration, EU executives thus overlaid the NEG mechanisms that mimicked TNC's labour control regimes with new governance tools that cannot be found in TNCs, namely, debt mutualisation and a pledge to strengthen the EU's social pillars.

A New Regime that Makes Countervailing Protest Action Still Difficult

In designing the post-Covid NEG regime, EU leaders nonetheless continued to deploy an institutional design that would still make it very difficult for unions and social movements to politicise the post-Covid NEG regime across borders, that is, even more intricate bureaucratic procedures, a sustained *country-specific* focus, stronger policy enforcement mechanisms, and policy formulation mechanisms that insulate national and EU executives even more effectively from their parliaments, unions, and social movements.

More intricate bureaucratic procedures: Not only have EU executives embedded the monitoring of the implementation of NRRPs' quantitative and qualitative measures in the European Semester process, but also the Commission's DG ECFIN produces and updates a specific biannual RRF scoreboard to monitor each EU member state's progress in implementing its NRRP as well as the NEG policy conditionalities specified in milestones and targets annexed to corresponding country-specific CIDs. The intricate European Semester process outlined in Chapter 2 has thus become further complicated through the addition of plenty of new NEG documents. To give national governments time to draft their original NRRPs, EU executives did not produce any CSRs in 2021. From 2022 onwards however, EU executives resumed issuing new CSRs, thereby adding new policy commitments for member states. Their implementation will be monitored by the Commission in the context of both the Semester process and the disbursement of RRF funds.

Sustained country-specific focus: It follows from the above that EU executives are still able to pursue their overarching supranational policy agenda through *country-specific* policy prescriptions. Hence, the post-Covid NEG regime remains a case of differentiated integration but not to accommodate economic, social, and cultural heterogeneity. Instead, the regime's country-specific policy prescriptions allow EU executives to realign member state policies in line with EU executives' supranational policy preferences.

Therefore, we have described the post-Covid NEG regime as a case of *reversed differentiated integration* (Stan and Erne, 2023; Chapter 3).

Reinforced coercive mechanisms: The RRF's 'money for reform' approach mirrors the NEG regime's most effective and thus most coercive policy enforcement mechanism, namely, the threat to withdraw EU funding if a member state's implementation of the MoU-related NEG prescriptions is perceived as inadequate. Although national governments usually implemented the MoU-related prescriptions that they received, the Commission has not always been satisfied with the implementation of SGP/MIP-related prescriptions, as outlined in Chapter 2. Although the Six-Pack laws gave EU executives ample fining powers, they shied away from actually using them against non-fully complying member states, given the unpredictable backlash effects of SPG/MIP-related sanctions' 'atomic bomb' character on the EU integration process (Chapter 2); and the implementation of NEG prescriptions was even weaker in countries not under a coercive arm of the NEG policy enforcement regime. EU legislators thus made EU structural funding in the 2014–2020 budget cycle conditional on the satisfactory implementation of NEG prescriptions (Regulation 1303/2013), but 'unlike the EU budget ... the recovery fund has a *continuous system of conditionality*, with tranches of money being disbursed after reform and investment milestones have been met' (emphasis added) (Cornago and Springford, 2021: 1). The policy conditionalities of RRF funding thus substantially increased the steering power of NRRP-related NEG prescriptions across all member states.[4] By contrast, EU executives were not that concerned about auditing 'the costs actually incurred' to ensure that the funds have been spent for the stated purpose, to the annoyance of the head of the European Court of Auditors (O'Leary, 2023).

Hence, the new policy conditionalities linked to the disbursement of RFF funds enables EU executives to demand policy changes even from countries that have not received NEG prescriptions that are linked to the NEG policy enforment regime of a very coercive MoU, or a coercive excessive deficit, or excessive macroeconomic imbalances procedure (see Table 5.1). This has been shown, for example, by the Commission's rejection of the German government's initial NRRP and the Commission's demand to rework the plan, namely, on structural reforms that would 'improve the sustainability of the pension system' (Holz, 2023: 219). De facto however, the coercive power

---

[4] In 2022, for example, the European Commission (2022) penalised the Hungarian Orbán government by withholding RRF funding for unsatisfactory implementation of a CSR on the independence of the Hungarian judiciary, which is a prescription that would have had only a weak coercive power before the EU's shift to the post-Covid NEG regime.

of NRRP-related NEG prescriptions still differs, as the relative share of RRF funding as a share of their GDP substantially varies across countries, reflecting once more the uneven nature of the EU political economy. Whereas Romania and Italy have received, and will continue to receive, grant transfers of about 6 and 4 per cent, respectively, of their 2020 GDP from 2020 up to 2026, the agreed RRF grant payments for Germany and Ireland amount to less than 1 per cent and are thus much less significant (Nguyern and Redeker, 2022: Figure 2).

Steering the EU's economies without much democratic scrutiny: The post-Covid NEG regime remains a technocratic process steered top-down by national and EU executives. The European and national parliaments are not involved in the formulation of NRRP-related policy prescriptions. Regarding social partners, their involvement is also very limited, as even supporters of the socialisation thesis have acknowledged (Vanhercke and Verdun, 2021). Although the RRF Regulation requires member states to include in their NRRPs a statement about the involvement of social partners and other stakeholders in drafting the plan, one of the EU's own agencies has demonstrated that this involvement has been uneven and weak 'in a relatively high number of countries' (Eurofound, 2022: 1).

In sum, the inclusion of transnational redistribution mechanisms shows that the post-Covid NEG regime moved away from the beggar-thy-neighbour governance mechanisms that TNCs use to control their subsidiaries and workforce. Instead of mimicking the corporate governance structures of TNCs, the post-Covid NEG regime resembles the mechanism of examination boards and commissions in schools and universities, which evaluate their students based on the exam grades awarded across different subject areas. Hence, the post-Covid NEG regime continues to defy established standards of democratic accountability (Crouch, 2004; Mair, 2013; Erne, 2015), as NEG policymaking continues to be steered by executives without the democratic participation of national and EU parliaments, unions, and social movements.

Although member states now need A grades in four subject areas, including two that potentially point in a decommodifying policy direction, we need to get a better idea of the policy orientation of the entire EU governance regime after Covid to ascertain its role as a trigger for countervailing collective action. We do that in Chapter 13 by assessing of the policy orientation of the NRRP- and CID-related prescriptions and the new EU laws in our policy areas (employment relations and public services) and sectors (transport, water, and healthcare), before providing an outlook on what might come next.

13

The Policy Orientation of the EU's Post-Covid NEG Regime and Its Discontents

13.1 INTRODUCTION

By adopting the Recovery and Resilience Facility (RRF) Regulation in 2021, European Union (EU) legislators added two new governance tools to the EU's new economic governance (NEG) regime. The first tool is the National Recovery and Resilience Plans (NRRPs) that governments must draft in close collaboration with the Commission to get RRF funding. The second tool is the Council Implementing Decisions (CIDs) of the Council (of finance ministers). With its CIDs, the Council endorses the Commission's assessment of an NRRP, including the timeline for the implementation of its milestones and targets. This is crucial, as the Commission will only release RRF funding – which comes in funding tranches up to twice a year – once the member state has met the milestones and targets outlined in the corresponding CID.

As the Commission possesses considerable leeway in assessing member states' progress in implementing their NRRPs, a full assessment of the post-Covid NEG regime's policy orientation will be possible only after 2026 when the NRRP phase of the NEG regime is completed. This flexibility stems from the RRF Regulation's qualitative evaluation criteria for NRRPs that give EU executives significant scope for interpretation when assessing governments' progress in meeting the CID benchmarks (Table 12.1). Furthermore, some governments, such as those of Ireland and Italy, sought EU executives' permission to amend their NRRPs to take account of changing circumstances, such as the Russian invasion of Ukraine in 2022, rising inflation, or unforeseen technical obstacles. Nevertheless, given the pivotal role of the EU's 2019 and 2020 country-specific recommendations (CSRs) for the drafting of NRRPs and the corresponding CIDs, we are already able to outline the likely policy orientation of the post-Covid NEG regime in our fields.

The RRF Regulation's evaluation scoreboard for NRRPs and their implementation includes four core assessment categories (Chapter 12). Of these, the CSR-related scoreboard category is the most important one. Whereas NRRPs must merely '*contribute*' to 'economic, social and territorial cohesion' and the 'green' and the 'digital transition', all NRRPs must '*address* ... all or a significant subset of challenges identified in CSRs' (RRF Regulation, quoted in Table 12.1, emphasis added).

In this chapter, our analysis of the EU's post-Covid economic governance regime based on a) the CSRs issued in the 2019 and 2020 cycles of the European Semester process, b) the targets and milestones included in the NRRP's CIDs, and c) recent EU laws. As in Chapters 6 to 10, we analyse the policy orientation of the post-Covid NEG prescriptions across two areas (employment relations and public services), three sectors (transport, water, and healthcare services), and four countries (Germany, Ireland, Italy, and Romania). Pursuing our methodology (Chapters 4 and 5), we do so by considering the NEG prescriptions included in CSRs and CIDs in their broader semantic, communicative, and policy contexts.

13.2 EU GOVERNANCE OF EMPLOYMENT RELATIONS: TOWARDS DECOMMODIFICATION?

As shown in Chapter 6, Ireland, Italy, and Romania recurrently received commodifying NEG prescriptions on wages, collective bargaining, and hiring and firing mechanisms until 2019. By contrast, EU executives asked German policymakers to pursue more expansionary wage policies – not, however, for social reasons but to rebalance the EU economy (Chapter 11). Hence, all NEG prescriptions on employment relations that EU executives issued after the financial crisis were compatible with NEG's overarching commodifying script – with the exception of the 2018 prescription that asked the Romanian government to enhance social dialogue and the earlier prescriptions that asked the German government to curtail the use of mini-jobs. This situation changed after the outbreak of the pandemic.

In April 2020, the Council created the SURE unemployment insurance support fund to back the creation and operation of short-time work schemes across the EU. This allowed employers to keep their workers on payroll during the Covid lockdowns (Chapter 12). Accordingly, the CSRs issued in 2020 encompassed NEG prescriptions that urged member states to prevent a rise in unemployment by developing flexible working arrangements and activation measures, including access to short-time work schemes (Rainone, 2020).

Two years later, the European Parliament and Council adopted the EU directive (2022/2041) on adequate minimum wages. This directive signified a real EU labour policy volte-face (Maccarrone, Erne, and Golden, 2023) that went even further than the Commission's 2020 proposal (COM (2020) 682 final). EU legislators specified the setting of a national minimum wage 'with the aim of achieving a decent standard of living, reducing in-work poverty, as well as promoting social cohesion and upward social convergence, and reducing the gender pay gap' (Art. 5(1) Directive 2022/2041). Whereas EU executives urged governments to curb wages after the crisis in 2008 (Chapter 6), the 2022 directive returns to what Marshall (1950: 69) called the right to a 'living wage', defined as 'the right of the citizen to a minimum standard of civilised living'. To monitor the implementation of this goal, the directive sets statutory EU reference values for national minimum wage levels: '60% of the gross median wage and 50% of the gross average wage' of a fulltime worker (Art. 5(4)). Following this, 18 per cent of the EU's workforce was in line to get a wage increase (Schulten and Müller, 2021: Table 1). Only in France were the statutory minimum wage levels higher than the new EU reference values (2021: Table 1).

Furthermore, EU legislators recognised that workers' wages would be set best through collective bargaining. Their Minimum Wage Directive thus also commits member states to increase the 'collective bargaining coverage' rate and to facilitate 'the exercise of the right to collective bargaining on wage-setting' (Art. 4(1)). To monitor the implementation of this goal, EU legislators again provided an EU reference value: an 80 per cent collective bargaining coverage rate in each member state. In 2022, only seven[1] of the twenty-seven member states reached this benchmark (Commission, Communication, COM (2023) 40 final: Graph 1). The Minimum Wage Directive thus obliges member states to (a) strengthen the social partners' capacity to engage in collective bargaining on wage-setting at sector or cross-industry level, (b) protect workers and union representatives from acts that discriminate against them, and (c) protect unions from any acts of interference by employers (or their agents) in their establishment, functioning, or administration (Art. 4(1)).

The directive's approval by a very large majority of the European Parliament and Council shocked North American and European business leaders (Erne, 2023b) and not just because the directive represents a U-turn in EU wage policy-making. Business leaders had been confident that they would be able to defeat any Commission proposal in this field,[2] as the EU would not

---

[1] Austria, Belgium, Denmark, Finland, France, Italy, and Sweden.
[2] Roland Erne, participant observation, seminar for visiting UCD and Cornell University students, Business Europe, Head Office, Brussels, 22 November 2019.

have the legal competence to legislate on it. After all, opponents of EU collective bargaining laws had effectively used such arguments in the past (Cooper, 2015). This time, however, their EU-competence arguments no longer worked,[3] paradoxically because Business Europe (2020b) and its national affiliates compromised them by their own actions during the financial crisis when they lobbied EU executives to prescribe wage cuts and to decentralise bargaining systems (Chapters 3 and 6; Maccarrone, 2020). Aptly, European trade union leaders simply flipped the EU competence argument by asking EU executives the following question: How can one say that the EU has no right to provide a framework for adequate minimum wages, after a decade of binding EU prescriptions that tasked governments to curb wages and to marketise collective bargaining mechanisms? (Erne, 2023b). Not only did arguments about the apparently lacking EU competences in the field no longer work to prevent the adoption of the EU Minimum Wage Directive, they also failed to stop the Commission from proposing additional directives in the field of pay and employment relations policy in 2021 and 2022, namely,

- the Pay Transparency Directive (COM (2021) 93 final) to strengthen the application of the principle of equal pay for equal work or work of equal value between men and women through pay transparency and equal pay enforcement mechanisms, which came into force on 10 May 2023 (Directive (EU) 2023/970);
- the Directive on Improving Working Conditions in Platform Work (COM (2021) 762 final) to make it harder for companies in the gig economy to impose bogus self-employment (which triggered fierce opposition from platform companies, such as Uber, and still had to be adopted by EU legislators at the time of writing);
- the Directive on Corporate Sustainability Due Diligence (COM (2022) 71 final), which obliges companies and their suppliers to adopt measures to curb human rights abuses (forced labour, child labour, inadequate workplace health and safety, exploitation of workers) and activities that negatively affect the environment and the climate. This proposal also triggered the opposition of some capital factions; and also still had to be adopted by EU legislators at the time of writing.

[3] Incidentally, Nordic trade unions initially also used such arguments. Finally however, 'Nordic unions overcame their long-held scepticism towards European labour regulations, and specifically their opposition to any mention of a minimum wage manifesting in European legislation' (Lillie, 2022: 499). Likewise, the French employer association, MEDEF, eventually supported the directive – unlike Business Europe (2020b) – to ensure a more level playing field in the EU's internal market.

These legislative proposals show that the European Commission reoriented its employment relations policy in a decommodifying policy direction. In the 2019 and 2020 CSRs for Germany, Ireland, Italy, and Romania, however, this policy shift was not yet very visible. In addition to the references to the short-time work schemes mentioned above, the CSRs issued to these four countries contained only two sets of prescriptions on employment relations.[4] The first tasked the Romanian and Irish governments to strengthen 'the resilience of the health system, in particular with regard to health workers'. The second tasked the Romanian government to 'improve the quality and effectiveness of public administration and the predictability of decision-making, including through *adequate involvement of social partners*' (Council Recommendation Romania 2020/C 282/23, emphasis added).

Prescriptions on employment relations were also largely absent in the four NRRPs. The Irish NRRP contained only one in relation to healthcare workers. Given the proposal to establish a single-tier healthcare system (see below), it stipulated public-only employment contracts for doctors, with increased salaries for new entrants. More important for Irish employment relations, however, were the new EU laws regarding pay. Consequent to the EU directive on adequate minimum wages, the Irish government announced the introduction of a statutory 'living wage' to be set at 60 per cent of the median wage, matching the EU directive's reference value. The government also set up a tripartite high level working group, which proposed a strengthening of Ireland's sectoral wage-setting mechanisms. These developments are significant, as they reversed measures implemented in the period of MoU conditionality after the financial crisis (Chapter 6; Maccarrone, Erne, and Regan, 2019).

The 2019 and 2020 CSRs for Italy did not entail any prescriptions on workers' terms and conditions while in employment. Even so, Italy's NRRP contained a decommodifying prescription on wages. It stipulated that procurement procedures for publicly funded cultural events would have to include social and environmental criteria, including decent wages. Surprisingly however, this prescription did not apply to all instances of public procurement. Instead, the plan tasked Italian policymakers to reduce the restrictions on subcontracting currently contained in the Public Procurement Code, potentially therefore putting labour standards under increased competitive pressures.

In their 2019 CSR, EU executives tasked German policymakers to support higher wage growth. Nonetheless, the NRRP did not include any such

---

[4] As throughout the book, we focus our analysis on prescriptions that affect workers' terms and conditions while in employment. Hence, we do not assess NRRP prescriptions on pension reforms, despite their salience in the Romanian case (*adz.ro*, 27 October 2022).

measure. The narrow victory of the SPD led by Olaf Scholz in the federal elections in September 2021, however, paved the way for a sizable increase in the minimum wage from €9.82 to €12 in October 2022. The €12 rate came very close to the 60 per cent of the median wage that the Commission had included in its 2020 proposal for an EU directive on adequate minimum wages, thereby facilitating the adoption of the EU Minimum Wage Directive by the German labour minister in the Council. However, although the government programme of the SPD's traffic-light coalition with the Greens and the neoliberal Free Democrats (FDP) included the one-off increase of the minimum wage to €12, the FDP prevented the inclusion of the EU's reference values in it. As a result, the German minimum wage commission was able to remove the 2022 gains of minimum wage workers by setting wage rises for 2024 and 2025 well below the EU's reference values for adequate minimum wages (*Zeit.de*, 1 July 2023). After all, German lawmakers had not yet transposed the new EU directive into German law.

EU executives repeatedly tasked the Romanian government to use 'objective criteria' for setting the minimum wage between 2014 and 2019. As outlined in Chapter 6, these prescriptions pointed in a commodifying direction, as EU executives had issued them to prevent unilateral wage increases by social democratic governments against the will of employers. After the approval of the EU Minimum Wage Directive however, the meaning of the term 'objective criteria' changed, as the implementation by March 2024 of the EU's new reference values for adequate minimum wages and the corresponding CID benchmark (Annex to the Council Implementing Decision … for Romania 12319/21 ADD 1: 449) may lead to significant minimum wage increases. In 2022, its government had already increased the minimum wage by 17.65 per cent, which was the third largest increase in the EU (Eurofound, 2023).

The Romanian NRRP also contained another prescription on wages, namely, a call to implement a unitary pay scale in the public sector. When Romania was under bailout conditionality, this call had been linked to budgetary retrenchment (Chapters 6 and 7). In 2022 however, its meaning changed when Romanian public sector unions, such as the healthcare workers' union Sanitas, were leveraging the NRRP prescription to demand the inclusion of the social partners 'in the process of designing the new law on the salaries of budgetary staff – which the government has assumed through the NRRP – so as to guarantee a direct correlation between salary income and purchasing power and the cost of living' (Sanitas, 2022).

In addition, Romania's NRRP included a prescription on hiring and firing mechanisms: the introduction of hourly tickets, or vouchers, which employers can use to pay domestic care workers in a tax compliant manner. The rationale provided in the plan is a decommodifying one, namely, 'to provide incentives to create formal employment for domestic workers who are currently recorded as unemployed or inactive' (Annex to the Council Implementing Decision ... for Romania 12319/21 ADD 1: 449). Given the Italian experiences with such vouchers however, their introduction might not end informal employment as such but only lead to a regularisation of some working hours. If used widely, they may even lead to more precarious employment, as vouchers create incentives for employers to use them instead of standard contracts of employment, given their lower costs (Anastasia, Bombelli, and Maschio, 2016).

Most importantly however, the CID also included a hard benchmark on intersectoral employment relations, as it tasked Romania's legislators to revise its collective labour law by the end of 2022 in order to secure the payment of the subsequent tranche of RRF funding:

> Q4 2022 Entry into force of a new law on social dialogue, negotiated with the social partners. The law shall address deficiencies in the social dialogue process as highlighted in the relevant Country Specific Recommendation and be in line with the International Labour Organisation recommendations issued in April 2018 and referred to in recital 25 of the 2020 Country Specific Recommendations. Also, the Law shall foresee a Revision of the definition of the economic sectors as a basis for sector level collective agreement.
> (Annex to the Council Implementing Decision ... for Romania 12319/21 ADD 1: 522)

This binding EU benchmark enabled the Romanian social democrats to overcome the opposition of their centre-right coalition partners from the Partidul Național Liberal (PNL), which initially resisted reversing the 2011 collective labour law reforms that the then centre-right Romanian government adopted under MoU conditionality (Chapter 6). Subsequently, on 22 December 2022, the Romanian legislators adopted a new Law on Social Dialogue ('Legea privind dialogul social' nr. 367/2022), which strengthened workers' and union rights[5] and re-established multi-employer bargaining structures at sectoral and intersectoral level. This may be a 'real

---

[5] The 2022 Social Dialogue Law lowered the minimum number of workers required to form a union, re-legalised strikes against socioeconomic government policies, facilitated union officials' access to unionised and non-unionised firms, reduced the representativeness threshold for unions at unit and sectoral level, allowed the self-employed and the unemployed to join unions, and increased the protection of union members against discrimination and union leaders against any form of coercion (De Spiegelaere, 2023; industriAll Europe, 2023).

game changer' (industriAll Europe, 2023), as sectoral collective bargaining broke down in almost all sectors following the adoption of the 2011 Social Dialogue Law (Chapter 6). This change would not have been possible without EU leaders' changing policy orientation, the persistent lobbying of the ETUC and its affiliates for the EU Minimum Wage Directive, and the concurring mobilisations of Romanian unions for the revision of the Romanian collective labour law. The latter included a five-day-long protest 'Caravan of Social Rights' by trade unionists from Bucharest to Brussels in July 2021, which politicised the EU Minimum Wage Directive, the Romanian NRRP, and its demand for reform of the Romanian labour law (Table 13.1). Powerful employers, such as all foreign-owned banks operating in Romania, accepted the return to sectoral bargaining too, to create a level playing field in 'a tight labor market' (De Spiegelaere, 2023: 9). National and EU policymakers, however, would hardly have shifted the direction of their labour policy interventions in a decommodifying direction had they not feared popular discontent and a revival of collective union action following the cost-of-living crisis that 'has pushed millions of people into poverty' (Vanhercke, Sabato, and Spasova, 2023: 7).

Overall, our assessment of the four NRRPs, the corresponding CIDs, and the recent EU laws has revealed a substantial change of direction in EU policymaking in the area of employment relations. Whereas EU executives prescribed wage cuts and commodifying reforms of collective bargaining and hiring and firing mechanisms after the financial crisis in 2008, the EU interventions in the field predominantly pointed in a decommodifying policy direction after the outbreak of the Covid pandemic. The same, however, cannot be said of their interventions in the field of public services, as we outline below.

13.3 EU GOVERNANCE OF PUBLIC SERVICES: PUBLIC INVESTMENT FOR PRIVATE GAIN

Before the pandemic, the EU NEG prescriptions had already shifted away from demanding a curtailing of resources for public service providers. Instead, EU executives prescribed greater investments in sectors that would be critical for economic development. Most of these expansionary quantitative NEG prescriptions, however, remained subordinated to NEG's overarching commodification script, given their semantic links to policy rationales – such as boost competitiveness and growth, rebalance the EU economy, and enhance private sector involvement (Table 11.2) – that are compatible with public service commodification.

TABLE 13.1 *Transnational protests politicising the EU governance of employment relations (2020–28 February 2023)*

Date	Location	Action type	Topic	Coordinators
25 February 2020	Brussels	Demonstration	Commission proposal for gender pay transparency legislation	ETUC
25 September 2020–25 June 2022	Online	ECI	Unconditional basic incomes (UBI) throughout the EU	Netzwerk Grundeinkommen
18 June 2021	Brussels	Demonstration	Gender Pay Transparency Directive	ETUC
1–5 July 2021	Multi-sited	Demonstration	Caravan of Social Rights: Bucharest to Brussels	Cartel Alfa
7 October 2021	Multi-sited	Demonstration, strike	World Day for Decent Work	ITUC, ETUC, national unions
23 June 2022	Multi-sited	Demonstration	World Public Service Day	EPSU
5 October 2022	Strasbourg	Demonstration	End the cost-of-living crisis. Increase wages, tax profits	ETUC, French unions
26 November 2022	Schengen	Demonstration	Against the neoliberal policy that has been implemented in Europe for decades	OGBL, DCB, ver.di, CGT, Younion, FGTB
30 November 2022	Brussels	Demonstration	Ban unpaid internships	ETUC

Source: Transnational Socioeconomic Protest Database (Erne and Nowak, 2023).
The table includes transnational protest events (1 January 2020–28 February 2023) targeting EU authorities in relation to employment relations, using the database's political category, excluding socioeconomic protests at company, sectoral, and systemic level.

Conversely, *all* qualitative NEG prescriptions pointed clearly in a commodifying policy direction across all four countries and all years until 2019 (Table 11.1). In the 2019 Semester cycle, EU executives tasked the Italian government to 'address restrictions to competition ... through a new annual competition law' (Council Recommendation 2019/C 301/12), and Romania was required to improve the efficiency of public procurement (Council Recommendation 2019/C 301/23). Italy was asked to reform its public administration, whereas the Romanian government was told to strengthen the corporate governance of state-owned enterprises (SOEs), 'with a view to upgrading operational performance, limiting risks to the government budget and improving their functioning in the economy' (Council Recommendation 2019/C 301/23).

In response to the Covid-19 pandemic, member states massively increased their public spending. EU leaders supported this response by temporarily suspending the Stability and Growth Pact (SGP) (Chapter 12). The Council's 2020 NEG prescriptions reflected this new reality, as most governments were told to take all necessary measures, in line with the SGP's general escape clause, to effectively address the crisis caused by the pandemic (Council Recommendations for Ireland (2020/C 282/07), Italy (2020/C 282/12), and Germany (2020/C 282/05)). Even so, EU executives toned down these expansionary prescriptions by requesting a return to restrictive fiscal policies once the situation improved. Furthermore, in 2020, EU executives expected the Romanian government to limit the public deficit with a view to bringing it below 3 per cent of GDP in 2022. After all, Romania had been made subject to an excessive deficit procedure just before the outbreak of the pandemic (Council Recommendation 2020/C 116/01). In 2021, EU executives nonetheless extended to 2024 the deadline to bring the deficit below the SGP threshold, given the negative impact of the pandemic on the Romanian economy (Commission SWD (2021) 530 final). This shows that the fiscal flexibility granted to governments was temporary and still constrained by the overarching EU fiscal framework. This, we expect, will clearly be the case if EU leaders re-enact a constraining SGP regime, a question to which we return below. In addition, EU executives did not ask governments to increase resources for *all* public service providers. Instead, they asked governments to 'front-load' approved public investment projects and to 'focus' investment on the green and digital transition (Council Recommendations for Ireland 2020/C 282/07, Italy 2020/C 282/12, and Germany 2020/C 282/05). As shown in Chapter 7, however, the prioritisation of investments in some areas at the expense of other areas does not have a decommodifying effect on public services in general. In addition, the prescriptions in the area of provider-level governance mechanisms issued to Italy and Romania also pointed in a commodifying direction, tasking the two governments to 'improve the effectiveness of public administration' (Council Recommendations for Romania 2020/C 282/23 and Italy 2020/C 282/12). Given that the pandemic's devastating impact underlined the importance of adequate and accessible public services, we expected to find more prescriptions in the 2020 Semester cycle on people's access to public services. However, only Romania received a prescription to extend the coverage of essential public services (Council Recommendation 2020/C 282/23), as in previous Semester cycles (Chapter 7).

The four NRRPs prescribed a similar policy mix, combining calls for more public investments with demands for marketising public sector reforms. These patterns were most notable in the Romanian and Italian NRRPs; this is hardly surprising, as EU executives matched those countries' greater share of RRF funding to more policy conditionalities. Given the RRF Regulation's evaluation criteria, the NRRPs channelled public expenditure towards capital (rather than personnel) spending and towards the green and digital transitions. Most green and digital investments were directed towards specific sectors, as we shall see below. If we look at green investments across sectors, only those for spending on the energy efficiency of Irish, Italian, and Romanian public buildings stand out in their respective NRRPs, in which, by contrast, digitalisation played a more prominent cross-sectoral role.

All four NRRPs first committed governments to digitalise public administrations and then operationalised the corresponding expenditure and reform targets in more detail. All plans prescribed measures to increase the digital delivery of public services, with the stated aim of increasing citizens' access to them. Other measures concerned the internal operation of public administration, such as the creation of shared cloud services and data centres or the provision of training on digital skills for public service workers. The Romanian NRRP also committed the government to automate laborious, repetitive, and rule-based tasks in the public sector. This could have a commodifying or a decommodifying impact, depending on whether automated services will be used to reduce the public sector workforce or to expand public services. All NRRPs presented digitalisation as a means to increase citizens' access to public services, but only Romania's plan foresaw additional measures to increase access to, and the quality of, local-level services. These measures mirrored the decommodifying prescriptions on the same issue that Romania received in the 2019 and 2020 Semester cycles. At the same time however, Romania's NRRP linked digitalisation to commodifying public services reforms, that is, to the creation of digital platforms for human resource management (HRM).

More generally, the Italian and Romanian NRRPs combined decommodifying (quantitative) prescriptions for more investments with prescriptions for commodifying (qualitative) public sector reforms. In the sector-level governance mechanisms category, the Italian NRRP committed the government to remove obstacles to competition in the services sector, both public and private, through the introduction of annual law to further competition. This had been a recurrent theme in the CSRs for the Italian government up to the 2019 cycle (Chapter 7). In the NRRP, the Italian government thus committed itself to foster competitive tendering for local public services; to curtail the possibility of in-house delivery of public services; and to reduce the length of public concessions contracts in several areas, such as ports, highways, electric charging stations, and hydropower. The Italian NRRP also required the simplification of Italy's procurement rules to accelerate the awarding of public contracts, which was a recurring theme in the NEG prescriptions for Italy, albeit not in the 2019 and 2020 cycles. The theme of increasing the efficiency of public procurement was very present in the NEG prescriptions for Romania too, including the 2019 ones. In turn, the Romanian NRRP committed the government to fully implement its National Public Procurement Strategy approved in 2015. Another commodifying measure of both the Italian and the Romanian NRRPs was the commitment to strengthen spending review procedures, mirroring NEG prescriptions that EU executives had already issued before the 2019 and 2020 Semester cycles (Chapter 7).

Both the Italian and Romanian NRRPs also contained prescriptions on provider-level governance mechanisms. The reform of HRM practices in public administration had been a long-standing theme in NEG prescriptions for Italy and Romania, including in the 2020 cycle. Accordingly, they featured prominently in the NRRPs too. The Italian NRRP prescribed an update in public sector job profiles, a reform of hiring procedures and career trajectories, and new provisions on public sector workers' horizontal and vertical mobility. In addition to these commodifying goals, the plan mentioned some decommodifying ones, including a stronger commitment to gender equality. In addition to the digitalisation of HRM practices discussed above, the Romanian plan prescribed a reform of the recruitment procedures for public sector workers and the introduction of a unitary pay system in the public sector, which may or may not be linked to budgetary retrenchment, depending on its implementation. Moreover, the Romanian NRRP addressed another recurring theme in NEG prescriptions, namely, the reform of governance mechanisms in SOEs. EU executives thus set implementation targets that tasked the Romanian government to insulate SOEs' senior management from government interventions by separating SOE ownership and regulatory functions and to 'remove any direct or indirect advantage that might derive

TABLE 13.2 *Transnational protests politicising the EU governance of public services (2020–28 February 2023)*

Date	Location	Action type	Topic	Coordinators
23 June 2021	Multi-sited	Demonstration, strike	World Public Service Day	EPSU
23 June 2022	Multi-sited	Demonstration	World Public Service Day	EPSU
26 November 2022	Schengen	Demonstration	Against the neoliberal policy that has been implemented in Europe for decades	OGBL, DGB, ver.di, CGT, Younion, FGTB

Source: Transnational Socioeconomic Protest Database (Erne and Nowak, 2023). The table includes intersectoral public sector protest events (1 January 2020–28 February 2023) across at least two public sectors targeting EU authorities, excluding those of European public servants (public EU).

from State ownership' (Annex to the Council Implementing Decision ... for Romania 12319/21 ADD 1: 474–475).

In sum, the post-Covid EU governance interventions on public services at cross-sectoral level very much mirrored the patterns of NEG prescriptions that EU executives had issued before the pandemic. The NRRPs committed governments to spend more in certain areas, but the quest for greater investments continued to be predominantly linked to policy rationales that did not question NEG's overarching commodification script in public services. The NRRPs' qualitative prescriptions on public services reforms largely pointed in the same commodifying direction as the qualitative NEG prescriptions that EU executives had issued before the pandemic (Chapter 11). Accordingly, unions and social movements tried to politicise EU economic governance interventions through transnational union protests in 2021 and 2022 also (Table 13.2).

As EU executives' commodifying public service NEG prescriptions continued to be country-specific, protest organisers used very general watchwords to mobilise people, such as 'no to privatisation and commercialisation', which somewhat shielded the specific NEG interventions – such as the NRRP commitment for Italy to liberalise local public services – from their politicisation in the transnational public sphere.

Having assessed the EU's post-Covid NEG prescriptions and the corresponding transnational actions by trade unions and social movements in our two intersectoral areas, we now turn to the analysis of the post-Covid prescriptions in our three public sectors.

13.4 EU GOVERNANCE OF TRANSPORT SERVICES: STILL COMMODIFYING

Before the pandemic, EU executives' prescriptions on resource levels for public services had already taken an expansionary turn, especially in sectors regarded as critical for economic growth, including transport and water services but not healthcare (Chapter 11). In the 2019 Semester cycle, they promoted investment in sustainable transport for Germany, Romania, and Ireland and quality infrastructure for Italy after the collapse of the Morandi Bridge (Chapter 8). The prescriptions also promoted investment to address regional disparities in Romania, Ireland, and Italy. These quantitative NEG prescriptions pointed in a decommodifying direction – although with some qualifications, given their semantic links to policy rationales such as 'enhance private sector involvement', which were compatible with NEG's commodification script (Table 11.4).

Conversely, *all* qualitative prescriptions on transport services issued in 2019 pointed in a commodifying direction (Table 11.3). EU executives tasked the Romanian government to reform governance of its SOEs and urged the Italian government to introduce each year a bespoke annual 'competition law' (Council Recommendation 2019/C 301/12) to expose in-house public service providers (namely, public transport and water services) to greater market competition.

The prescriptions issued by EU executives in the 2020 Semester cycle mirrored the patterns of previous years. All four countries received a decommodifying prescription for greater investment in the 'green and digital transition' (Council Recommendations Germany 2020/C 282/05, Ireland 2020/C 282/07, Italy 2020/C 282/12, Romania 2020/C 282/23). At the same time, EU executives again tasked the four governments to combine public *and* private investment, effectively diluting the decommodifying component in favour of commodification.

After the end of the Covid lockdowns and the return to workplaces, public transport operators faced challenges in terms of getting people back to using their services. Whereas private car usage surged with car manufacturers capitalising on public fears, a declining trend persisted in public transport. On account of the central role of transport in the transition to a green economy, however, it featured consistently across the four countries' NRRPs, channelling a substantial share of RRF funds into this sector. This is in line with the 2019–2020 CSRs on investment and, more generally, the 37 per cent minimum spending threshold on the green transition mandated by the RRF Regulation (Chapter 12).

Nevertheless, each NRRP differed in terms of the funds for transport and mobility, with the four countries planning to spend between 17 and 26 per cent of the RRF funds on them (European Parliament, 2022). The plans also differed in content. Whereas all NRRPs stipulated investments in railways, electrification was envisaged in the case of Ireland, and the Italian plan included the building of new rail connections, increasing capacity on (high-speed) passenger and freight rail transport, and upgrading regional rail lines. The German NRRP foresaw the replacement of old diesel trains with 280 new ones using alternative fuels and the roll-out of zero-emission buses. The Italian plan also envisaged greening regional fleets with 150 trains and, along with Romania's plan, investing in regional and urban transport networks. Both the Romanian and the Italian plan included cycle tracks in urban areas and the development of cycle routes to promote cycling tourism.

The NRRPs thus mirrored the quantitative expansionary prescriptions on transport that EU executives had issued in the 2019 and 2020 Semester cycles, but the plans also implemented the qualitative 2019 prescriptions that pointed clearly in a commodifying direction. The Italian plan included the implementation of the bespoke annual competition law, which EU executives had requested in 2019 and before without success, which will also affect local public transport services. The Romanian plan likewise included a clear commitment to reform the governance structures of SOEs, including in the transport sector. To that aim, the NRRP tasked the Romanian Ministry of Transport and Infrastructure to 'contract/select through competitive public procurement an International Financing Institution or an international auditing company, recognised for the competence and expertise in state-owned enterprises' performance. The recommendations from this independent assessment shall be implemented by 30 June 2023' (Annex to the Council Implementing Decision ... for Romania 12319/21 ADD 1: 103). The OECD provided the blueprint for such a corporate governance reform. It urged the government to further centralise control over SOEs by setting up an 'independent public agency ... not otherwise involved in the ownership and regulation of SOEs' and to create 'a level playing field with other [e.g., private] companies' (OECD, 2023b). On 28 June 2023, the Romanian president Klaus Iohannis promulgated the new law[6] that established such an agency (Agenția pentru Monitorizarea și Evaluarea Performanțelor Întreprinderilor Publice, AMEPIP) to be set up under the aegis of the government's general

---

[6] LEGE nr.187 din 28 iunie 2023 pentru modificarea si completarea Ordonantei de urgență a Guvernului nr. 109/2011 privind guvernanta corporativă a întreprinderilor publice.

secretary, who is also a member of Iohannis' centre-right PNL party (ADZ.ro, 06 July 2023).

After the pandemic, governance interventions by law also triggered some interesting developments. At national level, the German monthly €9 ticket valid on all local buses, trams, metros, and regional trains nationwide garnered considerable attention as a radical measure incentivising the use of public transport. Although the initiative lasted only three months, it put the question of green public transport front and centre. In May 2023, Germany's federal legislators therefore amended its regionalisation law (*Regionalisierungsgesetz*), in turn enabling its *Länder* to introduce a permanent successor ticket for €49. On the other hand, the largest NRRP investment in the German transport sector involves support for the purchase of electric vehicles, a ten-year tax exemption, and the establishment of a comprehensive charging infrastructure. In other words, car-dependent transport systems will continue to the detriment of alternative (public) transport modes, despite the climate emergency.

At EU level, in December 2020, the Commission published an ambitious legislative new transport policy agenda called 'Sustainable and Smart Mobility Strategy' (Commission, Communication, COM/2020/789 final). Although the Commission linked it to the green transition, the creation of a single EU transport *market* remained its principal goal. The Commission also opened proceedings against Europe's biggest publicly owned rail-based cargo operators, as the state aid that they had received would disadvantage their (road-based) competitors (Commission, Announcement (2023/C 131/13), *Fret SNCF*; Commission, Announcement (C/2022/639), *DB Cargo*). These actions are revealing, as a further weakening of the EU's biggest *rail* freight operators in the name of market competition will hardly reverse the ongoing decline of rail freight, which began in the 1990s after the EU started liberalising its transport policies (Chapter 8). How this will further the green transition is unclear.

The Commission's continuing quest for the marketisation of transport services has also informed its draft implementation guideline for a Public Service Obligation Regulation that was part of the fourth package of EU railways laws (Chapter 8), which infuriated the ETF (2023), as the Commission's draft guidelines wrongly insinuated that direct PSO concession awards of national and local governments to their public rail companies would no longer be legal. The Commission's draft implementation guideline triggered not only a response from the European Parliament in which it reiterated that it would not accept any attempt by the Commission to alter the spirit of the regulation without involving the Council and Parliament in a co-decision procedure but also a European demonstration of rail workers in Brussels (see Table 13.3).

TABLE 13.3 *Transnational protests politicising the EU governance of transport services (2020–28 February 2023)*

Date	Location	Action type	Topic	Coordinators
28 June 2022	Brussels	Strike, demonstration	Fair Transport rally: '30 years of liberalisation – it's enough'	ETF, CGT
28 June 2023	Brussels	Demonstration	Protests for democracy and against the Commission's unilateral attempt to force public transport liberalisation	ETF, Members of the European Parliament

Source: Transnational Socioeconomic Protest Database (Erne and Nowak, 2023).
The table includes transnational protest events (1 January 2020–28 February 2023) targeting EU authorities in relation to transport services.

Despite another transnational strike and demonstration day in June 2022 against the thirty years of transport liberalisation, commodifying policy objectives continued to shape the Commission's transport policy, regardless of the need to foster a green transition. On 11 July 2023, the Commission proposed its 'Greening freight for more economic gain' package of two draft EU laws, which included:

- the draft Monster Lorry Directive (COM (2023) 445/2), which aims to increase the productivity of road transport operators by removing the current maximum height and weight restrictions for low emission lorries (*Politico.eu*, 11 July 2023);
- the draft Rail Capacity Management Regulation (COM (2023) 443/2), which aims to make rail more attractive for cargo companies by replacing the current national rail capacity management systems that would hinder 'the functioning of the Single Market' by a single EU system that gives freight operators 'non-discriminatory' access to all railway lines according to an 'industry-led' rail capacity management plan for the entire 'single European railway area' (European Commission, 2023b).

In sum, neither Covid nor the climate emergency triggered major changes in the EU governance interventions in the transport sector. Although all NRRPs foresaw greater transport infrastructure investments, the NRRPs' policy conditionalities and the Commission's 2023 draft transport laws still clearly point in a commodifying, transport-service-marketisation direction.

13.5 EU GOVERNANCE OF WATER SERVICES: TOWARDS A NEW COMMODIFICATION PUSH?

In the 2019 and 2020 Semester cycles, EU executives explicitly prescribed more resources for local public services (including water services) for all four countries except Romania. As in preceding years, EU executives tasked the German authorities in 2019 to 'achieve a sustained upward trend in private and public investment, in particular at regional and municipal level' (Council Recommendation 2019/C 301/05). This is relevant for water services, as they are normally located at local level. Similarly, the 2019 and 2020 CSRs urged Ireland to focus investment on green transition in sustainable water services. These prescriptions followed up on earlier ones of 'investment prioritisation' issued since 2016. Italy received a similar prescription in 2020 to 'focus investment on the green and digital transition, in particular on ... waste and water management'. In 2019, Romania did not obtain any explicit prescriptions on higher resource levels, even though Recital 19 to its 2019 CSR lamented the country's deficiencies in water and wastewater infrastructure. Instead, it got a decommodifying prescription in 2020, which tasked the government to 'extend social protection measures and access to essential services for all'. Water was not mentioned in the main CSR text, but its Recital 19 considered water services as essential: 'Social and essential services remain largely insufficient, including in areas such as water and sanitation, energy and housing.' We categorised all these expansionary prescriptions as decommodifying, as they represented a shift away from the austerity cuts of 2009–2014 by advocating higher resource levels for public service providers or higher public service coverage levels (Chapters 9 and 11). When assessing the semantic links of the recent quantitative NEG prescriptions to their underlying policy rationale however, we found that most of the policy rationales behind the expansionary prescriptions, such as 'rebalance the EU economy', 'boost competitiveness and growth', or 'enhance private sector involvement', were compatible with NEG's commodification script (Table 11.4). Since 2018 however, the 'shift to a green economy' rationale has also gained traction in relation to these prescriptions.

Conversely, the qualitative prescriptions concerning the mechanisms governing the provision of water services continued to point in a commodifying direction. Despite the 2011 Italian referendum vote in favour of public local (water) services, and a subsequent 2016 Constitutional Court decision (Chapter 8), EU executives tasked the government to increase 'the efficiency and quality of local public services'. This prescription does not sound commodifying, but Recital 24 of the same CSR document clearly discloses its policy direction: 'A new legislative initiative is thus needed to promote the efficiency and quality of local public services, *including by prioritising competitive bids over in-house solutions or direct grants*' (emphasis added).

The four countries' NRRPs pursued commodifying qualitative and decommodifying quantitative objectives too. As mentioned in Chapter 12, each NRRP had to allocate at least 37 per cent of its RRF funds to support the green transition. According to the Commission's Recovery and Resilience Scoreboard,[7] member states promised to spend approximately 2 per cent of their RRF funds on the sustainable use and protection of water and marine resources. At the same time, the spending targets differed greatly across countries. Water did not feature in the German NRRP and was only marginally present in the Irish one, which mentioned wastewater management as part of the Irish River Basin Management plan. By contrast, the Italian and Romanian NRRPs included sections on the management of water services.

The Italian plan included several qualitative reform commitments. The first mirrored the commodifying prescriptions on the sector- and provider-level mechanisms governing local public services that Italy received in the 2019 and 2020 Semester cycles, namely, the commitment to adopt bespoke 'Annual Competition Laws in 2021, 2022, 2023 and 2024' to increase 'competitive procedures to award public service contracts for local public services', including 'transport' (see section 13.4) and 'water' services (Annex to the Revised Council Implementing Decision ... for Italy 10160/21 ADD 1 REV 1: 188–189). In addition, the plan criticises the fragmentation of the Italian water sector and sets out incentives to regional governments to integrate small water providers into single operators per at least 40,000 inhabitants. The Italian NRRP thus committed the Italian authorities to introduce new laws and regulations on water services that shall 'at least reduce the number of water service providers' and introduce new 'pricing policies ... to facilitate a more sustainable consumption of water' (Annex to the Revised Council Implementing Decision ... for Italy 10160/21 ADD 1 REV 1: 370–371). Hence, EU executives are again instrumentalising green arguments as a means to increase users' water charges, as happened earlier (Chapter 8). Water services also featured in the first component of Romania's NRRP, which included far-reaching governance reforms of the water sector and aimed to extend access to water services by 'support to families and single people with low incomes ... to cover the costs of connection to the public water supply and sanitation system' (Annex to the Council Implementing Decision ... for Romania 12319/21 ADD 1: 3). Whereas this prescription at face value points in a decommodifying policy direction, we must recall that

---

[7] Table: Climate tracking: Breakdown of expenditure towards climate objectives per policy area, https://ec.europa.eu/economy_finance/recovery-and-resilience-scoreboard/green.html.

Romania privatised its lucrative water service providers long ago (Chapter 9). This NRRP prescription thus amounts to a call to subsidise privately owned water providers to incentivise them to set up water services in rural areas that still have no access to any water and sanitation systems.

In sum, the quantitative measures prescribed in the CSRs and the NRRPs called for more public investment across all four countries, although the water sector played only a marginal role in the German and Irish cases. The same policy documents called for higher water service coverage levels for Romania to give more people access to drinking water and wastewater service grids. As shown in Chapter 11, calls for greater public investments can go hand in hand with qualitative prescriptions that point in a commodifying policy direction, as in the case of the Italian NRRP that prescribed several reforms that further advanced the commodification of the mechanisms governing the public provision of water services.

The future orientation of the post-Covid EU governance of water services will also depend on the outcome of the ongoing discussions about new EU laws in the field. In 2020, EU legislators adopted the Recast Drinking Water Directive (2020/2184). This directive contains a decommodifying provision on people's rights to access drinking water, thanks in part to political pressures created by the successful Right2Water European Citizens' Initiative (Chapter 9). More legislative changes are in the pipeline. In 2022, the Commission proposed a new Water Directive (COM (2022) 540 final) and the Recast Urban Wastewater Treatment Directive (COM (2022) 541 final). The former aims to reduce the pollution of groundwater and surface waters across the EU and the latter aims to set higher EU standards for the extraction of pollutants from wastewaters. If adopted, the latter in particular will require much higher investments in water treatment plants. So far, these proposals have not triggered any protest actions by public service advocates, but both public and privately owned water operators have lobbied EU lawmakers to force polluting industries to contribute more to their higher prospective wastewater treatment costs. Even so, the need to invest more in greener water treatment facilities may lead to a renewed push to privatise water services and renewed social protests later, namely, when EU leaders terminate the suspension of the SGP.

13.6 EU GOVERNANCE OF HEALTHCARE SERVICES: GROWING DISCONTENT

In the years preceding the pandemic, the prescriptions for our set of four countries displayed a combination of mostly commodifying healthcare prescriptions, with few decommodifying ones (Chapter 10). In 2019, in the first category, we saw prescriptions to shift from inpatient to outpatient care (Romania) and to increase cost-effectiveness (Ireland) and cost-efficiency (Romania) in healthcare; and in the second, the prescription to improve users' access to long-term care (Italy) and to healthcare (Romania).

After the outbreak of the Covid-19 pandemic, EU member states faced a significant increase in the numbers of patients in need of highly specialised care. In March 2020, the importance of well-equipped and well-staffed public hospital services became apparent to almost everyone. In response, in the 2020 Semester cycle, EU executives introduced a general prescription that urged member states to 'strengthen the resilience of the health system'. The concrete substance of the prescription remained vague however, as its language neither defined 'resilience' nor clearly outlined how it should be 'strengthened'. By considering other healthcare-related texts in CSRs and recitals, we tried to unearth the meaning of the 'strengthen the resilience of the health system' prescription, as indicated in brackets in Table A13.1 of the Online Appendix. This enabled us to establish that the prescriptions for the four countries to 'strengthen the resilience of the health system' were meant to direct more funding towards healthcare infrastructure and healthcare workers, to secure long-term financing (Germany) or investment in healthcare (Romania), to improve healthcare infrastructure (Ireland), and to address the needs of healthcare workers (Ireland) and their retention in the healthcare system (Germany, Italy, Romania). These prescriptions were thus quantitative and expansionary and pointed in a decommodifying policy direction. Nonetheless, in a context where healthcare systems in all the four countries had already been affected by service commodification before (Germany, Italy, Ireland) or after (Ireland, Romania) the 2008 crisis, greater public spending may actually benefit private providers more than public ones. Tellingly, the prescriptions referred to 'the health system' rather than to public health service providers. In this context, increased healthcare financing may also be used to boost the profits of private providers of medical services and products or of the builders of healthcare infrastructure.

In addition to these 2020 prescriptions on resource levels, we found several prescriptions on users' access to healthcare services to 'improve accessibility of the health system' and 'ensure universal coverage to primary care' (Ireland) and to 'improve access to healthcare' (Romania), all pointing in a decommodifying direction. These prescriptions are a continuation of similar exhortations in previous years in recitals for Ireland and in CSRs for Romania (Chapter 10; Online Appendix, Table A10.4). The same caveat applies to these prescriptions as to those seen above: in significantly commodified healthcare systems, calls to increase accessibility may also translate into measures seeking to redirect public funding towards private providers. Overall however, EU executives reoriented their quantitative NEG prescriptions in 2020 towards higher resource levels for healthcare providers and higher service coverage levels for its users, away from their curtailment. This development is notable, as healthcare did not profit from the earlier shift of EU executives' prescriptions in favour of more investment that occurred in allegedly more productive sectors (including transport and water) from 2016 onwards (Table 11.4).

Finally, the 2020 CSRs also included prescriptions on the sector-level governance of healthcare services. Germany was tasked to deploy e-health services, mirroring EU executives' earlier prescriptions calling for healthcare digitalisation to advance their commodifying agenda. As shown in Chapter 10, although e-health has been presented as a means for increasing patient choice, in practice it was introduced as a tool to reorganise health systems along managerialist financial control lines. Italy's prescription to 'enhance coordination between national and regional (healthcare) authorities', which we classified under the same category, leaves space for both commodifying and decommodifying possibilities inasmuch as neither the nature of this coordination nor the means to achieve it were specified.

The subsequent NRRPs had to address both 2019 and 2020 CSRs, and this is where both commodifying and decommodifying streams in healthcare prescriptions for the two years became relevant. On the decommodifying side, the 2020 prescriptions to 'strengthen the resilience of the health system' were translated in the CIDs of the corresponding NRRPs into very detailed measures seeking to improve healthcare infrastructure, service provision, and access to health services (Online Appendix, Table A13.2). On the infrastructure side (our category of resource levels for service providers), the four NRRPs included measures aimed at improving emergency services (Germany); de-institutionalised health services, the use of local pharmacies as health services, community health houses, homecare services, community hospitals, hospital equipment, and intensive care services (Italy); community health networks (Ireland); and GP practices, integrated community services, preventive services, long-term care services, and hospital infrastructure (Romania). In the area of users' access to services, NRRPs included measures to simplify access to health services for people with disabilities and the elderly (Italy) and to extend the range of services covered by the national insurance fund (Romania).

Prescriptions to 'strengthen the resilience of the health system' also led to measures concerning healthcare workers, which fell under our resource level category too. Its NRRP committed the Irish government to issue public-only healthcare service contracts for medical consultants, a measure that pointed in a decommodifying direction. Romania's NRRP in this area, however, was more ambivalent. On the one hand, pointing in a decommodifying direction, it committed its government to establish, and fund from the state budget, two skills and development training centres for healthcare workers and to build houses for healthcare professionals in marginalised communities. On the other hand, the plan obliged the government to fund skills and integrity training programmes, opening new business opportunities for private training operators. In addition, the plan required the government to introduce performance-based rewards mechanisms for health professionals, a clearly commodifying measure.

This brings us to the commodifying side of the NRRPs' healthcare-related measures, mirroring 2019 NEG prescriptions to increase 'cost-effectiveness' (Ireland) or 'cost-efficiency' (Romania), which meant marketising the provider- and sector-level governance mechanisms of healthcare services (Chapter 10). All NRRPs emphasise digitalisation, either in the form of digitalising hospitals (Germany and Italy) or in terms of digitalising healthcare data for the purpose of financial management (Italy, Ireland, Romania). In addition, the Italian NRRP committed the government to simplify public procurement rules, which is a measure seeking to commodify provider-level governance. In turn, the Romanian NRRP tasked the government to introduce further spending reviews in budgetary processes and additional performance-based mechanisms to finance healthcare providers. These measures sought to commodify the governance of healthcare services at sector level: the first sought to further entrench budgetary discipline in healthcare management, continuing the line traced by the prescriptions to strengthen budget control mechanisms for hospitals issued to Romania between 2011 and 2014; the second sought to generalise to all healthcare providers the prescription issued in 2013 to introduce performance-based payments in primary care (Chapter 10).

This commodifying orientation could be reinforced also by developments taking place through the ordinary legislative procedure, namely, the Commission's draft Regulation on the European Health Data Space (COM (2022) 197 final). The draft regulation not only obliges all healthcare practitioners to input their patients' data into a European database to facilitate the management of healthcare services and to create a European healthcare union but also entitles private companies to access the proposed European database for 'secondary use' to facilitate their commercial research and innovation. Although the big tech TNCs, the pharmaceutical industry, and private healthcare providers 'stand to benefit' from the draft regulation (*Politico.eu*, 27 October 2022) and despite the popular critiques of digital capitalism, for example by Shoshana Zuboff (2019), no transnational protests against the proposed regulation took place until February 2023 (Table 13.4). However,

TABLE 13.4 *Transnational protests politicising the EU governance of healthcare (2020–28 February 2023)*

Date	Location	Action type	Topic	Coordinators
7 April 2020	Brussels, multi-sited	Demonstration	World Health Day: European action against the commercialisation of health and social protection	ENPCHSP, PHM
30 November 2020–1 August 2022	Online	ECI	Right to cure. No profits on the pandemic	No profit on pandemic coalition
26–30 October 2020	Brussels, multi-sited	Demonstration	European Action Week 'Invest in care'. Fighting for health and care beyond the pandemic. Higher wages, more staff, quality care for all	EPSU, ENPCHSP, PHM Europe
7 April 2021	Brussels, multi-sited	Demonstration	World Health Day: Europe-wide mobilisation to defend access to vaccines	ENPCHSP, PHM Europe
29 October 2021	Brussels	Demonstration	Global Action Day for Care workers: 'Investment and decent work in care'	EPSU, PSI, ITUC, other global union federations
8 March 2022	Paris, Porto	Demonstration	For the right to care and the non-commercial nature of care	EPSU
7 April 2022	Brussels, multi-sited	Demonstration	World Health Day: European action against the commercialisation of health. "The other pandemic'	ENPCHSP, PHM Europe
9 December 2022	Brussels	Demonstration	#Applauseisnotenough. Higher pay – more staff – no commercialisation	EPSU

Source: Transnational Socioeconomic Protest Database (Erne and Nowak, 2023).
The table includes transnational protest events (1 January 2020–28 February 2023) targeting EU authorities in relation to healthcare services.

the EU's own in-house privacy regulator, the European Data Protection Board, raised concerns about the sharing of certain data with industry, echoing the disquiet of other not-for-profit organisations representing patients, healthcare professionals, hospital pharmacists, payers, and healthcare institutions that advocate for a 'society-centred digitisation of healthcare' (AIM et al., 2022). An EPSU (2022b) press release struck a similar tone: 'We cannot trust nor rely on an approach that would give commercial interests (from companies seeking profits) any role in a health data sharing space. Health is not a commodity and commercial interests can have no place in our public and private health issues.' Instead, however, of mobilising their members against the proposed European Health Data Space, EPSU, but also the rank-and-file European Network against Privatisation and Commercialisation of Health and Social Protection (ENPCHSP, or the European Network), organised several transnational protests that responded to the more burning challenges for health services and healthcare workers caused by the Covid-19 pandemic (see Table 13.4).

The pandemic made the negative consequences of NEG's insistence on cuts in healthcare spending more visible, notably in terms of public hospital bed, staff, and equipment shortages. Healthcare workers called for better working and employment conditions in response to the heavy toll that the pandemic had taken on them (Vandaele, 2021). The European Network held an action day in April 2020 called 'Against the commercialisation of health and social protection', but it had to be confined to actions on social media and a press conference because of Covid lockdowns. In October 2020, EPSU organised a European action day 'Fighting for health and care beyond the pandemic', which focused on 'higher wages, more staff and quality of care for all [Table 13.4]', mirroring the International Trade Union Confederation's call for a Global Day of Action on 'Investing in care now'. The European Network's 2021 action day focused on 'universally accessible and affordable' access to Covid-19 vaccines, in support of the 'No profit on pandemic' European Citizens' Initiative launched by members of the European Left and supported by both the European Network and EPSU. However, by embracing the cause of fighting the larger commodification of health by pharmaceutical companies, the European Network drifted away from the more specific issue of *healthcare* commodification, although the pandemic did not reverse the EU executives' healthcare commodification agenda. The fight against the 'commercialisation' of healthcare services nonetheless remained a central theme in the protests of European healthcare workers – as shown by the cover picture of this book, which was taken on 9 December 2022 at the EPSU demonstration before the Council and Commission buildings in Brussels.

13.7 CONTINUITY AND CHANGE IN EU ECONOMIC GOVERNANCE AFTER THE PANDEMIC

After the financial crisis, EU executives' NEG prescriptions followed similarly commodifying trajectories in employment relations and public services. After the Covid-19 emergency, however, the trajectories of their governance interventions on employment relations and public services clearly pointed in opposite directions. Whereas EU executives virtually stopped prescribing commodifying qualitative prescriptions in employment relations, public services continued to be targeted by commodifying qualitative prescriptions also after the pandemic.

In the employment relations area, the most relevant developments took place outside the NRRP framework, following the approval of the aforementioned EU directive on adequate minimum wages. Only the Romanian NRRP addressed the issue directly, namely, by prescribing the 2022 labour law reform that sought to increase collective bargaining coverage and better protect union and workers' rights and by reversing the commodifying 2011 Social Dialogue Law introduced under the EU–IMF economic adjustment programme. In Ireland, improvements to the legislation underpinning collective bargaining are also forthcoming, but as an effect of the Minimum Wage Directive and not of the NRRP. In October 2022, the Scholz government substantially increased the German minimum wage, through an ad hoc intervention, to €12, almost matching the reference values of the EU directive. So far however, given the opposition of the FDP, the German government has not yet proposed any national legal changes transposing the EU directive into German law; this explains why the German Minimum Wage Commission has been able to propose derisorily low minimum wage increases for 2023 and 2024. Nevertheless, both EU executives and legislators clearly adopted a decommodifying U-turn in their wages and collective bargaining policies, as they came to realise even before the advent of the pandemic that they could hardly re-establish some popular legitimacy for the EU integration process without attempting to re-integrate workers and trade unions into the process (Ryner, 2023).

At the same time, our analysis has shown that these attempts to increase the popular legitimacy of the EU integration process did not involve any significant deviation from the overarching commodifying policy script informing EU executives' NEG prescriptions on public services. Before 2019, NEG's overarching commodification script had already been more visible in the EU executives' prescriptions on public services compared with those on employment relations. Although EU executives tasked governments to pursue qualitative commodifying structural reforms in both areas up to 2019, they gradually adopted more expansionary prescriptions on wages and public service resource levels from 2016 onwards – not to address pressing social concerns but to rebalance the EU economy and to boost its growth and competitiveness.

Accordingly, EU executives committed member states to prioritising public investments in allegedly more productive public sectors, excluding, however, public healthcare services from the allegedly social investment turn in EU executives' NEG prescriptions (Tables 11.1–11.4). Whereas water and transport had already been identified in prescriptions as deserving more investment before 2020, healthcare had not (Chapter 11). This oversight, in turn, contributed to making healthcare systems less able to respond to the Covid-19 emergency (Stan and Erne, 2023). After the pandemic, even DG ECFIN Commission officials stopped perceiving healthcare expenditure primarily as a drag on healthy public finances, as they had done before the pandemic (Chapter 10). This, however, did not lead them to see public healthcare as a common good. Instead, they began their thematic analysis of the NRRPs in healthcare by stating the following: 'Healthcare services constitute one of the most important *economic* sectors in Europe, accounting for almost 10 per cent of GDP, 15 per cent of government expenditure and 8.3 per cent of the total workforce in the EU' (emphasis added) (European Commission, 2021: 2). Hence, healthcare also became a sector worth investing in, as it 'contributes to higher productivity and boosts economic growth' provided that the NRRP investments and reforms addressed the 'structural weaknesses in health systems across the EU' (2021: 2).

The policy orientation of the post-Covid NEG regime in public services thus did not shift dramatically. After the pandemic, EU executives reinforced trends detected in the previous empirical chapters and summarised in Chapter 11: combining expansionary prescriptions on resource levels with calls for commodifying structural reforms. However, although EU executives had already prescribed commodifying policy reforms, for example on the digital transition of public services, before the pandemic (Chapter 11), the EU funding conditionalities specified in the RRF Regulation significantly increased the coercive power of their corresponding prescriptions even in countries that were not subject to an excessive deficit procedure or a macroeconomic imbalance procedure (see Chapters 2 and 12).

In terms of the post-Covid NEG prescriptions on people's access to public services, we uncovered more continuity than change. Where there were decommodifying prescriptions before 2020 to increase the coverage levels of public services, they remained also after 2020, circumscribed to specific sectors or countries, namely, Romania. This is striking, as the pandemic showed the need for accessible public services across all sectors and countries. Calls for increased investment did not target public services in general but remained sector-focused. Among the sectors that we analysed, water and, especially, transport were obvious targets of increased investment in the green and digital transition in the NRRPs. Although healthcare investments were not shaped by concerns about the green transition (apart from the retrofitting of hospital buildings), they were meant to advance the sector's digitalisation.

Although we classify prescriptions aimed at increasing resources for public services as decommodifying, both pre- and post-Covid NEG prescriptions remained silent on whether increased public investment should go to public or to private services operators. It is too early to study the implementation of the NRRPs now but, to be able to fully assess the orientation of the post-pandemic NEG regime, this is something that future research will need to address. In light of the RRF funding criteria discussed in Chapter 12, however, it is indeed quite likely that the public money channelled through NRRPs will end up fuelling private profits (Bellofiore and Garibaldo, 2022).

Regarding qualitative NEG prescriptions on public services, this risk is even greater. Indeed, across the public transport, water, and healthcare sectors, as well as public services across sectors, almost all post-Covid prescriptions on sector- and provider-level governance mechanisms pointed in a commodifying policy direction. Both national and EU executives thus used RRF funding not only to address underinvestment but also as a leverage tool to advance additional commodifying, structural reforms of public services.

However, the picture concerning intersectoral employment relations differs. It is in relation to qualitative prescriptions on employment relations that a break with the pre-Covid NEG regime is most evident. In the 2019 and 2020 Semester cycles, EU executives issued only a few prescriptions on employment relations. Consequently, NRRPs addressed employment relations issues in only a few cases. More precisely, the Romanian NRRP included a commitment to reform Romania's 2011 collective labour law to foster social dialogue. The trajectory of EU interventions in employment relations shifted in a decommodifying direction, as shown also in the adoption of the EU Minimum Wage Directive in 2022. The directive not only set EU reference values that should lead to minimum wage increases in almost all EU member states but also shifted EU executives' views on decommodifying multi-employer collective bargaining mechanisms. In the public sector however, workers remain subject to post-Covid prescriptions advocating commodifying structural public sector reforms. The coercive power of these prescriptions has even increased significantly given the threat of withdrawal of RRF funding in the case of non-compliance.

Notwithstanding the change in EU executives' perspective in favour of healthcare investments after the Covid pandemic, the contribution of the €37bn of RRF healthcare funding directed at addressing the acute staff shortages in Europe's public healthcare systems was very limited, as 'support from the Facility shall not, unless in duly justified cases, substitute recurring national budgetary expenditure' (Art. 5(1) RRF Regulation). Accordingly, the RRF investments in this regard were typically limited to supporting staff training initiatives provided by public but also private operators. Moreover, all NRRPs directed a large amount of investment (€15bn) towards the 'digital transition in healthcare' to achieve 'the target of allocating at least 20% of their total budget to the digital transition' (European Commission, 2021: 3), a measure with the potential to use technology for the long-term replacement of staff – further indicating that public services have become a key site for capital accumulation (Huws, 2012).

13.8 CONCLUSION

In sum, the trajectories of the EU's post-Covid governance of employment relations and public services have increasingly pointed in opposite directions. The policy direction of forthcoming EU laws and NEG prescriptions governing employment relations and public services, but also the forthcoming EU laws on the revised Stability and Growth Pact, will determine whether we shall see a continuation of this polarising trend.

The recent strengthening of decommodifying EU labour law was certainly important. After all, EU executives did not dare to adopt NEG prescriptions that explicitly went against existing EU labour laws, even before the outbreak of the pandemic. By contrast, neither national law nor the EU Treaty's primary law on the EU's competences stopped EU executives from prescribing commodifying structural reforms across all policy areas (Chapter 3), for instance in relation to pay and collective bargaining (Chapter 6) or healthcare services (Chapter 10). For workers and unions, and for public services users and social movements, the policy direction of secondary EU law is thus of utmost importance.

Advocates of a more social Europe thus would be well advised to focus their energies on the fight for decommodifying EU laws; for example, new EU laws prioritising non-profit-oriented public services for the common good over private operators that seek to maximise their profits. We believe that this would be much more promising than the attempts to 'socialise' the NEG regime through the inclusion of social scoreboards in its technical procedures or the addition of a '"Social Imbalances Procedure" (SIP) *complementing* existing fiscal and macroeconomic procedures' (emphasis added) (Vanhercke, Sabato, and Spasova, 2023: 147).

Our analysis has also shown that any socialisation of the NEG regime is very difficult to achieve, given the exclusion of national parliaments, the European Parliament, unions, and social movements from the NEG (and even more so the post-Covid NEG) policymaking process. NEG's technocratic and country-specific design makes it indeed very difficult for unions and social movements to politicise its prescriptions in a transnational political sphere through collective action that can shift the balance of power in their favour (Erne, 2015).

At the same time, unions and social movements should politicise the NEG regime *as a whole*. The looming threat of EU executives re-enacting the full constraints of the Stability and Growth Pact in 2024 and the Commission's April 2022 proposal for a new package[8] of EU laws governing the NEG regime represent important opportunities to do that, notably given the latter's explicit goal to use greater leeway in terms of *quantitative* budgetary austerity as a tool to advance *qualitative* structural reforms. This will in turn substantially increase the capacity of national and EU executives to further enforce qualitative structural reforms, as has already happened in the case of the NEG prescriptions included in NRRPs and the corresponding CIDs analysed above.

---

[8] The package proposed by the Commission includes (1) a draft Regulation (COM (2023) 240 final) 'on the effective coordination of economic policies and multilateral budgetary surveillance', which is planned to replace the Stability and Growth Pact laws; (2) Annexes 1–7 to the above draft regulation, which, inter alia, specify its relationship to the CSRs, including those issued under the macroeconomic imbalance procedure, and the commitments made under the NRRPs; (3) draft Regulation (COM (2023) 241 final) amending Regulation (EC) No 1467/97 'on speeding up and clarifying the implementation of the excessive deficit procedure'; and (4) draft Directive (COM(2023) 242 final) amending Directive 2011/85/EU on requirements for member states' budgetary frameworks.

14

Conclusion

This book offers a novel theoretical and methodological approach to understanding the EU's new economic governance (NEG) regime in employment relations and public services (Chapters 2–5) and presents significant empirical findings (Chapters 6–13) that are crucial for understanding the prospects of the EU integration process, social justice, and democracy in Europe. The book makes three major analytical contributions.

First, we argue that to understand EU policies in employment relations and public services, we need to consider the actions not solely of EU institutional actors but also of trade unions and social movements (Chapter 3). In looking at EU executives' NEG interventions in employment and social policy areas from the perspective of labour politics, the book upscales insights on the historical role that trade unions and social movements have played in the development of democracy and social welfare states at national level, in order to shed light on corresponding processes at the supranational level of the EU polity. Our approach thus goes beyond the institutionalist studies of EU policymaking that focus their attention on institutional actors operating in national capitals and Brussels' EU quarter. Equally, our focus on collective action in the field of labour politics complements the EU politicisation studies that focus on media debates, opinion polls, and elections and referendums. This is vital, as social justice and the democratisation of the EU polity requires transnational collective action by social actors, including trade unions and social movements (Erne, 2008).

Second, we show that the introduction of the EU's NEG regime represents a crucial shift in the dominant mode of EU integration (Chapter 2), namely, from a market-driven mode of horizontal integration to a much more political mode of vertical integration (Chapter 3). This shift echoes the resurgence of a much more political form of capital accumulation across the globe, in which capitalists' rate of return increasingly hinges on political power (Harvey, 2004;

Crouch, 2016; Durand, 2020; Riley and Brenner, 2022). In Europe, this shift became very visible after the financial crisis of 2008 when European business and political leaders realised that the single market and monetary union did not lead to the desired market-driven convergence of national economic, employment relations, and social policies but to threatening macroeconomic imbalances. To insure the 'proper functioning' of the EU's economic and monetary union (Art. 2, Regulation No 1176/2011), its leaders consequently started a 'silent revolution' from above (Barroso cited in ANSA, 2010) that involved a significant upscaling of employment and social policymaking powers from national to EU level and the deployment of commodifying policy prescriptions, thereby further increasing social inequality and the EU's democratic deficit.

EU executives combined the shift to a supranational NEG regime of policy formation with a country-specific deployment of NEG prescriptions. Their NEG interventions thus offer contradictory possibilities for initiating countervailing trade union and social-movement action. The supranational location of the interventions' origin provides labour across countries with common targets. However, the country-specific deployment of the interventions, which mimics the governance modes of transnational corporations in relation to their subsidiaries, risks fragmenting collective action along national divides. Moreover, the shift from a horizontal to a vertical mode of EU integration has sapped the assumed autonomy of national labour and social policymaking institutions, rendering the methodological nationalism of the varieties of capitalism literature anachronistic (Chapter 3). We have therefore developed a novel comparative research design that can capture both the supranational formulation of NEG policies and the uneven deployment of NEG prescriptions across countries, years, areas, and sectors, as well as their uneven coercive power (Chapter 5).

Third, we argue that the key dimension of the policy orientation of NEG prescriptions in employment and social policy areas is commodification (Chapter 4). Given the historical role played by trade unions and social movements in the extension of social rights through the decommodification of employment relations and public services, commodification captures the fundamental stakes of labour movements in EU executives' NEG interventions in these policy areas (Chapter 3). Our focus on commodification also mirrors the fact that public services provision itself has become a key site of capital accumulation. Moreover, we distinguish between the qualitative and the quantitative dimensions of commodification to map the deployment and intertwining of curtailment (austerity) and marketisation (structural adjustment) in NEG prescriptions on employment relations and public services. This conceptual framework allowed us to overcome the methodological difficulties encountered by studies that selected other policy orientation dimensions (Chapter 4). This is important, as earlier studies' implicit focus on the quantitative aspects of NEG, whether in terms of social investment or austerity measures, made it difficult for them to capture the relevance of the structural changes stipulated by EU executives' NEG prescriptions, which, unlike their quantitative counterpart, are more difficult to reverse.

The book also makes three major empirical contributions. First, our research has revealed that the EU executives' NEG prescriptions are informed by an overarching commodification script, across the two areas (employment relations and public services), three sectors (transport, water, and healthcare), four countries (Germany, Italy, Ireland, and Romania), and eleven years (2009 to 2019) under consideration (Chapters 6–10). We have shown that commodifying NEG prescriptions mirrored an overarching commodification script not simply and solely because the commodifying prescriptions were more numerous than the decommodifying ones but also because the logic of their deployment was one of advancing commodification in the areas, sectors, and countries that, up to 2008, lagged behind others in terms of commodification. This makes NEG a mechanism of *reversed* differentiated integration (Chapters 3 and 11). The NEG regime enabled EU executives to issue a battery of prescriptions with significant coercive power in quantitative (curtailment) and qualitative (marketisation) terms, depending on the receiving countries' location in the uneven NEG enforcement regime. From the mid-2010s onwards however, their coercive power decreased, given the gradual recovery of European economies from the 2008 financial crisis. The number of commodifying quantitative NEG prescriptions also decreased, echoing a shift of EU executives' preferences in favour of a new policy mix blending qualitative marketising structural reforms with greater public investments. Our analysis shows that the latter did not amount to an alternative, decommodifying policy script that would vindicate those that saw a socialisation of the NEG regime. Rather, decommodifying prescriptions on investment were subordinated to the dominant commodification script, as most of them were semantically linked to commodifying policy rationales and had only a weak coercive power (Chapters 6–10, see Chapter 11 for a detailed comparative analysis).

Second, the book shows that NEG's commodifying script unleashed a plethora of countermovements, namely, in the public services that had been exposed to commodifying NEG prescriptions more consistently across countries. Unions and social movements politicised economic governance interventions not only at national and local level but also transnationally, as evidenced by the findings of our transnational socioeconomic protest database (Chapters 6–11). Unions and social movements framed their protests with reference to transnational political divides along the commodification–decommodification axis, rather than to divides along a national versus EU politics axis; for example, in the successful Right2Water European Citizens' Initiative (Chapter 9) or the yearly 'Our health is not for sale' European action days (Chapter 10). Despite these countermovements, EU executives maintained their course: from the mid-2010s on, they indeed softened the commodifying bent of their quantitative NEG prescriptions – but only to better keep the focus on commodifying structural reforms. Concretely, EU executives shifted the direction of quantitative prescriptions in public services from austerity to greater investments but limited the decommodifying potential of this shift by confining investment prescriptions to what they viewed as 'productive' public services (transport and water), by articulating such investment prescriptions with policy rationales compatible with the overarching commodification script that they pursued in NEG, and by ensuring that the sparse prescriptions with a truly decommodifying potential had only weak coercive power. In employment relations, the European Commission and Council agreed to open discussions on new EU instruments to secure stronger social pillars for the EU integration process, but until 2019 they kept their advancement at a snail's pace. Already at this stage, however, the UK's Brexit vote raised the spectre of responses to commodifying EU interventions taking a nationalist turn, which would ultimately mean the EU's implosion.

Finally, we show that, when the Covid-19 pandemic hit Europe, EU executives changed direction. With the suspension of the Stability and Growth Pact (SGP) in 2020 and the establishment of the Recovery and Resilience Facility (RRF) in 2021, they sought to mitigate this new crisis with an injection of public EU money also in areas that had not benefitted from their pre-Covid NEG prescriptions for more public investments, including healthcare. At the same time, EU leaders made the receipt of RRF funding conditional on the implementation of their NEG prescriptions, regardless of their unequal legal basis and the receiving country's location in NEG's policy enforcement regime. EU executives thus replaced, at least for the time being, the financial sanctioning mechanisms of the SGP with the threat of withholding RRF funding in the event of non-compliance with their NEG prescriptions (Chapter 12). As the amount of RRF funding at stake is substantial in many member states, the coercive power of post-Covid NEG prescriptions has increased further.

In employment relations, EU executives did not use the increased leverage of their post-Covid NEG prescriptions to demand commodifying reforms (Chapter 13). A telling example is the following. Whereas in 2011 they tasked the Romanian government to abolish intersectoral social dialogue and to decentralise multi-employer collective bargaining, in 2022 they prescribed a decommodifying reform of the 2011 Romanian labour law, which led in December 2022 to the adoption of a new law that restored trade union rights and intersectoral and sectoral collective bargaining. This policy shift mirrors continued union pressures, growing worries among EU executives about popular support for the EU integration project, and a more positive assessment of multi-employer bargaining by factions of organised capital (Chapter 13). EU executives' volte-face in this policy area also led to a resurgence of decommodifying EU laws, starting with the adoption of the EU directive on adequate minimum wages in 2022. By contrast, the post-Covid policy orientation of the NEG regime in public services has not changed so much. Given the institutional setup of the post-Covid NEG regime (Chapter 12), EU executives' continued insistence on public services marketisation through EU laws and NEG prescriptions (Chapter 13), and the legacy of decades-long marketising public sector reforms, it is highly likely that the massive RRF funding will boost private rather than public service providers.

The shift to NEG has posed direct threats to European democracy ever since its introduction in the wake of the 2008 financial crisis. Its technocratic governance design eschewed citizens' and workers' political rights to have a say in policymaking; and the commodifying bent of its prescriptions importantly eroded their social rights to be protected from the vagaries of the market. After the pandemic, the technocratic bent in the EU's economic governance nonetheless endured, as the National Recovery and Resilience Plans, which are the key documents for unlocking RRF funding, were co-designed by national and EU executives, without any meaningful input from trade unions and social movements and without the possibility of national parliaments and the European Parliament making any amendments. The commodifying direction of the post-Covid NEG regime also endured, albeit with some concessions, most notably in employment relations. In the last decades, EU executives embraced commodification; more recently though, they have had to face the prospect that the hollowing out of social rights, that resulted from commodification, is pushing important sections of electorates towards eurosceptic parties.

In the current unstable context, labour politics matters a lot. Trade unions and social movements are essential in framing the social and political struggles about the policy direction of EU economic governance along a commodification–decommodification axis, rather than a national–EU politics axis. Future research based on our transnational – but also context-specific – analytical approach on the role of labour politics in the next iteration of the EU's NEG regime is thus not only of academic interest but also of upmost importance for the future of the EU integration process and the prospects of democracy in Europe.

Glossary

ANALYTICAL TERMS

Federal: (from Latin *foedus* 'alliance') Organisational principle in which individual members (constituent member states) have a degree of autonomy and statehood but are united to form an overarching totality

Horizontal vs. vertical European integration: Typology that distinguishes market-driven horizontal and political vertical modes of European integration

Intergovernmental: (from Latin *inter* 'between') Intergovernmental relations are relations *between* governments

International: (from Latin *inter* 'between') International relations are relations *between* nation states

Politicising [something]: An activity that makes an issue become 'political' in character (see Erne, 2019)

Supranational: (from Latin *supra* 'above') Supranational law supersedes national law

Transnational: (from Latin *trans* 'across') Refers to social processes that transcend national boundaries and national systems

EUROPEAN INSTITUTIONS

Council (of the European Union): Co-legislator and co-executive of the EU, uniting the responsible national ministers (or governments' permanent representatives in Brussels)

Council of Europe (CoE): International organisation based in Strasbourg, created in 1949 to uphold human rights and democracy in Europe; not an EU institution

Directorates General (DG) (of the Commission): Government departments of the Commission in charge of various policy areas, e.g., economic and financial affairs (DG ECFIN), employment, social affairs, and inclusion (DG EMPL), health (DG SANTE), etc.
EU executives: The European Commission and Council
EU legislators: The European Parliament and Council
EU social partners: The representative organisations of management and labour that can act as co-legislators in the social policy field (Art. 154 and 155 TFEU)
European Commission: Principal executive arm of the EU composed of its President and its College of Commissioners and the EU's civil service
European Council: Institution uniting the heads of states and governments; it is not involved in everyday EU governance but defines its general direction, namely, in crisis situations
European Parliament: Directly elected co-legislator of the EU; no decision-making role in the EU's new economic governance (NEG) regime

LEGAL INSTRUMENTS OF THE EU

Decisions: Binding legal acts of EU institutions, e.g., on the allocation of EU funding
Directives: EU framework laws that must be transposed into national law to take effect
EU Treaties: Primary EU legislation, including Treaty on European Union (TEU) and Treaty on the Functioning of the European Union (TFEU)
Recommendations: Formally non-binding legal acts of EU institutions, which may still have significant coercive power in conjunction with other EU laws, such as the Six-Pack
Regulations: EU laws that do not need to be transposed into national laws to take effect

TOOLS OF THE EU'S NEW ECONOMIC GOVERNANCE (NEG) REGIME

Council Recommendations (on National Reform Programmes): containing a set number of country-specific recommendations (CSRs);

legal act outlining the NEG prescriptions that the Commission proposes in spring and the Council adopts in July every year

Europe 2020: Non-binding EU policy coordination and growth strategy adopted in 2010

European Semester: Yearly cycle of country-specific NEG prescriptions, surveillance, and enforcement, integrating MoU-, SGP-, MIP-, and Europe 2020-related NEG prescriptions in one document

European Stability Mechanism (ESM): Financial bailout mechanisms created in 2011 for EU member states in the eurozone

Macroeconomic Imbalance Procedure (MIP): Constraining EU economic governance tool institutionalised by the EU's Six-Pack laws of 2011

Memoranda of Understanding (MoUs): Very constraining EU economic governance tool outlining the policy conditionalities for the receipt of EU bailout funding

NEG prescription: Shortest segment of an MoU or a CSR outlining a specific policy instruction issued by EU executives' within the EU's NEG regime

Six-Pack (of EU laws on economic governance): Package of six EU laws that institutionalised the EU's NEG regime in 2011

Stability and Growth Pact (SGP): Constraining EU fiscal and economic governance tool created in 1997 and reinforced by the Six-Pack laws of 2011; EU executives temporarily suspended its application after the outbreak of the Covid-19 pandemic in March 2020

TOOLS OF EU'S POST-COVID NEW ECONOMIC GOVERNANCE (NEG) REGIME

National Recovery and Resilience Plan (NRRP): National government document used for applying for EU RRF funding; key document of the post-Covid NEG regime

Recovery and Resilience Facility (RRF) Regulation: EU law that in 2021 institutionalised the EU's post-Covid NEG regime and the conditionalities for the receipt of RRF funding

Council Implementing Decision (CID): Legal act endorsing the Commission's assessment of NRRPs and specifying the policy conditionalities for receipt of RRF funding

EU EMPLOYMENT RELATIONS AND SOCIAL POLICY

See the **European Industrial Relations Dictionary** of Eurofound, the EU's tripartite foundation for the improvement of Living and Working Conditions, https://www.eurofound.europa.eu/en/european-industrial-relations-dictionary

References

Adascalitei, D. and Muntean, A. (2019). Trade union strategies in the age of austerity. *European Journal of Industrial Relations*, 25(2): 113–128.
Afonso, A. (2019). State-led wage devaluation in Southern Europe in the wake of the Eurozone crisis. *European Journal of Political Research*, 58(3): 938–959.
Aglietta, M. (2019). *The Reform of Europe: A Political Guide to the Future*. Verso.
AIM, EAHP, EPF, EURODIS, and HOPE. (2022). Joint statement on the European Health Data Space Draft Proposal: A call for society-centred digitalisation of healthcare. https://epha.org/wp-content/uploads/2023/04/ngo_jointstatement_ehds.pdf
Akkermans, B. and Ramaekers, E. (2010). Article 345 TFEU (ex-Article 295 EC), its meanings and interpretations. *European Law Journal*, 16(3): 292–314.
Albert, M. (1997). Pas de regret pour le 'gouvernement économique européen'. *Commentaire*, 79: 584–588.
Al-Kadi, R. and Clauwaert, S. (2019). Socialising the European semester? Working Paper 2019.08. European Trade Union Institute.
Allais, M. (1960). *L'Europe Unie*. Calmann-Levy.
Allen, K. (2007). *The Corporate Takeover of Ireland*. Irish Academic Press.
Almond, P. and Connolly, H. (2020). A manifesto for 'slow' comparative research on work and employment. *European Journal of Industrial Relations*, 26(1): 59–74.
Anastasia, B., Bombelli, S., and Maschio, S. (2016). Il lavoro accessorio dal 2008 al 2015. Profili dei lavoratori e dei committenti. WorkINPS Paper.
Ancelovici, M. (2002). Organizing against globalization. *Politics & Society*, 30(3): 427–463.
Anderson, P. (2009). *New Old World*. Verso.
Andor, L. (2020). SURE – EU capacity for stabilising employment and incomes in the pandemic. *Intereconomics*, 55(3): 139–142.
Anner, M., Greer, I., Hauptmeier, M., Lillie, N., and Winchester, N. (2006). The industrial determinants of transnational solidarity. *European Journal of Industrial Relations*, 12(1): 7–27.
ANSA. (2010). Barroso, Stiamo facendo rivoluzione silenziosa. Press release, 18 June, Agenzia Nazionale Stampa Associata, Fiesole.
Appadurai, A. (1986). Introduction. In A. Appadurai (ed.), *The Social Life of Things*. Cambridge University Press, 3–63.

Appel, H. and Orenstein, M. (2018). *From Triumph to Crisis: Neoliberal Economic Reform in Postcommunist Countries*. Cambridge University Press.

Armeni, C. (2008). The right to water in Italy. IELRC briefing paper 2008-1. International Environmental Law Research Centre.

Armingeon, K., Guthmann, K., and Weisstanner, D. (2016). How the Euro divides the union: The effect of economic adjustment on support for democracy in Europe. *Socio-Economic Review*, 14(1): 1–26.

Armstrong, K. (2010). *Governing Social Inclusion: Europeanization through Policy Coordination*. Oxford University Press.

Armstrong, P., Armstrong, H., and Bourgeault, I. et al. (2000). *Heal Thyself*. Garamond.

Arnholtz, J. and Lillie, N. (2019). *Posted Work in the European Union*. Routledge.

Arrowsmith, J., Sisson, K., and Marginson, P. (2004). What can 'benchmarking' offer the open method of co-ordination? *Journal of European Public Policy*, 11(2): 311–328.

Artus, I., Birke, P., Kerber-Clasen, S., and Menz, W. (eds.). (2017). *Sorge-Kämpfe*. VSA.

Ashiagbor, D. (2013). Unravelling the embedded liberal bargain: Labour and social welfare law in the context of EU market integration. *European Law Journal*, 19 (3): 303–324.

Aspinwall, M. (1995). International integration or internal politics? *Journal of Common Market Studies*, 33(4): 475–499.

Baccaro, L. and Benassi, C. (2017). Throwing out the ballast: Growth models and the liberalization of German industrial relations. *Socio-Economic Review*, 15(1): 85–115.

Baccaro, L. and Howell, C. (2017). *Trajectories of Neoliberal Transformation: European Industrial Relations since the 1970s*. Cambridge University Press.

Bach, S. and Bordogna, L. (2013). Reframing public service employment relations: The impact of economic crisis and the new EU economic governance. *European Journal of Industrial Relations*, 19(4): 279–294.

Baeten, R. (2012). *Europeanization of National Health Systems. National Impact and EU Codification of the Patient Mobility Case Law*. EPSU.

Baeten, R. and Vanhercke, B. (2016). Inside the black box: The EU's economic surveillance of national healthcare systems. *Comparative European Politics*, 15 (3): 478–497.

Bajohr, S. (2015). *Die Schuldenbremse: Politische Kritik des Staatsschuldenrechts*. Springer.

Balme, R. and Chabanet, D. (2008). *European Governance and Democracy: Power and Protest in the EU*. Rowman & Littlefield.

Ban, C. (2014). *Dependență și dezvoltare: Economia politică a capitalismului românesc*. Editura Tact.

(2016). *Ruling Ideas: How Global Neoliberalism Goes Local*. Oxford University Press.

Barrett, G. (2020). *Judging the Eurozone*. Institute of International and European Affairs.

Bartlett, O. and Naumann, A. (2021). Reinterpreting the health in all policies obligation in Article 168 TFEU: The first step towards making enforcement a realistic prospect. *Health Economics, Policy and Law*, 16(1): 8–22.

Bartolini, S. (2000). *The Political Mobilization of the European Left, 1860–1980: The Class Cleavage*. Cambridge University Press.
  (2005). *Restructuring Europe: Centre Formation, System Building, and Political Structuring between the Nation State and the European Union*. Oxford University Press.
Basilicata, A. (2021). The Long-Term Care System in Italy. CRC 1342 Social Policy Country Briefs, issue 7.
Bauer, M. W. and Becker, S. (2014). The unexpected winner of the crisis: The European Commission's strengthened role in economic governance. *Journal of European Integration*, 36(3): 213–229.
BDA and BDI. (2010). Für eine neue europäische Stabilitätspolitik. Gemeinsame Erklärung von BDA und BDI. 29 June.
Beck, U. (2013). *German Europe*. Polity.
Bekker, S. (2015). *European Socioeconomic Governance in Action*. European Social Observatory.
  (2021). Hardening and softening of country-specific recommendations in the European Semester. *West European Politics*, 44(1): 114–133.
Bélanger, J., Berggren, C., Björkman, T., and Kähler, C. (eds.). (2000). *Being Local Worldwide: ABB and the Challenge of Global Management*. Cornell University Press.
Bellamy, R. and Kröger, S. (2017). A democratic justification of differentiated integration in a heterogeneous EU. *Journal of European Integration Studies*, 39(5): 625–639.
Bellofiore, R. and Garibaldo, F. (2022). *L'Ultimo Metrò. L'Europa tra Crisi Economica e Crisi Sanitaria*. Mimesis.
Béthoux, É., Erne, R., and Golden, D. (2018). A primordial attachment to the nation? French and Irish workers and trade unions in past EU referendum debates. *British Journal of Industrial Relations*, 56(3): 656–678.
Bickerton, C. J., Hodson, D., and Puetter, U. (2015). The new intergovernmentalism: European integration in the post-Maastricht era. *Journal of Common Market Studies*, 53(4): 703–722.
Bieler, A. (2006). *The Struggle for Social Europe: Trade Unions and EMU in Times of Global Restructuring*. Manchester University Press
  (2007). Co-option or resistance? Trade unions and neoliberal restructuring in Europe. *Capital & Class*, 31(3): 111–124.
  (2011). Labour, new social movements and the resistance to neoliberal restructuring in Europe. *New Political Economy*, 16(2): 163–183.
  (2015). 'Sic vos non vobis' (For you, but not yours): The struggle for public water in Italy. *Monthly Review*, 67(5): 35–50.
  (2017). Fighting for public water: The first successful European citizens' initiative, 'Water and sanitation are a human right'. *Interface*, 9(1): 300–326.
  (2021). *Fighting for Water*. Zed.
Bieler, A. and Erne, R. (2014). Transnational solidarity? The European working class in the Eurozone crisis. *Socialist Register*, 51: 157–177.
Bieler, A. and Jordan, J. (2018). Commodification and 'the commons'. *European Journal of International Relations*, 24(4): 934–957.

Bieler, A., Jordan, J., and Morton, A. D. (2019). EU aggregate demand as a way out of crisis? Engaging the post-Keynesian critique. *Journal of Common Market Studies*, 57(4): 805–822.

Bieler, A. and Morton, A. D. (2018). *Global Capitalism, Global War, Global Crisis*. Cambridge University Press.

Bieling, H.-J. and Deckwirth, C. (2008). Privatising public infrastructure within the EU: The interaction between supranational institutions, transnational forces and national governments. *Transfer*, 14(2): 237–257.

Bieling, H.-J. and Schulten, T. (2003). Competitive restructuring and industrial relations within the European Union: Corporatist involvement and beyond. In A. Cafruny and M. Ryner (eds.), *A Ruined Fortress?* Rowman & Littlefield, 231–260.

Bispinck R. and Schulten T. (2010) *Sector-level Bargaining and Possibilities for Deviations at Company Level: Germany*. Eurofound.

Blyth, M. (2013). *Austerity: The History of a Dangerous Idea*. Oxford University Press.

Boda, Z. and Scheiring, G. (2006). Water privatisation in the context of the transition. In D. Chavez (ed.), *Beyond the Market: The Future of Public Services*. Transnational Institute and Public Services International Research Unit, 95–101.

Böhlke, N., Greer, I., and Schulten, T. (2011). World champions in hospital privatisation: The effects of neoliberal reform on German employees and patients. In J. Lister (ed.), *Europe's Health for Sale*. Libri, 9–28.

Bohle, D. and Greskovits, B. (2012). *Capitalist Diversity on Europe's Periphery*. Cornell University Press.

Bojar, A., Bremer, B., Kriesi, H., and Wang, C. (2022). The effect of austerity packages on government popularity during the great recession. *British Journal of Political Science*, 52(1): 181–199.

Bolkestein, F. (2002). Speech by Frits Bolkestein Member of the European Commission in charge of the Internal Market and Taxation. Nuclear energy needed more than ever. Address to the Institute of Economic Affairs London, 7 November. Speech/02/543.

Bonelli, M. and Claes, M. (2018). Judicial serendipity: How Portuguese judges came to the rescue of the Polish judiciary: ECJ 27 February 2018, Case C-64/16, Associação Sindical dos Juízes Portugueses. *European Constitutional Law Review*, 14(3): 622–643.

Bourdieu, P. (1989). Social space and symbolic power. *Sociological Theory*, 7(1): 14–25.

(1994). Rethinking the state: Genesis and structure of the bureaucratic field. *Sociological Theory*, 12(1): 1–18.

(2008). *Political Interventions: Social Science and Political Action*. Verso.

Bovis, C. H. (2005). The application of state aid rules to the European Union transport sectors. *Columbia Journal of European Law*, 11(3): 556–604.

Boyer, R. and Dehove, M. (2001). Du 'gouvernement économique' au gouvernement tout court. *Critique Internationale*, 11: 179–195.

Brenner, N., Peck, J., and Theodore, N. (2010). Variegated neoliberalization: Geographies, modalities, pathways. *Global Networks*, 10(2): 182–222.

Brookes, M. (2019). *The New Politics of Transnational Labor*. Cornell University Press.

Brooks, E. (2016). Public Health, Free Movement and Macroeconomic Coordination: Mapping the Evolving Governance of European Union Health Policy. PhD thesis, Lancaster University.

Bruff, I. (2010). Germany's Agenda 2010 reforms: Passive revolution at the crossroads. *Capital & Class*, 34(3): 409–428.
  (2014). The rise of authoritarian neoliberalism. *Rethinking Marxism*, 26(1): 113–129.
Buch-Hansen, H. and Wigger, A. (2011). *The Politics of European Competition Regulation*. Routledge.
Büchs, M. (2007). *New Governance in European Social Policy*. Palgrave Macmillan.
Bulfone, F. and Afonso, A. (2020). Business against markets: Employer resistance to collective bargaining liberalization during the Eurozone crisis. *Comparative Political Studies*, 53(5): 809–846.
Bundesministerium für Wirtschaft und Energie. (2017). *Nationales Reformprogramm*. BMWi.
Bündnis Krankenhaus statt Fabrik. (2020). Wie weit geht der Einfluss der Europäischen Union im Gesundheitswesen? EU-Vorgaben für Finanzierung und Subventionierung von Krankenhäusern. In *Das Fallpauschalensystem und die Ökonomisierung der Krankenhäuser*. Maintal, 143–145. www.krankenhaus-statt-fabrik.de/53187.
Burawoy, M. (2000). Introduction. In M. Burawoy et al. (eds.), *Global Ethnography*. University of California Press, 1–40.
  (2010). From Polanyi to Pollyanna: The false optimism of global labor studies. *Global Labour Journal*, 1(2): 301–313.
  (2022). The necessity of real Utopias. *Global Dialogue*, 12:(2). https://globaldialogue.isa-sociology.org/articles/the-necessity-of-real-utopias.
Burke, S., Thomas, S., Barry, S., and Keegan, C. (2014). Indicators of health system coverage and activity in Ireland during the economic crisis 2008–2014 – From 'more with less' to 'less with less'. *Health Policy*, 117: 275–278.
Buschak, W. (2014). *Die Vereinigten Staaten von Europa sind unser Ziel*. Klartext.
Business Europe. (2010). Improving Euro-area Governance. 10 June.
  (2020a). Business Europe Proposals for a European Economic Recovery Plan, 30 April.
  (2020b). Proposal for an EU Directive on Fair Minimum Wages. www.businesseurope.eu/sites/buseur/files/media/position_papers/social/2020-12-04_pp_minimum_wages.pdf.
Busse, R. and Blümel, M. (2014). Germany: Health system review. *Health Systems in Transition*, 16(2): 1–296.
Buti, M. and Turrini, A. (2017). Overcoming Eurozone wage inertia. *Vox.EU*, 6 October.
Buti, M. and van den Noord, P. (2004). Fiscal policy in EMU: Rules, discretion and political incentives. *European Economy*, No. 206, July.
Calmfors, L. (2012). Can the Eurozone develop into a well-functioning fiscal union? *CESifo Forum* 13(1): 10–16.
Cartabellotta, N., Cottafava, E., Luceri, R., and Mosti, M. (2019). *4° Rapporto GIMBE*. Fondazione GIMBE.
Cecchini, P., Catinat, M., and Jacquemin, A. (1988). *The European Challenge, 1992: The Benefits of a Single Market*. Gower.
Celi, G., Ginzburg, A., Guarascio, D., and Simonazzi, A. (2018). *Crisis in the European Monetary Union: A Core-Periphery Perspective*. Routledge.

CER (2011). *CER Proposed Amendments: Recast of the First Railway Package*. Community of European Railways.

Chivu, L. (2011). *Romania: Industrial Relations in the Health Care Sector*. Eurofound.

Clarke, J., Gewirtz, S., and McLaughlin, E. (2010). *New Managerialism, New Welfare?* Sage.

Clauwaert, S. (2018). *The Country Specific Recommendations (CSRs) in the Social Field. An Overview and Comparison. Update Including the CSRs 2018–2019*. ETUI.

Clegg, S., Geppert, M., and Hollinshead, G. (2018). Politicization and political contests in and around contemporary multinational corporations. *Human Relations*, 71(6): 745–765.

Clifton, J., Comín, F., and Diaz Fuentes, D. (2003). *Privatisation in the European Union Public Enterprises and Integration*. Springer.

Clifton, J., Comín, F., and Díaz Fuentes, D. (2006). Privatizing public enterprises in the European Union 1960–2002: Ideological, pragmatic, inevitable? *Journal of European Public Policy*, 13(5): 736–756.

Comte, E. (2019). Promising more to give less: International disputes between core and periphery around European posted labor, 1955–2018. *Labor History*, 60(6): 749–764.

Cooper, I. (2015). A yellow card for the striker: National parliaments and the defeat of EU legislation on the right to strike. *Journal of European Public Policy*, 22(10): 1406–1425.

Copeland, P. (2014). *EU Enlargement, the Clash of Capitalisms and the European Social Dimension*. Manchester University Press.

(2020). *Governance and the European Social Dimension: Politics, Power and the Social Deficit in a Post-2010 EU*. Routledge.

Copeland, P. and Daly, M. (2018). The European Semester and EU social policy. *Journal of Common Market Studies*, 56(5): 1001–1018.

Cornago E. and Springford J. (2021). Why the EU's Recovery Fund Should Be Permanent, 11 November. www.cer.eu/publications/archive/policy-brief/2021/why-eus-recovery-fund.

Costamagna, F. and Miglio, A. (2021). Sanctions in the EMU economic pillar. In S. Montaldo, F. Costamagna, and A. Miglio (eds.), *EU Law Enforcement*. Routledge, 139–160.

Council of the EU. (2020). Statement of EU Ministers of Finance on the Stability and Growth Pact in Light of the COVID-19 Crisis. Press release, 23 March.

Cova, J. (2022). Reconsidering the drivers of country-specific recommendations: The Commission's ideological preferences on wage policies. *European Union Politics*, 23(4): 639–661.

Cox, L. and Nilsen, A. G. (2014). *We Make our Own History*. Pluto.

Cremona, M. (ed.). (2011). *Market Integration and Public Services in the European Union*. Oxford University Press.

Crespy, A. (2012). *Qui A Peur de Bolkestein? Conflit, Résistances et Démocratie dans l'Union Européenne*. Economica.

(2016). *Welfare Markets in Europe: The Democratic Challenge of European Integration*. Palgrave Macmillan.

Crespy, A. and Schmidt, V. (2017). The EU's economic governance in 2016: Beyond austerity? In B. Vanhercke, S. Sabato, and D. Bouget (eds.), *Social Policy in the European Union. State of the Play 2017*. ETUI and OSE, 99–114.

Crespy, A. and Vanheuverzwijn, P. (2019). What 'Brussels' means by structural reforms: Empty signifier or constructive ambiguity? *Comparative European Politics*, 17: 92–111.

Crochemore, K. (2014). Syndicalisme International et Régionalisation du Monde : L'ITF Face à la Construction de l'Europe (1943–2013). PhD thesis, Université du Havre and ULB, Bruxelles.

Crouch, C. (1999). *Social Change in Western Europe*. Oxford University Press.

— (2000). The snakes and ladders of 21st-century trade unionism. *Oxford Review of Economic Policy*, 16(1): 70–83.

— (2004). *Post-Democracy*. Polity.

— (2005). *Capitalist Diversity and Change: Recombinant Governance and Institutional Entrepreneurs*. Oxford University Press.

— (2011). *The Strange Non-death of Neo-Liberalism*. Polity.

— (2015). *Governing Social Risks in Post-crisis Europe*. Edward Elgar.

— (2016). The paradoxes of privatisation and public service outsourcing. *The Political Quarterly*, 86(1): 156–171.

Crouch, C. and Farrell, H. (2004). Breaking the path of institutional development? Alternatives to the new determinism. *Rationality and Society*, 16(1): 5–43.

Crouch, C. and Pizzorno, A. (eds.). (1978). *The Resurgence of Class Conflict in Western Europe since 1968*. MacMillan.

Daly, M. (2012). Paradigms in EU social policy: A critical account of Europe 2020. *Transfer*, 18(3): 273–284.

Darvas, Z. and Leandro, A. (2015). The limitations of policy coordination in the Euro area under the European Semester. *Bruegel Policy Summary*, 19, November: 1–19.

Dawson, M. (2018). New governance and the displacement of Social Europe. *European Constitutional Law Review*, 14(1): 191–209.

de Búrca, G. (2015). Conclusion. In D. Kochenov, G. de Búrca, and A. Williams (eds.), *Europe's Justice Deficit?* Bloomsbury, 459–463.

De Francesco, F. and Castro, G. (2018). Beyond legal transposition. *Journal of European Public Policy*, 25(3): 369–388.

Degli Abbati, C. (1987). *Transport and European Integration*. Commission of the European Communities.

Degryse, C., Jepsen, M., and Pochet, P. (2013). The Euro crisis and its impact on national and European social policies. Working paper 2013.05. ETUI.

Degryse, C. and Tilly, P. (2013). *1973–2013: 40 Years of History of the European Trade Union Confederation*. ETUI.

de la Porte, C. and Heins, E. (2016). A new era of European integration? Governance of labour market and social policy since the sovereign debt crisis. In C. de la Porte and E. Heins (eds.), *The Sovereign Debt Crisis, the EU and Welfare State Reform*. Palgrave Macmillan, 15–42.

de la Porte, C. and Jensen, M.D. (2021). The next generation EU: An analysis of the dimensions of conflict behind the deal. *Social Policy & Administration*, 55(2): 388–402.

de la Porte, C. and Natali, D. (2014). Altered Europeanisation of pension reform in the context of the great recession: Denmark and Italy compared. *West European Politics*, 37(4): 732–749.
  (2018). Agents of institutional change in EU policy: The social investment moment. *Journal of European Public Policy*, 25(6): 828–843.
della Porta, D. and Caiani, M. (2009). *Social Movements and Europeanization*. Oxford University Press.
Delors, J., Fernandes, S., and Mermet, E. (2011). The European Semester: Only a first step. *Notre Europe Policy Brief*, no. 22, February.
De Ruijter, A. (2019). *EU Health Law and Policy. The Expansion of EU Power in Public Health and Health Care*. Oxford University Press.
De Spiegelaere, S. (2023). Back on track: Are we seeing a renaissance of collective bargaining in Romania? *HesaMag* 27 (Spring): 8–11.
Diani, M. and Bison, I. (2004). Organizations, coalitions, and movements. *Theory and Society*, 33(3): 281–309.
Digital Europe. (2020). How to spend it: A digital investment plan for Europe. 22 October.
Di Giulio, M. and Galanti, M. T. (2015). Varieties of regulation? Implementing the regional governance of local utilities in Italy. *Network Industries Quarterly*, 17(4): 6–10.
Dobner, P. (2010). *Wasserpolitik. Zur politischen Theorie, Praxis und Kritik globaler Governance*. Suhrkamp.
Dølvik, J. E. (1995). Nordic trade unions, the EU and European works councils. *Transfer*, 1(2): 216–228.
  (1997). *Redrawing Boundaries of Solidarity? ETUC, Social Dialogue and the Europeanisation of Trade Unions in the 1990s*. Arena and FAFO.
  (2004). Industrial relations in EMU. In A. Martin and G. Ross (eds.), *Euros and Europeans*. Cambridge University Press, 278–308.
Dølvik, J. E. and Visser, J. (2009). Free movement, equal treatment and workers' rights. *Industrial Relations Journal*, 40(6): 491–509.
Doherty, M. and Erne, R. (2010). Mind the gap: National and local partnership in the Irish public sector. *Industrial Relations Journal*, 41(5): 461–478.
Draghi, M. and Trichet, J.-C. (2011). Letter to the Prime Minister of Italy, 5 August. www.corriere.it/economia/11_settembre_29/trichet_draghi_inglese_304a5f1e-ea59-11e0-ae06-4da866778017.shtml.
Dribbusch, H. (2015). Where is the European general strike? Understanding the challenges of trans-European trade union action against austerity. *Transfer*, 21 (2): 171–185.
Dufresne, A. (2015). The trade union response to the European economic governance regime: Transnational mobilization and wage coordination. *Transfer*, 21(2): 141–156.
Dufresne, A. and Pernot, J.-M. (2013). Les syndicats européens à l'épreuve de la nouvelle gouvernance économique. *Chronique Internationale de l'IRES*, 143/144: 3–29.
Dukelow, F. (2015). 'Pushing against an open door': Reinforcing the neo-liberal policy paradigm in Ireland and the impact of EU intrusion. *Comparative European Politics*, 13(1): 93–111.

Durand, C. (2020). *Techno-féodalisme: Critique de l'économie numérique*. La Découverte.
Dyrhauge, H. (2013). *EU Railway Policymaking: On Track?* Palgrave Macmillan.
  (2022). Transforming a steam train: A historical institutionalist analysis of EU railway policy. *Journal of European Integration*, 44(6): 855–870.
Edwards, T. and Kuruvilla, S. (2005). International HRM: National business systems, organizational politics and the international division of labour in MNCs. *International Journal of Human Resource Management*, 16(1): 1–21.
Efstathiou, K. and Wolff, G. (2018). Is the European Semester effective and useful? *Policy Contribution*, 9, June: 1–15.
Ekman, J., Møller Stahl, R., and Ryner, M. (2023). Northern Realignment? Conference paper, 29th International Conference of Europeanists, Reykjavik, 27–29 June.
ENPCHSP. (European Network against Privatisation and Commercialisation of Health and Social Protection) (2014a). Political statements. 24 September. http://europe-health-network.net/spip.php?article45.
  (2014b). History. 1 September. http://europe-health-network.net/spip.php?article21.
EPSU. (2008). EPSU comments on the European Commission (EC) proposal for a directive on the application of patients' rights in cross-border healthcare. Press briefing.
  (2021). *The Fight for the Human Right to Water in Europe*. EPSU.
  (2022a). Europe's health and care workers demand action over growing staff shortage crisis. Press release, 5 December.
  (2022b). European Health Data Space needs to protect patients and workers' rights. Press release, 5 April.
Erdmenger, J. (1983). *The European Community Transport Policy: Towards a Common Transport Policy*. Gower.
Erne, R. (2008). *European Unions. Labor's Quest for Transnational Democracy*. Cornell University Press.
  (2012a). European unions after the global crisis. In L. Burroni, M. Keune, and G. Meardi (eds.), *Economy and Society in Europe*. Edward Elgar, 124–139.
  (2012b). European industrial relations after the crisis. In S. Smismans (ed.), *The European Union and Industrial Relations*. Manchester University Press, 225–235.
  (2012c). European unions after the crisis. In L. Burroni, M. Keune, and G. Meardi (eds.), *Economy and Society in Europe*. Edward Elgar, 124–139.
  (2015). A supranational regime that nationalizes social conflict. Explaining European trade unions' difficulties in politicizing European economic governance. *Labor History*, 56(3): 345–368.
  (2018). Labour politics and the EU's new economic governance regime. *Transfer*, 24(2): 237–247.
  (2019). How to analyse a supranational regime that nationalises social conflict? The European crisis, labour politics and methodological nationalism. In E. Nanopoulos and F. Vergis (eds.), *The Crisis Behind the Euro-Crisis*. Cambridge University Press, 346–368.
  (2020). Interest groups. In D. Caramani (ed.), *Comparative Politics*. Oxford University Press, 5th ed., 252–266.

(2023a). Interest groups. In D. Caramani (ed.), *Comparative Politics*. Oxford University Press, 6th ed., 277–293.

(2023b). Zur EU-Mindestlohnrichtlinie. *Express*, 61(3–4): 19.

Erne, R., Bieler, A., and Golden, D. et al. (2015). Introduction: Politicizing the transnational. *Labor History*, 56(3): 237–245.

Erne, R. and Blaser, M. (2018). Direct democracy and trade union action. *Transfer*, 24 (2): 217–232.

Erne, R., Gross, A., Kaufmann, B., and Kleger, H. (eds.). (1995). *Transnationale Demokratie. Impulse für ein demokratisch verfasstes Europa*. Realotopia. https://researchrepository.ucd.ie/handle/10197/5685.

Erne, R. and Nowak, J. (2022). Structural determinants of transnational solidarity. Explaining the rise in socioeconomic protests across European borders since 1997. Working Paper No. 11, ERC Project 'European Unions'. www.erc-europeanunions.eu/working-papers/.

(2023). Transnational Socioeconomic Protest Database. Version 06/2023. ERC Project 'European Unions'. University College Dublin. http://hdl.handle.net/10197/24708.

Esping-Andersen, G. (1990). *The Three Worlds of Welfare Capitalism*. Princeton University Press.

ETF. (2010). *A Trade Union Guide to The PSO Regulation*. ETF.

(2012). *Modern Slavery in Modern Europe? An ETF Account on the Working and Living Conditions of Professional Drivers in Europe*. ETF.

(2014). Petition to the Council of Transport Ministers' Meeting, 8 October.

(2015a). ETF comments on the common approach of the EU Transport Council on the 4th Railway Package.

(2015b). Vision paper 'Fair Transport Europe' ETF vision for the future of European transport.

(2016). Letter to affiliates regarding Fair Transport Europe campaign. 16 September.

(2018). A line in the sand for transport liberalisation: European Parliament rejects harsh proposals on pay and rest time for drivers. Press Release, 4 July.

(2023). Transport workers and unions rally for democracy: ETF protests European Commission's attempt to force public transport liberalisation. 28 February. www.etf-europe.org/activity/public-service-obligations-pso-guidelines-the-european-commissions-push-for-liberalisation/.

ETUC. (2013). A new path for Europe: ETUC plan for investment, sustainable growth and quality jobs. 7 November.

(2019). Action programme 2019–2023.

ETUC, Business Europe, CEEP, and SME United. (2019). European Parliament elections 2019: Statement of the European Social Partners, 18 March. www.etuc.org/en/document/european-parliament-elections-2019-statement-european-social-partners.

Eurofound. (2022). Involvement of social partners in the national recovery and resilience plans. Publications Office of the European Union.

(2023). Minimum wage hikes struggle to offset inflation. www.eurofound.europa.eu/publications/article/2023/minimum-wage-hikes-struggle-to-offset-inflation

European Commission. (1972). *First Report on Competition Policy*. Commission of the European Communities.

(1990). *One Market, One Money: An Evaluation of the Potential Benefits and Costs of Forming an Economic and Monetary Union*. European Commission, DG for Economic and Financial Affairs.

(2003). Internal Market Strategy Priorities 2003–2006. Communication from the Commission to the Council, the European Parliament and the Economic and Social Committee.

(2010a). Surveillance of intra-Euro-area competitiveness and imbalances. *European Economy*, 1.

(2010b). *Industrial Relations in Europe*. Publications Office of the European Union.

(2010c). Joint report on health systems prepared by the European Commission and the Economic Policy Committee. European Economy. Occasional Paper 74.

(2011). Medical Tourism Directive. DG Internal Market, Industry, Entrepreneurship and SMEs.

(2012). A blueprint to safeguard europe's water resources.

(2013). Overall assessment of the two balance-of-payments assistance programmes for Romania, 2009–2013. DG ECFIN Occasional Papers 156, July 2013.

(2014a). Romania: Balance-of-payments assistance programme mission report (22 October–5 November 2013).

(2014b). Assessment of the 2014 national reform programme and convergence programme for Romania.

(2014c). Post-Programme Surveillance for Ireland Spring 2014 Report. European Commission. DG ECFIN.

(2015a). Macroeconomic imbalances country report – Italy 2015. DG ECFIN Occasional Papers 219.

(2015b). Balance of payments assistance programme Romania, 2013–2015. DG ECFIN Institutional Paper 012.

(2016a). State-owned enterprises in the EU: Lessons learnt and ways forward in a post-crisis context. European Economy Institutional Paper 031.

(2016b). *Cost-Containment Policies in Hospital Expenditure in the European Union*. DG ECFIN.

(2020a). Schuman declaration. https://european-union.europa.eu/principles-coun tries-history/history-eu/1945-59/schuman-declaration-may-1950_en.

(2020b). Europe's moment: Repair and prepare for the next generation, 27 May. https://ec.europa.eu/commission/presscorner/detail/en/ip_20_940.

(2021). Recovery and resilience scoreboard. Thematic analysis. Healthcare. DG ECFIN.

(2022). Commission finds that Hungary has not progressed enough in its reforms and must meet essential milestones for its recovery and resilience funds. Press release, 30 November.

(2023a). DG Energy's reply to the freedom of information request of Felix Syrovatka 'Stakeholder and the hydrogen strategie' [sic]. www.asktheeu.org/en/request/stake holder_and_the_hydrogen_str#outgoing-20223.

(2023b). Greening freight for more economic gain with less environmental impact. 11 July. DG Transport.

European Council. (2000). Presidency conclusions. Lisbon European Council, 23–24 March. www.europarl.europa.eu/summits/lis1_en.htm.

(2001). Presidency conclusions. Laeken European Council, 14–15 December. www.consilium.europa.eu/media/20950/68827.pdf.

European Court of Auditors. (2020). The European Semester. Special Report. ECA.

European Environment Agency. (2013). Assessment of Cost Recovery through Water Pricing. Publications Office of the European Union.

European Parliament. (2022). Transport trends in national recovery and resilience plans. www.europarl.europa.eu/thinktank/en/document/EPRS_BRI(2021)698765.

European Parliament, Wolff, G., Sousa, C., Terzi, A., and Sapir, A. (2014) The Troika and financial assistance in the euro area. https://data.europa.eu/doi/10.2861/52615.

Fabbrini, S. (2022). Governmental change in 2019 Italy: Domestic factors or European constraints? *Journal of Contemporary European Studies*, 30(3): 433–444.

Faniel, J. (2012). Crisis behind the figures? Belgian trade unions between strength, paralysis and revitalisation. *Management Revue*, 23(1): 14–31.

Ferre, F., de Belvis, A. G., and Valerio, L. et al. (2014). Italy: Health system review. *Health Systems in Transition*, 16(4): 1–168.

Ferrera, M. (2021). Round table. From Lisbon to Porto: Taking stock of developments in EU social policy. *Transfer*, 27(4): 505–511.

Ferrera, M. and Gualmini, E. (2004). *Rescued by Europe? Social and Labour Market Reforms in Italy from Maastricht to Berlusconi*. Amsterdam University Press.

Fillon, J.-C. (2009). Cross-border healthcare. In Y. Jorens (ed.), *50 Years of Social Security Coordination*. DG for Employment, Social Affairs and Equal Opportunities, 213–236.

Finger, M. and Messulam, P. (2015). Rail economics and regulation. In M. Finger and P. Messulam (eds.), *Rail Economics, Policy and Regulation in Europe*. Edward Elgar, 1–21.

Fischbach-Pyttel, C. (2017). *Building the European Federation of Public Service Unions: The History of EPSU (1978–2016)*. ETUI, EPSU.

Flecker, J. and Hermann, C. (2012). Company responses to liberalisation and privatisation and consequences for employment and working conditions. In C. Hermann and J. Flecker (eds.), *Privatization of Public Services. Impacts for Employment, Working Conditions, and Service Quality in Europe*. Routledge, 109–123.

Florio, M. (2013). *Network Industries and Social Welfare: The Experiment That Reshuffled European Utilities*. Oxford University Press.

Foot, P. (2005). *The Vote: How It Was Won and How It Was Undermined*. Penguin.

Fox-Hodess K. (2017). (Re-)locating the local and national in the global: Multi-scalar political alignment in transnational European dockworker union campaigns. *British Journal of Industrial Relations*, 55(3): 626–647.

France, G., Taroni F., and Donatini, A. (2005). The Italian health-care system. *Health Economics*, 14: 187–202.

Frangakis, M., Hermann, C., Huff Schmidd, J., and Lóránt, K. (eds.). (2009). *Privatisation against the European Social Model. A Critique of European Policies and Proposals for Alternatives*. Palgrave Macmillan.

Friedberg, M. W., Safran, D. G., and Coltin, K. et al. (2010). Paying for performance in primary care. *Health Affairs*, 29(5), 926–932.

Furåker, B. and Larsson, B. (2020). Revision of the EU Posting of Workers Directive, social dumping and trade unions' position. In B. Furåker and B. Larsson (eds.), *Trade Union Cooperation in Europe*. Springer, 109–139.

Galanti, C. (2023). The Struggle for Healthcare under the European Union's New Economic Governance Regime. Trade Union and Grassroots Mobilisations in Response to Healthcare Commodification in Italy and Romania (2008–2022). PhD thesis, University College Dublin.

Galbraith, J. K. (1952). *American Capitalism: The Concept of Countervailing Power*. Transaction.

Galetto, M., Marginson, P., and Spieser, C. (2014). Collective bargaining and reforms to hospital healthcare provision. *European Journal of Industrial Relations*, 20(2): 131–147.

Garben, S. (2017). The constitutional (im)balance between 'the market' and 'the social' in the European Union. *European Constitutional Law Review*, 13(1): 23–61.

Gasseau, G. and Maccarrone, V. (2023). The people's budget? *Global Political Economy*, 2(2): 185–205.

Gélédan, A. (ed.). (1993). *Le bilan économique des années Mitterrand*. Le Monde éditions.

Gentile, A. and Tarrow, S. (2009). Charles Tilly, globalization, and labor's citizen rights. *European Political Science Review*, 1(3): 465–493.

Gessler, T. and Schulte-Cloos, J. (2020). The return of the economy? Issue contention in the protest arena. In H. Kriesi, J. Lorenzini, B. Wüest, and S. Hausermann (eds.), *Contention in Times of Crisis*. Cambridge University Press, 128–145.

Gevaers, R., Maes, J., Van de Voorde, E., and Vanelslander, T. (2015). Incumbents and new entrants in European rail freight. In M. Finger and P. Messulam (eds.), *Rail Economics*. Edward Elgar, 138–170.

Gill, S. (1998). European governance and new constitutionalism: Economic and monetary union and alternatives to disciplinary neoliberalism in Europe. *New Political Economy*, 3(1): 5–26.

Giubboni, S. (2006). *Social Rights and Market Freedom in the European Constitution*. Cambridge University Press.

Glynn, A. (2006). *Capitalism Unleashed*. Oxford University Press.

Gobin, C. (1996). Consultation et Concertation Sociales à l'Échelle de la Communauté Économique Européenne. Étude des Positions et Stratégies de la Confédération Européenne des Syndicats (1958–1991). PhD thesis, Université libre de Bruxelles.

Golden, D. (2015). Challenging the Pro-European Consensus: Explaining the Uneven Trajectory of Euroscepticism in Irish and Italian Unions Across Time. PhD thesis, University College Dublin.

  (2019). A fairer Europe for workers ... or else? Some observations from the ETUC Congress 2019, Vienna, 21–24 May 2019. *Transfer*, 25(4): 489–493.

  (2024). *Labour Euroscepticism: Italian and Irish Unions' Changing Preferences towards the EU*. ECPR Press.

Golden, D. and Erne, R. (2022). Ryanair pilots: Unlikely pioneers of transnational collective action. *European Journal of Industrial Relations*, 28(4): 451–469.

Golden, D., Szabó, I., and Erne, R. (2021). The EU's new economic governance prescriptions for German, Irish, Italian and Romanian public transport and water

services from 2009 to 2019. Working Paper 10. ERC Project 'European Unions'. www.erc-europeanunions.eu/working-papers/.
Gordon-Walker, S. and Marr, S. (2002). *Study on the Application of the Competition Rules to the Water Sector in the European Community*. WRc PLC/Ecologic – Institute for International and European Environmental Policy.
Greer, I. (2015). Welfare reform, precarity and the re-commodification of labour. *Work, Employment and Society*, 30(1): 162–173.
Greer, I. and Hauptmeier, M. (2016). Management whipsawing: The staging of labor competition under globalization. *ILR Review*, 69(1): 29–52.
Greer, S. (2014). The three faces of European Union health policy: Policy, markets, and austerity. *Policy and Society*, 33(1): 13–24.
Greer, S. and Brooks, E. (2021). Termites of solidarity: Undermining fiscal governance in the European Union. *Journal of Health Politics, Policy and Law*, 46(1): 71–92.
Greer, S., Jarman, H., and Baeten, R. (2016). The new political economy of health care in the European Union. *International Journal of Health Services*, 46(2): 262–282.
Greer, S. and Rauscher, S. (2011). When does market-making make markets? EU health services policy at work in the United Kingdom and Germany. *Journal of Common Market Studies*, 49(4): 797–822.
Griffith-Jones, S., Ocampo, J. A., and Stiglitz, J. E. (eds.). (2010). *Time for a Visible Hand: Lessons from the 2008 World Financial Crisis*. Oxford University Press.
Griffiths, R. T. (1994). Europe's first constitution: The European political community, 1952–1954. In S. Martin (ed.), *The Construction of Europe*. Kluwer, 19–39.
Grote, J. R. and Schmitter, P. C. (1999). The renaissance of national corporatism. *Transfer*, 5(1–2): 34–63.
Guérin-Schneider, L., Breuil, L., and Lupton, S. (2014). Liberalization of water services in Europe: The end of the French water exception? In G. Schneier-Madanes (ed.), *Globalized Water*. Dordrecht, 77–93.
Guilhot, N. (2005). *The Democracy Makers. Human Rights and the Politics of Global Order*. Columbia University Press.
Gumbrell-McCormick, R. and Hyman, R. (2013). *Trade Unions in Western Europe: Hard Times, Hard Choices*. Oxford University Press.
Haas, E. B. (1958 [2004]). *The Uniting of Europe: Political, Social, and Economic Forces 1950–1957*. University of Notre Dame Press.
Haas, T., Syrovatka, F., and Jürgens, I. (2022). The European Green Deal and the limits of ecological modernisation. *Culture, Practice & Europeanization*, 7(2): 247–261.
Habermas, J. (1992). Staatsbürgerschaft und nationale Identität. In *Faktizität und Geltung*. Suhrkamp, 632–660. (In English: Habermas, J. (1996). Citizenship and national identity. In *Between Facts and Norms*. MIT Press, 491–515.
  (2011). Die Konstruktionsfehler der Währungsunion. *Blätter für deutsche und internationale Politik*, 56(5): 64–66.
Hall, D. and Lobina, E. (2007). International actors and multinational water company strategies in Europe, 1990–2003. *Utilities Policy*, 15: 64–77.
Hall, D., Lanz, K., Lobina, E., and de la Motte, R. (2004). *International Context Report. Watertime Project*. University of Greenwich.

Hall, P. A. and Soskice, D. (eds.). (2001). *Varieties of Capitalism: The Institutional Foundations of Comparative Advantage*. Oxford University Press.
Hardiman, N. and MacCarthaigh, M. (2011). The un-politics of new public management in Ireland. In J.-M. Eymeri-Douzans and J. Pierre (eds.), *Administrative Reforms and Democratic Governance*. Routledge, 73–85.
Hardy, J. (2009). *Poland's New Capitalism*. Pluto.
Harvey, D. (2003). *The New Imperialism*. Oxford University Press.
  (2004). The 'new' imperialism: Accumulation by dispossession. *Socialist Register*, 40: 63–87.
  (2005). *A Brief History of Neoliberalism*. Oxford University Press.
  (2010). *The Enigma of Capital and the Crises of Capitalism*. Oxford University Press.
Harvey, G. and Turnbull, P. (2015). Can labor arrest the 'sky pirates'? Transnational trade unionism in the European civil aviation industry. *Labor History*, 56(3): 308–326.
Hatzopoulos, V. (2005). Health law and policy: The impact of the EU. In G. de Búrca (ed.), *EU Law and the Welfare State*. Oxford University Press, 123–160.
Heimberger, P., Huber, J., and Kapeller, J. (2020). The power of economic models. *Socio-Economic Review*, 18(2): 337–366.
Heipertz, M. and Verdun, A. (2010). *Ruling Europe: The Politics of the Stability and Growth Pact*. Cambridge University Press.
Henrich-Franke, C. (2008). Mobility and European integration: Politicians, professionals and the foundation of the ECMT. *Journal of Transport History*, 29(1): 64–84.
Héritier, A. (1997). Market-making policy in Europe: Its impact on member state policies. The case of road haulage in Britain, the Netherlands, Germany and Italy. *Journal of European Public Policy*, 4(4): 539–555.
  (2001). The politics of public services in European regulation. *Journal of European Public Policy*, 8(5): 825–852.
Hermann, C. (2021). *The Critique of Commodification. Contours of a Post-Capitalist Society*. Oxford University Press.
Hermann, C. and Verhoest, K. (2012). The process of liberalisation, privatisation and marketisation. In C. Hermann and J. Flecker (eds.), *Privatization of Public Services*. Routledge, 6–32.
Hervey, T. and McHale, J. (2015). *European Union Health Law. Themes and Implications*. Cambridge University Press.
Hilal, N. (2009). L'Europe. Nouvelle figure de la crise syndicale: Les syndicats face à la libéralisation du rail en Europe. *Politique Européenne*, 27(1): 75–103.
Hilliard, M. (2018). Irish Water timeline: From March 2011 to July 2018. *The Irish Times*.
Hinarejos, A. (2015). *The Euro Area Crisis in Constitutional Perspective*. Oxford University Press.
Hirschman, A. O. (1970). *Exit, Voice, and Loyalty: Responses to Decline in Firms, Organizations, and States*. Harvard University Press.

Hix, S. and Høyland, B. (2013). Empowerment of the European Parliament. *Annual Review of Political Science*, 16: 171–189.
Hochschild, A. R. (2000). Global care chains and emotional surplus value. In W. Hutton and A. Giddens (eds.), *On the Edge: Living with Global Capitalism*. Jonathan Cape, 130–146.
Hoedeman, O. (2020). Wakeup call for the European Commission in its failed power grab over local services. CEO. https://corporateeurope.org/en/2020/11/wakeup-call-european-commission-its-failed-power-grab-over-local-services.
Holz, A. (2023). Politische Konditionalitäten in der EU. Vom Aufstieg neuer Governance-Instrumente in den Europäischen Struktur- und Investitionsfonds. PhD thesis, Universität zu Köln.
Höpner, M. and Schäfer, A. (2010). A new phase of European integration: Organized capitalisms in post-Ricardian Europe. *West European Politics*, 33(2): 344–368.
Höpner, M. and Seeliger, M. (2018). Transnationale Lohnkoordination zur Stabilisierung des Euro? *KZfSS Kölner Zeitschrift für Soziologie und Sozialpsychologie*, 70(1): 415–437.
Hollingsworth, J. R. and Boyer, R. (eds.). (1997). *Contemporary Capitalism. The Embeddedness of Institutions*. Cambridge University Press.
Hollingsworth, J. R. and Lindberg, L. N. (eds.). (1991). *Governance of the American Economy*. Cambridge University Press.
Holman, O. (2001). The enlargement of the European Union towards Central and Eastern Europe: The role of supranational and transnational actors. In A. Bieler and A. D. Morton (eds.), *Social Forces in the Making of the New Europe*. Palgrave, 161–184.
Hooghe, L. and Marks, G. (2001). *Multi-Level Governance and European Integration*. Rowman & Littlefield.
Horn, L. (2012). Anatomy of a 'critical friendship': Organized labour and the European state formation. *Globalizations*, 9(4): 577–592.
Hugree, C., Penissat, E., and Spire, A. (2020). *Social Class in Europe*. Verso.
Huws, U. (2012). Crisis as capitalist opportunity: New accumulation through public service commodification. *Socialist Register*, 48: 64–84.
Hyman, R. (2001). Trade union research and cross-national comparison. *European Journal of Industrial Relations*, 7(2): 203–232.
  (2005). Trade unions and the politics of the European social model. *Economic and Industrial Democracy*, 26(1): 9–40.
Hynes M. and Malone, P. (2020). The utility of public transport in Ireland. UCD Geary Institute for Public Policy. https://publicpolicy.ie/papers/the-utility-of-public-transport-in-ireland-post-covid-19-lockdown-and-beyond/.
ICTU. (2022). No compulsory transfers of staff to Irish Water. Irish Congress of Trade Unions News. June 25. www.ictu.ie/news/no-compulsory-transfers-staff-irish-water.
industriAll Europe. (2023). Romania. https://news.industriall-europe.eu/documents/upload/2023/1/638092006538236088_RO_-_Reformed_social_dialogue.pdf.
INS (Institutul National de Statistica). (2018). Activitatea unitatilor sanitare in anul 2017.
Jabko, N. (2006). *Playing the Market: A Political Strategy for Uniting Europe, 1985–2005*. Cornell University Press.

Jensen, O. and Richardson, T. (2004). *Making European Space: Mobility, Power and Territorial Identity*. Routledge.

Joerges, C. (2002). 'Deliberative supranationalism' – two defences. *European Law Journal*, 8(1): 133–151.

(2013). Brother, can you paradigm? *Governance*, 26(2): 189–192.

(2016). Integration through law and the crisis of law in Europe's emergency. In C. Joerges, D. Chalmers, and M. Jachtenfuchs (eds.), *The End of the Eurocrats' Dream*. Cambridge University Press, 299–338.

Johnson, M. and Ghiglione, D. (2020). Coronavirus 'tsunami' pushes Italy's hospitals to breaking point. *Financial Times*, 11 March

Jordan, J., Maccarrone, V., and Erne, R. (2021). Towards a socialisation of the EU's new economic governance regime? EU labour policy interventions in Germany, Italy, Ireland and Romania (2009–2019). *British Journal of Industrial Relations*, 59(1): 191–213.

Jouen, M. (2015). The macro-economic conditionality. Policy Paper, no. 131. http://institutdelors.eu/wp-content/uploads/2018/01/macroeconomicconditionnality-jouen-jdi-march15.pdf.

Juncker, J.-C. (2016). State of the Union address. https://data.europa.eu/doi/10.2775/968989.

Juncker, J.-C., with Tusk, D., Dijsselbloem, J., Draghi, M., and Schulz, M. (2015). *Completing Economic and Monetary Union*. European Commission.

Kaeding, M. (2007). *Better Regulation in the European Union: Lost in Translation or Full Steam Ahead? The Transportation of EU Transport Directives Across Member States*. Leiden University Press.

Kahancová, M. and Szabó, I. G. (2015). Hospital bargaining in the wake of management reforms: Hungary and Slovakia compared. *European Journal of Industrial Relations*, 21(4): 335–352.

Karp, B. (1954). The draft constitution for a European political community. *International Organization*, 8(2): 181–202.

Kassim, H. and Stevens, H. (2010). *Air Transport and the European Union Europeanization and Its Limits*. Palgrave Macmillan.

Kelemen, D.R. (2011). *Eurolegalism: The Transformation of Law and Regulation in the European Union*. Harvard University Press.

Kelly, J. (2012 [1998]). *Rethinking Industrial Relations: Mobilisation, Collectivism and Long Waves*. Routledge.

Kerwer, D. and Teutsch, M. (2001). Transport policy in the EU. In A. Windhoff-Héritier et al. (eds.), *Differential Europe*. Rowman & Littlefield, 23–55.

Keune, M., Leschke, J., and Watt, A. (eds.). (2008). *Privatisation and Liberalisation of Public Services in Europe: An Analysis of Economic and Labour Market Impacts*. ETUI.

Kilpatrick, C. (2017). The EU and its sovereign debt programmes: The challenges of liminal legality. *Current Legal Problems*, 70(1): 337–363.

Kilpatrick, C. and Scott, J. (eds.). (2021). *Contemporary Challenges to EU Legality*. Oxford University Press.

Kirhensteine, I., Clarke, S., Oosterhuis, F., and Munk Sorensen, M. (2010). *Managing Scarce Water Resources – Implementing the Pricing Policies of the Water Framework Directive*. ENTEC UK, European Commission.

Kishimoto, S., Gendall, S., and Lobina, E. (eds.). (2015). *Our Public Water Future: The Global Experience with Remunicipalisation*. Transnational Institute, Public Services International Research Unit, and EPSU.

Knill, C. and Lehmkuhl, D. (2002). The national impact of European Union regulatory policy. *European Journal of Political Research*, 41(2): 255–280.

Kochenov, D. (2019). The oxymoron of 'market citizenship' and the future of the union. In F. Amtenbrink, G. Davies, D. Kochenov, and J. Lindeboom (eds.), *The Internal Market and the Future of European Integration*. Cambridge University Press, 217–230.

Kölliker, A. (2006). *Flexibility and European Unification: The Logic of Differentiated Integration*. Rowman & Littlefield.

Kohler-Koch, B. and Quittkat, C. (2013). *De-Mystification of Participatory Democracy: EU-Governance and Civil Society*. Oxford University Press.

Kohler-Koch, B. and Rittberger, B. (2006). The 'governance turn' in EU studies. *Journal of Common Market Studies*, 44(1): 27–49.

Kostakopoulou, D. (2007). European Union citizenship. *European Law Journal*, 13 (5): 623–646.

Krachler, N., Auffenberg, J., and Wolf, L. (2021). The role of organizational factors in mobilizing professionals: Evidence from nurse unions in the United States and Germany. *British Journal of Industrial Relations*, 59(3): 643–668.

Krachler, N., Greer, I., and Umney, C. (2022). Can public healthcare afford marketization? Market principles, mechanisms, and effects in five health systems. *Public Administration Review*, 82(5): 876–886.

Kreuder-Sonnen, C. and White, J. (2022). Europe and the transnational politics of emergency. *Journal of European Public Policy*, 29(6): 953–965.

Kriesi, H., Lorenzini, J., Wüest, B., and Häusermann, S. (2020). *Contention in Times of Crisis*. Cambridge University Press.

Kriesi, H. and Wüest, B. (2020). Conclusion. In H. Kriesi, J. Lorenzini, B. Wüest, and S. Hausermann (eds.), *Contention in Times of Crisis*. Cambridge University Press, 276–290.

Kunkel, K. (2021). Die politische Ökonomie des Fallpauschalensystems zur Krankenhaus-finanzierung. *PROKLA. Zeitschrift für kritische Sozialwissenschaft*, 51(205): 631–651.

Kunzlik, P. (2013). Neoliberalism and the European public procurement regime. *Cambridge Yearbook of European Legal Studies*, 15: 283–356.

Lanchester, J. (2014). *How to Speak Money*. Faber & Faber.

Lascoumes, P. and Le Galès, P. (eds.). (2004). *Gouverner par les Instruments*. Presses de Sciences Po.

Lavenda, R. and Schultz, E. (2020). *Core Concepts in Cultural Anthropology*. Oxford University Press.

Lefébure, P. and Lagneau, E. (2001). Dynamics of Europrotest. In D. Imig and S. Tarrow (eds.), *Contentious Europeans: Protest and Politics in an Emerging Polity*. Rowman & Littlefield, 187–204.

Lehndorff, S. (2015). Acting in different worlds. Challenges to transnational trade union cooperation in the eurozone crisis. *Transfer*, 21(2): 157–170.

Leibfried, S. (2015). Social policy: Left to judges and the market? In H. Wallace, M. A. Pollack, and A. R. Young (eds.), *Policy-Making in the European Union*. Oxford University Press, 7th ed., 263–292.

Leiren, M.D. (2015). Scope of negative integration: A comparative analysis of post, public transport and port services. *Journal of Common Market Studies*, 53(3): 609–626.
Leisink, P. and Hyman, R. (2005). Introduction: The dual evolution of Europeanization and varieties of governance. *European Journal of Industrial Relations*, 11(3): 277–286.
Léonard, E., Erne, R., Marginson, P., and Smismans, S. (with the collaboration of P. Tilly). (2007). *New Structures, Forms and Processes of Governance in European Industrial Relations*. Eurofound/Office for the Official Publications of the European Communities.
Lethbridge, J. (2013). *Expansion and Consolidation?* PSIRU, EPSU.
Leuffen, D., Rittberger, B., and Schimmelfennig, F. (2022). *Integration and Differentiation in the European Union*. Springer, 2nd ed.
Lillie, N. (2022). Round table. Nordic unions and the European Minimum Wage Directive. *Transfer*, 28(4): 499–504.
Lindberg, L. and Scheingold, S. (1970). *Europe's Would-Be Polity*. Prentice Hall.
Lübker, M. (2019). *Europäischer Tarifbericht des WSI 2018/2019*. WSI.
Lutz, H. and Palenga-Mollenbeck, E. (2010). Care work migration in Germany. *Social Policy and Society*, 9(3): 419–430.
Maccarrone, V. (2020). *A Tale of Two Countries? The Impact of the New European Economic Governance Regime on Irish and Italian Industrial Relations*. PhD thesis, University College Dublin.
Maccarrone, V. and Erne, R. (2023). 'Ireland: Trade unions recovering after being tipped off balance by the Great Recession?. In J. Waddington, T. Müller and K: Vandaele (eds.) *Trade unions in the European Union: Picking up the pieces from the neoliberal challenge*. Brussels: Peter Lang, 585–624.
Maccarrone, V., Erne, R., and Golden, D. (2023). The European Union: A significant player in labour policymaking. In D. Clegg and N. Durazzi (eds.), *The Handbook of Labour Market Policy in Advanced Democracies*. Edward Elgar, 219–233.
Maccarrone, V., Erne, R., and Regan, A. (2019). Ireland: Life after social partnership. In T. Müller, K. Vandaele, and J. Waddington (eds.), *Collective Bargaining in Europe*. ETUI, vol. II, 315–335.
MacCarthaigh, M. (2017). *Public Sector Reform in Ireland: Countering Crisis*. Palgrave.
MacCarthaigh, M. and Hardiman, N. (2020). Exploiting conditionality: EU and international actors and post-NPM reform in Ireland. *Public Policy and Administration*, 35(2): 179–200.
Maher, I. (2021a). Revisiting soft law governance, regulation and networks. In M. Eliantonio, E. Korkea-aho, and O. Stefan (eds.), *EU Soft Law in the Member States: Theoretical Findings and Empirical Evidence*. Bloomsbury.
(2021b). Competition law: Convergence through law and networks. In P. Craig and G. de Búrca (eds.), *The Evolution of EU Law*. Oxford University Press, 824–846.
Mainil, T. (2012). *Transnational Healthcare and Medical Tourism*. PhD thesis, NHTV Breda University of Applied Sciences.
Mair, P. (2013). *Ruling the Void: The Hollowing of Western Democracy*. Verso.

Majone, G. (1994). The rise of the regulatory state in Europe. *West European Politics*, 17(3): 77–101.
Mallet, V., Chazan, G., and Fleming, S. (2020). The chain of events that led to Germany's change over Europe's recovery fund. *Financial Times*, 22 May.
Marginson, P. and Sisson, K. (2004). *European Integration and Industrial Relations: Multi-Level Governance in the Making*. Palgrave Macmillan.
Marginson, P. and Welz, C. (2015). European wage-setting mechanisms under pressure. *Transfer*, 21(4): 429–450.
Markakis, M. and Dermine, P. (2018). Bailouts, the legal status of Memoranda of Understanding, and the scope of application of the EU Charter. *Common Market Law Review*, 55(2): 643–671.
Marks, G., Scharpf, F., Schmitter, P. C., and Streeck, W. (1996). *Governance in the European Union*. Sage.
Marshall, T. H. (1950). *Citizenship and Social Class and Other Essays*. Cambridge University Press.
Martin, A. and Ross, G. (eds.). (1999). *The Brave New World of European Labor: European Trade Unions at the Millennium*. Berghahn.
Martinsen, D. S. and Vrangbaek, K. (2008). The Europeanisation of health care governance. *Public Administration*, 86(1): 169–184.
Marx, K. (2005 [1867]). *Capital. Volume One*. Marxists Internet Archive. www.marxists.org/archive/marx/works/1867-c1/cho1.htm.
Mazzucato, M. (2013). *The Entrepreneurial State: Debunking Public Vs. Private Sector Myths*. Anthem.
McAlevey, J. (2016). *No Shortcuts: Organizing for Power in the New Gilded Age*. Oxford University Press.
McDaid, D., Wiley, M., Maresso, A., and Mossialos, E. (2009). Ireland. Health system review. *Health Systems in Transition*, 11(4): 1–267.
McDonough, T. and Dundon, T. (2010). Thatcherism delayed? The Irish crisis and the paradox of social partnership. *Industrial Relations Journal*, 41(6): 544–562.
McGann, M. (2021). 'Double activation': Workfare meets marketization. *Administration*, 69(2): 19–42.
Meardi, G. (2013). *Social Failures of EU Enlargement: A Case of Workers Voting with Their Feet*. Routledge.
 (2014). Employment relations under external pressure: Italian and Spanish reforms during the great recession. In M. Hauptmeier and M. Vidal (eds.), *Comparative Political Economy of Work*. Palgrave Macmillan, 332–350.
 (2016). The fate of the 'hard' and 'soft' acquis communautaires in the new member states. In V. Delteil and V. N. Kirov (eds.), *Labour and Social Transformation in Central and Eastern Europe*. Routledge, 137–162.
Ménard, C. (2009). From technical integrity to institutional coherence: Regulatory challenges in the water sector. In C. Ménard and M. Ghertman (eds.), *Regulation, Deregulation, Reregulation: Institutional Perspectives*. Edward Elgar, 83–108.
Menz, G. (2015). Whatever happened to social Europe? The three-pronged attack on European social policy. In G. Menz and A. Crespy (eds.), *Social Policy and the Euro Crisis: Quo Vadis Social Europe*. Palgrave, 45–62.

Mercille, J. (2018). Privatization in the Irish hospital sector since 1980. *Journal of Public Health*, 40(4): 863–870.
Mercille, J. and Murphy, E. (2016). Conceptualising European privatisation processes after the great recession. *Antipode*, 48(3): 685–704.
  (2017). What is privatization? A political economy framework. *Environment and Planning*, 49(5): 1040–1059.
Mercille, J., Turner, B., and Lucey, D. S. (2022). Ireland's takeover of private hospitals during the COVID-19 pandemic. *Health Economics, Policy and Law*, 17(2): 232–237.
Messulam, P. and Finger, M. (2015). Rail access charges. In M. Finger and P. Messulam (eds.), *Rail Economics, Policy and Regulation in Europe*. Edward Elgar, 323–340.
Mihailovic, N., Kocic, S., and Jakovljevic, M. (2016). Review of diagnosis-related group-based financing of hospital care. *Health Services Research and Managerial Epidemiology*, 3: 1–8.
Miller, P. and Rose, N. (1990). Governing economic life. *Economy and Society*, 19(1): 1–31.
Mills, C. W. (2000 [1959]). *The Sociological Imagination*. Oxford University Press.
Milward, A. (1999). *The European Rescue of the Nation State*. Routledge.
Millward, R. (2005). *Private and Public Enterprise in Europe: Energy, Telecommunications and Transport, 1830–1990*. Cambridge University Press.
Miró, J. (2021). In the name of competitiveness: A discursive institutionalist analysis of the EU's approach to labour market structural reform. *Socio-Economic Review*, 19(2): 711–733.
Molina, O. and Rhodes, M. (2002). Corporatism: The past, present, and future of a concept. *Annual Review of Political Science*, 5: 305–331.
Monti, M. (2010). A new strategy for the single market. Report to the President of the European Commission, 9 May.
Moore, M. (2018). *Wellsprings of Resistance. Struggles over Water in Europe*. Rosa Luxemburg Stiftung.
  (2023). *Water Struggles as Resistance to Neoliberal Capitalism: A Time of Reproductive Unrest*. Manchester University Press.
Moravcsik, A. (1993). Preferences and power in the European Community: A liberal intergovernmentalist approach. *Journal of Common Market Studies*, 31(4): 473–524.
  (1998). *The Choice for Europe Social Purpose and State Power from Messina to Maastricht*. Routledge.
Moretti, F. and Pestre, D. (2015). Bankspeak: The language of World Bank reports. *New Left Review*, 92(2): 75–99.
Morgan, G. and Kristensen, P. H. (2006). The contested space of multinationals: Varieties of institutionalism, varieties of capitalism. *Human Relations*, 59(11): 1467–1490.
Mouffe, C. (2011). *On the Political*. Routledge.
Müller, T. and Platzer, H.-W. (2017). The European trade union federations. In S. Lehndorff, H. Dribbusch, and T. Schulten (eds.), *Rough Waters. European Trade Unions in a Time of Crisis*. ETUI, 289–314.

Murphy, C. and O'Sullivan, M. (2021). Running to stand still? Two decades of trade union activity in the Irish long-term care sector. *Transfer*, 27(3): 383–397.
Murphy, N. (2019). Overview of the anti-water privatisation campaign in Ireland. http://europeanwater.org/actions/country-city-focus/899-anti-water-privatisation-campaign-in-ireland.
Nanetti, R. (1996). EU cohesion and territorial restructuring in the member states. In L. Hooghe (ed.), *Cohesion Policy and European Integration*. Oxford University Press, 59–88.
Naughton, M. (2021). Mobilising societal power: Understanding public support for nursing strikes. *Industrial Relations Journal*, 53(2): 93–109.
   (2023). Protest in Response to the Commodification of Healthcare in the Era of the European Union's New Economic Governance Regime. PhD thesis, University College Dublin.
Nguyen, T. and Redeker, N. (2022). How to make the marriage work: Wedding the Recovery and Resilience Facility and the European Semester. Policy Brief, 31 January. Hertie School.
Niemann, A., Lefkofridi, Z., and Schmitter, P. C. (2019). Neofunctionalism. In A. Wiener, T. Börzel, and T. Risse (eds.), *European Integration Theory*. Oxford University Press, 3rd ed., 43–63.
Nowak, J. and Erne, R. (2024). Unions and politics. In G. Gall (ed.), *The Handbook of the Past, Present and Future of Labour Unions*. Agenda.
Nunes, R. (2021). *Neither Vertical nor Horizontal: A Theory of Political Organization*. Verso.
O'Donnell, G. and Schmitter, P. C. (2013 [1986]). *Transitions from Authoritarian Rule: Tentative Conclusions about Uncertain Democracies*. Johns Hopkins University Press.
OECD. (2016). Contracts covered by the Public Procurement Directives. Brief 4. Public Procurement, September. OECD. www.sigmaweb.org/publications/Public-Procurement-Policy-Brief-4-200117.pdf.
   (2020). Health Care Resources. https://stats.oecd.org/Index.aspx?DataSetCode=HEALTH_REAC#.
   (2022). OECD/AIAS ICTWSS Database. www.oecd.org/employment/ictwss-database.htm.
   (2023a). Health Care Resources. https://stats.oecd.org/Index.aspx?DataSetCode=HEALTH_REAC.
   (2023b). Review of the Corporate Governance of State-Owned Enterprises in Romania. 27 January. https://doi.org/10.1787/fabf20a8-en.
Offe, C. and Wiesenthal, H. (1980). Two logics of collective action: Theoretical notes on social class and organizational form. *Political Power and Social Theory*, 1(1): 67–115.
O'Leary, N. (2023). Will the EU's Covid-19 stimulus money be wasted? *The Irish Times*, 9 March.
Ó Riain, S. (2014). *The Rise and Fall of Ireland's Celtic Tiger*. Cambridge University Press.
Orwell, G. (2013 [1946]). *Politics and the English Language*. Penguin.

Page, B. and Kaika, M. (2003). The EU Water Framework Directive: Part 2. Policy innovation and the shifting choreography of governance. *Environmental Policy and Governance*, 13(6): 328–343.

Palcic, D. and Reeves, E. (2013). State-owned enterprise policy and the loss of economic sovereignty: The case of Ireland. *Public Organization Review*, 13: 117–130.

  (2018). State-owned enterprise sector, 2017. *Administration*, 66(1): 59–68.

Panitch, L. (2015). Capital and politics. *Perspectives on Politics*, 13(4): 1075–1083.

Parks, L. (2015). *Social Movement Campaigns on EU Policy: In the Corridors and in the Streets*. Palgrave Macmillan.

Patel, K. K. and Schot, J. (2011). Twisted paths to European integration: Comparing agriculture and transport policies in a transnational perspective. *Contemporary European History*, 20(4): 383–403.

Pautz, H. (2008). Think-tanks in Germany: The Bertelsmann Foundation's role in labour market reform. *Zeitschrift für Politikberatung*, 1(3): 437–456.

Petrini, F. (2010). Vincolo esterno e lotte sociali: Gli industriali italiani e la fine dell'età dell'oro. In I. Del Biondo, L. Mechi, and F. Petrini (eds.), *Fra Mercato Comune e Globalizzazione*. Franco Angeli, 15–44.

  (2013). Demanding democracy in the workplace. The European Trade Union Confederation and the struggle to regulate multinationals. In W. Kaiser and J.-H. Meyer (eds.), *Societal Actors in European Integration*. Palgrave, 151–172.

Pinder, J. (1968). Positive integration and negative integration: Some problems of economic union in the EEC. *The World Today*, 24(3): 88–110.

Pochet, P. (2019). *A la Recherche de l'Europe Sociale*. Presses universitaires de France.

Pochet, P. and Degryse, C. (2013). Monetary union and the stakes for democracy and social policy. *Transfer*, 19(1): 103–116.

Polanyi, K. (2001 [1944]). *The Great Transformation: The Political and Economic Origins of our Time*. Beacon Press, 2nd ed.

Pollack, M. A. (1998). The engines of integration? Supranational autonomy and influence in the European Union. In W. Sandholtz and A. Stone Sweet (eds.), *European Integration and Supranational Governance*. Oxford University Press, 217–249.

Pontusson, J. (2006). *Inequality and Prosperity: Social Europe vs Liberal America*. Cornell University Press.

Porcher, S. and Saussier, S. (2018). Public versus private management in water public services: Taking stock, looking ahead. Working paper. http://cadmus.eui.eu//handle/1814/60066.

Poulantzas, N. (1980). *State, Power, Socialism*. Verso.

PPI Project Database. (2016). PPI project summary: Romania, Bucharest – Concession agreement for water and sanitation services. https://ppp.worldbank.org/public-private-partnership/ppi-project-summary-romania-bucharest-concession-agreement-water-and-sanitation-services.

Prosser, T. (2016). Dualization or liberalization? Investigating precarious work in eight European countries. *Work, Employment & Society*, 30(6): 949–965.

Przeworski, A. and Teune, H. (1970). *The Logic of Comparative Social Inquiry*. Wiley.

Pulignano, V., Carrieri, D., and Baccaro, L. (2018). Industrial relations in Italy in the twenty-first century. *Employee Relations*, 40(4): 654–673.

Pulignano, V., Tregaskis, O., Doerflinger, N., and Bélanger, J. (2018). The distinctiveness of employment relations within multinationals: Political games and social compromises within multinationals' subsidiaries in Germany and Belgium. *Journal of Industrial Relations*, 60(4): 465–491.
Radaelli, C. M. (1999). *Technocracy in the European Union*. Routledge.
Rainone, S. (2018). Labour rights in the making of the EU and in the CJEU case law: A case study on the Transfer of Undertakings Directive. *European Labour Law Journal*, 9(3): 299–325.
— (2020). An overview of the 2020–2021 country-specific recommendations (CSRs) in the social field. The impact of Covid-19. ETUI, 5 November.
— (2022). From deregulatory pressure to laissez faire: The (moderate) social implications of the EU recovery strategy. *Italian Labour Law e-Journal*, 15(1S): 31–52.
Regan, A. and Brazys, S. (2017). Celtic phoenix or leprechaun economics? *New Political Economy*, 23(2): 223–238.
Regling, K. (2021). Reforming the ESM: Implications for European financial stability and resilience. Speech to Institute of International and European Affairs, Dublin, 3 February.
Review Group on State Assets and Liabilities. (2011). Final Report. April 2011. http://cdn.thejournal.ie/media/2011/04/stateassetsrep.pdf.
Rhodes, M. (2000). The political economy of social pacts: 'Competitive corporatism' and European welfare reform. In P. Pierson (ed.), *The New Politics of the Welfare State*. Oxford University Press, 165–194.
Riley, D. and Brenner, R. (2022). Seven theses on American politics. *New Left Review*, 138: 21–27.
Rocca, M. (2022). Introduction: The EU new economic governance, labour law and labour lawyers. *European Labour Law Journal*, 13(2): 141–155.
Roche, W. K. (2007). Social partnership in Ireland and new social pacts. *Industrial Relations: A Journal of Economy and Society*, 46(3): 395–425.
Roche, W. K. and Geary, J. F. (2006). *Partnership at Work: The Quest for Radical Organizational Change*. Routledge.
Roche, W. K., O'Connell, P. J., and Prothero, A. (eds.). (2016). *Austerity and Recovery in Ireland: Europe's Poster Child and the Great Recession*. Oxford University Press.
Rokkan, S. (1999). *State Formation, Nation-Building, and Mass Politics in Europe*. Clarendon.
Romair Consulting. (2009). Management of Infrastructure Projects for Hospitals in Romania. https://ec.europa.eu/regional_policy/sources/docgener/evaluation/library/romania/0910_hospital_infra_eval_en.pdf.
Rone, J. (2020). *Contesting Austerity and Free Trade in the EU*. Routledge.
Rubery, J. and Piasna, A. (2016). Labour market segmentation and the EU reform agenda: Developing alternatives to the mainstream. ETUI Working Paper 2016.10.
Rueschemeyer, D., Huber Stephens, E., and Stephens, J. (1992). *Capitalist Development and Democracy*. Polity.
Ruggie, J. G. (1982). International regimes, transactions, and change: Embedded liberalism in the postwar economic order. *International Organization*, 36(2): 379–415.

Rutherford, T. and Frangi, L. (2018). Overturning Italy's Article 18. *Economic and Industrial Democracy*, 39(3): 439–457.
Ryner, J.M. (2023). Silent revolution/passive revolution: Europe's COVID-19 recovery plan and green deal. *Globalizations*, 20(4): 628–643.
Sanitas (2022). SANITAS cere Guvernului României aplicarea integrală a Legii salarizării bugetare, aflată în vigoare. Press release, 29 November.
Saurugger, S. (2016). Sociological approaches to the European Union in times of turmoil. *Journal of Common Market Studies*, 54(1): 70–86.
Savage, J. D. (2005). *Making the EMU*. Oxford University Press.
Scharpf, F. W. (1999). *Governing in Europe: Effective and Democratic?* Oxford University Press.
  (2006). The joint-decision trap revisited. *Journal of Common Market Studies*, 44(4): 845–864.
  (2021). Forced structural convergence in the Eurozone. In A. Hassel and B. Palier (eds.), *Growth and Welfare in Advanced Capitalist Economies: How Have Growth Regimes Evolved?* Oxford University Press, 161–200.
Schiek, D. (2012). *Economic and Social Integration: The Challenge for EU Constitutional Law*. Edward Elgar.
Schmid, A., Cacace, M., Gotze, R., and Rothgang, H. (2010). Explaining health care system change: Problem pressure and the emergence of 'hybrid' health care systems. *Journal of Health Politics, Policy and Law*, 35(4): 455–486.
Schmidt, S. K. (1996). Sterile debates and dubious generalizations: European integration theory tested by telecommunications and electricity. *Journal of Public Policy*, 16: 233–271.
  (2002). The impact of mutual recognition: Inbuilt limits and domestic responses to the single market. *Journal of European Public Policy*, 9(6): 935–953.
Schmidt, V. A. (2020). *Europe's Crisis of Legitimacy. Governing by Rules and Ruling by Numbers in the Eurozone*. Oxford University Press.
  (2022). European emergency politics and the question of legitimacy. *Journal of European Public Policy*, 29(6): 979–993.
Schmitter, P. C. (2000). *How to Democratize the European Union . . . and Why Bother?* Rowman & Littlefield.
  (2012) European disintegration? A way forward? *Journal of Democracy*, 23(4): 39–46.
Schmitter, P. and Grote, J. (1997). The corporatist Sisyphus: Past, present and future. EUI Working Paper SPS, 97(4). https://cadmus.eui.eu/bitstream/handle/1814/284/97_4.pdf.
Schneider, E. (2023). NextGenerationEU and the future of the European monetary union: Shifting interests and new fractures in the German power bloc. *Journal of Common Market Studies*. https://doi.org/10.1111/jcms.13465.
Schneider, E. and Syrovatka, F. (2020). Corona und die nächste Eurokrise. *PROKLA. Zeitschrift für kritische Sozialwissenschaft*, 50(199): 335–344.
Schot, J. and Schipper, F. (2011). Experts and European transport integration. *Journal of European Public Policy*, 18(2): 274–303.
Schulten, T. (2002). A European solidaristic wage policy? *European Journal of Industrial Relations*, 8(2): 173–196.

(2006). *Liberalisation, Privatisation and Regulation in the German Healthcare Sector/Hospitals*. Hans-Böckler-Stiftung.
Schulten, T. and Müller, T. (2015). European economic governance and its intervention in national wage development and collective bargaining. In S. Lehndorff (ed.), *Divisive Integration. The Triumph of Failed Ideas in Europe – Revisited*. ETUI, 331–363.
(2020). Kurzarbeitergeld in der Corona-Krise. WSI Policy Brief, no. 38, April.
(2021). A paradigm shift towards Social Europe? *Italian Labour Law e-Journal*, 14(1): 1–19.
Schulz-Forberg, H. and Stråth, B. (2014). *The Political History of European Integration: The Hypocrisy of Democracy-through-Market*. Routledge.
Schweitzer, H. (2011). Services of general economic interest: European law's impact on the role of markets and of member states. In M. Cremona (ed.), *Market Integration and Public Services in the European Union*. Oxford University Press, 11–62.
Sciarra, S. (2003). New discourses in labour law. Part-time work and the paradigm of flexibility. EUI Working Paper Law 2003/14.
Scordamaglia, D. and Katsarova, I. (2016). *The Fourth Railway Package*. European Parliament.
Seeliger, M. and Wagner, I. (2020). A socialization paradox: Trade union policy cooperation in the case of the enforcement directive of the Posting of Workers Directive. *Socio-Economic Review*, 18(4): 1113–1131.
Simonazzi, A., Ginzburg, A., and Nocella, G. (2013). Economic relations between Germany and southern Europe. *Cambridge Journal of Economics*, 37(3): 653–675.
Smith, M. P. (2005). *States of Liberalization: Redefining the Public Sector in Integrated Europe*. State University of New York Press.
Snyder, F. (1993). The effectiveness of European Community law: Institutions, processes, tools and techniques. *Modern Law Review*, 56(1): 19–54.
Spinelli, A. and Rossi, E. (2013 [1941]). *The Ventotene Manifesto*. www.cvce.eu/obj/the_manifesto_of_ventotene_1941-en-316aa96c-e7ff-4b9e-b43a-958e96afbecc.html.
Spradley, J. (2016). *The Ethnographic Interview*. Waveland.
Stamati, F. and Baeten, R. (2015). *Health Care Reforms and the Crisis*. ETUI.
Stan, S. (2018). Neoliberal citizenship and the politics of corruption: Redefining informal exchange in Romanian healthcare. In J. Carrier (ed.), *Economy, Crime and Wrong in a Neoliberal Era*. Berghahn, 172–194.
Stan, S. and Erne, R. (2014). Explaining Romanian labor migration: From development gaps to development trajectories. *Labor History*, 55(1): 21–46.
(2016). Is migration from Central and Eastern Europe an opportunity for trade unions to demand higher wages? Evidence from the Romanian health sector. *European Journal of Industrial Relations*, 22(2): 167–183.
(2018/2019). A new methodology for analysing NEG prescriptions on healthcare. From counting CSRs to mapping semantic fields. Working Paper No. 3, ERC Project 'European Unions', www.erc-europeanunions.eu/working-papers/.
(2021a). Time for a paradigm change? Incorporating transnational processes into the analysis of the emerging European health-care system. *Transfer*, 27(3): 289–302.

(2021b). Bringing society back into our understanding of European cross-border care. *Journal of European Social Policy*, 31(4): 432–439.

(2023). Pursuing an overarching commodification script through country-specific interventions? The EU's New Economic Governance prescriptions in healthcare (2009–2019). *Socio-Economic Review*. https://doi.org/10.1093/ser/mwad053.

Stan, S., Erne, R., and Gannon, S. (2021). Bringing EU citizens together or taking them apart? The European Health Insurance Card, east–west mobility and the failed promise of European social integration. *Journal of European Social Policy*, 31(4): 409–423.

Stan, S., Helle, I., and Erne, R. (2015). European collective action in times of crisis. *Transfer: European Review of Labour and Research*, 21(2): 131–139.

Stan, S. and Toma, V.-V. (2019). Accumulation by dispossession and public–private biomedical pluralism in Romanian health care. *Medical Anthropology*, 38(1): 85–99.

Statham, P. and Trenz, H. J. (2013). *The Politicization of Europe*. Routledge.

Sterkel, G., Schulten, T., and Wiedemuth, J. (eds.). (2004). *Autonomie im Laufstall? Gewerkschaftliche Lohnpolitik im Euroland*. VSA.

Stevens, H. (2004). *Transport Policy in the European Union*. Palgrave Macmillan, 3rd ed.

Stiglitz, J. E. (2002). Employment, social justice and societal well-being. *International Labour Review*, 141(1–2): 9–29.

(2010). *Freefall: America, Free Markets, and the Sinking of the World Economy*. Norton.

Streeck, W. (1992). National diversity, regime competition and institutional deadlock: Problems in forming a European industrial relations system. *Journal of Public Policy*, 12(4): 301–330.

(1998). The internationalization of industrial relations in Europe: Prospects and problems. *Politics & Society*, 26(4): 429–459.

(2014). *Buying Time: The Delayed Crisis of Democratic Capitalism*. Verso.

Streeck, W. and Schmitter, P. C. (1991). From national corporatism to transnational pluralism: Organized interests in the single European market. *Politics & Society*, 19(2): 133–164.

Sultana, F. and Loftus, A. (eds.). (2012). *The Right to Water: Politics, Governance and Social Struggles*. Earthscan, 1st ed.

Supiot, A. (2013). Grandeur and misery of the social state. *New Left Review*, 82: 99–113.

(2017). *Governance by Numbers*. Bloomsbury.

Sweeney, P. (2004). *Selling Out? Privatisation in Ireland*. New Island.

Syrovatka, F. (2021). Labour market policy under the new European economic governance: France in the focus of the new European labour market policy. *Capital & Class*, 45(2): 283–309.

(2022a). *Neue Europäische Arbeitspolitik: Umkämpfte Integration in der Eurokrise*. Campus.

(2022b). The emergence of a new European labour policy regime: Continuity and change since the euro crisis. *Competition & Change*, 26(5): 575–602.

Szabó, I. (2018). Trade unions and the sovereign power of the state. A comparative analysis of employer offensives in the Danish and Irish public sectors. *Transfer*, 24(2):163–178.

(2020). Professionals on the road to contention: Social movement unionism in healthcare labour disputes across Europe. *Economic and Industrial Democracy*, 43(1): 410–430.

(2022). The wages of reconstruction – the EU's new budget and the public service staff shortage crisis on the EU's eastern periphery. *Transfer*, 28(1): 141–145.

Szabó, I., Golden, D., and Erne, R. (2022). Why do some labour alliances succeed in politicizing Europe across borders? A comparison of the Right2Water and Fair Transport European Citizens' Initiatives. *Journal of Common Market Studies*, 60(3): 634–652.

Szypulewska-Porczyńska, A. (2020). Changes in the EU legal framework on the provision of services in the internal market in the past decade. In A. M. Kowalski and M. A. Weresa (eds.), *Poland Competitiveness Report 2020*. SGH, 29–42.

Tarrow, S. (1994). *Power in Movement*. Cambridge University Press.

Taylor, R. (1999). Some comments on the Blair/Schroeder 'Third Way/Neue Mitte' manifesto. *Transfer*, 5(3): 411–414.

Thelen, K. (2001). Varieties of labor politics in the developed democracies. In P. A. Hall and D. Soskice (eds.), *Varieties of Capitalism*. Oxford University Press, 76–92.

(2014). *Varieties of Liberalization and the New Politics of Social Solidarity*. Cambridge University Press.

Tilly, C. (1992). *Coercion, Capital, and European States, AD 990–1992*. Blackwell.

Tinbergen, J. (1965). *International Economic Integration*. Elsevier, 2nd rev. ed.

Tindemans, L. (1976). Report by Mr. Leo Tindemans, Prime Minister of Belgium, to the European Council. *Bulletin of the European Communities*, Supplement 1/76.

Tooze, A. (2018). *Crashed: How a Decade of Financial Crises Changed the World*. Penguin.

(2023). EU green policy must bring the population with it. *Financial Times*, 7 April.

Transfer. (2002). European Commission view on liberalisation of network industries. *Transfer*, 8(2): 292–295.

Traxler, F. and Adam, G. (2008). *Representativeness of the European Social Partner Organisations: Railways Sector*. Eurofound.

Tricart, J. P. (2019). Legislative implementation of European social partner agreements: Challenges and debates. ETUI Research Paper–Working Paper No. 2019-9. DOI: 10.2139/ssrn.3402880.

Trichet, J. C. (2006). EMU after seven years: Successes and challenges. Speech made at the Frankfurt Chamber of Industry and Commerce in Frankfurt, 5 May.

Trif, A. (2016). Surviving frontal assault on collective bargaining institutions in Romania. *European Journal of Industrial Relations*, 22(3): 221–234.

Trif, A. and Paolucci, V. (2018). Romania: From legal support to frontal assault. In T. Müller, K. Vandaele, and J. Waddington (eds.), *Collective Bargaining in Europe: Towards an Endgame*. European Trade Union Institute, 505–523.

Turnbull, P. (2006). The war on Europe's waterfront. *British Journal of Industrial Relations*, 44(2): 305–326.

(2000). Contesting globalization on the waterfront. *Politics & Society*, 28(3): 367–391.

(2010). From social conflict to social dialogue: Counter-mobilization on the European waterfront. *European Journal of Industrial Relations*, 16(4): 333–349.
Turner, T. (1994). Bodies and anti-bodies: Flesh and fetish in contemporary social theory. In T. Csordas (ed.), *Embodiment and Experience*. Cambridge University Press, 27–47.
Unite. (2016). Submission to the Committee-on-Transport, Dublin.
van Apeldoorn, B. (2002). *Transnational Capitalism and the Struggle over European Integration*. Routledge.
Vandaele, K. (2021). Applauded 'nightingales' voicing discontent. Exploring labour unrest in health and social care in Europe before and since the COVID-19 pandemic. *Transfer*, 27(3): 399–411.
van den Berge, J., Boelens, R., and Vos, J. (2018). Uniting diversity to build Europe's Right2Water movement. In R. Boelens, T. Perreault, and J. Vos (eds.), *Water Justice*. Cambridge University Press, 226–245.
van de Velde, D. (2015). European railway reform. In M. Finger and P. Messulam (eds.), *Rail Economics, Policy and Regulation in Europe*. Edward Elgar, 52–88.
Vanhercke, B. (2016). Inside the Social Open Method of Coordination: The Hard Politics of 'Soft' Governance. PhD thesis, Amsterdam Institute for Social Science Research.
Vanhercke, B., Sabato, S., and Spasova, S. (eds.). (2023). *Social Policy in the European Union: State of Play 2022*. OSE, ETUI.
Vanhercke, B. and Verdun, A. (2021). From the European Semester to the Recovery and Resilience Facility. Working Paper 2021.13, ETUI.
van Middelaar, L. (2021). *Das europäische Pandämonium. Was die Pandemie über den Zustand der EU enthüllt*. Suhrkamp.
Vanpool, C. and Vanpool, T. (2009). The semantics of local knowledge. *Journal of Anthropological Research*, 65(4): 529–554.
ver.di. (2010). Wasserwirtschaft muss für Qualität und Nachhaltigkeit stehen. Bundesvorstand Vereinte Dienstleistungsgewerkschaft'. Press release, 22 March.
von der Leyen, U. (2019). Speech to European Parliament plenary on the occasion of the presentation of her College of Commissioners and their programme, 27 November. SPEECH_19_6408.
Wagner, I. (2020). *Workers Without Borders: Posted Work and Precarity in the EU*. Cornell University Press.
Wahl, A. (2011). *The Rise and Fall of the Welfare State*. Pluto.
Walsh, J. (2019). *The Globalist: Peter Sutherland. His Life and Legacy*. Harper Collins.
Warlouzet, L. (2018). *Governing Europe in a Globalizing World: Neoliberalism and Its Alternatives Following the 1973 Oil Crisis*. Routledge.
Welz, C. (2008). *The European Social Dialogue under Articles 138 and 139 of the EC Treaty*. Kluwer Law International.
Whelan, K. (2014). Ireland's economic crisis: The good, the bad and the ugly. *Journal of Macroeconomics*, 39: 424–440.
Wickham, J. and Latniak, E. (2010). European urban public transport: Towards a single European employment model? *Work Organisation, Labour and Globalisation*, 4(1): 160–174.

Wigger, A. (2019). The new EU industrial policy: Authoritarian neoliberal structural adjustment and the case for alternatives. *Globalizations*, 16(3): 353–369.

Wilks, S. and McGowan, L. (1996). Competition policy in the European Union: Creating a federal agency? In S. Wilks and G. B. Doern (eds.), *Comparative Competition Policy*. Clarendon Press, 225–267.

Wise, P. (2021). Spain reaches deal with employers and unions on labour reforms. *Financial Times*, 7 April.

Woolfson, C. and Sommers, J. (2006). Labour mobility in construction: European implications of the Laval un Partneri dispute with Swedish labour. *European Journal of Industrial Relations*, 12(1): 49–68.

Würth, R. (2020). Fünf Billionen für Euro-Bonds wären angebracht. *Handelsblatt*, 10–13 April: 6–7.

Zeitlin, J. and Vanhercke, B. (2018). Socializing the European Semester: EU social and economic policy co-ordination in crisis and beyond. *Journal of European Public Policy*, 25(2): 149–174.

Zuboff, S. (2019). *The Age of Surveillance Capitalism: The Fight for a Human Future at the New Frontier of Power*. Profile.

Zürn, M. (2016). Opening up Europe: Next steps in politicisation research. *West European Politics*, 39(1): 164–182.

Index

access to public services. *See* coverage levels of public services, NEG prescriptions on
accession policies. *See* EU enlargement
Adequate Minimum Wage Directive. *See also* minimum wage regulation; post-Covid NEG regime
    adoption of, 39, 128–130, 325–326, 357
    collective bargaining provisions, 130, 325
    minimum wage-setting provisions, 130, 324–325
    significance, 130–131, 306, 350
Albert, Michel, 26
Andriessen, Frans, 135
austerity policies. *See* expenditure on public services, NEG prescriptions on
aviation services. *See* civil aviation services

bailout programmes for banks, 1–2, 27–28
bailout programmes for Member States, 27–29, 35–36, 313–314, 361
Ban, Cornel, 103–104
Barrett, Gavin, 28, 39
Barroso, José Manuel, 2, 29
Bartolini, Stefano, 22
Beck, Ulrich, 26, 38
Belgian Platform for Action on Health and Solidarity, 259
Bellamy, Richard, 42–43, 254, 297
Berlusconi, Silvio, 104, 113, 117
Bieler, Andreas, 159, 192–193
Blair, Tony, 103–104
Bolkestein Directive. *See* service trade liberalisation via Services Directive
Bolkestein, Frits, 50, 138–139, 208
Bourdieu, Pierre, 78–79
Boyer, Robert, 26

Boylan, Lynn, 228
Brexit, 49, 131, 312, 356
Broad Economic Policy Guidelines, 24, 31, 35, 44, 104
broadband services. *See* telecommunications services
Brooks, Eleanor, 54, 241–243, 253, 256
Büchs, Milena, 105
Burawoy, Michael, 45, 50
bus services, Ireland, 180, 187
Byrne, David, 240

Calmfors, Lars, 32
capitalist accumulation
    by dispossession, 47–49
    marketisation of public services. *See* public services marketisation
    NEG regime based on logic of, 28–29, 40, 353–354
    solidaristic employment and welfare arrangements, tempering function, 21–22, 46–47, 233
carers' rights regulation, 102, 128
Centrale nationale des employés (CNE) (Belgian trade union), 259
CFR Infrastructura (Romanian railway infrastructure company), 184, 186
CFR Marfă (Romanian state-owned freight railway company), 185
CGT (Confédération Générale du Travail) (French trade union), 262
childcare services, NEG prescriptions on, 148, 156
CIDs (Council Implementing Decisions), 323, 361–362

civil aviation services. *See also* transport services
  European Aviation and Safety Agency, 183
  Ireland, commodification of, 177–180
  liberalisation (pre-2008), 169–170
CNE (Centrale nationale des employés) (Belgian trade union), 259
coercive power of NEG prescriptions
  concept and taxonomy, 80–81, 85, 109–111
  employment relations prescriptions, 111, 113–114, 118
  EU funds, NEG conditionalities
    RRF funds. *See* Resilience and Recovery Facility (RRF)
    social and cohesion funds, 32, 185, 190, 321
  Europe 2020 strategy, weakness of, 2, 35
  MIP's coercive power, 85, 278–279
    fines for compliance failures, 30–32, 35, 321
    post-Covid prescriptions, 321–322
  public services prescriptions. *See* coercive power of public services NEG prescriptions
  SGP's coercive power, 85, 278
    Covid-19 pandemic suspension, 9, 232, 265, 306–309, 313, 356
    fines for compliance failures, 29–32, 35
    synthesising assessment, 276, 280–281, 355
    uneven coercive power, challenge for transnational protests, 304–306
coercive power of public services NEG prescriptions
  generally, 142, 154–155, 292
  on healthcare services, 243, 249
  on transport, 177, 183, 188, 202
  on water services, 211–213, 220, 229
cohesion funds, 32, 175, 185, 190, 206, 321
collective action, transnational. *See* transnational collective action
collective bargaining. *See also* trade unions; wages
  Adequate Minimum Wage Directive on, 130, 325
  Germany, healthcare worker protests over, 258
  Laval Quartet rulings, 106, 120, 128
  NEG prescriptions on, 114–116, 283, 329–330, 357
    commodifying or decommodifying potential, 62–65, 114, 119–120, 281

pre-2008 wage negotiations, 17, 31, 45, 100–101, 103–104, 121
Commission. *See* European Commission
commodifying or decommodifying potential of NEG prescriptions
  comparative analyses. *See* comparative analyses of commodifying or decommodifying potential
  conceptual framework, 58–60, 85, 108–109, 354–355
  employment relations prescriptions, 6–7, 108–109, 114, 116, 118–120, 276–277, 283–284
    NRRPs and post-Covid prescriptions, 324–330, 348, 356–357
  healthcare services prescriptions, 8, 231–232, 242–243, 253–257
    NRRPs and post-Covid prescriptions, 265–266, 343–347, 349, 351
  public services prescriptions generally, 7, 142, 147–149, 154–157, 160, 163–164, 276–277
    NRRPs and post-Covid prescriptions, 330–335, 348–350, 357
  transport services prescriptions, 7, 176–177, 187–190, 200–202
    NRRPs and post-Covid prescriptions, 336–338
  water services prescriptions, 7–8, 209–210, 213–214, 218–221, 229–230
    NRRPs and post-Covid prescriptions, 340–342
comparative analyses of commodifying or decommodifying potential
  employment relations and public services prescriptions
    expenditure boosts, 279–281
    expenditure curtailments, 277–279
    generally, 276–277, 283–285, 351
    marketising prescriptions, 281–283
  public services sectoral prescriptions
    expenditure boosts, 291–293
    expenditure curtailments, 290–291
    generally, 285–290, 296–298
    marketising prescriptions, 293–296
  quantitative and qualitative prescriptions distinguished, 8–9, 59, 271–276
competitive tendering liberalisation. *See* public services marketisation
Concessions Directive
  healthcare services under, 242, 258, 295

Index

social clause, 163
transport services exclusion from, 295
water services exclusion from, 158, 221–222, 226–227, 305
Confédération Générale du Travail (CGT) (French trade union), 262
Constitutional Treaty and Lisbon Treaty referendums, 24, 139, 320
consultation rights, 102, 116–117
Conte, Giuseppe, 32
contracts of employment. *See* employment protection
Copeland, Paul, 46–47, 57, 60
Copenhagen accession criteria, 16–17, 137, 235
Cornago, Elisabetta, 321
Corporate Sustainability Due Diligence Directive, 326
corporatisation of public service providers, 69–70
cost-coverage mechanisms, 71–72, 154, 214–215, 252–253. *See also* coverage levels of public services, NEG prescriptions on
Council of Europe, 19, 360
Council of the European Union
 CIDs (Council Implementing Decisions), 323, 361–362
 Council of finance ministers, 27, 29–31, 43–44, 104, 107, 189, 191, 219, 231–232
 Council of transport ministers, 167–168, 189–191, 200, 294
 European Council and Council of Europe distinguished from, 359–360
 NEG Recommendations of, 33–35
 QMV in. *See* qualified majority voting (QMV) in Council
country-specific nature of NEG prescriptions
 country-specific recommendations defined, 360–361
 national countermovements triggered by, 41, 44, 49, 305, 311–312
 post-Covid prescriptions, 320–321
 research implications, 4, 42–44, 52, 62, 80–83, 354
 specific country studies. *See* Germany; Ireland; Italy; Romania
 synthesising assessments. *See* coercive power of NEG prescriptions; commodifying or decommodifying potential of NEG prescriptions

transnational collective action, challenge for, 96, 127, 164, 232, 264–265, 304–305, 354
coverage levels of public services, NEG prescriptions on
 healthcare services, 251–253
 public services generally, 153–154, 349–350
 quantitative and qualitative prescriptions distinguished, 71–72
 transport services, 187
 water services, 214–216
Covid-19 pandemic. *See also* post-Covid NEG regime
 employment relations impact, 130–131
 Eurogroup crisis loans, 309–310
 hospital bed and equipment shortages, 254–255, 307, 309, 343, 347, 349
 lockdowns, 307, 317–318
 NRRPs issued during. *See* National Resilience and Recovery Plans (NRRPs)
 road haulage services in, 200
 RRF funds. *See* Resilience and Recovery Facility (RRF)
 SGP suspended during, 9, 232, 265, 306–309, 313, 356
 state aid rules suspended during, 309
 transnational collective action during, 347–348
Crespy, Amandine, 56–57, 71, 241–242
cross-border healthcare services
 commercial route, 239–240, 256
 Cross-Border Care Directive, 157, 241–242, 257–258, 264
 social security route, 234–235
Crouch, Colin, 40

Daly, Mary, 57
Dawson, Mark, 55, 80
De Spiegelaere, Stan, 330
decommodifying potential of NEG prescriptions. *See* commodifying or decommodifying potential of NEG prescriptions
Degli Abbati, Carlo, 172
Degryse, Christophe, 35
Dehove, Mario, 26
Delors, Jacques, 99, 101, 121
democracy
 EU policymaking democratisation, 23–25
 European Citizens' Initiatives, 24, 198

democracy (cont.)
  QMV reforms. *See* qualified majority
    voting (QMV) in Council
  NEG's democratic deficit. *See* democratic
    deficit of NEG regime
  referendums. *See* referendums
  social policies and democratisation, 21–22,
    46
democratic deficit of NEG regime
  alternative methods of governance. *See*
    governance
  European Parliament's role limited, 31,
    160–164, 256, 263, 313
  necessity rationale, 38, 308
  popular protests against, 41, 44, 49, 305,
    311–312, 356
  post-Covid prescriptions, 322
  transnational protests against. *See*
    transnational collective action
  transport prescriptions example, 201
demonstrations, transnational. *See*
    transnational collective action
Deutsche Bahn (German state railway
    company), 173–174, 184, 188,
    191–192, 294
Díaz, Yolanda, 319
differentiated integration, NEG as reversed
    form of, 42–43, 254, 297, 304,
    320–321, 355
digitalisation policies, 317–318, 333, 349. *See*
    also e-health systems
dockworkers' strikes, 193, 198, 203, 304
Drinking Water Directives, 205–207, 222, 227,
    342
Dublin Bus, 180, 187
Dyrhauge, Helene, 175, 184, 190

EASA (European Aviation and Safety Agency),
    183
economic and monetary union (EMU)
  accession criteria, 17, 100–101, 136
    transport services commodification via,
      174–176
  Broad Economic Policy Guidelines, 24, 31,
    35, 44, 104
  core and periphery Member States,
    differentiated impacts, 17–18
  Covid-19 pandemic, Eurogroup response,
    309–310
  labour and public services impacts, 16–17,
    95, 103, 235–237

  Maastricht Treaty on. *See* Maastricht Treaty
  soveriegn debt crisis. *See* eurozone crisis
economic governance, EU
  post-2008. *See* NEG (new economic
    governance) regime
  pre-2008. *See* EU economic governance
    (pre-2008)
EDP (excessive deficit procedure) of SGP,
    29–30, 32–33, 136, 278–279, 332
e-health systems
  European Health Data Space Regulation
    (draft), 345–347
  NEG prescriptions on, 70, 76, 251, 296,
    317, 344
EHIC (European Health Insurance Card),
    234–235, 242
employee information and consultation rights,
    102, 116–117
employment protection
  flexible working rights, 102, 128, 324
  flexicurity policies (pre-2008), 25, 105
  Germany, mini-jobs, 118, 282–283, 324
  information and consultation rights, 102,
    116–117
  Italy, Jobs Act, 117, 153, 281
  NEG prescriptions on, 31, 36, 117,
    282–283, 328–329
    commodifying or decommodifying
      potential, 65–66, 118–119, 281
  for pregnant workers, 102, 128
  self-employed worker status, 131, 326
employment relations
  commodification of. *See* labour
    commodification
  democratisation of, 21–22, 46
  dimensions of. *See* collective bargaining;
    employment protection; wages
  EU governance pre-2008. *See* employment
    relations governance (pre-2008)
  MIP social indicators, 31–32
  NEG, labour politics of, 3, 13–14, 44–46,
    306, 311–312, 353, 357–358
  transnational collective action. *See*
    transnational collective action
  post-Covid. *See* Adequate Minimum Wage
    Directive; post-Covid NEG regime
  self-employed worker status, 131, 326
  trade unions. *See* trade unions
employment relations governance (pre-2008)
  approaches characterising, 1, 20–21, 25
  flexicurity policies, 25, 105

Index

health and safety policies. *See* occupational health and safety
phases, 97, 120–121, 129
   1950s–1980s, 97–99
   1980s–1990s, 99–103
   2000–2008, 103–107
   wage moderation policies, 17, 31, 100–101, 103–104
employment security. *See* employment protection
EMU. *See* economic and monetary union (EMU)
enhancing social inclusion policies. *See* social inclusion policies
enlargement policies. *See* EU enlargement process
ENPCHSP. *See* European Network Against Privatisation and Commercialisation of Health and Social Protection (ENPCHSP)
environmental policies
   EU's competence for, 207
   green economy policy rationale, 156, 202, 221, 292, 316–317, 340
   post-Covid transport measures, 338–340
   post-Covid water service measures, 341–342
EPSU. *See* European Public Service Union (EPSU)
Erne, Roland, 39, 49, 85, 95, 127, 160, 308–309
   writing with Béthoux and Golden, 50, 121, 139, 174, 311–312, 320
   writing with Jordan and Maccarrone, 9, 35, 39, 83, 85, 271, 278
   writing with Maccarrone and Golden, 16, 324–325
   writing with Maccarrone and Regan, 88, 112, 115, 153, 182, 327
   writing with Nowak, 4, 9, 46, 62, 89–91, 121, 193, 223
   writing with Stan, 3, 45, 83, 88, 104, 232, 234–235, 309, 349
   writing with Szabó and Golden, 5, 24, 39, 45, 50, 88, 137, 158, 193, 198, 202–203, 210, 216, 226, 230, 306
ESM (European Stability Mechanism), 310, 361
ETF. *See* European Transport Workers' Federation (ETF)
ETUC. *See* European Trade Union Confederation (ETUC)

EU competence
   'competence creep' strategies and arguments, 28–29, 38, 105, 108, 158, 318–319
   for decommodifying measures, arguments for, 38–39, 130, 325–326
   for environmental policies, 207
EU economic governance (post-2008). *See* NEG (new economic governance) regime
EU economic governance (pre-2008)
   asymmetry of economic and social integration, 14–16, 18
   employment relations governance. *See* employment relations governance (pre-2008)
   EMU. *See* economic and monetary union (EMU)
   'governance' term, 41–42
   neoliberalism, emergence of, 134–135, 169–170
   political dynamics, 18–25
   public services governance. *See* public services governance (pre-2008)
   service trade liberalisation. *See* service trade liberalisation via Services Directive
   single market. *See* single market project
EU enlargement
   Copenhagen accession criteria, 16–17, 136–137, 235
   core and periphery Member States, differentiated impacts, 17–18
   public services commodification and, 136–137, 193
   water governance and, 206–207
   workers' free movement restrictions, 99–100
EU integration. *See* single market project
EU legal instruments, 360
Euratom (European Atomic Energy Community), 20
Europe 2020 strategy, 2, 33, 35, 361
European Atomic Energy Community (Euratom), 20
European Aviation and Safety Agency (EASA), 183
European Central Bank, 27–29, 103
European Citizens' Initiatives, 24, 198
   examples. *See* Fair Transport; Right2Water
European Coal and Steel Community, 19–20
European Commission
   bank bailout approvals, 1–2, 27

398 Index

European Commission (cont.)
  Covid-19 pandemic relief programmes,
    309–310, 312
  definition, 360
  democratisation of policymaking, 23–24
  eurozone crisis role, 27–29
  NEG enforcement powers, 29–32
  NEG implementation assessments by, 36
  NRRP implementation assessments by,
    313–320, 323–324
  rail services, competition enforcement
    action, 191–192
  state aid regulation. *See* state aid regulation
  wage policy competence claim, 108
European Council
  Council of the European Union and
    Council of Europe distinguished from,
    359–360
  EU Constitution, call for, 23
  role, 20
European Federation of Salaried Doctors, 262
European Health Data Space Regulation
  (draft), 345–347
European Health Insurance Card (EHIC),
  234–235, 242
European Network Against Privatisation and
  Commercialisation of Health and
  Social Protection (ENPCHSP)
  establishment, 8, 259, 265
  membership, 259, 263
  'Our health is not for sale' annual days of
    action, 259–264, 306, 356
  post-Covid protests organisation, 347–348
European Parliament
  definition, 360
  legislative role, 18, 20, 171
  NEG regime, role limited, 31, 160–164,
    256, 263, 313
  service trade liberalisation opposition, 24,
    139–140
European Pillar of Social Rights, 127–128,
  160, 222, 316
European Public Service Union (EPSU)
  Cross-Border Care Directive opposition,
    257–258, 264
  European Health Data Space Regulation
    response, 347
  healthcare commodification protests,
    support for, 262–264
  healthcare workers' protests organisation
    (post-Covid), 347–348

NEG regime protests organisation, 8, 159,
  302
Right2Water. *See* Right2Water
  (European Citizens' Initiative)
Procurement Directive protests organisation,
  222, 239, 258
Services Directive protests organisation,
  223–226, 257, 302
European Semester process
  NEG prescriptions integration role, 2,
    34–35
  NRRP, Commission assessments, 313–320,
    323–324
  outlined, 209, 361
  trade union participation in, 127
European Stability Mechanism (ESM), 310,
  361
European Trade Union Confederation
  (ETUC)
  establishment, 98
  in pre-2008 period, 99, 101–102, 121
  NEG regime protests organisation, 121, 127,
    159–160
  NEG regime social dialogue, 127–129, 160,
    264–265
European Transport Workers' Federation
  (ETF)
  aim, 192–193
  Fair Transport (European Citizens'
    Initiative), 7, 198–200, 202–203
  pre-2008 period protests, 202, 301–302, 304
  Public Services Obligation Regulation
    welcomed by, 172
  rail services measures, concerns about, 191
  road haulage workers' rights initiatives, 200
Eurosceptic politics, 44, 49, 305, 311–312,
  356
eurozone crisis
  German opposition to debt mutualisation
    policies, 310–311
  Member State bailout programmes, 27–29,
    35–36, 313–314, 361
  NEG adoption during, 1–2, 13, 25–27,
    37–38, 95–96, 107
excessive deficit procedure of SGP, 29–30,
  32–33, 136, 278–279, 332
expenditure on public services, NEG
  prescriptions on
  cross-sectoral synthesising assessment,
    290–293
  general public spending, 66–68, 146–149

healthcare services spending, 243–248, 290–291, 318
  in Covid-19 pandemic and post-Covid period, 332–333, 350
  public sector wages. *See* public sector wages
  transport spending, 180–182, 187–188
  water services spending, 218

Fair Transport (European Citizens' Initiative), 7, 198–200, 202–203
female labour market participation, prescriptions on, 148, 156, 248, 293
Ferrovie dello Stato (Italian state railway company), 184, 186
Finger, Matthias, 175, 189
Fiscal Treaty (Treaty on Stability, Coordination, and Governance in the Economic and Monetary Union), 30, 121, 147
Fischbach-Pyttel, Carola, 257
flexible working rights, 102, 128, 324
flexicurity policies (pre-2008), 25, 105
Forum Italiano dei Movimenti per L'acqua, 91, 184–185, 227–228
France
  Constitutional Treaty referendum, 24, 139, 320
  NEG prescriptions for, 35
  public services tradition, 133
  state aid provision, 137–138

gender equality policies, 99, 131
Germany
  business associations
    Covid-19 resilience and recovery funds, support for, 310–312
    opposition to NEG, 27, 311
  Deutsche Bahn (state railway company), 173–174, 184, 188, 191–192, 294
  employment relations prescriptions. *See* Germany, employment relations prescriptions
  healthcare services, EMU convergence criteria impact, 236–237, 251
  mini-jobs, 118, 282–283, 324
  minimum wage regulation, 327–328, 348
  MIP's wage policy, reception in, 107–108
  NRRP for. *See* Germany, NRRP (National Resilience and Recovery Plan)
  private hospitals, 254, 258
  public services prescriptions. *See* Germany, public services prescriptions
  public services tradition, 133
  rail services liberalisation, resistance to, 173–174
  road haulage regulation, 171
  transport reform, post-Covid, 338
  wage moderation policies (pre-2008), 31, 103–104, 119, 284
  water charges, protests against, 226–227
Germany, employment relations prescriptions
  on collective bargaining, 64, 115–116, 281
  on employment protection, 118–119, 281–283
  on public sector wages, 279
  on wage levels, 111, 113, 119–120, 324
Germany, NRRP (National Resilience and Recovery Plan)
  on healthcare services, 344–345
  on transport services, 337–338
Germany, public services prescriptions
  on expenditure, 147–149, 156, 181–182, 218, 279
  on healthcare services, 78, 82, 247, 249–250, 290–291, 344
  on public procurement, 148–150, 155, 216–217, 222, 227
  on public sector wages, 279
  on transport, 148, 181–184, 188–189, 202
  on water services, 216–220, 340
  rebalance the EU economy rationale, 6, 113, 220, 279–280, 293, 324
global financial crisis, 1–2, 27. *See also* eurozone crisis
glossary of terms, 359–362
Golden, Darragh, 128, 258, 263
  writing with Béthoux and Erne, 50, 121, 139, 174, 311–312, 320
  writing with Maccarrone and Erne, 16, 324–325
  writing with Szabó and Erne, 5, 24, 39, 45, 50, 88, 137, 158, 193, 198, 202–203, 209–210, 216, 226, 230, 306
governance
  by ad hoc prescriptions. *See* NEG prescriptions
  by law, 87, 188, 221–223, 257, 276, 338
  by numbers, 24, 29, 70
    MIP's scoreboard of indicators, 31–32, 107–108, 112, 278–279

Index

governance (cont.)
    ULCs (unit labour costs) benchmark, 107, 112, 119, 276–279, 284, 296
    NEG model, TNC corporate governance analogy, 3, 5, 42–46, 305, 319
    pre-2008 period. *See* employment relations governance (pre-2008); EU economic governance (pre-2008); public services governance (pre-2008)
    technocratic, 13–14, 33, 51, 55, 357
    term, 41–42
green economy policy rationale, 156, 202, 221, 292, 316–317, 340. *See also* environmental policies
Greer, Ian, 69, 71
Greer, Scott L., 54
Griffith-Jones, Stephany, 26

Haas, Ernst, 20
Hall, David, 206
Harvey, David, 47–48, 59
health and safety regulation. *See* occupational health and safety
healthcare services. *See also* Covid-19 pandemic; social welfare
    commodifying or decommodifying potential of prescriptions, 8, 231–232, 242–243, 253–257
    NRRPs and post-Covid prescriptions, 265–266, 343–347, 349, 351
    coverage level prescriptions, 251–253
    cross-border provision. *See* cross-border healthcare services
    e-health systems
        European Health Data Space Regulation (draft), 345–347
        NEG prescriptions on, 70, 76, 251, 296, 317, 344
    EMU convergence criteria, impact on, 235–237, 251, 264
    EU governance (pre-2008), 231–232
        1950s–1990s, 232–235
        1990s–2000, 235–237, 264
        2000–2008, 140, 237–242
    expenditure, prescriptions on, 243–248, 290–291, 318
    Germany, prescriptions on, 78, 82, 247, 249–250, 290–291, 344
    hospitals, private services and privatisations, 60, 254–255, 258
    Ireland, prescriptions on. *See* Ireland, healthcare services prescriptions
    Italy, prescriptions on, 77–78, 82, 248–249, 252, 293
    marketisation reforms (pre-2008), 140, 237–242, 256
    NEG application, socialisation thesis on, 54
    provider-level governance, prescriptions on, 250–251, 295–296
    Romania, prescriptions on. *See* Romania, healthcare services prescriptions
    sector-level governance, prescriptions on, 248–250, 295–296
healthcare services, transnational collective action on
healthcare worker protests (post-Covid), 347–348
    NEG regime protests, 239, 257–265, 306, 356
    Services Directive inclusion protests, 8, 232, 238–240, 256–257
Henrich-Franke, Christian, 168
Héritier, Adrienne, 171
hiring and firing mechanisms. *See* employment protection
Höpner, Martin, 120
horizontal–vertical EU integration paradigm
    adoption of, 37–41, 95–96, 353–354
    democratic deficit of. *See* democratic deficit of NEG regime
    labour politics of NEG, 2–3, 13–14, 44–46, 306, 311–312, 353, 357–358
    transnational collective action. *See* transnational collective action
    modes distinguished, 39–40, 44, 359
    prescriptions, country-specific nature. *See* country-specific nature of NEG prescriptions
Horn, Laura, 121
Huws, Ursula, 305–306
Hyman, Richard, 84, 106

information and consultation rights, 102, 116–117
Insurance Directive, 242
internal market. *See* single market project
International Monetary Fund, 27–29, 42
Ireland
    bus services, 180, 187
    corporatist agreements (pre-2008), 100–101

employment relations prescriptions. *See*
    Ireland, employment relations
    prescriptions
healthcare services, EMU convergence
    criteria impact, 236–237
healthcare workers' protests, 258–259
industrial cluster policies (pre-2008), 17–18
NRRP for. *See* Ireland, NRRP (National
    Resilience and Recovery Plan)
private hospitals, 254–255, 266
privatisations, 153
public services prescriptions. *See* Ireland,
    public services prescriptions
Ireland, employment relations prescriptions
    employment protection, no specific
        prescriptions, 117–118
    on collective bargaining, 115
    on healthcare workers (post-Covid), 327
    on public sector wages, 111–112, 146,
        277–278
    on wage levels generally, 119, 327
Ireland, healthcare services prescriptions
    cost-efficiency and managerialism, 76–78,
        249–251, 254–255, 295–296
    generally, 82, 247, 291
    post-Covid prescriptions, 327, 343
    sector-level governance mechanisms, 249
Ireland, NRRP (National Resilience and
    Recovery Plan)
    on healthcare services, 327, 344
    on transport services, 337
    on water services, 341
Ireland, public services prescriptions
    digitalisation measures, 333
    on expenditure, 147, 163–164, 181, 277–278
    social infrastructure investments,
        148–149, 156, 202, 279–280
    on healthcare services. *See* Ireland,
        healthcare services prescriptions
    on privatisation, 151
    on public procurement, 340–341
    on public sector wages, 111–112, 146,
        277–278
    on water services. *See* Ireland, water services
        prescriptions
    transport, no specific prescriptions, 176,
        182–183, 189
Ireland, water services prescriptions
    cost-coverage mechanisms, 214–215, 219,
        223, 294–295
    investment prescriptions, 218, 220–221, 340

Irish Water incorporation, 214–216
    national protests against, 215–216, 223, 228,
        230, 306
Italian Water Movements Forum, 91,
    184–185, 227–228
Italy
    Commission enforcement action against, 32
    corporatist agreements (pre-2008), 100–101
    employment relations prescriptions. *See* Italy,
        employment relations prescriptions
    general strike (2002), 104, 117
    healthcare services, EMU convergence
        criteria impact, 236–237, 251
    Jobs Act, 117, 153, 281
    NRRP for. *See* Italy, NRRP (National
        Resilience and Recovery Plan)
    private hospitals, 254
    public services prescriptions. *See* Italy,
        public services prescriptions
    public services tradition, 133
    rail services liberalisation, resistance to,
        173–174
    Right2Water campaign support in, 227–228
    road haulage regulation, 171
Italy, employment relations prescriptions
    on collective bargaining, 115
    on employment protection, 31, 36, 117, 119
    on public sector wages, 112–113, 146–147
    on wages generally, 327
Italy, NRRP (National Resilience and
    Recovery Plan)
    on healthcare services, 327, 344–345
    on public administration, 334
    on public procurement, 334
    on transport services, 337
    on water services, 341
Italy, public services prescriptions
    on expenditure, 147–149, 163–164, 182,
        248, 279–280
    on healthcare services, 77–78, 82, 248–249,
        252, 293, 344
    on privatisation, 152, 185–186, 192, 281–282
    on professional services liberalisation,
        77–78, 150
    on public administration, 152–153
    on public procurement, 150–151, 155–156,
        184–185, 201, 217–218, 336
    on public sector wages, 112–113, 146–147
    on SOE governance, 152, 186–187, 216
    on transport, 148, 182–184, 189, 294
    on water services, 217–219

Jobs Act (Italy), 117, 153, 281
Jordan, Jamie, 85
Juncker, Jean-Claude, 127–128, 199, 202, 280, 304

Kaeding, Michael, 167, 170
Kallas, Siim, 174
Kerwer, Dieter, 170
Kölliker, Alkuin, 43
Krachler, Nick, 69, 71
Kriesi, Hanspeter, 89, 159
Kröger, Sandra, 42–43, 254, 297
Kyprianou, Markos, 240

labour commodification. *See also* employment relations
  coercive power of NEG prescriptions, 111, 113–114, 118
  commodifying or decommodifying potential of NEG prescriptions, 6–7, 108–109, 114, 116, 118–120, 276–277
  post-Covid prescriptions, 324–330, 348
  conceptual framework, 58–60, 85, 108–109, 354–355
  dimensions of. *See under* collective bargaining; employment protection; wages
  in pre-2008 period, 18, 22, 48, 103–107
  negative–positive EU integration, effects on, 15–16, 22
  neoliberalism driving, 46–49, 81–83
  overview, 60–61
  public sector employment. *See* public sector wages
  specific country studies. *See* Germany, employment relations prescriptions; Ireland, employment relations prescriptions; Italy, employment relations prescriptions; Romania, employment relations prescriptions
  transnational action resisting. *See* transnational collective action
labour politics of NEG regime, 2–3, 13–14, 44–46, 306, 311–312, 353, 357–358. *See also* transnational collective action
Laval Quartet rulings, 106, 120, 128
legal instruments of EU, 360
Leisink, Peter, 106
Leyen, Ursula von der, 130, 202, 307, 316
Lindberg, Leon N., 169
Lisbon Strategy, 24–25

Lisbon Treaty and Constitutional Treaty referendums, 24, 139, 320
Lobina, Emanuele, 206

Maastricht Treaty
  as multilevel governance regime, 20–21, 23–24
  Broad Economic Policy Guidelines introduced by, 24, 31, 35, 44, 104
  EMU accession criteria, 17, 100–101, 136
  environmental governance competence under, 207
  healthcare services impact, 235–237
  QMV (qualified majority voting) rules, 20, 23, 101
  Social Protocol, 16, 23, 101–103
Maccarrone, Vincenzo, 46, 319, 326
  writing with Erne and Golden, 16, 324–325
  writing with Erne and Jordan, 9, 35, 39, 83, 85, 271, 278
  writing with Erne and Regan, 88, 112, 115, 153, 182, 327
Macroeconomic Imbalance Procedure (MIP)
  aim, 35
  coercive power, 85, 278–279
  fines for compliance failures, 30–32, 35, 321
  definition, 361
  scoreboard of indicators, 31–32, 107–108, 112, 278–279
  Social Imbalances Procedure counterpart proposal, 351–352
  wage policy, 107–108
macroeconomic imbalances
  definition, 2, 30–31
  eurozone crisis. *See* eurozone crisis
  German prescriptions, rebalance the EU economy rationale, 6, 113, 220, 279–280, 293, 324
MIP. *See* Macroeconomic Imbalance Procedure (MIP)
Macron, Emmanuel, 310
Majone, Giandomenico, 13
managerialisation of public service providers, 70, 72
marketisation of public services. *See* public services marketisation
Martin, Andrew, 45, 299
Marx, Karl, 44–45, 47
Mazzucato, Mariana, 202, 292

Index

McAlevey, Jane, 51
McGowan, Lee, 172
Memoranda of Understanding (MoUs), bailout programmes under, 27–29, 35–36, 313–314, 361
Merkel, Angela, 310–312
Messulam, Pierre, 175, 189
mini-jobs (Germany), 118, 282–283, 324
minimum wage regulation. *See also* wages
   Directive on. *See* Adequate Minimum Wage Directive
   generally, 62
   Germany, adoption of, 327–328, 348
   Ireland, prescriptions on, 112, 119, 327
   for posted workers, 128
   Romania, prescriptions on, 112
MIP. *See* Macroeconomic Imbalance Procedure (MIP)
Miró, Joan, 56–57
Monti, Mario, 117, 132, 192, 282
Morandi Bridge disaster (2018), 182, 336
Morton, Adam David, 192
MoUs (Memoranda of Understanding), bailout programmes under, 27–29, 35–36, 313–314, 361

Nanetti, Raffaella Y., 175
national protests against NEG regime, 41, 44, 49, 305, 311–312, 356
National Resilience and Recovery Plans (NRRPs)
   background to adoption, 310–312
   characteristics, 320–322, 357
   Commission's assessments of, 313–319, 323–324
   definition, 361
   on employment relations, 328–329, 348, 350
   on healthcare services, 343–347, 349, 351
   on transport services, 336–338
   on water services, 341–342
   policy orientation of. *See* post-Covid NEG regime
nationalisation policies, 134, 138. *See also* public services privatisation
NEG (new economic governance) regime
   adoption of, 1–2, 13, 25–27, 37–38, 95–96, 107
   analytical contributions of study, 353–358
   in Covid-19 pandemic and post-Covid period. *See* Covid-19 pandemic; post-Covid NEG regime

   democratic deficit. *See* democratic deficit of NEG regime
   Europe 2020 strategy, 2, 33, 35, 361
   European Semester process. *See* European Semester process
   horizontal–vertical paradigm. *See* horizontal–vertical EU integration paradigm
   legality questionable, 28, 38–39
   MIP strand. *See* Macroeconomic Imbalance Procedure (MIP)
   MoU strand (bailout programmes), 27–29, 35–36, 313–314, 361
   policy orientation, commodification–decommodification axis. *See* commodifying or decommodifying potential of NEG prescriptions; labour commodification; post-Covid NEG regime; public services commodification
   policy orientation, socialisation thesis, 53–55, 79, 160
   politicisation of. *See* politicisation
   prescriptions. *See* NEG prescriptions
   research design and methodology. *See* NEG regime, research design and methodology
   SGP strand. *See* Stability and Growth Pact (SGP)
   Six-Pack laws, 13–14, 29–30, 39, 83–84, 147, 361
   social dialogue on, 127–129, 160, 264–265
   TNC corporate governance analogy, 3, 5, 42–46, 305, 319
   Two-Pack laws, 29–30, 147
NEG prescriptions
   bailout programmes, 27–29, 35–36, 313–314, 361
   coercive power. *See* coercive power of NEG prescriptions
   commodifying or decommodifying potential. *See* commodifying or decommodifying potential of NEG prescriptions
   communicative contexts of, 78–81
   country-specific nature. *See* country-specific nature of NEG prescriptions
   in Covid-19 pandemic and post-Covid period. *See* National Resilience and Recovery Plans (NRRPs); post-Covid NEG regime

NEG prescriptions (cont.)
  definition, 2, 361
  European Semester process integrating. *See* European Semester process
  implementation, Commission's assessments, 36
  MIP indicators, linkage to, 31
  policy contexts, 81–83
  policy rationales. *See* policy rationales of NEG prescriptions
  quantitative and qualitative types. *See* quantitative and qualitative NEG prescriptions
  semantic analysis of, 55–57, 74–78, 85
NEG regime, research design and methodology
  case selection and analytical strategy, 84–85, 87–88, 141–142
  coercive power, taxonomy of, 80–81, 85, 109–111
  country-specific prescriptions, research implications, 4, 42–44, 52, 62, 80–83, 354
  data collection and sources, 88–91
  overview, 4–6, 73–74, 83–84
  semantic analysis of prescriptions, 55–57, 74–78, 85
negative–positive EU integration paradigm, 15–16, 39–40
neoliberalism
  commodification and, 1, 46–49, 81–83
  emergence in EU governance, 134–135, 169–170
  network services liberalisation, 23, 135–136, 172–173
Nowak, Jörg, 4, 9, 46, 62, 89–91, 121, 193, 223
NRRPs. *See* National Resilience and Recovery Plans (NRRPs)

Ocampo, José Antonio, 26
occupational health and safety
  pregnant workers, 102, 128
  Single European Act, measures under, 23, 101
  working time regulation, 102, 128
Open Method of Coordination, 24, 35, 44, 105, 120
Orbán, Viktor, 318–319, 321
ordinary legislative procedure, 23, 32–33, 41, 158, 221, 263
outsourcing of public services, 69

Palacio, Loyola de, 171
parental rights regulation, 102, 128
Patel, Kiran Klaus, 168–169
Pay Transparency Directive (proposed), 326
People's Health Movement (PHM) Europe, 91, 259, 262
platform companies, 131, 317–318, 326
Pochet, Philippe, 35
Polanyi, Karl, 50, 61
policy rationales of NEG prescriptions
  to boost competitiveness and growth, 155, 163, 220, 280
  digitalisation policies, 317–318, 333, 349
  enhancing social inclusion. *See* social inclusion policies
  generally, 271, 291–293, 330–332, 340, 356
  green economy, 156, 202, 221, 292, 316–317, 340
  labour market participation expansion, 148, 156, 248, 255, 293
  payroll taxes reduction, 255, 296
  private sector involvement in public services promotion, 155–156, 280, 336
  to rebalance the EU economy, 6–7, 113, 220, 229, 279–280, 293, 324
political will of EU executives, 295
politicisation
  depoliticised policymaking of NEG. *See* governance
  of EU integration, 18–19, 22, 49
  labour politics of NEG regime, 2–3, 13–14, 44–46, 306, 311–312, 353, 357–358
  by social movements and trade unions. *See* transnational collective action
  term, 359
  theory on, 5–6, 46, 50–51
popular protests against NEG regime, 41, 44, 49, 305, 311–312, 356
Port Services Directives, 193, 199, 202, 269–270
positive–negative EU integration paradigm, 15–16, 39–40
post-Covid NEG regime
  characteristics of prescriptions, 320–322
  employment relations prescriptions, 324–330, 348, 356–357
  healthcare services governance, 342–347
  minimum wage regulation. *See* Adequate Minimum Wage Directive
  policy orientation, synthesising assessment, 348–351

public service prescriptions generally, 330–335, 348–350, 357
transnational collective action against, 335, 338–339, 347
transport governance, 338–340
water services governance, 340–342
posted workers' rights, 102, 106, 128, 200
power relations, study of, 6, 42, 53, 57, 82, 84–85
PPPs (public–private partnerships), 60, 69, 137, 202, 207, 222
pregnant workers' rights, 102, 128
privatisation policies. *See* public services privatisation
Procurement Directives
healthcare services under, 242, 258
social and environmental content, 140, 163, 222
transnational collection action against, 193, 222, 239, 258
transport services under, 169
professional services liberalisation prescription, Italy, 77–78, 150
protests, transnational. *See* transnational collective action
public procurement policies. *See* public services marketisation
public sector wages
commodifying or decommodifying policies, 66, 108, 277–281
Germany, prescriptions on, 279
healthcare worker protests, 258, 347–348
Ireland, prescriptions on, 111–112, 146, 216, 277–278
Italy, prescriptions on, 112–113, 146–147, 149
Romania, prescriptions on, 112, 146, 277–278, 328, 334
public services commodification
comparative analysis of NEG prescriptions. *See* coercive power of public services NEG prescriptions; commodifying or decommodifying potential of NEG prescriptions
conceptual framework, 58–60, 85, 108–109, 354–355
coverage level dimension. *See* coverage levels of public services, NEG prescriptions on
EU enlargement process driving, 136–137
in pre-2008 period, 17, 22, 48

marketisation policies, 8, 106–107, 137, 140, 237–242
via Services Directive. *See* service trade liberalisation via Services Directive
neoliberalism driving, 46–49, 81–83
overview, 66, 72
public sector employment. *See* public sector wages
resource level dimension. *See* expenditure on public services, NEG prescriptions on
sectors analysed. *See* healthcare services; transport services; water services
specific country studies. *See* Germany, public services prescriptions; Ireland, public services prescriptions; Italy, public services prescriptions; Romania, public services prescriptions
transnational action resisting. *See* transnational collective action
via marketisation. *See* public services marketisation
via privatisation. *See* public services privatisation
public services governance (pre-2008)
approaches characterising, 1, 20–21, 25, 132, 137
marketisation policies, 8, 106–107, 137, 140, 237–242
network services liberalisation, 23, 135–136, 172–173
phases, 133, 163
1950s–1980s, 133–134
1980s–1990s, 134–138
2000–2008, 138–141
privatisation policies, 59–60, 136–137, 173
service trade liberalisation. *See* service trade liberalisation via Services Directive
specific sectors. *See* healthcare services; transport services; water services
state aid regulation. *See* state aid regulation
public services marketisation
concept, 68–69, 71–72
EU laws on. *See* Concessions Directive; Procurement Directives
Germany, prescriptions on. *See under* Germany, public services prescriptions
healthcare marketisation reforms. *See under* healthcare services
in pre-2008 period, 8, 106–107, 137, 140, 237–242

public services marketisation (cont.)
  Ireland, prescriptions on, 340–341
  Italy, prescriptions on. See under Italy, public services prescriptions
  managerialisation of providers, 70, 72
  NEG prescriptions on, synthesising assessment, 281–283, 293–296
  outsourcing, 69
  post-Covid prescriptions on, 333–335
  PPPs (public–private partnerships), 60, 69, 137, 202, 207, 222
  privatisation. See public services privatisation
  Romania, prescriptions on, 150–152, 184
  SOEs, corporate governance prescriptions, 152, 186–187, 216, 332, 334–335, 337–338
  transport services, 172, 182–185, 188–190, 201, 338
  water services, 216–218
public services privatisation
  generally, 48
  'implicit' privatisation, 68
  in Ireland, 153
  marketisation via, 72
  NEG prescriptions on, 151–152, 185–186, 192, 201, 254–255, 281–282, 294
  in pre-2008 period, 59–60, 136–137, 173, 175, 254
  private hospitals, 60, 254–255, 258
  privatisation types, 70
public transport services. See transport services

qualified majority voting (QMV) in Council
  health and safety measures adopted by, 23, 101–102
  Lisbon Treaty reforms, 169, 174
  Maastricht Treaty reforms, 20, 23, 101
  reversed QMV on NEG fines on compliance failures, 29–30
  Single European Act reforms, 20, 101–102, 135, 170
quantitative and qualitative NEG prescriptions
  employment relations prescriptions, 61
  generally, 8–9, 59, 271–276
  public services prescriptions, 66–72, 285

Radaelli, Claudio M., 188
rail services. See also transport services
  Commission competition enforcement action, 191–192
  commodification via NEG prescriptions, 175, 294
  EU laws on (post-2008), 183–191, 193, 338–340
  EU laws on (pre-2008), 170–174, 176, 200
  Germany, prescriptions on, 184, 188–189
  Ireland, NRRP on, 337
  Italy, prescriptions on, 294, 337
  privatisations, 185–186, 192, 201, 294
  Romania, prescriptions on, 180–181, 183, 186, 189, 201, 294
referendums
  generally, 49
  on Constitutional Treaty and Lisbon Treaty ratification, 24, 139, 320
  on Italian compulsory competitive tendering rules, 184–185, 201, 217–218, 227–228
Regling, Klaus, 314
regulatory independence of public services, 68
Rehn, Olli, 39
remuneration. See wages
Renzi, Matteo, 117, 152–153, 186–187
research design and methodology. See NEG regime, research design and methodology
Resilience and Recovery Facility (RRF). See also National Resilience and Recovery Plans (NRRPs)
  background to adoption, 310–312, 361
  healthcare commodification, potential effect on, 265–266, 351
  NEG conditionalities, 9, 185, 321–322, 349–351, 356
  NRRP implementation assessments, 313–320, 323–324
  post-Covid prescriptions related to, 320–322
resource level prescriptions. See expenditure on public services, NEG prescriptions on
reversed differentiated integration, NEG as, 42–43, 254, 297, 304, 320–321, 355
reversed qualified majority voting (QMV) on NEG fines, 29–30
Right2Water (European Citizens' Initiative)
  Citizens' Initiatives generally, 24, 198
  country-level support for, 227–228
  effects of, 158, 199–200, 203, 226–227, 230, 305–306
  reasons for success, 199, 226
road haulage services, 170–171, 200

Rokkan, Stein, 22
Romania
  employment relations prescriptions. See
    Romania, employment relations
    prescriptions
  healthcare services prescriptions. See
    Romania, healthcare services
    prescriptions
  hospital privatisations, 60, 254, 258
  Labour Code (2003), 103–104, 114
  NRRP for. See Romania, NRRP (National
    Resilience and Recovery Plan)
  public services prescriptions. See Romania,
    public services prescriptions
Romania, employment relations prescriptions
  on collective bargaining, 114–115, 119–120,
    283, 329–330, 356–357
  on employment protection, 116–117, 119
  on public sector wages, 112, 146, 277–278,
    328, 334
  on wage levels generally, 112
Romania, healthcare services prescriptions
  cost-efficiency and managerialism, 78, 85,
    248–251, 254–255, 295–296
  coverage levels, 251–253, 291–293, 296
  generally, 82
  post-Covid prescriptions, 327, 343
  resource levels, 243–247, 290–291
Romania, NRRP (National Resilience and
  Recovery Plan)
  on employment relations, 328–329, 348,
    350
  on healthcare services, 344–345
  on public procurement, 334
  on public services digitalisation, 333–334
  on SOE governance, 332, 334–335,
    337–338
  on water services, 341–342
Romania, public services prescriptions
  on expenditure, 147–149, 163–164,
    243–247, 277–280, 332
  on healthcare services. See Romania,
    healthcare services prescriptions
  on privatisation, 151–152, 185, 281–282
  on public administration, 152, 327
  on public procurement, 150–151, 184
  on public sector wages, 112, 146, 277–278,
    328, 334
  rural areas, prescriptions affecting, 147–148,
    153–154, 156, 215–216, 221, 229
  on SOE governance, 152, 186
  on transport, 148, 180–181, 183, 185–186,
    189, 201, 294
  on water services, 215–216, 218–221, 229,
    340
Ross, George, 45, 299
RRF. See Resilience and Recovery Facility
  (RRF)
Rüffert case, 106–107, 140
Ryanair, 23, 180, 183

Sabato, Sebastiano, 330, 351–352
salaries. See wages
Sarkozy, Nicolas, 138
Savage, James D., 175
Scharpf, Fritz, 15–16, 23, 39–40
Scheingold, Stuart A., 169
Schmid, Achim, 68
Schmidt, Vivien A., 265, 307–308
Schmitter, Philippe C., 41
Scholz, Olaf, 312, 328
Schot, Johan, 168–169
Schröder, Gerhard, 103–104, 236
Schulten, Thorsten, 45
Schuman, Robert, 20
security of employment tenure. See
  employment protection
Seeliger, Martin, 120
self-employed worker status, 131, 326
service trade liberalisation via Services
  Directive
  background to, 17
  consequences of failure, 24, 41
  opposition to. See Services Directive
    opposition
Services Notification Procedure Directive
  (proposal), 157–158, 230
Services Directive opposition
  country-of-origin principle controversies,
    105–106, 139, 208–209
  generally, 24, 96, 121, 139–141, 158–159,
    284, 320
  to healthcare services inclusion, 8, 232,
    238–240, 256–257
  private sector unions' support for, 302–303
  to water services inclusion, 209,
    223–226
services of general economic interest (SGEI),
  133–134, 138, 172, 208–209, 237–238.
  See also state aid regulation
SGP. See Stability and Growth Pact (SGP)
silent revolution, 2, 25–27, 29, 37–38, 243

single currency. *See* economic and monetary union (EMU)
Single European Act
  mutual recognition principle, 99
  negative integration approach, 16, 22, 41, 45
  occupational health and safety measures, 23, 101
  QMV (qualified majority voting) rules, 20, 101–102, 135, 170
single market project
  core and periphery Member States, differentiated impacts, 17–18
  cross-border healthcare. *See* cross-border healthcare services
  economic and social integration differentiated, 14–16, 18
  free movement of workers, competitive pressures from, 17–18, 22, 45, 95, 99–100
  freedoms, commodifying effect of, 106–107
  marketisation reforms. *See* public services marketisation
  negative–positive integration paradigm, 15–16, 39–40
  political integration initiatives, 18–21
  SEA on. *See* Single European Act
  service trade liberalisation. *See* service trade liberalisation via Services Directive
  social policies, 16–17, 23, 99, 101–103, 233
  state aid regulation. *See* state aid regulation
Six-Pack laws, 13–14, 29–30, 39, 83–84, 147, 361
social and cohesion funds, 32, 175, 185, 190, 206, 321
social inclusion policies
  for rural areas in Romania, 147–148, 153–154, 156, 215–216, 221, 229
  generally, 111, 255–256, 292–293
Social Protocol, Maastricht Treaty, 16, 23, 101–103
social reproduction of labour, 46–47, 60–62, 97–98
Social Rights, European Pillar of, 127–128, 160, 222, 316
social welfare. *See also* healthcare services
  benefits levels, 62
  cross-border healthcare, social security route, 234–235
  democratisation, link to, 21–22, 46
  EU citizens' benefits rights, 233
  MIP social indicators, 31–32

socialisation thesis (on NEG policy orientation), 53–55, 79, 160
SOEs, corporate governance prescriptions, 152, 186–187, 216, 332, 334–335, 337–338
solidaristic employment and welfare arrangements
  capitalist accumulation, tempering function, 21–22, 46–47, 233
  decommodifying potential of prescriptions. *See* commodifying or decommodifying potential of NEG prescriptions
Spasova, Slavina, 330, 351–352
spending on public services. *See* expenditure on public services, NEG prescriptions on
Springford, John, 321
Stability and Growth Pact (SGP)
  aim, 35, 136
  coercive power, 85, 278
  fines for compliance failures, 29–32, 35
  Covid-19 pandemic, suspension during, 9, 232, 265, 306–309, 313, 356
  definition, 361
  EDP (excessive deficit procedure), 29–30, 32–33, 136, 278–279, 332
  greater fiscal flexibility, calls for, 127, 332
  'Growth' element added, 57
Stan, Sabina, 60, 237, 253
  writing with Erne, 3, 45, 83, 88, 104, 232, 234–235, 309, 349
state aid regulation
  bank bailouts, exemptions for, 27
  Covid-19 pandemic, suspension during, 309
  Directive 80/723/EEC, 134–135
  healthcare sector and, 238
  SGEI (services of general economic interest) concept, 133–134, 138, 172, 208–209, 237–238
  transport sector and, 169
state-owned enterprises, NEG prescriptions on, 152, 186–187, 216, 332, 334–335, 337–338
Sterkel, Gabriele, 45
Stevens, Handley, 169–170
Stiglitz, Joseph E., 26, 62
Streeck, Wolfgang, 16, 23, 50, 120
strikes, transnational. *See* transnational collective action
structure-agency nexus, 54–55
SUD-Health Social (French trade union), 259

Supiot, Alain, 38
SURE funds, 324
Sutherland, Peter, 135
Sweden, collective bargaining in, 64
Szabó, Imre, 66, 112, 318–319
  writing with Golden and Erne, 5, 24, 39, 45, 50, 88, 137, 158, 193, 198, 202–203, 209–210, 216, 226, 230, 306
  writing with Kahancová, 216, 258

technocratic governance, 13–14, 33, 51, 55, 357
telecommunications services
  Italy, prescription on, 148
  Romania, prescription on, 148
  sector liberalisation, 23, 135
Teutsch, Michael, 170
TNCs. See transnational corporations (TNCs)
Tooze, Adam, 316
trade unions
  collective bargaining by. See collective bargaining
  EPSU. See European Public Service Union (EPSU)
  ETF. See European Transport Workers' Federation (ETF)
  ETUC. See European Trade Union Confederation (ETUC)
  EU's competence for decommodifying measures, union arguments on, 38–39, 130, 325–326
  Laval Quartet rulings, 106, 120, 128
  Lisbon strategy response, 25
  market integration competitive pressures faced by, 16–18, 22, 45, 95, 99–100
  NEG policies, perceptions of, 26, 91
  rights under EU law, 62
  Services Directive, opposition to, 24, 96, 105–106
  transnational collective action by. See transnational collective action
transnational collective action
  agency-oriented factors affecting, 269
  commodifying script prerequisite, 269–270, 303, 355–356
  country-specific nature of prescriptions, challenge for, 96, 127, 164, 232, 264–265, 304–305, 354
  cross-border competition, challenge for, 193, 198
  in Covid-19 pandemic, 347–348

EPSU-organised. See European Public Service Union (EPSU)
ETUC-organised. See European Trade Union Confederation (ETUC)
EU actors targeted, explanations for, 301–303
European Parliament's limited NEG role, challenge for, 160–164, 263
future priorities, 9
healthcare commodification protests, 258–265, 306, 356
labour politics of NEG regime, 2–3, 13–14, 44–46, 306, 311–312, 353, 357–358
lists of NEG regime protests, 159–160
post-Covid period, 335, 338–339, 347–348
pre-2008 period, 299
  dockworkers' strikes, 193, 198, 203, 304
  Procurement Directives protests, 193, 222, 239, 258
  Services Directive protests. See Services Directive opposition
private and nation state actors targeted, dearth of protests, 299–301
research data on, 89–91
structural factors affecting, 49–52, 160–163
transport commodification protests, 7, 192–200, 202–203, 338–339
uneven coercive power of prescriptions, challenge for, 304–306
water rights campaign. See Right2Water (European Citizens' Initiative)
transnational corporations (TNCs)
  corporate governance, NEG regime compared, 3, 5, 42–46, 305, 319
  digital platform companies, 131, 317–318, 326
  ETUC promoting democracy in. See European Trade Union Confederation (ETUC)
  healthcare service and pharmaceutical companies, 256–257, 345–347
  water companies, 206–207, 222, 226
transport services
  buses, 180, 187
  civil aviation. See civil aviation services
  commodification via EMU accession criteria, 174–176
  commodifying or decommodifying potential of prescriptions, 7, 176–177, 187–190, 200–202
  NRRPs and post-Covid prescriptions, 336–338

transport services (cont.)
  compulsory competitive tendering rules, 172
  coverage level prescriptions, 187
  EU governance (pre-2008), 167–168, 200
    1950s–1970s, 168–169
    1980s–1990s, 169–171
    2000–2008, 171–174
  EU laws on (post-2008), 190–193, 338–340
  expenditure, prescriptions on, 180–182, 187–188
  Germany, prescriptions on, 148, 181–184, 188–189, 202
  Ireland, no specific prescriptions on, 176, 182–183, 189
  Italy, prescriptions on, 148, 182–184, 189, 294, 337
  provider-level governance, prescriptions on, 185–187, 201
  railways. *See* rail services
  Romania, prescriptions on, 148, 180–181, 183, 185–186, 189, 201, 294
  sector-level governance, prescriptions on, 182–185, 188–190, 201, 294
  transnational collective action on, 7, 192–200, 202–203, 338–339
Treaty on Stability, Coordination, and Governance in the Economic and Monetary Union (Fiscal Treaty), 30, 121, 147
Turnbull, Peter, 193
Two-Pack laws, 29–30, 147

Umney, Charles, 69, 71
unit labour costs (ULCs) benchmark, 107, 112, 119, 276–279, 284, 296
United Kingdom
  Brexit, 49, 131, 312, 356
  collective bargaining in, 63–64
  Maastricht Treaty Social Protocol rejection, 101
  privatisation policies, 59–60, 136
unjustified dismissal protections. *See* employment protection
Urban Waste-Water Treatment Directives, 206–207, 342
utilities
  commodification. *See* public services commodification
  network services liberalisation, 23, 135–136, 172–173
  sectors analysed. *See* transport services; water services

Vanhercke, Bart, 54, 78, 330, 351–352
Vanheuverzwijn, Pierre, 56–57
Vanpool, Christine and Todd, 74–75
Velde, Didier van de, 173
Veolia (transnational water and transport services corporation), 180, 213, 226
ver.di (German trade union), 91, 226
vertical integration. *See* horizontal–vertical EU integration paradigm
Viking and *Laval* cases, 106, 120, 128

wages
  collective bargaining of. *See* collective bargaining
  gender equality policies, 99, 131
  minimum wage regulation. *See* Adequate Minimum Wage Directive; minimum wage regulation
  MIP's wage policy, 107–108
  moderation policies (pre-2008), 17, 31, 100–101, 103–104, 284
  NEG prescriptions on, 61–62, 111–114, 119–120, 277–281, 327–328
  of public sector workers. *See* public sector wages
Pay Transparency Directive (proposed), 326
Water Framework Directive, 206–208, 295
water services
  commodification via Services Directive inclusion, 208–209, 219, 223–226
  commodifying or decommodifying potential of prescriptions, 7–8, 209–214, 218–221, 229–230
  NRRPs and post-Covid prescriptions, 340–342
  coverage level prescriptions, 214–216
  EU governance (pre-2008), 204–205
    1970s–1990s, 205–206, 229
    1990s–2000, 206–208, 229
    2000–08, 208–209, 219, 229
  EU laws on (post-2008), 221–223, 226–227, 342
  expenditure, prescriptions on, 218
  Germany, prescriptions on, 216–220, 340
  Ireland, prescriptions on. *See* Ireland, water services prescriptions
  Italy, prescriptions on, 217–219
  PPPs (public–private partnerships) for, 60, 207
  provider-level governance, prescriptions on, 216, 294–295

Romania, prescriptions on, 215–216, 218–221, 229, 340
sector-level governance, prescriptions on, 216–218, 294–295
transnational campaign on. *See* Right2Water (European Citizens' Initiative)
welfare services. *See* social welfare
Wiedemuth, Jörg, 45
Wilks, Stephen, 172

women's labour market participation, prescriptions on, 148, 156, 248, 293
workplace health and safety regulation. *See* occupational health and safety
World Bank's 'good governance' interventions, 42
Wüest, Bruno, 89
Würth, Reinhold, 311

Zeitlin, Jonathan, 54, 78
Zuboff, Shoshana, 345

For EU product safety concerns, contact us at Calle de José Abascal, 56–1°, 28003 Madrid, Spain or eugpsr@cambridge.org.